ADVANCED FINANCIAL ACCOUNTING

FIFTH EDITION

ADVANCED FINANCIAL ACCOUNTING

Richard E. Baker
Northern Illinois University

Valdean C. Lembke
University of Iowa

Thomas E. King
*Southern Illinois University
at Edwardsville*

Boston   Burr Ridge, IL   Dubuque, IA   Madison, WI   New York   San Francisco   St. Louis
Bangkok   Bogotá   Caracas   Kuala Lumpur   Lisbon   London   Madrid   Mexico City
Milan   Montreal   New Delhi   Santiago   Seoul   Singapore   Sydney   Taipei   Toronto

McGraw-Hill Higher Education

A Division of The **McGraw-Hill** *Companies*

ADVANCED FINANCIAL ACCOUNTING

Published by McGraw-Hill/Irwin, an imprint of The McGraw-Hill Companies, Inc. 1221 Avenue of the Americas, New York, NY, 10020. Copyright © 2002, 1999, 1996, 1993, 1989 by The McGraw-Hill Companies, Inc. All rights reserved. No part of this publication may be reproduced or distributed in any form or by any means or stored in a database or retrieval system, without the prior written consent of The McGraw-Hill Companies, Inc., including, but not limited to, in any network or other electronic storage or transmission, or broadcast for distance learning. Some ancillaries, including electronic and print components, may not be available to customers outside the United States..

Materials from the Certified Management Accountant Examinations, Copyright 1974, 1975, 1976, 1977, 1979, 1980, 1981, 1982, 1983, 1984, 1985, 1986, 1987, 1988, 1989, by the Institute of Certified Management Accountants, are reprinted and/or adapted with permission.

Material from the Uniform CPA Examinations and Unofficial Answers, copyright 1969, 1970, 1972, 1973, 1974, 1975, 1976, 1977, 1978, 1979, 1980, 1981, 1982, 1983, 1984, 1985, 1986, 1987, 1988, 1989, 1990, 1991, 1992, 1993, 1994, 1995, 1996, 1997, 1998, by the American Institute of Certified Public Accountants, Inc., is reprinted (or adapted) with permission.

This book is printed on acid-free paper.

4 5 6 7 8 9 0 CCW/CCW 0 9 8 7 6 5 4 3 2

ISBN 0-07-244412-6

Publisher: *Brent Gordon*
Sponsoring editor: *Steve DeLancey*
Developmental editor: *Kelly Odom*
Marketing manager: *Rich Kolasa*
Project manager: *Christina Thornton-Villagomez*
Production supervisor: *Debra R. Sylvester*
Coordinator freelance designer: *Mary L. Christianson*
Freelance cover design: *e3 design group*
Cover photograph: *© Ralph Mercer Photography*
Lead supplement coordinator: *Cathy Tepper*
Producer, Media technology: *Ed Przyzcki*
Compositor: *GAC Indianapolis*
Typeface: *10.5/12.5 Times Roman*
Printer: *Courier Westord*

Library of Congress Cataloging-in-Publication Data

Baker, Richard E.
     Advanced financial accounting / Richard E. Baker, Valdean C. Lembke, Thomas E.
King. — 5th ed.
        p.   cm.
     Includes bibliographical references and index.
     ISBN 0-07-244412-6 (alk. paper)
     1. Accounting.   I. Lembke, Valdean C.   II. King, Thomas E. III. Title.
HF5635.B165   2002
657'.046—dc21   2001030527

http://www.mhhe.com

ABOUT THE AUTHORS

RICHARD E. BAKER is the Ernst & Young LLP Distinguished Professor of Accountancy at Northern Illinois University. He has been recognized as an inaugural University Presidential Teaching Professor, the highest teaching recognition of his university. He received his B.S. degree from the University of Wisconsin at River Falls and his MBA and Ph.D. from the University of Wisconsin at Madison. His activities in the American Accounting Association include serving as the 1997–99 Director of Education of the AAA, the 1994–95 Chair of the Teaching and Curriculum Section, and the 1988–89 President of the Midwest Region. His service to the Federation of Schools of Accountancy (FSA) includes serving as the 2001 president, the 2000 vice president, and the 1996–97 secretary of the FSA. Many of his committee service efforts have involved research in assessing teaching and learning outcomes, and promoting the integration of computing into the accounting classroom. Professor Baker is serving as an associate editor for *Issues in Accounting Education,* and previously served as a reviewer for this journal for several years. He has served as an associate editor of *The Journal of Accounting Education* and as a reviewer for *Accounting Education, Accounting Horizons,* and *Advances in Accounting Education.* He has received numerous teaching awards at both the undergraduate and graduate levels and was selected as the Illinois CPA Society's 1993 Outstanding Accounting Educator. His most recent published research studies have concentrated on ways to make the learning/teaching experience as effective as possible. Other published research includes studies in financial reporting and mergers and acquisitions. Professor Baker's major teaching areas are advanced financial accounting, financial theory, and financial statement analysis. He is a CPA and also teaches advanced financial accounting topics in CPA examination review courses.

VALDEAN C. LEMBKE is professor of accounting in the College of Business Administration at the University of Iowa. He received his B.S. degree from Iowa State University and his MBA and Ph.D. from the University of Michigan. He has internal audit and public accounting experience. He has been active in the American Accounting Association, including serving as president of the Midwest Region and book review editor for *Issues in Accounting Education.* Professor Lembke has been a faculty member at the University of Iowa for 25 years, where he was named the first recipient of the Gilbert P. Maynard Excellence in Accounting Instruction award. He has served two terms as department head and is currently head of the Professional Program in Accounting. Professor Lembke has authored or coauthored articles in journals such as *The Accounting Review,* the *Journal of Accounting, Auditing and Finance,* the *Journal of Accountancy,* and the *Internal Auditor.* He also coauthored *Financial Accounting: A Decision-Making Approach,* an introductory accounting text, and a chapter on business combinations and consolidated financial statements in the *Accountant's Encyclopedia.* His teaching has been primarily in undergraduate and graduate coursework in financial accounting and in governmental and not-for-profit accounting.

THOMAS E. KING is professor of accounting in the School of Business at Southern Illinois University at Edwardsville. He received his B.S. degree from California State University, Northridge, and his MBA and Ph.D. from the University of California, Los Angeles. He is a CPA and received an Elijah Watt Sells Award and the Illinois gold medal for his scores on the Uniform CPA Examination. He has a number of years of business and consulting experience and has been teaching for more than 20 years. Professor King coauthored with Valdean Lembke the chapter on business combinations and consolidated financial statements in the *Accountant's Encyclopedia,* and he has authored or coauthored numerous articles appearing in journals such as *The Accounting Review, Accounting Horizons,* the *Journal of Accountancy,* the *Journal of Accounting, Auditing and Finance, Advances in Accounting,* the *Journal of Accounting Education,* and *Financial Executive.* He also coauthored *Financial Accounting: A Decision-Making Approach,* an introductory accounting text. He currently serves on the editorial boards of *Advances in Accounting* and *Advances in Accounting Education.* Professor King has served two terms on the board of governors of the St. Louis Chapter of the Institute of Internal Auditors, and he has been active in the Financial Executives Institute, Institute of Management Accountants, and the Illinois CPA Society. Professor King teaches primarily in the area of financial accounting.

PREFACE

The fifth edition of *Advanced Financial Accounting* is a comprehensive and highly illustrated presentation of the accounting and reporting principles used in a variety of business entities. The daily business press carries many stories about the merger and acquisition mania of multicorporate entities, the foreign activities of multinational firms, the operations of governmental and nonprofit entities, and other topics typically included in advanced accounting. Accountants must know how to deal with the accounting and reporting ramifications of these activities.

Overview

The fifth edition of *Advanced Financial Accounting* continues to provide strong coverage of advanced accounting topics, clarity of presentation, and integrated coverage based on continuous case examples. The text is highly illustrated with complete presentations of worksheets, schedules, and financial statements so that students can see the development of each new topic. Inclusion of all recent FASB and GASB pronouncements and their continuing deliberations provides a current and contemporary text for students preparing for the CPA examination and current practice. In the chapters covering consolidation subsequent to the date of combination, the three alternative methods of accounting for the parent's investment in the subsidiary are presented in each chapter (basic equity) and appendixes (cost and fully adjusted equity) to provide the opportunity for exploring the differences in the methods and seeing that the consolidated financial statements are the same regardless of the method the parent company uses to account for the investment.

Key Features

The key strengths of this book are the clear and readable discussions of concepts and the detailed demonstrations of these concepts through illustrations and explanations. The many favorable responses to earlier editions from both students and instructors confirm our belief that clear presentation and comprehensive illustrations are essential to learning the sophisticated topics in an advanced accounting course. Key features of the fifth edition include:

• **A building-block approach based on a strong conceptual foundation.** For each major topic area, students are provided with a thorough conceptual understanding before advancing to the procedures. The discussion begins with the fundamental concepts and why they are important. These fundamentals are then illustrated, giving students a basic example before progressing. Once this conceptual foundation is set, the complexities are layered gradually in successive steps. The authors developed this methodology through years of teaching the course. Many adopters have commented favorably on the effectiveness of this approach.

• **The use of a continuous case for each major subject matter area.** The comprehensive case of Peerless Products Corporation and its subsidiary, Special Foods, Inc., has been continued. Using a continuous case provides several benefits. First, students need only become familiar with one set of data and can then move more quickly through the subsequent discussion and illustrations without having to absorb a new set of data. Second, the case adds realism to the study of advanced accounting and permits students to see the effects of each successive step on the financial reports of a company. Finally, comparing and contrasting alternative methods using a continuous case allows students to evaluate different methods and outcomes more readily.

• **Extensive illustrations of key concepts.** The book is heavily illustrated with complete, not partial, workpapers, financial statements, and other computations and comparisons useful for demonstrating each topic. The illustrations are cross-referenced to the relevant text discussion. Each of the three major methods of accounting for the investment in a subsidiary—the cost method, the basic equity method, and the full equity method—are fully discussed and illustrated. Workpaper entries presented in the consolidations chapter are separately identified with an (E) and are shaded to clearly differentiate them from book entries. The extensive use of illustrations makes the learning process more efficient by allowing students to see quickly and readily the applications of the concepts. In addition, the illustrations reinforce understanding of the concepts by demonstrating the effects on the financial statements. In this manner, students understand that the many workpaper procedures typically covered in advanced accounting are the means to a desired end, not the end themselves.

• **Comprehensive coverage with significant flexibility.** The subject matter of advanced accounting is expanding at an unprecedented rate. New topics are being added, and traditional topics require more extensive coverage. Flexibility is therefore essential in an advanced accounting text. Most one-term courses are unable to cover all the topics included in this text. In recognition of time constraints, this text is structured to provide the most efficient use of the time available. The self-contained units of subject matter allow for substantial flexibility in sequencing the course materials. In addition, individual chapters are organized to allow for opportunities to go into greater depth on some topics through the use of the "Additional Considerations" sections. Several chapters include appendixes containing discussions of alternative accounting procedures or illustrations of procedures or concepts that are of a supplemental nature.

• **Extensive end-of-chapter materials.** A large number of questions, cases, exercises, and problems at the end of each chapter provide the opportunity to solidify understanding of the chapter material and assess mastery of the subject matter. The end-of-chapter materials progress from simple, focused exercises to more complex, integrated problems. Cases provide opportunities for extending thought and for gaining exposure to different sources of accounting-related information.

Organization: The Story of Peerless Products Corporation and Special Foods, Inc.

This textbook presents the complete story of a company, Peerless Products Corporation, from its beginning, through its growth to a multinational consolidated entity, and finally to its end. At each stage of the entity's development, including the acquisition of a subsidiary, Special Foods, Inc., the textbook presents comprehensive examples and discussions of the accounting and financial reporting issues that accountants face. In this edition, discussions tied to the case are easily identified by the company logos in the margin:

The following list describes how the text is organized and how the company unfolds to demonstrate many of the topics:

Business Combinations, Intercorporate Equity Investments, and Consolidation Concepts

Chapters 1 and 2 of the textbook introduce the issues of accounting for business combinations and intercorporate investments. Chapter 3 provides a conceptual foundation for the study of consolidated financial statements.

Consolidation at Date of Combination

Chapter 4 initiates the story of Peerless Products Corporation, which purchases the stock of Special Foods, Inc. and maintains Special Foods as a subsidiary. Basic consolidation procedures are presented, and the preparation of a consolidated balance sheet as of the date of combination is illustrated for Peerless Products and Special Foods.

Consolidation Subsequent to Combination

Chapter 5 continues the development of Peerless Products and Special Foods through the first two years of combined operations. This chapter introduces the three-part consolidation workpaper and considers the procedures used to develop a complete set of consolidated financial statements for the combined entity.

Intercompany Transactions

As is common for affiliated companies, Peerless and Special Foods engage in a number of intercompany transactions. Chapters 6, 7, and 8 discuss intercorporate transfers of noncurrent assets, intercompany inventory transactions, and intercompany indebtedness, respectively.

Complex Ownership Issues

Chapter 9 examines the special consolidation problems that arise from complex ownership structures. Included are the accounting issues that arise if: (1) Special Foods issues preferred stock, (2) Peerless decreases its percentage of ownership in Special Foods by selling some of its stock investment in Special Foods to a party outside the consolidated entity, or increases its ownership percentage by acquiring additional stock of Special Foods, (3) Special Foods acquires some of Peerless Products' stock, and (4) Special Foods issues stock dividends.

Consolidation Reporting Issues

Chapter 10 completes the discussion of consolidated reporting by presenting several additional consolidation issues encountered by Peerless and Special Foods. First, the preparation of a consolidated cash flow statement is discussed and illustrated for Peerless and Special Foods. Second, the manner in which the subsequent consolidation process and consolidated financial statements would be different if a business combination is treated as a pooling rather than a purchase is discussed. Next, the impact of interim acquisitions on consolidated financial statements is examined. The chapter also discusses tax considerations related to consolidated entities and the computation of consolidated earnings per share.

Multinational Accounting

Chapters 11 and 12 present the accounting and reporting issues that arise when Peerless enters the multinational business environment. First, Peerless extends its sales to international customers and begins dealing in foreign currency transactions. To manage its risk, Peerless uses forward exchange contracts and other financial derivatives for hedging purposes. Comprehensive appendixes are presented that discuss using the time value of derivatives and accounting for other forms of derivatives. In Chapter 12, Peerless acquires a subsidiary located in Germany. The German company reports its operations in European euros, and Peerless must restate the subsidiary's trial balance to U.S. dollars to consolidate the operations of its German subsidiary.

Segment and Interim Reporting

Chapter 13 discusses segment reporting requirements and examines the segment and related disclosures that Peerless must make in its consolidated financial statements. Interim financial reporting also is discussed in this chapter and is illustrated with Peerless's interim reports.

SEC Reporting

Chapter 14 presents a discussion of the issues that Peerless must understand if it wishes to "go public" and issue stock or debt in the capital markets. The Securities and Exchange Commission has many specific rules, procedures, and reporting requirements that companies must follow if their securities are going to trade publicly.

Partnership Accounting

Chapters 15 and 16 step back in chronology to review the origins of Peerless Products. The process begins with C. Alt starting a software development business. Alt then forms a partnership with Blue, and, after operating for a year, the two partners bring Cha into the partnership because they need her business expertise. Accounting issues associated with partnership accounting are presented in these two chapters. After operating the partnership for several years, the partners incorporate their business under the name of Peerless Products Corporation.

Governmental and Nonprofit Accounting

Chapters 17 and 18 present the accounting and financial reporting for Sol City, the city in which Peerless Products is located. C. Alt serves on the city council, and the chapters present the accounting information needed by Alt to represent his constituents. Chapter 19 presents the accounting and financial reporting requirements for Sol City University and for Sol City Community Hospital along with several other nonprofit agencies in Sol City.

Corporation in Financial Difficulty

Chapter 20 closes the story of Peerless Products and Special Foods. Because of the poor health of C. Alt, the consolidated entity experiences a variety of financial problems. Attempts are made to restructure its debt and to reorganize with the help of a court-appointed receiver. However, the company has too many financial problems and is forced to enter into bankruptcy.

Changes for the Fifth Edition

Each of the chapters in the text has been revised to include comprehensive discussion and full illustration of recent FASB and GASB standards. In addition, end-of-chapter materials have been developed and added that best illustrate and explore these new standards.

1. The chapter on business combinations has been updated to include discussion of the recent FASB deliberations on business combinations and intangible assets. The FASB's stated intention to eliminate the pooling method of accounting for business combinations is reflected in Chapter 1 by separating and slightly reducing the coverage of pooling accounting. However, because of the effects of prior poolings, inclusion of this topic is still important. In addition, the chapters on business combinations and consolidated financial statements have been revised in light of the FASB's discussions on how goodwill is treated subsequent to purchase-type business combinations. These chapters, and the related end-of-chapter materials, have been revised to be consistent with the changes presented in the proposed new standards.

2. End-of-chapter homework material has been enhanced with additional exercises and problems, while also maintaining the best of the end-of-chapter material from the fourth edition. Adopters and reviewers have provided numerous positive comments on the breadth and variety of the end-of-chapter materials.

3. The material on accounting for branch operations has been removed from the text, reflecting its narrower application and coverage in advanced financial accounting courses and on the CPA examination. It is available, however, through custom publishing by contacting your McGraw-Hill/Irwin representative.

4. Chapter 11, Multinational Accounting: Foreign Currency Transactions and Financial Instruments, has been extensively revised and extended to include much more presentation of the accounting and reporting of derivative and hedging transactions. Instructors have indicated the increasing importance of this topic for advanced financial accounting courses.

5. Chapters 17 and 18, Governmental Entities, have both been completed revised to include **GASB 34** on the new reporting model and other recent GASB standards (including **GASB 33**) that specify numerous changes to the governmental accounting and reporting model. Both fund-based and government-wide financial statements are fully developed and completely presented in the continuous case format so that students can easily determine the accounting for transactions and how the transactions are then reported in the required financial disclosures. Additional other-objective-answer-format (OOAF) exercises and problems have been added to reflect the coverage of governmental accounting on the CPA examination.

6. Chapter 19 covers accounting for not-for-profit entities. The chapter begins with accounting for special-purpose entities, and then presents the accounting for both private and public colleges and universities. **GASB 35,** which presents the new accounting and reporting standards for public universities, has been fully integrated into this chapter. In addition, the chapter discusses **FASB 136,** which provides the accounting requirements for transfers of assets to not-for-profit organizations that raise or hold contributions for others. The chapter provides full presentations of the required financial statements, with extensive discussion of the accounting and reporting requirements for these important entities. The end-of-chapter materials have been enhanced to cover the new standards in such a way that students will be prepared for these areas on the CPA examination.

7. A chapter on estate and trust accounting has been added to the book's website for those who wish to expand their knowledge of these areas. The chapter presents the material in the same comprehensive and clear manner for which the text is well known.

Retained Features

1. The comprehensive continuous case approach has been retained because it provides students with the ability to see how each successive step affects the financial reporting model of an entity. The Peerless Products and Special Foods case is robust and serves as a foundation for the building-block approach used throughout the text.

2. Although each chapter has been revised to some extent to reflect recent FASB and GASB standards, as well as to refine and focus the discussion and presentations, extensive efforts were made to retain the clear writing style in the text that faculty and students have valued very highly.

3. The full coverage of the FASB and GASB standards that have direct applicability to the topics in advanced financial accounting, including **FASB 130** on comprehensive income and **FASB 131** on segment disclosures, has been maintained.

4. Cases at the end of each chapter requiring students to write essay-type responses reflecting alternative viewpoints or justifying a specific accounting choice has been retained and updated. Students are asked to explain their reasoning and often are asked to use library or Internet research tools and materials in support of their answers. These cases require students to go beyond the computational level in addressing the topics in advanced financial accounting.

5. The end-of-chapter materials have been enhanced while also retaining the wide variety of homework materials for which the text is known.

6. The Internet-based cases and exercises introduced in the fourth edition have been enhanced to provide students with additional opportunities to access real-world data sources in conjunction with their coverage of the topics.

7. The study guide for the text is written by the three authors of the text to ensure full integration and compatible presentation of the topics. The study guide for the fifth edition has been extensively revised to reflect all the updates and enhancements in the textbook coverage as a result of the new GASB and FASB standards, and every effort has been made to provide a terrific learning tool for students.

8. Because advanced financial accounting is often taken by students who plan to take the CPA examination, numerous end-of-chapter materials are provided in the formats used for testing on the CPA examination. A wide variety of multiple-choice questions, cases requiring written presentations, and other objective answer format (OOAF) materials is provided.

Supplements

This text is accompanied by a full ancillary program with items designed to enhance the learning process. Supplemental materials are available from Irwin/McGraw-Hill.

For the Student

Study Guide. Closely coordinated with the text, the study guide contains summaries of the key concepts presented in each chapter and provides self-diagnostic and review materials in the form of multiple-choice, true/false, and fill-in-the-blank questions, as well as both short and comprehensive exercises and problems. The solutions are provided so that achievement levels can be assessed readily and topics that need further review can be identified.

Accounting Workpapers. The accounting workpapers provide useful forms for solving many of the end-of-chapter problems in the text. To increase efficiency, the forms already contain trial balances, other opening data, and column headings.

Check Figures. A list of answers is provided separately for many of the end-of-chapter materials in the text.

For the Instructor

Solutions Manual. Solutions are provided for all questions, cases, exercises, and problems in the text. Solutions are carefully explained and logically presented.

Answers to many of the multiple-choice questions include computations and explanations. Instructors can prepare transparencies directly from the solutions manual or can choose from the overhead transparencies available for selected exercises and problems.

Solutions Transparencies. Large-type transparencies have been prepared for approximately 175 exercises and problems in the text.

Test Bank. This comprehensive collection of both conceptual and procedural test items has been completely revised and expanded by Eddy Birrer of Gonzaga University. The material is organized by chapter and includes a large variety of multiple-choice questions and exercises and problems that can be used to measure student achievement in the topics in each chapter. The test items are closely coordinated with the text to ensure consistency.

Ready Shows. A Power Point presentation has been prepared by Douglas Cloud of Pepperdine University to accompany each chapter in the text. These slides are available on the text's website.

Website

The text's website address is http://www.mhhe.com/business/accounting/baker5e. Both students and instructors will find a variety of materials for the book and features to enhance the students' learning in *Advanced Financial Accounting*.

Acknowledgments

This text includes the thoughts and contributions of many individuals, and we wish to express our sincere appreciation to them. First, and foremost, we thank all the students in our advanced accounting classes, from whom we have learned so much. In many respects, this text is an outcome of the learning experiences we have shared with our students. Second, we wish to thank the many outstanding teachers we have had in our educational programs, from whom we learned the joy of the educational process. We are indebted to our colleagues in advanced accounting for helping us reach our goal of writing the best possible advanced financial accounting text. We appreciate the many valuable comments and suggestions from the instructors who used earlier editions of the text. Their comments and suggestions have contributed to making this text a more effective learning tool. We especially wish to thank: David Angelovich, San Francisco State University; Mark Bettner, Bucknell University; Dennis Bline, Bryant College; Bruce Bradford, Fairfield University; Bobby Carmichael, Texas A & M; Charles Christianson, Luther College; Steve Czarsty, Mary Washington College; David Doran, Pennsylvania State University, Erie; John Engstrom, Northern Illinois University; David Gotlob, Indiana University—Purdue University at Fort Wayne; Wayne Higley, Buena Vista College; Sharron Hoffmans, University of Texas at El Paso; James Hopkins, Morningside College; Gordon Hosch, University of New Orleans; David Karmon, Central Michigan University; Aubrey Kosson; James Lahey, Northern Illinois University; May H. Lo, Western New England College; Mary Maury, St. John's University; Ralph McQuade, Jr., Bentley College; David Meeting, Cleveland State University; Philip Meyer, Boston University; Jon Nance, Southwest Missouri State University; Scott Newman, Western State College of Colorado; Larry Prober,

Rider University; Rong Qui, CUNY-Baruch College; Terence Reilly, Albright College; Max Rexroad, Illinois State University; Andrew Rosman, University of Connecticut; Eugene Rozanski, Illinois State University; Norlin Rueschhoff, University of Notre Dame; Victoria Rymer, University of Maryland at College Park; Ted Skekel, University of Texas, San Antonio; Pam Smith, Northern Illinois University; James Stice, Brigham Young University; Mack Tennyson, University of Charleston; Stuart Webster, University of Wyoming; Scott Whisenant, Georgetown University.

We also wish to thank John R. Simon from Northern Illinois University for his assistance in revising end-of-chapter materials of several chapters in the text. Typing assistance was provided by Carol Denton, Northern Illinois University. James Hopkins, Morningside University, served as a comprehensive problem-checker and reviewed solutions to end-of-chapter materials for both accuracy and completeness. Lois Lembke has provided invaluable assistance in assuring accuracy and clarity in providing camera ready copy of the solutions manual.

We are grateful for the assistance and direction of the McGraw-Hill/Irwin team, especially our publisher, Jeffery Shelstad; our editor, Steve DeLancey; our developmental editor, Kelly Odom; our project manager, Christina Thornton-Villagomez; and our supplements coordinator, Cathy Tepper, who all worked hard to champion our book through the production process.

Permission has been received from the Institute of Certified Management Accountants of the Institute of Management Accountants to use questions and/or unofficial answers from past CMA examinations. We appreciate the cooperation of the American Institute of Certified Public Accountants for providing permission to adapt and use materials from past Uniform CPA Examinations.

Above all, we extend our deepest appreciation to our families who continue to provide the encouragement and support necessary for this textbook project.

Richard E. Baker
Valdean C. Lembke
Thomas E. King

BRIEF CONTENTS

CONTENTS

4 Consolidation as of the Date of Acquisition   155

CORPORATE EXPANSION AND ACCOUNTING FOR BUSINESS COMBINATIONS

The business environment in the United States is perhaps the most dynamic and vibrant in the world. Each day, new companies and new products enter the marketplace, and others are forced to leave or to change substantially in order to survive. In this setting, existing companies often find it necessary to combine their operations with those of other companies or to establish new operating units in emerging areas of business activity.

In recent years, the business world has witnessed many corporate acquisitions and combinations, often involving some of the nation's largest and best-known companies. Some of these combinations have captured the attention of the public because of the personalities involved, the daring strategies employed, and the huge sums of money at stake.

A *business combination* occurs when two or more companies join under common control. The concept of *control* relates to the ability to direct policies and management. Traditionally, control over a company has been gained by acquiring a majority of the company's outstanding voting stock. However, the diversity of financial and operating arrangements employed in recent years also raises the possibility of gaining control with less than majority ownership.

A number of accounting and reporting issues arise when two or more companies join under common ownership. One set of issues involves how to account for the business combination. The procedures used can have a substantial effect on financial statements prepared subsequent to the combination. Other issues involve how to account for intercorporate ownership interests in periods following an acquisition and how to report the results of operations and the financial positions of related companies.

The first 10 chapters of this text focus on accounting and financial reporting when two or more companies are involved. Chapter 1 deals explicitly with accounting and reporting issues related to business combinations. The second chapter focuses on accounting and reporting for stock ownership in other companies. The next eight chapters systematically develop the reporting procedures used by related companies to prepare financial statements as if the companies actually were a single company. Financial statements prepared for two or more legally separate, but related, corporations as if they actually were a single company are referred to as *consolidated financial statements.*

The Development of Multicorporate Entities

The simple business setting in which one company has two or three manufacturing plants and produces products for a local or regional market is much less common now than it was several decades ago. As companies have grown in size, they often have developed complex organizational and ownership structures.

Reasons for Corporate Expansion

Both corporate shareholders and management tend to have an interest in seeing a company grow in size. Economies of scale often exist with regard to production and distribution costs. By expanding into new markets or acquiring other companies already in those markets, companies can develop new earning potential, and those in cyclical industries can add greater stability to earnings through diversification. As an example, Boeing, a company very strong in commercial aviation, acquired McDonnell Douglas, a company weak in commercial aviation but very strong in military aviation and other defense and space applications. In some cases, companies expand the scope of their operations in response to governmental incentives, such as those encouraging trade with certain countries.

Corporate management often is rewarded with higher salaries as company size increases. In addition, prestige frequently increases with the size of a company and with a reputation for the successful acquisition of other companies. As a result, corporate management often finds it personally advantageous to increase company size.

Forms of Corporate Expansion

Companies historically have attempted to grow through a combination of new product development and expansion of existing product lines into new markets. In many cases, however, entry into new product areas or geographic regions is more easily accomplished by acquiring or combining with other companies. As a result, many companies have entered into business combinations over the past several decades as a means of attaining growth and diversification. For example, SBC Communications, a major telecommunications company, significantly increased its service area by combining with Pacific Telesis and Ameritech.

Business combinations may take one of several legal forms, as illustrated in Figure 1–1. A *statutory merger* is a type of business combination in which only one of the combining companies survives and the other loses its separate identity. The assets and liabilities of the acquired company are transferred to the acquiring company, and the acquired company is dissolved, or *liquidated*. The operations of the previously separate companies are carried on in a single legal entity following the merger.

A *statutory consolidation* is a business combination in which both the combining companies are dissolved and the assets and liabilities of both companies are transferred to a newly created corporation. The operations of the previously separate companies are carried on in a single legal entity, and neither of the combining companies remains in existence after a statutory consolidation. In many situations, however, the resulting corporation is new in form only, while in substance it actually is one of the combining companies reincorporated with a new name.

A *stock acquisition* occurs when one company acquires the voting shares of another company and the two companies continue to operate as separate, but related, legal entities. Because neither of the combining companies is liquidated, the acquiring

Figure 1–1   Types of Business Combinations

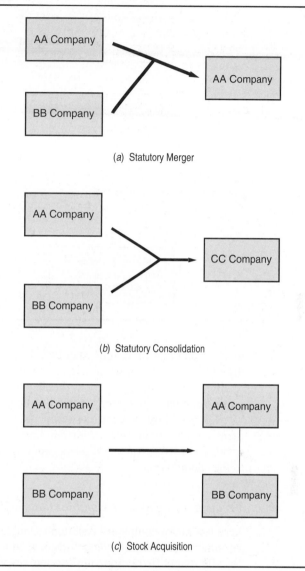

(*a*) Statutory Merger

(*b*) Statutory Consolidation

(*c*) Stock Acquisition

company accounts for its ownership interest in the other company as an investment. In a stock acquisition, the acquiring company need not acquire all the other company's stock to gain control.

The relationship that is created in a stock acquisition is referred to as a ***parent-subsidiary relationship.*** A ***parent company*** is one that controls another company, referred to as a ***subsidiary,*** usually through majority ownership of common stock. For general-purpose financial reporting, a parent company and its subsidiaries present consolidated financial statements that appear largely as if the companies had actually merged into one.

As illustrated in Figure 1–2, a stock acquisition occurs when one company acquires a majority of the voting stock of another company and both companies remain in existence as separate legal entities following the business combination. Statutory

FIGURE 1–2   Determining the Type of Business Combination

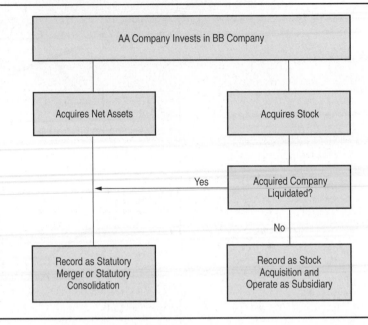

mergers and consolidations may be effected through acquisition of stock as well as through acquisition of net assets. To complete a statutory merger or consolidation following an acquisition of stock, the acquired company is liquidated and only the acquiring company or a newly created company remains in existence.

The legal form of a business combination, the substance of the combination agreement, and the circumstances surrounding the combination all affect how the combination is recorded initially and the accounting and reporting procedures used subsequent to the combination.

Frequency of Business Combinations and Multicorporate Entities

Very few major companies function as single legal entities in our modern business environment. Virtually all companies have at least one subsidiary, with more than a few broadly diversified companies having several hundred subsidiaries. In some cases, subsidiaries are created to separately incorporate part of the ongoing operations previously conducted within the parent company. Other subsidiaries are acquired through business combinations.

Business combinations are a continuing and frequent part of the business environment. A merger boom occurred in the 1960s. This period was characterized by frantic and, in some cases, disorganized merger binges, resulting in creation of a large number of conglomerates, or companies operating in many different industries. Because many of the resulting companies lacked coherence in their operations, they often were less successful than anticipated, and many of the acquisitions of the 1960s have since been sold or abandoned. In the 1980s, the number of business combinations again increased. That period saw many leveraged buyouts, but the resulting debt has plagued many of those companies over the years. The number of business combinations through the 1990s dwarfed previous merger booms, with all records for merger activity shattered. The fast pace of merger activity has continued into the new century, often involving some of the country's, and the world's, largest companies.

Mergers in recent years have been frequent in telecommunications, defense, banking and financial services, health care, entertainment, and natural resources. Companies involved in recent business combinations include such well-known names as Travelers Group, Citicorp, Bank of America, NationsBank, AT&T, SBC Communications, Ameritech, GTE, Bell Atlantic, Chrysler Corporation, Daimler-Benz, British Petroleum, Amoco, Chevron, Texaco, AOL, and Time Warner.

Expansion through Business Combinations

The types of business combinations found in today's business environment and the terms of the combination agreements are as diverse as the firms involved. Some knowledge of the form and the substance of various types of combinations is needed to appreciate the accounting issues that arise in dealing with business combinations.

Types of Business Combinations

Companies enter into various types of formal and informal arrangements that may have at least some of the characteristics of a business combination. Most companies tend to avoid recording informal agreements on their books because of the potential difficulty of enforcing them. In fact, some types of informal arrangements, such as those aimed at fixing prices or apportioning potential customers, are illegal. Formal agreements generally are enforceable and are more likely to be recognized on the books of the participants.

Informal Arrangements.   Informal arrangements take many different forms. A simple gentlemen's agreement may be all that is needed to establish an amiable long-term relationship in a joint business venture. In other cases, companies with complementary products or services develop implicit working relationships. For example, a building contractor might always use a particular electrical or plumbing subcontractor. Some companies form *strategic alliances* for working together on a somewhat more formal basis. For example, Washington Mutual, the country's largest thrift organization, formed a strategic alliance with SAFECO Corporation to distribute SAFECO annuities through Washington Mutual's multistate branch network, and Continental Airlines and Northwest Airlines entered a strategic agreement for route sharing. Companies that are partially dependent on each other may use interlocking directorates, in which one or more members serve on the boards of directors of both companies, as a means of providing a degree of mutual direction without taking formal steps to join together.

The informality and freedom that make informal arrangements workable also are strong factors against combining financial statements and treating the companies as if they were a single entity. Another key factor in most informal arrangements is the continuing separation of ownership and the ease with which the informal arrangements can be terminated. Without some type of combined ownership, the essentials of a business combination generally are absent.

Formal Agreements.   Formal business combinations usually are accompanied by written agreements. These agreements specify the terms of the combination, including the form of the combined company, the consideration to be exchanged, the disposition of outstanding securities, and the rights and responsibilities of the participants. Consummation of such an agreement requires recognition on the books of one or more of the companies that are a party to the combination.

In some cases, a formal agreement may be equivalent in substance to a business combination, yet different in form. For example, a company entering into an agreement to lease all the assets of another company for a period of several decades is, in effect, acquiring the other company. Similarly, an operating agreement giving one company full management authority over the operations of another company for an extended period of time may be viewed as a means of effecting a business combination. In spite of the substance of these types of agreements, they usually are not treated as business combinations from an accounting perspective.

Methods of Effecting Business Combinations

A business combination involves joining under common ownership two or more previously separate companies. Business combinations can be characterized as either friendly or unfriendly combinations. In a friendly combination, the managements of the companies involved come to agreement on the terms of the combination and recommend approval by the stockholders. Such combinations usually are effected in a single transaction involving an exchange of assets or voting shares. In an unfriendly combination, or hostile takeover, the managements of the companies involved are unable to agree on the terms of a combination, and the management of one of the companies makes a **tender offer** directly to the shareholders of the other company. A tender offer invites the shareholders of the other company to "tender," or exchange, their shares for securities or assets of the acquiring company. If sufficient shares are tendered, the acquiring company gains voting control of the other company and can install its own management by exercising its voting rights.

A business combination can be effected by one company's acquiring either the assets or the voting stock of another company.

Acquisition of Assets.   Sometimes one company acquires another company's assets through direct negotiations with its management. The agreement also may involve the acquiring company's assuming the other company's liabilities. Combinations of this sort take forms *(a)* or *(b)* in Figure 1–1. The selling company generally distributes to its stockholders the assets or securities received in the combination from the acquiring company and liquidates, leaving only the acquiring company as the surviving legal entity.

The acquiring company accounts for the combination by recording each asset acquired, each liability assumed, and the consideration given in exchange.

Acquisition of Stock.   A business combination effected through a stock acquisition does not necessarily have to involve the acquisition of all of a company's outstanding voting shares. For one company to gain control over another through stock ownership, a majority (i.e., more than 50 percent) of the outstanding voting shares usually is required. An acquisition of less than a majority of the outstanding voting shares typically is not regarded as a business combination. When a majority of the voting stock is held by a single stockholder, the remaining shares are referred to as the ***minority interest*** or ***noncontrolling interest.***

In those cases where control of another company is acquired and both companies remain in existence as separate legal entities following the business combination, the stock of the acquired company is recorded on the books of the acquiring company as an investment and subsequently is accounted for as an intercorporate investment. Alternatively, the acquired company may be liquidated and the assets and liabilities transferred to the acquiring company or a newly created company. To do so, all or substantially all of the voting stock of the acquired company must be obtained. An acquisition of stock and subsequent liquidation of the acquired company is equivalent to an acquisition of assets.

Valuation of Business Entities

All parties involved in a business combination must feel there is an opportunity to benefit before they will agree to participate. Determining whether a particular combination proposal is advantageous can be difficult. Both the value of a company's assets and its future earning potential are important in assessing the value of the company.

Value of Individual Assets and Liabilities. The value of a company's individual assets and liabilities is usually determined by appraisal. For some items, the value may be determined with relative ease, such as investments that are traded actively in the securities markets, or short-term payables. For other items the appraisal may be much more subjective, such as the value of land located in an area where there have been few recent sales. In addition, certain intangibles typically are not reported on the balance sheet. For example, the costs of developing new ideas, new products, and new production methods normally are expensed as research and development costs in the period incurred.

Current liabilities often are viewed as having fair values equal to their book values because they will be paid at face amount within a short time. Long-term liabilities, however, must be valued based on current interest rates if different from the effective rates at the issue dates of the liabilities. For example, if $100,000 of 10-year, 6 percent bonds, paying interest annually, had been issued at par three years ago, and the current market rate of interest for the same type of security is 10 percent, the value of the liability currently is computed as follows:

Present value for 7 years at 10% of principal payment of $100,000 ($100,000 × .51316)	$51,316
Present value at 10% of 7 interest payments of $6,000 ($6,000 × 4.86842)	29,211
Present value of bond	$80,527

Although accurate assessments of the value of assets and liabilities may be difficult, they form an important part of the overall determination of the value of an enterprise.

Value of Potential Earnings. In many cases, assets operated together as a group have a value that exceeds the sum of their individual values. This "going-concern value" makes it desirable to operate the assets as an ongoing entity rather than sell them individually. A company's earning power as an ongoing enterprise is of obvious importance in valuing that company.

There are different approaches to measuring the value of a company's future earnings. Sometimes companies are valued based on a multiple of their current earnings. For example, if Bargain Company reports earnings of $35,000 for the current year, the value of the company based on a multiple of 10 times current earnings is $350,000. The appropriate multiple to use is a matter of judgment and is based on factors such as the riskiness and variability of the earnings and the anticipated degree of growth.

Another method of valuing a company is to compute the present value of the anticipated future net cash flows generated by the company. This requires assessing the amount and timing of future cash flows and discounting them back to the present value at the discount rate determined to be appropriate for the type of enterprise. For example, if Bargain Company is expected to generate cash flows of $35,000 for each of the next 25 years, the present value of the firm at a discount rate of 10 percent is $317,696, computed as follows:

Annual cash flow generated	$ 35,000
Present value factor for an annuity of 25 annual payments at 10%	× 9.07704
Present value of future earnings	$ 317,696

Estimating the potential for future earnings requires numerous assumptions and estimates. Not surprisingly, the buyer and seller often have difficulty agreeing on the value of a company's expected earnings.

Valuation of Consideration Exchanged.   When one company acquires another, a value must be placed on the consideration given in the exchange. Little difficulty is encountered when cash is used in an acquisition, but valuation may be more difficult when securities are exchanged, particularly new untraded securities or securities with unusual features. For example, General Motors completed an acquisition a number of years ago using a new Series B common stock that paid dividends based on subsequent earnings of the acquired company rather than on the earnings of General Motors as a whole. Some companies have used non-interest-bearing bonds (zero coupon bonds), which have a fair value sufficiently below par value to compensate the holder for interest. Other companies have used various types of convertible securities. Unless these securities, or others that are considered equivalent, are being traded in the market, estimates must be made of their value. The approach generally followed is to use the value of some similar security with a determinable market value and adjust for the estimated value of the differences in the features of the two securities.

Accounting and Reporting Alternatives

For more than half a century, two methods of accounting for business combinations have been found in practice: *purchase* and *pooling of interests.* The central idea underlying purchase accounting for business combinations, and all through accounting, is a change of ownership. When one company purchases another business, as when it purchases any asset, ownership shifts from the seller(s) to the purchaser. The central idea of pooling of interests accounting has been continuity of ownership; that is, the owners of the combining companies become the owners of the combined company.

Thus, poolings could occur only when one company issued its common stock to acquire the assets or stock of another company.

Throughout the history of pooling of interests accounting, authoritative bodies have tried to restrict its use because of perceived shortcomings and abuses. Company managements, however, have shown a strong preference for pooling accounting in many instances and have resisted attempts to eliminate its use. Recently, the Financial Accounting Standards Board (FASB) issued Statement No. 141 (FASB 141), "Business Combinations." This standard eliminates pooling of interests as an acceptable method of accounting for business combinations initiated after June 30, 2001, and leaves purchase accounting as the only acceptable method. Even with the elimination of pooling of interests accounting as an acceptable method for future business combinations, however, so many business combinations have been treated as poolings that the effects will be found in financial statements for years to come. Accordingly, accountants will need to be knowledgeable about both methods of accounting for business combinations well into the future.

The major difference between purchase accounting and pooling of interests accounting has to do with a change in the basis of accounting. Because purchase accounting is based on a change in ownership, the basis of accounting changes for assets acquired and liabilities assumed in a business combination. Assets and liabilities acquired in a purchase-type business combination are reported subsequent to the combination based on their fair values at the date of combination. In addition, an intangible asset, goodwill, usually rises in a purchase-type business combination and is equal to the excess of the purchase price of the acquired company over the fair value of its net identifiable assets. On the other hand, pooling of interests accounting assumes a continuity of ownership and no change in the basis of accounting. Thus, assets and liabilities are reported subsequent to the business combination based on their previous book values, and no goodwill from the combination is recorded. In addition, because a continuity of ownership is assumed, the retained earnings balances of both combining companies are carried forward.

Accounting for business combinations under the two traditional methods is summarized in Figure 1–3. Note from the diagram that the choice of purchase or pooling accounting has been independent of whether the acquiring company acquired the net assets or the common stock of the other company. In general, an acquisition of net assets is associated with a statutory merger or consolidation, and an acquisition of stock is associated with the companies remaining as separate legal entities in a parent-subsidiary relationship. However, the choice of legal form has not been the major factor in determining whether purchase or pooling of interests treatment has been used in recording a business combination. The consideration given by the acquiring company in the exchange has been the key factor in determining the appropriate accounting method.

Part I—Purchase Accounting

All business combinations were treated as purchases before pooling of interests accounting was adopted as an acceptable alternative in the mid-twentieth century. Although pooling of interests accounting was very widespread through the 1960s, the issuance in 1970 of **APB Opinion No. 16,** "Business Combinations" (APB 16), significantly restricted the use of pooling. Following the issuance of **APB 16,** the number

FIGURE 1–3   Traditional Business Combination Alternatives

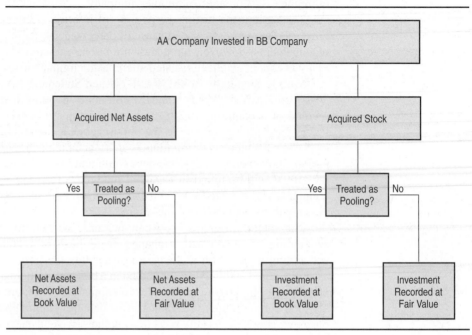

of poolings fell to only about 10 percent of business combinations. In the mid-1990s, however, economic conditions became very favorable for business acquisitions effected through stock issuances, and the number of poolings increased dramatically. In 2000, the proportion of business combinations accounted for as poolings declined in anticipation of the FASB's elimination of pooling as an acceptable method.

Nature of Purchase Treatment

When an asset is purchased, consideration is given in exchange for the ownership rights to the item acquired. Thus, purchase treatment is appropriate for business combinations in which owners of one or more of the combining companies give up their ownership rights.

Whenever an asset is purchased, the buyer records the asset at the total cost incurred in acquiring that asset. If a collection of assets is purchased for a single lump-sum purchase price, the total cost must be allocated to the individual assets acquired based on their fair values. The same principles apply to the purchase of an ongoing business as to the purchase of individual assets or groups of assets.

Determining the Purchase Price

In a business combination treated as a purchase, the purchaser considers all the costs associated with acquiring the net assets or stock of the other company as part of the total purchase price. The value of the consideration given to the owners of the acquired company normally constitutes the largest part of the total cost, but other costs also may be significant. There are three types of other costs that may be incurred in effecting a business combination: direct costs, costs of issuing securities, and indirect and general costs.

All direct costs associated with purchasing another company are treated as part of the total cost of the acquired company. For example, finders' fees often are paid to firms specializing in locating companies that meet the particular needs of the acquiring company. In addition, business combinations often result in substantial accounting, legal, and appraisal fees. Under purchase accounting, all of these costs are capitalized as part of the total purchase price of the acquired company.

Those costs incurred in issuing equity securities in connection with a purchase-type business combination should be treated as a reduction in the issue price of the securities rather than as an addition to the purchase price of the acquired company. Such costs include listing fees, audit and legal fees related to stock registration, and brokers' commissions. Costs incurred in issuing bonds payable as part of a purchase-type business combination should be accounted for as bond issue costs and amortized over the term of the bonds.

All indirect and general costs related to a business combination or to the issuance of securities in a combination should be expensed as incurred. For example, the salary costs of accountants on the staff of the acquiring company in a business combination would be expensed, even though some of their time was spent on matters related to the combination.

To illustrate the treatment of the costs incurred in a purchase-type business combination, assume that on January 1, 20X1, Point Corporation purchases all the assets and liabilities of Sharp Company in a statutory merger by issuing to Sharp 10,000 shares of $10 par common stock. The shares issued have a total market value of $600,000. Point incurs legal and appraisal fees of $40,000 in connection with the combination and stock issue costs of $25,000. The total purchase price is equal to the value of the shares issued by Point plus the additional costs incurred related to the acquisition of assets:

Fair value of stock issued	$600,000
Other acquisition costs	40,000
Total purchase price	$640,000

The stock issued by Point to effect the combination is valued at its fair value minus the issue costs:

Fair value of stock issued	$600,000
Stock issue costs	(25,000)
Recorded amount of stock	$575,000

Combination Effected through Purchase of Net Assets

When one company acquires the net assets of another in a purchase-type business combination, the acquiring company records on its books the individual assets and liabilities acquired in the combination and the consideration given in exchange. Once the

FIGURE 1–4   Sharp Company Balance Sheet Information, December 31, 20X0

Assets, Liabilities, and Equities	Book Value	Fair Value
Cash and Receivables	$ 45,000	$ 45,000
Inventory	65,000	75,000
Land	40,000	70,000
Buildings and Equipment	400,000	350,000
Accumulated Depreciation	(150,000)	
Patent		80,000
Total Assets	$400,000	$620,000
Current Liabilities	$100,000	$110,000
Common Stock ($5 par)	100,000	
Additional Paid-In Capital	50,000	
Retained Earnings	150,000	
Total Liabilities and Equities	$400,000	
Fair Value of Net Assets		$510,000

total purchase price of an acquisition has been determined, it must be assigned to the individual assets and liabilities acquired. Each identifiable asset and liability acquired is valued at its fair value at the date of combination. Any amount of the purchase price in excess of the fair value of the identifiable assets and liabilities acquired is viewed as the price paid for *goodwill.* In theory, goodwill is the excess earning power of the acquired company; in practice, goodwill represents the premium paid to acquire control.

In the Sharp Company acquisition, the total purchase price was computed to be $640,000. Assume the book values and fair values of Sharp's individual assets and liabilities given in Figure 1–4. When transferred to Point, these individual assets and liabilities must be recorded on Point's books at their fair values at the date of the business combination.

The relationship between the total purchase price paid for the net assets of Sharp, the fair value of Sharp's net assets, and the book value of Sharp's net assets is illustrated in the following diagram:

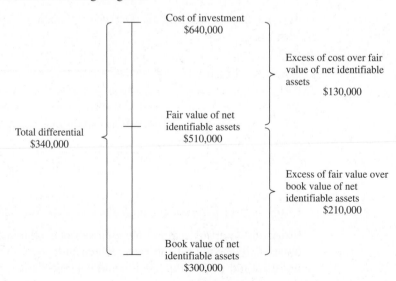

The $40,000 of other acquisition costs associated with the combination and the $25,000 of stock issue costs normally would be incurred before the time that the assets of Sharp are received by Point. To facilitate accumulating these amounts before recording the combination, they may be recorded by Point in separate temporary "suspense" accounts as incurred:

(1)	Deferred Merger Costs	40,000	
	Cash		40,000
	Record costs related to purchase of Sharp Company.		
(2)	Deferred Stock Issue Costs	25,000	
	Cash		25,000
	Record costs related to issuance of common stock.		

(*Note:* Journal entries used in the text to illustrate the various accounting procedures are numbered sequentially within individual chapters for easy reference. Each journal entry number appears only once in a chapter.)

On the date of combination, Point records the combination with the following entry:

(3)	Cash and Receivables	45,000	
	Inventory	75,000	
	Land	70,000	
	Buildings and Equipment	350,000	
	Patent	80,000	
	Goodwill	130,000	
	Current Liabilities		110,000
	Common Stock		100,000
	Additional Paid-In Capital		475,000
	Deferred Merger Costs		40,000
	Deferred Stock Issue Costs		25,000
	Record purchase of Sharp Company.		

Entry (3) records all the individual assets and liabilities of Sharp, both tangible and intangible, on Point's books at their fair values on the date of combination. The fair value of Sharp's net assets recorded is $510,000 ($620,000 − $110,000). The $130,000 difference between the total purchase price of $640,000 ($600,000 + $40,000), as computed earlier, and the fair value of Sharp's net assets is recorded as goodwill.

In recording the purchase-type business combination, Sharp's book values are not relevant to Point; only the fair values are recorded. Because a change in ownership has occurred, the basis of accounting used by the acquired company is not relevant to the purchaser. Consistent with this view, accumulated depreciation recorded by Sharp on its buildings and equipment is not relevant to Point and is not recorded. In other words, the assets and liabilities acquired are recorded by the purchaser in the same way as if there were no business combination and they were purchased as a group for a lump-sum purchase price.

The costs incurred in bringing about the merger are recorded in a separate temporary account entitled Deferred Merger Costs until the transfer of assets to Point is recorded. Because the merger costs are considered part of the total purchase price, the temporary account must be closed with entry (3) and these costs assigned, along with the remainder of the purchase price, to the net assets recorded. Similarly, the stock issue costs are recorded in a temporary account and then treated as a reduction in the proceeds received from the issuance of the stock by reducing the amount of additional paid-in capital recorded. Thus, the stock issued is recorded at its $600,000 fair value less the $25,000 of issue costs, with the $100,000 par value recorded in the common stock account and the remaining $475,000 recorded as additional paid-in capital.

Temporary accounts normally are used to accumulate the merger and stock issue costs because numerous individual costs often are incurred at different times before a business combination. Merger costs incurred after a combination is recorded may be debited directly to goodwill, while stock issue costs incurred subsequently are charged against additional paid-in capital.

Entries Recorded by Acquired Company.   On the date of the combination, Sharp records the following entry to recognize receipt of the Point shares and the transfer of all individual assets and liabilities to Point:

(4)	Investment in Point Stock	600,000	
	Current Liabilities	100,000	
	Accumulated Depreciation	150,000	
	Cash and Receivables		45,000
	Inventory		65,000
	Land		40,000
	Buildings and Equipment		400,000
	Gain on Sale of Net Assets		300,000
	Record transfer of assets to Point Corporation.		

The fair value of Point Corporation shares is recognized by Sharp at the time of the exchange, and a gain of $300,000 is recorded. The distribution of Point shares and the liquidation of Sharp are recorded on Sharp's books with the following entry:

(5)	Common Stock	100,000	
	Additional Paid-In Capital	50,000	
	Retained Earnings	150,000	
	Gain on Sale of Net Assets	300,000	
	Investment in Point Stock		600,000
	Record distribution of Point Corporation stock.		

Recording Goodwill.   Goodwill is viewed in accounting as the combination of all those factors that permit a company to earn above-average profits. As with any asset, goodwill is valued based on its original cost to the purchaser, where objectively determinable. Because expenditures for "self-developed" goodwill often are not distinguishable from current operating costs, such expenditures are required to be expensed as incurred. When goodwill is purchased in connection with a business combination, however, the amount of the expenditure is viewed as objectively determinable and is capitalized. In a purchase-type business combination, the cost of goodwill purchased is measured as the excess of the total purchase price over the fair value of the net identifiable assets acquired. The goodwill recorded when Point purchases Sharp Company is valued at $130,000, the difference between the total purchase price of $640,000 and the $510,000 fair value of Sharp's net identifiable assets.

Once goodwill resulting from a business combination has been recorded, the required procedure for the past several decades has been to amortize that goodwill over the time to be benefitted, not to exceed 40 years. For many business combinations, this amortization has had a significantly negative effect on earnings of the combined company subsequent to the combination. Recently, however, the FASB prohibited the amortization of goodwill with the issuance of FASB Statement No. 142, "Goodwill and Other Intangible Assets." Rather than amortizing goodwill, the FASB now requires companies to evaluate goodwill for impairment of value and to write off an appropriate amount of the asset when the evidence indicates it has been impaired (but not otherwise).

Negative Goodwill.   Sometimes the purchase price of an acquired company is less than the fair value of the net identifiable assets acquired. This difference often is referred to as *negative goodwill.*

The existence of negative goodwill might be viewed as implying that the acquired company should be liquidated because the assets and liabilities are worth more individually than together as an ongoing enterprise. On the other hand, the view usually adopted in practice is that the acquisition represents a *bargain purchase.*

With the issuance of FASB 141, the approach to accounting for negative goodwill has changed somewhat from previous practice. Any excess of the fair value of acquired net assets over the cost of the acquired entity (negative goodwill) is to be "allocated as a pro rata reduction of the amounts that otherwise would have been assigned to all of the acquired assets except (a) financial assets other than investments accounted for by the equity method, (b) assets to be disposed of by sale, (c) deferred tax assets, (d) prepaid assets relating to pension or other postretirement benefit plans, and (e) any other current assets."[1] Any amount remaining after reducing these acquired assets to zero would be recognized as an extraordinary gain.

To illustrate the treatment of negative goodwill, assume that Point Corporation purchases all the assets and liabilities of Sharp Company at a total cost of $460,000 rather than the $640,000 assumed previously. In this case, the relationship between the total purchase price paid for the stock of Sharp, the fair value of Sharp's net assets, and the book value of Sharp's net assets is illustrated in the following diagram:

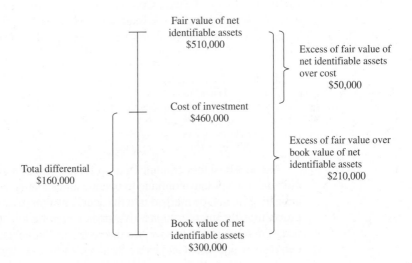

The fair values of Sharp's assets and liabilities total $510,000. The $510,000 total fair value of the net identifiable assets acquired exceeds the $460,000 purchase price by $50,000. This $50,000 of negative goodwill is apportioned as follows:

---

[1]*Financial Accounting Standards Board Statement No. 141,* "Business Combinations," June 2001, para. 44.

Item	Book Value	Fair Value	Reduction	Amount Recorded
Cash and Receivables	$ 45,000	$ 45,000		$ 45,000
Inventory	65,000	75,000		75,000
Land	40,000	70,000	70/500 × $50,000 = $ 7,000	63,000
Buildings and Equipment (net)	250,000	350,000	350/500 × 50,000 = 35,000	315,000
Patent		80,000	80/500 × 50,000 = 8,000	72,000
Total Identifiable Assets	$400,000	$620,000	$50,000	$570,000
Current Liabilities	100,000	110,000		110,000
Net Identifiable Assets	$300,000	$510,000		$460,000

Combination Effected through Purchase of Stock

Many business combinations are effected by purchasing the voting stock of another company rather than by acquiring its net assets. In such a situation, the acquired company continues to exist, and the purchasing company records an investment in the common stock of the acquired company rather than the individual assets and liabilities. As with the purchase of the assets and liabilities, the cost of the investment is based on the total value of the consideration given in purchasing the shares, together with any additional costs incurred in bringing about the combination. For example, if Point Corporation *(a)* exchanges 10,000 shares of its stock with a total market value of $600,000 for all the shares of Sharp Company in a purchase transaction and *(b)* incurs merger costs of $40,000 and stock issue costs of $25,000, previously recorded in deferred charge accounts, the following entry is recorded by Point upon receipt of the Sharp stock:

(6) Investment in Sharp Stock	640,000	
Common Stock		100,000
Additional Paid-In Capital		475,000
Deferred Merger Costs		40,000
Deferred Stock Issue Costs		25,000
Record purchase of Sharp Company stock.		

When a business combination is effected through an acquisition of stock, the acquired company may continue to operate as a separate company or it may lose its separate identity and be merged into the acquiring company. The accounting and reporting procedures for intercorporate investments in common stock where the acquired company continues in existence are discussed in the next nine chapters. If the acquired company is liquidated and its assets and liabilities are transferred to the acquiring company, the dollar amounts recorded would be identical to those in entry (3).

Financial Reporting Subsequent to a Purchase

Financial statements prepared subsequent to a purchase-type business combination reflect the combined entity only from the date of combination. When a combination occurs during a fiscal period, income earned by the acquired company prior to the combination is not reported in the income statement of the combined enterprise. If the combined company presents comparative financial statements that include statements for periods before the combination, those statements include only the activities and financial position of the acquiring company and not those of the acquired company.

To illustrate financial reporting subsequent to a purchase-type business combination, assume the following information for Point Corporation and Sharp Company:

	20X0	20X1
Point Corporation:		
Separate Income (excluding any income from Sharp)	$300,000	$300,000
Shares Outstanding, December 31	30,000	40,000
Sharp Company:		
Net Income	$ 60,000	$ 60,000

Point Corporation acquires all the stock of Sharp Company at book value on January 1, 20X1, in a purchase-type business combination by issuing 10,000 shares of common stock. Subsequently, Point Corporation presents comparative financial statements for the years 20X0 and 20X1. The net income and earnings per share that Point presents in its comparative financial statements for the two years are as follows:

20X0:	
Net Income	$300,000
Earnings per Share ($300,000/30,000 shares)	$ 10.00
20X1:	
Net Income ($300,000 + $60,000)	$360,000
Earnings per Share ($360,000/40,000 shares)	$ 9.00

If Point Corporation had purchased Sharp Company in the middle of 20X1 instead of at the beginning, Point would include only Sharp's earnings subsequent to acquisition in its 20X1 income statement. If Sharp earned $25,000 in 20X1 before acquisition by Point and $35,000 after the combination, Point would report total net income for 20X1 of $335,000 ($300,000 + $35,000).

If a business combination results in goodwill, the FASB now requires that the goodwill be reported as a separate line item in the balance sheet and any goodwill impairment loss be reported as a separate line item in the operating section of the income statement.

Disclosure Requirements

A number of disclosures are required following a business combination to provide financial statement readers with information about the combination and the expected effects of the combination on operating results. **APB 16** requires the following disclosures in the notes to the financial statements when purchase treatment is used:[2]

1. The name and a brief description of the acquired company.
2. A statement that purchase treatment has been used.

---

[2]*Accounting Principles Board Opinion No. 16,* "Business Combinations," August 1970, par. 95.

3. Information on the total cost incurred in making the purchase. When an exchange of stock occurs, the number of shares issued and remaining to be issued should be disclosed, along with the dollar amount assigned to the shares.
4. The portion of the year for which operating results of the acquired company have been included.
5. Information on any contingent payments or commitments and their accounting treatment.

Pro forma financial statement data also should be presented to provide statement readers with a better understanding of the potential operating impact of the business combination. At a minimum, supplemental information should be provided to show:

1. Operating results as if the acquisition had been made at the start of the period.
2. When comparative financial statements are presented, operating results for the preceding period as if the acquisition had occurred at the start of that period.

In addition to the requirements of **APB 16,** the FASB now requires disclosures that include the primary reason for a business combination and a description of the factors leading to positive or negative goodwill. In the period in which significant goodwill is acquired in a business combination, the amount of the goodwill and the amount that is deductible for tax purposes must be disclosed. Subsequently, the amount of any goodwill impairment loss must be disclosed, along with a description of the circumstances leading to the loss.

Part II—Pooling of Interests Accounting

Pooling of interests accounting is the other primary method that has been used to account for business combinations. Against the wishes of the companies involved, pooling of interests accounting was first applied to public utilities by regulatory bodies more than half a century ago. Owners of companies subject to rate regulation typically are permitted to earn a fair return on their asset base. If assets are written up, the owners are allowed to earn a higher dollar return because of the higher asset base. The term *pooling* first was used in 1943 in describing the required carryforward of book values for rate-making purposes when two companies had merged, even though the managements of the companies wanted to restate the assets of the acquired company. Not long thereafter, the first nonregulated companies voluntarily opted to use pooling treatment. Before that time, all business combinations were considered to be purchases.

Excluding rate-making situations, the managements of companies involved in business combinations have often preferred accounting for the combinations as poolings because of the impact on the financial statements subsequent to the combination. Purchase accounting requires the purchased assets and liabilities to be valued at their fair values. In many cases, the fair values of an acquired company's assets are higher than the previous book values, and if the assets have limited lives, these higher fair values must be amortized. Under pooling of interests accounting, the book values of both the acquiring company and the acquired company are carried forward. Therefore, income often is higher subsequent to the combination under pooling accounting than under purchase accounting because of lower depreciation and amortization charges.

Further, the higher asset values recorded under purchase accounting negatively impact ratios such as return on investment because of the lower income amount in the numerator and the higher asset amount in the denominator. In addition, the carryforward of the acquired company's retained earnings under pooling accounting may give management more flexibility with respect to dividends subsequent to the combination.

Pooling procedures may lead to "instant earnings" when combinations are consummated late in the fiscal year, because the earnings of the pooled companies are combined for the entire year. Additional earnings also could be created if assets acquired in the pooling are sold at amounts considerably greater than their book values. For example, a piece of land with a book value of $40,000 and a fair value of $60,000 might be acquired in a business combination and immediately sold for $60,000. If the combination is treated as a pooling, the combined company recognizes a $20,000 gain ($60,000 − $40,000) on the sale; if the combination is treated as a purchase, no gain ($60,000 − $60,000) is recognized at the time of sale.

Attempts to restrict the use of pooling of interests accounting were notably unsuccessful before the issuance of **APB 16** in 1970. Thus, before **APB 16** became effective, companies had rather broad latitude in recording business combinations, and there were many abuses of pooling of interests accounting. For example, some combinations were recorded as "part purchase, part pooling" combinations because they seemed to involve elements of both. Others were treated originally as purchases and later changed to "retroactive poolings" as the standards eroded.

APB 16 set very stringent requirements for the use of pooling of interests accounting. Many of the rules established in **APB 16** are quite complex and exist primarily to eliminate the previous abuses of pooling accounting. More recently, the FASB has studied the issues surrounding accounting for business combinations for quite some time but has had difficulty agreeing on new standards that would be acceptable to all parties involved. The FASB has now decided to eliminate pooling of interests as an acceptable alternative for accounting for business combinations and to require all business combinations be treated as purchases. The FASB argued that using only purchase accounting provides more complete and useful information about business combinations and results in greater uniformity of accounting for similar transactions. In addition, the elimination of pooling brings U.S. accounting standards closer to those standards used internationally. Few other countries permit pooling, and then usually only in very specific situations. Only the future will tell if the FASB is successful in permanently eliminating pooling.

Regardless of whether pooling is eliminated or revived as a method of accounting for business combinations, the effects of past poolings will affect financial statements for many years in the future. Thus, an examination of pooling of interests accounting is warranted.

Nature of Pooling Treatment

The notion of continuity of ownership is central to the pooling of interests concept. Therefore, an exchange of voting common stock is essential for a combination to be viewed as a pooling of interests. Through the exchange of stock, the shareholder groups of two previously separate companies are joined together, in effect, pooling their interests to share jointly the rewards and risks of ownership from that point forward. Pooling is viewed as different from purchase accounting in that no new assets are invested, nor do the original owners withdraw assets or give up their ownership rights when participating in the exchange. A pooling is simply a coming together of previously separate owners. Following this line of thought, there is no purchase or sale of ownership, and there are no grounds for establishing a new basis of accountability.

The requirements of **APB 16** for use of pooling accounting aim at ensuring a continuity of ownership. In particular, pooling of interests accounting has been acceptable only in combinations where one company exchanged its voting common stock for at least 90 percent of the other company's common stock or for all its net assets. Numerous other conditions, presented later in the chapter, also were established in **APB 16** for pooling of interests accounting.

Distinguishing Characteristics of Pooling

Pooling of interests accounting treats a business combination as a "nonevent" in that the combining companies are viewed as if they had always been together. The unique attributes of pooling of interests accounting are the carryforward of assets and liabilities at book value and the carryforward of retained earnings. This contrasts with purchase accounting, in which the acquired assets and liabilities are recorded at their fair values and retained earnings of the acquired company is not recorded. Further, under pooling of interests accounting, no goodwill is recorded as arising from the combination, while under purchase accounting goodwill often is recorded.

Consistent with the view that the combining companies have always been together, comparative financial statements for periods before a combination that are included in financial reports issued subsequent to the combination are retroactively restated as if the companies had always been combined. All costs associated with the combination or with issuing the stock used in the combination are expensed as incurred; none of the costs of bringing about the combination are capitalized, nor are the stock issue costs deducted from the recorded amount of the stock.

Combination Effected through Acquisition of Net Assets

When one company is merged into another in a pooling of interests, the assets and liabilities of that company are recorded on the books of the continuing company at their book values. The stock issued is recorded at the book value of the net assets received in exchange. Thus, the stockholders' equity accounts of the continuing company are increased so that the total stockholders' equity of the combined company after the combination is equal to the sum of the stockholders' equity accounts of the combining companies before the combination.

Pooling of interests accounting can be illustrated with the merger of Point Corporation and Sharp Company. Balance sheet data as of December 31, 20X0, are presented for the two companies in Figure 1–5. Note that, while fair values may be relevant for determining the amount of stock to be exchanged in the combination, only book values are needed for recording the combination.

Assume that on January 1, 20X1, in a statutory merger accounted for as a pooling of interests, Point Corporation issues 10,000 shares of its $10 par common stock in exchange for all the assets and liabilities of Sharp Company. Sharp distributes the shares to its shareholders and retires its own stock. The entry to record the combination on Point's books is as follows:

FIGURE 1–5　　**Point Corporation and Sharp Company Balance Sheets, December 31, 20X0**

	Book Values	
Assets, Liabilities, and Equities	Point	Sharp
Cash and Receivables	$ 75,000	$ 45,000
Inventory	125,000	65,000
Land	100,000	40,000
Buildings and Equipment	600,000	400,000
Accumulated Depreciation	(200,000)	(150,000)
Total Assets	$700,000	$400,000
Current Liabilities	$150,000	$100,000
Common Stock		
Point Corporation ($10 par)	300,000	
Sharp Company ($5 par)		100,000
Additional Paid-In Capital	30,000	50,000
Retained Earnings	220,000	150,000
Total Liabilities and Equities	$700,000	$400,000

(7)	Cash and Receivables	45,000	
	Inventory	65,000	
	Land	40,000	
	Buildings and Equipment	400,000	
	Accumulated Depreciation		150,000
	Current Liabilities		100,000
	Common Stock (Point Corporation)		100,000
	Additional Paid-In Capital		50,000
	Retained Earnings		150,000
	Record pooling-type merger with Sharp.		

Point simply records the assets, liabilities, and contra accounts of Sharp on its books using the book values carried by Sharp. Similarly, the stockholders' equity amounts of Sharp are carried over to Point's books. In this example, the total par value of Point's stock issued for Sharp's assets and liabilities is $100,000 and is the same as the total par value of Sharp's stock. Point's common stock issued in the combination replaces that of Sharp, and the other stockholders' equity accounts of Sharp are brought on to Point's books.

The total stockholders' equity of the combined company is always equal to the sum of the stockholders' equity accounts of the combining companies in a pooling of interests. In this example, the individual stockholders' equity accounts of the combined company also are equal to the sums of the individual stockholders' equity accounts of the combining companies. This occurs only because the total par value of the stock issued in the combination by Point is equal to the total par value of Sharp's stock that is retired. If the total par values were different, total stockholders' equity would not change but the totals of individual stockholders' equity items would.

Note that any merger costs or stock issue costs incurred in effecting the combination would have been expensed as incurred.

Entries Recorded by Acquired Company.   On the date of combination, Sharp records the following entry to recognize receipt of the Point shares and the transfer of all individual assets and liabilities to Point:

(8)	Investment in Point Stock	300,000	
	Current Liabilities	100,000	
	Accumulated Depreciation	150,000	
	Cash and Receivables		45,000
	Inventory		65,000
	Land		40,000
	Buildings and Equipment		400,000
	Record transfer of assets to Point Corporation.		

The amount recorded by Sharp as its investment in Point Corporation shares is based on the book value of Sharp's net assets in the pooling case. The distribution of Point shares and the liquidation of Sharp are recorded on Sharp's books with the following entry:

(9)	Common Stock	100,000	
	Additional Paid-In Capital	50,000	
	Retained Earnings	150,000	
	Investment in Point Stock		300,000
	Record distribution of Point Corporation stock.		

Differences in Total Par Value

In most poolings, the total par value of the shares issued in the combination is different from the total par value of the stock acquired. This occurs because the number of shares issued usually is different from the number of shares acquired and the per-share par values often are different.

    If the total par value of the stock issued in the combination is different from the total par value of the stock acquired, the combined stockholders' equity amounts cannot be determined by a simple summing of the individual stockholders' equity accounts of the combining companies. In determining the composition of the stockholders' equity section of the combined entity, the total par value of shares issued by the acquiring company must be determined first. Then, the combined additional paid-in capital must be reduced by any excess of the total par value of the shares issued in the combination over the par value of the shares acquired or increased by the excess of the total par value of the shares acquired over the par value of the shares issued. To illustrate, the following bar graph can be constructed by summing the individual stockholders' equity accounts of the combining companies:

Combined Stockholders' Equity

Premium records the combination with the following journal entry:

(16)	Investment in Standard Stock	240,000	
	Common Stock		40,000
	Additional Paid-In Capital		200,000
	Record purchase of Standard stock.		

The transfer of the assets and liabilities of Standard to Premium and the retirement of Standard's stock are recorded by Premium with the following entry:

(17)	Accounts Receivable	10,000	
	Inventory	55,000	
	Land	30,000	
	Buildings and Equipment	125,000	
	Goodwill	60,000	
	Accounts Payable		40,000
	Investment in Standard Stock		240,000
	Record assets acquired and liabilities assumed in purchase of Standard Company.		

The $60,000 difference between the $240,000 purchase price and the $180,000 fair value of the net identifiable assets received is recorded as goodwill. The resulting balance sheet for the combined entity is presented in Figure 1–8. As is always true in a purchase-type business combination, the retained earnings of the combined company is the retained earnings of the acquiring company; the retained earnings of the acquired company is not carried over to the acquiring company.

Pooling of Interests Accounting

When pooling of interests accounting is used to record the combination, the book values of the assets and liabilities and the retained earnings of the combining companies are carried over to the combined company. Premium records the pooling-type business combination with the following entry:

(18)	Investment in Standard Stock	150,000	
	Common Stock		40,000
	Additional Paid-In Capital		20,000
	Retained Earnings		90,000
	Record pooling-type combination with Standard.		

The resulting $10,000 reduction in total par value of the shares outstanding is added to additional paid-in capital, and the full balance of Standard's retained earnings is carried over to Premium's books.

Premium records the transfer of the individual assets and liabilities from Standard with the following entry:

(19)	Accounts Receivable	10,000	
	Inventory	35,000	
	Land	45,000	
	Buildings and Equipment	120,000	
	Accumulated Depreciation		20,000
	Accounts Payable		40,000
	Investment in Standard Stock		150,000
	Record assets acquired and liabilities assumed in pooling-type combination.		

The resulting balance sheet, shown in Figure 1–8, reflects the carryforward of accumulated depreciation and retained earnings from Standard, along with the other book values of Standard.

FIGURE 1–8   Balance Sheets for Premium Corporation and Standard Company Combined, January 1, 20X2

Assets, Liabilities, and Equities	Purchase	Pooling
Accounts Receivable	$110,000	$110,000
Inventory	255,000	235,000
Land	80,000	95,000
Buildings and Equipment	575,000	570,000
Accumulated Depreciation	(150,000)	(170,000)
Goodwill	60,000	
Total Assets	$930,000	$840,000
Accounts Payable	$ 90,000	$ 90,000
Common Stock ($10 par)	240,000	240,000
Additional Paid-In Capital	230,000	50,000
Retained Earnings	370,000	460,000
Total Liabilities and Equities	$930,000	$840,000

The stockholders' equity section of the combined balance sheet in Figure 1–8 is based on Premium Corporation's issuing 4,000 shares of its $10 par stock to acquire 100 percent of Standard's stock. If 7,300 shares are issued by Premium instead, the $23,000 increase ($73,000 − $50,000) in the par value of shares outstanding precludes the carryforward of Standard's $10,000 of additional paid-in capital and causes a reduction of $13,000 in the additional paid-in capital already carried on the books of Premium. The entry recorded by Premium in this case is:

(20)	Investment in Standard Stock	150,000	
	Additional Paid-In Capital	13,000	
	Common Stock		73,000
	Retained Earnings		90,000
	Record pooling-type combination with Standard.		

If Premium issues 11,000 shares in the combination, the increase in the total par value of the shares outstanding is $60,000 ($110,000 – $50,000). In this case, no additional paid-in capital is carried over from Standard, all Premium's additional paid-in capital is eliminated, and combined retained earnings must be reduced by $20,000. Therefore, only $70,000 ($90,000 – $20,000) of Standard's retained earnings is carried over to Premium's books. The combination is recorded by the following entry on Premium's books:

(21)	Investment in Standard Stock	150,000	
	Additional Paid-In Capital	30,000	
	Common Stock		110,000
	Retained Earnings		70,000
	Record pooling-type combination with Standard.		

Earnings Subsequent to Combination

Income of the combined company subsequent to the combination generally is affected by the method used to account for the combination. To illustrate, assume that the combined company reports net income of $200,000 for 20X2 after accounting for the January 1 combination of Premium and Standard as a pooling of interests. If the combination had been treated as a purchase, several adjustments to income would be needed. If all Standard's inventory at the date of combination is sold in 20X2, the additional cost of that inventory to Premium would have to be reflected in cost of goods sold. If Standard's buildings and equipment had a five-year remaining life from the date of combination, the $25,000 additional cost to Premium would have to be amortized over the remaining life. In addition, assume that based on management's evaluation, a $6,000 goodwill impairment loss must be recognized. Thus, the combined company's income for 20X2 would be $31,000 less under purchase treatment than under pooling, as follows:

Income following pooling of interests	$200,000
Goodwill impairment loss	(6,000)
Additional depreciation ($25,000/5)	(5,000)
Excess over book value of inventory	(20,000)
Income following purchase	$169,000

Questions—Part I

Q1–1 Describe each of the three legal forms that a business combination might take.

Q1–2 What does continuity of ownership mean, and how is it important in business combinations?

Q1–3 How does goodwill arise in a business combination? Under what conditions is it recorded?

Q1–4 When a purchase-type business combination occurs after the beginning of the year, the income earned by the acquired company between the beginning of the year and the date of combination is excluded from the net income reported by the combined company for the year. Why?

Q1–5 What is the maximum balance in retained earnings that can be reported by the combined entity following a business combination under purchase treatment?

Q1–6 What factors may make it attractive for a company to complete a business combination by acquiring the stock of another company and operating it as a subsidiary?

Q1–7 How does negative goodwill arise in a business combination? How is it normally treated for financial reporting purposes?

Q1–8 How is the amount of additional paid-in capital determined when purchase treatment is used in recording a business combination?

Q1–9 How is a business combination likely to be recorded if convertible preferred stock is used to acquire the voting common shares of another company? Why?

Q1–10 How are prior-period financial statement data of the acquired company reported by the combined company following a business combination recorded as a purchase? Why?

Q1–11 Which of the costs incurred in completing a business combination can be capitalized under purchase treatment?

Q1–12 Which of the costs incurred in completing a business combination should be treated as a reduction of additional paid-in capital under purchase treatment?

Questions—Part II

Q1–13 What are the major differences between purchase and pooling of interests treatment in recording a business combination?

Q1–14   Why is it considered appropriate to carry forward retained earnings of all the combining companies in a pooling of interests?

Q1–15   When a business combination occurs after the beginning of the year, how is the income earned by the acquired company between the beginning of the year and the date of combination reported by the combined company for the year when the combination is accounted for as a pooling? Why?

Q1–16   What is the maximum balance in retained earnings that can be reported by the combined entity following a business combination under pooling of interests treatment?

Q1–17   How is the amount of additional paid-in capital determined when pooling of interests treatment is used in recording a business combination?

Q1–18   How is prior-period financial statement data of the acquired company reported by the combined company following a business combination recorded as a pooling of interests?

Q1–19   Which of the costs incurred in completing a business combination can be capitalized under pooling of interests treatment?

Q1–20   Which of the costs incurred in completing a business combination should be treated as a reduction of additional paid-in capital under pooling of interests treatment?

Cases

C1–1   **Reporting Alternatives and International Harmonization**

Accounting procedures for business combinations differ among countries. In most countries, pooling of interests accounting is unacceptable, while accounting standards in some countries permit goodwill to be written off directly against stockholders' equity at the time of a business combination treated as a purchase.

Required

a. Over the years, many U.S. companies complained they were at a disadvantage when competing against foreign companies in purchasing other business enterprises because, unlike U.S. companies, most foreign companies did not need to capitalize goodwill. Why were U.S. companies opposed to capitalizing goodwill?

b. What arguments can be made to support the elimination of pooling of interests accounting and requiring all business combinations to be treated as purchases?

c. Should U.S. companies care about accounting standards other than those that are generally accepted in the United States? Explain.

C1–2   **Goodwill and the Effects of Purchase versus Pooling of Interests Treatment**

Midvale Corporation plans to acquire ownership of Bostwick Corporation in an exchange of common shares to take place in the middle of the current year. The president of Midvale Corporation is attempting to anticipate the financial statement impact of acquiring Bostwick Corporation and is particularly interested in the goodwill that might arise in the business combination.

a. From an accounting perspective, explain the nature of goodwill. Is goodwill an asset? Explain. Under what conditions is goodwill recorded and at what amount?

b. After it is recorded, how is goodwill treated?

c. Other than goodwill, what dollar amounts will be reported differently in the financial statements of the combined company prepared subsequent to the combination if the combination is recorded as a pooling of interests rather than a purchase?

d. Which method of accounting for the business combination is likely to result in higher reported net income for the combined company in the year of the combination? Why?

C1–3   **Differences between Purchase and Pooling of Interests [AICPA Adapted]**

Flavin Company entered into a business combination with Stevens Company in the middle of the year. The combination was accounted for as a pooling of interests. Both companies use the same methods of accounting.

Flavin Company acquired all the assets and liabilities of Rubin Company in the middle of the year. This combination was accounted for as a purchase and resulted in goodwill. Both companies use the same methods of accounting.

Flavin Company effected both combinations through the issuance of equity securities, and registration fees for the equity securities involved in the combinations were incurred. There were no intercompany transactions before or after the combinations.

Required

a. (1) In the business combination accounted for as a pooling of interests, how should the recorded assets and liabilities of the separate companies be accounted for? What is the rationale for accounting for a business combination as a pooling of interests?

   (2) In the business combination accounted for as a pooling of interests, how should the registration fees and direct costs related to effecting the business combination be accounted for?

   (3) In the business combination accounted for as a pooling of interests, how should the results of operations for the year in which the business combination occurred be reported?

b. (1) In the business combination accounted for as a purchase, how should the assets acquired and liabilities assumed be recorded? What is the rationale for accounting for a business combination as a purchase?

   (2) In the business combination accounted for as a purchase, how should the registration fees and direct costs related to effecting the business combination be accounted for?

   (3) In the business combination accounted for as a purchase, how should the results of operations of the acquired company for the year in which the business combination occurred be reported?

C1–4 Business Combinations

A merger boom comparable to those of the 1960s and mid-1980s occurred in the 1990s and into the new century. The merger activity of the 1960s was associated with increasing stock prices and heavy use of pooling of interests accounting. The mid-1980s activity was associated with a number of leveraged buyouts and acquisitions involving junk bonds. Merger activity in the early 1990s, on the other hand, appeared to involve primarily purchases with cash and standard debt instruments. By the mid-1990s, however, many business combinations were being effected through exchanges of stock.

a. Which factors do you feel were the most prominent in encouraging business combinations in the 1990s? Which of these was the most important? Explain why.

b. If a major review of the tax laws were undertaken, would it be wise or unwise public policy to establish greater tax incentives for corporate mergers? Propose three incentives that might be used.

c. If the FASB were interested in encouraging more mergers, what action should it take with regard to revising or eliminating existing accounting standards? Explain.

d. Why were so many of the business combinations in the middle and late 1990s effected through exchanges of stock?

C1–5 Reasons for Business Combinations

Particular factors within individual industries often lead to an unusual number of business combinations occurring within those industries over a relatively short period of time. Three industries that have been notable in that regard over the past few years are defense, banking and financial services, and telecommunications.

Required

a. For one of these three industries, select a major company in that industry that has been involved in one or more business combinations during the past five years. Describe the business combination or combinations and discuss the parties involved, the form of the combination or combinations, the consideration exchanged, the accounting method or methods employed, the reasons for the combination or combinations, and any general business strategy that is evident.

b. In what ways are general economic conditions or industry factors relevant to the company's business combination activities?

c. Do you anticipate that the company will be involved in additional business combinations in the near future? Explain.

C1–6   Planning for Acquisitions: Cisco Systems and Quaker Oats

Companies often have different reasons for and approaches to expansion through business combinations. Cisco Systems is a company that is thought to acquire other companies to fill identifiable niches, with the specific role of each acquisition planned in advance. On the other hand, the Quaker Oats Company has not always been viewed in the same way. For example, when Quaker Oats acquired Snapple in 1994, some viewed Quaker Oats as simply "purchasing earnings" rather than making a strategic acquisition. The two companies have had varying degrees of success with their acquisitions.

Required

a. Describe the nature of the business of Cisco Systems.

b. Describe the nature of the business of Quaker Oats.

c. What evidence can you find that indicates that Cisco's business acquisitions are made for a specific purpose?

d. What evidence can you find that indicates that Quaker Oats' business acquisitions are or are not always the result of well-considered strategic planning in terms of the role that each will play in the overall company?

e. How has Cisco Systems and its acquisitions fared? How successful was the acquisition of Snapple by Quaker Oats? What action did Quaker Oats ultimately take with respect to Snapple?

C1–7   Companies Built through Business Combinations: MCI WorldCom and Citigroup

Some companies grow large through internal expansion. Other companies rise to be among the largest in their industries through a series of business combinations. Two major companies that have followed the latter route are MCI WorldCom Inc. and Citigroup Inc.

Required

a. What are the primary businesses of MCI WorldCom and Citigroup?

b. Trace recent major acquisitions of both companies, and provide a brief history of how the two companies reached their current positions. What consideration (e.g., cash, stock) was used in their acquisitions? What was the apparent strategy in the growth of the two companies?

c. Who are Sanford Weill, John Reed, and Bernard Ebbers? What roles have they played in the growth of MCI WorldCom and Citigroup?

C1–8   Assignment of the Difference between Cost and Book Value

When a company purchases another company for an amount different than the book value of the acquired company's net assets, the difference must be allocated in the manner prescribed by generally accepted accounting principles. Often the treatment is relatively straightforward, but sometimes less clear-cut issues arise.

Required

a. What is the nature of the goodwill associated with Centrex Corporation's Home Building subsidiary's fiscal 1997 combination transaction with Vista Properties? How was this amount treated subsequent to the combination?

b. When one company purchases another, the other company may have research and development efforts underway, referred to as "in-process research and development." If these research and development efforts of the acquired company have value to the acquiring company, a portion of the purchase price must be assigned to them. How do Compaq Computer, Analog Devices, and Mylan Laboratories account for the cost they assign to in-process research and development when they purchase other companies? What justification can be given for this treatment?

Exercises—Part I

E1–1 **Multiple-Choice Questions on Recording Business Combinations [AICPA Adapted]**

Select the correct answer for each of the following questions.

1. Goodwill represents the excess of the cost of an acquired company over the:

   a. Sum of the fair values assigned to identifiable assets acquired less liabilities assumed.

   b. Sum of the fair values assigned to tangible assets acquired less liabilities assumed.

   c. Sum of the fair values assigned to intangible assets acquired less liabilities assumed.

   d. Book value of an acquired company.

2. In a business combination accounted for as a purchase, costs of registering equity securities to be issued by the acquiring company are a(n):

   a. Expense of the combined company for the period in which the costs were incurred.

   b. Direct addition to stockholders' equity of the combined company.

   c. Reduction of the otherwise determinable fair value of the securities.

   d. Addition to goodwill.

3. Which of the following is the appropriate basis for valuing fixed assets acquired in a business combination accounted for as a purchase carried out by exchanging cash for common stock?

   a. Historical cost.

   b. Book value.

   c. Cost plus any excess of purchase price over book value of assets acquired.

   d. Fair value.

4. In a business combination accounted for as a purchase, the appraisal value of the identifiable assets acquired exceeds the acquisition price. The excess appraisal value should be reported as a:

   a. Deferred credit.

   b. Reduction of the values assigned to current assets and a deferred credit for any unallocated portion.

   c. Pro rata reduction of the values assigned to current and noncurrent assets and a deferred credit for any unallocated portion.

   d. No answer listed is correct.

5. On June 30, 20X2, Pane Corporation exchanged 150,000 shares of its $20 par value common stock for all of Sky Corporation's common stock. At that date, the fair value of Pane's common stock issued was equal to the book value of Sky's net assets. Both corporations continued to operate as separate businesses, maintaining accounting records with years ending December 31. Information from separate company operations follows:

	Pane	Sky
Retained earnings, Dec. 31, 20X1	$3,200,000	$925,000
Net income, 6 months ended June 30, 20X2	800,000	275,000
Dividends paid, March 25, 20X2	750,000	—

If the business combination is accounted for as a purchase, what amount of retained earnings would Pane report in its June 30, 20X2, consolidated balance sheet?

  a. $5,200,000.
  b. $4,450,000.
  c. $3,525,000.
  d. $3,250,000.

6. A and B Companies have been operating separately for five years. Each company has a minimal amount of liabilities and a simple capital structure consisting solely of voting common stock. A Company, in exchange for 40 percent of its voting stock, acquires 80 percent of the common stock of B Company. This was a "tax-free" stock-for-stock (type B) exchange for tax purposes. B Company assets have a total net fair market value of $800,000 and a total net book value of $580,000. The fair market value of the A stock used in the exchange was $700,000. The goodwill on this acquisition would be:

  a. Zero.
  b. $60,000.
  c. $120,000.
  d. $236,000.

E1–2   Multiple-Choice Questions on Reported Balances [AICPA Adapted]

Select the correct answer for each of the following questions.

1. On December 31, 20X3, Saxe Corporation was merged into Poe Corporation. In the business combination, Poe issued 200,000 shares of its $10 par common stock, with a market price of $18 a share, for all of Saxe's common stock. The stockholders' equity section of each company's balance sheet immediately before the combination was:

	Poe	*Saxe*
Common Stock	$3,000,000	$1,500,000
Additional Paid-In Capital	1,300,000	150,000
Retained Earnings	2,500,000	850,000
	$6,800,000	$2,500,000

Assume the merger qualifies for treatment as a purchase. In the December 31, 20X3, consolidated balance sheet, additional paid-in capital should be reported at:

  a. $950,000.
  b. $1,300,000.
  c. $1,450,000.
  d. $2,900,000.

2. On January 1, 20X1, Rolan Corporation issued 10,000 shares of common stock in exchange for all Sandin Corporation's outstanding stock. Condensed balance sheets of Rolan and Sandin immediately before the combination are as follows:

	Rolan	*Sandin*
Total Assets	$1,000,000	$500,000
Liabilities	$ 300,000	$150,000
Common Stock ($10 par)	200,000	100,000
Retained Earnings	500,000	250,000
Total Liabilities and Equities	$1,000,000	$500,000

Rolan's common stock had a market price of $60 per share on January 1, 20X1. The market price of Sandin's stock was not readily ascertainable.

Assuming that the combination of Rolan and Sandin qualifies as a purchase, Rolan's investment in Sandin's stock will be stated in Rolan's balance sheet immediately after the combination in the amount of:

a. $100,000.

b. $350,000.

c. $500,000.

d. $600,000.

3. On February 15, 20X1, Reed Corporation paid $1,500,000 for all the issued and outstanding common stock of Cord Inc. in a transaction properly accounted for as a purchase. The book values and fair values of Cord's assets and liabilities on February 15, 20X1, were as follows:

	Book Value	Fair Value
Cash	$ 160,000	$ 160,000
Receivables	180,000	180,000
Inventory	290,000	270,000
Property, Plant, and Equipment	870,000	960,000
Liabilities	(350,000)	(350,000)
Net Worth	$1,150,000	$1,220,000

What is the amount of goodwill resulting from the business combination?

a. $0.

b. $70,000.

c. $280,000.

d. $350,000.

4. On April 1, 20X2, the Jack Company paid $800,000 for all the issued and outstanding common stock of Ann Corporation in a transaction properly accounted for as a purchase. The recorded assets and liabilities of Ann Corporation on April 1, 20X2, were as follows:

Cash	$ 80,000
Inventory	240,000
Property and Equipment (net of accumulated depreciation of $320,000)	480,000
Liabilities	(180,000)

On April 1, 20X2, it was determined that the inventory of Ann had a fair value of $190,000 and that the property and equipment had a fair value of $560,000. What is the amount of goodwill resulting from the business combination?

a. $0.

b. $50,000.

c. $150,000.

d. $180,000.

5. The Action Corporation issued nonvoting preferred stock with a fair market value of $4,000,000 in exchange for all the outstanding common stock of Master Corporation. On the date of the exchange, Master had tangible net assets with a book value of $2,000,000 and a fair value of

$2,500,000. In addition, Action issued preferred stock valued at $400,000 to an individual as a finder's fee in arranging the transaction. As a result of this transaction, Action should record an increase in net assets of:

    a. $2,000,000.

    b. $2,500,000.

    c. $2,900,000.

    d. $4,400,000.

E1–3   Stock Acquisition

McDermott Corporation has been in the midst of a major expansion program. Much of its growth had been internal, but in 20X1 McDermott decided to continue its expansion through the acquisition of other companies. The first company acquired was Tippy Inc., a small manufacturer of inertial guidance systems for aircraft and missiles. On June 10, 20X1, McDermott issued 17,000 shares of its $25 par common stock for all 40,000 of Tippy's $10 par common shares. At the date of combination, Tippy reported additional paid-in capital of $100,000 and retained earnings of $350,000. McDermott's stock was selling for $58 per share immediately prior to the combination. Subsequent to the combination, Tippy operated as a subsidiary of McDermott.

Required

Present the journal entry or entries that McDermott would make to record the business combination with Tippy as a purchase.

E1–4   Balances Reported under Purchase Treatment

Elm Corporation and Maple Company have announced terms of an exchange agreement under which Elm will issue 8,000 shares of its $10 par value common stock to acquire all the assets of Maple Company. Elm shares currently are trading at $50, and Maple $5 par value shares are trading at $18 each. Historical cost and fair value balance sheet data on January 1, 20X2, are as follows:

	Elm Corporation		Maple Company	
Balance Sheet Item	*Book Value*	*Fair Value*	*Book Value*	*Fair Value*
Cash and Receivables	$150,000	$150,000	$ 40,000	$ 40,000
Land	100,000	170,000	50,000	85,000
Buildings and Equipment (net)	300,000	400,000	160,000	230,000
Total Assets	$550,000	$720,000	$250,000	$355,000
Common Stock	$200,000		$100,000	
Additional Paid-In Capital	20,000		10,000	
Retained Earnings	330,000		140,000	
Total Equities	$550,000		$250,000	

Required

What will be the amount reported immediately following the business combination for each of the following items in the combined company's balance sheet under purchase treatment?

    a. Common Stock.

    b. Cash and Receivables.

    c. Land.

    d. Buildings and Equipment (net).

    e. Goodwill.

    f. Additional Paid-In Capital.

    g. Retained Earnings.

E1–5   Goodwill Recognition

Spur Corporation reported the following balance sheet amounts on December 31, 20X1:

Balance Sheet Item	Historical Cost	Fair Value
Cash and Receivables	$ 50,000	$ 40,000
Inventory	100,000	150,000
Land	40,000	30,000
Plant and Equipment	400,000	350,000
Less: Accumulated Depreciation	(150,000)	
Patent		130,000
Total Assets	$440,000	$700,000
Accounts Payable	$ 80,000	$ 85,000
Common Stock	200,000	
Additional Paid-In Capital	20,000	
Retained Earnings	140,000	
Total Liabilities and Equities	$440,000	

Required

Blanket Company purchases the assets and liabilities of Spur Corporation for $670,000 cash on December 31, 20X1. Give the entry made by Blanket Company to record the purchase.

E1–6   Negative Goodwill

Musial Corporation used debentures with a par value of $580,000 to acquire 100 percent of the net assets of Sorden Company on January 1, 20X2. On that date, the fair value of the bonds issued by Musial Corporation was $564,000, and the following balance sheet data were reported by Sorden Company:

Balance Sheet Item	Historical Cost	Fair Value
Cash and Receivables	$ 55,000	$ 50,000
Inventory	105,000	200,000
Land	60,000	100,000
Plant and Equipment	400,000	300,000
Less: Accumulated Depreciation	(150,000)	
Goodwill	10,000	
Total Assets	$480,000	$650,000
Accounts Payable	$ 50,000	$ 50,000
Common Stock	100,000	
Additional Paid-In Capital	60,000	
Retained Earnings	270,000	
Total Liabilities and Equities	$480,000	

Required

Give the journal entry recorded by Musial Corporation at the time of exchange.

E1–7   Computation of Fair Value

Grant Company acquired all of the assets and liabilities of Bedford Corporation on January 1, 20X2, in a business combination recorded as a purchase. At that date, Bedford reported assets with a book value of $624,000 and liabilities of $356,000. Grant noted that Bedford had $40,000 of research and development costs on its books at the date of acquisition that did not appear to be of value. Grant also determined that patents developed by Bedford had a fair value of $120,000 but were not recorded by Bedford. Except for buildings and equipment, Grant determined the fair value of all other assets and liabilities reported by Bedford approximated the recorded amounts. In recording the transfer of assets and liabilties to Grant's books, Grant recorded goodwill of $93,000. Grant paid $517,000 to aquire the assets and liabilities of Bedford Corporation. If the book value of Bedford's buildings and equipment was $341,000 at the date of acquisition, what was their fair value?

E1–8   Computation of Shares Issued and Goodwill

Allsap Company was acquired by Dunyain Corporation on January 1, 20X1, through an exchange of common shares in a business combination recorded as a purchase. All of Allsap's assets and liabilities were immediately transferred to Dunyain Corporation. Dunyain reported total par value of shares outstanding of $218,400 and $327,600 and additional paid-in capital of $370,000 and $650,800 immediately before and after the business combination, respectively.

a. Assuming Dunyain's common stock had a market value of $25 per share at the time of exchange, what number of shares were issued?

b. What is the par value per share of Dunyain's common stock?

c. Assuming Allsap's identifiable assets had a fair value of $476,000 and its liabilities had a fair value of $120,000, what amount of goodwill did Dunyain record at the time of the business combination?

E1–9   Combined Balance Sheet under Purchase Treatment

The following balance sheets were prepared for Adam Corporation and Best Company on January 1, 20X2, just before they entered into a business combination:

	Adam Corporation		Best Company	
Item	Book Value	Fair Value	Book Value	Fair Value
Cash and Receivables	$150,000	$150,000	$ 90,000	$ 90,000
Inventory	300,000	380,000	70,000	160,000
Buildings and Equipment	600,000	430,000	250,000	240,000
Less: Accumulated Depreciation	(250,000)		(80,000)	
Total Assets	$800,000	$960,000	$330,000	$490,000
Accounts Payable	$ 75,000	$ 75,000	$ 50,000	$ 50,000
Notes Payable	200,000	215,000	30,000	35,000
Common Stock:				
$8 par value	180,000			
$6 par value			90,000	
Additional Paid-In Capital	140,000		55,000	
Retained Earnings	205,000		105,000	
Total Liabilities and Equities	$800,000		$330,000	

Adam acquired all of the assets and liabilities of Best Company on January 1, 20X2, in an exchange of common shares treated as a purchase. Adam issued 8,000 shares of stock to complete the business transaction.

Required

Prepare a balance sheet of the combined company immediately following the acquisition assuming the market price of Adam's shares was:

a. $60 at the date of issue.

b. $48 at the date of issue.

E1–10 **Recording a Business Combination**

The following financial statement information was prepared for Blue Corporation and Sparse Company at December 31, 20X2:

Balance Sheets
December 31, 20X2

	Blue Corporation		Sparse Company	
Cash		$ 140,000		$ 70,000
Accounts Receivable		170,000		110,000
Inventory		250,000		180,000
Land		80,000		100,000
Buildings and Equipment	$680,000		$450,000	
Less: Accumulated Depreciation	(320,000)	360,000	(230,000)	220,000
Goodwill		70,000		20,000
Total Assets		$1,070,000		$700,000
Accounts Payable		$ 70,000		$195,000
Bonds Payable		320,000		100,000
Bond Premium				10,000
Common Stock		120,000		150,000
Additional Paid-In Capital		170,000		60,000
Retained Earnings		390,000		185,000
Total Liabilities and Equities		$1,070,000		$700,000

Blue Corporation and Sparse Company agreed to combine as of January 1, 20X3. In completing the merger, Blue Corporation paid finder's fees of $30,000, audit fees of $15,000, legal fees of $24,000, stock registration fees of $8,000, and stock listing application fees of $6,000.

At January 1, 20X3, the book values of Sparse Company's assets and liabilities approximated market value except for inventory with a market value of $200,000, buildings and equipment with a market value of $350,000, and bonds payable with a market value of $105,000. All assets and liabilities were immediately recorded on the books of Blue Corporation.

Required

Give all journal entries recorded by Blue Corporation assuming:

a. Blue Corporation issued 40,000 shares of $8 par value common stock to acquire all the assets and liabilities of Sparse Company in a business combination recorded as a purchase. Blue Corporation common stock was trading at $14 per share on January 1, 20X3.

b. Blue Corporation issued 8,000 shares of $10 par value preferred stock to acquire all the assets and liabilities of Sparse Company in a business combination recorded as a purchase. Blue Corporation preferred stock was determined to have a market value of $50 per share at the time of issue.

E1–11 **Reporting Income**

On July 1, 20X2, Alan Enterprises merged with Cherry Corporation through an exchange of stock and subsequent liquidation of Cherry. Alan issued 200,000 shares of its stock to effect the combination. The book values of Cherry's assets and liabilities were equal to their fair values at the date of combination, and the value of the shares exchanged was equal to the book value of Cherry Corporation. Information relating to income for the companies is as follows:

	20X1	*January 1–June 30, 20X2*	*July 1–December 31, 20X2*
Net Income:			
Alan Enterprises	$4,460,000	$2,500,000	$3,528,000
Cherry Corporation	1,300,000	692,000	—

Alan Enterprises had 1,000,000 shares of stock outstanding prior to the combination.

Required

Compute the net income and earnings-per-share amounts that would be reported in Alan's 20X2 comparative income statements for both 20X2 and 20X1, assuming the business combination is treated as a purchase.

Exercises—Part II

E1–12 **Multiple-Choice Questions on Recording Business Combinations [AICPA Adapted]**
Select the correct answer for each of the following questions.

1. Cedar Company's planned combination with Birch Company on January 1, 20X2, can be structured as either a purchase or a pooling of interests. In a purchase, Cedar would acquire Birch's identifiable net assets at less than their book values. These book values approximate fair values. Birch's assets consist of current assets and depreciable noncurrent assets. How would the combined entity's 20X2 net income and operating cash flows under purchase accounting compare to those under pooling of interests accounting? Ignore costs required to effect the combination and income tax expense.

Purchase Accounting Net Income	**Purchase Accounting Operating Cash Flows**
a. Equal to pooling	Greater than pooling
b. Equal to pooling	Equal to pooling
c. Greater than pooling	Greater than pooling
d. Greater than pooling	Equal to pooling

2. In a business combination accounted for as a pooling of interests, the combined corporation's retained earnings usually equals the sum of the retained earnings of the individual combining corporations. Assuming there is *no* contributed capital other than capital stock at par value, which of the following describes a situation where the combined retained earnings must be increased or decreased?

    a. Increased if the par value dollar amount of the outstanding shares of the combined corporation exceeds the total capital stock of the separate combining companies.

    b. Increased if the par value dollar amount of the outstanding shares of the combined corporation is less than the total capital stock of the combining companies.

    c. Decreased if the par value dollar amount of the outstanding shares of the combined corporation exceeds the total capital stock of the separate combining companies.

    d. Decreased if the par value dollar amount of the outstanding shares of the combined corporation is less than the total capital stock of the separate combining companies.

3. Two calendar-year corporations combine on July 1, 20X1. The combination is properly accounted for as a pooling of interests. How should the results of operations have been reported for the year ended December 31, 20X1?

a. Combined from July 1 to December 31 and disclosed for the separate companies from January 1 to June 30.

b. Combined from July 1 to December 31 and disclosed for the separate companies for the entire year.

c. Combined for the entire year and disclosed for the separate companies from January 1 to June 30.

d. Combined for the entire year and disclosed for the separate companies for the entire year.

4. Costs incurred in effecting a business combination accounted for as a pooling of interests should be:

a. Added to the cost of the investment account of the parent corporation.

b. Deducted from additional paid-in capital of the combined corporation.

c. Deducted in determining net income of the combined corporation for the period in which the costs were incurred.

d. Capitalized and subsequently amortized over a period not exceeding 40 years.

E1–13   **Multiple-Choice Questions on Pooling Treatment [AICPA Adapted]**

Select the correct answer for each of the following questions.

1. On June 30, 20X2, Pane Corporation exchanged 150,000 shares of its $20 par value common stock for all of Sky Corporation's common stock. At that date, the fair value of Pane's common stock issued was equal to the book value of Sky's net assets. Both corporations continued to operate as separate businesses, maintaining accounting records with years ending December 31. Information from separate company operations follows:

	Pane	Sky
Retained earnings, Dec. 31, 20X1	$3,200,000	$925,000
Net income, 6 months ended June 30, 20X2	800,000	275,000
Dividends paid, March 25, 20X2	750,000	—

If the business combination is accounted for as a pooling of interests, what amount of retained earnings would Pane report in its June 30, 20X2, consolidated balance sheet?

a. $5,200,000.

b. $4,450,000.

c. $3,525,000.

d. $3,250,000.

2. Ethel Corporation issued voting common stock with a stated value of $90,000 in exchange for *all* the outstanding common stock of Lum Company. The combination was properly accounted for as a pooling of interests. The stockholders' equity section of Lum Company at the date of the combination was as follows:

Common Stock	$ 70,000
Capital Contributed in Excess of Stated Value	7,000
Retained Earnings	50,000
	$127,000

What should the increase in stockholders' equity of Ethel Corporation be at the date of acquisition as a result of the business combination?

a. $0.

b. $37,000.

c. $90,000.

d. $127,000.

3. In a business combination, how should plant and equipment of the acquired corporation generally be reported under each of the following methods?

Pooling of Interests	Purchase
a. Fair value	Recorded value
b. Fair value	Fair value
c. Recorded value	Recorded value
d. Recorded value	Fair value

4. A supportive argument for the pooling of interests method of accounting for a business combination is that:

a. It was developed within the boundaries of the historical cost system and is compatible with it.

b. One company is clearly the dominant and continuing entity.

c. Goodwill is generally a part of any acquisition.

d. A portion of the total cost is assigned to individual assets acquired on the basis of their fair values.

5. On December 31, 20X3, Saxe Corporation was merged into Poe Corporation. In the business combination, Poe issued 200,000 shares of its $10 par common stock, with a market price of $18 a share, for all of Saxe's common stock. The stockholders' equity section of each company's balance sheet immediately before the combination was:

	Poe	Saxe
Common Stock	$3,000,000	$1,500,000
Additional Paid-In Capital	1,300,000	150,000
Retained Earnings	2,500,000	850,000
	$6,800,000	$2,500,000

Assume the merger qualifies for treatment as a pooling of interest. In the December 31, 20X3, consolidated balance sheet, additional paid-in capital should be reported at:

a. $950,000.

b. $1,300,000.

c. $1,450,000.

d. $2,900,000.

6. On January 1, 20X1, Rolan Corporation issued 10,000 shares of common stock in exchange for all Sandin Corporation's outstanding stock. Condensed balance sheets of Rolan and Sandin immediately before the combination are as follows:

	Rolan	Sandin
Total Assets	$1,000,000	$500,000
Liabilities	$ 300,000	$150,000
Common Stock ($10 par)	200,000	100,000
Retained Earnings	500,000	250,000
Total Liabilities and Equities	$1,000,000	$500,000

Rolan's common stock had a market price of $60 per share on January 1, 20X1. The market price of Sandin's stock was not readily ascertainable. Assuming that the combination of Rolan and Sandin qualifies as a pooling of interests, rather than as a purchase, what should be reported as retained earnings in the consolidated balance sheet immediately after the combination?

a. $500,000.

b. $600,000.

c. $750,000.

d. $850,000.

E1–14 Stock Acquisition

McDermott Corporation has been in the midst of a major expansion program. Much of its growth had been internal, but in 20X1 McDermott decided to continue its expansion through the acquisition of other companies. The first company acquired was Tippy Inc., a small manufacturer of inertial guidance systems for aircraft and missiles. On June 10, 20X1, McDermott issued 17,000 shares of its $25 par common stock for all 40,000 of Tippy's $10 par common shares. At the date of combination, Tippy reported additional paid-in capital of $100,000 and retained earnings of $350,000. McDermott's stock was selling for $58 per share immediately prior to the combination. Subsequent to the combination, Tippy operated as a subsidiary of McDermott.

Required

Present the journal entry or entries that McDermott would make to record the business combination with Tippy as a pooling of interests.

E1–15 Stockholders' Equity Amounts under Pooling Treatment

Center Company and North Corporation agreed to merge on January 1, 20X1, in a business combination recorded as a pooling of interests. Abbreviated balance sheet data for the two companies included the following:

Balance Sheet Item	Center Company	North Corporation
Net Assets	$550,000	$250,000
Common Stock	$200,000	$100,000
Additional Paid-In Capital	20,000	10,000
Retained Earnings	330,000	140,000
Total Equities	$550,000	$250,000

The acquisition is completed by exchanging shares of Center Company's $10 par value common stock for the net assets of North Corporation.

Required

Prepare the stockholders' equity section of the balance sheet for the combined company if Center Company issues the following number of shares:

a. 8,000 shares.

b. 12,000 shares.

c. 16,000 shares.

E1–16   Recording Pooling of Interests

Reed Company exchanged shares of its $1 par common stock for all of the assets and liabilities of Bradford Corporation in a merger treated as a pooling of interests. Immediately prior to the combination, Bradford's balance sheet appeared as follows:

Assets	
Current Assets	$ 600,000
Plant and Equipment	1,610,000
Total Assets	$2,210,000

Liabilities and Equities	
Current Liabilities	$ 110,000
Long-Term Debt	1,000,000
Common Stock ($5 par)	500,000
Additional Paid-In Capital	200,000
Retained Earnings	400,000
Total Liabilities and Equities	$2,210,000

Before the combination, Reed reported additional paid-in capital of $350,000 and retained earnings of $700,000.

Required

Prepare the journal entries that would appear on Reed's books to record the combination if Reed issued the following number of shares in the combination:

a. 450,000 shares.

b. 600,000 shares.

c. 1,100,000 shares.

E1–17   Combining Balance Sheets under Pooling Treatment

The balance sheets of Regal Company and Sour Corporation contained the following balances on January 1, 20X1:

	Regal Company **Balance Sheet** **January 1, 20X1**		
Cash and Receivables	$100,000	Accounts Payable	$ 50,000
Inventory	200,000	Common Stock	
Land	50,000	($10 par value)	300,000
Buildings and Equipment	400,000	Additional Paid-In Capital	100,000
Less: Accumulated		Retained Earnings	150,000
Depreciation	(150,000)		
Total Assets	$600,000	Total Liabilities and Equities	$600,000

Sour Corporation
Balance Sheet
January 1, 20X1

Cash and Receivables	$ 40,000	Accounts Payable	$ 10,000
Inventory	100,000	Common Stock	
Land	60,000	($5 par value)	100,000
Buildings and Equipment	700,000	Additional Paid-In Capital	50,000
Less: Accumulated		Retained Earnings	490,000
Depreciation	(250,000)		
Total Assets	$650,000	Total Liabilities and Equities	$650,000

Required

Prepare a balance sheet for the combined entity immediately after Regal Company acquires the net assets of Sour Corporation on January 1, 20X1, by issuing 8,000 shares of its voting common stock in a pooling of interests.

E1–18   Combined Balance Sheet under Pooling of Interests Treatment

The following balance sheets were prepared for Adam Corporation and Best Company on January 1, 20X2, just before they entered into a business combination:

	Adam Corporation		Best Company	
Item	*Book Value*	*Fair Value*	*Book Value*	*Fair Value*
Cash and Receivables	$150,000	$150,000	$ 90,000	$ 90,000
Inventory	300,000	380,000	70,000	160,000
Buildings and Equipment	600,000	430,000	250,000	240,000
Less: Accumulated Depreciation	(250,000)		(80,000)	
Total Assets	$800,000	$960,000	$330,000	$490,000
Accounts Payable	$ 75,000	$ 75,000	$ 50,000	$ 50,000
Notes Payable	200,000	215,000	30,000	35,000
Common Stock:				
$8 par value	180,000			
$6 par value			90,000	
Additional Paid-In Capital	140,000		55,000	
Retained Earnings	205,000		105,000	
Total Liabilities and Equities	$800,000		$330,000	

Adam acquired all of the assets and liabilities of Best Company on January 1, 20X2, in an exchange of common shares treated as a pooling of interests. Adam issued 8,000 shares of stock to complete the business combination. Adam's stock was selling at $60 per share at the date of issue.

Required

Prepare a balance sheet for the combined company immediately following the acquisition.

E1–19   Recording a Business Combination

The following financial statement information was prepared for Blue Corporation and Sparse Company at December 31, 20X2:

Balance Sheets
December 31, 20X2

	Blue Corporation		Sparse Company	
Cash		$ 140,000		$ 70,000
Accounts Receivable		170,000		110,000
Inventory		250,000		180,000
Land		80,000		100,000
Buildings and Equipment	$680,000		$450,000	
Less: Accumulated Depreciation	(320,000)	360,000	(230,000)	220,000
Goodwill		70,000		20,000
Total Assets		$1,070,000		$700,000
Accounts Payable		$ 70,000		$195,000
Bonds Payable		320,000		100,000
Bond Premium				10,000
Common Stock		120,000		150,000
Additional Paid-In Capital		170,000		60,000
Retained Earnings		390,000		185,000
Total Liabilities and Equities		$1,070,000		$700,000

Blue Corporation and Sparse Company agreed to combine as of January 1, 20X3. In completing the merger, Blue Corporation paid finder's fees of $30,000, audit fees of $15,000, legal fees of $24,000, stock registration fees of $8,000, and stock listing application fees of $6,000.

At January 1, 20X3, the book values of Sparse Company's assets and liabilities approximated market value except for inventory with a market value of $200,000, equipment with a market value of $350,000, and bonds payable with a market value of $105,000. All assets and liabilities were immediately recorded on the books of Blue Corporation.

Required

Give all journal entries recorded by Blue Corporation assuming Blue Corporation issued 40,000 shares of its $8 par value common stock to acquire all the assets and liabilities of Sparse in a business combination recorded as a pooling of interests. Blue Corporation common stock was trading at $14 per share on January 1, 20X3.

E1–20   Reporting Income
On July 1, 20X2, Alan Enterprises merged with Cherry Corporation through an exchange of stock and subsequent liquidation of Cherry. Alan issued 200,000 shares of its stock to effect the combination. The book values of Cherry's assets and liabilities were equal to their fair values at the date of combination, and the value of the shares exchanged was equal to the book value of Cherry Corporation. Information relating to income for the companies is as follows:

	20X1	January 1–June 30, 20X2	July 1–December 31, 20X2
Net Income:			
Alan Enterprises	$4,460,000	$2,500,000	$3,528,000
Cherry Corporation	$1,300,000	$ 692,000	—

Alan Enterprises had 1,000,000 shares of stock outstanding prior to the combination.

Required

Compute the net income and earnings-per-share amounts that would be reported in Alan's 20X2 comparative income statements for both 20X1 and 20X2, assuming the business combination is treated as a pooling of interests.

Problems—Part I

P1–21 **Journal Entries—Purchase Treatment**

On January 1, 20X2, Frost Company acquired all of the assets and liabilities of TKK Corporation by issuing 24,000 shares of its $4 par value common stock. At that date, Frost Company shares were selling at $22 per share. Historical cost and fair value balance sheet data for TKK Corporation at the time of acquisition were as follows:

Balance Sheet Item	Historical Cost	Fair Value
Cash and Receivables	$ 28,000	$ 28,000
Inventory	94,000	122,000
Buildings and Equipment	600,000	470,000
Less: Accumulated Depreciation	(240,000)	
Total Assets	$482,000	$620,000
Accounts Payable	$ 41,000	$ 41,000
Notes Payable	65,000	63,000
Common Stock ($10 par value)	160,000	
Retained Earnings	216,000	
Total Liabilities and Equities	$482,000	

Frost Company paid legal fees for the transfer of assets and liabilties of $14,000, audit fees of $21,000, and listing application fees for the new shares of $7,000.

Required

Prepare the journal entries made by Frost to record the business combination assuming purchase treatment was used.

P1–22 **Recording Business Combinations**

Taylor Corporation exchanged shares of its $2 par common stock for all of the assets and liabilities of Mark Company in a planned merger. Immediately prior to the combination, Mark's assets and liabilities were as follows:

Assets	
Cash and Equivalents	$ 41,000
Accounts Receivable	73,000
Inventory	144,000
Land	200,000
Buildings	1,520,000
Equipment	638,000
Accumulated Depreciation	(431,000)
Total Assets	$2,185,000

Liabilities and Equities	
Accounts Payable	$ 35,000
Short-Term Notes Payable	50,000
Bonds Payable	500,000
Common Stock ($10 par)	1,000,000
Additional Paid-In Capital	325,000
Retained Earnings	275,000
Total Liabilities and Equities	$2,185,000

Immediately prior to the combination, Taylor reported additional paid-in capital of $250,000 and retained earnings of $1,350,000. The fair values of Mark's assets and liabilities were equal to their book values on the date of combination except that Mark's buildings were worth $1,500,000 and its equipment was worth $300,000. Costs associated with planning and completing the business combination totaled $38,000, and stock issue costs totaled $22,000. The market value of Taylor's stock at the date of combination was $4 per share.

Required

Prepare the journal entries that would appear on Taylor's books to record the combination under purchase accounting if Taylor issued the following number of shares in the combination:

a. 400,000 shares.

b. 900,000 shares.

P1–23   Purchase Treatment with Goodwill

Anchor Corporation paid cash of $178,000 to acquire the net assets of Zink Company on February 1, 20X3. The balance sheet data for the two companies and fair value information for Zink Company immediately before the business combination were:

	Anchor Corporation	Zink Company	
Balance Sheet Item	*Book Value*	*Book Value*	*Fair Value*
Cash	$240,000	$ 20,000	$ 20,000
Accounts Receivable	140,000	35,000	35,000
Inventory	170,000	30,000	50,000
Patents	80,000	40,000	60,000
Buildings and Equipment	380,000	310,000	150,000
Less: Accumulated Depreciation	(190,000)	(200,000)	
Total Assets	$820,000	$235,000	$315,000

Accounts Payable	$ 85,000	$ 55,000	$ 55,000
Notes Payable	150,000	120,000	120,000
Common Stock:			
$10 par value	200,000		
$6 par value		18,000	
Additional Paid-In Capital	160,000	10,000	
Retained Earnings	225,000	32,000	
Total Liabilities and Equities	$820,000	$235,000	

Required

a. Give the journal entry to be recorded by Anchor Corporation at the time it purchases the net assets of Zink Company.

b. Prepare a balance sheet for Anchor Corporation immediately following the acquisition.

c. Give the journal entry to be recorded by Anchor Corporation if it purchases all of Zink's common stock for $178,000.

P1–24 Negative Goodwill

Eagle Company purchased the net assets of Lark Corporation on January 3, 20X2, for $565,000 cash. In addition, $5,000 of direct costs were incurred in consummating the combination. At the time of acquisition Lark Corporation reported the following historical cost and current market data:

Balance Sheet Item	Book Value	Fair Value
Cash and Receivables	$ 50,000	$ 50,000
Inventory	100,000	150,000
Buildings and Equipment (net)	200,000	300,000
Patent	—	200,000
Total Assets	$350,000	$700,000
Accounts Payable	$ 30,000	$ 30,000
Common Stock	100,000	
Additional Paid-In Capital	80,000	
Retained Earnings	140,000	
Total Liabilities and Equities	$350,000	

Required

Give the journal entry or entries recorded by Eagle Company to record its purchase of the net assets of Lark Corporation.

P1–25 Journal Entries—Purchase Treatment

On January 1, 20X3, More Products Corporation issues 12,000 shares of its $10 par value stock to acquire the net assets of Light Steel Company. Underlying book value and fair value information for the balance sheet items of Light Steel Company at the time of acquisition are as follows:

Balance Sheet Item	Book Value	Fair Value
Cash	$ 60,000	$ 60,000
Accounts Receivable	100,000	100,000
Inventory (LIFO basis)	60,000	115,000
Land	50,000	70,000
Buildings and Equipment	400,000	350,000
Less: Accumulated Depreciation	(150,000)	—
Total Assets	$520,000	$695,000
Accounts Payable	$ 10,000	$ 10,000
Bonds Payable	200,000	180,000
Common Stock ($5 par value)	150,000	
Additional Paid-In Capital	70,000	
Retained Earnings	90,000	
Total Liabilities and Equities	$520,000	

Light Steel shares were selling at $18 and More Products shares were selling at $50 just before the merger announcement. Additional cash payments made by More Corporation in completing the acquisition were:

Finder's fee paid to firm that located Light Steel	$10,000
Audit fee for stock issued by More Products	3,000
Stock registration fee for new shares of More Products	5,000
Legal fees paid to assist in transfer of net assets	9,000
Cost of SEC registration of More Products shares	1,000

Required

Prepare all journal entries to be recorded on More Products' books assuming the business combination is recorded as a purchase.

P1–26   Purchase at More Than Book Value

Ramrod Manufacturing acquired all the assets and liabilities of Stafford Industries on January 1, 20X2, in exchange for 4,000 shares of its $20 par value common stock. Balance sheet data for both companies just before the merger are given as follows:

	Ramrod Manufacturing		Stafford Industries	
Balance Sheet Items	Book Value	Fair Value	Book Value	Fair Value
Cash	$ 70,000	$ 70,000	$ 30,000	$ 30,000
Accounts Receivable	100,000	100,000	60,000	60,000
Inventory	200,000	375,000	100,000	160,000
Land	50,000	80,000	40,000	30,000
Buildings and Equipment	600,000		400,000	
Less: Accumulated Depreciation	(250,000)	540,000	(150,000)	350,000
Total Assets	$770,000	$1,165,000	$480,000	$630,000

Accounts Payable	$ 50,000	$ 50,000	$ 10,000	$ 10,000
Bonds Payable	300,000	310,000	150,000	145,000
Common Stock:				
$20 par value	200,000			
$5 par value			100,000	
Additional Paid-In Capital	40,000		20,000	
Retained Earnings	180,000		200,000	
Total Liabilities and Equities	$770,000		$480,000	

Ramrod shares were selling for $150 on the date of acquisition.

Required

Assuming purchase accounting is appropriate for the business combination, prepare the following:

a. Journal entries to record the acquisition on Ramrod's books.

b. A balance sheet for the combined enterprise immediately following the business combination.

P1–27   Business Combination
Below are the balance sheets of the Boogie Musical Corporation and the Toot-Toot Tuba Company as of December 31, 20X5.

Boogie Musical Corporation
Balance Sheet
December 31, 20X5

Assets		*Liabilities and Equities*	
Cash	$ 23,000	Accounts Payable	$ 48,000
Accounts Receivable	85,000	Notes Payable	65,000
Allowance for Uncollectible Accounts	(1,200)	Mortgage Payable	200,000
Inventory	192,000	Bonds Payable	200,000
Plant and Equipment	980,000	Capital Stock ($10 par)	500,000
Accumulated Depreciation	(160,000)	Premium on Capital Stock	1,000
Other Assets	14,000	Retained Earnings	118,800
Total Assets	$1,132,800	Total Liabilities and Equities	$1,132,800

Toot-Toot Tuba Company
Balance Sheet
December 31, 20X5

Assets		*Liabilities and Equities*	
Cash	$ 300	Accounts Payable	$ 8,200
Accounts Receivable	17,000	Notes Payable	10,000
Allowance for Uncollectible Accounts	(600)	Mortgage Payable	50,000
Inventory	78,500	Bonds Payable	100,000
Plant and Equipment	451,000	Capital Stock ($50 par)	100,000
Accumulated Depreciation	(225,000)	Premium on Capital Stock	150,000
Other Assets	25,800	Retained Earnings	(71,200)
Total Assets	$347,000	Total Liabilities and Equities	$347,000

In preparation for a possible business combination, a team of experts from Boogie Musical made a thorough examination and audit of Toot-Toot Tuba. They found that Toot-Toot's assets and liabilities were correctly stated except that they estimated uncollectible accounts at $1,400. They also estimated the market value of the inventory at $35,000 and the market value of the plant and equipment at $500,000. The business combination took place on January 1, 20X6, and on that date Boogie Musical acquired all the assets and liabilities of Toot-Toot Tuba. On that date, Boogie's common stock was selling for $55 per share.

Required

Record the combination on Boogie's books assuming that the combination was treated as a purchase and Boogie issued 9,000 of its $10 par common shares in exchange for Toot-Toot's assets and liabilities.

P1–28 Combined Balance Sheet under Purchase Treatment

Bilge Pumpworks and Seaworthy Rope Company agreed to merge on January 1, 20X3. On the date of the merger agreement, the companies report the following data:

	Bilge Pumpworks		Seaworthy Rope Company	
Balance Sheet Items	*Book Value*	*Fair Value*	*Book Value*	*Fair Value*
Cash and Receivables	$ 90,000	$ 90,000	$ 20,000	$ 20,000
Inventory	100,000	150,000	30,000	42,000
Land	100,000	140,000	10,000	15,000
Plant and Equipment	400,000		200,000	
Less: Accumulated Depreciation	(150,000)	300,000	(80,000)	140,000
Total Assets	$540,000	$680,000	$180,000	$217,000
Current Liabilities	$ 80,000	$ 80,000	$ 20,000	$ 20,000
Capital Stock	200,000		20,000	
Capital in Excess of Par Value	20,000		5,000	
Retained Earnings	240,000		135,000	
Total Liabilities and Equities	$540,000		$180,000	

Bilge Pumpworks has 10,000 shares of its $20 par value shares outstanding on January 1, 20X3, and Seaworthy has 4,000 shares of $5 par value stock outstanding. The market values of the shares are $300 and $50, respectively.

Required

a. Bilge issues 700 shares of stock in exchange for all the net assets of Seaworthy. Prepare a balance sheet for the combined entity immediately following the merger assuming the acquisition is recorded as a purchase.

b. Prepare the stockholders' equity section of the combined company's balance sheet under purchase treatment assuming Bilge acquires all the net assets of Seaworthy by issuing:

(1) 1,100 shares of common.

(2) 1,800 shares of common.

(3) 3,000 shares of common.

P1–29 Incomplete Data Problem

On January 1, 20X2, End Corporation acquired all of the assets and liabilities of Cork Corporation by issuing shares of its common stock in a business combination recorded as a purchase. Partial balance sheet data for the companies prior to the business combination and immediately following the combination are as follows:

	End Corp.	Cork Corp.	Combined Entity
	Book Value	Book Value	
Cash	$ 40,000	$ 10,000	$ 50,000
Accounts Receivable	60,000	30,000	88,000
Inventory	50,000	35,000	96,000
Buildings & Equipment (net)	300,000	110,000	430,000
Goodwill			?
Total Assets	$450,000	$185,000	$?
Accounts Payable	$ 32,000	$ 14,000	$ 46,000
Bonds Payable	150,000	70,000	220,000
Bond Premium	6,000		6,000
Common Stock, $5 par	100,000	40,000	126,000
Additional Paid-In Capital	65,000	28,000	247,000
Retained Earnings	97,000	33,000	?
Total Liabilities and Equities	$450,000	$185,000	$?

Required

a. What number of shares did End Corporation issue to acquire the shares of Cork Corporation?

b. What was the market value of the shares issued by End Corporation?

c. What was the fair value of the inventory held by Cork Corporation at the date of combination?

d. What was the fair value of the net assets held by Cork Corporation at the date of combination?

e. What amount of goodwill, if any, will be reported by the combined entity immediately following the combination?

f. What balance in retained earnings will be reported by the combined entity immediately following the combination?

g. If the depreciable assets held by Cork Corporation had an average remaining life of 10 years at the date of acquisition, what amount of depreciation expense will be reported on those assets in 20X2?

P1–30 Incomplete Data Following Purchase

On January 1, 20X1, Alpha Corporation acquired all of the assets and liabilities of Bravo Company by issuing shares of its $3 par value stock to the owners of Bravo Company in an exchange recorded as a purchase. Alpha also made a cash payment to Banker Corporation as a finder's fee. Partial balance sheet data for Alpha and Bravo before the cash payment and issuance of shares and a combined balance sheet following the business combination are as follows:

	Alpha Company	Bravo Company		Combined Entity
	Book Value	Book Value	Fair Value	
Cash	$ 65,000	$ 15,000	$ 15,000	$ 56,000
Accounts Receivable	105,000	30,000	30,000	135,000
Inventory	210,000	90,000	?	320,000
Buildings and Equipment (net)	400,000	210,000	293,000	693,000
Goodwill				?
Total Assets	$780,000	$345,000	$448,000	$?

Accounts Payable	$ 56,000	$ 22,000	$ 22,000	$ 78,000
Bonds Payable	200,000	120,000	120,000	320,000
Common Stock	96,000	70,000		117,000
Additional Paid-In Capital	234,000	42,000		577,000
Retained Earnings	194,000	91,000		?
Total Liabilities and Equities	$780,000	$345,000	$142,000	$?

Required

a. What number of its $5 par value shares did Bravo Company have outstanding at January 1, 20X1?

b. Assuming all of Bravo's shares were issued when the company was started, what was the price per share received at the time of issue?

c. How many shares of Alpha Company were issued at the date of combination?

d. What was the market value of the shares of Alpha Company issued at the date of combination?

e. What amount of cash did Alpha pay to Banker Corporation as a finder's fee?

f. What was the fair value of Bravo's inventory at the date of combination?

g. What was the fair value of Bravo's net assets at the date of combination?

h. What amount of goodwill, if any, will be reported in the combined balance sheet following the combination?

P1–31   Comprehensive Problem: Purchase Accounting

Integrated Industries Inc. entered into a business combination agreement with Hydrolized Chemical Corporation (HCC) to assure an uninterrupted supply of key raw materials and to realize certain economies from combining the operating processes and the marketing efforts of the two companies. Under the terms of the agreement, Integrated Industries issued 180,000 shares of its $1 par common stock in exchange for all the assets and liabilities of HCC. The Integrated Industries shares then were distributed to the shareholders of HCC, and HCC was liquidated.

Immediately prior to the combination, HCC's balance sheet appeared as follows, with fair values also indicated:

	Book Values	Fair Values
Assets		
Cash	$ 28,000	$ 28,000
Accounts Receivable	258,000	251,500
Less: Allowance for Bad Debts	(6,500)	
Inventory	381,000	395,000
Long-Term Investments	150,000	175,000
Land	55,000	100,000
Rolling Stock	130,000	63,000
Plant and Equipment	2,425,000	2,500,000
Less: Accumulated Depreciation	(614,000)	
Patents	125,000	500,000
Special Licenses	95,800	100,000
Total Assets	$3,027,300	$4,112,500
Liabilities		
Current Payables	$ 137,200	$ 137,200
Mortgages Payable	500,000	520,000
Equipment Trust Notes	100,000	95,000
Debentures Payable	1,000,000	950,000
Less: Discount on Debentures	(40,000)	
Total Liabilities	$1,697,200	$1,702,200

Stockholders' Equity

Common Stock ($5 par)	600,000
Additional Paid-In Capital from Common Stock	500,000
Additional Paid-In Capital from Retirement	
of Preferred Stock	22,000
Retained Earnings	220,100
Less: Treasury Stock (1,500 shares)	(12,000)
Total Liabilities and Equity	$3,027,300

Immediately prior to the combination, Integrated Industries common stock was selling for $14 per share. Integrated Industries incurred direct costs of $135,000 in arranging the business combination and $42,000 of costs associated with registering and issuing the common stock used in the combination.

Required

a. Prepare all journal entries that Integrated Industries should have entered on its books to record the combination as a purchase.

b. Present all journal entries that should have been entered on the books of HCC to record the combination and the distribution of the stock received, assuming the combination was treated as a purchase.

Problems—Part II

P1–32   Recording Procedures under Pooling of Interests Treatment

Obscure Advertising and Brown Company are considering joining forces in a business combination to be recorded as a pooling of interests. The balance sheet data of the two companies at the time of merger are as follows:

Balance Sheet Item	Obscure Advertising	Brown Company
Cash	$ 75,000	$ 10,000
Accounts Receivable	5,000	7,000
Inventory	70,000	60,000
Land	5,000	8,000
Buildings and Equipment	100,000	150,000
Less: Accumulated Depreciation	(40,000)	(120,000)
Total Assets	$215,000	$115,000
Accounts Payable	$ 75,000	$ 70,000
Common Stock	50,000	30,000
Additional Paid-In Capital	8,000	4,000
Retained Earnings	82,000	11,000
Total Liabilities and Equities	$215,000	$115,000

The shareholders of Brown Company agree to accept 4,000 shares of Obscure Advertising's $10 par value shares in exchange for the net assets of Brown Company in a business combination considered to be a pooling of interests.

Required

a. Give the journal entry to be recorded by Obscure Advertising when it issues its shares in exchange for the net assets of Brown Company.

b. Prepare the balance sheet for Obscure Advertising immediately following the merger.

c. Give the journal entry to be recorded by Obscure Advertising if it issues its 4,000 shares in exchange for all of the common stock of Brown Company, instead of for Brown's net assets, and if both companies remain as separate corporations.

P1–33   Journal Entries—Pooling Treatment

Required

Using the data presented in Problem 1–21, prepare the journal entries made by Frost Company to record the business combination as a pooling of interests.

P1–34   Recording Business Combinations

Required

Using the data presented in Problem 1–22, prepare the journal entries made by Taylor Corporation to record the business combination as a pooling of interests.

P1–35   Journal Entries—Pooling of Interests

Required

Using the data presented in Problem 1–25, prepare all journal entries to be recorded on More Products Corporation's books assuming the business combination is recorded as a pooling of interests.

P1–36   Pooling Treatment

Required

Using the data presented in Problem 1–26, *(a)* prepare all journal entries to record the acquisition on Ramrod Manufacturing's books, and *(b)* prepare a balance sheet immediately following the business combination when pooling of interests accounting is used in recording the acquisition.

P1–37   Business Combinations

Required

Use the data presented in Problem 1–27 to do the following:

a. Record the combination on Boogie Musical Corporation's books assuming that the combination was treated as a pooling of interests and Boogie issued 9,000 of its $10 par common shares in exchange for Toot-Toot Tuba Company's assets and liabilities.

b. Present the capital section of Boogie's balance sheet immediately after the combination, assuming that the combination was treated as a pooling of interests and Boogie issued 26,000 shares of its common stock in exchange for all the assets and liabilities of Toot-Toot.

c. Record the combination on Boogie's books assuming that the combination was treated as a pooling of interests and Boogie issued 9,000 of its $10 par common shares to acquire all Toot-Toot's common stock. Both companies retain their separate identities subsequent to the combination.

P1–38   Combined Balance Sheet under Pooling Treatment

Required

Use the data presented in Problem 1–28 to do the following:

a. Prepare a balance sheet for the combined entity immediately following the merger assuming Bilge Pumpworks issues 700 shares of its stock in exchange for the net assets of Seaworthy in a business combination recorded as a pooling of interests.

b. Prepare the stockholders' equity section of the combined balance sheet under pooling of interests treatment assuming Bilge acquires all of the net assets of Seaworthy by issuing the following shares:

(1) 1,100 shares of common.

(2) 1,800 shares of common.

(3) 3,000 shares of common.

P1–39 **Comprehensive Problem with Incomplete Data**

On January 1, 20X1, Speedy Plumbers issued shares of its $5 par value stock to acquire all the shares of Flash Heating Company, which was liquidated immediately thereafter. The balance sheet for Speedy Plumbers and balance sheets for the combined company under both purchase and pooling of interests treatment are presented.

Balance Sheet Item	Speedy Plumbers	Combined Company Pooling	Combined Company Purchase
Cash	$ 70,000	$100,000	$ 100,000
Accounts Receivable	130,000	180,000	180,000
Inventory	100,000	170,000	220,000
Land	100,000	160,000	175,000
Buildings and Equipment	400,000	600,000	550,000
Less: Accumulated Depreciation	(150,000)	(230,000)	(150,000)
Goodwill			55,000
Total Assets	$650,000	$980,000	$1,130,000
Accounts Payable	$ 40,000	$ 60,000	$ 60,000
Bonds Payable	100,000	160,000	160,000
Common Stock	200,000	240,000	240,000
Additional Paid-In Capital	60,000	130,000	420,000
Retained Earnings	250,000	390,000	250,000
Total Liabilities and Equities	$650,000	$980,000	$1,130,000

Required

Shortly after the above information was compiled, a fire destroyed the accounting records. You have been employed to determine the answers to a number of questions raised by the owners of the newly combined company.

a. What was the value of the shares issued by Speedy Plumbers to acquire Flash Heating Company?

b. What was the fair value of the net assets held by Flash Heating immediately before the combination?

c. How many shares of Speedy Plumbers were issued in completing the combination?

d. What was the market price per share of Speedy Plumbers stock at the date of combination?

e. Was the full retained earnings balance of Flash Heating carried forward in the pooling case? How do you know?

f. What was the book value of the net assets of Flash Heating at combination?

g. Flash Heating uses a LIFO inventory basis. How much did its inventory increase in value between the date purchased and the time of the business combination?

h. What was the balance in working capital reported by Flash Heating before the business combination?

P1–40   Incomplete Data for Purchase and Pooling

On May 6, 20X1, Roto Corporation acquired all the assets and liabilities of Spice Company by issuing its $5 par voting common stock in exchange. Spice's $10 par value common shares had a market price of $55 each at the time of combination. Partial balance sheet data for the companies prior to the business combination and immediately following the combination are as follows:

	Roto	Totals for Spice Company		Combined Entity	
	Book Value	Book Value	Fair Value	Pooling	Purchase
Cash	$ 50,000	$ 20,000	$ 20,000	$ 70,000	$ 70,000
Accounts Receivable	?	55,000	55,000	145,000	145,000
Inventory	100,000	?	110,000	170,000	210,000
Buildings and Equipment (net)	350,000	140,000	?	490,000	570,000
Goodwill	30,000	?		70,000	?
Total Assets	$620,000	$325,000	$?	$945,000	$1,077,000
Accounts Payable	$ 70,000	$ 30,000	$ 30,000	$100,000	$ 100,000
Bonds Payable	300,000	100,000	?	400,000	400,000
Bond Premium					5,000
Common Stock	120,000	50,000		190,000	190,000
Additional Paid-In Capital	10,000	?		45,000	262,000
Retained Earnings	120,000	?		210,000	?
Total Liabilities and Equities	$620,000	$325,000	$?	$945,000	$1,077,000

Required

a. What was the book value of Spice's inventory at the date of combination?

b. What was the fair value of total assets reported by Spice at the date of combination?

c. What was the market value of Spice's bonds at the date of combination?

d. How many shares of common stock did Roto issue in completing the acquisition of Spice?

e. What was the market price per share of Roto's stock at the date of combination?

f. What amount of goodwill, if any, did Spice have on its books prior to the business combination?

g. What amount of goodwill will be reported following the business combination if the combination is a purchase?

h. What amount of retained earnings did Spice report immediately before the combination?

i. What amount of retained earnings will be reported following the business combination if the combination is recorded as a purchase?

j. What amount of additional paid-in capital did Spice report at the date of combination?

k. Assume that prior to the time the business combination was completed, Roto paid audit fees of $3,500, finder's fees of $5,000, stock registration fees of $4,000, legal fees for property transfers of $12,000, and stock transfer fees of $2,300 in connection with the combination.

   (1) Give the journal entry or entries recorded by Roto for these costs if the business combination is recorded as a pooling of interests.

   (2) Give the journal entry or entries recorded by Roto for these costs if the business combination is recorded as a purchase.

   (3) Taking these additional costs into consideration and assuming the business combination is recorded as a purchase, what amount of goodwill will be reported by the combined entity following the business combination?

(4) Taking these additional costs into consideration and assuming the business combination is recorded as a purchase, what amount of additional paid-in capital will be reported by the combined entity following the business combination?

(5) If the business combination is recorded as a pooling of interests, what effect will these costs have on the amounts reported as goodwill and additional paid-in capital by the combined entity? Explain.

P1–41   **Reporting Results of Operations**

On July 1, 20X2, Amalgamated Transport acquired all of the assets and liabilities of the Swamp Island Railroad by issuing 25,000 common shares. At the date of acquisition, Amalgamated's stock was selling for $96 per share; the net book value of the Swamp Island Railroad on that date was $2,200,000. All the excess of the purchase price over Swamp Island's net book value was attributable to equipment with a life of five years from the date of combination. The following annual results of operations were reported by Amalgamated and Swamp Island prior to the combination and by the combined company subsequent to the combination:

	20X1	*20X2*	*20X3*
Revenue:			
Amalgamated	$1,400,000	$2,000,000	$2,100,000
Swamp Island	350,000		
Net Income:			
Amalgamated	500,000	620,000	700,000
Swamp Island	100,000		

These results of operations reflect the amounts actually reported for each year; the amounts reported for periods subsequent to the combination are based on the combination's having been treated as a pooling of interests.

The revenues and income for both companies have been earned evenly throughout individual years. For the first half of 20X2, Amalgamated earned net income of $255,000 on revenue of $800,000; Swamp Island earned $55,000 on revenue of $200,000. There were no intercompany transactions between the two companies at any time. Amalgamated had 100,000 shares of common stock outstanding prior to the combination.

Required

Present the amounts that would appear for 20X1, 20X2, and 20X3 in Amalgamated Transport's comparative income statement prepared at the end of its fiscal year on December 31, 20X3, for (1) revenues, (2) net income, and (3) earnings per share assuming the business combination was treated as a:

a. Pooling of interests.

b. Purchase.

P1–42   **Comprehensive Problem: Pooling of Interests**

Required

Use the data presented in P1–31 to do the following:

a. Prepare all journal entries that Integrated Industries should have entered on its books to record the combination as a pooling of interests.

b. Present all journal entries that should have been entered on the books of HCC to record the combination and the distribution of the stock received, assuming the combination was treated as a pooling of interests.

REPORTING INTERCORPORATE INVESTMENTS IN COMMON STOCK

Many companies invest in the common stock of other corporations. Some companies invest in common stock to earn a favorable return by taking advantage of potentially profitable situations. Others acquire common stock to *(a)* gain control over other companies, *(b)* enter new market or product areas through companies established in those areas, *(c)* ensure a supply of raw materials or other production inputs, *(d)* ensure a customer for production output, *(e)* gain economies associated with greater size, *(f)* diversify, *(g)* gain new technology, or *(h)* lessen competition. Examples of intercorporate investments include IBM's acquisition of a sizable portion of Intel's stock to ensure a supply of computer components, AT&T's purchase of the stock of McCaw Cellular Communications to gain a foothold in the cellular phone market, and Texaco's acquisition of Getty Oil's stock to acquire oil and gas reserves.

There are a number of aspects of accounting for intercorporate investments in common stock that differ from accounting for other types of investments. This chapter presents the accounting and reporting procedures for investments in common stock.

Methods of Reporting Investments in Common Stock

Ownership of intercorporate investments in common stock can lead to the preparation of consolidated financial statements or to use of the equity method or cost method (adjusted to market, if appropriate) for financial reporting purposes. The method used depends on the level of influence or control that the investor is able to exercise over the investee.

Consolidation involves combining for financial reporting the individual assets, liabilities, revenues, and expenses of two or more related companies as if they were part of a single company. This process includes the elimination of all intercompany ownership and activities. Consolidation normally is appropriate where one company, referred to as the *parent,* controls another company, referred to as a *subsidiary.* The specific requirements for consolidation are discussed in Chapter 3. A subsidiary that is not consolidated with the parent is referred to as an *unconsolidated subsidiary* and is shown as an investment on the parent's balance sheet. Under current accounting standards, most subsidiaries are consolidated.

20X3

12/31/X3 — Smallco reports a net loss for 20X3 of $10,000.

	Debit	Credit
Loss from Investee	2,000	
Investment in Smallco Stock		2,000

12/31/X3 — Big Company amortizes the differential ($5,000/10).

	Debit	Credit
Loss from Investee	500	
Investment in Smallco Stock		500

12/31/X3 — Smallco declares and pays a $35,000 dividend. (Excess of Big's share of dividends over Big's share of earnings since 12/31/X1 is $17,000 – $16,000 = $1,000.)

Cost method:

	Debit	Credit
Cash	7,000	
Dividend Income		6,000
Investment in Smallco Stock		1,000

Equity method:

	Debit	Credit
Cash	7,000	
Investment in Smallco Stock		7,000

20X4

12/31/X4 — Smallco reports net income of $80,000 for 20X4.

	Debit	Credit
Investment in Smallco Stock	16,000	
Income from Investee		16,000

12/31/X4 — Big Company amortizes the differential ($5,000/10).

	Debit	Credit
Income from Investee	500	
Investment in Smallco Stock		500

12/31/X4 — Smallco declares and pays its regular annual dividend of $50,000.

Cost method:

	Debit	Credit
Cash	10,000	
Dividend Income		10,000

Equity method:

	Debit	Credit
Cash	10,000	
Investment in Smallco Stock		10,000

Summary

Cost

Dividend Income

20X1	$ 8,000
20X2	10,000
20X3	6,000
20X4	10,000

Investment in Smallco Stock

7/1/X1	$100,000
12/31/X1	98,000
12/31/X2	98,000
12/31/X3	97,000
12/31/X4	97,000

Equity

Income (Loss) from Investee

20X1	$ 7,750
20X2	17,500
20X3	(2,500)
20X4	15,500

Investment in Smallco Stock

7/1/X1	$100,000
12/31/X1	97,750
12/31/X2	105,250
12/31/X3	95,750
12/31/X4	101,250

reported is considerably different under the equity method than with consolidation. For example, an investor would report the same equity-method income from the following two investees even though their income statements are quite different in composition:

	Investee 1	Investee 2
Sales	$50,000	$ 500,000
Operating Expenses	(30,000)	(620,000)
Operating Income (Loss)	$20,000	$(120,000)
Gain on Sale of Land		140,000
Net Income	$20,000	$ 20,000

Similarly, an investment in the stock of another company is reported under the equity method as a single amount in the balance sheet of the investor regardless of the asset and capital structure of the investee. In the past, some companies borrowed heavily through unconsolidated subsidiaries and reported their investments in the subsidiaries using the equity method. Because the debt was not reported in these situations, concerns were raised over the use of the equity method to facilitate "off-balance sheet" financing.

As a result of these concerns, the Financial Accounting Standards Board eliminated the use of the equity method for reporting investments in subsidiaries by requiring the consolidation of virtually all majority-owned subsidiaries. The FASB is continuing to study the use of the equity method for investments in corporate joint ventures and other types of investees.

Additional Considerations Relating to the Equity Method

Determination of Significant Influence

The general rule established in **APB 18** is that the equity method is appropriate where the investor, by virtue of its common stock interest in an investee, is able to exercise significant influence over the operating and financial policies of the investee. In the absence of other evidence, common stock ownership of 20 percent or more is viewed as indicating that the investor is able to exercise significant influence over the investee. However, the APB also stated a number of factors that could constitute other evidence of the ability to exercise significant influence:[4]

1. Representation on board of directors.
2. Participation in policy making.
3. Material intercompany transactions.
4. Interchange of managerial personnel.
5. Technological dependency.
6. Size of investment in relation to concentration of other shareholdings.

[4]**APB 18,** par. 17.

FASB Interpretation No. 35, "Criteria for Applying the Equity Method of Accounting for Investments in Common Stock" (FIN 35), provides some examples of evidence that an investor is unable to exercise significant influence over an investee:[5]

1. Opposition by the investee, such as litigation or complaints to governmental regulatory authorities, challenges the investor's ability to exercise significant influence.

2. The investor and investee sign an agreement under which the investor surrenders significant rights as a shareholder.

3. Majority ownership of the investee is concentrated among a small group of shareholders who operate the investee without regard to the views of the investor.

4. The investor needs or wants more financial information to apply the equity method than is available to the investee's other shareholders (for example, the investor wants quarterly financial information from an investee that publicly reports only annually), tries to obtain that information, and fails.

5. The investor tries and fails to obtain representation on the investee's board of directors.

These lists are not meant to be exhaustive but are intended to indicate the types of factors that must be considered in determining whether the investor has the ability to significantly influence the investee.

Unrealized Intercompany Profits

The equity method as applied under **APB 18** often is referred to as a ***one-line consolidation*** because (*a*) the investor's income and stockholders' equity are the same as if the investee were consolidated and (*b*) all equity method adjustments are made through the investment and related income accounts, which are reported in only a single line in the balance sheet and a single line in the income statement.[6] The view currently taken in consolidation is that intercompany sales do not result in the realization of income until the intercompany profit is confirmed in some way, usually through a transaction with an unrelated third party. For example, if a parent company sells inventory to a subsidiary at a profit, that profit cannot be recognized in the consolidated financial statements until it is confirmed by resale of the inventory to an external party. Because profits from sales to related companies are viewed from a consolidated perspective as being unrealized until there is a resale to unrelated parties, such profits must be eliminated when preparing consolidated financial statements.

The consolidated financial statements are not the only ones affected, however, because **APB 18** requires that the income of an investor that reports an investment using the equity method must be the same as if the investee were consolidated. Therefore, the investor's equity-method income from the investee must be adjusted for unconfirmed profits on intercompany sales as well. The term for the application of the equity method that includes the adjustment for unrealized profit on sales to affiliates is ***fully adjusted equity method.***

---

[5]*Financial Accounting Standards Board Interpretation No. 35,* "Criteria for Applying the Equity Method of Accounting for Investments in Common Stock," May 1981, par. 4.

[6]Although **APB 18** established the requirement for an equity-method investor's income and stockholders' equity to be the same as if the investee were consolidated, the FASB's recent decision to not permit the write-off of equity method goodwill may lead to differences in situations in which such goodwill has been impaired.

Adjusting for Unrealized Intercompany Profits.   An intercompany sale normally is recorded on the books of the selling affiliate in the same manner as any other sale, including the recognition of profit. In applying the equity method, any intercompany profit remaining unrealized at the end of the period must be deducted from the amount of income that otherwise would be reported.

Under the one-line consolidation approach, the income recognized from the investment and the carrying amount of the investment are reduced to remove the effects of the unrealized intercompany profits. In future periods when the intercompany profit actually is realized, the entry is reversed.

Unrealized Profit Adjustments Illustrated.   To illustrate the adjustment for unrealized intercompany profits under the equity method, assume that Palit Corporation owns 40 percent of the common stock of Label Manufacturing. During 20X1, Palit sells inventory to Label for $10,000; the inventory originally cost Palit $7,000. Label resells one-third of the inventory to outsiders during 20X1 and retains the other two-thirds in its ending inventory. The amount of unrealized profit is computed as follows:

Total intercompany profit:	$10,000 − $7,000 = $3,000
Unrealized portion:	$3,000 × ⅔ = $2,000

Assuming that Label reports net income of $60,000 for 20X1 and declares no dividends, the following entries are recorded on Palit's books at the end of 20X1:

December 31, 20X1
(21)	Investment in Label Manufacturing Stock	24,000	
	Income from Label Manufacturing		24,000
	Record equity-method income:		
	$60,000 × .40		
(22)	Income from Label Manufacturing	2,000	
	Investment in Label Manufacturing Stock		2,000
	Remove unrealized intercompany profit.		

If all the remaining inventory is sold in 20X2, the following entry is made on Palit's books at the end of 20X2 to record the realization of the previously unrealized intercompany profit:

December 31, 20X2
(23)	Investment in Label Manufacturing Stock	2,000	
	Income from Label Manufacturing		2,000
	Recognize realized intercompany profit.		

Additional Requirements of APB 18

APB 18, the governing pronouncement dealing with equity-method reporting, includes several additional requirements:

1. The investor's share of the investee's extraordinary items, prior-period adjustments, and cumulative adjustments due to changes in accounting principles should be reported as such by the investor, if material.

2. If an investor's share of investee losses exceeds the carrying amount of the investment, the equity method should be discontinued once the investment has been reduced to zero. No further losses are to be recognized by the investor unless the investor is committed to provide further financial support for the investee or unless the investee's imminent return to profitability appears assured. If, after the equity method has been suspended, the investee reports net income, the investor again should apply the equity method, but only after the investor's share of net income equals its share of losses not previously recognized.

3. Preferred dividends of the investee should be deducted from the investee's net income if declared or, whether declared or not, if the preferred stock is cumulative, before the investor computes its share of investee earnings.

APB 18 also includes a number of required financial statement disclosures. When using the equity method, the investor must disclose:

1. The name and percentage ownership of each investee.
2. The investor's accounting policies with respect to its investments in common stock, including the reasons for any departures from the 20 percent criterion established by **APB 18.**
3. The amount and accounting treatment of any differential.
4. The aggregate market value of each identified nonsubsidiary investment where a quoted market price is available.
5. Either separate statements for or summarized information as to assets, liabilities, and results of operations of corporate joint ventures of the investor, if material in the aggregate.

Investor's Share of Other Comprehensive Income

When an investor uses the equity method to account for its investment in another company, the investor's comprehensive income should include its proportionate share of each of the amounts reported as "Other Comprehensive Income" by the investee. For example, assume Ajax Corporation purchases 40 percent of the common stock of Barclay Company on January 1, 20X1. For the year 20X1, Barclay reports net income of $80,000 and comprehensive income of $115,000, which includes other comprehensive income (in addition to net income) of $35,000. This other comprehensive income (OCI) reflects an unrealized $35,000 gain (net of tax) resulting from an increase in the fair value of an investment in stock classified as available-for-sale under the criteria established by **FASB 115.** In addition to recording the normal equity-method entries, Ajax recognizes its proportionate share of the unrealized gain on available-for-sale securities reported by Barclay during 20X1 with the following entry:

(24)	Investment in Barclay Stock	14,000	
	Unrealized Gain on Investments of Investee (OCI)		14,000
	Recognize share of investee's unrealized gain on available-for-sale securities.		

Entry (24) has no effect on Ajax's net income for 20X1, but it does increase Ajax's other comprehensive income, and thus its total comprehensive income, by $14,000. Ajax will make a similar entry at the end of each period for its proportionate share of any increase or decrease in Barclay's accumulated unrealized holding gain.

Tax Allocation Procedures

Intercompany income accruals and dividend transfers must be taken into consideration in computing income tax expense for the period. The impact will depend on the level of ownership and the filing status of the companies. Because corporations generally are permitted to deduct 80 percent of the dividends received (100 percent if at least 80 percent of all voting stock is owned), they are taxed at relatively low effective tax rates (20 percent times the marginal tax rate) on those dividends.

When an investor and an investee file a consolidated tax return, intercompany dividends and income accruals are eliminated in determining taxable income. Because these items are eliminated, there is no need to provide deferred tax accruals when temporary differences occur between the recognition of investment income by the investor and realization through dividend transfers from the investee. Those situations in which a consolidated return may be filed are relatively limited. The investor must own at least 80 percent of the stock of the investee and must elect to file a consolidated return. In all other cases separate returns must be filed.

If an investor and an investee file separate tax returns, the investor is taxed on the dividends received from the investee rather than on the amount of investment income reported. The amount of tax expense reported in the income statement of the investor each period should be based on income from the investor's own operations as well as on income recognized from its intercompany investments. **FASB Statement No. 109,** "Accounting for Income Taxes" (FASB 109), specifies those situations in which additional deferred tax accruals are required as a result of temporary differences in the recognition of income for financial reporting purposes and that used in determining taxable income.

Tax Expense under the Cost Method.   If the investor reports its investment using the cost method, income tax expense recorded by the investor on the investment income and the amount of taxes actually paid both are based on dividends received from the investee. No interperiod income tax allocation is required under the cost method because the income is recognized in the same period for both financial reporting and tax purposes; there are no temporary differences.

Tax Expense under the Equity Method.   If the investment is reported using the equity method and separate tax returns are filed, the investor reports its share of the investee's income in the income statement but reports only its share of the investee's dividends in the tax return. When the amount of the investee's dividends is different from its earnings, a temporary difference arises and interperiod tax allocation is required for the investor. In this situation, deferred income taxes must be recognized on the difference between the equity-method income reported by the investor in its income statement and the dividend income reported in its tax return. Current accounting standards generally require that the investor's reported income tax expense be computed as if all the investment income recognized by the investor under the equity method actually had been received. Thus, the investor's tax expense is recorded in excess of the taxes actually paid when the investee's earnings are greater than its dividends and normally is recorded at less than taxes actually paid when dividends are greater than earnings.

The requirements for computing the investor's income tax expense on income from intercorporate investments in common stock are summarized in Figure 2–4.

4. Investor Inc. owns 40 percent of Alimand Corporation. During the calendar year 20X5, Alimand had net earnings of $100,000 and paid dividends of $10,000. Investor mistakenly recorded these transactions using the cost method rather than the equity method of accounting. What effect would this have on the investment account, net earnings, and retained earnings, respectively?

   a. Understate, overstate, overstate.

   b. Overstate, understate, understate.

   c. Overstate, overstate, overstate.

   d. Understate, understate, understate.

5. A corporation using the equity method of accounting for its investment in a 40 percent-owned investee, which earned $20,000 and paid $5,000 in dividends, made the following entries:

Investment in Investee	8,000	
Equity in Earnings of Investee		8,000
Cash	2,000	
Dividend Revenue		2,000

   What effect will these entries have on the investor's statement of financial position?

   a. Financial position will be fairly stated.

   b. Investment in the investee will be overstated, retained earnings understated.

   c. Investment in the investee will be understated, retained earnings understated.

   d. Investment in the investee will be overstated, retained earnings overstated.

E2–3   **Multiple-Choice Questions on Equity-Method Reporting [AICPA Adapted]**
Select the correct answer for each of the following questions.

1. On January 1, 20X5, the Swing Company purchased at book value 100,000 shares (20 percent) of the voting common stock of Harpo Instruments Inc. for $1,200,000. Direct costs associated with the purchase were $50,000. On December 1, 20X5, the board of directors of Harpo declared a dividend of $2 per share payable to holders of record on December 28, 20X5. The net income of Harpo for the year ended December 31, 20X5, was $1,600,000. What should be the balance in Swing's Investment in Harpo Instruments Inc. account on December 31, 20X5?

   a. $1,200,000.

   b. $1,250,000.

   c. $1,370,000.

   d. $1,520,000.

2. Cox Company received dividends from its common stock investments during the year ended December 31, 20X4, as follows:

   • A cash dividend of $5,000 from West Corporation, in which Cox owns a 2 percent interest.

   • A cash dividend of $50,000 from Bell Corporation, in which Cox owns a 30 percent interest. A majority of Cox's directors are also directors of Bell.

   • A stock dividend of 300 shares from Mill Corporation, received on December 10, 20X4, on which date the quoted market value of Mill's shares was $10 per share. Cox owns less than 1 percent of Mill's common stock.

   How much dividend income should Cox report in its 20X4 income statement?

   a. $5,000.

   b. $8,000.

   c. $55,000.

   d. $58,000.

3. Grant Inc. acquired 30 percent of South Company's voting stock for $200,000 on January 2, 20X3. Grant's 30 percent interest in South gave Grant the ability to exercise significant

influence over South's operating and financial policies. During 20X3, South earned $80,000 and paid dividends of $50,000. South reported earnings of $100,000 for the six months ended June 30, 20X4, and $200,000 for the year ended December 31, 20X4. On July 1, 20X4, Grant sold half of its stock in South for $150,000 cash. South paid dividends of $60,000 on October 1, 20X4. In its 20X4 income statement, what amount should Grant report as the gain from the sale of half of its investment?

   a. $24,500.

   b. $30,500.

   c. $35,000.

   d. $45,500.

4. Park Company uses the equity method to account for its January 1, 20X6, purchase of Tun Inc.'s common stock. On January 1, 20X6, the fair value of Tun's FIFO inventory and land exceeded their carrying amounts. How do these excesses of fair values over carrying amounts affect Park's reported equity in Tun's 20X6 earnings?

	Inventory Excess	Land Excess
a.	Decrease	Decrease
b.	Increase	Increase
c.	Decrease	No effect
d.	Increase	No effect

5. On July 1, 20X8, Denver Corporation purchased 3,000 shares of Eagle Company's 10,000 outstanding shares of common stock for $20 per share. On December 15, 20X8, Eagle paid $40,000 in dividends to its common stockholders. Eagle's net income for the year ended December 31, 20X8, was $120,000, earned evenly throughout the year. In its 20X8 income statement, what amount of income from this investment should Denver report?

   a. $36,000.

   b. $18,000.

   c. $12,000.

   d. $6,000.

E2–4   **Cost versus Equity Reporting**

Roller Corporation purchased 20 percent ownership of Steam Company on January 1, 20X5, for $70,000. On that date, the book value of net assets reported by Steam Company was $200,000. The excess over book value paid is attributable to depreciable assets with a remaining useful life of 10 years. Net income and dividend payments of Steam Company in the following periods were:

Year	Net Income	Dividends
20X5	$20,000	$ 5,000
20X6	40,000	15,000
20X7	20,000	35,000

Required

Prepare journal entries on the books of Roller Corporation relating to its investment in Steam Company for each of the three years, assuming it accounts for the investment using (*a*) the cost method and (*b*) the equity method.

E2–5   **Cost versus Equity Reporting**

Winston Corporation purchased 40 percent of the stock of Fullbright Company on January 1, 20X2, at underlying book value. The companies reported the following operating results and dividend payments during the first three years of intercorporate ownership:

	Winston Corporation		Fullbright Company	
Year	Operating Income	Dividends	Net Income	Dividends
20X2	$100,000	$ 40,000	$70,000	$30,000
20X3	60,000	80,000	40,000	60,000
20X4	250,000	120,000	25,000	50,000

Required

Compute the net income reported by Winston Corporation for each of the three years, assuming it accounts for its investment in Fullbright Company using (*a*) the cost method and (*b*) the equity method.

E2–6   Acquisition Price

Phillips Company bought 40 percent ownership in Jones Bag Company on January 1, 20X1, at underlying book value. In 20X1, 20X2, and 20X3, Jones Bag reported net income of $8,000, $12,000, $20,000, and dividends of $15,000, $10,000, and $10,000, respectively. The balance in the investment account of Phillips Company on December 31, 20X3, was $54,000.

Required

In each of the following independent cases, determine the amount that Phillips Company paid for its investment in Jones Bag stock assuming that Phillips accounted for its investment using the (*a*) cost method and (*b*) equity method.

E2–7   Investment Income

Ravine Corporation purchased 30 percent ownership of Valley Industries for $90,000 on January 1, 20X6, when Valley had capital stock of $240,000 and retained earnings of $60,000. The following data were reported by the companies for the years 20X6 through 20X9:

			Dividends Declared	
Year	Operating Income, Ravine Corporation	Net Income, Valley Industries	Ravine	Valley
20X6	$140,000	$30,000	$ 70,000	$20,000
20X7	80,000	50,000	70,000	40,000
20X8	220,000	10,000	90,000	40,000
20X9	160,000	40,000	100,000	20,000

Required

a. What net income would have been reported by Ravine Corporation for each of the years, assuming Ravine accounts for the intercorporate investment using (1) the cost method and (2) the equity method?

b. Give all appropriate journal entries for 20X8 made by Ravine Corporation under both the cost and the equity methods.

E2–8   Differential Assigned to Patents

Power Corporation purchased 35 percent of the common stock of Snow Corporation on January 1, 20X2, by issuing 15,000 shares of its $6 par value common stock. The market price of Power's shares at the date of issue was $24. Snow Corporation reported net assets with a book value of $980,000 on that date. The amount paid in excess of the book value of Snow Corporation's net assets was attributed to the increased value of patents held by Snow with a remaining useful life of eight years. Snow Corporation reported net income of $56,000 and paid dividends of $20,000 in 20X2 and reported net loss of $44,000 and paid dividends of $10,000 in 20X3.

Required

Assuming Power Corporation uses the equity method in accounting for its investment in Snow Corporation, prepare all journal entries for Snow Corporation for 20X2 and 20X3.

E2–9   Differential Assigned to Copyrights

Best Corporation acquired 25 percent of the voting common stock of Flair Company on January 1, 20X7, by issuing bonds with a par value and fair value of $170,000 and making a cash payment of $26,000. At the date of acquisition, Flair Company reported assets of $740,000 and liabilities of $140,000. The book values and fair values of Flair's net assets were equal, except for land and copyrights. Flair's land had a fair value $16,000 greater than its book value. All of the remaining purchase price was attributable to the increased value of Flair's copyrights with a remaining useful life of eight years. Flair company reported a loss of $88,000 in 20X7 and net income of $120,000 in 20X8. Flair paid dividends of $24,000 each year.

Required

Assuming Best Corporation uses the equity method in accounting for its investment in Flair Company, prepare all journal entries for Best Corporation for 20X7 and 20X8.

E2–10   Purchase Differential Attributable to Depreciable Assets

Capital Corporation purchased 40 percent of the stock of Cook Company on January 1, 20X4, for $136,000. On that date Cook Company reported net assets of $300,000 valued at historical cost and $340,000 stated at fair value. The difference was due to the increased value of buildings with a remaining life of 10 years. During 20X4 and 20X5 Cook Company reported net income of $10,000 and $20,000 and paid dividends of $6,000 and $9,000, respectively.

Required

Assuming Capital Corporation uses (*a*) the equity method and (*b*) the cost method in accounting for its ownership of Cook Company, give the journal entries recorded by Capital Corporation in 20X4 and 20X5.

E2–11   Investment Income

Brindle Company purchased 25 percent of the voting common stock of Monroe Company for $162,000 on January 1, 20X4. At that date, Monroe reported assets of $690,000 and liabilities of $230,000. The book values and fair values of Monroe were equal except for land which had a fair value $30,000 greater than book value and equipment which had a fair value $80,000 greater than book value. The remaining economic life of all depreciable assets at January 1, 20X4, was five years. The amount of the differential assigned to goodwill is not amortized. Monroe reported net income of $68,000 and paid dividends of $34,000 in 20X4.

Required

Compute the amount of investment income to be reported by Brindle for 20X4.

E2–12   Income from Investee

Spone Corporation purchased 40 percent of the voting common stock of Hall Corporation on January 1, 20X8, for $133,400. Hall Corporation reported net income of $55,000 for 20X8 and paid dividends of $25,000 on December 30, 20X8. At the date of acquisition, Hall reported assets of $345,000 and liabilities of $105,000. A total of $24,000 of the purchase differential was assigned to buildings with a remaining economic life of 10 years at January 1, 20X8. In addition, $8,000 of the

	Twelve Months Ended December 31, 20X3	Six Months Ended December 31, 20X3
Net income	$300,000	$160,000
Dividends declared and paid	190,000	100,000

In its income statement for the year ended December 31, 20X3, how much income should Barker report from this investment?

a. $20,000.

b. $32,000.

c. $38,000.

d. $60,000.

2. On January 1, 20X3, Miller Company purchased 25 percent of Wall Corporation's common stock; no goodwill resulted from the purchase. Miller appropriately carries this investment at equity, and the balance in Miller's investment account was $190,000 on December 31, 20X3. Wall reported net income of $120,000 for the year ended December 31, 20X3, and paid dividends on its common stock totaling $48,000 during 20X3. How much did Miller pay for its 25 percent interest in Wall?

a. $172,000.

b. $202,000.

c. $208,000.

d. $232,000.

3. On January 1, 20X7, the Robohn Company purchased for cash 40 percent of the 300,000 shares of voting common stock of the Lowell Company for $1,800,000 when 40 percent of the underlying equity in the net assets of Lowell was $1,740,000. The payment in excess of underlying equity was assigned to amortizable assets with a remaining life of six years. The amortization is not deductible for income tax reporting. As a result of this transaction, Robohn has the ability to exercise significant influence over the operating and financial policies of Lowell. Lowell's net income for the year ended December 31, 20X7, was $600,000. During 20X7, Lowell paid $325,000 in dividends to its shareholders. The income reported by Robohn for its investment in Lowell should be:

a. $120,000.

b. $130,000.

c. $230,000.

d. $240,000.

4. In January 20X0, Farley Corporation acquired 20 percent of the outstanding common stock of Davis Company for $800,000. This investment gave Farley the ability to exercise significant influence over Davis. The book value of the acquired shares was $600,000. The excess of cost over book value was attributed to an identifiable intangible asset, which was undervalued on Davis's balance sheet and which had a remaining economic life of 10 years. For the year ended December 31, 20X0, Davis reported net income of $180,000 and paid cash dividends of $40,000 on its common stock. What is the proper carrying value of Farley's investment in Davis on December 31, 20X0?

a. $772,000.

b. $780,000.

c. $800,000.

d. $808,000.

P2–26   Cost versus Equity Reporting

Dagger Company purchased 25 percent of the voting common stock of Lurch Corporation on July 1, 20X6, at $10,000 over underlying book value. The excess all relates to amortizable assets with a remaining life of 10 years. Both companies report on a calendar-year basis and pay dividends at the end of the year. All income is earned evenly throughout the year. The following income and dividend information is provided by the companies at the end of 20X9:

Year	Operating Income, Dagger Company	Net Income, Lurch Corporation	Dividends Paid — Dagger Company	Dividends Paid — Lurch Corporation
20X6	$50,000	$10,000	$20,000	$ 4,000
20X7	50,000	30,000	10,000	20,000
20X8	50,000	22,000	20,000	30,000
20X9	50,000	40,000	10,000	20,000

Required

Compute net income for Dagger Company for each of the years using (*a*) the cost method and (*b*) the equity method.

P2–27   Amortization of Purchase Differential

Ball Corporation purchased 30 percent of the common stock of Krown Company on January 1, 20X5, by issuing preferred stock with a par value of $50,000 and a market price of $120,000. The following amounts relate to the balance sheet items of Krown Company at that date:

	Book Value	Fair Value
Cash and Receivables	$200,000	$200,000
Buildings and Equipment	400,000	360,000
Less: Accumulated Depreciation	(100,000)	
Total Assets	$500,000	
Accounts Payable	$ 50,000	50,000
Bonds Payable	200,000	200,000
Common Stock	100,000	
Retained Earnings	150,000	
Total Liabilities and Equities	$500,000	

Buildings and equipment were purchased by Krown Company on January 1, 20X0, with an expected economic life of 20 years. No change in overall expected economic life occurred as a result of the acquisition of stock by Ball Corporation. The amount paid in excess of the fair value of the reported net assets of Krown Company is attributed to unrecorded copyrights with a remaining useful life of eight years. During 20X5, Krown Company reported net income of $40,000 and paid dividends of $10,000.

Required

Give all journal entries to be recorded on the books of Ball Corporation during 20X5, assuming it uses the equity method in accounting for its ownership of Krown Company.

to sell a recently acquired investment in a subsidiary in the near future or an investee's treasury stock transactions cause an investor's stockholdings temporarily to represent a majority of the outstanding common stock. This requirement maintains consistency in the financial reporting picture over time.

Differences in Fiscal Periods and Accounting Methods

A difference in the fiscal periods of a parent and subsidiary should not preclude consolidation of that subsidiary. Often the fiscal period of the subsidiary, if different from the parent's, is changed to coincide with that of the parent. Another alternative is to adjust the financial statement data of the subsidiary each period to place the data on a basis consistent with the fiscal period of the parent. Both the Securities and Exchange Commission and current accounting standards permit the consolidation of a subsidiary's financial statements without adjusting the fiscal period of the subsidiary if that period does not differ from the parent's by more than three months and if recognition is given to intervening events that have a material effect on financial position or results of operations.

A difference in accounting methods between a parent and its subsidiary generally should have no effect on the decision to consolidate that subsidiary. In any event, adequate disclosure of the various accounting methods used must be given in the notes to the financial statements.

The Changing Concept of the Reporting Entity

For nearly three decades, **ARB 51** served without significant revision as the primary source of consolidation policy. Over those years, many changes occurred in the business environment, including widespread diversification of companies and the increased emphasis on financial services by manufacturing and merchandising companies such as General Electric.

In addition, the criteria used in determining whether to consolidate specific subsidiaries were subject to varying interpretations. Companies exercised great latitude in selecting which subsidiaries to consolidate and which to report as intercorporate investments. The lack of consistency in consolidation policy became of increasing concern as many manufacturing and merchandising companies engaged in "off-balance sheet financing" by borrowing heavily through finance subsidiaries and then excluding those subsidiaries from consolidation.

In 1982, the FASB began a project aimed at developing a comprehensive consolidation policy. In 1987, **FASB 94,** requiring consolidation of all majority-owned subsidiaries, was issued to eliminate the inconsistencies found in practice until a more comprehensive standard could be issued. Unfortunately, the issues have been more difficult to resolve than anticipated, and, after grappling with these issues for two decades, the FASB finally may be approaching agreement on a comprehensive set of consolidation policies and procedures.

The primary focus of the FASB's deliberations has been on the concept of control. The FASB is expected to require consolidation of all controlled entities. However, defining the meaning of control with sufficient precision for consistent application in practice has been extremely difficult. The FASB has moved beyond the traditional view of *legal control* to one of *effective control* as "the nonshared decision-making ability of one entity to direct the policies and management that guide the ongoing activities of another entity so as to increase its benefits and limit its losses from that other entity's activities."[1] This view of control is much broader than the traditional reliance on strict legal control based on majority ownership, but numerous aspects must be clarified for implementation in practice. This broader view of control has important implications because (1) it means that consolidation will be required in some situations when less than a majority of a company's voting stock is owned; (2) it applies to noncorporate entities, such as partnerships and trusts, as well as corporations; and (3) it includes not-for-profit entities as well as business enterprises. In addition, a broader view of control is more consistent with the consolidation standards of many other countries, and the international harmonization of accounting standards is of increasing importance.

Overview of the Consolidation Process

The consolidation process adds together the financial statements of two or more legally separate companies, creating a single set of financial statements. The specific procedures used to produce consolidated financial statements are discussed in considerable detail in the following chapters. An understanding of the procedures is important because they facilitate the accurate and efficient preparation of consolidated statements. However, while these procedures are being learned, the focus should continue to be on the end product, the financial statements. The procedures are intended to produce financial statements that appear as if the consolidated companies are actually a single company.

The separate financial statements of the companies involved serve as the starting point each time consolidated statements are prepared. These separate statements are added together, after some adjustments and eliminations, to generate consolidated statements.

After all the consolidation procedures have been applied, the preparer should review the resulting statements and ask: "Do these statements appear as if the consolidated companies were actually a single company?" To answer this question, two other questions must be answered:

1. Are there items included in the statements that would not appear, or that would be stated at different amounts, in the statements of a single company?
2. Are there items that do not appear in these statements that would appear if the consolidated entity were actually a single company?

These questions are answered based not on a knowledge of consolidation procedures, but on a thorough knowledge of generally accepted accounting principles. If the statements are not equivalent to those of a single company, additional procedures must be completed to provide statements as they would be presented by a single reporting entity.

The Consolidation Process Illustrated

The basic concepts that apply to the preparation of consolidated financial statements are illustrated in the following example. On January 1, 20X1, Popper Company purchases at book value all the common stock of Sun Corporation. At the end of 20X1, the balance sheets of the two companies appear as follows:

---

[1]Financial Accounting Standards Board, *Consolidations—Policy and Procedures,* "Project Summary," January 12, 2001.

Balance Sheets
December 31, 20X1

	Popper	Sun
Assets		
Cash	$ 5,000	$ 3,000
Receivables (net)	84,000	30,000
Inventory	95,000	60,000
Fixed Assets (net)	375,000	250,000
Other Assets	25,000	15,000
Investment in Sun Stock	300,000	
Total Assets	$884,000	$358,000
Liabilities and Equities		
Short-Term Payables	$ 60,000	$ 8,000
Long-Term Payables	200,000	50,000
Common Stock	500,000	200,000
Retained Earnings	124,000	100,000
Total Liabilities and Equities	$884,000	$358,000

Additional information regarding Popper and Sun is as follows:

1. Popper uses the basic equity method to account for its investment in Sun. The investment account is carried at the book value of Sun's net assets and is adjusted for Popper's share of Sun's earnings and dividends.
2. Sun owes Popper $1,000 on account at the end of the year.
3. Sun purchases $6,000 of inventory from Popper during 20X1. The inventory originally cost Popper $4,000. Sun still holds all the inventory at the end of the year.

The Consolidated Entity

The following diagram can be helpful in understanding the consolidated entity:

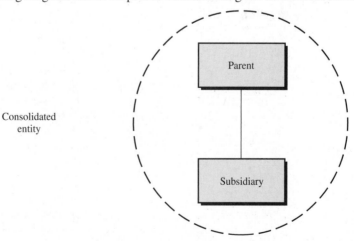

Consolidated
entity

The boxes representing the parent and the subsidiary indicate legal entities. Transactions are recorded in the accounts of these legal entities. The dashed circular line can be viewed as defining the consolidated entity, which encompasses both the parent and the subsidiary. This consolidated entity has no legal existence but is considered to have economic reality. Transactions or ownership relations that cross over the dashed line can be viewed as involving outsiders and are properly reflected in the consolidated financial statements. Those transactions or relations that are entirely within the consolidated entity are not reflected in the consolidated financial statements because they do not involve outsiders. Instead, they are viewed as occurring within a single accounting entity and, therefore, do not qualify for inclusion in the consolidated statements.

The consolidated balance sheet for Popper and Sun appears in Figure 3–1, along with the computations used in deriving the balances reported. The like accounts from the parent and subsidiary financial statements are added together and then adjusted, where appropriate, to remove the effects of intercompany ownership and transactions. For example, the totals reported for cash, fixed assets, other assets, and long-term payables in this example are derived by simply adding together the amounts reported by the two companies. An adjustment is required to reduce receivables (net) and short-term payables for intercompany debt. Similarly, inventory and retained earnings are adjusted to remove the write-up in carrying value which occurred when Sun purchased the inventory from Popper. For corporate ownership, only the stockholders' equity balances of Popper, as the parent company, are included in the consolidated balance sheet. A discussion of the rationale for each of the adjustments is presented in the sections that follow.

In the Popper and Sun example, several items need to be given special attention to ensure that the consolidated financial statements appear as if they are the statements of a single company:

1. Intercorporate stockholdings.
2. Intercompany receivables and payables.
3. Profits on intercompany sales.

Intercorporate Stockholdings.   In the example given, Popper Company's common stock is held by those outside the consolidated entity and is properly viewed as the common stock of the entire entity. The common stock of Sun, on the other hand, is held entirely within the consolidated entity and is not stock outstanding from a consolidated viewpoint. These relationships are illustrated as follows:

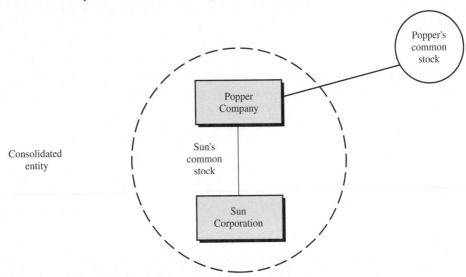

Because a company cannot report in its financial statements an investment in itself, Sun's common stock and Popper's investment in that stock both must be eliminated. Popper's common stock remains as the common stock of the consolidated entity.

FIGURE 3–1 **Consolidated Balance Sheet**

<table>
<tr><td colspan="4" align="center">**Popper Company**
Consolidated Balance Sheet
December 31, 20X1</td></tr>
<tr><td>**Assets**</td><td></td><td>**Liabilities and Equities**</td><td></td></tr>
<tr><td>Cash</td><td>$ 8,000[a]</td><td>Short-Term Payables</td><td>$ 67,000[f]</td></tr>
<tr><td>Receivables (net)</td><td>113,000[b]</td><td>Long-Term Payables</td><td>250,000[g]</td></tr>
<tr><td>Inventory</td><td>153,000[c]</td><td></td><td></td></tr>
<tr><td>Fixed Assets (net)</td><td>625,000[d]</td><td>Common Stock</td><td>500,000[h]</td></tr>
<tr><td>Other Assets</td><td>40,000[e]</td><td>Retained Earnings</td><td>122,000[i]</td></tr>
<tr><td>Total Assets</td><td>$939,000</td><td>Total Liabilities and Equities</td><td>$939,000</td></tr>
</table>

The consolidated balances were obtained as follows:

(a) Cash: $5,000 + $3,000 = $8,000

(b) Receivables (net): $84,000 + $30,000 − $1,000 = $113,000

(c) Inventory: $95,000 + $60,000 − $2,000 = $153,000

(d) Fixed Assets (net): $375,000 + $250,000 = $625,000

(e) Other Assets: $25,000 + $15,000 = $40,000

(f) Short-Term Payables: $60,000 + $8,000 − $1,000 = $67,000

(g) Long-Term Payables: $200,000 + $50,000 = $250,000

(h) Common Stock: $500,000 + $200,000 − $200,000 = $500,000

(i) Retained Earnings: $124,000 + $100,000 − $100,000 − $2,000 = $122,000

Only the retained earnings of Popper Company is included in the consolidated balance sheet shown in Figure 3–1. The retained earnings of Sun is not reported in the consolidated balance sheet because it relates to an ownership interest held entirely within the consolidated entity. The retained earnings of Popper, on the other hand, represents a claim of the parent's shareholders, viewed as the residual owners of the consolidated entity. Popper's retained earnings (less the unrealized intercompany profit) indicates the amount of undistributed past earnings of the consolidated entity accruing to the stockholders of the parent company and, therefore, is reported as consolidated retained earnings.

Intercompany Receivables and Payables. The intercompany receivable/payable can be viewed as follows:

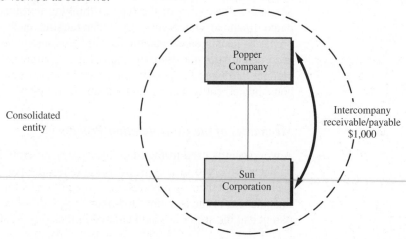

A single company cannot owe itself money. While as separate companies Popper properly reports a $1,000 trade receivable from Sun and Sun properly reports a $1,000 trade payable to Popper, such a receivable/payable does not exist from a consolidated viewpoint. Therefore, the $1,000 is eliminated from both receivables and payables in preparing the consolidated balance sheet.

Profits on Intercompany Sales.   The sale of inventory from Popper to Sun also must be viewed in the context of a single entity, as illustrated in the following diagram:

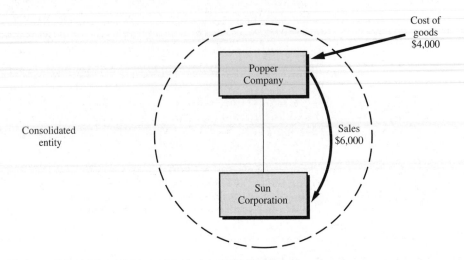

A single company may not recognize a profit and write up its inventory simply because the inventory is transferred from one department or division to another. This also applies to intercompany sales within a consolidated entity. In this example, the intercompany inventory remaining at the end of the period ($6,000) must be restated to its original cost to the consolidated entity, the $4,000 paid by Popper. Similarly, the $2,000 profit recognized on the intercompany sale and included in Popper's retained earnings may not be included in the consolidated amounts. Therefore, both the inventory and the consolidated retained earnings must be reduced by the $2,000 unrealized intercompany profit when preparing the consolidated balance sheet.

Single-Entity Viewpoint.   The various adjustments discussed in this simplified example are illustrative of the type of thinking involved in the preparation of consolidated financial statements. In understanding each of the adjustments needed in preparing consolidated statements, the focus should be on (1) identifying the treatment accorded a particular item by each of the separate companies and (2) identifying the amount that would appear in the financial statements with respect to that item if the consolidated entity were actually a single company.

Mechanics of the Consolidation Process

A worksheet is used to facilitate the process of combining and adjusting the account balances involved in a consolidation. While the parent company and the subsidiary each maintain their own books, there are no books for the consolidated entity. Instead, the balances of the accounts are taken at the end of each period from the books of the parent and the subsidiary and entered in the consolidation workpaper.

A consolidation workpaper for the preparation of Popper Company's consolidated balance sheet appears in Figure 3–2. The account balances for Popper and Sun, taken from their separate books, are listed in the first two columns beside one another so the amounts for each asset, liability, and equity item may be added across to obtain the consolidated balances.

Where the simple adding of the amounts from the two companies leads to a consolidated figure different from the amount that would appear if the two companies were actually one, the combined amount must be adjusted to the desired figure. This is done through the preparation of *eliminating entries.* Separate debit and credit columns are provided for the eliminating entries in the workpaper in Figure 3–2. The final column in the workpaper presents the amounts to appear in the consolidated balance sheet. These amounts are obtained by summing across each line and including the effects of each debit or credit elimination or adjustment. The consolidated amounts then appear in the consolidated balance sheet as in Figure 3–1.

Consolidation workpapers and eliminating entries are discussed in more detail in the following chapters. The consolidation procedures and workpapers are important because they facilitate the preparation of the consolidated statements, help ensure clerical accuracy, and provide a trail for the verification of the account balances in the consolidated statements. At this point, however, the reader should focus on understanding what numbers appear in the financial statements when adopting a single-entity viewpoint rather than concentrating on specific procedures or workpaper techniques.

Noncontrolling Interest

When one company acquires the common stock of another in a business combination, it does not always acquire 100 percent of the other company's outstanding shares. For the parent to consolidate the subsidiary, only a controlling interest is needed. Those shareholders of the subsidiary other than the parent are referred to as "noncontrolling" or "minority" shareholders. The claim of these shareholders on the income and net assets of the subsidiary is referred to as the *noncontrolling interest* or the *minority interest.*

The noncontrolling shareholders clearly have a claim on the assets and earnings of the subsidiary by virtue of their stock ownership. Because all the assets, liabilities, and earnings of the subsidiary normally are included in the consolidated statements, the noncontrolling shareholders' claim on these items must be reported. The portion of subsidiary net income assigned to the noncontrolling interest normally is deducted from earnings available to all shareholders to arrive at consolidated net income in the consolidated income statement. The noncontrolling shareholders' claim on the net assets of the subsidiary is shown most commonly with liabilities or between liabilities and stockholders' equity in the consolidated balance sheet.

Several different theories of consolidation have been proposed which affect differently the treatment of the noncontrolling interest. These theories are discussed briefly later in the chapter. The FASB favors treating the noncontrolling interest as an ownership interest, with the noncontrolling interest's claim on subsidiary assets reported in consolidated stockholders' equity and the claim on subsidiary net income reported as an allocation of consolidated net income. However, practice has traditionally favored the income deduction-liability approach. For example, Century Telephone specifically refers to the minority interest's share of income as an expense in its notes to its consolidated financial statements.

FIGURE 3–2   **Consolidated Balance Sheet Workpaper**

Popper Company and Subsidiary
Consolidated Balance Sheet Workpaper
December 31, 20X1

Item	Popper Company	Sun Corporation	Eliminations Debit	Eliminations Credit	Consolidated
Cash	5,000	3,000			8,000
Receivables (net)	84,000	30,000		(a) 1,000	113,000
Inventory	95,000	60,000		(b) 2,000	153,000
Fixed Assets (net)	375,000	250,000			625,000
Other Assets	25,000	15,000			40,000
Investment in Sun Stock	300,000			(c) 300,000	
	884,000	358,000			939,000
Short-Term Payables	60,000	8,000	(a) 1,000		67,000
Long-Term Payables	200,000	50,000			250,000
Common Stock	500,000	200,000	(c) 200,000		500,000
Retained Earnings	124,000	100,000	(c) 100,000		
			(b) 2,000		122,000
	884,000	358,000	303,000	303,000	939,000

(a) Eliminate intercompany receivable/payable.
(b) Eliminate unrealized intercompany profit included in ending inventory against consolidated retained earnings.
(c) Eliminate intercorporate investment against subsidiary's stockholders' equity.

In uncomplicated situations, the amount of noncontrolling interest is a simple proportionate share of the relevant subsidiary amounts. For example, if a subsidiary has net income of $150,000 and the noncontrolling shareholders own 10 percent of the subsidiary's common stock, their share of income is $15,000 ($150,000 × .10). Similarly, if the subsidiary's only stockholders' equity accounts are common stock of $600,000 and retained earnings of $200,000, the total noncontrolling interest, reflecting the noncontrolling shareholders' claim on the net assets of the subsidiary, is computed as follows:

Subsidiary common stock	$600,000
Subsidiary retained earnings	200,000
Book value of subsidiary	$800,000
Noncontrolling stockholders' proportionate share	× .10
Noncontrolling interest	$ 80,000

Effect of Purchase versus Pooling Accounting on Consolidation

As discussed in Chapter 1, the purchase and pooling of interests accounting methods often lead to significantly different balances being reported in financial statements prepared after a business combination. While the two accounting methods result in different amounts being reported in the consolidated financial statements, these differences arise because of differences in the amounts at which the balance sheet items were recorded on the date of combination rather than because of any differences in consolidation concepts or procedures. In general, the same consolidation procedures apply whether the combination has been treated as a purchase or pooling of interests.

The differences in the consolidated financial statements due to the differences in purchase and pooling accounting fall largely into two areas. First, retained earnings is a residual and, therefore, can never be purchased. The existing retained earnings of a company acquired in a purchase-type business combination cannot become part of consolidated retained earnings. Instead, the amount of the subsidiary's retained earnings at the date of acquisition must be eliminated each time consolidated financial statements are prepared. If the combination originally was accounted for as a pooling of interests, the combining companies are viewed as always having been together and the retained earnings balance of the subsidiary at the date of the combination is included along with the parent's retained earnings.

The second area of difference involves the valuation of the subsidiary's assets and liabilities in the consolidated financial statements. If the subsidiary was purchased, its assets and liabilities must be valued for consolidation purposes based on their fair values at the date of combination. When this is not done on the subsidiary's books, the consolidation procedures must provide for this revaluation and any associated amortization of the revalued amounts. For a combination that was treated as a pooling of interests, no revaluation is needed; instead, the book values of the parent's and subsidiary's assets and liabilities are combined.

In those cases where a subsidiary is purchased and the purchase price exceeds the fair value of the net identifiable assets of the acquired company at the date of combination, the excess is considered as a payment for goodwill. This goodwill normally is not recorded on the subsidiary's books; therefore, the consolidation procedures include recognizing the goodwill in the consolidated financial statements. Goodwill is never created as a result of a pooling of interests.

The following chapters emphasize consolidation procedures following a purchase-type business combination. Specific consolidation procedures following a pooling of interests are discussed in Chapter 10.

Combined Financial Statements

Financial statements sometimes are prepared for a group of companies when no one company in the group owns a majority of the common stock of any other company in the group. Financial statements that include a group of related companies without including the parent company or other owner are referred to as *combined financial statements.*

Combined financial statements are commonly prepared when an individual, rather than a corporation, owns or controls a number of companies and wishes to include them all in a single set of financial statements. In some cases, a parent company may prepare financial statements that include only its subsidiaries and not the parent. In other cases, a parent may prepare financial statements for its subsidiaries by operating group, with all the subsidiaries engaged in a particular type of operation, or those located in a particular geographical region, reported together.

The procedures used to prepare combined financial statements are essentially the same as those used in preparing consolidated financial statements. All intercompany receivables and payables, intercompany transactions, and unrealized intercompany profits and losses must be eliminated in the same manner as in the preparation of consolidated statements. Although no parent company is included in the reporting entity, any intercompany ownership, and the associated portion of stockholders' equity, must be eliminated in the same way as the parent's investment in a subsidiary is eliminated in preparing consolidated financial statements. The remaining stockholders' equity of the companies in the reporting entity is divided into the portions accruing to the controlling and noncontrolling interests.

Additional Considerations—Different Approaches to Consolidation

The previous sections gave a brief overview of the concepts, issues, and procedures to be discussed in Chapters 4 through 10. Before these matters are covered in detail in subsequent chapters, this section addresses the various theories underlying the consolidation process.

Several different theories exist that might serve as a basis for preparing consolidated financial statements. The choice of consolidation theory can have a significant impact on the consolidated financial statements in those cases where the parent company owns less than 100 percent of the subsidiary's common stock. The discussion included in this section of the chapter is intended to provide a basic understanding of the major differences between the theories.

This discussion focuses on three alternative theories of consolidation: (1) proprietary, (2) parent company, and (3) entity. The proprietary and entity theories may be viewed as falling near opposite ends of a spectrum, with the parent company theory falling somewhere in between:

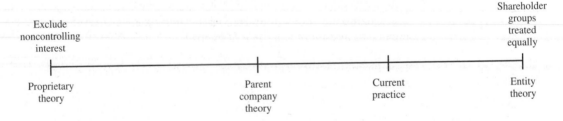

While no one of the three theories has been adopted in its entirety by the accounting profession, the consolidation procedures traditionally used in practice come closest to the parent company approach.

Proprietary Theory

The **proprietary theory** of accounting views the firm as an extension of its owners. The assets and liabilities of the firm are considered to be assets and liabilities of the owners themselves. Similarly, revenue of the firm is viewed as increasing the wealth of the owners, while expenses decrease the wealth of the owners.

When applied to the preparation of consolidated financial statements, the proprietary concept results in what is referred to as a **pro rata consolidation.** The parent company consolidates only its proportionate share of the assets and liabilities of the subsidiary. For a subsidiary acquired in a purchase-type business combination, the consolidated amounts are determined at the date of combination by adding the parent's proportionate share of the fair value of each of the subsidiary's identifiable assets and liabilities to the book values of the parent's individual assets and liabilities. In addition, the amount paid by the parent in excess of the fair value of the parent's share of the subsidiary's net identifiable assets is reported as goodwill in the consolidated balance sheet. The portion of the subsidiary's identifiable assets and liabilities assignable to the noncontrolling interest is excluded from the consolidated statements, as is any implied goodwill assignable to the noncontrolling interest. The amount of net assets of the subsidiary included in the consolidated financial statements is shown by the shaded area in the left portion of the following diagram:

Proprietary Theory

Recognition of Subsidiary
Net Assets

Parent's share / Noncontrolling share

Goodwill

Fair value increment

Book value

Recognition of Subsidiary
Net Income

Parent's share / Noncontrolling share

Revenues

Expenses

Net income

Portion included in consolidated financial statements.

In a manner similar to the treatment of assets and liabilities, only the parent's share of individual revenues and expenses reported by the subsidiary subsequent to the purchase is combined with the parent's revenues and expenses in preparing the consolidated income statement. As indicated in the diagram, that portion of the subsidiary's revenues and expenses assignable to the noncontrolling shareholders is omitted from the consolidated income statement.

Parent Company Theory

The ***parent company theory*** is perhaps better suited to the modern corporation and the preparation of consolidated financial statements than is the proprietary approach. The parent company theory recognizes that although the parent does not have direct ownership of the assets or direct responsibility for the liabilities of the subsidiary, it has the ability to exercise effective control over all of the subsidiary's assets and liabilities, not simply a proportionate share. Thus, all the assets and liabilities of the subsidiary are reported in the consolidated balance sheet by combining them with the assets and liabilities of the parent. Similarly, all the revenues and expenses of the subsidiary are included in the consolidated income statement. Under this approach, separate recognition is given in the consolidated balance sheet to the noncontrolling interest's claim on the net assets of the subsidiary and in the consolidated income statement to the earnings assigned to the noncontrolling shareholders.

The full amount of the book value of the subsidiary's net assets is included in the consolidated balance sheet when the parent company method is used. In those cases where the parent pays more than book value for its share of the subsidiary's ownership in a purchase-type business combination, the parent's portion of the fair value increment and goodwill is included in the consolidated statements. As a result, subsidiary assets are included at their fair values only in those cases where the parent purchases full ownership. The noncontrolling shareholders are assigned a proportionate share of book value of the subsidiary's net assets in preparing the consolidated balance sheet, as shown in the following diagram:

Parent Company Theory

Recognition of Subsidiary Net Assets		Recognition of Subsidiary Net Income	
Parent's share	Noncontrolling share	Parent's share	Noncontrolling share

Goodwill

Fair value increment

Book value

Revenues

Expenses

Net income

 Portion included in consolidated financial statements.

While the full book values of the assets of the subsidiary are included in the consolidated balance sheet under this approach, amounts less than the full fair values of identifiable assets and the full amount of goodwill are reported whenever the parent does not purchase all of the subsidiary ownership.

With the parent company theory, the full amounts of subsidiary revenues and expenses are included in the consolidated income statement; however, only the portion of subsidiary income assignable to the parent company is included in consolidated net income. Income assigned to the noncontrolling shareholders is treated as a deduction in the consolidated income statement in arriving at consolidated net income.

Entity Theory

As a general ownership theory, the **entity theory** focuses on the firm as a separate economic ... er than on the ownership rights of the shareholders of the parent or ... sis under the entity approach is on the consolidated entity itself, with ... d noncontrolling shareholders viewed as two separate groups, each ... in the consolidated entity. Neither of the two groups is emphasized ... over the consolidated entity.

... arent and subsidiary together are viewed as a single entity under the ... he full amounts of the assets and liabilities of both the parent and sub- ... ned in the consolidated balance sheet. Assuming the subsidiary was ... ness combination accounted for as a purchase, all the assets and lia- ... sidiary and any goodwill are reflected in the consolidated balance ... fair values on the date of combination regardless of the actual per- ... ship acquired, as shown in the following diagram:

Entity Theory

f Subsidiary ssets		Recognition of Subsidiary Net Income	
nt's re	Noncon- trolling share	Parent's share	Noncon- trolling share

Revenues

Expenses

Net income

Portion included in consolidated financial statements.

The consolidated income statement under the entity approach contains the revenues and expenses of both the parent and the subsidiary companies. Because the parent and subsidiary are viewed as constituting a single entity, consolidated net income is a combined figure that is allocated between the controlling and noncontrolling ownership groups.

Current Practice

The procedures used in practice represent a blending of the parent company and entity approaches. The amount of subsidiary net assets recognized in the consolidated balance sheet at acquisition is the same in practice as under the parent company approach. On the other hand, the determination of consolidated net income is a combination of the entity and parent company approaches.

No specific presentation of noncontrolling (minority) interest is required in the official pronouncement, and there is less than complete uniformity in the presentations found in practice. Most companies deduct the noncontrolling interest's share of subsidiary net income in the consolidated income statement to obtain consolidated net income. This expense-type treatment views the computation of consolidated net income from the parent company's point of view and seems to be consistent with the view of consolidated net income adopted by **APB 18.**

The dollar amount reported as noncontrolling interest in the consolidated balance sheet is presented in any one of three ways. Most companies show the noncontrolling interest either as part of the liabilities section or between the liabilities and stockholders' equity sections of the balance sheet. The liability treatment is consistent with the parent company approach and with deducting the noncontrolling interest's share of income as an expense. The in-between treatment amounts to no classification at all. A few companies classify the noncontrolling interest as a stockholders' equity item. This presentation is consistent with the entity approach and with the treatment of the noncontrolling interest's share of income as an allocation of consolidated net income rather than as a deduction to obtain consolidated net income.

Future Practice

The FASB has indicated its preference to move to an entity approach in practice. If this approach is implemented, the noncontrolling shareholders' claims on the net assets of the subsidiary will be reported in the stockholders' equity section of the consolidated balance sheet. Similarly, consolidated net income will be reported without deducting the noncontrolling interest's share of subsidiary income. Instead, consolidated net income will be presented in the consolidated income statement, followed by the allocation of that amount to the controlling and noncontrolling interests.

Some other issues relating to the entity approach may be more difficult to resolve. For example, most companies oppose valuing subsidiary assets at full fair value at the date of a less-than-wholly-owned acquisition rather than just recognizing the parent's proportionate fair value increment because of the negative effect the additional amortization and write-offs would have on future earnings.

Summary of Key Concepts and Terms

Consolidated financial statements present the financial position and results of operations of a parent and one or more subsidiaries as if they were actually a single company. As a result, a group of legally separate companies is portrayed as a single economic entity by the consolidated financial statements. All indications of intercorporate ownership and the effects of all intercompany transactions are excluded from the consolidated statements. The basic approach to the preparation of consolidated financial statements is to combine the separate financial statements of the individual consolidating companies and then to eliminate or adjust those items that would not appear, or that would appear differently, if the companies actually were one.

Current consolidation standards require that the consolidated financial statements include all companies under common control unless control is questionable or temporary. Consolidated financial statements are prepared primarily for those with a long-run interest in the parent company, especially the stockholders and long-term creditors of the parent. While consolidated financial statements allow interested parties to view a group of related companies as a single economic entity, such statements have some limitations. In particular, information about the characteristics and operations of the individual companies within the consolidated entity is lost in the process of combining financial statements.

Several different theories or approaches underlie the preparation of consolidated financial statements, and the approach used can significantly affect the consolidated statements when the subsidiaries are not wholly owned. The proprietary and entity theories can be viewed as lying at opposite ends of a spectrum, with the parent company theory in the middle. Current practice tends to fall closest to the parent company theory, with some characteristics of the entity theory. The FASB has indicated that a move toward the entity approach in practice is likely.

Combined financial statements	Noncontrolling interest
Consolidated financial statements	Parent
Direct control	Parent company theory
Effective control	Proprietary theory
Eliminating entries	Pro rata consolidation
Entity theory	Related companies
Indirect control	Separate legal entities
Legal control	Subsidiary
Minority interest	

Questions

Q3–1   What is the basic idea underlying the preparation of consolidated financial statements?

Q3–2   How might consolidated statements help an investor assess the desirability of purchasing shares of the parent company?

Q3–3   Are consolidated financial statements likely to be more useful to the owners of the parent company or to the noncontrolling owners of the subsidiaries? Why?

Q3–4   What is meant by "parent company"? When is a company considered to be a parent?

Q3–5   Are consolidated financial statements likely to be more useful to the creditors of the parent company or to the creditors of the subsidiaries? Why?

Q3–6   Why is ownership of a majority of the common stock of another company considered important in consolidation?

Q3–7   What major criteria must be met before a company is consolidated?

Q3–8   When is consolidation considered inappropriate even though the parent holds a majority of the voting common shares of another company?

Q3–9   What is meant by "indirect control"? Give an illustration.

Q3–10   What means other than majority ownership might be used to gain control over a company? Can consolidation occur if control is gained by other means?

Q3–11   Why must intercompany receivables and payables be eliminated when consolidated financial statements are prepared?

Q3–12   Why are subsidiary shares not reported as stock outstanding in the consolidated balance sheet?

Q3–13 What must be done if the fiscal periods of the parent and its subsidiary are not the same?

Q3–14 What is the noncontrolling interest in a subsidiary?

Q3–15 What is the difference between consolidated and combined financial statements?

Q3–16* How does the proprietary theory of consolidation differ from current accounting practice?

Q3–17* How does the entity theory of consolidation differ from current accounting practice?

Q3–18* Which theory of consolidation is closest to current accounting practice?

Cases

C3–1 **Computation of Total Asset Values**

A reader of the consolidated financial statements of Gigantic Company received copies from another source of the financial statements of the individual companies included in the consolidation. He is confused by the fact that the total assets in the consolidated balance sheet differ rather substantially from the sum of the asset totals reported by the individual companies.

Required

Will this relationship always be true? What factors may cause this difference to occur?

C3–2 **Accounting Entity [AICPA Adapted]**

The concept of the accounting entity often is considered to be the most fundamental of accounting concepts, one that pervades all of accounting.

Required

a. (1) What is an accounting entity? Explain.

(2) Explain why the accounting entity concept is so fundamental that it pervades all of accounting.

b. For each of the following, indicate whether the accounting concept of the entity is applicable; discuss and give illustrations.

(1) A unit created by or under law.

(2) The product-line segment of an enterprise.

(3) A combination of legal units.

(4) All the activities of an owner or a group of owners.

(5) The economy of the United States.

C3–3 **Consolidation Effects**

Crumple Car Corporation produces fuel-efficient automobiles and sells them through a vast dealer network. It has two wholly owned subsidiaries. One subsidiary provides financing for approximately 70 percent of all automobile sales of the parent company and its dealers. The other subsidiary purchases approximately 15 percent of the parent company's production and leases the cars to other companies. Until recently, the parent company accounted for both subsidiaries using the equity method and reported them in its consolidated financial statements as intercorporate investments. It is now fully consolidating both subsidiaries.

Required

a. What specific accounts or items within the consolidated financial statements could be expected to be different when both subsidiaries are fully consolidated?

---

*Indicates that the item relates to "Additional Considerations."

    c. Cost of goods sold for 20X3.

    d. Sales for 20X2.

    e. Sales for 20X3.

P3–24   **Determining Net Income of Consolidated Entity**

Placer Corporation purchased 75 percent of the common stock of Murdokk Enterprises on January 1, 20X1, for $20,000 more than underlying book value. The excess payment is assigned to increased value of equipment which had a remaining life of eight years at the date of the business combination. Placer Corporation reported net income of $110,000 and paid dividends of $30,000 in 20X1. Murdokk Enterprises reported net income of $24,000 and paid dividends of $14,000 in 20X1. Placer Corporation accounts for its ownership of Murdokk using the cost method.

Required

Determine the amount of consolidated net income to be reported for 20X1 for Placer Corporation and its subsidiary.

P3–25   **Determining Net Income of Parent Company**

Consolidated net income of $164,300 was reported for 20X2 by Tally Corporation and its subsidiary. Tally had purchased 60 percent of the common shares of its subsidiary at underlying book value. Noncontrolling interest was assigned income of $15,200 in the consolidated income statement for 20X2.

Required

Determine the amount of separate operating income reported by Tally Corporation for 20X2.

P3–26   **Consolidated Income Statement Data**

Slender Products Corporation purchased 80 percent ownership of LoCal Bakeries on January 1, 20X3, for $40,000 more than its portion of LoCal's underlying book value. The full additional payment is assigned to depreciable assets with an eight-year economic life. Income statement data for the two companies for 20X3 included the following:

	Slender Products		LoCal Bakeries	
Sales		$300,000		$200,000
Cost of Goods Sold	$200,000		$130,000	
Depreciation Expense	40,000	(240,000)	30,000	(160,000)
Income before Income from Subsidiary		$ 60,000		
Net Income				$ 40,000

During 20X3, Slender Products Corporation purchased a special imported yeast for $35,000 and resold it to LoCal Bakeries for $50,000. None of the yeast was resold by LoCal Bakeries before year-end.

Required

Determine the amounts to be reported in the consolidated income statement for 20X3 for each of the following items:

a. Sales.

b. Investment income from LoCal Bakeries.

c. Cost of goods sold.

d. Depreciation expense.

P3–27   Incomplete Company and Consolidated Data

Beryl Corporation purchased 100 percent of the common stock of Stargel Enterprises on December 31, 20X4. At that date, the book values and fair values of Stargel's identifiable assets and liabilities were identical. Balance sheet data for the individual companies and consolidated entity on January 1, 20X5, are as follows:

	Beryl Corporation	Stargel Enterprises	Consolidated Entity
Cash	$ 60,000	$ 35,000	$ 95,000
Accounts Receivable	90,000	50,000	130,000
Inventory	120,000	90,000	?
Land	70,000	50,000	105,000
Buildings and Equipment	340,000	220,000	560,000
Less: Accumulated Depreciation	(180,000)	(90,000)	(270,000)
Investment in Stargel Enterprises Stock	110,000		
Goodwill			30,000
Total Assets	$610,000	$355,000	$?
Accounts Payable	$ 75,000	$ 55,000	?
Wages Payable	30,000	20,000	50,000
Notes Payable	250,000	200,000	450,000
Common Stock	?	30,000	100,000
Retained Earnings	155,000	50,000	140,000
Total Liabilities and Stockholders' Equity	$610,000	$355,000	$?

Required

a. Assuming there were no inventory transactions between the companies, what balance should be reported as inventory in the consolidated balance sheet?

b. What amount did Beryl pay to acquire ownership of Stargel? Was this amount equal to underlying book value, greater than underlying book value, or less than underlying book value? How do you know?

c. Beryl sold land it had purchased 12 years earlier for $10,000 to Stargel immediately after it acquired ownership of Stargel. At what price did Beryl sell the land to Stargel? How do you know?

d. What balance will be reported as accounts payable in the consolidated balance sheet?

e. What is the par value of Beryl Corporation's common stock outstanding at January 1, 20X5?

P3–28   Consolidation Following Intercompany Sale of Equipment

Potash Company owns 100 percent of the common stock of Bortz Corporation, which it acquired on December 31, 20X4, at underlying book value. Potash uses the equity method in accounting for its investment in Bortz. On December 31, 20X6, Potash sold equipment with a book value of $85,000 to Bortz for $110,000. Bortz made immediate payment of $93,000 and will pay the remainder on March 15, 20X7. Balance sheet data on January 1, 20X7, are as follows:

	Potash Company	Bortz Corporation
Cash	$ 50,000	$ 35,000
Accounts Receivable	110,000	60,000
Merchandise Inventory	95,000	75,000
Equipment (net)	230,000	105,000
Investment in Bortz Corporation Stock	140,000	
Total Assets	$625,000	$275,000
Accounts Payable	$ 82,000	$ 28,000
Notes Payable	200,000	107,000
Common Stock	180,000	50,000
Additional Paid-In Capital		25,000
Retained Earnings	163,000	65,000
Total Liabilities and Stockholders' Equity	$625,000	$275,000

Required

Prepare a consolidated balance sheet for Potash Company as of January 1, 20X7.

P3–29 **Parent Company and Consolidated Amounts**

Quoton Corporation purchased 80 percent of the common stock of Tempro Company on December 31, 20X5, at underlying book value. The following trial balance data was provided by Tempro Company at December 31, 20X5:

	Debit	Credit
Cash	$ 28,000	
Accounts Receivable	65,000	
Inventory	90,000	
Buildings and Equipment (net)	210,000	
Cost of Goods Sold	105,000	
Depreciation Expense	24,000	
Other Operating Expenses	31,000	
Dividends Declared	15,000	
Accounts Payable		$ 33,000
Notes Payable		120,000
Common Stock		90,000
Retained Earnings		130,000
Sales		195,000
Total	$568,000	$568,000

Required

a. How much did Quoton Corporation pay in purchasing its shares of Tempro Company?

b. If consolidated financial statements are prepared at December 31, 20X5, what amount will be assigned to the noncontrolling interest in the consolidated balance sheet?

c. If Quoton Corporation reported income of $143,000 from its separate operations for 20X5, what amount of consolidated net income will be reported for 20X5?

d. If Quoton Corporation had purchased its ownership of Tempro on January 1, 20X5, at underlying book value and Quoton reported income of $143,000 from its separate operations for 20X5, what amount of consolidated net income will be reported for 20X5?

P3–30 Purchase versus Pooling of Interests

Smart Corporation acquires 100 percent of the common stock of Wisner Company on January 1, 20X8, by issuing 50,000 shares of $4 par value common stock. Smart Corporation shares are selling for $11 at the time of issue. Balance sheet data of the two companies just before the acquisition are summarized as follows:

	Smart Corporation		Wisner Company	
	Book Value	*Fair Value*	*Book Value*	*Fair Value*
Total Assets	$800,000	$970,000	$400,000	$610,000
Total Liabilities	$200,000	215,000	$100,000	110,000
Total Stockholders' Equity	600,000		300,000	
Total Liabilities and Stockholders' Equity	$800,000		$400,000	

Required

Indicate the dollar amounts to be reported in the consolidated balance sheet for each of the following items under the alternatives indicated.

a. Acquisition of shares by Smart Corporation recorded as a pooling of interests:
   (1) Total assets.
   (2) Total liabilities.
   (3) Total stockholders' equity.

b. Acquisition of shares by Smart Corporation recorded as a purchase:
   (1) Total assets.
   (2) Total liabilities.
   (3) Total stockholders' equity.

P3–31 Parent Company and Consolidated Balances

Exacto Company reported net assets of $260,000 on January 1, 20X5, and reported the following net income and dividends for the years indicated:

Year	Net Income	Dividends
20X5	$35,000	$12,000
20X6	45,000	20,000
20X7	30,000	14,000

True Corporation purchased 75 percent of the common stock of Exacto Company on January 1, 20X5, and reported a balance in its investment account of $259,800 on December 31, 20X7. The excess of the purchase price paid by True Corporation over book value of the shares acquired was assigned to equipment with an economic life of 10 years remaining at January 1, 20X5.

Required

a. What amount was paid in excess of book value by True Corporation when it purchased the shares of Exacto?

b. What amount will be added to buildings and equipment when the consolidated balance sheet is prepared at December 31, 20X7?

c. What amount will be added to accumulated depreciation when the consolidated balance sheet is prepared at December 31, 20X7?

d. What amount will be assigned to the noncontrolling shareholders in the consolidated balance sheet prepared at December 31, 20X7?

P3–32   Fair Value Greater than Cost

Delkart Products Company acquired 100 percent of the common shares of Angel Company on January 1, 20X2, by issuing 6,000 shares of its $10 par common stock. At the time of the business combination, Delkart's stock was selling for $70 per share. Balance sheets for the two companies as of December 31, 20X1, with fair values included, were as follows:

	Delkart Products Co.		Angel Company	
	Book Value	*Fair Value*	*Book Value*	*Fair Value*
Cash and Receivables	$ 80,000	$ 80,000	$ 75,000	$ 75,000
Inventory	240,000	260,000	125,000	145,000
Equipment (net)	480,000	560,000	300,000	340,000
Total Assets	$800,000	$900,000	$500,000	$560,000
Current Payables	$ 50,000	$ 50,000	$ 30,000	$ 30,000
Notes Payable	200,000	220,000	100,000	100,000
Common Stock	300,000		200,000	
Retained Earnings	250,000		170,000	
Total Liabilities and Equity	$800,000		$500,000	

On December 31, 20X1, Angel owed Delkart $25,000 on a one-year note; although the interest was paid on December 31, the principal was still outstanding on January 1, 20X2.

Required

Prepare a consolidated balance sheet for Delkart Products Company and its subsidiary as of January 1, 20X2:

a. Assuming the combination is treated as a pooling of interests.

b. Assuming the combination is treated as a purchase.

P3–33   Indirect Ownership

Purple Corporation recently attempted to expand by purchasing ownership in Green Company. The following ownership structure was reported on December 31, 20X9:

Investor	*Investee*	*Percentage of Ownership Held*
Purple Corporation	Green Company	70
Green Company	Orange Corporation	10
Orange Corporation	Blue Company	60
Green Company	Yellow Company	40

The following income from operations (excluding investment income) and dividend payments were reported by the companies during 20X9:

Company	Operating Income	Dividends Paid
Purple Corporation	$ 90,000	$60,000
Green Company	20,000	10,000
Orange Corporation	40,000	30,000
Blue Company	100,000	80,000
Yellow Company	60,000	40,000

Required

Compute the amount of consolidated net income reported for 20X9.

P3–34 Comprehensive Problem: Consolidated Financial Statements

Bishop Enterprises purchased 100 percent of the common shares of Mangle Manufacturing Company on January 1, 20X7, for $1,250,000, a price that was $55,000 in excess of the book value of the shares acquired. All of the excess of the cost over book value was related to goodwill except for $25,000 related to equipment with a five-year remaining life at the date of combination. The amount of the differential attributed to goodwill as a result of the purchase of Mangle Manufacturing shares is not amortized.

Balance sheets for the two companies as of December 31, 20X7, were as follows:

	Bishop Enterprises	Mangle Manufacturing
Cash	$ 71,000	$ 33,000
Receivables (net)	431,000	122,000
Inventory	909,000	370,000
Investment in Mangle Stock (at cost)	1,250,000	—
Land	510,000	100,000
Buildings (net)	1,303,000	250,000
Equipment (net)	1,528,000	475,000
Total Assets	$6,002,000	$1,350,000
Current Payables	$ 227,000	$ 95,000
Bonds Payable	500,000	—
Common Stock	1,000,000	500,000
Additional Paid-In Capital	3,550,000	400,000
Retained Earnings	725,000	355,000
Total Liabilities and Equity	$6,002,000	$1,350,000

For the year 20X7, the separate income statements of Bishop and Mangle included, among other items, the following:

	Bishop Enterprises	Mangle Manufacturing
Sales Revenue	$8,325,000	$2,980,000
Cost of Goods Sold	5,150,000	2,010,000
Depreciation Expense	302,000	85,000

The only intercompany transaction during 20X7 was a sale of inventory at the end of the year from Bishop to Mangle. Bishop originally purchased the goods for $34,000 and sold them to Mangle for $45,000 on account. All of the goods still were in Mangle's inventory at year-end, and the account had not yet been paid by Mangle.

Required

Indicate the amount at which each of the following items would be reported in the 20X7 consolidated financial statements of Bishop Enterprises and its subsidiary:

a. Cash.
b. Receivables (net).
c. Inventory.
d. Investment in Mangle Stock.
e. Equipment (net).
f. Goodwill.
g. Current Payables.
h. Common Stock (par).
i. Sales Revenue.
j. Cost of Goods Sold.
k. Depreciation Expense.

P3–35*   Balance Sheet Amounts under Alternative Accounting Theories

Parsons Corporation purchased 75 percent ownership of Tumble Company on December 31, 20X7, for $210,000. Summarized balance sheet amounts for the companies on December 31, 20X7, prior to the purchase, were as follows:

	Parsons Corporation	Tumble Company Book Value	Fair Value
Cash and Inventory	$300,000	$ 80,000	$ 80,000
Buildings and Equipment (net)	400,000	120,000	180,000
Total Assets	$700,000	$200,000	$260,000
Common Stock	$380,000	$ 90,000	
Retained Earnings	320,000	110,000	
Total Liabilities and Stockholders' Equity	$700,000	$200,000	

Required

If consolidated financial statements are prepared, determine the amounts that would be reported as cash and inventory, buildings and equipment (net), and goodwill using the following consolidation alternatives:

a. Proprietary theory.

b. Parent company theory.

c. Entity theory.

d. Current accounting practice.

CONSOLIDATION AS OF THE DATE OF ACQUISITION

Consolidated and unconsolidated financial statements are prepared using the same generally accepted accounting principles. The unique aspect of consolidated statements is that they bring together the operating results and financial positions of two or more separate legal entities into a single set of statements for the economic entity as a whole. To accomplish this, the consolidation process includes procedures that eliminate all effects of intercorporate ownership and intercompany transactions. Only transactions with parties external to the economic entity are reported in the consolidated financial statements.

The procedures used in accounting for intercorporate investments were discussed in Chapter 2. These procedures are important for the preparation of consolidated statements because the specific consolidation procedures depend on the way in which the parent accounts for its investment in a subsidiary. The consolidated statements, however, are the same regardless of the method used by the parent company to account for its investment.

This chapter and the next provide a thorough introduction to the process by which consolidated financial statements are prepared. After introducing the consolidation workpaper, this chapter provides the foundation for an understanding of the preparation of consolidated financial statements by discussing the preparation of a consolidated balance sheet immediately following the establishment of a parent-subsidiary relationship. The process is extended in Chapter 5 to include the preparation of a full set of consolidated financial statements in subsequent periods. Then, using a building-block approach, Chapters 6 through 10 deal with intercorporate transfers and other more complex issues.

Consolidation Workpapers

The *consolidation workpaper* provides a mechanism for efficiently combining the accounts of the separate companies involved in the consolidation and for adjusting the combined balances to the amounts that would be reported if all the consolidating companies were actually a single company. Keep in mind that there is no set of books for the consolidated entity. The parent and its subsidiaries, as separate legal and accounting entities, each maintain their own books. When consolidated financial statements are prepared, the account balances are taken from the separate books of the parent and

FIGURE 4–1   Format for Consolidation Workpaper

Account Titles	Trial Balance Data		Elimination Entries		Consolidated
	Parent	Subsidiary	Debits	Credits	

Work flow →

each subsidiary and placed in the consolidation workpaper. The consolidated statements are prepared, after adjustments and eliminations, from the amounts in the consolidation workpaper.

Workpaper Format

The basic form of the consolidation workpaper is shown in Figure 4–1. The titles of the accounts of the consolidating companies are listed in the first column of the workpaper. The account balances from the books or trial balances of the individual companies are listed in the next set of columns, with a separate column for each company included in the consolidation. Entries are made in the columns labeled "Elimination Entries" to adjust or eliminate balances so that the resulting amounts are those that would appear in the financial statements if all the consolidating companies actually formed a single company. The balances in the last column are obtained by summing all amounts algebraically across the workpaper by account. These are the balances that appear in the consolidated financial statements.

Nature of Eliminating Entries

Eliminating entries are used in the consolidation workpaper to adjust the totals of the individual account balances of the separate consolidating companies to reflect the amounts that would appear if all the legally separate companies were actually a single company. Eliminating entries appear only in the consolidating workpapers and do not affect the books of the separate companies.

For the most part, companies that are to be consolidated record their transactions during the period without regard to the consolidated entity. Transactions with related companies tend to be recorded in the same manner as those with unrelated parties, although intercompany transactions may be recorded in separate accounts or other records may be kept to facilitate the later elimination of intercompany transactions. Each of the consolidating companies also prepares its adjusting and closing entries at the end of the period in the normal manner. The resulting balances are entered in the consolidation workpaper and combined to arrive at the consolidated totals. Eliminating entries are used to increase or decrease in the workpaper the combined totals for individual accounts so that only transactions with external parties are reflected in the consolidated amounts.

Some eliminating entries are required at the end of one period but not at the end of subsequent periods. For example, a loan from a parent to a subsidiary in December 20X1, repaid in February 20X2, requires an entry to eliminate the intercompany receivable and payable on December 31, 20X1, but not at the end of 20X2. Some other eliminating entries need to be placed in the consolidation workpapers each time consolidated statements are prepared for a period of years. For example, if a parent company sells land to a subsidiary for $5,000 above the cost to the parent, a workpaper entry is needed to reduce the land amount by $5,000 each time a consolidated balance sheet is prepared, for as long as the land is held by an affiliate. It is important to remember that eliminating entries, because they are not made on the books of any company, do not carry over from period to period.

Preparation of Consolidated Balance Sheet Immediately Following Acquisition of Full Ownership

The simplest consolidation setting occurs when the financial statements of related companies are consolidated immediately after a parent-subsidiary relationship is established through a business combination. A series of examples follows that illustrates the preparation of a consolidated balance sheet in various situations that might arise when the business combination is treated as a purchase. In each example, Peerless Products Corporation purchases all or part of the capital stock of Special Foods Inc. on January 1, 20X1, and immediately prepares a consolidated balance sheet. The separate balance sheets of the two companies immediately before the combination appear in Figure 4–2.

In the material that follows, all journal entries and workpaper eliminating entries are numbered sequentially throughout the chapter. Eliminating entries appearing in the workpapers are also discussed in the text of the chapter. To avoid confusing the eliminating entries with journal entries that appear on the separate books of the parent or subsidiary, all workpaper eliminating entries appearing in the text are shaded and designated by an entry number preceded by an "E."

Full Ownership Purchased at Book Value

In the first example, Peerless purchases all of Special Foods' outstanding common stock for $300,000. On the date of combination, the fair values of Special Foods' individual assets and liabilities are equal to their book values shown in Figure 4–2.

FIGURE 4–2   **Balance Sheets of Peerless Products and Special Foods, January 1, 20X1, Immediately before Combination**

	Peerless Products	*Special Foods*
Assets		
Cash	$ 350,000	$ 50,000
Accounts Receivable	75,000	50,000
Inventory	100,000	60,000
Land	175,000	40,000
Buildings and Equipment	800,000	600,000
Accumulated Depreciation	(400,000)	(300,000)
Total Assets	$1,100,000	$500,000
Liabilities and Stockholders' Equity		
Accounts Payable	$ 100,000	$100,000
Bonds Payable	200,000	100,000
Common Stock	500,000	200,000
Retained Earnings	300,000	100,000
Total Liabilities and Equity	$1,100,000	$500,000

Because Peerless acquires all of Special Foods' common stock and because Special Foods has only the one class of stock outstanding, the total book value of the shares acquired is equal to the total stockholders' equity of Special Foods ($200,000 + $100,000). The purchase price of $300,000 is equal to the book value of the shares acquired. This ownership situation can be characterized as follows:

(P)	Investment cost		$300,000
	Book value		
1/1/X1	Common stock—Special Foods	$200,000	
100%	Retained earnings—Special Foods	100,000	
		$300,000	
(S)	Peerless's share	× 1.00	(300,000)
	Difference between cost and book value		$ -0-

Peerless records the stock acquisition on its books with the following entry on the date of combination:

January 1, 20X1
(1) Investment in Special Foods Stock   300,000
          Cash   300,000
     Record purchase of Special Foods stock.

The separate financial statements of Peerless and Special Foods immediately after the combination appear in Figure 4–3. Special Foods' balance sheet in Figure 4–3 is the same as in Figure 4–2, but the balance sheet of Peerless has changed to reflect the $300,000 reduction in cash and the recording of the investment in Special Foods stock for the same amount.

FIGURE 4–3 **Balance Sheets of Peerless Products and Special Foods, January 1, 20X1, Immediately after Combination**

	Peerless Products	Special Foods
Assets		
Cash	$ 50,000	$ 50,000
Accounts Receivable	75,000	50,000
Inventory	100,000	60,000
Land	175,000	40,000
Buildings and Equipment	800,000	600,000
Accumulated Depreciation	(400,000)	(300,000)
Investment in Special Foods Stock	300,000	
Total Assets	$1,100,000	$500,000
Liabilities and Stockholders' Equity		
Accounts Payable	$ 100,000	$100,000
Bonds Payable	200,000	100,000
Common Stock	500,000	200,000
Retained Earnings	300,000	100,000
Total Liabilities and Equity	$1,100,000	$500,000

Consolidation Workpaper. The workpaper for the preparation of a consolidated balance sheet immediately following the acquisition is presented in Figure 4–4. The first two columns of the workpaper in Figure 4–4 are the account balances taken from the books of Peerless and Special Foods, as shown in Figure 4–3. The balances of like accounts are placed side by side so that they may be added together. If more than two companies were to be consolidated, a separate column would be included in the workpaper for each additional subsidiary.

The accounts are placed in the workpaper so that those having debit balances are in the upper half of the workpaper and those having credit balances are in the lower half. Total debit items must equal total credit items for each of the companies and for the consolidated totals.

The two columns labeled "Eliminations" in Figure 4–4 are used to adjust the amounts reported by the individual companies to the amounts appropriate for the consolidated statement. All eliminations made in the workpapers are made in double-entry form; the debit amounts of each entry must equal the credit amounts. All parts of the same eliminating entry are "keyed" with the same number or other symbol so that whole entries can be identified. When the workpaper is completed, total debits entered in the Debit Eliminations column must equal total credits entered in the Credit Eliminations column. After the appropriate eliminating entries have been entered in the Eliminations columns, summing algebraically across the individual accounts provides the consolidated totals.

The Investment Elimination Entry. The only eliminating entry in the workpaper in Figure 4–4 is that needed to eliminate the Investment in Special Foods Stock account and the subsidiary's stockholders' equity accounts. This is accomplished through entry E(2) in the workpaper:

FIGURE 4–4   **Workpaper for Consolidated Balance Sheet, January 1, 20X1, Date of Combination; 100 Percent Purchase at Book Value**

Item	Peerless Products	Special Foods	Eliminations Debit	Eliminations Credit	Consolidated
Cash	50,000	50,000			100,000
Accounts Receivable	75,000	50,000			125,000
Inventory	100,000	60,000			160,000
Land	175,000	40,000			215,000
Buildings and Equipment	800,000	600,000			1,400,000
Investment in Special Foods Stock	300,000			(2) 300,000	
Total Debits	1,500,000	800,000			2,000,000
Accumulated Depreciation	400,000	300,000			700,000
Accounts Payable	100,000	100,000			200,000
Bonds Payable	200,000	100,000			300,000
Common Stock	500,000	200,000	(2) 200,000		500,000
Retained Earnings	300,000	100,000	(2) 100,000		300,000
Total Credits	1,500,000	800,000	300,000	300,000	2,000,000

Elimination entry:

(2) Eliminate investment balance and stockholders' equity of Special Foods.

(*Note:* Elimination entries are keyed to those in the text; all entries are numbered sequentially throughout the chapter.)

E(2) Common Stock—Special Foods	200,000	
Retained Earnings	100,000	
Investment in Special Foods Stock		300,000
Eliminate investment balance.		

Remember that this entry is made in the consolidation workpaper, not on the books of either the parent or the subsidiary, and is presented here in general journal form only for instructional purposes.

The investment account must be eliminated because, from a single entity viewpoint, a company cannot hold an investment in itself. The subsidiary's stock and the related stockholders' equity accounts must be eliminated because the stock of the subsidiary is held entirely within the consolidated entity and none represents claims by outsiders.

From a somewhat different viewpoint, the investment account on the parent's books can be thought of as a single account representing the parent's investment in the net assets of the subsidiary, a so-called *one-line consolidation*. In a full consolidation, the individual assets and liabilities of the subsidiary are combined with those of the parent. Including both the net assets of the subsidiary, as represented by the balance in the investment account, and the subsidiary's individual assets and liabilities would double-count the same set of assets. Therefore, the investment account is eliminated and not carried to the consolidated balance sheet.

The Consolidated Balance Sheet.   The consolidated balance sheet presented in Figure 4–5 is prepared directly from the last column of the consolidation workpaper in Figure 4–4. The total debit and credit balances shown on the balance sheet differ from

FIGURE 4–5 **Consolidated Balance Sheet, January 1, 20X1, Date of Combination; 100 Percent Purchase at Book Value**

Peerless Products Corporation and Subsidiary Consolidated Balance Sheet January 1, 20X1				
Assets			Liabilities	
Cash		$ 100,000	Accounts Payable	$ 200,000
Accounts Receivable		125,000	Bonds Payable	300,000
Inventory		160,000		
Land		215,000	Stockholders' Equity:	
Buildings and Equipment	$1,400,000		Common Stock	500,000
Accumulated Depreciation	(700,000)	700,000	Retained Earnings	300,000
Total Assets		$1,300,000	Total Liabilities and Equity	$1,300,000

the debit and credit totals given in the workpaper because contra asset accounts are included with the credits in the workpaper but are offset against the related assets in the consolidated balance sheet. Because the combination was treated as a purchase and there were no operations between the date of combination and the preparation of the consolidated balance sheet, the stockholders' equity section of the consolidated balance sheet is identical with that of Peerless given in Figure 4–2.

Full Ownership Purchased at More than Book Value

The price of the stock of a company is influenced by many factors, including net asset values, enterprise earning power, and general market conditions. When one company purchases another, there is no reason to expect that the purchase price necessarily will be equal to the book value of the stock acquired. The process used to prepare the consolidated balance sheet is complicated only slightly when 100 percent of the stock of a company is purchased at a price different from its book value.

To illustrate the purchase of a subsidiary at a price greater than book value, assume that Peerless purchases all of Special Foods' outstanding capital stock for $340,000 in cash on January 1, 20X1. In doing so, Peerless pays $40,000 in excess of the book value of that stock. The resulting ownership situation can be viewed as follows:

(P)	Investment cost			$340,000
	Book value			
1/1/X1	Common stock—Special Foods	$200,000		
100%	Retained earnings—Special Foods	100,000		
		$300,000		
(S)	Peerless's share	× 1.00	(300,000)	
	Differential			$ 40,000

Peerless records the stock acquisition by making the following entry:

January 1, 20X1		
(3) Investment in Special Foods Stock	340,000	
Cash		340,000
Record purchase of Special Foods stock.		

In a business combination accounted for as a purchase, the purchase price must be allocated to the assets and liabilities acquired. Therefore, the full amount paid by Peerless must be assigned to individual assets and liabilities of Special Foods when preparing consolidated financial statements.

The workpaper procedures used in adjusting to the proper consolidated amounts follow a consistent pattern. The first eliminating entry prepared in each case involves the elimination of the investor's investment account balance and each of the common stockholders' equity accounts of the investee. When the purchase price is above the underlying book value of the stock acquired, the first eliminating entry includes a debit to a workpaper clearing account to balance the entry. This clearing account is referred to as the **purchase differential,** or just *differential*. The differential represents the difference between the cost of the investment as recorded on the books of the parent and the book value of the shares acquired based on the stockholders' equity accounts of the subsidiary.

The workpaper entry to eliminate the investment account of Peerless Products and the stockholders' equity accounts of Special Foods is as follows:

E(4)	Common Stock—Special Foods	200,000	
	Retained Earnings	100,000	
	Differential	40,000	
	Investment in Special Foods Stock		340,000
	Eliminate investment balance.		

The balance assigned to Differential in this initial eliminating entry is subsequently cleared from that account through one or more additional workpaper entries. These additional workpaper entries adjust the various account balances to reflect the fair values of the subsidiary's assets and liabilities at the time the parent acquired the subsidiary.

Treatment of a Positive Differential

There are several reasons the purchase price of a company's stock might exceed the stock's book value:

1. Errors or omissions on the books of the subsidiary.
2. Excess of fair value over the book value of the subsidiary's net identifiable assets.
3. Existence of goodwill.
4. Other reasons.

Errors or Omissions on the Books of the Subsidiary.   An examination of the books of an acquired company may reveal material errors. In some cases, assets may have been expensed rather than capitalized by the acquired company or, for other reasons, omitted from the books. An acquired company that previously had been closely held may not have followed generally accepted accounting principles in maintaining its accounting records. In some cases, there may simply have been inadequate record-keeping.

Where such errors or omissions exist, corrections should be made directly on the books of the subsidiary as of the date of acquisition. These corrections are treated as prior-period adjustments in accordance with **FASB Statement No. 16,** "Prior Period Adjustments" (FASB 16). Once the books of the subsidiary are stated in accordance with generally accepted accounting principles, that portion of the differential attributable to the errors or omissions would no longer exist.

Excess of Fair Value over Book Value of Subsidiary's Net Identifiable Assets. The fair value of a company's assets is an important factor in the overall determination of the purchase price of the company. In many cases, the fair value of an acquired company's net assets exceeds the book value. Consequently, the purchase price may exceed the book value of the stock acquired. Consistent with the accounting treatment required for purchase-type business combinations, the procedures used in preparing the consolidated balance sheet should lead to reporting all the assets and liabilities of the acquired company based on their fair values on the date of combination. This valuation may be accomplished in one of two ways: (1) the assets and liabilities of the subsidiary may be revalued directly on the books of the subsidiary, or (2) the accounting basis of the subsidiary may be maintained and the revaluations made each period in the consolidation workpaper.

Revaluing the assets and liabilities on the books of the subsidiary generally is the simplest approach if all the common stock of the subsidiary is acquired. On the other hand, it generally is not appropriate to revalue the assets and liabilities on the books of the subsidiary if there is a significant noncontrolling interest in that subsidiary. From a noncontrolling shareholder's point of view, the subsidiary is a continuing company, and the basis of accounting should not change. More difficult to resolve is the situation where the parent acquires all the common stock of the subsidiary but continues to issue separate financial statements of the subsidiary to holders of the subsidiary's bonds or preferred stock. Revaluing the assets and liabilities of the subsidiary directly on the subsidiary's books is referred to as ***push-down accounting*** and is discussed later in this chapter.

When the assets and liabilities are revalued directly on the subsidiary's books, that portion of the differential no longer exists. However, if the assets and liabilities are not revalued on the subsidiary's books, an entry to revalue those assets and allocate the differential is needed in the consolidation workpaper each time consolidated financial statements are prepared, for as long as the related assets are held.

In the example introduced earlier, Peerless Products acquired all the stock of Special Foods for $340,000, giving rise to a $40,000 debit differential. In a consolidated balance sheet prepared immediately after acquisition, the investment elimination entry appearing in the consolidation workpaper is (as given earlier):

E(4)	Common Stock—Special Foods	200,000	
	Retained Earnings	100,000	
	Differential	40,000	
	Investment in Special Foods Stock		340,000
	Eliminate investment balance.		

If the fair value of Special Foods' land is determined to be $40,000 greater than its book value, and all other assets and liabilities have fair values equal to their book values, the entire amount of the differential is allocated to the subsidiary's land. This allocation of the differential is made in the consolidation workpaper with the following entry:

FIGURE 4–6   Workpaper for Consolidated Balance Sheet, January 1, 20X1, Date of Combination; 100 Percent Purchase at More than Book Value

Item	Peerless Products	Special Foods	Eliminations Debit		Eliminations Credit		Consolidated
Cash	10,000	50,000					60,000
Accounts Receivable	75,000	50,000					125,000
Inventory	100,000	60,000					160,000
Land	175,000	40,000	(5)	40,000			255,000
Buildings and Equipment	800,000	600,000					1,400,000
Investment in Special Foods Stock	340,000				(4)	340,000	
Differential			(4)	40,000	(5)	40,000	
Total Debits	1,500,000	800,000					2,000,000
Accumulated Depreciation	400,000	300,000					700,000
Accounts Payable	100,000	100,000					200,000
Bonds Payable	200,000	100,000					300,000
Common Stock	500,000	200,000	(4)	200,000			500,000
Retained Earnings	300,000	100,000	(4)	100,000			300,000
Total Credits	1,500,000	800,000		380,000		380,000	2,000,000

Elimination entries:

(4) Eliminate investment balance and stockholders' equity of Special Foods.

(5) Assign differential to land.

E(5)	Land	40,000	
	Differential		40,000
	Assign differential to land.		

The consolidation workpaper reflecting the allocation of the differential to the subsidiary's land is illustrated in Figure 4–6. The workpaper is based on the data in Figure 4–2 and a purchase price of $340,000 for the stock of Special Foods.

The amounts reported in the consolidated balance sheet are those in the consolidated column of the workpaper in Figure 4–6. Land is included in the consolidated balance sheet at $255,000, the amount carried on Peerless's books ($175,000) plus the amount carried on Special Foods' books ($40,000) plus the differential reflecting the increased value of Special Foods' land ($40,000).

This example is sufficiently simple that the assignment of the differential to land could be made directly in eliminating entry E(4) rather than through the use of the differential clearing account. In practice, however, the differential often relates to more than a single asset, and the allocation of the differential may be considerably more complex than in this example. The possibilities for clerical errors are reduced in complex situations by making two separate entries rather than one complicated entry.

Existence of Goodwill.   If a company purchases a subsidiary at a price in excess of the total of the fair values of the subsidiary's net identifiable assets, the additional amount generally is considered to be a payment for the excess earning power of the acquired company, referred to as "goodwill." Thus, once the identifiable assets of the subsidiary are restated to their fair values, any remaining debit differential normally is allocated to goodwill.

If, in the example of Peerless and Special Foods, the fair values of Special Foods' assets and liabilities are equal to their book values, and the $40,000 differential is considered a payment for goodwill, the following elimination entry is needed in the consolidation workpaper:

E(6) Goodwill	40,000	
Differential		40,000
Assign differential to goodwill.		

The consolidation workpaper would appear as in Figure 4–6 except that elimination entry E(6) would replace elimination entry E(5). Goodwill, which does not appear on the books of either Peerless or Special Foods, would appear in the consolidated balance sheet immediately after acquisition at $40,000.

Other Reasons.   The amounts assigned to identifiable assets and goodwill should be reasonable when viewed in light of the existing circumstances and the conditions of the purchase. The reason for all or part of a debit differential is not always clear, however. In these cases, management sometimes chooses to carry a portion of the differential directly to the consolidated balance sheet with a title such as "Excess of Purchase Price over Fair Value of Subsidiary's Net Assets."

Cases where the reason for a debit differential is not determinable should be rare. Normally, the management of the parent company is expected to know why it paid a particular price for the subsidiary, and the differential should be allocated accordingly.

In practice, companies sometimes do not attempt to allocate any of the differential, and simply report the entire amount in the consolidated balance sheet as a deferred charge. Usually this amount is given a title such as "Excess of Purchase Price over Book Value of Investment in Subsidiary Stock." While expedient, such an approach is inappropriate because it is not consistent with the idea of a single economic entity.

Illustration of Treatment of Debit Differential

In many situations, the differential relates to a number of different assets and liabilities. As a means of illustrating the allocation of the differential to various assets and liabilities, assume the book values and fair values of Special Foods' assets and liabilities are as shown in Figure 4–7. The inventory and land have fair values in excess of their book values, while the buildings and equipment are worth less than their book values.

Bond prices fluctuate as interest rates change. In this example, the value of Special Foods' bonds payable is greater than the book value. This indicates that the nominal interest rate on the bonds is higher than the current market rate of interest, and, therefore, investors are willing to pay a price higher than par for the bonds. With the fluctuations in interest rates in recent years, considerable emphasis has been placed on valuing acquired liabilities at their fair values. In determining a purchase price for Special Foods, Peerless must recognize that it is assuming a liability that pays an interest rate higher than the current market rate and will pay a lower price for Special Foods than if the liability carried a lower interest rate. The resulting consolidated financial

FIGURE 4–7   **Balance Sheet for Special Foods Inc., January 1, 20X1, Date of Combination**

		Book Value	Fair Value	Difference between Fair Value and Book Value
Cash		$ 50,000	$ 50,000	
Accounts Receivable		50,000	50,000	
Inventory		60,000	75,000	$15,000
Land		40,000	100,000	60,000
Buildings and Equipment	$600,000			
Accumulated Depreciation	(300,000)	300,000	290,000	(10,000)
		$500,000	$565,000	
Accounts Payable		$100,000	$100,000	
Bonds Payable		100,000	135,000	(35,000)
Common Stock		200,000		
Retained Earnings		100,000		
		$500,000	$235,000	$30,000

statements, therefore, should recognize the fair values rather than the book values of Special Foods' liabilities.

Assume that Peerless Products acquires all Special Foods' capital stock for $400,000 on January 1, 20X1, by issuing $100,000 of 9 percent first mortgage bonds and paying cash of $300,000. The resulting ownership situation can be pictured as follows:

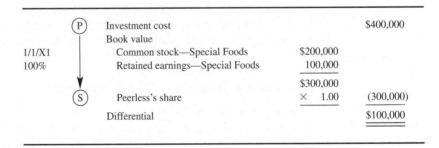

Peerless records the investment on its books with the following entry:

January 1, 20X1
  (7) Investment in Special Foods Stock   400,000
             Bonds Payable   100,000
             Cash   300,000
     Record purchase of Special Foods stock.

The relationship between the total purchase price paid for the stock of Special Foods, the fair value of Special Foods' net assets, and the book value of Special Foods' net assets is as follows:

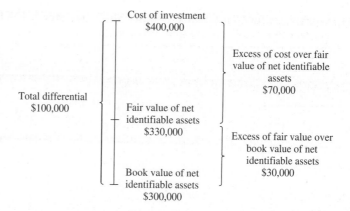

The total purchase price of $400,000 exceeds by $100,000 the book value of Special Foods' net assets (assets of $500,000 less liabilities of $200,000). Thus, there is a total purchase differential of $100,000. The total fair value of the net identifiable assets acquired in the combination is $330,000 ($565,000 − $235,000), based on the data in Figure 4–7. The amount by which the total purchase price of $400,000 exceeds the $330,000 fair value of the net identifiable assets is $70,000, and that amount is assigned to goodwill in the consolidated balance sheet.

The eliminations entered in the consolidation workpaper in preparing the consolidated balance sheet immediately after the combination are:

E(8)	Common Stock—Special Foods	200,000	
	Retained Earnings	100,000	
	Differential	100,000	
	Investment in Special Foods Stock		400,000
	Eliminate investment balance.		
E(9)	Inventory	15,000	
	Land	60,000	
	Goodwill	70,000	
	Buildings and Equipment		10,000
	Premium on Bonds Payable		35,000
	Differential		100,000
	Assign differential.		

These entries are reflected in the workpaper in Figure 4–8. While entry E(9) is somewhat more complex than those in the previous examples, there is no conceptual difference. In each case, the end result is a consolidated balance sheet with the assets and liabilities of the subsidiary valued at their fair values at the date of combination.

Full Ownership Purchased at Less than Book Value

There have been numerous cases of companies with common stock trading in the market at prices less than book value. Often the companies are singled out as prime acquisition targets. When one company acquires the stock of another at less than book value, there may be several reasons for the negative, or credit, differential:

1. Errors or omissions on the books of the subsidiary.

FIGURE 4–8 Workpaper for Consolidated Balance Sheet, January 1, 20X1, Date of Combination; 100 Percent Purchase at More than Book Value

	Peerless Products	Special Foods	Eliminations Debit		Eliminations Credit		Consolidated
Item							
Cash	50,000	50,000					100,000
Accounts Receivable	75,000	50,000					125,000
Inventory	100,000	60,000	(9)	15,000			175,000
Land	175,000	40,000	(9)	60,000			275,000
Buildings and Equipment	800,000	600,000			(9)	10,000	1,390,000
Goodwill			(9)	70,000			70,000
Investment in Special Foods Stock	400,000				(8)	400,000	
Differential			(8)	100,000	(9)	100,000	
Total Debits	1,600,000	800,000					2,135,000
Accumulated Depreciation	400,000	300,000					700,000
Accounts Payable	100,000	100,000					200,000
Bonds Payable	300,000	100,000					400,000
Premium on Bonds Payable					(9)	35,000	35,000
Common Stock	500,000	200,000	(8)	200,000			500,000
Retained Earnings	300,000	100,000	(8)	100,000			300,000
Total Credits	1,600,000	800,000		545,000		545,000	2,135,000

Elimination entries:

(8) Eliminate investment balance and stockholders' equity of Special Foods.

(9) Assign differential.

2. Excess of book value over the fair value of the subsidiary's net identifiable assets.

3. Diminution of previously recorded goodwill.

4. Bargain purchase.

Errors or Omissions on the Books of the Subsidiary. As in the case of a debit differential, errors or omissions on the subsidiary's books should be corrected directly on those books. Often this involves recognizing previously unrecorded liabilities incurred by the subsidiary. Once these corrections are made on the books of the subsidiary, that portion of the differential will no longer exist.

Excess of Book Value over Fair Value of Subsidiary's Net Identifiable Assets. Because in a purchase-type business combination all assets and liabilities of the acquired company are to be valued at their fair values as of the date of combination, adjustments are needed for any of the acquired company's assets and liabilities carried at amounts other than their current fair values. Assets with fair values less than their book values are written down on the subsidiary's books if push-down accounting is used, or in the consolidation workpaper.

Diminution of Previously Recorded Goodwill. If the subsidiary has goodwill carried on its books from a previous business combination, the credit differential may be

The balance sheet of Decibel at acquisition contained the following balances:

Decibel Studios
Balance Sheet
January 1, 20X2

Cash and Receivables	$ 40,000	Accounts Payable	$ 90,000
Inventory	180,000	Notes Payable	250,000
Buildings and Equipment (net)	350,000	Common Stock	100,000
Goodwill	30,000	Additional Paid-In Capital	200,000
		Retained Earnings	(40,000)
Total Assets	$600,000	Total Liabilities and Stockholders' Equity	$600,000

On the date of combination, the inventory held by Decibel Studios had a fair value of $170,000, and its buildings and recording equipment had a value of $375,000. Goodwill reported by Decibel resulted from a purchase of Sound Stage Enterprises in 20X1.Sound Stage was liquidated and its assets and liabilities were brought onto Decibel's books.

Required

Compute the balances to be reported in the consolidated statements for:

a. Inventory.

b. Buildings and Equipment (net).

c. Investment in Decibel Stock.

d. Goodwill.

e. Common Stock.

f. Retained Earnings.

P4–21 **Majority-Owned Subsidiary Purchased at Book Value**

Cameron Corporation purchased 70 percent of the common stock of Darla Corporation on December 31, 20X4, for $87,500. Data from the balance sheets of the two companies included the following amounts as of the date of acquisition:

Item	Cameron Corporation	Darla Corporation
Cash	$ 65,000	$ 21,000
Accounts Receivable	90,000	44,000
Inventory	130,000	75,000
Land	60,000	30,000
Buildings and Equipment	410,000	250,000
Less: Accumulated Depreciation	(150,000)	(80,000)
Investment in Darla Corporation Stock	87,500	
Total Assets	$692,500	$340,000
Accounts Payable	$152,500	$ 35,000
Mortgage Payable	250,000	180,000
Common Stock	80,000	40,000
Retained Earnings	210,000	85,000
Total Liabilities and Stockholders' Equity	$692,500	$340,000

At the date of the business combination, the book values of Darla Corporation's assets and liabilities approximated fair value. At December 31, 20X4, Cameron Corporation reported accounts payable of $12,500 to Darla Corporation and Darla Corporation reported an equal amount in its accounts receivable.

Required

a. Give the eliminating entry or entries needed to prepare a consolidated balance sheet immediately following the business combination.

b. Prepare a consolidated balance sheet workpaper.

c. Prepare a consolidated balance sheet in good form.

P4–22   Majority-Owned Subsidiary Purchased at Greater than Book Value

Cameron Corporation purchased 70 percent of the common stock of Darla Corporation on December 31, 20X4, for $102,200. Data from the balance sheets of the two companies included the following amounts as of the date of acquisition:

Item	Cameron Corporation	Darla Corporation
Cash	$ 50,300	$ 21,000
Accounts Receivable	90,000	44,000
Inventory	130,000	75,000
Land	60,000	30,000
Buildings and Equipment	410,000	250,000
Less: Accumulated Depreciation	(150,000)	(80,000)
Investment in Darla Corporation Stock	102,200	
Total Assets	$692,500	$340,000
Accounts Payable	$152,500	$ 35,000
Mortgage Payable	250,000	180,000
Common Stock	80,000	40,000
Retained Earnings	210,000	85,000
Total Liabilities and Stockholders' Equity	$692,500	$340,000

At the date of the business combination, the book values of Darla Corporation's assets and liabilities approximated fair value except for inventory, which had a fair value of $81,000, and buildings and equipment, which had a fair value of $185,000. At December 31, 20X4, Cameron Corporation reported accounts payable of $12,500 to Darla Corporation and Darla Corporation reported an equal amount in its accounts receivable.

Required

a. Give the eliminating entry or entries needed to prepare a consolidated balance sheet immediately following the business combination.

b. Prepare a consolidated balance sheet workpaper.

c. Prepare a consolidated balance sheet in good form.

P4–23   Consolidation of Majority-Owned Subsidiary with Differential

Forward Company was 75 percent acquired by Quinn Company on January 1, 20X9. The following balance sheet information was provided by the companies at the time:

Item	Quinn Company Book Value	Forward Company Book Value	Forward Company Fair Value
Cash	$ 166,000	$ 50,000	$ 50,000
Accounts Receivable	170,000	90,000	90,000
Inventory	220,000	180,000	240,000
Land	120,000	80,000	110,000
Buildings and Equipment	700,000	400,000	300,000
Less: Accumulated Depreciation	(290,000)	(150,000)	
Investment in Forward Co. Stock	397,000		
Total	$1,483,000	$650,000	$790,000
Accounts Payable	$ 110,000	$ 50,000	$ 50,000
Bonds Payable	440,000	250,000	240,000
Common Stock	300,000	140,000	
Additional Paid-In Capital	230,000	60,000	
Retained Earnings	403,000	150,000	
Total	$1,483,000	$650,000	$290,000

Required

a. Give all eliminating entries to prepare a consolidated balance sheet as of the date of acquisition.

b. Prepare a consolidated balance sheet workpaper.

c. Prepare a consolidated balance sheet in good form.

P4–24   Consolidation of Majority-Owned Subsidiary with Differential

Skyhigh Airlines acquired 80 percent of the stock of Klunker Car Rentals for $285,000 on January 1, 20X2. Summarized balance sheets for the two companies on January 1, 20X2, are presented below:

Klunker Car Rentals
Balance Sheet
January 1, 20X2

Cash and Receivables	$ 90,000	Accounts Payable	$ 60,000
Inventory	60,000	Taxes Payable	30,000
Land	30,000	Notes Payable	100,000
Buildings and Equipment (net)	230,000	Common Stock	200,000
Marketable Securities	80,000	Retained Earnings	100,000
Total Assets	$490,000	Total Liabilities and Stockholders' Equity	$490,000

Skyhigh Airlines
Balance Sheet
January 1, 20X2

Cash and Receivables	$ 140,000	Acounts Payable	$ 190,000
Inventory	30,000	Taxes Payable	15,000
Land	70,000	Bonds Payable	600,000
Planes and Equipment (net)	790,000	Common Stock	200,000
Investment in Klunker Car Rentals	285,000	Retained Earnings	310,000
Total Assets	$1,315,000	Total Liabilities and Stockholders' Equity	$1,315,000

At the time of acquisition, Klunker's land had an estimated value of $40,000, its buildings and equipment had a value of $250,000, and its notes payable had a fair value of $108,000. Book values and fair values were approximately equal for all other assets and liabilities.

Required

a. Give all eliminating entries needed to prepare a consolidated balance sheet for January 1, 20X2.

b. Complete a consolidated balance sheet workpaper.

c. Prepare a consolidated balance sheet in good form.

P4–25   Multiple-Choice Questions on Consolidated Balances

Whitehurst Electronics published the following balance sheet for December 31, 20X5:

Whitehurst Electronics
Balance Sheet
December 31, 20X5

Cash	$ 100,000	Accounts Payable	$ 70,000
Accounts Receivable	210,000	Taxes Payable	130,000
Inventory	360,000	Notes Payable	500,000
Buildings and Equipment	800,000	Common Stock	600,000
Less: Accumulated Depreciation	(320,000)	Additional Paid-In Capital	120,000
Goodwill	100,000	Retained Earnings	360,000
Investment in Shocker Manufacturing	530,000		
Total Assets	$1,780,000	Total Liabilities and Stockholders' Equity	$1,780,000

The balance sheet for Shocker Manufacturing for December 31, 20X5, appeared as follows:

Shocker Manufacturing
Balance Sheet
December 31, 20X5

Cash	$ 40,000	Accounts Payable	$ 10,000
Accounts Receivable	80,000	Taxes Payable	60,000
Inventory	120,000	Notes Payable	130,000
Buildings and Equipment	300,000	Common Stock	200,000
Less: Accumulated Depreciation	(90,000)	Retained Earnings	100,000
Marketable Securities	50,000		
Total Assets	$500,000	Total Liabilities and Stockholders' Equity	$500,000

Whitehurst acquired 80 percent of Shocker's common stock on December 31, 20X5. The fair values of Shocker's identifiable assets and liabilities were equal to book values, except for the following:

	Book Value	Fair Value
Inventory	$120,000	$190,000
Buildings and Equipment (net)	210,000	410,000
Notes Payable	130,000	120,000

Required

Select the correct answer for each of the following questions.

1. What will be the balance reported for consolidated retained earnings on December 31, 20X5?
    a. $360,000.
    b. $380,000.
    c. $440,000.
    d. $460,000.

2. What balance will be reported for common stock in the consolidated balance sheet?
    a. $600,000.
    b. $640,000.
    c. $760,000.
    d. $800,000.

3. What amount of notes payable will be reported by the consolidated entity?
    a. $596,000.
    b. $620,000.
    c. $622,000.
    d. $630,000.

4. What inventory balance will be reported in the consolidated balance sheet?
    a. $480,000.
    b. $512,000.
    c. $536,000.
    d. $550,000.

5. What amount of goodwill will be reported in the consolidated balance sheet?
    a. $100,000.
    b. $166,000.
    c. $330,000.
    d. $390,000.

6. What balance will be reported for the noncontrolling interest?
    a. $0.
    b. $40,000.
    c. $60,000.
    d. $112,000.

7. What amount of accounts payable will be reported in the consolidated balance sheet?
    a. $70,000.
    b. $72,000.
    c. $78,000.
    d. $80,000.

8. Total assets in the consolidated balance sheet will be:
    a. $1,750,000.
    b. $2,032,000.
    c. $2,180,000.
    d. $2,250,000.

9. Total stockholders' equity in the consolidated balance sheet will be:
    a. $1,080,000.
    b. $1,140,000.
    c. $1,320,000.
    d. $1,380,000.

10. Total liabilities reported in the consolidated balance sheet will be:
    a. $200,000.
    b. $700,000.
    c. $892,000.
    d. $900,000.

P4–26   Intercorporate Receivables and Payables

Astor Corporation acquired 60 percent of the outstanding shares of Shield Company on January 1, 20X7. Balance sheet data for the two companies immediately following the purchase were as follows:

	Astor Corporation	Shield Company
Cash	$ 70,000	$ 35,000
Accounts Receivable	90,000	65,000
Inventory	184,000	80,000
Buildings and Equipment	400,000	300,000
Less: Accumulated Depreciation	(160,000)	(75,000)
Investment in Shield Company Stock	191,000	
Investment in Shield Company Bonds	50,000	
Total Assets	$825,000	$405,000
Accounts Payable	$ 50,000	$ 20,000
Bonds Payable	200,000	100,000
Common Stock	300,000	150,000
Capital in Excess of Par		140,000
Retained Earnings	275,000	(5,000)
Total Liabilities and Equities	$825,000	$405,000

As indicated in the parent company balance sheet, Astor purchased $50,000 of Shield Company bonds from the subsidiary immediately after it purchased the stock. An analysis of intercompany receivables and payables also indicates that the subsidiary owes the parent $10,000. On the date of combination, the book values and fair values of Shield's assets and liabilities were the same.

Required

a. Give all eliminating entries needed to prepare a consolidated balance sheet for January 1, 20X7.
b. Complete a consolidated balance sheet workpaper.
c. Prepare a consolidated balance sheet in good form.

P4–27   Comprehensive Problem: Consolidation of Majority-Owned Subsidiary

On January 2, 20X8, B.N. Counter Corporation purchased 75 percent of the outstanding common stock of Ticken Tie Company. In exchange for Ticken Tie's stock, B.N. Counter issued bonds payable with a par and fair value of $500,000 directly to the selling stockholders of Ticken Tie. The two companies continued to operate as separate entities subsequent to the combination.

Immediately prior to the combination, the book values and fair values of the companies' assets and liabilities were as follows:

	B.N. Counter		Ticken Tie	
	Book Value	*Fair Value*	*Book Value*	*Fair Value*
Cash	$ 12,000	$ 12,000	$ 9,000	$ 9,000
Receivables	41,000	39,000	31,000	30,000
Allowance for Bad Debts	(2,000)		(1,000)	
Inventory	86,000	89,000	68,000	72,000
Land	55,000	200,000	50,000	70,000
Buildings and Equipment	960,000	650,000	670,000	500,000
Accumulated Depreciation	(411,000)		(220,000)	
Patent				40,000
Total Assets	$741,000	$990,000	$607,000	$721,000
Current Payables	$ 38,000	$ 38,000	$ 29,000	$ 29,000
Bonds Payable	200,000	210,000	100,000	90,000
Common Stock	300,000		200,000	
Additional Paid-In Capital	100,000		130,000	
Retained Earnings	103,000		148,000	
Total Liabilities and Equity	$741,000		$607,000	

At the date of combination, Ticken Tie owed B.N. Counter $6,000 plus accrued interest of $500 on a short-term note. These amounts have been properly recorded by both companies.

Required

a. Record the business combination on the books of B.N. Counter Corporation.

b. Present in general journal form all elimination entries that would be needed in a workpaper to prepare a consolidated balance sheet immediately following the business combination on January 2, 20X8.

c. Prepare and complete a consolidated balance sheet workpaper as of January 2, 20X8, immediately following the business combination.

d. Present a consolidated balance sheet for B.N. Counter and its subsidiary as of January 2, 20X8.

5

CONSOLIDATION FOLLOWING ACQUISITION

The procedures used to prepare a consolidated balance sheet as of the date of acquisition were introduced in the preceding chapter. More than a consolidated balance sheet, however, is needed to provide a comprehensive picture of the consolidated entity's activities following acquisition. As with a single company, the set of basic financial statements for a consolidated entity consists of a balance sheet, an income statement, a statement of changes in retained earnings, and a statement of cash flows.

The purpose of this chapter is to present the procedures used in the preparation of a consolidated balance sheet, income statement, and retained earnings statement subsequent to the date of combination. The preparation of a consolidated statement of cash flows is discussed in Chapter 10.

This chapter first deals with the important concepts of consolidated net income and consolidated retained earnings, followed by a description of the workpaper format used to facilitate the preparation of a full set of consolidated financial statements. The remainder of the chapter deals with the specific procedures used to prepare consolidated financial statements subsequent to the date of combination.

The discussion in the chapter focuses on procedures for consolidation when the parent company accounts for its investment in subsidiary stock using the equity method. If the parent accounts for its investment using the cost method, the general approach to the preparation of consolidated financial statements is the same, but the specific procedures differ somewhat. The consolidation procedures following use of the cost method are discussed in Appendix 5A. Regardless of the method used by the parent to account for its subsidiary investment, however, the consolidated statements will be the same because the investment and related accounts are eliminated in the consolidation process.

Overview of the Consolidation Process

The approach followed to prepare a complete set of consolidated financial statements subsequent to a business combination is quite similar to that used to prepare a consolidated balance sheet as of the date of combination. However, in addition to the assets and liabilities, the revenues and expenses of the consolidating companies must be combined. As the accounts are combined, eliminations must be made in the consolidation workpaper so that the consolidated financial statements appear as if they are the financial statements of a single company.

Because consolidation subsequent to acquisition of a subsidiary involves changes that take place over time, the resulting financial statements rest heavily on the concepts of consolidated net income and consolidated retained earnings. The consolidation approach that has traditionally been used in practice in the United States and Canada is essentially the parent company approach, which emphasizes the income and retained earnings of the consolidated entity accruing to the parent.

Consolidated Net Income

All revenues and expenses of the individual consolidating companies arising from transactions with nonaffiliated companies are included in the consolidated income statement. The amount reported as ***consolidated net income*** is that part of the income of the total enterprise that is assigned to the shareholders of the parent company. When all subsidiaries are wholly owned by the parent, all income of the parent and its subsidiaries accrues to the shareholders of the parent company. In this case, consolidated net income is the difference between consolidated revenues and expenses. When a subsidiary is less than wholly owned, a portion of its income accrues to its noncontrolling shareholders and is excluded from consolidated net income. A subsidiary's income available for common shareholders is divided between the controlling and noncontrolling shareholders on the basis of their relative common stock ownership of the subsidiary. For example, if a parent owns 80 percent of the common stock of a subsidiary, and the subsidiary earns net income of $100,000, 80 percent of the income accrues to the parent and the remaining $20,000 is allocated to the noncontrolling interest.

Approaches to Computing Consolidated Net Income.   Consolidated net income is computed through an *additive approach* by adding together the parent's income from its own operations (i.e., excluding any income from consolidated subsidiaries recognized by the parent) and the parent's proportionate share of the net income of each subsidiary adjusted for differential write-off, where appropriate. This is the same approach used to compute the parent's equity-method net income. In the absence of unrealized profits from intercompany transactions, consolidated net income and the parent's equity-method net income are normally equal.

In the workpaper to prepare a complete set of consolidated financial statements, consolidated net income is determined using a *residual approach*. The revenues and expenses of the separate consolidating companies are included, and those elements that should not be included are eliminated. Consolidated net income, in simple cases, is equal to the total earnings for all companies consolidated, less any income recorded by the parent from the consolidating companies and any income assigned to noncontrolling shareholders. Intercorporate investment income included in the parent's net income must be removed in computing consolidated net income in order to avoid double counting.

Computation of Consolidated Net Income Illustrated.   To illustrate the computation of consolidated net income under the two approaches, assume that Push Corporation owns 80 percent of the stock of Shove Company, which was purchased at book value. During 20X1, Shove reports net income of $25,000, while Push reports earnings of $100,000 from its own operations and equity-method investment income of $20,000. Consolidated net income for 20X1 is computed as follows:

Additive Computation		
Separate operating income of Push		$100,000
Net income of Shove	$ 25,000	
Push's proportionate share	× .80	20,000
Consolidated net income		$120,000
Residual Computation		
Net income of Push	$120,000	
Less: Income from subsidiary	(20,000)	$100,000
Net income of Shove		25,000
		$125,000
Less: Income to noncontrolling interest	$ 25,000	
	× .20	(5,000)
Consolidated net income		$120,000

Note that both methods of computing consolidated net income lead to the same result; the two methods simply represent different approaches to reaching the same end.

Consolidated Retained Earnings

Consolidated retained earnings must be measured on a basis consistent with that used in determining consolidated net income. *Consolidated retained earnings* is that portion of the undistributed earnings of the consolidated enterprise accruing to the shareholders of the parent company. As with a single company, ending consolidated retained earnings is equal to the beginning consolidated retained earnings balance plus consolidated net income, less consolidated dividends.

Only those dividends paid to the owners of the consolidated entity can be included in the consolidated retained earnings statement. Because the owners of the parent company are considered to be the owners of the consolidated entity, only dividends paid by the parent company to its shareholders are treated as a deduction in the consolidated retained earnings statement; dividends of the subsidiary are not included.

Computing Consolidated Retained Earnings.   Consolidated retained earnings is computed by adding together the parent's retained earnings from its own operations (i.e., excluding any income from consolidated subsidiaries recognized by the parent) and the parent's proportionate share of the net income of each subsidiary since the date of acquisition, adjusted for differential write-off and goodwill impairment. This is the same approach used to compute the parent's retained earnings when the parent accounts for consolidated subsidiaries using the equity method on its books. In the absence of unrealized profits from intercompany transactions, consolidated retained earnings and the parent's equity-method retained earnings are normally equal.

If the parent uses the equity method on its books, the retained earnings of each subsidiary is completely eliminated when the subsidiary is consolidated. This is necessary because (1) retained earnings cannot be purchased, and so subsidiary retained earnings at the date of a purchase-type business combination cannot be included in the retained earnings of the combined company; (2) the parent's share of the subsidiary's income since acquisition is already included in the parent's equity-method retained earnings; and (3) the noncontrolling interest's share of the subsidiary's retained earnings is not included in consolidated retained earnings.

Consolidation—Controlling Ownership Purchased at Book Value

Because total ownership of a subsidiary is not required for consolidation, consolidated financial statements often include one or more subsidiaries that are less than wholly owned. Whenever the parent company holds less than total ownership of a subsidiary and consolidated financial statements are prepared, the claim of the noncontrolling shareholders must be reflected in the statements.

When a subsidiary is less than wholly owned, the consolidation procedures must be modified slightly from those discussed previously to include recognition of the noncontrolling interest. To illustrate, assume that on January 1, 20X1, Peerless Products purchases 80 percent of the common stock of Special Foods for $240,000. All other data are the same as those used in the previous example and presented in Figure 5–2. Because Special Foods has stockholders' equity of $300,000 on the date of combination, the purchase of 80 percent of Special Foods' outstanding stock for $240,000 is at underlying book value ($300,000 × .80). The resulting ownership situation can be characterized as follows:

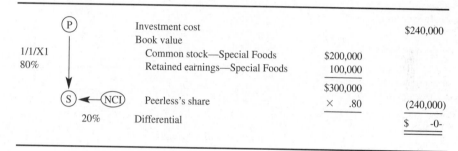

	Investment cost		$240,000
1/1/X1	Book value		
80%	Common stock—Special Foods	$200,000	
	Retained earnings—Special Foods	100,000	
		$300,000	
	Peerless's share	× .80	(240,000)
20%	Differential		$ -0-

Year of Combination

On January 1, 20X1, Peerless records its purchase of Special Foods common stock with the following entry:

January 1, 20X1

(10)	Investment in Special Foods Stock	240,000	
	Cash		240,000
	Record purchase of Special Foods stock.		

During 20X1, Peerless earns $140,000 from its own separate operations and declares dividends of $60,000. Special Foods reports net income of $50,000 and declares dividends of $30,000.

Parent Company Entries.   Peerless carries its investment in Special Foods stock using the equity method and, therefore, records its 80 percent share of Special Foods' 20X1 income and dividends with the following entries:

(11)	Investment in Special Foods Stock	40,000	
	Income from Subsidiary		40,000
	Record equity-method income:		
	$50,000 × .80		

(12)	Cash	24,000	
	Investment in Special Foods Stock		24,000
	Record dividends from Special Foods:		
	$30,000 × .80		

FIGURE 5–5   December 31, 20X1, Equity-Method Workpaper for Consolidated Financial Statements, Year of Combination; 80 Percent Purchase at Book Value

Item	Peerless Products	Special Foods	Eliminations Debit		Eliminations Credit		Consolidated
Sales	400,000	200,000					600,000
Income from Subsidiary	40,000		(13)	40,000			
Credits	440,000	200,000					600,000
Cost of Goods Sold	170,000	115,000					285,000
Depreciation and Amortization	50,000	20,000					70,000
Other Expenses	40,000	15,000					55,000
Debits	(260,000)	(150,000)					(410,000)
							190,000
Income to Noncontrolling Interest			(14)	10,000			(10,000)
Net Income, carry forward	180,000	50,000		50,000			180,000
Retained Earnings, January 1	300,000	100,000	(15)	100,000			300,000
Net Income, from above	180,000	50,000		50,000			180,000
	480,000	150,000					480,000
Dividends Declared	(60,000)	(30,000)			(13)	24,000	
					(14)	6,000	(60,000)
Retained Earnings, December 31, carry forward	420,000	120,000		150,000		30,000	420,000
Cash	264,000	75,000					339,000
Accounts Receivable	75,000	50,000					125,000
Inventory	100,000	75,000					175,000
Land	175,000	40,000					215,000
Buildings and Equipment	800,000	600,000					1,400,000
Investment in Special Foods Stock	256,000				(13)	16,000	
					(15)	240,000	
Debits	1,670,000	840,000					2,254,000
Accumulated Depreciation	450,000	320,000					770,000
Accounts Payable	100,000	100,000					200,000
Bonds Payable	200,000	100,000					300,000
Common Stock	500,000	200,000	(15)	200,000			500,000
Retained Earnings, from above	420,000	120,000		150,000		30,000	420,000
Noncontrolling interest					(14)	4,000	
					(15)	60,000	64,000
Credits	1,670,000	840,000		350,000		350,000	2,254,000

Elimination entries:
(13) Eliminate income from subsidiary.
(14) Assign income to noncontrolling interest.
(15) Eliminate beginning investment balance.

As a result of the entries recorded on the books of Peerless during 20X1, the balance in the investment account is $256,000 on December 31, 20X1. The trial balance data for Peerless and Special Foods at December 31, 20X1, appear in the workpaper in Figure 5–5. The amounts presented in Figure 5–5 for Peerless Products differ from those presented in Figure 5–3 as a result of the decrease in the percentage of Special Foods stock purchased and the correspondingly lower purchase price. Less cash was used in making the purchase, and a smaller share of income and dividends from Special Foods is recorded during 20X1 by Peerless. The trial balance for Special

Foods is unaffected by the level of ownership purchased by Peerless and therefore is the same as in Figure 5–3.

Consolidation Workpaper—Year of Combination. When a subsidiary is not wholly owned, the eliminating entries needed to prepare consolidated financial statements differ from those presented earlier in that these eliminating entries must establish the amount of the noncontrolling interest in the workpaper. Three eliminating entries are needed in this particular case. In the first eliminating entry, Peerless's share (80 percent) of Special Foods' income and dividends is eliminated in the normal manner:

E(13)	Income from Subsidiary	40,000	
	Dividends Declared		24,000
	Investment in Special Foods Stock		16,000
	Eliminate income from subsidiary.		

The difference between income and dividends is credited to the investment account and eliminates the change in the investment balance for 20X1. Except for the difference in the dollar amounts due to the difference in the percentage of ownership, this entry is identical with the entry used in the earlier illustration in which the subsidiary was 100 percent owned.

All three of the consolidated statements are affected by the existence of noncontrolling shareholders. The primary change in the consolidated income statement is that a portion of the income of the subsidiary is assigned to the noncontrolling interest and, in turn, is deducted in computing consolidated net income.

Individual revenue and expense items of the consolidating companies are included in the consolidated income statement at their full amounts regardless of the percentage ownership held by the parent. Including only the parent's share of revenue and expenses of partially owned subsidiaries would be inconsistent with the idea of a single economic entity. Thus, consolidated revenue and expenses are the same as in Figure 5–3 even though the ownership levels differ. Consolidated net income, on the other hand, is not the same, because it includes only the income assignable to parent company shareholders. Consolidated net income is reduced as the parent's ownership is reduced.

The amount of income assignable to noncontrolling shareholders of the subsidiary must be computed and deducted in arriving at consolidated net income each time consolidated statements are prepared. The share of Special Foods' income accruing to its noncontrolling shareholders is $10,000, the subsidiary's net income times the noncontrolling ownership percentage ($50,000 × .20). This amount is deducted in the workpaper to arrive at consolidated net income.

A separate entry is placed in the workpaper to establish the amount of income allocated to noncontrolling shareholders and to enter the increase in their claim on the net assets of the subsidiary during the period:

E(14)	Income to Noncontrolling Interest	10,000	
	Dividends Declared		6,000
	Noncontrolling Interest		4,000
	Assign income to noncontrolling interest.		

Income is assigned to the noncontrolling shareholders by entering a debit in the income statement portion of the workpaper. After summing across, this amount is subtracted in the consolidated column to arrive at consolidated net income.

Subsidiary dividends do not represent the dividends of the consolidated entity and therefore need to be eliminated fully. Workpaper entry E(13) eliminates only the parent's portion of subsidiary dividends. Entry E(14) eliminates the noncontrolling interest's share of subsidiary dividends. The difference between the noncontrolling stockholders' share of subsidiary income and their share of subsidiary dividends represents the change in their claim on the net assets of the subsidiary for the period and becomes part of the ending balance sheet amount of the noncontrolling interest.

The third workpaper entry in Figure 5–5 eliminates the stockholders' equity accounts of the subsidiary and the investment account balance shown by the parent at the beginning of the period. This entry also establishes the amount of the noncontrolling interest at the beginning of the period:

E(15)	Common Stock—Special Foods	200,000	
	Retained Earnings, January 1	100,000	
	Investment in Special Foods Stock		240,000
	Noncontrolling Interest		60,000
	Eliminate beginning investment balance.		

Noncontrolling Interest.   The total credits to noncontrolling interest in the eliminating entries equal $64,000. They consist of the noncontrolling stockholders' share of subsidiary net assets at the beginning of the period, established in entry E(15), and the noncontrolling stockholders' portion of the undistributed 20X1 earnings of the subsidiary, established in entry E(14). This $64,000 amount appears on the consolidated balance sheet prepared as of December 31, 20X1, as the total noncontrolling interest. The noncontrolling interest balance can be verified by multiplying the common stockholders' equity of the subsidiary on December 31, 20X1, by the noncontrolling interest's ownership ratio of 20 percent:

Special Foods common stock, December 31, 20X1	$200,000
Special Foods retained earnings, December 31, 20X1	120,000
Book value of Special Foods, December 31, 20X1	$320,000
Proportion of stock held by noncontrolling shareholders	× .20
Noncontrolling interest, December 31, 20X1	$ 64,000

Second Year of Ownership

Consolidation in the second year follows the same procedures as in the first year. From the data for Peerless and Special Foods outlined in Figure 5–2, it can be seen that Peerless earns separate operating income of $160,000 and pays dividends of $60,000 in 20X2. Special Foods reports net income of $75,000 and pays dividends of $40,000 in 20X2.

Parent Company Entries.   Peerless makes the following entries in 20X2 to record its 80 percent share of Special Foods' net income and dividends:

(16)	Investment in Special Foods Stock	60,000	
	Income from Subsidiary		60,000
	Record equity-method income:		
	$75,000 × .80		
(17)	Cash	32,000	
	Investment in Special Foods Stock		32,000
	Record dividends from Special Foods:		
	$40,000 × .80		

FIGURE 5–6 December 31, 20X2, Equity-Method Workpaper for Consolidated Financial Statements, Second Year following Combination; 80 Percent Purchase at Book Value

Item	Peerless Products	Special Foods	Eliminations Debit		Eliminations Credit		Consolidated
Sales	450,000	300,000					750,000
Income from Subsidiary	60,000		(18)	60,000			
Credits	510,000	300,000					750,000
Cost of Goods Sold	180,000	160,000					340,000
Depreciation and Amortization	50,000	20,000					70,000
Other Expenses	60,000	45,000					105,000
Debits	(290,000)	(225,000)					(515,000)
							235,000
Income to Noncontrolling Interest			(19)	15,000			(15,000)
Net Income, carry forward	220,000	75,000		75,000			220,000
Retained Earnings, January 1	420,000	120,000	(20)	120,000			420,000
Net Income, from above	220,000	75,000		75,000			220,000
	640,000	195,000					640,000
Dividends Declared	(60,000)	(40,000)			(18)	32,000	
					(19)	8,000	(60,000)
Retained Earnings, December 31, carry forward	580,000	155,000		195,000		40,000	580,000
Cash	291,000	85,000					376,000
Accounts Receivable	150,000	80,000					230,000
Inventory	180,000	90,000					270,000
Land	175,000	40,000					215,000
Buildings and Equipment	800,000	600,000					1,400,000
Investment in Special Foods Stock	284,000				(18)	28,000	
					(20)	256,000	
Debits	1,880,000	895,000					2,491,000
Accumulated Depreciation	500,000	340,000					840,000
Accounts Payable	100,000	100,000					200,000
Bonds Payable	200,000	100,000					300,000
Common Stock	500,000	200,000	(20)	200,000			500,000
Retained Earnings, from above	580,000	155,000		195,000		40,000	580,000
Noncontrolling interest					(19)	7,000	
					(20)	64,000	71,000
Credits	1,880,000	895,000		395,000		395,000	2,491,000

Elimination entries:
(18) Eliminate income from subsidiary.
(19) Assign income to noncontrolling interest.
(20) Eliminate beginning investment balance.

These entries increase the balance in Peerless's investment account by $28,000 during 20X2, resulting in an ending balance of $284,000.

Consolidation Workpaper—Second Year Following Combination. The three-part workpaper to prepare consolidated financial statements for 20X2 appears in Figure 5–6.

Three eliminating entries are needed to complete the workpaper:

E(18)	Income from Subsidiary	60,000	
	Dividends Declared		32,000
	Investment in Special Foods Stock		28,000
	Eliminate income from subsidiary.		
E(19)	Income to Noncontrolling Interest	15,000	
	Dividends Declared		8,000
	Noncontrolling Interest		7,000
	Assign income to noncontrolling interest.		
E(20)	Common Stock—Special Foods	200,000	
	Retained Earnings, January 1	120,000	
	Investment in Special Foods Stock		256,000
	Noncontrolling Interest		64,000
	Eliminate beginning investment balance.		

The first eliminating entry removes the income that Peerless has recognized from Special Foods, Peerless's share (80 percent) of Special Foods' dividends, and the $28,000 change in the investment account that occurred during 20X2.

Elimination entry E(19) assigns $15,000 of subsidiary income to the noncontrolling shareholders, based on subsidiary income of $75,000 and a 20 percent noncontrolling interest. The entry also eliminates the noncontrolling interest's share of Special Foods' dividends. Finally, this entry establishes in the workpaper the increase in the noncontrolling interest for the period.

Entry E(20) eliminates the stockholders' equity accounts of the subsidiary and the investment account balance reported by the parent at the beginning of the year and establishes the amount of the noncontrolling interest's claim on the net assets of the subsidiary at the beginning of the year.

The credits to noncontrolling interest in elimination entries E(19) and E(20) result in a total noncontrolling interest reported in the consolidated balance sheet on December 31, 20X2, of $71,000 ($7,000 + $64,000). This amount is equal to 20 percent of the stockholders' equity balance of Special Foods on that date [($200,000 + $155,000) × .20].

Consolidation—Controlling Ownership Purchased at More than Book Value

In many cases a controlling investment in another company is purchased at an amount in excess of the book value of the shares acquired. As discussed in Chapter 4, the excess of the purchase price over the book value of the net identifiable assets purchased must be allocated to those assets and liabilities acquired, including any purchased goodwill. If this revaluation is not accomplished on the separate books of the subsidiary through the use of push-down accounting, as illustrated in Appendix 5B, it must be made in the consolidation workpaper each time consolidated statements are prepared. In addition, if the revaluations relate to assets or liabilities that must be depreciated, amortized, or otherwise written off, appropriate entries must be made in the consolidation workpaper to reduce consolidated net income accordingly.

When the equity method is applied, as illustrated in Chapter 2, the amount of differential viewed as expiring during the period is recorded by the investor as a reduction in the income recognized from the investee. In consolidation, the purchase differential is assigned to the asset and liability balances, and the amounts expiring during the period are included in the appropriate expense categories (e.g., depreciation expense).

Year of Combination

To illustrate the purchase of less than total ownership at an amount greater than book value, assume that Peerless Products purchases 80 percent of the common stock of Special Foods on January 1, 20X1, for $310,000. The resulting ownership situation is as follows:

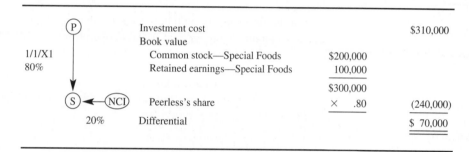

Investment cost		$310,000
Book value		
Common stock—Special Foods	$200,000	
Retained earnings—Special Foods	100,000	
	$300,000	
Peerless's share	× .80	(240,000)
Differential		$ 70,000

1/1/X1
80%
20%

The total book value of Special Foods stock on the date of combination is $300,000, and the book value of the stock acquired by Peerless is $240,000 ($300,000 × .80). The difference between the total purchase price of $310,000 and the book value of the shares acquired is $70,000.

On the date of combination, all assets and liabilities of Special Foods have fair values equal to their book values, except as follows:

	Book Value	Fair Value	Fair Value Increment	Peerless's 80% Portion
Inventory	$ 60,000	$ 65,000	$ 5,000	$ 4,000
Land	40,000	50,000	10,000	8,000
Buildings and Equipment	300,000	360,000	60,000	48,000
	$400,000	$475,000	$75,000	$60,000

Of the $70,000 total differential, $60,000 relates to identifiable assets of Special Foods. The remaining $10,000 is attributable to goodwill. The apportionment of the differential appears as follows:

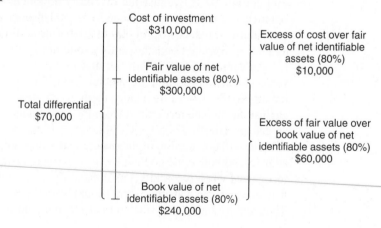

All the inventory to which the differential relates is sold during 20X1; none is left in ending inventory. The buildings and equipment have a remaining economic life of 10 years from the date of combination, and straight-line depreciation is used. At the end of 20X1, the management of Peerless determines that the goodwill acquired in the combination with Special Foods has been impaired. Management determines that a $2,500 goodwill impairment loss should be recognized in the consolidated income statement.

For the first year immediately after the date of combination, 20X1, Peerless Products earns income from its own separate operations of $140,000 and pays dividends of $60,000. Special Foods reports net income of $50,000 and pays dividends of $30,000.

Parent Company Entries.   During 20X1, Peerless makes the normal equity-method entries on its books to record its purchase of Special Foods stock and its share of Special Foods' net income and dividends:

(21)	Investment in Special Foods Stock	310,000	
	Cash		310,000
	Record purchase of Special Foods stock.		
(22)	Investment in Special Foods Stock	40,000	
	Income from Subsidiary		40,000
	Record equity-method income:		
	$50,000 \times .80$		
(23)	Cash	24,000	
	Investment in Special Foods Stock		24,000
	Record dividends from Special Foods:		
	$30,000 \times .80$		

Entries (22) and (23) are the same as if Peerless had acquired its 80 percent investment at underlying book value. In addition, however, entries are needed on Peerless's books to recognize the write-off of the differential:

(24)	Income from Subsidiary	4,000	
	Investment in Special Foods Stock		4,000
	Adjust income for differential related to inventory sold:		
	$5,000 \times .80$		
(25)	Income from Subsidiary	4,800	
	Investment in Special Foods Stock		4,800
	Amortize differential related to buildings and equipment.		

A portion of the differential, $4,000, relates to inventory of Special Foods that is sold during 20X1. Because the inventory no longer is held by Special Foods, the investment account must be reduced by $4,000 through entry (24). Further, Peerless's income must be reduced by $4,000 to reflect the additional amount paid by Peerless for its share of Special Foods' inventory sold during 20X1.

An additional $48,000 of the differential is attributable to the excess of the fair value over the book value of Special Foods' buildings and equipment with a 10-year remaining life. Use of the equity method requires the matching of the additional cost against the income recognized from the investment, and this is accomplished through annual amortization of $4,800 ($48,000 ÷ 10 years) in entry (25).

The $10,000 portion of the differential representing equity method goodwill is not adjusted. Although the goodwill will be written down and a goodwill impairment loss recognized when preparing consolidated financial statements, the FASB has indicated that no equity-method adjustment should be made to reflect this impairment of goodwill. Thus, the parent's equity-method net income (and retained earnings) will be different than consolidated net income (and retained earnings) when an impairment of goodwill has occurred.

Consolidation Workpaper—Year of Combination.   After the subsidiary income accruals are entered on the books of Peerless, the adjusted trial balance data of the consolidating companies are entered in the three-part consolidation workpaper as shown in Figure 5–7.

As before, the first three workpaper entries eliminate the subsidiary income and dividends recorded by Peerless, eliminate the investment account and the stockholders' equity accounts of Special Foods, and establish the noncontrolling interest:

E(26)	Income from Subsidiary	31,200	
	Dividends Declared		24,000
	Investment in Special Foods Stock		7,200
	Eliminate income from subsidiary.		
E(27)	Income to Noncontrolling Interest	10,000	
	Dividends Declared		6,000
	Noncontrolling Interest		4,000
	Assign income to noncontrolling interest.		
E(28)	Common Stock—Special Foods	200,000	
	Retained Earnings, January 1	100,000	
	Differential	70,000	
	Investment in Special Foods Stock		310,000
	Noncontrolling Interest		60,000
	Eliminate beginning investment balance.		

Entry E(26) removes the net effect of the income accrual recorded by the parent during 20X1 in entries (22), (24), and (25) and removes the parent's portion of dividends declared by the subsidiary during the period, as recorded in entry (23). Elimination entry E(27) places the noncontrolling interest's share of subsidiary income ($50,000 × .20) in the workpaper, eliminates the noncontrolling interest's share of subsidiary dividends ($30,000 × .20), and recognizes the increase in the noncontrolling interest during 20X1. The $4,000 increase in the claim of the noncontrolling shareholders for the period is included in the balance assigned to the noncontrolling interest in the bottom portion of the balance sheet section of the workpaper.

The third elimination entry, E(28), removes the stockholders' equity balances of the subsidiary and the investment account of the parent as of the beginning of the period and establishes the amount of the noncontrolling shareholders' claim as of the beginning of the period. Because the purchase price of the investment exceeded its book value, a purchase differential appears as the balancing figure in this entry. The differential established in this entry represents the unamortized amount as of the beginning of the period. Because the combination occurred on the first day of 20X1, the amount is equal to the differential on the date of combination, $70,000. As in Chapter 4, the differential account serves as a clearing account in the workpaper and is entered in the balance sheet portion of the workpaper at the bottom of the asset section.

Noncontrolling interest is credited for $60,000 ($300,000 × .20) in entry E(28), representing 20 percent of Special Foods' stockholders' equity at the beginning of the year. The noncontrolling interest totals $64,000 at the end of the period as a result of elimination entries E(27) and E(28). The amount assigned to the noncontrolling interest is based on the underlying book value of the subsidiary's net assets and is not affected by the amount paid by the parent in purchasing the subsidiary's stock. Thus, the noncontrolling shareholders' claim in Figure 5–7 is identical to that reported in Figure 5–5.

FIGURE 5–7 **December 31, 20X1, Equity-Method Workpaper for Consolidated Financial Statements, Year of Combination; 80 Percent Purchase at More than Book Value**

Item	Peerless Products	Special Foods	Eliminations Debit		Eliminations Credit		Consolidated
Sales	400,000	200,000					600,000
Income from Subsidiary	31,200		(26)	31,200			
Credits	431,200	200,000					600,000
Cost of Goods Sold	170,000	115,000	(29)	4,000			289,000
Depreciation and Amortization	50,000	20,000	(30)	4,800			74,800
Goodwill Impairment Loss			(31)	2,500			2,500
Other Expenses	40,000	15,000					55,000
Debits	(260,000)	(150,000)					(421,300)
							178,700
Income to Noncontrolling Interest			(27)	10,000			(10,000)
Net Income, carry forward	171,200	50,000		52,500			168,700
Retained Earnings, January 1	300,000	100,000	(28)	100,000			300,000
Net Income, from above	171,200	50,000		52,500			168,700
	471,200	150,000					468,700
Dividends Declared	(60,000)	(30,000)			(26)	24,000	
					(27)	6,000	(60,000)
Retained Earnings, December 31, carry forward	411,200	120,000		152,500		30,000	408,700
Cash	194,000	75,000					269,000
Accounts Receivable	75,000	50,000					125,000
Inventory	100,000	75,000					175,000
Land	175,000	40,000	(29)	8,000			223,000
Buildings and Equipment	800,000	600,000	(29)	48,000			1,448,000
Investment in Special Foods Stock	317,200				(26)	7,200	
					(28)	310,000	
Goodwill			(29)	10,000	(31)	2,500	7,500
Differential			(28)	70,000	(29)	70,000	
Debits	1,661,200	840,000					2,247,500
Accumulated Depreciation	450,000	320,000			(30)	4,800	774,800
Accounts Payable	100,000	100,000					200,000
Bonds Payable	200,000	100,000					300,000
Common Stock	500,000	200,000	(28)	200,000			500,000
Retained Earnings, from above	411,200	120,000		152,500		30,000	408,700
Noncontrolling interest					(27)	4,000	
					(28)	60,000	64,000
Credits	1,661,200	840,000		488,500		488,500	2,247,500

Elimination entries:
(26) Eliminate income from subsidiary.
(27) Assign income to noncontrolling interest.
(28) Eliminate beginning investment balance.
(29) Assign beginning differential.
(30) Amortize differential related to buildings and equipment.
(31) Write down goodwill for impairment.

Three additional eliminating entries are needed in the workpaper in Figure 5–7 to allocate and write down the differential:

E(29)	Cost of Goods Sold	4,000	
	Land	8,000	
	Buildings and Equipment	48,000	
	Goodwill	10,000	
	Differential		70,000
	Assign beginning differential.		
E(30)	Depreciation Expense	4,800	
	Accumulated Depreciation		4,800
	Amortize differential related to buildings and equipment:		
	$48,000 ÷ 10 years		
E(31)	Goodwill Impairment Loss	2,500	
	Goodwill		2,500
	Write down goodwill for impairment.		

Entry E(29) assigns the original amount of the differential to the appropriate asset and expense accounts based on the fair value differences computed previously.

Because all the inventory on hand on the date of combination has been sold during the year, the $4,000 of differential applicable to inventory is allocated directly to cost of goods sold. The cost of goods sold recorded on the books of Special Foods is correct for that company's separate financial statements. However, the cost of the inventory to the consolidated entity is viewed as being $4,000 higher, and this additional cost must be included in consolidated cost of goods sold.

No workpaper entry is needed in future periods with respect to the inventory because the inventory has been expensed and no longer is on the books of the subsidiary. The portion of the differential related to the inventory no longer exists on Peerless's books after 20X1 because it is removed from the investment account by entry (24).

The difference between the $310,000 total purchase price paid by Peerless and the $300,000 fair value of Peerless's share of the net identifiable assets acquired is assumed to be payment for the excess earning power of Special Foods. This difference is entered in the workpaper with entry E(29) as goodwill of $10,000.

The differential assigned to depreciable assets in entry E(29) must be charged to depreciation expense over the remaining lives of those assets. From a consolidated viewpoint, the parent's additional payment is part of the total cost of the depreciable assets. Depreciation already is recorded on the subsidiary's books based on the original cost of the assets to the subsidiary, and these amounts are carried to the consolidated workpaper as depreciation expense. Depreciation on the additional cost of those assets to the consolidated entity is entered in the consolidation workpaper through entry E(30). The impairment in the value of the goodwill acquired when Peerless purchased Special Foods is recognized with eliminating entry E(31). Although goodwill is not amortized, it must be written down when its value is impaired. This entry reduces the amount of goodwill to be reported in the consolidated balance sheet and establishes a loss to be reported in the consolidated income statement.

A distinction must be made between journal entries recorded on the parent's books under equity-method reporting and the eliminating entries needed in the workpaper to prepare the consolidated financial statements. The eliminating entry to record depreciation expense in the workpaper is needed even though Peerless amortizes the purchase differential on its books at the end of 20X1 with entry (25). The entry on Peerless's books alters the balance in its investment account and the amount of income recognized from Special Foods. However, both account balances are eliminated in the

FIGURE 5–8   Consolidated Net Income and Retained Earnings, 20X1; 80 Percent Purchase at More than Book Value

Consolidated net income, 20X1:	
Peerless's separate operating income	$140,000
Peerless's share of Special Foods' net income: $50,000 × .80	40,000
Write-off of differential related to inventory sold during 20X1	(4,000)
Amortization of differential related to buildings and equipment in 20X1	(4,800)
Goodwill impairment loss	(2,500)
Consolidated net income, 20X1	$168,700
Consolidated retained earnings, December 31, 20X1:	
Peerless's retained earnings on date of combination, January 1, 20X1	$300,000
Peerless's separate operating income, 20X1	140,000
Peerless's share of Special Foods' 20X1 net income: $50,000 × .80	40,000
Write-off of differential related to inventory sold during 20X1	(4,000)
Amortization of differential related to buildings and equipment in 20X1	(4,800)
Goodwill impairment loss	(2,500)
Dividends declared by Peerless, 20X1	(60,000)
Consolidated retained earnings, December 31, 20X1	$408,700

consolidation process, thereby removing any effect of entry (25) on the consolidated totals. Consequently, consolidated income does not reflect the amortization of the differential unless eliminating entry (30) is made.

Once the appropriate eliminating entries are placed in the consolidation workpaper in Figure 5–7, the workpaper is completed by summing each row across, taking into consideration the debit or credit effect of the eliminations.

Consolidated Net Income and Retained Earnings.   As can be seen from the workpaper, consolidated net income for 20X1 is $168,700 and consolidated retained earnings on December 31, 20X1, is $408,700. These amounts can be computed as shown in Figure 5–8. Note that both consolidated net income and retained earnings are reduced by the write-off of the purchase differential and the impairment of goodwill.

Second Year of Ownership

The consolidation procedures employed at the end of the second year, and in periods thereafter, are basically the same as those used at the end of the first year. Consolidation two years after acquisition is illustrated by continuing the example used for 20X1. During 20X2, Peerless Products earns income from its own separate operations of $160,000 and pays dividends of $60,000; Special Foods reports net income of $75,000 and pays dividends of $40,000. No further impairment of the goodwill acquired in the business combination occurs during 20X2.

Parent Company Entries.   Peerless Products records the following entries on its separate books during 20X2:

(32)	Investment in Special Foods Stock	60,000	
	Income from Subsidiary		60,000
	Record equity-method income:		
	$75,000 × .80		
(33)	Cash	32,000	
	Investment in Special Foods Stock		32,000
	Record dividends from Special Foods:		
	$40,000 × .80		

(34) Income from Subsidiary	4,800	
Investment in Special Foods Stock		4,800
Amortize differential related to buildings and equipment.		

Entry (34) to record the 20X2 amortization of the purchase differential related to buildings and equipment is identical to entry (25) recorded by Peerless in 2001 because the straight-line method is used.

The changes in the parent's investment account for 20X1 and 20X2 can be summarized as follows:

	20X1		20X2	
Balance at start of year		$310,000		$317,200
Income from subsidiary:				
Parent's share of subsidiary's income	$40,000		$60,000	
Differential write-off for inventory sold	(4,000)			
Amortization of differential	(4,800)		(4,800)	
		31,200		55,200
Less: Dividends received from subsidiary		(24,000)		(32,000)
Balance at end of year		$317,200		$340,400

Consolidation Workpaper—Second Year Following Combination. The workpaper to prepare a complete set of consolidated financial statements for the year 20X2 is illustrated in Figure 5–9. Eliminating entries at the end of 20X2 are similar to those at the end of 20X1.

The first workpaper entry, E(35), eliminates Peerless's income from Special Foods and Peerless's share of Special Foods' dividends for 20X2:

E(35) Income from Subsidiary	55,200	
Dividends Declared		32,000
Investment in Special Foods Stock		23,200
Eliminate income from subsidiary.		

The net credit to the investment account of $23,200 represents the increase in the account balance during the period and takes the account balance back to the amount on January 1, 20X2, the beginning of the second year.

The amount of subsidiary income assigned to the noncontrolling shareholders in 20X2 is $15,000 ($75,000 × .20), and this amount enters the workpaper through entry E(36):

E(36) Income to Noncontrolling Interest	15,000	
Dividends Declared		8,000
Noncontrolling Interest		7,000
Assign income to noncontrolling interest.		

The $15,000 of subsidiary income assigned to the noncontrolling interest is subtracted to arrive at consolidated net income in the income statement portion of the workpaper. Entry E(36) also includes a credit to Dividends Declared to eliminate the noncontrolling interest's portion of Special Foods' dividends. Entries E(35) and E(36) together totally eliminate the dividends of Special Foods. The $7,000 difference between the noncontrolling stockholders' share of subsidiary income and dividends represents the increase in the noncontrolling interest for 20X2 and is placed in the balance sheet portion of the workpaper.

FIGURE 5–9 December 31, 20X2, Equity-Method Workpaper for Consolidated Financial Statements, Second Year Following Combination; 80 Percent Purchase at More than Book Value

Item	Peerless Products	Special Foods	Eliminations Debit		Eliminations Credit		Consolidated
Sales	450,000	300,000					750,000
Income from Subsidiary	55,200		(35)	55,200			
Credits	505,200	300,000					750,000
Cost of Goods Sold	180,000	160,000					340,000
Depreciation and Amortization	50,000	20,000	(39)	4,800			74,800
Other Expenses	60,000	45,000					105,000
Debits	(290,000)	(225,000)					(519,800)
							230,200
Income to Noncontrolling Interest			(36)	15,000			(15,000)
Net Income, carry forward	215,200	75,000		75,000			215,200
Retained Earnings, January 1	411,200	120,000	(37)	120,000			
			(40)	2,500			408,700
Net Income, from above	215,200	75,000		75,000			215,200
	626,400	195,000					623,900
Dividends Declared	(60,000)	(40,000)			(35)	32,000	
					(36)	8,000	(60,000)
Retained Earnings, December 31, carry forward	566,400	155,000		197,500		40,000	563,900
Cash	221,000	85,000					306,000
Accounts Receivable	150,000	80,000					230,000
Inventory	180,000	90,000					270,000
Land	175,000	40,000	(38)	8,000			223,000
Buildings and Equipment	800,000	600,000	(38)	48,000			1,448,000
Investment in Special Foods Stock	340,400				(35)	23,200	
					(37)	317,200	
Goodwill			(38)	10,000	(40)	2,500	7,500
Differential			(37)	61,200	(38)	61,200	
Debits	1,866,400	895,000					2,484,500
Accumulated Depreciation	500,000	340,000			(38)	4,800	
					(39)	4,800	849,600
Accounts Payable	100,000	100,000					200,000
Bonds Payable	200,000	100,000					300,000
Common Stock	500,000	200,000	(37)	200,000			500,000
Retained Earnings, from above	566,400	155,000		197,500		40,000	563,900
Noncontrolling interest					(36)	7,000	
					(37)	64,000	71,000
Credits	1,866,400	895,000		524,700		524,700	2,484,500

Elimination entries:
 (35) Eliminate income from subsidiary.
 (36) Assign income to noncontrolling interest.
 (37) Eliminate beginning investment balance.
 (38) Assign beginning differential.
 (39) Amortize differential related to buildings and equipment.
 (40) Adjust for 20X1 impairment of goodwill.

Entry E(37) eliminates the balances in Peerless's investment account and Special Foods' stockholders' equity accounts as of the beginning of the period:

E(37)	Common Stock—Special Foods	200,000	
	Retained Earnings, January 1	120,000	
	Differential	61,200	
	Investment in Special Foods Stock		317,200
	Noncontrolling Interest		64,000
	Eliminate beginning investment balance.		

Together, entries E(35) and E(37) fully eliminate the ending balance in the parent's investment account. The noncontrolling interest is credited for its proportionate share of the book value of the subsidiary at the beginning of the period ($320,000 × .20). This amount is added to the 20X2 increase in noncontrolling interest established in entry E(36), and the total is reported in the consolidated balance sheet.

Entry E(37) also establishes the purchase differential as of the beginning of 20X2. The differential at the beginning of 20X1, the date of combination, was $70,000 and was reduced by the amounts written off during 20X1. During 20X1, Peerless wrote off the $4,000 of the differential related to the inventory sold in 20X1 and amortized $4,800 of the differential related to buildings and equipment. Therefore, the unamortized balance of the differential at the beginning of 20X2, is $61,200 ($70,000 − $4,000 − $4,800).

In the consolidation workpaper, allocation of the purchase differential in 20X2 is different from the allocation in the first year in several respects:

1. No allocation is made to inventory or cost of goods sold.
2. The balance in the goodwill account in 20X2 should be only $7,500 because of the $2,500 write-off of goodwill in 20X1 to reflect an impairment loss. However, because the purchase differential was not written down on Peerless's books to reflect the goodwill impairment and goodwill is not amortized (in accordance with the FASB's requirements), the original $10,000 amount of goodwill is established in the workpaper. The prior period's impairment is then recognized in a separate entry.
3. Accumulated depreciation must be entered in the workpaper to reflect the additional depreciation on the buildings and equipment taken in the 20X1 consolidation workpaper. This should be part of the 20X2 consolidated total, but it does not automatically carry forward from the previous year's workpaper.

Entry E(38) assigns the January 1, 20X2, purchase differential:

E(38)	Land	8,000	
	Buildings and Equipment	48,000	
	Goodwill	10,000	
	Differential		61,200
	Accumulated Depreciation		4,800
	Assign beginning differential.		

Because each year's workpaper is prepared from the trial balance data reported by the separate companies and not from the previous year's workpaper, the $4,800 of accumulated depreciation entered in the consolidation workpaper at the end of 20X1 does not automatically carry over to the 20X2 workpaper. Thus, the workpaper entry to allocate the differential each time also must establish the accumulated depreciation for all prior years on any differential amounts assigned to depreciable assets.

FIGURE 5–10   Consolidated Net Income and Retained Earnings, 20X2;
80 Percent Purchase at More than Book Value

Consolidated net income, 20X2:	
Peerless's separate operating income	$160,000
Peerless's share of Special Foods' net income: $75,000 × .80	60,000
Amortization of differential related to buildings and equipment in 20X2	(4,800)
Consolidated net income, 20X2	$215,200
Consolidated retained earnings, December 31, 20X2:	
Consolidated retained earnings, December 31, 20X1	$408,700
Peerless's separate operating income, 20X2	160,000
Peerless's share of Special Foods' 20X2 net income: $75,000 × .80	60,000
Amortization of differential related to buildings and equipment in 20X2	(4,800)
Dividends declared by Peerless, 20X2	(60,000)
Consolidated retained earnings, December 31, 20X2	$563,900

The 20X2 depreciation of the portion of the differential assigned to buildings and equipment is given in entry E(39):

E(39) Depreciation Expense	4,800	
Accumulated Depreciation		4,800
Amortize differential related to buildings and equipment:		
$48,000 ÷ 10 years		

The amount of additional depreciation expense each period remains the same from year to year unless (1) a depreciation method other than straight-line is used, or (2) some of the underlying assets are sold, or (3) some of the assets become fully depreciated.

Entry E(40) corrects the beginning consolidated retained earnings and the goodwill balance for the impairment loss recognized in the 20X1 consolidated income statement:

E (40) Retained Earnings, January 1	2,500	
Goodwill		2,500
Adjust for 20X1 impairment of goodwill.		

Because the purchase differential on Peerless's books is not written down under the equity method to reflect the 20X1 impairment of goodwill, the differential established in the 20X2 workpaper through entry E(37) includes the full $10,000 differential originally representing goodwill. Also, because the impairment loss did not affect Peerless's equity-method net income, and Peerless's retained earnings becomes consolidated retained earnings, beginning consolidated retained earnings will be overstated unless it is reduced by the amount of the prior period's impairment loss. Thus, both beginning consolidated retained earnings and goodwill must be reduced each period in the consolidated workpaper for the 20X1 impairment.

Consolidated Net Income and Retained Earnings.   The computation of 20X2 consolidated net income and consolidated retained earnings at the end of 20X2 is shown in Figure 5–10.

Consolidated Financial Statements.   A consolidated income statement and retained earnings statement for the year 20X2 and a consolidated balance sheet as of December 31, 20X2, are presented in Figure 5–11.

FIGURE 5–11   Consolidated Financial Statements for Peerless Products Corporation and Special Foods Inc., 20X2

Peerless Products Corporation and Subsidiary
Consolidated Income Statement
For the Year Ended December 31, 20X2

Sales		$750,000
Cost of Goods Sold		(340,000)
Gross Margin		$410,000
Expenses:		
Depreciation and amortization	$ 74,800	
Other Expenses	105,000	
Total Expenses		(179,800)
		$230,200
Income to Noncontrolling Interest		(15,000)
Consolidated Net Income		$215,200

Peerless Products Corporation and Subsidiary
Consolidated Retained Earnings Statement
For the Year Ended December 31, 20X2

Consolidated Retained Earnings, January 1, 20X2	$408,700
Consolidated Net Income, 20X2	215,200
Dividends Declared, 20X2	(60,000)
Consolidated Retained Earnings, December 31, 20X2	$563,900

Peerless Products Corporation and Subsidiary
Consolidated Balance Sheet
December 31, 20X2

Assets:			Liabilities:		
Cash		$ 306,000	Accounts Payable	$200,000	
Accounts Receivable		230,000	Bonds Payable	300,000	
Inventory		270,000			$ 500,000
Land		223,000	Noncontrolling Interest		71,000
Buildings and Equipment	$1,448,000		Stockholders' Equity		
Accumulated Depreciation	(849,600)		Common Stock	$500,000	
		598,400	Retained Earnings	563,900	
Goodwill		7,500			1,063,900
Total		$1,634,900	Total		$1,634,900

Treatment of Other Comprehensive Income

In **FASB Statement No. 130**, "Reporting Comprehensive Income," the FASB established a new category for financial reporting, *other comprehensive income,* which includes all revenues, expenses, gains, and losses that under generally accepted accounting principles are excluded from net income.[1] **FASB 130** permits companies to

---

[1]Under **FASB 130,** comprehensive income is the total of net income and other comprehensive income. Currently, the major elements of other comprehensive income are (1) foreign currency translation adjustments, (2) unrealized gains and losses on investments in certain securities, and (3) certain minimum pension liability adjustments.

present either a single statement of income and comprehensive income or a separate income statement and statement of comprehensive income.[2] In the latter case, the income statement is unchanged, and an additional statement of comprehensive income is added. The consolidation process is the same whether a combined statement or separate statements are prepared.

Other comprehensive income accounts are temporary accounts that are closed at the end of each period. Instead of being closed to Retained Earnings as revenue and expense accounts are, other comprehensive income accounts are closed to a special stockholders' equity account, Accumulated Other Comprehensive Income.

Modification of the Consolidation Workpaper

When a parent or subsidiary has recorded other comprehensive income, the consolidation workpaper normally includes an additional section for other comprehensive income. This section of the workpaper facilitates computation of the amount of other comprehensive income to be reported in the consolidated income statement or statement of comprehensive income, the portion, if any, of other comprehensive income to be assigned to the noncontrolling interest, and the amount of accumulated other comprehensive income to be reported in the consolidated balance sheet. Although this extra section of the workpaper for comprehensive income could be placed after the income statement section of the standard workpaper, the format used here is to place it at the bottom of the workpaper. If neither the parent nor any subsidiary reports other comprehensive income, the section can be omitted from the workpaper. When other comprehensive income is reported, the workpaper is prepared in the normal manner, with the additional section added to the bottom. The only modification within the standard workpaper is an additional stockholders' equity account included in the balance sheet portion of the workpaper for the cumulative effects of the other comprehensive income.

To illustrate the consolidation process when a subsidiary reports other comprehensive income, assume that during 20X2 Special Foods purchases $20,000 of investments classified as available for sale.[3] By December 31, 20X2, the fair value of the securities increases to $30,000. Other than the effects of accounting for Special Foods' investment in securities, the financial statement information reported by Peerless Products and Special Foods at December 31, 20X2, is identical to that presented in Figure 5–9.

Adjusting Entry Recorded by Subsidiary

At December 31, 20X2, Special Foods recognizes the increase in the fair value of its available-for-sale securities by recording the following adjusting entry:

(41)	Investment in Available-for-Sale Securities	10,000	
	Unrealized Gain on Investments (OCI)		10,000
	Record increase in fair value of available-for-sale securities.		

The unrealized gain is not included in the subsidiary's net income but is reported by the subsidiary as an element of other comprehensive income.

---

[2]**FASB 130** also permits reporting other comprehensive income elements only in the statement of stockholders' equity, but it does not recommend this approach.

[3]*FASB Statement No. 115*, "Accounting for Certain Investments in Debt and Equity Securities," requires that most investments in debt and equity securities be classified as (1) trading securities, (2) available-for-sale securities, or (3) held-to-maturity securities (debt securities only). **FASB 130** affects reporting only for those investments classified as available for sale.

Adjusting Entry Recorded by Parent Company

In 20X2, Peerless records all its normal entries [(32) through (34)] relating to its investment in Special Foods, as if the subsidiary had not reported other comprehensive income. In addition, at December 31, 20X2, Peerless products separately recognizes its proportionate share of the subsidiary's unrealized gain from the increase in the value of the available-for-sale securities:

(34a)	Investment in Special Foods Stock	8,000	
	Other Comprehensive Income from Subsidiary—Unrealized		
	Gain on Investments (OCI)		8,000
	Record Peerless's proportionate share of the increase in value of		
	available-for-sale securities held by subsidiary.		

Consolidation Workpaper—Second Year following Combination

The workpaper to prepare a complete set of consolidated financial statements for the year 20X2 is illustrated in Figure 5–12. In the workpaper, Peerless's balance of the Investment in Special Foods Stock account is greater than in Figure 5–9 because of entry (34a), and Peerless's $8,000 proportionate share of Special Foods' unrealized gain is included in the separate section of the workpaper for comprehensive income (Other Comprehensive Income from Subsidiary—Unrealized Gain on Investments). Special Foods' trial balance has been changed to reflect (1) the reduction in the cash balance resulting from the investment acquisition, (2) the investment in available-for-sale securities, and (3) an unrealized gain of $10,000 on the investment.

Consolidation Procedures

Eliminating entries E(35) through E(40) were used in preparing the consolidation workpaper for 20X2 presented in Figure 5–9. When other comprehensive income is introduced, the parent's income from its subsidiary is eliminated in the normal manner with entry E(35), and a proportionate share of the subsidiary's income is allocated to the noncontrolling interest with entry E(36); both of these entries are as shown in Figure 5–9. Entry E(37) in Figure 5–9 eliminates the beginning balances of the investment account and the beginning stockholders' equity balances of the subsidiary. Although this entry remains unchanged in this example, it would have included the elimination of the beginning balance of the subsidiary's accumulated other comprehensive income if the subsidiary had had a balance as of the beginning of the period because that account is properly included in the subsidiary's stockholders' equity; further, a portion of the balance of that account would have been allocated to the beginning noncontrolling interest, as with the other stockholders' equity accounts of the subsidiary.

Eliminating entries E(38) through E(40) dealing with the differential also are unchanged from Figure 5–9. However, two additional entries are needed for the treatment of the subsidiary's other comprehensive income. First, the proportionate share of the subsidiary's other comprehensive income recorded by the parent with entry (34a) must be eliminated to avoid double counting the subsidiary's other comprehensive income. Thus, entry (34a) is reversed:

E(42)	Other Comprehensive Income from Subsidiary—Unrealized		
	Gain on Investments (OCI)	8,000	
	Investment in Special Foods Stock		8,000
	Eliminate other comprehensive income from subsidiary.		

FIGURE 5–12 **December 31, 20X2, Comprehensive Income Illustration, Second Year Following Combination; 80 Percent Purchase at More than Book Value**

Item	Peerless Products	Special Foods	Eliminations Debit		Eliminations Credit		Consolidated
Sales	450,000	300,000					750,000
Income from Subsidiary	55,200		(35)	55,200			
Credits	505,200	300,000					750,000
Cost of Goods Sold	180,000	160,000					340,000
Depreciation and Amortization	50,000	20,000	(39)	4,800			74,800
Other Expenses	60,000	45,000					105,000
Debits	(290,000)	(225,000)					(519,800)
							230,200
Income to Noncontrolling Interest			(36)	15,000			(15,000)
Net Income, carry forward	215,200	75,000		75,000			215,200
Retained Earnings, January 1	411,200	120,000	(37)	120,000			
			(40)	2,500			408,700
Net Income, from above	215,200	75,000		75,000			215,200
	626,400	195,000					623,900
Dividends Declared	(60,000)	(40,000)			(35)	32,000	
					(36)	8,000	(60,000)
Retained Earnings, December 31, carry forward	566,400	155,000		197,500		40,000	563,900
Cash	221,000	65,000					286,000
Accounts Receivable	150,000	80,000					230,000
Inventory	180,000	90,000					270,000
Land	175,000	40,000	(38)	8,000			223,000
Buildings and Equipment	800,000	600,000	(38)	48,000			1,448,000
Investment in AFS Securities		30,000					30,000
Investment in Special Foods Stock	348,400				(35)	23,200	
					(37)	317,200	
					(42)	8,000	
Goodwill			(38)	10,000	(40)	2,500	7,500
Differential			(37)	61,200	(38)	61,200	
Debits	1,874,400	905,000					2,494,500
Accumulated Depreciation	500,000	340,000			(38)	4,800	
					(39)	4,800	849,600
Accounts Payable	100,000	100,000					200,000
Bonds Payable	200,000	100,000					300,000
Common Stock	500,000	200,000	(37)	200,000			500,000
Retained Earnings, from above	566,400	155,000		197,500		40,000	563,900
Accumulated Other Comprehensive Income, from below	8,000	10,000		10,000			8,000
Noncontrolling interest					(36)	7,000	
					(37)	64,000	
					(43)	2,000	73,000
Credits	1,874,400	905,000		534,700		534,700	2,494,500
Other Comprehensive Income:							
OCI from Subsidiary—Unrealized Gain on Investments	8,000		(42)	8,000			
Unrealized gain on Investments		10,000					10,000
Other Comprehensive Income to Noncontrolling Interest			(43)	2,000			(2,000)
Accumulated Other Comprehensive Income, January 1							
Accumulated Other Comprehensive Income, December 31, carry up	8,000	10,000		10,000			8,000

Elimination entries:
(35) Eliminate income from subsidiary.
(36) Assign income to noncontrolling interest.
(37) Eliminate beginning investment balance.
(38) Assign beginning differential.
(39) Amortize differential related to buildings and equipment.
(40) Adjust for 20X1 impairment of goodwill.
(42) Eliminate other comprehensive income from subsidiary.
(43) Assign other comprehensive income to noncontrolling interest.

Second, a proportionate share of the subsidiary's other comprehensive income must be allocated to the noncontrolling interest, just as is done with the subsidiary's net income:

E(43) Other Comprehensive Income to Noncontrolling Interest	2,000	
Noncontrolling Interest		2,000
Assign other comprehensive income to noncontrolling interest.		

Thus, the amount of other comprehensive income reported in the consolidated financial statements is equal to the parent's 80 percent share of the subsidiary's $10,000 of other comprehensive income; the remaining $2,000 is included in the noncontrolling interest.

While consolidated net income is the same in Figure 5–12 as in Figure 5–9, the other comprehensive income section of the workpaper in Figure 5–12 gives explicit recognition to the unrealized gain on available-for-sale securities held by Special Foods. This permits the preparation of either a single statement of net income and comprehensive income or separate statements of income and comprehensive income. Consolidated financial statements are presented in Figure 5–13.

Consolidation Workpaper—Comprehensive Income in Subsequent Years

Each year following 20X2, Special Foods will adjust the unrealized gain on investments on its books for the change in fair value of the available-for-sale securities. For example, if the investment held by Special Foods increased in value by an additional $5,000 during 20X3, Special Foods would increase by $5,000 the carrying amount of its investment in securities and recognize as an element of 20X3's other comprehensive income an unrealized gain of $5,000. Under equity-method recording, Peerless would increase its Investment in Special Foods' Stock account and record its $4,000 share of the subsidiary's other comprehensive income.

The eliminating entries required to prepare the consolidation workpaper at December 31, 20X3, would include those corresponding to E(35) to eliminate the income from the subsidiary recorded by the parent, E(36) to allocate a proportionate share of subsidiary income to the noncontrolling interest, and E(38) through E(40) relating to the differential. In addition, an eliminating entry corresponding to E(37) would be made to eliminate the beginning investment balance and the beginning stockholders' equity balances of the subsidiary, including the subsidiary's $10,000 beginning Accumulated Other Comprehensive Income balance, and to increase the noncontrolling interest by its proportionate share of the subsidiary's beginning Accumulated Other Comprehensive Income amount ($10,000 × .20). Two additional eliminating entries also would be needed:

E(42a) Other Comprehensive Income from Subsidiary—Unrealized		
Gain on Investments (OCI)	4,000	
Investment in Special Foods Stock		4,000
Eliminate other comprehensive income from subsidiary.		
E(43a) Other Comprehensive Income to Noncontrolling Interest	1,000	
Noncontrolling Interest		1,000
Assign other comprehensive income to noncontrolling interest.		

Entry E(42a) would eliminate the share of the subsidiary's other comprehensive income for the period recorded by the parent, and entry (43a) would allocate a portion of the subsidiary's other comprehensive income for the period to the noncontrolling interest.

FIGURE 5–13 **Consolidated Financial Statements, for Peerless Products Corporation and Special Foods Inc., 20X2, Including Other Comprehensive Income**

Peerless Products Corporation and Subsidiary
Consolidated Statement of Income
For the Year Ended December 31, 20X2

Sales		$750,000
Cost of Goods Sold		(340,000)
Gross Margin		$410,000
Expenses:		
Depreciation and Amortization	$ 74,800	
Other Expenses	105,000	
Total Expenses		(179,800)
Entity Net Income		$230,200
Income to Noncontrolling Interest		(15,000)
Consolidated Net Income		$215,200

Peerless Products Corporation and Subsidiary
Consolidated Statement of Comprehensive Income
For the Year Ended December 31, 20X2

Consolidated Net Income		$215,200
Other Comprehensive Income:		
Unrealized Gain on Investments Held by Subsidiary	$10,000	
Other Comprehensive Income to Noncontrolling Interest	(2,000)	
Other Comprehensive Income to Controlling Interest		8,000
Consolidated Comprehensive Income		$223,200

Peerless Products Corporation and Subsidiary
Consolidated Statement of Financial Position
December 31, 20X2

Assets		
Cash		$ 286,000
Accounts Receivable		230,000
Inventory		270,000
Investment in Available-for-Sale Securities		30,000
Land		223,000
Buildings and Equipment	$1,448,000	
Accumulated Depreciation	(849,600)	
		598,400
Goodwill		7,500
Total Assets		$1,644,900
Liabilities		
Accounts Payable	$ 200,000	
Bonds Payable	300,000	
Total Liabilities		$ 500,000
Noncontrolling Interest		73,000
Stockholders' Equity		
Common Stock	$ 500,000	
Retained Earnings	563,900	
Accumulated Other Comprehensive Income	8,000	
Total Stockholders' Equity		1,071,900
Total Liabilities and Stockholders' Equity		$1,644,900

Discontinuance of Consolidation

A subsidiary that previously has been consolidated but no longer meets the conditions for consolidation normally must be reported as an investment under the cost method in the consolidated financial statements. For example, if a previously consolidated subsidiary declared bankruptcy and the appointment of a receiver by the courts prevented the parent from exercising control, the subsidiary would not qualify for consolidation. A change in the specific companies for which consolidated statements are prepared is viewed as a change in the accounting entity. **Accounting Principles Board Opinion No. 20,** "Accounting Changes" (APB 20), requires financial statements of all prior periods presented for comparative purposes to be restated to exclude from the consolidation the nonqualifying subsidiary and to reflect the new reporting entity. In addition, the financial statements for the period of the change must disclose if the change is material, the nature of the change and the reason for it, and the effect of the change on income before extraordinary items, net income, and related per-share amounts.

Additional Considerations Relating to the Assignment of Differential

Although the assignment of a purchase differential in the consolidation workpaper usually is straightforward, special attention is needed when differential-related assets are sold and when the differential is assigned to liabilities.

Disposal of Differential-Related Assets by Subsidiary

When a subsidiary disposes of an asset, it recognizes a gain or loss on the disposal equal to the difference between the proceeds received and the book value of the asset given up. If the asset is one to which a differential is assigned in the consolidation workpaper, both equity-method income recorded by the parent and consolidated net income are affected. The unamortized portion of a positive purchase differential that applies to the asset sold or written off must be treated under the equity method as a reduction of both the parent's income from the subsidiary and the investment account. In consolidation, the unamortized part of the purchase differential must be recognized as an adjustment to the gain or loss on the disposal of the asset.

Inventory.   Any inventory-related differential is assigned to inventory for as long as the inventory units are held by the subsidiary. In the period in which the inventory units are sold, the inventory-related differential is assigned to cost of goods sold, as illustrated previously in Figure 5–7.

The choice of inventory method used by the subsidiary determines the period in which the differential cost of goods sold is recognized. When FIFO inventory costing is used by the subsidiary, the inventory units on hand on the date of combination are viewed as being the first units sold after the combination. Therefore, the differential normally is assigned to cost of goods sold in the period immediately after the combination. When the subsidiary uses LIFO inventory costing, the inventory units on the date of combination are viewed as remaining in the subsidiary's inventory. Only if the inventory level drops below the level at the date of combination is a portion of the differential assigned to cost of goods sold.

Fixed Assets.   A purchase differential related to land held by a subsidiary is added to the land balance in the consolidation workpaper each time a consolidated balance sheet is prepared. If the subsidiary sells the land to which the differential relates, the differential is treated in the consolidation workpaper as an adjustment to the gain or loss on the sale of the land in the period of the sale.

To illustrate, assume that on January 1, 20X1, Bright purchases all the common stock of Star at $10,000 more than book value. All the differential relates to land that Star had purchased earlier for $25,000. So long as Star continues to hold the land, the $10,000 differential is assigned to the land in the consolidation workpaper. If Star sells the land to an unrelated company for $40,000, the following entry is recorded on Star's books:

(44) Cash	40,000	
Land		25,000
Gain on Sale of Land		15,000
Record sale of land.		

While a gain of $15,000 is appropriate for Star to report, the land cost the consolidated entity $35,000 ($25,000 + $10,000). Therefore, the consolidated enterprise must report a gain of only $5,000. To reduce the $15,000 gain reported by Star to the $5,000 gain that should be reported by the consolidated entity, the following elimination is included in the consolidation workpaper for the year of the sale:

E(45) Gain on Sale of Land	10,000	
Differential		10,000
Assign beginning differential.		

If, instead, Star sells the land for $32,000, the $7,000 ($32,000 − $25,000) gain recorded by Star is eliminated and a loss of $3,000 ($32,000 − $35,000) is recognized in the consolidated income statement. The eliminating entry in this case is:

E(46) Gain on Sale of Land	7,000	
Loss on Sale of Land	3,000	
Differential		10,000
Assign beginning differential.		

When the equity method is used on the parent's books, the parent must adjust the carrying amount of the investment and its equity-method income in the period of the sale to write off the differential. Thereafter, the $10,000 differential no longer exists.

The sale of differential-related equipment is treated in the same manner as land except that the amortization for the current and previous periods must be considered.

Differential Assigned to Liabilities

With the considerable swings in interest rates over the past decade, companies often find that liabilities assumed in a business combination have fair values different from their book values. As with assets acquired, liabilities assumed in a purchase-type combination must be valued at their fair values. Thus, a portion of the differential arising in the consolidation workpaper often relates to liabilities.

To better understand this, assume that Bright purchases all the common stock of Star on January 1, 20X1, for an amount $19,473 in excess of book value, all relating to Star's 6 percent bonds payable. The bonds were issued three years ago at their par value of $100,000 and mature seven years from the date of combination. The bonds pay interest once each year on December 31. The current market rate of interest is 10 percent. The present value of the bonds on the date of combination is computed as follows:

Present value of $100,000 at 10 percent for 7 years ($100,000 × .51316)	$51,316
Present value at 10 percent of an annuity of seven payments of $6,000 each ($6,000 × 4.86842)	29,211
Present value of bonds	$80,527

The $19,473 difference between the $100,000 book value of the bonds and the $80,527 fair value is considered a discount on the bonds from a consolidated viewpoint. In a consolidation workpaper prepared on the date of combination, the entire $19,473 differential is assigned to the discount on bonds payable. In preparing consolidated statements subsequent to the date of combination, the bond discount differential must be amortized. For 20X1, the amount of amortization to be entered in the consolidation workpaper using effective-interest amortization is computed as follows:

Par value of bonds	$100,000
Imputed discount	(19,473)
Fair value of bonds on January 1, 20X1	$ 80,527
Effective interest rate	× .10
Interest expense for 20X1	$ 8,053
Cash interest payment ($100,000 × .06)	(6,000)
Amortization of bond discount	$ 2,053

The entry to assign the differential in the consolidation workpaper prepared for December 31, 20X1, is:

E(47)	Interest Expense	2,053	
	Discount on Bonds Payable	17,420	
	Differential		19,473
	Assign beginning differential.		

Because the differential also is amortized on the parent's books under the equity method, the differential and the amount assigned to the discount will be smaller by $2,053 in the workpaper prepared at the end of 20X2. The remaining $17,420 of discount will be charged to consolidated interest expense over the remaining life of the bonds.

Summary of Key Concepts and Terms

As with single-corporate reporting entities, a full set of consolidated financial statements includes a balance sheet, income statement, statement of retained earnings, and statement of cash flows. In the preparation of consolidated financial statements subsequent to the date that a company acquires a subsidiary, a comprehensive three-part consolidation workpaper is used. The workpaper is similar to that used in preparing only a consolidated balance sheet, but it also includes sections for the income statement and retained earnings statement in addition to the section for the balance sheet. If the parent or a subsidiary records any elements of other comprehensive income, an other comprehensive income section can be added to the workpaper.

For periods subsequent to the purchase of a subsidiary, workpaper elimination entries are needed to (1) eliminate the parent's intercorporate investment balance and the stockholders' equity accounts of the subsidiary, (2) eliminate income from the subsidiary recognized by the parent during the period and dividends declared by the subsidiary, (3) eliminate intercompany receivables and payables, (4) assign any differential to specific assets and liabilities, and (5) amortize or write off a portion of a differential, if appropriate. In addition, if a noncontrolling interest exists, the noncontrolling shareholders' claim on the income and net assets of the subsidiary must be recognized.

Consolidated net income normally is computed as the total of the parent's income from its own separate operations and the parent's proportionate share of the net income of the subsidiary. Consolidated retained earnings normally is computed as the total of the parent's cumulative earnings, excluding any income from the subsidiary, plus the parent's proportionate share of the subsidiary's cumulative net income since acquisition, minus all dividends declared by the parent.

> Consolidated net income
>
> Consolidated retained earnings
>
> Other comprehensive income

APPENDIX 5A CONSOLIDATION AND THE COST METHOD

Not all parent companies use the equity method to account for their subsidiary investments that are to be consolidated. The choice of the cost or equity method has no effect on the consolidated financial statements. This is because the balance in the parent's investment account, the parent's income from the subsidiary, and related items are eliminated in preparing the consolidated statements. Thus, the parent is free to use on its separate books either the cost method or some version of the equity method in accounting for investments in subsidiaries that are to be consolidated.

Impact on the Consolidation Process

While the parent's net income and retained earnings under the equity method usually equals the consolidated amounts, this equality usually does not exist when the cost method is used. Because the cost method uses different parent-company entries than the equity method, it also requires different eliminating entries in preparing the consolidation workpaper. Keep in mind that the consolidated financial statements appear the same regardless of whether the parent uses the cost or the equity method on its separate books.

Consolidation—Year of Combination

To illustrate the preparation of consolidated financial statements when the parent company carries its investment in the subsidiary using the cost method, the Peerless Products and Special Foods example is used once again. Assume that Peerless purchases 80 percent of the common stock of Special Foods on January 1, 20X1, for $310,000. The purchase price is $70,000 in excess of the book value of the stock acquired. Of the total differential, $8,000 relates to land, $48,000 relates to buildings and equipment having a remaining life of 10 years from the date of combination, $4,000 relates to inventory that is sold during 20X1, and $10,000 relates to goodwill that is reduced by a $2,500 impairment loss in 20X1 and remains constant thereafter. All other data are the same as presented in Figure 5–2. Peerless earns income from its own separate operations of $140,000 in 20X1 and declares dividends of $60,000; Special Foods reports net income of $50,000 in 20X1 and pays dividends of $30,000.

Parent Company Cost-Method Entries.   When the cost method is used, only two journal entries are recorded by Peerless during 20X1 related to its investment in Special Foods. Entry (48) records Peerless's purchase of Special Foods stock; entry (49) recognizes dividend income based on the $24,000 ($30,000 × .80) of dividends received during the period:

(48)	Investment in Special Foods Stock	310,000	
	Cash		310,000
	Record purchase of Special Foods stock.		

(49)	Cash	24,000	
	Dividend Income		24,000
	Record dividends from Special Foods:		
	$30,000 × .80		

No entries are made on the parent's books to amortize or write off the portion of the purchase differential that expires during 20X1, as would be done under the equity method.

Consolidation Workpaper—Year of Combination. The workpaper to prepare consolidated financial statements for December 31, 20X1, is shown in Figure 5–14. The trial balance data for Peerless and Special Foods included in the workpaper in Figure 5–14 differ from those presented in Figure 5–7 only by the effects of using the cost method rather than the equity method on Peerless's books.

Five eliminating entries are used to prepare the consolidation workpaper:

E(50)	Dividend Income	24,000	
	Dividends Declared		24,000
	Eliminate dividend income from subsidiary.		
E(51)	Income to Noncontrolling Interest	10,000	
	Dividends Declared		6,000
	Noncontrolling Interest		4,000
	Assign income to noncontrolling interest.		
E(52)	Common Stock—Special Foods	200,000	
	Retained Earnings, January 1	100,000	
	Differential	70,000	
	Investment in Special Foods Stock		310,000
	Noncontrolling Interest		60,000
	Eliminate investment balance at date of acquisition.		
E(53)	Cost of Goods Sold	4,000	
	Land	8,000	
	Buildings and Equipment	48,000	
	Goodwill	10,000	
	Differential		70,000
	Assign differential at date of acquisition.		
E(54)	Depreciation Expense	4,800	
	Goodwill Impairment Loss	2,500	
	Accumulated Depreciation		4,800
	Goodwill		2,500
	Amortize differential related to buildings and equipment ($4,800) and reduce goodwill for impairment ($2,500).		

Entry E(50) eliminates the dividend income recorded by Peerless during the period along with Special Foods' dividend declaration related to the stockholdings of Peerless. Entry E(51) assigns income to the noncontrolling shareholders ($50,000 × .20) and eliminates their portion of the subsidiary dividends ($30,000 × .20). This entry is the same as the one under the equity method and is not affected by the method used on the parent's books.

Entry E(52) eliminates the balances in the stockholders' equity accounts of Special Foods and the balance in Peerless's investment account as of the date of combination. A differential clearing account is established, representing the $70,000 purchase differential at that date. Entry E(53) assigns the differential to the appropriate expense and asset categories. Entry E(54) recognizes the additional depreciation related to the portion of the differential assigned to buildings and equipment. This entry also establishes in the workpaper the loss from the impairment of the goodwill included in the differential and reduces the goodwill by the amount of the impairment.

FIGURE 5–14   **December 31, 20X1, Cost-Method Workpaper for Consolidated Financial Statements, Year of Combination; 80 Percent Purchase at More than Book Value**

Item	Peerless Products	Special Foods	Eliminations Debit		Eliminations Credit		Consolidated
Sales	400,000	200,000					600,000
Dividend Income	24,000		(50)	24,000			
Credits	424,000	200,000					600,000
Cost of Goods Sold	170,000	115,000	(53)	4,000			289,000
Depreciation and Amortization	50,000	20,000	(54)	4,800			74,800
Goodwill Impairment Loss			(54)	2,500			2,500
Other Expenses	40,000	15,000					55,000
Debits	(260,000)	(150,000)					(421,300)
							178,700
Income to Noncontrolling Interest			(51)	10,000			(10,000)
Net Income, carry forward	164,000	50,000		45,300			168,700
Retained Earnings, January 1	300,000	100,000	(52)	100,000			300,000
Net Income, from above	164,000	50,000		45,300			168,700
	464,000	150,000					468,700
Dividends Declared	(60,000)	(30,000)			(50)	24,000	
					(51)	6,000	(60,000)
Retained Earnings, December 31, carry forward	404,000	120,000		145,300		30,000	408,700
Cash	194,000	75,000					269,000
Accounts Receivable	75,000	50,000					125,000
Inventory	100,000	75,000					175,000
Land	175,000	40,000	(53)	8,000			223,000
Buildings and Equipment	800,000	600,000	(53)	48,000			1,448,000
Investment in Special Foods Stock	310,000				(52)	310,000	
Goodwill			(53)	10,000	(54)	2,500	7,500
Differential			(52)	70,000	(53)	70,000	
Debits	1,654,000	840,000					2,247,500
Accumulated Depreciation	450,000	320,000			(54)	4,800	774,800
Accounts Payable	100,000	100,000					200,000
Bonds Payable	200,000	100,000					300,000
Common Stock	500,000	200,000	(52)	200,000			500,000
Retained Earnings, from above	404,000	120,000		145,300		30,000	408,700
Noncontrolling interest					(51)	4,000	
					(52)	60,000	64,000
Credits	1,654,000	840,000		481,300		481,300	2,247,500

Elimination entries:
  (50) Eliminate dividend income from subsidiary.
  (51) Assign income to noncontrolling interest.
  (52) Eliminate investment balance at date of acquisition.
  (53) Assign differential at date of acquisition.
  (54) Amortize differential and reduce goodwill for impairment.

The investment elimination entry, E(52), is the same as the corresponding entry made when using the equity method. This occurs only in the year of acquisition because the balances eliminated are those at the beginning of the year, the date of combination. The balances on the date of combination are the same regardless of the method used to account for the investment subsequent to the combina-

E5–13   **Computation of Income Reported by Subsidiary**

Blithe Company purchased 60 percent of the stock of Spirit Company for $100,000 on January 1, 20X6, when Spirit reported $120,000 of common stock outstanding and retained earnings of $25,000. On December 31, 20X8, Blithe reported its investment in Spirit at $126,100 using equity-method accounting for its investment. Blithe received dividends from Spirit totaling $15,000 over the three-year period. The purchase differential is amortized over 10 years.

Required

Determine the amount of net income reported by Spirit Company over the three-year period.

E5–14   **Computation of Parent Company and Consolidated Balances**

Jersey Company purchased 80 percent of the common stock of Briar Company at the beginning of the current year. On the date of acquisition, Briar Company reported common stock outstanding of $80,000 and retained earnings of $140,000, and Jersey reported common stock outstanding of $350,000 and retained earnings of $520,000.

   During the first year of ownership Briar Company reported net income of $35,000 and paid dividends of $15,000. Jersey reported earnings from its separate operations of $95,000 and paid dividends of $46,000. Jersey uses the equity method in accounting for its investment in Briar.

Required

a. Assuming Jersey Company purchased the stock for $176,000, compute the following:

   (1) Consolidated net income for the year.

   (2) The balance in the investment account at year-end.

   (3) Income assigned to noncontrolling interest in the consolidated income statement for the year.

b. Assume Jersey Company purchased the stock for $216,000 and that $30,000 of the differential is attributed to depreciable assets with an economic life of eight years at the date of acquisition. At the end of the year, management reviewed the portion of the differential assigned to goodwill and concluded goodwill had been impaired and should be reported at $2,000. Compute the following:

   (1) Consolidated net income for the year.

   (2) The balance in the investment account at year-end.

   (3) Income assigned to noncontrolling interest in the consolidated income statement for the year.

E5–15   **Consolidation Following Three Years of Ownership**

Boxwell Corporation purchased 60 percent of the ownership of Conway Company on January 1, 20X7, for $277,500. Conway reported the following net income and dividend payments:

Year	Net Income	Dividends Paid
20X7	$45,000	$25,000
20X8	55,000	35,000
20X9	30,000	10,000

On January 1, 20X7, Conway had $250,000 of $5 par value common stock outstanding and retained earnings of $150,000. At that date, Conway held land with a book value of $22,500 and a market value of $30,000 and equipment with a book value of $320,000 and market value of $360,000. All of the remainder of the purchase price was attributable to an increase in the value of patents which had a remaining useful life of 10 years. All depreciable assets held by Conway at the date of acquisition had a remaining economic life of six years.

Required

a. Prepare the eliminating entries needed at January 1, 20X7, to prepare a consolidated balance sheet.

b. Compute the balance reported by Boxwell Corporation as its investment in Conway at January 1, 20X9.

c. Prepare the journal entries recorded by Boxwell with regard to its investment in Conway during 20X9.

d. Prepare the eliminating entries needed at December 31, 20X9, to prepare a three-part consolidation workpaper.

E5–16   Computation of Consolidated Balances in Subsequent Period

Asp Corporation holds 60 percent ownership of Parry Company, which it acquired on January 1, 20X1. Asp Corporation paid $226,000 for its ownership of Parry. At acquisition, Parry had retained earnings of $50,000 and $200,000 of stock outstanding. Book values approximated market values on some of Parry's assets and liabilities at the date of combination. However, the following amounts were not in full agreement:

	Book Value	Fair Value
Inventory (FIFO basis)	$ 40,000	$ 50,000
Land	40,000	60,000
Buildings and Equipment	150,000	200,000

Parry's depreciable assets should be expensed over 15 years. Management has reviewed the amount attributed to goodwill at the end of each year for impairment. At December 31, 20X2, management concluded a goodwill impairment loss of $12,000 had occurred during 20X2. No other impairment of goodwill has taken place.

The balance sheets of the companies on December 31, 20X4, included the following amounts:

	Asp Corporation	Parry Company
Cash	$ 10,000	$ 30,000
Accounts Receivable	48,000	100,000
Inventory	230,000	80,000
Land	150,000	40,000
Buildings and Equipment	400,000	240,000
Less: Accumulated Depreciation	(180,000)	(90,000)
Investment in Parry Stock	242,000	
	$900,000	$400,000
Accounts Payable	$ 60,000	$ 10,000
Bonds Payable	300,000	90,000
Common Stock	400,000	200,000
Retained Earnings	140,000	100,000
	$900,000	$400,000

Required

Give the amounts to be reported in the consolidated balance sheet as of December 31, 20X4, for the following accounts:

    a. Inventory.

    b. Land.

    c. Buildings and Equipment.

    d. Accumulated Depreciation.

    e. Investment in Parry Company.

    f. Goodwill.

    g. Common Stock.

    h. Retained Earnings.

E5–17   **Multiple-Choice Questions on Consolidated Balances**

Farrow Corporation acquired 70 percent of the stock of Rand Company on January 1, 20X7, for $300,000. Other relevant data are as follows:

	Farrow	Rand
Common stock outstanding	$200,000	$250,000
Retained earnings, January 1, 20X7	240,000	150,000
Net income for 20X7		40,000
Operating income, excluding investment income	180,000	
Dividends declared	35,000	10,000

The excess of purchase price over book value was assigned to depreciable assets with a remaining economic life of five years.

Required

Select the correct answer for each of the following:

1. What amount of investment income will Farrow report for 20X7 on its investment in Rand?

    a. $36,000.

    b. $28,000.

    c. $25,200.

    d. $24,000.

2. What amount of consolidated net income will be reported for 20X7?

    a. $220,000.

    b. $216,000.

    c. $208,000.

    d. $204,000.

3. What amount of income will be assigned to the noncontrolling interest in the 20X7 consolidated income statement?

    a. $66,000.

    b $12,000.

    c. $10,800.

    d. $9,000.

4. What amount will be reported as dividend payments by the consolidated entity for 20X7?

    a. $45,000.

    b $42,000.

    c. $38,000.

    d. $35,000.

5. What amount will be reported as common stock outstanding in the consolidated balance sheet prepared at December 31, 20X7?

a. $200,000.

b. $275,000.

c. $375,000.

d. $450,000.

6. What amount will be reported in the consolidated balance sheet prepared at December 31, 20X7, as the balance in retained earnings?

a. $240,000.

b. $390,000.

c. $409,000.

d. $589,000.

7. What amount will Farrow show as its investment in Rand at December 31, 20X7?

a. $300,000.

b. $317,000.

c. $314,000.

d. $328,000.

E5–18   Basic Consolidation Workpaper

Blake Corporation acquired 100 percent of the voting shares of Shaw Corporation on January 1, 20X3, at underlying book value. Blake uses the equity method in accounting for its investment in Shaw Corporation. Adjusted trial balances for Blake Corporation and Shaw Corporation on December 31, 20X3, are as follows:

	Blake Corporation		Shaw Corporation	
Item	Debit	Credit	Debit	Credit
Current Assets	$145,000		$105,000	
Depreciable Assets (net)	325,000		225,000	
Investment in Shaw Corporation Stock	170,000			
Depreciation Expense	25,000		15,000	
Other Expenses	105,000		75,000	
Dividends Declared	40,000		10,000	
Current Liabilities		$ 50,000		$ 40,000
Long-Term Debt		100,000		120,000
Common Stock		200,000		100,000
Retained Earnings		230,000		50,000
Sales		200,000		120,000
Income from Subsidiary		30,000		
	$810,000	$810,000	$430,000	$430,000

Required

a. Give all the eliminating entries required on December 31, 20X3, to prepare consolidated financial statements.

b. Prepare a three-part consolidation workpaper as of December 31, 20X3.

E5–19   Basic Consolidation Workpaper for Second Year

Blake Corporation acquired 100 percent of the voting shares of Shaw Corporation on January 1, 20X3, at underlying book value. Blake uses the equity method in accounting for its investment in Shaw Corporation. Adjusted trial balances for Blake Corporation and Shaw Corporation on December 31, 20X4, are as follows:

	Blake Corporation		Shaw Corporation	
Item	Debit	Credit	Debit	Credit
Current Assets	$210,000		$150,000	
Depreciable Assets (net)	300,000		210,000	
Investment in Shaw Corporation Stock	190,000			
Depreciation Expense	25,000		15,000	
Other Expenses	150,000		90,000	
Dividends Declared	50,000		15,000	
Current Liabilities		$ 70,000		$ 50,000
Long-Term Debt		100,000		120,000
Common Stock		200,000		100,000
Retained Earnings		290,000		70,000
Sales		230,000		140,000
Income from Subsidiary		35,000		
	$925,000	$925,000	$480,000	$480,000

Required

a. Give all eliminating entries required on December 31, 20X4, to prepare consolidated financial statements.

b. Prepare a three-part consolidation workpaper as of December 31, 20X4.

E5–20 **Consolidation Workpaper with Differential**

Kennelly Corporation purchased all the common shares of Short Company on January 1, 20X5, for $180,000. On that date, the book value of the net assets reported by Short Company was $150,000. The entire purchase differential was assigned to depreciable assets with a six-year remaining economic life from January 1, 20X5.

The adjusted trial balances for the two companies on December 31, 20X5, are as follows:

	Kennelly Corporation		Short Company	
Item	Debit	Credit	Debit	Credit
Cash	$ 15,000		$ 5,000	
Accounts Receivable	30,000		40,000	
Inventory	70,000		60,000	
Depreciable Assets (net)	325,000		225,000	
Investment in Short Company Stock	195,000			
Depreciation Expense	25,000		15,000	
Other Expenses	105,000		75,000	
Dividends Declared	40,000		10,000	
Accounts Payable		$ 50,000		$ 40,000
Notes Payable		100,000		120,000
Common Stock		200,000		100,000
Retained Earnings		230,000		50,000
Sales		200,000		120,000
Income from Subsidiary		25,000		
	$805,000	$805,000	$430,000	$430,000

Kennelly Corporation uses the equity method in accounting for its investment in Short Company. Short Company dividends were declared and paid on December 31, 20X5.

Required

a. Prepare the eliminating entries needed as of December 31, 20X5, to complete a consolidation workpaper.

b. Prepare a three-part consolidation workpaper as of December 31, 20X5.

E5–21   Consolidation Workpaper for Majority-Owned Subsidiary

Proud Corporation purchased 80 percent of the voting stock of Stergis Company on January 1, 20X3, at underlying book value. Proud Corporation uses the equity method in accounting for its ownership of Stergis during 20X3. On December 31, 20X3, the trial balances of the two companies are as follows:

	Proud Corporation		Stergis Company	
Item	*Debit*	*Credit*	*Debit*	*Credit*
Current Assets	$173,000		$105,000	
Depreciable Asset	500,000		300,000	
Investment in Stergis Company Stock	136,000			
Depreciation Expense	25,000		15,000	
Other Expenses	105,000		75,000	
Dividends Declared	40,000		10,000	
Accumulated Depreciation		$175,000		$ 75,000
Current Liabilities		50,000		40,000
Long-Term Debt		100,000		120,000
Common Stock		200,000		100,000
Retained Earnings		230,000		50,000
Sales		200,000		120,000
Income from Subsidiary		24,000		
	$979,000	$979,000	$505,000	$505,000

Required

a. Give all eliminating entries required as of December 31, 20X3, to prepare consolidated financial statements.

b. Prepare a three-part consolidation workpaper.

c. Prepare a consolidated balance sheet, income statement, and retained earnings statement for 20X3.

E5–22   Consolidation Workpaper for Majority-Owned Subsidiary for Second Year

Proud Corporation purchased 80 percent of the voting stock of Stergis Company on January 1, 20X3, at underlying book value. Proud Corporation uses the equity method in accounting for its ownership of Stergis. On December 31, 20X4, the trial balances of the two companies are as follows:

Item	Proud Corporation		Stergis Company	
	Debit	*Credit*	*Debit*	*Credit*
Current Assets	$ 235,000		$150,000	
Depreciable Assets (net)	500,000		300,000	
Investment in Stergis Company Stock	152,000			
Depreciation Expense	25,000		15,000	
Other Expenses	150,000		90,000	
Dividends Declared	50,000		15,000	
Accumulated Depreciation		$ 200,000		$ 90,000
Current Liabilities		70,000		50,000
Long-Term Debt		100,000		120,000
Common Stock		200,000		100,000
Retained Earnings		284,000		70,000
Sales		230,000		140,000
Income from Subsidiary		28,000		
	$1,112,000	$1,112,000	$570,000	$570,000

Required

a. Give all eliminating entries required on December 31, 20X4, to prepare consolidated financial statements.

b. Prepare a three-part consolidation workpaper as of December 31, 20X4.

E5–23 Preparation of Stockholders' Equity Section with Other Comprehensive Income

Tollway Corporation purchased 75 percent of the common stock of Stem Corporation on January 1, 20X8, for $435,000. At that date, Stem reported common stock outstanding of $300,000 and retained earnings of $200,000. The purchase differential is assigned to other intangible assets and amortized over 10 years. Tollway and Stem reported the following data for 20X8 and 20X9.

Year	Stem Corporation			Tollway Corporation	
	Net Income	*Comprehensive Income*	*Dividends Paid*	*Operating Income*	*Dividends Paid*
20X8	$40,000	$50,000	$15,000	$120,000	$70,000
20X9	60,000	65,000	30,000	140,000	70,000

Required

a. Compute consolidated net income for 20X8 and 20X9.

b. Compute consolidated comprehensive income for 20X8 and 20X9.

c. Assuming Tollway Corporation reported capital stock outstanding of $320,000 and retained earnings of $430,000 at January 1, 20X8, prepare the stockholders' equity section of the consolidated balance sheet at December 31, 20X8 and 20X9.

E5–24 **Eliminating Entries for Subsidiary with Other Comprehensive Income**

Palmer Corporation purchased 70 percent of the ownership of Krown Corporation on January 1, 20X8, for $140,000. At that date Krown reported capital stock outstanding of $120,000 and retained earnings of $80,000. During 20X8, Krown reported net income of $30,000, comprehensive income of $36,000, and paid dividends of $25,000.

Required

a. Present all entries that would have been recorded by Palmer Corporation in accounting for its investment in Krown Corporation during 20X8.

b. Present all eliminating entries needed at December 31, 20X8, to prepare a complete set of consolidated financial statements for Palmer Corporation and its subsidiary.

E5–25* **Complex Assignment of Differential**

On December 31, 20X4, Holly Corporation purchased 90 percent of the common stock of Brinker Inc. for $888,000, a price that was $240,000 in excess of the book value of the shares acquired. Of the $240,000 differential, $5,000 related to the increased value of Brinker's inventory, $75,000 related to the increased value of Brinker's land, $60,000 related to the increased value of Brinker's equipment, and $50,000 was associated with a change in the value of Brinker's notes payable due to increasing interest rates. Brinker's equipment had a remaining life of 15 years from the date of combination. The amount of the differential assigned to goodwill is not amortized. All of the inventory held by Brinker at the end of 20X4 was sold during 20X5; the land to which the differential related also was sold during the year for a large gain. The amortization of the differential relating to Brinker's notes payable was $7,500 for 20X5.

At the date of combination, Brinker reported retained earnings of $120,000, common stock outstanding of $500,000, and premium on common stock of $100,000. For the year 20X5, Brinker reported net income of $68,000, but paid no dividends. Holly accounts for its investment in Brinker using the equity method.

Required

a. Present all entries that would have been recorded by Holly during 20X5 with respect to its investment in Brinker.

b. Present all elimination entries that would have been included in the workpaper to prepare a full set of consolidated financial statements for the year 20X5.

E5–26A **Consolidation Using Cost-Method Accounting**

City Touring Company holds 70 percent ownership of Country Playgrounds Inc. and uses the cost method in accounting for its investment. During 20X5, Country Playgrounds reported net income of $70,000 and paid dividends of $40,000. City Touring reported net income (including dividend income) of $130,000 and paid dividends of $50,000. There was no differential at the time of investment.

Required

a. What amount of consolidated net income will be reported for 20X5?

b. What amount of income will be assigned to the noncontrolling interest in the consolidated income statement?

c. What additional factors must be known to compute consolidated retained earnings for December 31, 20X5?

E5–27A **Computation of Consolidated Balances Using the Cost Method**

Cable Corporation purchased 70 percent of the ownership of Brush Company on January 1, 20X5, and paid $220,000. At that date, Brush Company reported the book value of its net assets as

---

*Indicates that the item relates to "Additional Considerations."

$280,000 and a remaining useful life of 10 years for those assets to which the purchase differential is assigned. The companies reported the following data for 20X9:

	Retained Earnings January 1, 20X9	20X9 Net Income	20X9 Dividends
Cable Corporation	$520,000	$120,000	$50,000
Brush Company	230,000	25,000	10,000

Cable Corporation uses the cost method in accounting for its investment in Brush. The following entry was included in the eliminating entries used to prepare the consolidated financial statements at December 31, 20X9:

E(3) Retained Earnings	21,000	
Noncontrolling Interest		21,000

Required

a. What amount of retained earnings did Brush report at January 1, 20X5?

b. What amount should be reported as consolidated retained earnings at January 1, 20X9?

c. What amount should be reported as consolidated net income for 20X9?

d. What amount should be reported as consolidated retained earnings at December 31, 20X9?

E5–28A **Basic Cost-Method Workpaper**

Blake Corporation purchased 100 percent of the voting shares of Shaw Corporation on January 1, 20X3, at underlying book value. Blake uses the cost method in accounting for its investment in Shaw Corporation. Shaw Corporation retained earnings, as shown in the 20X3 trial balance, was $50,000 on January 1, 20X3. On December 31, 20X3, the trial balance data for the two companies are as follows:

	Blake Corporation		Shaw Corporation	
Item	Debit	Credit	Debit	Credit
Current Assets	$145,000		$105,000	
Depreciable Assets (net)	325,000		225,000	
Investment in Shaw Corporation Stock	150,000			
Depreciation Expense	25,000		15,000	
Other Expenses	105,000		75,000	
Dividends Declared	40,000		10,000	
Current Liabilities		$ 50,000		$ 40,000
Long-Term Debt		100,000		120,000
Common Stock		200,000		100,000
Retained Earnings		230,000		50,000
Sales		200,000		120,000
Dividend Income		10,000		
	$790,000	$790,000	$430,000	$430,000

Required

a. Give all eliminating entries needed to prepare a three-part consolidation workpaper as of December 31, 20X3.

b. Prepare the workpaper in good form.

E5–29A   Cost-Method Workpaper in Subsequent Period

The trial balances for Blake Corporation and Shaw Corporation as of December 31, 20X4, are as follows:

Item	Blake Corporation Debit	Blake Corporation Credit	Shaw Corporation Debit	Shaw Corporation Credit
Current Assets	$170,000		$110,000	
Depreciable Assets (net)	300,000		210,000	
Investment in Shaw Corporation Stock	150,000			
Depreciation Expense	25,000		15,000	
Other Expenses	250,000		160,000	
Dividends Declared	20,000		15,000	
Current Liabilities		$ 30,000		$ 20,000
Long-Term Debt		100,000		120,000
Common Stock		200,000		100,000
Retained Earnings		270,000		70,000
Sales		300,000		200,000
Dividend Income		15,000		
	$915,000	$915,000	$510,000	$510,000

Blake purchased 100 percent ownership of Shaw Corporation on January 1, 20X3, at a cost of $150,000. Shaw reported $50,000 of retained earnings at acquisition. Blake uses the cost method in accounting for its investment in Shaw Corporation.

Required

a. Give all eliminating entries required to prepare a full set of consolidated statements for 20X4.

b. Prepare a three-part consolidation workpaper in good form as of December 31, 20X4.

E5–30A   Cost-Method Consolidation for Majority-Owned Subsidiary

Lintner Corporation purchased 80 percent of the voting stock of Knight Company on January 1, 20X6, at underlying book value. Lintner uses the cost method in accounting for its investment in Knight Company. Knight reported $50,000 of retained earnings at the time of acquisition. Trial balance data for the two companies on December 31, 20X7, are as follows:

Item	Lintner Corporation Debit	Lintner Corporation Credit	Knight Company Debit	Knight Company Credit
Current Assets	$ 183,000		$ 80,000	
Depreciable Assets	500,000		300,000	
Investment in Knight Company Stock	120,000			
Depreciation Expense	25,000		15,000	
Other Expenses	251,000		155,000	
Dividends Declared	25,000		20,000	
Accumulated Depreciation		$ 200,000		$ 90,000
Accounts Payable		120,000		110,000
Common Stock		200,000		100,000
Retained Earnings		268,000		70,000
Sales		300,000		200,000
Dividend Income		16,000		
	$1,104,000	$1,104,000	$570,000	$570,000

Required

a. Prepare eliminating entries as of December 31, 20X7, for a full set of consolidated statements.

b. Prepare a three-part consolidation workpaper as of December 31, 20X7.

c. Prepare a consolidated income statement, balance sheet, and retained earnings statement for 20X7.

Problems

P5–31 **Consolidated Balances [AICPA Adapted]**

The separate condensed balance sheets and income statements of Purl Corporation and its wholly owned subsidiary, Scott Corporation, are as follows:

Balance Sheets
December 31, 20X0

	Purl		Scott	
Current Assets				
Cash	$ 80,000		$ 60,000	
Accounts Receivable (net)	140,000		25,000	
Inventories	90,000		50,000	
Total Current Assets		$ 310,000		$135,000
Property, Plant & Equipment (net)		625,000		280,000
Investment in Scott (equity method)		390,000		
Total Assets		$1,325,000		$415,000
Current Liabilities				
Accounts Payable		$ 160,000		$ 95,000
Accrued Liabilities		110,000		30,000
Total Current Liabilities		$ 270,000		$125,000
Stockholders' Equity				
Common Stock ($10 par)	$300,000		$ 50,000	
Additional Paid-In Capital			10,000	
Retained Earnings	755,000		230,000	
Total Stockholders' Equity		1,055,000		290,000
Total Liabilities and Stockholders' Equity		$1,325,000		$415,000

Income Statement
Year Ended December 31, 20X0

	Purl	Scott
Sales	$2,000,000	$750,000
Cost of Goods Sold	(1,540,000)	(500,000)
Gross Margin	$ 460,000	$250,000
Operating Expenses	(260,000)	(150,000)
Operating Income	$ 200,000	$100,000
Equity in Earnings of Scott	60,000	
Income Before Taxes	$ 260,000	$100,000
Provision for Income Taxes	(60,000)	(30,000)
Net Income	$ 200,000	$ 70,000

Additional Information

- On January 1, 20X0, Purl purchased for $360,000 all of Scott's $10 par, voting common stock. On January 1, 20X0, the fair value of Scott's assets and liabilities equaled their carrying amount of $410,000 and $160,000, respectively, except that the fair values of certain items identifiable in Scott's inventory were $10,000 more than their carrying amounts and Scott held unrecorded copyrights with a fair value of $100,000 and a remaining useful life of 10 years. The inventory items were still on hand at December 31, 20X0.

- During 20X0, Purl and Scott paid cash dividends of $100,000 and $30,000, respectively. For tax purposes, Purl receives the 100 percent exclusion for dividends received from Scott.

- There were no intercompany transactions, except for Purl's receipt of dividends from Scott and Purl's recording of its share of Scott's earnings. Both Purl and Scott paid income taxes at the rate of 30 percent.

In the December 31, 20X0, consolidated financial statements of Purl and its subsidiary:

1. Total current assets should be:
    a. $455,000.
    b. $445,000.
    c. $310,000.
    d. $135,000.

2. Total assets should be:
    a. $1,740,000.
    b. $1,450,000.
    c. $1,350,000.
    d. $1,325,000.

3. Total retained earnings should be:
    a. $985,000.
    b. $825,000.
    c. $795,000.
    d. $755,000.

4. Net income should be:
    a. $270,000.
    b. $200,000.
    c. $190,000.
    d. $170,000.

5. Copyright amortization expense should be:
    a. $20,000.
    b. $10,000.
    c. $6,000.
    d. $0.

P5–32   Ownership Balances

Penn Corporation acquired 75 percent of the voting common stock of Eastland Company on January 1, 20X2, for $648,000. The purchase differential was assigned to equipment with a remaining economic life of eight years at the date of acquisition. On that date, Eastland reported the following stockholders' equity balances:

Common Stock, $10 par value	$300,000
Additional Paid-In Capital	180,000
Retained Earnings	320,000

Penn Corporation reported retained earnings of $485,000 at January 1, 20X2, and operating income of $65,000, $80,000, and $50,000 in 20X2, 20X3, and 20X4, respectively. Penn and Eastland paid dividends of $30,000 and $20,000, respectively, each of the three years. Eastland had 30,000 shares of common stock outstanding throughout the three-year period. In the consolidated balance sheet prepared at December 31, 20X4, noncontrolling interest was reported at $227,500.

Required

a. Compute the balance in retained earnings reported by Eastland Company on December 31, 20X4.

b. Compute the balance in the investment account reported by Penn Corporation on December 31, 20X4, assuming Penn uses the equity method in accounting for its ownership of Eastland.

c. Compute the balance in consolidated retained earnings on December 31, 20X4.

P5–33   **Consolidated Income and Retained Earnings**

Bolt Corporation is 80 percent owned by Allied Foundries Inc. The shares of Bolt were acquired by Allied on January 1, 20X2, for $160,000. Selected stockholders' equity balances for the companies are as follows:

	Allied Foundries Inc.	Bolt Corporation
Common Stock	$400,000	$100,000
Additional Paid-In Capital	150,000	40,000
Retained Earnings, January 1, 20X2	350,000	60,000
Retained Earnings, January 1, 20X4	548,000	130,000
Retained Earnings, December 31, 20X4	642,000	150,000

Allied operates the subsidiary as an independent company and uses the equity method to account for its ownership interest. Operating results for the two enterprises are as follows:

	Allied Foundries Inc.		Bolt Corporation	
Year	Operating Income	Dividends	Net Income	Dividends
20X2	$100,000	$20,000	$40,000	$10,000
20X3	50,000	20,000	70,000	30,000
20X4	90,000	20,000	30,000	10,000

Operating income for Allied Foundries includes all revenue and expenses except for investment income from Bolt Corporation.

Required

a. Compute consolidated net income for 20X4.

b. Compute consolidated retained earnings as of December 31, 20X4.

c. Compute the amount reported as noncontrolling interest in the consolidated balance sheet on December 31, 20X4.

d. Prepare a consolidated retained earnings statement for 20X4.

P5–34   **Income and Retained Earnings**

Quill Corporation purchased 70 percent of the stock of North Company on January 1, 20X9, for $105,000. The following stockholders' equity balances were reported by the companies immediately after the acquisition:

	Quill Corporation	North Company
Common Stock	$120,000	$ 30,000
Additional Paid-In Capital	230,000	80,000
Retained Earnings	290,000	40,000
Total	$640,000	$150,000

Quill and North reported 20X9 operating incomes of $90,000 and $35,000 and dividend payments of $30,000 and $10,000, respectively.

Required

a. Compute the amount reported as net income by each company for 20X9, assuming Quill uses equity-method accounting for its investment in North.

b. Compute consolidated net income for 20X9.

c. Compute the reported balance in retained earnings at December 31, 20X9, for both companies.

d. Compute consolidated retained earnings at December 31, 20X9.

e. How would the computation of consolidated retained earnings at December 31, 20X9, change if Quill uses the cost method in accounting for its investment in North Company?

P5–35   **Eliminating Entries for Consolidated Balance Sheet**

Rise Corporation purchased 60 percent of the voting common stock of Doughboy Company on January 1, 20X7, for $400,000. At the date of acquisition, Doughboy reported common stock outstanding of $240,000 and retained earnings of $310,000. The purchase price included a differential entirely assignable to equipment with a remaining economic life of seven years. The balance sheet of Doughboy at December 31, 20X9, contained the following amounts:

Doughboy Company
Balance Sheet
December 31, 20X9

Cash	$ 90,000	Accounts Payable	$125,000
Accounts Receivable	170,000	Bonds Payable	200,000
Land	150,000	Common Stock	240,000
Buildings and Equipment	650,000	Retained Earnings	395,000
Less: Accumulated Depreciation	(100,000)		
	$960,000		$960,000

Required

a. Compute the balance in the investment account reported by Rise Corporation at December 31, 20X9.

b. Give all eliminating entries needed to prepare a consolidated balance sheet at December 31, 20X9.

P5–43 **Comprehensive Problem: Differential Apportionment**
Bigelow Corporation purchased 80 percent of Granite Company on January 1, 20X7, for $173,000. The trial balances for the two companies on December 31, 20X7, included the following amounts:

	Bigelow Corporation		Granite Company	
Item	*Debit*	*Credit*	*Debit*	*Credit*
Cash	$ 38,000		$ 25,000	
Accounts Receivable	50,000		55,000	
Inventory	240,000		100,000	
Land	80,000		20,000	
Buildings and Equipment	500,000		150,000	
Investment in Granite Company Stock	202,000			
Cost of Goods Sold	500,000		250,000	
Depreciation Expense	25,000		15,000	
Other Expenses	75,000		75,000	
Dividends Declared	50,000		20,000	
Accumulated Depreciation		$ 155,000		$ 75,000
Accounts Payable		70,000		35,000
Mortgages Payable		200,000		50,000
Common Stock		300,000		50,000
Retained Earnings		290,000		100,000
Sales		700,000		400,000
Income from Subsidiary		45,000		
	$1,760,000	$1,760,000	$710,000	$710,000

Additional Information

1. On January 1, 20X7, Granite Company reported net assets with a book value of $150,000. A total of $20,000 of the purchase price is applied to goodwill which was not impaired in 20X7.

2. Granite Company depreciable assets had an estimated economic life of 11 years on the date of combination. The difference between fair value and book value of tangible assets is related entirely to depreciable assets.

3. Bigelow Corporation used the equity method in accounting for its investment in Granite.

4. Detailed analysis of receivables and payables showed that Granite owed Bigelow Corporation $16,000 on December 31, 20X7.

Required

a. Give all journal entries recorded by Bigelow Corporation with regard to its investment in Granite Company during 20X7.

b. Give all eliminating entries needed to prepare a full set of consolidated financial statements for 20X7.

c. Prepare a three-part consolidation workpaper as of December 31, 20X7.

P5–44 **Comprehensive Problem: Differential Apportionment in Subsequent Period**
Bigelow Corporation purchased 80 percent of Granite Corporation on January 1, 20X7, for $173,000. The trial balances for the two companies on December 31, 20X8, included the following amounts:

Item	Bigelow Corporation		Granite Company	
	Debit	Credit	Debit	Credit
Cash	$ 59,000		$ 31,000	
Accounts Receivable	83,000		71,000	
Inventory	275,000		118,000	
Land	80,000		30,000	
Buildings and Equipment	500,000		150,000	
Investment in Granite Company Stock	215,000			
Cost of Goods Sold	490,000		310,000	
Depreciation Expense	25,000		15,000	
Other Expenses	62,000		100,000	
Dividends Declared	45,000		25,000	
Accumulated Depreciation		$ 180,000		$ 90,000
Accounts Payable		86,000		30,000
Mortgages Payable		200,000		70,000
Common Stock		300,000		50,000
Retained Earnings		385,000		140,000
Sales		650,000		470,000
Income from Subsidiary		33,000		
	$1,834,000	$1,834,000	$850,000	$850,000

Additional Information

1. On January 1, 20X7, Granite Company reported net assets with a book value of $150,000. A total of $20,000 of the purchase price is applied to goodwill. At December 31, 20X8, the management of Bigelow reviewed the amount attributed to goodwill and concluded goodwill was impaired and should be reduced to $6,000.

2. Granite Company depreciable assets had an estimated economic life of 11 years on the date of combination. The difference between fair value and book value of tangible assets is related entirely to depreciable assets.

3. Bigelow Corporation used the equity method in accounting for its investment in Granite.

4. Detailed analysis of receivables and payable showed that Bigelow owed Granite $9,000 on December 31, 20X8.

Required

a. Give all journal entries recorded by Bigelow Corporation with regard to its investment in Granite Company during 20X8.

b. Give all eliminating entries needed to prepare a full set of consolidated financial statements for 20X8.

c. Prepare a three-part consolidation workpaper as of December 31, 20X8.

P5–45   Analyzing Consolidated Data

Buckman Corporation and Eckel Mining Company reported the following balance sheet data as of December 31, 20X3:

Buckman Corporation
Balance Sheet
December 31, 20X3

Current Assets	$ 81,000	Current Liabilities	$ 70,000
Long-Term Assets (net)	400,000	Bonds Payable	100,000
Investment in Eckel Mining Company	120,000	Common Stock	200,000
		Retained Earnings	231,000
Total	$601,000	Total	$601,000

Eckel Mining Company
Balance Sheet
December 31, 20X3

Current Assets	$ 50,000	Current Liabilities	$ 30,000
Long-Term Assets (net)	200,000	Bonds Payable	50,000
		Common Stock	100,000
		Retained Earnings	70,000
Total	$250,000	Total	$250,000

Buckman Corporation purchased controlling ownership of Eckel Mining Company on January 1, 20X3. Buckman Corporation uses the equity method in accounting for its ownership in Eckel Mining. Since Buckman has more than 50 percent ownership of Eckel Mining, it prepared consolidated statements for 20X3 as follows:

Buckman Corporation and Subsidiary
Consolidated Balance Sheet
December 31, 20X3

Current Assets	$ 91,000	Current Liabilities	$ 60,000
Long-Term Assets (net)	600,000	Bonds Payable	150,000
Patents	18,000	Noncontrolling Interest	68,000
		Common Stock	200,000
		Retained Earnings	231,000
Total	$709,000	Total	$709,000

Buckman Corporation and Subsidiary
Consolidated Income Statement
For the Year Ended December 31, 20X3

Sales		$400,000
Cost of Goods Sold	$260,000	
Other Expenses	57,000	(317,000)
		$ 83,000
Income to Noncontrolling Interest		(12,000)
Consolidated Net Income		$ 71,000

All intangible assets are amortized over a 10-year life.

Required

a. What percentage of Eckel Mining Company's common stock does Buckman hold?

b. Was the stock purchase made at underlying book value or at some other amount? If at another amount, how much more or less than book value was paid?

c. What amount of net income was reported by Eckel Mining Company for 20X3?

d. If Eckel Mining Company paid dividends of $10,000 in 20X3, (1) what was the balance of the noncontrolling interest on January 1, 20X3, and (2) what amount did Buckman pay to purchase the Eckel Mining Company shares on January 1, 20X3?

e. Were there any intercompany receivables or payables on December 31, 20X3? If so, what amount?

P5–46 **Subsidiary with Other Comprehensive Income in Year of Acquisition**

Amber Corporation acquired 60 percent ownership of Sparta Company on January 1, 20X8, at underlying book value. Trial balance data at December 31, 20X8, for Amber and Sparta are as follows:

Amber Corporation and Sparta Company
Balance Sheets
December 31, 20X8

Items	Amber Corporation Debit	Amber Corporation Credit	Sparta Company Debit	Sparta Company Credit
Cash	$ 27,000		$ 8,000	
Accounts Receivable	65,000		22,000	
Inventory	40,000		30,000	
Buildings and Equipment	500,000		235,000	
Investment in Row Company Securities			40,000	
Investment in Sparta Company	108,000			
Cost of Goods Sold	150,000		110,000	
Depreciation Expense	30,000		10,000	
Interest Expense	8,000		3,000	
Dividends Declared	24,000		15,000	
Accumulated Depreciation		$140,000		$ 85,000
Accounts Payable		63,000		20,000
Bonds Payable		100,000		50,000
Common Stock		200,000		100,000
Retained Earnings		208,000		60,000
Other Comprehensive Income from Subsidiary (OCI)—Unrealized Gain on Investments		6,000		
Unrealized Gain on Investments (OCI)				10,000
Sales		220,000		148,000
Income from Subsidiary		15,000		
	$952,000	$952,000	$473,000	$473,000

Additional Information

Sparta Company purchased stock of Row Company on January 1, 20X8, for $30,000 and classified the investment as available-for-sale securities. The value of the Row Company securities increased to $40,000 at December 31, 20X8.

Required

a. Give all eliminating entries needed to prepare a three-part consolidation workpaper as of December 31, 20X8.

b. Prepare a three-part consolidation workpaper for 20X8 in good form.

c. Prepare a consolidated balance sheet, income statement, and statement of comprehensive income for 20X8.

P5–47 **Subsidiary with Other Comprehensive Income in Year Following Acquisition**

Amber Corporation acquired 60 percent ownership of Sparta Company on January 1, 20X8, at underlying book value. Trial balance data at December 31, 20X9, for Amber and Sparta are as follows:

Amber Corporation and Sparta Company
Balance Sheets
December 31, 20X9

	Amber Corporation		Sparta Company	
Items	*Debit*	*Credit*	*Debit*	*Credit*
Cash	$ 18,000		$ 11,000	
Accounts Receivable	45,000		21,000	
Inventory	40,000		30,000	
Buildings and Equipment	585,000		257,000	
Investment in Row Company Securities			44,000	
Investment in Sparta Company	116,400			
Cost of Goods Sold	170,000		97,000	
Depreciation Expense	30,000		10,000	
Interest Expense	8,000		3,000	
Dividends Declared	40,000		20,000	
Accumulated Depreciation		$ 170,000		$ 95,000
Accounts Payable		75,000		24,000
Bonds Payable		100,000		50,000
Common Stock		200,000		100,000
Retained Earnings		231,000		70,000
Accumulated Other Comprehensive Income		6,000		10,000
Other Comprehensive Income from Subsidiary (OCI)—Unrealized Gain on Investments		2,400		
Unrealized Gain on Investments (OCI)				4,000
Sales		250,000		140,000
Income from Subsidiary		18,000		
	$1,052,400	$1,052,400	$493,000	$493,000

Additional Information

Sparta Company purchased stock of Row Company on January 1, 20X8, for $30,000 and classified the investment as available-for-sale securities. The value of the Row Company securities increased to $40,000 and $44,000, respectively, at December 31, 20X8, and 20X9.

Required

a. Give all eliminating entries needed to prepare a three-part consolidation workpaper as of December 31, 20X9.

b. Prepare a three-part consolidation workpaper for 20X9 in good form.

P5–48A **Computation of Balances When Cost Method Is Used**
Pine Corporation purchased 70 percent of the stock of Spike Company on January 1, 20X3, at $50,000 more than underlying book value due to the increased value of buildings held by Spike. At that date, Spike reported $200,000 par value common shares outstanding and $100,000 of retained earnings. All depreciable and amortizable assets of Spike were assumed to have a remaining useful life of 10 year at the date of acquisition.

On January 1, 20X9, Pine and Spike reported retained earnings balances of $500,000 and $300,000, respectively. During 20X9, Pine reported income from its separate operations of $85,000 and paid dividends of $40,000. Spike reported 20X9 net income of $50,000 and paid dividends of $30,000.

Pine uses the cost method in accounting for its investment in Spike.

Required

a. What balance will Pine report as its investment in Spike at January 1, 20X9?

b. What amount will Pine Corporation report as net income for 20X9?

c. What amount will be reported as consolidated net income for 20X9?

d. What amount will Pine report as retained earnings in its balance sheet prepared at December 31, 20X9?

e. What amount will be reported as retained earnings in the consolidated balance sheet prepared at December 31, 20X9?

P5–49A **Cost-Method Workpaper with Differential**
Trial balance data for Light Corporation and Star Company on December 31, 20X5, are as follows:

	Light Corporation		Star Company	
Item	Debit	Credit	Debit	Credit
Cash	$ 37,000		$ 20,000	
Accounts Receivable	50,000		30,000	
Inventory	70,000		60,000	
Buildings and Equipment	300,000		240,000	
Investment in Star Company Stock	220,000			
Cost of Goods Sold	210,000		85,000	
Depreciation Expense	25,000		20,000	
Other Expenses	23,000		25,000	
Dividends Declared	20,000		10,000	
Accumulated Depreciation		$105,000		$ 65,000
Accounts Payable		40,000		20,000
Taxes Payable		70,000		55,000
Common Stock		200,000		150,000
Retained Earnings, January 1		230,000		50,000
Sales		300,000		150,000
Dividend Income		10,000		
	$955,000	$955,000	$490,000	$490,000

Light Corporation purchased all the shares of Star Company on January 1, 20X5, for $220,000. The full purchase differential is assigned to goodwill. At December 31, 20X5, the management of Light reviewed the amount attributed to goodwill and concluded goodwill had been impaired and should be reported at $8,000. Light uses the cost method in accounting for its investment in Star.

Required

Present all eliminating entries needed to prepare consolidated financial statements for the year 20X5, and prepare a three-part consolidation workpaper in good form as of December 31, 20X5.

P5–50A   **Cost-Method Consolidation in Subsequent Period**

Trial balance data for Light Corporation and Star Company on December 31, 20X6, are as follows:

Item	Light Corporation		Star Company	
	Debit	*Credit*	*Debit*	*Credit*
Cash	$ 46,000		$ 30,000	
Accounts Receivable	55,000		40,000	
Inventory	75,000		65,000	
Buildings and Equipment	300,000		240,000	
Investment in Star Company (at cost)	220,000			
Cost of Goods Sold	270,000		135,000	
Depreciation Expense	25,000		20,000	
Other Expenses	21,000		10,000	
Dividends Declared	20,000		20,000	
Accumulated Depreciation		$ 130,000		$ 85,000
Accounts Payable		20,000		30,000
Taxes Payable		50,000		35,000
Common Stock		200,000		150,000
Retained Earnings, January 1		262,000		60,000
Sales		350,000		200,000
Dividend Income		20,000		
	$1,032,000	$1,032,000	$560,000	$560,000

Light Corporation purchased all the shares of Star Company on January 1, 20X5, for $220,000. The retained earnings balance of Star Company at the date of acquisition was $50,000. The full purchase differential is assigned to goodwill. At December 31, 20X5, the management of Light reviewed the amount attributed to goodwill and concluded goodwill had been impaired and should be reported at $8,000. No further impairment occurred during 20X6. Light uses the cost method in accounting for its investment in Star.

Required

Prepare all eliminating entries needed to prepare consolidated financial statements for the year 20X6, and prepare a three-part consolidation workpaper in good form as of December 31, 20X6.

P5–51A Cost-Method Consolidation of Majority-Owned Subsidiary

Rapid Delivery Corporation was created on January 1, 20X2, and quickly became successful. On January 1, 20X6, the owner sold 80 percent of the stock to Samuelson Company at underlying book value. Samuelson has continued to operate the subsidiary as a separate legal entity and uses the cost method in recording investment income.

Trial balance data for the two companies on December 31, 20X6, consist of the following:

Item	Samuelson Company Debit	Credit	Rapid Delivery Corporation Debit	Credit
Cash and Receivables	$ 141,000		$ 80,000	
Inventory	240,000		100,000	
Land	80,000		20,000	
Buildings and Equipment	500,000		150,000	
Investment in Rapid Delivery Stock	120,000			
Cost of Goods Sold	500,000		250,000	
Depreciation Expense	25,000		15,000	
Wage Expense	45,000		35,000	
Other Expenses	30,000		40,000	
Dividends Declared	50,000		20,000	
Accumulated Depreciation		$ 155,000		$ 75,000
Accounts Payable		70,000		35,000
Notes Payable		200,000		50,000
Common Stock		300,000		50,000
Retained Earnings		290,000		100,000
Sales		700,000		400,000
Dividend Income		16,000		
	$1,731,000	$1,731,000	$710,000	$710,000

Retained earnings of Rapid Delivery Corporation on the date of acquisition was $100,000.

Required

You have been asked by the controller of Samuelson Company to prepare a three-part consolidation workpaper in good form and to prepare a consolidated income statement, balance sheet, and statement of changes in retained earnings for the year 20X6.

P5–52A Comprehensive Cost-Method Consolidation Problem

Pillar Corporation acquired 80 percent ownership of Stanley Wood Products Company on January 1, 20X1, for $160,000. On that date Stanley Wood Products reported retained earnings of $50,000 and had $100,000 of common stock outstanding. Pillar has used the cost method in recording its investment in Stanley.

Trial balance data for the two companies on December 31, 20X5, are as follows:

E(4) Gain on Sale of Land	15,000	
Land		15,000
Eliminate unrealized gain on sale of land.		

Assignment of Unrealized Profit Elimination

A gain or loss on an intercompany transfer is recognized by the selling affiliate and ultimately accrues to the stockholders of that affiliate. When a sale is from a parent to a subsidiary, referred to as a ***downstream sale,*** any gain or loss on the transfer accrues to the stockholders of the parent company. When the sale is from a subsidiary to its parent, an ***upstream sale,*** any gain or loss accrues to the stockholders of the subsidiary. If the subsidiary is wholly owned, all the gain or loss ultimately accrues to the parent company as the sole stockholder. If, however, the selling subsidiary is not wholly owned, the gain or loss is apportioned between the parent company and the noncontrolling shareholders.

Generally, gains and losses are not considered realized by the consolidated entity until a sale is made to an external party. Unrealized gains and losses are eliminated in preparing consolidated financial statements against the interests of those shareholders who recognized the gains and losses in the first place: the shareholders of the selling affiliate. Therefore, the direction of the sale determines which shareholder group absorbs the elimination of unrealized intercompany gains and losses. Specifically, unrealized intercompany gains and losses are eliminated in the following ways:

Sale	*Elimination*
Downstream (parent to subsidiary)	Against controlling interest
Upstream (subsidiary to parent):	
Wholly owned subsidiary	Against controlling interest
Majority-owned subsidiary	Proportionally against controlling and noncontrolling interests

As an illustration, assume that Purity Company owns 75 percent of the common stock of Southern Corporation. Purity reports operating income from its own activities, excluding any investment income from Southern, of $100,000; Southern reports net income of $60,000. Included in the income of the selling affiliate is an unrealized gain of $10,000 on the intercompany transfer of an asset. If the sale is a downstream transfer, all the unrealized profit is eliminated from the controlling interest's share of income when consolidated statements are prepared. Thus, consolidated net income is computed as follows:

Purity's separate income		$100,000
Less: Unrealized intercompany profit on downstream asset sale		(10,000)
Purity's separate realized income		$ 90,000
Purity's share of Southern's income:		
Southern's net income	$60,000	
Purity's proportionate share	× .75	45,000
Consolidated net income		$135,000

If, instead, the intercompany transfer is from subsidiary to parent, the unrealized profit on the upstream sale is eliminated proportionately from the interests of the controlling and noncontrolling shareholders. In this situation, consolidated net income is computed as follows:

Purity's separate income		$100,000
Purity's share of Southern's realized income:		
Southern's net income	$60,000	
Less: Unrealized intercompany profit on upstream asset sale	(10,000)	
Southern's realized income	$50,000	
Purity's proportionate share	× .75	37,500
Consolidated net income		$137,500

Consolidated net income is $2,500 greater in the upstream case because 25 percent of the unrealized profit elimination is deducted from the noncontrolling interest rather than deducting the full amount from the controlling interest as in the downstream case.

Note that unrealized intercompany gains and losses always are fully eliminated in preparing consolidated financial statements. The existence of a noncontrolling interest in a selling subsidiary affects only the allocation of the eliminated unrealized gain or loss and not the amount eliminated.

Income to Noncontrolling Interest.   The income assigned to the noncontrolling interest is the noncontrolling interest's proportionate share of the subsidiary's income realized in transactions with parties external to the consolidated entity. Income assigned to the noncontrolling interest in the downstream example is computed as follows:

Southern's net income	$60,000
Proportionate share to noncontrolling interest	× .25
Income assigned to noncontrolling interest	$15,000

Income assigned to the noncontrolling interest in the upstream example is computed as follows:

Southern's net income	$ 60,000
Less: Unrealized gain on upstream sale of asset	(10,000)
Southern's realized net income	$ 50,000
Proportionate share to noncontrolling interest	× .25
Income assigned to noncontrolling interest	$ 12,500

In the downstream example, the $10,000 of unrealized intercompany profit is recognized on the parent company's books; therefore, the noncontrolling interest is not affected by the unrealized gain on the downstream intercompany transaction. The entire

$60,000 of the subsidiary's income is realized in transactions with parties external to the consolidated entity. In the upstream example, the subsidiary's income includes $10,000 of unrealized intercompany profit. The amount of the subsidiary's income realized in transactions with external parties is only $50,000 ($60,000 less $10,000 of unrealized intercompany profit).

Downstream Sale

To illustrate more fully the treatment of unrealized intercompany profits, assume the following with respect to the Peerless-Special Foods example used previously:

1. Peerless Products Corporation purchases 80 percent of the stock of Special Foods Inc. on December 31, 20X0, at the stock's book value of $240,000.

2. On July 1, 20X1, Peerless sells land to Special Foods for $35,000. The land originally had been purchased by Peerless on January 1, 20X1, for $20,000. Special Foods continues to hold the land through 20X1 and subsequent years.

3. During 20X1, Peerless reports separate income of $155,000, consisting of income from regular operations of $140,000 and a $15,000 gain on the sale of land; Peerless declares dividends of $60,000. Special Foods reports net income of $50,000 and declares dividends of $30,000.

4. Peerless accounts for its investment in Special Foods using the basic equity method, under which it records its share of Special Foods' net income and dividends but does not adjust for unrealized intercompany profits.

Peerless records the sale of the land and the resulting gain of $15,000 ($35,000 − $20,000) with entry (2), given previously. Special Foods records the purchase of the land for $35,000 with entry (3).

Basic Equity-Method Entries—20X1.   During 20X1, Peerless records its share of income and dividends from Special Foods with the usual entries under the basic equity method:

(5)	Investment in Special Foods Stock	40,000	
	Income from Subsidiary		40,000
	Record equity-method income:		
	$50,000 × .80		
(6)	Cash	24,000	
	Investment in Special Foods Stock		24,000
	Record dividends from Special Foods:		
	$30,000 × .80		

On December 31, 20X1, the investment account on Peerless's books appears as follows:

Investment in Special Foods Stock				
Original cost	240,000			
(5) Equity accrual			(6) Dividends	
($50,000 × .80)	40,000		($30,000 × .80)	24,000
Balance, 12/31/X1	256,000			

FIGURE 6–3   December 31, 20X1, Consolidation Workpaper, Period of Intercompany Sale; Downstream Sale of Land

Item	Peerless Products	Special Foods	Eliminations Debit		Eliminations Credit		Consolidated
Sales	400,000	200,000					600,000
Gain on Sale of Land	15,000		(10)	15,000			
Income from Subsidiary	40,000		(7)	40,000			
Credits	455,000	200,000					600,000
Cost of Goods Sold	170,000	115,000					285,000
Depreciation and Amortization	50,000	20,000					70,000
Other Expenses	40,000	15,000					55,000
Debits	(260,000)	(150,000)					(410,000)
							190,000
Income to Noncontrolling Interest			(8)	10,000			(10,000)
Net Income, carry forward	195,000	50,000		65,000			180,000
Retained Earnings, January 1	300,000	100,000	(9)	100,000			300,000
Net Income, from above	195,000	50,000		65,000			180,000
	495,000	150,000					480,000
Dividends Declared	(60,000)	(30,000)			(7)	24,000	
					(8)	6,000	(60,000)
Retained Earnings, December 31, carry forward	435,000	(120,000)		165,000		30,000	420,000
Cash	299,000	40,000					339,000
Accounts Receivable	75,000	50,000					125,000
Inventory	100,000	75,000					175,000
Land	155,000	75,000			(10)	15,000	215,000
Buildings and Equipment	800,000	600,000					1,400,000
Investment in Special Foods Stock	256,000				(7)	16,000	
					(9)	240,000	
Debits	1,685,000	840,000					2,254,000
Accumulated Depreciation	450,000	320,000					770,000
Accounts Payable	100,000	100,000					200,000
Bonds Payable	200,000	100,000					300,000
Common Stock	500,000	200,000	(9)	200,000			500,000
Retained Earnings, from above	435,000	120,000		165,000		30,000	420,000
Noncontrolling Interest					(8)	4,000	
					(9)	60,000	64,000
Credits	1,685,000	840,000		365,000		365,000	2,254,000

Elimination entries:

(7) Eliminate income from subsidiary.

(8) Assign income to noncontrolling interest.

(9) Eliminate beginning investment balance.

(10) Eliminate unrealized gain on sale of land.

Consolidation Workpaper—20X1.   The consolidation workpaper used in preparing consolidated financial statements for 20X1 is shown in Figure 6–3. The normal workpaper entries are included:

E(7)	Income from Subsidiary	40,000	
	Dividends Declared		24,000
	Investment in Special Foods Stock		16,000
	Eliminate income from subsidiary.		
E(8)	Income to Noncontrolling Interest	10,000	
	Dividends Declared		6,000
	Noncontrolling Interest		4,000
	Assign income to noncontrolling interest:		
	$10,000 = $50,000 × .20		
	$6,000 = $30,000 × .20		
E(9)	Common Stock—Special Foods	200,000	
	Retained Earnings, January 1	100,000	
	Investment in Special Foods Stock		240,000
	Noncontrolling Interest		60,000
	Eliminate beginning investment balance.		

Entry E(7) eliminates the changes in Peerless's investment account for the year, the income from Special Foods recognized by Peerless in entry (5), and Peerless's share of Special Foods' dividends recognized in entry (6). Entry E(8) assigns a share of Special Foods' income to the noncontrolling stockholders ($50,000 × .20) and eliminates their share of Special Foods' dividends. The noncontrolling interest is not affected by the unrealized intercompany gain because the transfer was a downstream sale. Entry E(9) eliminates Peerless's beginning investment balance and the beginning stockholders' equity amounts of Special Foods, and establishes the noncontrolling interest as of the beginning of the year.

One additional entry is needed to eliminate the unrealized gain on the intercompany sale of the land:

E(10)	Gain on Sale of Land	15,000	
	Land		15,000
	Eliminate unrealized gain on downstream sale of land.		

Because the land still is held within the consolidated entity, the $15,000 gain recognized on Peerless's books must be eliminated in the consolidation workpaper so that it does not appear in the consolidated income statement. Similarly, the land must appear in the consolidated balance sheet at its $20,000 original cost to the consolidated entity and, therefore, must be reduced from the $35,000 amount carried on Special Foods' books.

Consolidated Net Income.   The 20X1 consolidated net income is computed as follows:

Peerless's separate income		$155,000
Less: Unrealized intercompany profit on downstream land sale		(15,000)
Peerless's separate realized income		$140,000
Peerless's share of Special Foods' income:		
Special Foods' net income	$50,000	
Peerless's proportionate share	× .80	40,000
Consolidated net income, 20X1		$180,000

Noncontrolling Interest. The noncontrolling stockholders' share of the income of the consolidated entity is limited to their proportionate share of the subsidiary's income. Special Foods' net income for 20X1 is $50,000, and the noncontrolling stockholders' ownership interest is 20 percent. Therefore, income of $10,000 ($50,000 × .20) is allocated to the noncontrolling interest.

As shown in Figure 6–3, the total noncontrolling interest at the end of 20X1 is $64,000, which represents the noncontrolling stockholders' proportionate share of the total book value of the subsidiary:

Book value of Special Foods, December 31, 20X1:	
Common stock	$200,000
Retained earnings	120,000
Total book value	$320,000
Noncontrolling stockholders' proportionate share	× .20
Noncontrolling interest, December 31, 20X1	$ 64,000

The noncontrolling interest is unaffected by the unrealized gain on the downstream sale.

Upstream Sale

An upstream sale results in the recording of intercompany profits on the books of the subsidiary. If the profits are unrealized from a consolidated viewpoint, they must not be included in the consolidated financial statements. The unrealized intercompany profits are eliminated from the consolidation workpaper in the same manner as in the downstream case. However, the profit elimination reduces both the controlling and the noncontrolling interests in proportion to their ownership.

The treatment of an upstream sale may be illustrated with the same example used to illustrate a downstream sale. In this case, Special Foods recognizes a $15,000 gain from selling the land to Peerless in addition to the $50,000 of income earned from its regular operations; thus, Special Foods' net income for 20X1 is $65,000. Peerless's separate income is $140,000 and comes entirely from its normal operations.

The upstream sale from Special Foods to Peerless is as follows:

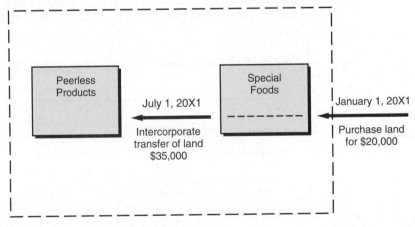

Consolidated Entity

Basic Equity-Method Entries—20X1.   During 20X1, Peerless records the normal entries under the basic equity method, reflecting its share of Special Foods' income and dividends:

(11)	Investment in Special Foods Stock	52,000	
	Income from Subsidiary		52,000
	Record equity-method income:		
	$65,000 \times .80$		
(12)	Cash	24,000	
	Investment in Special Foods Stock		24,000
	Record dividends from Special Foods:		
	$30,000 \times .80$		

Note that Peerless's equity accrual in entry (11) includes its share of both Special Foods' operating income and Special Foods' gain on the transfer of the land.

The investment account on Peerless's books appears as follows at the end of 20X1:

Investment in Special Foods Stock

Original cost	240,000			
(11) Equity accrual			(12) Dividends	
($65,000 \times .80$)	52,000		($30,000 \times .80$)	24,000
Balance, 12/31/X1	268,000			

Consolidation Workpaper—20X1.   The consolidation workpaper prepared at the end of 20X1 appears in Figure 6–4. The four eliminating entries needed to prepare consolidated statements in the upstream case are nearly identical with those in the downstream case:

E(13)	Income from Subsidiary	52,000	
	Dividends Declared		24,000
	Investment in Special Foods Stock		28,000
	Eliminate income from subsidiary.		
E(14)	Income to Noncontrolling Interest	10,000	
	Dividends Declared		6,000
	Noncontrolling Interest		4,000
	Assign income to noncontrolling interest:		
	$10,000 = ($65,000 - $15,000) \times .20$		
	$6,000 = $30,000 \times .20$		
E(15)	Common Stock—Special Foods	200,000	
	Retained Earnings, January 1	100,000	
	Investment in Special Foods Stock		240,000
	Noncontrolling Interest		60,000
	Eliminate beginning investment balance.		
E(16)	Gain on Sale of Land	15,000	
	Land		15,000
	Eliminate unrealized gain on upstream sale of land.		

The only difference between these elimination entries and those in the downstream example is in entry E(13). This difference results from the subsidiary's reporting $65,000 as its income in the upstream example rather than the $50,000 reported in the downstream example, with the additional $15,000 being the gain on the sale of the land.

FIGURE 6–4   December 31, 20X1, Consolidation Workpaper, Period of Intercompany Sale; Upstream Sale of Land

Item	Peerless Products	Special Foods	Eliminations Debit		Eliminations Credit		Consolidated
Sales	400,000	200,000					600,000
Gain on Sale of Land		15,000	(16)	15,000			
Income from Subsidiary	52,000		(13)	52,000			
Credits	452,000	215,000					600,000
Cost of Goods Sold	170,000	115,000					285,000
Depreciation and Amortization	50,000	20,000					70,000
Other Expenses	40,000	15,000					55,000
Debits	(260,000)	(150,000)					(410,000)
							190,000
Income to Noncontrolling Interest			(14)	10,000			(10,000)
Net Income, carry forward	192,000	65,000		77,000			180,000
Retained Earnings, January 1	300,000	100,000	(15)	100,000			300,000
Net Income, from above	192,000	65,000		77,000			180,000
	492,000	165,000					480,000
Dividends Declared	(60,000)	(30,000)			(13)	24,000	
					(14)	6,000	(60,000)
Retained Earnings, December 31, carry forward	432,000	135,000		177,000		30,000	420,000
Cash	229,000	110,000					339,000
Accounts Receivable	75,000	50,000					125,000
Inventory	100,000	75,000					175,000
Land	210,000	20,000			(16)	15,000	215,000
Buildings and Equipment	800,000	600,000					1,400,000
Investment in Special Foods Stock	268,000				(13)	28,000	
					(15)	240,000	
Debits	1,682,000	855,000					2,254,000
Accumulated Depreciation	450,000	320,000					770,000
Accounts Payable	100,000	100,000					200,000
Bonds Payable	200,000	100,000					300,000
Common Stock	500,000	200,000	(15)	200,000			500,000
Retained Earnings, from above	432,000	135,000		177,000		30,000	420,000
Noncontrolling Interest					(14)	4,000	
					(15)	60,000	64,000
Credits	1,682,000	855,000		377,000		377,000	2,254,000

Elimination entries:
  (13) Eliminate income from subsidiary.
  (14) Assign income to noncontrolling interest.
  (15) Eliminate beginning investment balance.
  (16) Eliminate unrealized gain on sale of land.

Entry E(14), which assigns income to the noncontrolling interest, is the same as in the downstream example. The assignment of income to the controlling and noncontrolling interests is based on the realized income of the subsidiary, which is the same in both cases, $50,000.

The only procedural difference in the upstream and downstream elimination process is that unrealized intercompany profits of the subsidiary from upstream sales are eliminated proportionately against the controlling and noncontrolling interests, while unrealized intercompany profits of the parent from downstream sales are eliminated totally against the controlling interest. Thus, in the downstream example, the entire $15,000 unrealized intercompany gain was eliminated against the controlling interest's share of income to derive consolidated net income. In the upstream case, $3,000 of the unrealized intercompany gain is subtracted from the noncontrolling stockholders' share of income. The noncontrolling stockholders' share of the subsidiary's total net income is $13,000 ($65,000 × .20), but is reduced by their $3,000 ($15,000 × .20) share of the unrealized gain on the intercompany sale.

Particularly note that the elimination of the unrealized intercompany profit is the same for the upstream case in entry E(16) as for the downstream case, entry E(10). The full amount of the unrealized intercompany profit, $15,000 in this example, is always eliminated. The only difference between the upstream and downstream cases involves how the income reduction for unrealized profit is allocated between the controlling and noncontrolling interests.

Consolidated Net Income. When intercompany profits that are unrealized from a consolidated point of view are included in the income of a subsidiary, consolidated net income and the noncontrolling stockholders' share of income both must be adjusted for the unrealized profits. Consolidated net income for 20X1 is computed as follows:

Peerless's separate income		$140,000
Peerless's share of Special Foods realized income:		
Special Foods' net income	$65,000	
Less: Unrealized intercompany profit on upstream land sale	(15,000)	
Special Foods' realized income	$50,000	
Peerless's proportionate share	× .80	40,000
Consolidated net income, 20X1		$180,000

This amount appears in the workpaper in Figure 6–4 as the result of the income eliminations and the assignment of income to the noncontrolling interest:

Peerless's net income		$192,000
Special Foods' net income		65,000
		$257,000
Eliminations:		
Peerless's income from Special Foods	$52,000	
Unrealized gain on sale of land	15,000	
		(67,000)
		$190,000
Noncontrolling stockholders' share of income		(10,000)
Consolidated net income, 20X1		$180,000

Consolidated net income in this year is the same whether or not there is an intercompany sale because the gain is unrealized. The unrealized gain must be eliminated fully, with consolidated net income based only on the realized income of the two affiliates.

Noncontrolling Interest.   The income assigned to the noncontrolling shareholders is computed as their proportionate share of the realized income of Special Foods, $10,000 ($50,000 × .20). Total noncontrolling interest is computed as the noncontrolling stockholders' proportionate share of the stockholders' equity of Special Foods, excluding unrealized gains and losses. On December 31, 20X1, noncontrolling interest totals $64,000, computed as follows:

Book value of Special Foods, December 31, 20X1:	
Common stock	$200,000
Retained earnings	135,000
Total book value	$335,000
Unrealized intercompany gain on upstream land sale	(15,000)
Realized book value of Special Foods	$320,000
Noncontrolling stockholders' proportionate share	× .20
Noncontrolling interest, December 31, 20X1	$ 64,000

Eliminating Unrealized Profits after the First Year

In the period in which an intercorporate sale occurs, workpaper eliminating entries are used in the consolidation process to remove the gain or loss recorded by the seller and to adjust the reported amount of the asset back to the price originally paid by the selling affiliate. Each period thereafter while the asset is held by the purchasing affiliate, the reported asset balance and the shareholder claims of the selling affiliate are adjusted to remove the effects of the unrealized gain or loss.

In the case of a downstream sale, the profit on the intercompany transfer is recognized entirely by the parent and is included in the parent's retained earnings in subsequent years. Therefore, the following eliminating entry is needed in the consolidation workpaper each year after the year of the downstream sale of the land, for as long as the land is held by the subsidiary:

E(17) Retained Earnings, January 1	15,000	
Land		15,000
Eliminate unrealized gain on prior-period downstream sale of land.		

This entry reduces beginning consolidated retained earnings and the reported balance of the land to exclude the unrealized intercompany gain.

In the upstream case, the intercompany profit is recognized by the subsidiary. The parent recognizes its proportionate share of the gain, and that amount is included in the parent's beginning retained earnings in subsequent years. In the consolidation workpaper prepared in years subsequent to the intercompany transfer while the land is held by the parent, the unrealized intercompany gain is eliminated from the reported balance of the land and proportionately from the subsidiary ownership interests with the following entry:

E(18)	Retained Earnings, January 1	12,000	
	Noncontrolling Interest	3,000	
	Land		15,000
	Eliminate unrealized gain on prior-period upstream sale of land.		

Thus, in periods subsequent to an upstream intercompany transfer, consolidated retained earnings is reduced by the parent's share of the unrealized intercompany gain, and the noncontrolling interest is reduced by the remainder. All other elimination entries are made as if there is no unrealized intercompany gain.

Subsequent Disposition of Asset

Unrealized profits on intercompany sales of assets are viewed as being realized at the time the assets are resold to external parties. For consolidation purposes, the gain or loss recognized by the affiliate selling to the external party must be adjusted for the previously unrealized intercompany gain or loss. While the seller's reported profit on the external sale is based on that affiliate's cost, the gain or loss reported by the consolidated entity is based on the cost of the asset to the consolidated entity, which is the cost incurred by the affiliate that purchased the asset originally from an outside party.

When previously unrealized intercompany profits are realized, the effects of the profit elimination process must be reversed. At the time of realization, the full amount of the deferred intercompany profit is added back into the consolidated income computation and assigned to the shareholder interests from which it originally was eliminated.

To illustrate the treatment of unrealized intercompany profits once the transferred asset is resold, assume that Peerless purchases land from an outside party for $20,000 on January 1, 20X1, and sells the land to Special Foods on July 1, 20X1, for $35,000. Special Foods subsequently sells the land to an outside party on March 1, 20X5, for $45,000, as follows:

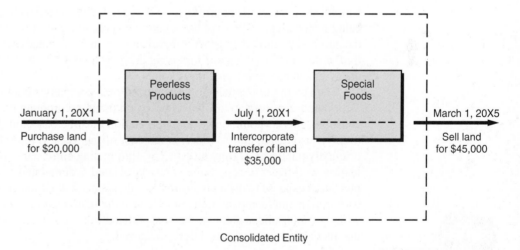

Consolidated Entity

Special Foods recognizes a gain on the sale to the outside party of $10,000 ($45,000 − $35,000). From a consolidated viewpoint, however, the gain is $25,000, the difference between the price at which the land left the consolidated entity ($45,000) and the price at which the land entered the consolidated entity ($20,000) when purchased originally by Peerless.

In the consolidation workpaper, the land no longer needs to be reduced by the unrealized intercompany gain because the gain now is realized and the land no longer is held by the consolidated entity. Instead, the $10,000 gain recognized by Special Foods on the sale of the land to an outsider must be adjusted to reflect a total gain for the consolidated entity of $25,000. Thus, the following eliminating entry is made in the consolidation workpaper prepared at the end of 20X5:

E(19) Retained Earnings, January 1	15,000	
Gain on Sale of Land		15,000
Adjust for previously unrealized intercompany gain on sale of land.		

In addition to adjusting the gain, this entry reduces beginning consolidated retained earnings by the amount of the unrealized intercompany gain previously recognized by Peerless. All other elimination entries are the same as if there were no unrealized intercompany profits at the beginning of the period.

No additional consideration need be given the intercompany transfer in periods subsequent to the external sale. From a consolidated viewpoint, all aspects of the transaction are complete, and the profit is realized once the sale to an external party occurs.

In the example, if the sale to the external party had been made by Peerless following an upstream intercompany transfer from Special Foods, the workpaper treatment would be the same as in the case of the downstream transfer except that the debit in elimination entry E(19) would be prorated between beginning retained earnings ($12,000) and the noncontrolling interest ($3,000) based on the relative ownership interests.

Asset Transfers Involving Depreciable Assets

Unrealized intercompany profits on a depreciable or amortizable asset are viewed as being realized gradually over the remaining economic life of the asset as it is used by the purchasing affiliate in generating revenue from unaffiliated parties. In effect, a portion of the unrealized gain or loss is realized each period as benefits are derived from the asset and its service potential expires.

The amount of depreciation recognized on a company's books each period on an asset purchased from an affiliate is based on the intercorporate transfer price. From a consolidated viewpoint, however, depreciation must be based on the cost of the asset to the consolidated entity, which is the cost of the asset to the related company that originally purchased it from an outsider. Eliminating entries are needed in the consolidation workpaper to restate the asset, associated accumulated depreciation, and depreciation expense to the amounts that would appear in the financial statements if there had been no intercompany transfer. Because the intercompany sale takes place totally within the consolidated entity, the consolidated financial statements must appear as if the intercompany transfer had never occurred.

Downstream Sale

The example of Peerless Products and Special Foods is modified to illustrate the downstream sale of a depreciable asset. Assume that Peerless sells equipment to Special Foods on December 31, 20X1, for $7,000, as follows:

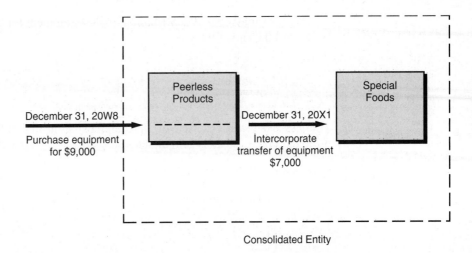

Consolidated Entity

The equipment originally cost Peerless $9,000 when purchased on December 31, 20W8, three years before December 31, 20X1, and is being depreciated over a total life of 10 years using straight-line depreciation with no residual value. The book value of the equipment immediately before the sale by Peerless is computed as follows:

Original cost to Peerless		$9,000
Accumulated depreciation on December 31, 20X1:		
Annual depreciation ($9,000 ÷ 10 years)	$900	
Number of years	× 3	
		(2,700)
Book value on December 31, 20X1		$6,300

The gain recognized by Peerless on the intercompany sale of the equipment is:

Sale price of the equipment	$7,000
Book value of the equipment	(6,300)
Gain on sale of the equipment	$ 700

Separate-Company Entries—20X1. Special Foods records the purchase of the equipment at its cost:

December 31, 20X1		
(20) Equipment		7,000
Cash		7,000
Record purchase of equipment.		

Special Foods does not depreciate the equipment during 20X1 because the equipment is purchased at the very end of 20X1.

Peerless must record depreciation on the equipment for 20X1 because it held the asset until the end of the year:

December 31, 20X1

(21) Depreciation Expense	900	
Accumulated Depreciation		900
Record 20X1 depreciation expense on equipment sold.		

Peerless also records the sale of the equipment at the end of 20X1 and recognizes the $700 ($7,000 − $6,300) gain on the sale:

December 31, 20X1

(22) Cash	7,000	
Accumulated Depreciation	2,700	
Equipment		9,000
Gain on Sale of Equipment		700
Record sale of equipment.		

In addition, Peerless records the normal basic equity-method entries to recognize its share of Special Foods' income and dividends for 20X1:

(23) Investment in Special Foods Stock	40,000	
Income from Subsidiary		40,000
Record equity-method income:		
$50,000 × .80		

(24) Cash	24,000	
Investment in Special Foods Stock		24,000
Record dividends from Special Foods:		
$30,000 × .80		

Consolidation Workpaper—20X1.   The workpaper to prepare consolidated financial statements at the end of 20X1 appears in Figure 6–5. The first three elimination entries in the workpaper are the normal entries to (1) eliminate the income and dividends from Special Foods recognized by Peerless and the change in the investment account for the year, (2) assign income to the noncontrolling interest, and (3) eliminate the stockholders' equity accounts of Special Foods and the investment account as of the beginning of the year:

E(25) Income from Subsidiary	40,000	
Dividends Declared		24,000
Investment in Special Foods Stock		16,000
Eliminate income from subsidiary.		
E(26) Income to Noncontrolling Interest	10,000	
Dividends Declared		6,000
Noncontrolling Interest		4,000
Assign income to noncontrolling interest:		
$10,000 = $50,000 × .20		
E(27) Common Stock—Special Foods	200,000	
Retained Earnings, January 1	100,000	
Investment in Special Foods Stock		240,000
Noncontrolling Interest		60,000
Eliminate beginning investment balance.		

An additional workpaper entry is needed to eliminate the unrealized intercompany gain on the sale of the equipment from consolidated net income and to restate the

FIGURE 6–5   **December 31, 20X1, Consolidation Workpaper, Period of Intercompany Sale; Downstream Sale of Equipment**

Item	Peerless Products	Special Foods	Eliminations Debit		Eliminations Credit		Consolidated
Sales	400,000	200,000					600,000
Gain on Sale of Equipment	700		(28)	700			
Income from Subsidiary	40,000		(25)	40,000			
Credits	440,700	200,000					600,000
Cost of Goods Sold	170,000	115,000					285,000
Depreciation and Amortization	50,000	20,000					70,000
Other Expenses	40,000	15,000					55,000
Debits	(260,000)	(150,000)					(410,000)
							190,000
Income to Noncontrolling Interest			(26)	10,000			(10,000)
Net Income, carry forward	180,700	50,000		50,700			180,000
Retained Earnings, January 1	300,000	100,000	(27)	100,000			300,000
Net Income, from above	180,700	50,000		50,700			180,000
	480,700	150,000					480,000
Dividends Declared	(60,000)	(30,000)			(25)	24,000	
					(26)	6,000	(60,000)
Retained Earnings, December 31, carry forward	420,700	120,000		150,700		30,000	420,000
Cash	271,000	68,000					339,000
Accounts Receivable	75,000	50,000					125,000
Inventory	100,000	75,000					175,000
Land	175,000	40,000					215,000
Buildings and Equipment	791,000	607,000	(28)	2,000			1,400,000
Investment in Special Foods Stock	256,000				(25)	16,000	
					(27)	240,000	
Debits	1,668,000	840,000					2,254,000
Accumulated Depreciation	447,300	320,000			(28)	2,700	770,000
Accounts Payable	100,000	100,000					200,000
Bonds Payable	200,000	100,000					300,000
Common Stock	500,000	200,000	(27)	200,000			500,000
Retained Earnings, from above	420,700	120,000		150,700		30,000	420,000
Noncontrolling Interest					(26)	4,000	
					(27)	60,000	64,000
Credits	1,668,000	840,000		352,700		352,700	2,254,000

Elimination entries:

(25) Eliminate income from subsidiary.

(26) Assign income to noncontrolling interest.

(27) Eliminate beginning investment balance.

(28) Eliminate unrealized gain on sale of equipment.

equipment to the amounts that would appear in the consolidated statements if there had been no intercompany sale. The amounts in the trial balances of the parent and subsidiary include the effects of the intercompany transfer and need to be adjusted in the consolidation workpaper to the balances immediately before the transfer:

	Amounts from Trial Balances	Elimination	Consolidated Amounts
Buildings and equipment	$7,000	$2,000	$9,000
Accumulated depreciation	-0-	(2,700)	(2,700)
Gain on sale of equipment	(700)	700	-0-

Thus, the following entry is needed in the workpaper:

E(28)	Buildings and Equipment	2,000	
	Gain on Sale of Equipment	700	
	Accumulated Depreciation		2,700
	Eliminate unrealized gain on downstream sale of equipment.		

As a result of this entry, the equipment, stated at $7,000 on Special Foods' books, is reported in the consolidated balance sheet at $9,000 ($7,000 + $2,000), its original cost to Peerless. While Special Foods has not depreciated the equipment, elimination entry E(28) provides for $2,700 of accumulated depreciation ($900 × 3), the amount that would have shown on Peerless's books had the equipment not been sold. Entry E(28) also eliminates the $700 intercompany gain that is unrealized and cannot appear when Peerless and Special Foods are viewed together as a single entity. The overall effect of entry E(28) is to report exactly the same numbers in the consolidated financial statements as if the parent company had continued to own the equipment and there had been no intercompany transfer.

Separate-Company Entries—20X2.   During 20X2, Special Foods begins depreciating the $7,000 cost of the equipment acquired from Peerless Products over its remaining life of seven years using straight-line depreciation. The resulting depreciation is $1,000 per year ($7,000 ÷ 7 years):

(29)	Depreciation Expense	1,000	
	Accumulated Depreciation		1,000
	Record depreciation expense for 20X2.		

This amount is $100 more per year than the depreciation that would have been recorded each year if Peerless had continued to hold the equipment.

Peerless records its normal equity-method entries for 20X2 to reflect its share of Special Foods' $74,000 income and dividends of $40,000:

(30)	Investment in Special Foods Stock	59,200	
	Income from Subsidiary		59,200
	Record equity-method income:		
	$74,000 × .80		

(31)	Cash	32,000	
	Investment in Special Foods Stock		32,000
	Record dividends from Special Foods:		
	$40,000 × .80		

Special Foods' net income is only $74,000 in 20X2 because it has been reduced by the $1,000 of depreciation on the transferred asset. Accordingly, Peerless's share of that income is $59,200 ($74,000 × .80).

The investment account on Peerless's books appears as follows:

Investment in Special Foods Stock			
Original cost	240,000		
(23) 20X1 equity accrual ($50,000 × .80)	40,000	(24) 20X1 dividends ($30,000 × .80)	24,000
Balance, 12/31/X1	256,000		
(30) 20X2 equity accrual ($74,000 × .80)	59,200	(31) 20X2 dividends ($40,000 × .80)	32,000
Balance, 12/31/X2	283,200		

Consolidation Workpaper—20X2.   The consolidation workpaper for 20X2 is presented in Figure 6–6. The trial balance amounts from the basic example have been adjusted to reflect the intercompany asset sale. The first three elimination entries are the normal entries to eliminate income and dividends from the subsidiary, the investment account, and the stockholders' equity accounts of the subsidiary, and to establish the noncontrolling interest in the workpaper:

E(32)	Income from Subsidiary	59,200	
	Dividends Declared		32,000
	Investment in Special Foods Stock		27,200
	Eliminate income from subsidiary.		
E(33)	Income to Noncontrolling Interest	14,800	
	Dividends Declared		8,000
	Noncontrolling Interest		6,800
	Assign income to noncontrolling interest: $14,800 = $74,000 × .20		
E(34)	Common Stock—Special Foods	200,000	
	Retained Earnings, January 1	120,000	
	Investment in Special Foods Stock		256,000
	Noncontrolling Interest		64,000
	Eliminate beginning investment balance.		

Entry E(33) assigns the noncontrolling interest its full 20 percent of the $74,000 reported income of Special Foods, given that the unrealized profits are on the books of the parent.

In addition to the normal elimination entries, entry E(35) is needed to eliminate the effects of the 20X1 intercompany transaction as of the beginning of 20X2:

E(35)	Buildings and Equipment	2,000	
	Retained Earnings, January 1	700	
	Accumulated Depreciation		2,700
	Eliminate unrealized gain on equipment.		

Entry E(35) restates the balance of the equipment to $9,000 ($7,000 + $2,000), the original cost to the consolidated entity when purchased by Peerless. Accumulated depreciation on the equipment is credited for $2,700. This is the amount at which accumulated depreciation would have been stated as of January 1, 20X2, if the asset had not been transferred to Special Foods:

FIGURE 6–6   December 31, 20X2, Consolidated Workpaper, Next Period Following Intercompany Sale; Downstream Sale of Equipment

Item	Peerless Products	Special Foods	Eliminations Debit		Eliminations Credit		Consolidated
Sales	450,000	300,000					750,000
Income from Subsidiary	59,200		(32)	59,200			
Credits	509,200	300,000					750,000
Cost of Goods Sold	180,000	160,000					340,000
Depreciation and Amortization	49,100	21,000			(36)	100	70,000
Other Expenses	60,000	45,000					105,000
Debits	(289,100)	(226,000)					(515,000)
							235,000
Income to Noncontrolling Interest			(33)	14,800			(14,800)
Net Income, carry forward	220,100	74,000		74,000		100	220,200
Retained Earnings, January 1	420,700	120,000	(34)	120,000			
			(35)	700			420,000
Net Income, from above	220,100	74,000		74,000		100	220,200
	640,800	194,000					640,200
Dividends Declared	(60,000)	(40,000)			(32)	32,000	
					(33)	8,000	(60,000)
Retained Earnings, December 31, carry forward	580,800	154,000		194,700		40,100	580,200
Cash	298,000	78,000					376,000
Accounts Receivable	150,000	80,000					230,000
Inventory	180,000	90,000					270,000
Land	175,000	40,000					215,000
Buildings and Equipment	791,000	607,000	(35)	2,000			1,400,000
Investment in Special Foods Stock	283,200				(32)	27,200	
					(34)	256,000	
Debits	1,877,200	895,000					2,491,000
Accumulated Depreciation	496,400	341,000	(36)	100	(35)	2,700	840,000
Accounts Payable	100,000	100,000					200,000
Bonds Payable	200,000	100,000					300,000
Common Stock	500,000	200,000	(34)	200,000			500,000
Retained Earnings, from above	580,800	154,000		194,700		40,100	580,200
Noncontrolling Interest					(33)	6,800	
					(34)	64,000	70,800
Credits	1,877,200	895,000		396,800		396,800	2,491,000

Elimination entries:

(32) Eliminate income from subsidiary.

(33) Assign income to noncontrolling interest.

(34) Eliminate beginning investment balance.

(35) Eliminate unrealized gain on equipment.

(36) Adjust depreciation for realization of intercompany gain.

only the amount of income from the subsidiary recognized by Peerless and the balance in the investment account. These balances, in turn, are eliminated by entries E(59) and E(61). The gain account entered on Special Foods' books at the time the equipment is sold is unaffected by the entries recorded by Peerless and, therefore, carries over to the consolidation workpaper unless eliminated. Entry E(62) is needed to prevent the gain from appearing in the consolidated income statement.

Note that in the workpaper shown in Figure 6–9, the parent's net income is equal to consolidated net income and the parent's retained earnings is equal to consolidated retained earnings.

Fully Adjusted Equity-Method Entries—20X2.   In 20X2, Peerless records its share of Special Foods' $75,900 income and $40,000 of dividends with the following entries:

(63)	Investment in Special Foods Stock	60,720	
	Income from Subsidiary		60,720
	Record equity-method income:		
	$75,900 × .80		
(64)	Cash	32,000	
	Investment in Special Foods Stock		32,000
	Record dividends from Special Foods:		
	$40,000 × .80		

An additional entry is recorded by Peerless under the fully adjusted equity method to increase income for the partial realization of the unrealized intercompany gain:

(65)	Investment in Special Foods Stock	80	
	Income from Subsidiary		80
	Recognize portion of gain on sale of equipment:		
	($700 ÷ 7 years) × .80		

The gain on the 20X1 intercompany transfer is viewed as being realized over a seven-year period. The $100 of intercompany gain realized each year is equal to the difference between the amount of depreciation recorded by Peerless ($1,000) and the amount that would have been recorded by Special Foods had there been no intercompany transfer ($900). Because depreciation expense will be adjusted in the preparation of consolidated financial statements to the amount that would have been reported if there had been no intercompany transfer, total income in the workpaper will be increased by $100. This increase will be allocated between the controlling and noncontrolling interests in the upstream case, leading to an increase of $80 ($100 × .80) in consolidated net income.

Entry (65) adds into Peerless's equity-method income a proportionate share of the part of the gain considered realized during 20X2. Recall that Peerless's 20X1 income was reduced by a proportionate share of the unrealized gain. Therefore, Peerless's portion of the realized part of the gain ($100 × .80) is put back into Peerless's income and the investment account in 20X2. Consistent with the idea of a one-line consolidation, entry (65) makes Peerless's fully adjusted equity-method net income equal to consolidated net income.

Consolidation Workpaper—20X2.   The consolidation workpaper for 20X2 is shown in Figure 6–10. The following elimination entries are included in the workpaper:

E(66)	Income from Subsidiary	60,800	
	Dividends Declared		32,000
	Investment in Special Foods Stock		28,800
	Eliminate income from subsidiary:		
	$60,800 = ($75,900 + $100) × .80		
E(67)	Income to Noncontrolling Interest	15,200	
	Dividends Declared		8,000
	Noncontrolling Interest		7,200
	Assign income to noncontrolling interest:		
	$15,200 = ($75,900 + $100) × .20		

FIGURE 6–10 December 31, 20X2, Fully Adjusted Equity-Method Consolidation Workpaper, Next Period Following Intercompany Sale; Upstream Sale of Equipment

Item	Peerless Products	Special Foods	Eliminations Debit		Eliminations Credit		Consolidated
Sales	450,000	300,000					750,000
Income from Subsidiary	60,800		(66)	60,800			
Credits	510,800	300,000					750,000
Cost of Goods Sold	180,000	160,000					340,000
Depreciation and Amortization	51,000	19,100			(70)	100	70,000
Other Expenses	60,000	45,000					105,000
Debits	(291,000)	(224,100)					(515,000)
							235,000
Income to Noncontrolling Interest			(67)	15,200			(15,200)
Net Income, carry forward	219,800	75,900		76,000		100	219,800
Retained Earnings, January 1	420,000	120,700	(68)	120,700			420,000
Net Income, from above	219,800	75,900		76,000		100	219,800
	639,800	196,600					639,800
Dividends Declared	(60,000)	(40,000)			(66)	32,000	
					(67)	8,000	(60,000)
Retained Earnings, December 31, carry forward	579,800	156,600		196,700		40,100	579,800
Cash	284,000	92,000					376,000
Accounts Receivable	150,000	80,000					230,000
Inventory	180,000	90,000					270,000
Land	175,000	40,000					215,000
Buildings and Equipment	807,000	591,000	(69)	2,000			1,400,000
Investment in Special Foods Stock	284,800		(69)	560	(66)	28,800	
					(68)	256,560	
Debits	1,880,800	893,000					2,491,000
Accumulated Depreciation	501,000	336,400	(70)	100	(69)	2,700	840,000
Accounts Payable	100,000	100,000					200,000
Bonds Payable	200,000	100,000					300,000
Common Stock	500,000	200,000	(68)	200,000			500,000
Retained Earnings, from above	579,800	156,600		196,700		40,100	579,800
Noncontrolling Interest			(69)	140	(67)	7,200	
					(68)	64,140	71,200
Credits	1,880,800	893,000		399,500		399,500	2,491,000

Elimination entries:

(66) Eliminate income from subsidiary.

(67) Assign income to noncontrolling interest.

(68) Eliminate beginning investment balance.

(69) Eliminate unrealized gain on equipment.

(70) Adjust depreciation for realization of intercompany gain.

E(68)	Common Stock—Special Foods	200,000	
	Retained Earnings, January 1	120,700	
	Investment in Special Foods Stock		256,560
	Noncontrolling Interest		64,140
	Eliminate beginning investment balance:		
	$256,560 = ($200,000 + $120,700) \times .80$		
	$64,140 = ($200,000 + $120,700) \times .20$		
E(69)	Buildings and Equipment	2,000	
	Investment in Special Foods Stock	560	
	Noncontrolling Interest	140	
	Accumulated Depreciation		2,700
	Eliminate unrealized gain on upstream sale of equipment.		
E(70)	Accumulated Depreciation	100	
	Depreciation Expense		100
	Adjust depreciation for realization of intercompany gain.		

These entries are the same as the eliminating entries used following application of the basic equity method, with two differences. First, entry E(66) eliminates Special Foods' income and dividends recognized by Peerless. Because the income recognized by Peerless under the fully adjusted equity method includes Peerless's share of the realized 20X1 intercompany gain, which is not included when using the basic equity method, the income elimination is $80 ($100 \times .80$) greater following use of the fully adjusted equity method.

The second difference is in entry E(69). When the basic equity method is used, the parent's share of the intercompany gain unrealized at the beginning of 20X2 is included in its retained earnings and must be eliminated when consolidating. This was accomplished in the basic equity illustration through entry E(51). When the fully adjusted equity method is used, however, the parent's share of the unrealized gain is deducted from income on the parent's books in the year of the intercompany transfer and subsequently is not included in retained earnings. Therefore, no additional elimination of retained earnings is needed.

Replacing the debit to Retained Earnings in entry E(51) is a debit to the investment account in entry E(69). Because the investment account is reduced at the same time that the unrealized income is deducted from the parent's income, eliminating entry E(68), which credits the investment account for an amount equal to the parent's proportionate share of the beginning subsidiary stockholders' equity balances, eliminates an amount greater than the actual beginning investment account balance. The additional amount is equal to the parent's share of the intercompany gain unrealized at the beginning of the year. Entry E(69) debits the investment account for that amount, and the two entries together, E(68) and E(69), fully eliminate the beginning balance of the investment.

All other eliminations are the same under both the basic and the fully adjusted equity methods.

Cost Method

When using the cost method of accounting for an investment in a subsidiary, the parent records dividends received from the subsidiary during the period as income. No entries are made under the cost method to record the parent's share of undistributed subsidiary earnings, amortize differential, or remove unrealized intercompany profits.

To illustrate consolidation following an intercompany sale of equipment when the parent accounts for its subsidiary investment using the cost method, assume the same facts as in previous illustrations of an upstream sale.

Consolidation Workpaper—20X1. The workpaper illustrated in Figure 6–11 is used in preparing consolidated financial statements for 20X1 following the upstream sale of equipment to Peerless by Special Foods. The following elimination entries appear in the workpaper, assuming Peerless uses the cost method to account for its investment:

FIGURE 6–11   December 31, 20X1, Cost-Method Consolidation Workpaper, Period of Intercompany Sale; Upstream Sale of Equipment

Item	Peerless Products	Special Foods	Eliminations Debit		Eliminations Credit		Consolidated
Sales	400,000	200,000					600,000
Gain on Sale of Equipment		700	(74)	700			
Dividend Income	24,000		(71)	24,000			
Credits	424,000	200,700					600,000
Cost of Goods Sold	170,000	115,000					285,000
Depreciation and Amortization	50,000	20,000					70,000
Other Expenses	40,000	15,000					55,000
Debits	(260,000)	(150,000)					(410,000)
							190,000
Income to Noncontrolling Interest			(72)	10,000			(10,000)
Net Income, carry forward	164,000	50,700		34,700			180,000
Retained Earnings, January 1	300,000	100,000	(73)	100,000			300,000
Net Income, from above	164,000	50,700		34,700			180,000
	464,000	150,700					480,000
Dividends Declared	(60,000)	(30,000)			(71)	24,000	
					(72)	6,000	(60,000)
Retained Earnings, December 31, carry forward	404,000	120,700		134,700		30,000	420,000
Cash	257,000	82,000					339,000
Accounts Receivable	75,000	50,000					125,000
Inventory	100,000	75,000					175,000
Land	175,000	40,000					215,000
Buildings and Equipment	807,000	591,000	(74)	2,000			1,400,000
Investment in Special Foods Stock	240,000				(73)	240,000	
Debits	1,654,000	838,000					2,254,000
Accumulated Depreciation	450,000	317,300			(74)	2,700	770,000
Accounts Payable	100,000	100,000					200,000
Bonds Payable	200,000	100,000					300,000
Common Stock	500,000	200,000	(73)	200,000			500,000
Retained Earnings, from above	404,000	120,700		134,700		30,000	420,000
Noncontrolling Interest					(72)	4,000	
					(73)	60,000	64,000
Credits	1,654,000	838,000		336,700		336,700	2,254,000

Elimination entries:

(71) Eliminate dividend income from subsidiary.

(72) Assign income to noncontrolling interest.

(73) Eliminate investment balance at date of acquisition.

(74) Eliminate unrealized gain on equipment.

E(71)	Dividend Income	24,000	
	Dividends Declared		24,000
	Eliminate dividend income from subsidiary:		
	$30,000 × .80		
E(72)	Income to Noncontrolling Interest	10,000	
	Dividends Declared		6,000
	Noncontrolling Interest		4,000
	Assign income to noncontrolling interest:		
	$10,000 = ($50,700 − $700) × .20		
E(73)	Common Stock—Special Foods	200,000	
	Retained Earnings, January 1	100,000	
	Investment in Special Foods Stock		240,000
	Noncontrolling Interest		60,000
	Eliminate investment balance at date of acquisition.		
E(74)	Buildings and Equipment	2,000	
	Gain on Sale of Equipment	700	
	Accumulated Depreciation		2,700
	Eliminate unrealized gain on equipment.		

Entry E(71) eliminates Peerless's share of Special Foods' 20X1 dividends. All other eliminating entries are the same as under the basic equity method in the year of acquisition.

Consolidation Workpaper—20X2. The consolidation workpaper prepared for December 31, 20X2, is presented in Figure 6–12. The following eliminating entries are needed in the workpaper:

E(75)	Dividend Income	32,000	
	Dividends Declared		32,000
	Eliminate dividend income from subsidiary:		
	$40,000 × .80		
E(76)	Income to Noncontrolling Interest	15,200	
	Dividends Declared		8,000
	Noncontrolling Interest		7,200
	Assign income to noncontrolling interest:		
	$15,200 = ($75,900 + $100) × .20		
E(77)	Common Stock—Special Foods	200,000	
	Retained Earnings, January 1	100,000	
	Investment in Special Foods Stock		240,000
	Noncontrolling Interest		60,000
	Eliminate investment balance at date of acquisition.		
E(78)	Retained Earnings, January 1	4,140	
	Noncontrolling Interest		4,140
	Assign undistributed prior earnings of subsidiary to		
	noncontrolling interest: ($120,700 − $100,000) × .20		
E(79)	Buildings and Equipment	2,000	
	Retained Earnings, January 1	560	
	Noncontrolling Interest	140	
	Accumulated Depreciation		2,700
	Eliminate unrealized gain on equipment.		
E(80)	Accumulated Depreciation	100	
	Depreciation Expense		100
	Adjust depreciation for realization of intercompany gain.		

Entry E(75) eliminates Peerless's share of Special Foods' dividends. Entry E(76) assigns income to the noncontrolling interest in the normal manner, taking into consideration a proportionate share

FIGURE 6–12   December 31, 20X2, Cost-Method Consolidation Workpaper, Next Period Following
Intercompany Sale; Upstream Sale of Equipment

Item	Peerless Products	Special Foods	Eliminations				Consolidated
			Debit		Credit		
Sales	450,000	300,000					750,000
Dividend Income	32,000		(75)	32,000			
Credits	482,000	300,000					750,000
Cost of Goods Sold	180,000	160,000					340,000
Depreciation and Amortization	51,000	19,100			(80)	100	70,000
Other Expenses	60,000	45,000					105,000
Debits	(291,000)	(224,100)					(515,000)
							235,000
Income to Noncontrolling Interest			(76)	15,200			(15,200)
Net Income, carry forward	191,000	75,900		47,200		100	219,800
Retained Earnings, January 1	404,000	120,700	(77)	100,000			
			(78)	4,140			
			(79)	560			420,000
Net Income, from above	191,000	75,900		47,200		100	219,800
	595,000	196,600					639,800
Dividends Declared	(60,000)	(40,000)			(75)	32,000	
					(76)	8,000	(60,000)
Retained Earnings, December 31, carry forward	535,000	156,600		151,900		40,100	579,800
Cash	284,000	92,000					376,000
Accounts Receivable	150,000	80,000					230,000
Inventory	180,000	90,000					270,000
Land	175,000	40,000					215,000
Buildings and Equipment	807,000	591,000	(79)	2,000			1,400,000
Investment in Special Foods Stock	240,000				(77)	240,000	
Debits	1,836,000	893,000					2,491,000
Accumulated Depreciation	501,000	336,400	(80)	100	(79)	2,700	840,000
Accounts Payable	100,000	100,000					200,000
Bonds Payable	200,000	100,000					300,000
Common Stock	500,000	200,000	(77)	200,000			500,000
Retained Earnings, from above	535,000	156,600		151,900		40,100	579,800
Noncontrolling Interest			(79)	140	(76)	7,200	
					(77)	60,000	
					(78)	4,140	71,200
Credits	1,836,000	893,000		354,140		354,140	2,491,000

Elimination entries:

(75) Eliminate dividend income from subsidiary.

(76) Assign income to noncontrolling interest.

(77) Eliminate investment balance at date of acquisition.

(78) Assign undistributed prior earnings of subsidiary to noncontrolling interest.

(79) Eliminate unrealized gain on equipment.

(80) Adjust depreciation for realization of intercompany gain.

common stock outstanding. Prime uses the basic equity method in accounting for its investment in Lane Company.

Trial balance data for the two companies on December 31, 20X7, are as follows:

Item	Prime Company		Lane Company	
	Debit	Credit	Debit	Credit
Cash and Accounts Receivable	$ 151,000		$ 55,000	
Inventory	240,000		100,000	
Land	100,000		80,000	
Buildings and Equipment	500,000		150,000	
Investment in Lane Company Stock	240,000			
Cost of Goods Sold	160,000		80,000	
Depreciation and Amortization	25,000		15,000	
Other Expenses	20,000		10,000	
Dividends Declared	60,000		35,000	
Accumulated Depreciation		$ 230,000		$ 60,000
Accounts Payable		60,000		25,000
Bonds Payable		200,000		50,000
Common Stock		300,000		100,000
Retained Earnings		420,000		140,000
Sales		250,000		150,000
Income from Subsidiary		36,000		
Total	$1,496,000	$1,496,000	$525,000	$525,000

Additional Information

1. At the date of combination, the book values and fair values of all separably identifiable assets of Lane Company were the same. At December 31, 20X6, the management of Prime Company reviewed the amount attributed to goodwill as a result of its purchase of Lane Company stock and recognized an impairment loss of $25,000. No further impairment occurred in 20X7.

2. On January 1, 20X5, Lane Company sold land that had cost $8,000 to Prime Company for $18,000.

3. On January 1, 20X6, Prime Company sold to Lane Company equipment that it had purchased for $75,000 on January 1, 20X1. The equipment has a total economic life of 15 years and was sold to Lane Company for $70,000. Both companies use straight-line depreciation.

4. Intercorporate receivables and payables total $4,000 on December 31, 20X7.

Required

a. Show how Prime's income from its subsidiary is computed for 20X7.

b. Prepare a reconciliation between the balance in the investment in subsidiary account reported by Prime Company on December 31, 20X7, and the underlying book value of Lane Company.

c. Prepare all workpaper eliminating entries needed as of December 31, 20X7, and complete a three-part consolidation workpaper for 20X7.

P6–36   Incomplete Data

Partial trial balance data for Phantom Corporation and Shadow Company at December 31, 20X7, are as follows:

Phantom Corporation and Shadow Company
Trial Balance Data
December 31, 20X7

Item	Phantom Corporation	Shadow Company	Consolidated Entity
Cash	$ 66,500	$ 25,000	$ 91,500
Accounts Receivable	(d)	35,000	126,000
Inventory	160,000	75,000	235,000
Buildings and Equipment	345,000	150,000	(i)
Land	70,000	90,000	153,000
Investment in Shadow Company Stock	(f)		
Cost of Goods Sold	230,000	195,000	425,000
Depreciation Expense	45,000	10,000	52,000
Amortization Expense			(e)
Miscellaneous Expense	18,000	15,000	33,000
Dividends Declared	25,000	20,000	25,000
Income to Noncontrolling Interest			(l)
Copyrights			5,000
Total Debits	$1,190,500	$615,000	$1,671,200
Accumulated Depreciation	$ 180,000	$ 80,000	$ (j)
Accounts Payable	25,000	85,000	101,000
Common Stock	100,000	50,000	(a)
Additional Paid-In Capital	(b)	70,000	140,000
Retained Earnings	380,000	80,000	(k)
Income from Subsidiary	15,500		
Sales	343,000	(c)	593,000
Gain on Sale of Land	(g)		(h)
Noncontrolling Interest			82,800
Total Credits	$1,190,500	$615,000	$1,671,200

Additional Information

1. Phantom Corporation purchased 60 percent ownership of Shadow Company on January 1, 20X4, for $105,000. Shadow reported retained earnings of $30,000 on January 1, 20X4. The purchase differential is assigned to copyrights that are being amortized over a six-year life.

2. On August 13, 20X7, Phantom sold land to Shadow for $28,000. Phantom also has accounts receivable from Shadow on services performed prior to the end of 20X7.

3. Equipment purchased by Shadow for $60,000 on January 1, 20X4, was sold to Phantom on January 1, 20X6, for $45,000. The equipment is depreciated on a straight-line basis and had a total expected useful life of five years when purchased by Shadow Company. No change in life expectancy resulted from the intercompany transfer.

Required

Compute the dollar amount for each of the balances indicated by a letter.

P6–37   Multiple-Choice Questions—Computation of Various Account Balances

Kendel Manufacturing Corporation purchased 60 percent of the outstanding stock of Trendy Products Corporation on January 1, 20X2. Trendy reported retained earnings of $120,000 at the date of acquisition. The price paid for Trendy's stock included $30,000 that was attributable to identifiable intangible assets with a remaining life of 10 years. Summarized balance sheet data for December 31, 20X4, are as follows:

	Kendel Manufacturing	Trendy Products
Current Assets	$200,000	$100,000
Land	120,000	80,000
Buildings and Equipment (net)	300,000	200,000
Investment in Trendy Products Corporation Stock	201,000	
Total Assets	$821,000	$380,000
Liabilities	$150,000	$ 80,000
Common Stock	150,000	90,000
Additional Paid-In Capital	100,000	10,000
Retained Earnings	421,000	200,000
Total Liabilities and Equity	$821,000	$380,000

Kendel Manufacturing uses the basic equity method in accounting for its investment in Trendy Products. For the year ended December 31, 20X4, Trendy Products reported net income of $40,000 and paid dividends of $15,000; Kendel Manufacturing reported income from its separate operations of $75,000 and paid dividends of $55,000.

Kendel Manufacturing sold land that it had purchased for $25,000 to Trendy Products for $45,000 on December 31, 20X3. On January 1, 20X4, Trendy Products sold equipment with a book value of $48,000 to Kendel Manufacturing for $58,000. The equipment had an estimated economic life of five years at the time of intercorporate transfer.

Required

1. What amount of income will be assigned to noncontrolling shareholders in the 20X4 consolidated income statement?

   a. $4,000.

   b. $12,000.

   c. $12,800.

   d. $16,800.

2. What amount will be reported as identifiable intangible assets in the consolidated balance sheet on December 31, 20X4?

   a. $12,600.

   b. $21,000.

   c. $24,000.

   d. $30,000.

3. What amount of buildings and equipment (net) will be reported in the consolidated balance sheet on December 31, 20X4?

   a. $490,000.

   b. $492,000.

   c. $494,000.

   d. $495,000.

   e. $500,000.

4. What amount of land will be reported in the consolidated balance sheet on December 31, 20X4?

   a. $120,000.

   b. $180,000.

   c. $188,000.

   d. $200,000.

5. What amount of consolidated net income will be reported for 20X4?

   a. $91,200.

   b. $99,000.

   c. $104,000.

   d. $112,000.

   e. $115,000.

6. What amount of consolidated retained earnings will be reported in the consolidated balance sheet on December 31, 20X4?

   a. $396,200.

   b. $516,200.

   c. $566,200.

   d. $568,200.

   e. $596,200.

7. What balance will be reported for the noncontrolling interest in the December 31, 20X4, consolidated balance sheet?

   a. $108,000.

   b. $116,000.

   c. $116,800.

   d. $120,000.

8. What amount was reported as noncontrolling interest in the consolidated balance sheet prepared as of December 31, 20X3?

   a. $102,000.

   b. $110,000.

   c. $120,000.

   d. $122,000.

P6–38   Intercompany Sale of Equipment in Prior Period at a Loss

Block Corporation was created on January 1, 20X0, to develop computer software. On January 1, 20X5, Foster Company purchased 90 percent of the common stock of Block Corporation at underlying book value. Trial balances for Foster Company and Block Corporation on December 31, 20X9, are as follows:

20X9 Trial Balance Data

	Foster Company		Block Corporation	
	Debit	*Credit*	*Debit*	*Credit*
Cash	$ 82,000		$ 32,400	
Accounts Receivable	80,000		90,000	
Other Receivables	40,000		10,000	
Inventory	200,000		130,000	
Land	80,000		60,000	
Buildings and Equipment	500,000		250,000	
Investment in Block Corporation Stock	216,000			
Cost of Goods Sold	500,000		250,000	
Depreciation Expense	45,000		15,000	
Other Expense	95,000		75,000	
Dividends Declared	40,000		20,000	
Accumulated Depreciation		$ 155,000		$ 75,000
Accounts Payable		63,000		35,000
Other Payables		95,000		20,000
Bonds Payable		250,000		200,000
Bond Premium				2,400
Common Stock		210,000		50,000
Additional Paid-In Capital		110,000		
Retained Earnings		235,000		150,000
Sales		680,000		385,000
Other Income		26,000		15,000
Income from Subsidiary		54,000		
Total	$1,878,000	$1,878,000	$932,400	$932,400

On January 1, 20X7, Block Corporation sold equipment to Foster Company for $48,000. The equipment had been purchased for $90,000 on January 1, 20X5, by Block Company and was depreciated on a straight-line basis with an expected life of 10 years and no anticipated scrap value. The total expected life of the equipment is unchanged as a result of the intercompany sale.

Required

a. Give all eliminating entries required to prepare a three-part consolidated working paper at December 31, 20X9.

b. Prepare a three-part workpaper for 20X9 in good form.

P6–39 **Comprehensive Problem: Intercorporate Transfers**

Rossman Corporation holds 75 percent of the common stock of Schmid Distributors Inc. The stock originally was purchased on December 31, 20X1, for $2,340,000. At the date of acquisition, Schmid reported common stock with a par value of $1,000,000, additional paid-in capital of $1,350,000, and retained earnings of $620,000. The differential at acquisition was attributable to the following items:

Inventory (sold in 20X2)	$ 22,500
Land	40,000
Goodwill	50,000
Total Differential	$112,500

During 20X2, Rossman sold to Schmid at a gain of $23,000 a piece of land that it had purchased several years before; Schmid continues to hold the land. In 20X6, Rossman and Schmid entered into a five-year contract under which Rossman provides management consulting services to Schmid on a continuing basis; Schmid pays Rossman a fixed fee of $80,000 per year for these services. At December 31, 20X8, Schmid owed Rossman $20,000 as the final 20X8 quarterly payment under the contract.

On January 2, 20X8, Rossman purchased from Schmid for $250,000 equipment that Schmid was then carrying at $290,000. That equipment had been purchased by Schmid on December 27, 20X2, for $435,000. The equipment is expected to have a total life of 15 years and no salvage value. The amount of the differential assigned to goodwill is not amortized.

At December 31, 20X8, trial balances for Rossman and Schmid appeared as follows:

	Rossman Corporation		Schmid Distributors	
Item	*Debit*	*Credit*	*Debit*	*Credit*
Cash	$ 50,700		$ 38,000	
Current Receivables	101,800		89,400	
Inventory	286,000		218,900	
Investment in Schmid Stock	2,970,000			
Land	400,000		1,200,000	
Buildings and Equipment	2,400,000		2,990,000	
Cost of Goods Sold	2,193,000		525,000	
Depreciation and Amortization	202,000		88,000	
Other Expenses	1,381,000		227,000	
Dividends Declared	50,000		20,000	
Accumulated Depreciation		$ 1,105,000		$ 420,000
Current Payables		86,200		76,300
Bonds Payable		1,000,000		200,000
Common Stock		100,000		1,000,000
Additional Paid-In Capital		1,272,000		1,350,000
Retained Earnings, January 1		1,497,800		1,400,000
Sales		4,801,000		985,000
Other Income or Loss		90,000	35,000	
Income from Subsidiary		82,500		
Total	$10,034,500	$10,034,500	$5,431,300	$5,431,300

As of December 31, 20X8, Schmid had declared but not yet paid its fourth-quarter dividend of $5,000. Both companies use straight-line depreciation and amortization. Rossman uses the basic equity method to account for its investment in Schmid Distributors.

Required

a. Compute the amount of the differential as of January 1, 20X8.

b. Verify the balance in Rossman's Investment in Schmid Stock account as of December 31, 20X8.

c. Present all elimination entries that would appear in a three-part consolidation workpaper as of December 31, 20X8.

d. Prepare and complete a three-part workpaper for the preparation of consolidated financial statements for 20X8.

P6–40A   **Fully Adjusted Equity Method**

On December 31, 20X7, Prime Company recorded the following entry on its books to adjust its investment in Lane Company from the basic equity method to the fully adjusted equity method:

Retained Earnings	26,000	
Income from Subsidiary		2,000
Investment in Lane Company Stock		24,000

Required

a. Adjust the data reported by Prime Company in the trial balance contained in Problem 6–35 for the effects of the adjusting entry presented above.

b. Prepare the journal entries that would have been recorded on the books of Prime Company during 20X7 if it had always used the fully adjusted equity method.

c. Prepare all eliminating entries needed to complete a consolidation workpaper as of December 31, 20X7, assuming Prime has used the fully adjusted equity method.

d. Complete a three-part consolidation workpaper as of December 31, 20X7.

P6–41A   **Cost Method**

The trial balance data presented in Problem 6–35 can be converted to reflect use of the cost method by inserting the following amounts in place of those presented for Prime Company:

Investment in Lane Company Stock	$160,000
Retained Earnings	348,000
Income from Subsidiary	-0-
Dividend Income	28,000

Required

a. Prepare the journal entries that would have been recorded on the books of Prime Company during 20X7 under the cost method.

b. Prepare all eliminating entries needed to complete a consolidation workpaper as of December 31, 20X7, assuming Prime has used the cost method.

c. Complete a three-part consolidation workpaper as of December 31, 20X7.

INTERCOMPANY INVENTORY TRANSACTIONS

Inventory transactions are the most common form of intercorporate exchange. Conceptually, the elimination of inventory transfers between related companies is no different than for other types of intercompany transactions. All revenue and expense items recorded by the participants must be eliminated fully in preparing the consolidated income statement, and all profits and losses recorded on the transfers are deferred until the items are sold to a nonaffiliate.

The record-keeping process for intercorporate transfers of inventory may be more complex than for other forms of transfers. There often are many different types of inventory items, and some may be transferred from affiliate to affiliate. Also, the problems of keeping tabs on which items have been resold and which items still are on hand are greater in the case of inventory transactions because part of a shipment may be sold immediately by the purchasing company and other units may remain on hand for several accounting periods. Nevertheless, the consolidation procedures relating to inventory transfers are quite similar to those discussed in Chapter 6 relating to fixed assets.

General Overview

The workpaper eliminating entries used in preparing consolidated financial statements must eliminate fully the effects of all transactions between related companies. When there have been intercompany inventory transactions, eliminating entries are needed to remove the revenue and expenses related to the intercompany transfers recorded by the individual companies. The eliminations ensure that only the historical cost of the inventory to the consolidated entity is included in the consolidated balance sheet when the inventory is still on hand and is charged to cost of goods sold in the period the inventory is resold to nonaffiliates.

Transfers at Cost

Merchandise sometimes is sold to related companies at the seller's cost or carrying value. When an intercorporate sale includes no profit or loss, the balance sheet inventory amounts at the end of the period require no adjustment for consolidation because the carrying amount of the inventory for the purchasing affiliate is the same as the cost to the transferring affiliate and the consolidated entity. At the time the inventory is resold to a nonaffiliate, the amount charged to cost of goods sold by the affiliate making the outside sale is the cost to the consolidated entity.

Even when the intercorporate sale includes no profit or loss, however, an eliminating entry is needed to remove both the revenue from the intercorporate sale and the related cost of goods sold recorded by the seller. This avoids overstating these two accounts. Consolidated net income is not affected by the eliminating entry when the transfer is made at cost because both revenue and cost of goods sold are reduced by the same amount.

Transfers at a Profit or Loss

Companies use many different approaches in setting intercorporate transfer prices. In some companies, the sale price to an affiliate is the same as the price to any other customer. Some companies routinely mark up inventory transferred to affiliates by a certain percentage of cost. For example, a company might mark up inventory transferred to affiliates by 50 percent of cost, selling inventory that cost $2,000 to an affiliate for $3,000. Other companies have elaborate transfer pricing policies designed to encourage internal sales. Regardless of the method used in setting intercorporate transfer prices, the elimination process must remove the effects of such sales from the consolidated statements.

When intercorporate sales include profits or losses, there are two aspects of the workpaper eliminations needed in the period of transfer to prepare consolidated financial statements:

1. Elimination of the income statement effects of the intercorporate sale in the period in which the sale occurs, including the sales revenue from the intercorporate sale and the related cost of goods sold recorded by the transferring affiliate.
2. Elimination from the inventory on the balance sheet of any profit or loss on the intercompany sale that has not been confirmed by resale of the inventory to outsiders.

Inventory reported in the consolidated balance sheet must be reported at the cost to the consolidated entity. Therefore, if profits or losses have been recorded on inventory acquired in an intercompany transfer, those profits or losses must be eliminated to state the inventory in the consolidated balance sheet at its cost to the consolidated entity. The result is the same as if the intercompany transfer had not occurred.

Effect of Type of Inventory System

Most companies use either a perpetual or a periodic inventory control system to keep track of inventory and cost of goods sold. Under a perpetual inventory system, a purchase of merchandise is debited directly to the inventory account; a sale requires a debit to cost of goods sold and a credit to inventory for the cost of the item. When a periodic system is used, a purchase of merchandise is debited to a purchases account rather than to inventory, and no entry is made to recognize cost of goods sold until the end of the accounting period.

The choice between periodic and perpetual inventory systems results in different entries on the books of the individual companies and, therefore, slightly different workpaper eliminating entries in preparing consolidated financial statements. Because most companies use perpetual inventory systems, the discussion in the chapter focuses on the consolidation procedures used in connection with perpetual inventories. Procedures related to periodic inventory systems are discussed in Appendix 7A.

Downstream Sale—Perpetual Inventory System

For consolidation purposes, profits recorded on an intercorporate inventory sale are recognized in the period in which the inventory is resold to an unrelated party. Until the point of resale, all intercorporate profits must be deferred. Consolidated net income must be based on the realized income of the transferring affiliate. Because intercompany profits from downstream sales are on the books of the parent, consolidated net income and the overall claim of parent company shareholders must be reduced by the full amount of the unrealized profits.

When a company sells an inventory item to an affiliate, one of three situations results: (1) the item is resold to a nonaffiliate during the same period, (2) the item is resold to a nonaffiliate during the next period, or (3) the item is held for two or more periods by the purchasing affiliate. The continuing example of Peerless Products Corporation and Special Foods Inc. is used to illustrate the consolidation process under each of the alternatives. As in Chapter 6, assume that Peerless Products purchases 80 percent of the common stock of Special Foods on December 31, 20X0, for its book value of $240,000.

As an illustration of the effects of a downstream sale, assume that on March 1, 20X1, Peerless buys inventory for $7,000 and resells it to Special Foods for $10,000 on April 1. Peerless records the following entries on its books:

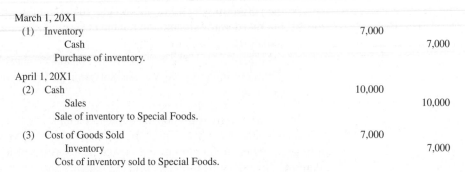

March 1, 20X1		
(1) Inventory	7,000	
Cash		7,000
Purchase of inventory.		
April 1, 20X1		
(2) Cash	10,000	
Sales		10,000
Sale of inventory to Special Foods.		
(3) Cost of Goods Sold	7,000	
Inventory		7,000
Cost of inventory sold to Special Foods.		

Special Foods records the purchase of the inventory from Peerless with the following entry:

April 1, 20X1		
(4) Inventory	10,000	
Cash		10,000
Purchase of inventory from Peerless.		

Resale in Period of Intercorporate Transfer

To illustrate consolidation when inventory is sold to an affiliate and then resold to a nonaffiliate during the same period, assume that on November 5, 20X1, Special Foods sells the inventory purchased from Peerless to Nonaffiliated Corporation for $15,000, as follows:

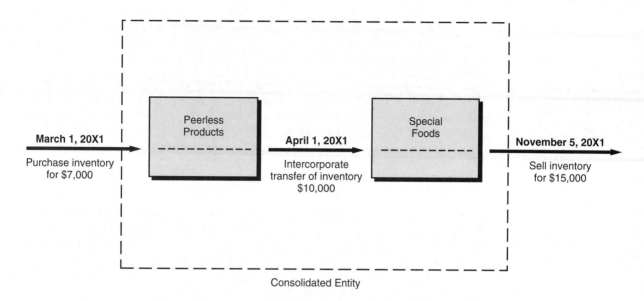

Consolidated Entity

Special Foods records the sale to Nonaffiliated with the following entries:

November 5, 20X1

(5)	Cash	15,000	
	Sales		15,000
	Sale of inventory to Nonaffiliated.		
(6)	Cost of Goods Sold	10,000	
	Inventory		10,000
	Cost of inventory sold to Nonaffiliated.		

A review of all entries recorded by the individual companies indicates that incorrect balances will be reported in the consolidated income statement if the effects of the intercorporate sale are not removed:

Item	Peerless Products	Special Foods	Unadjusted Totals	Consolidated Amounts
Sales	$10,000	$15,000	$25,000	$15,000
Cost of Goods Sold	(7,000)	(10,000)	(17,000)	(7,000)
Gross Profit	$ 3,000	$ 5,000	$ 8,000	$ 8,000

While consolidated gross profit is correct even if no adjustments are made, the totals for sales and cost of goods sold derived by simply adding the amounts on the books of Peerless and Special Foods are overstated for the consolidated entity. The selling price of the inventory to Nonaffiliated Corporation is $15,000, and the original cost to Peerless Products is $7,000. Thus, gross profit of $8,000 is correct from a consolidated viewpoint, but consolidated sales and cost of goods sold should be $15,000 and $7,000, respectively, rather than $25,000 and $17,000. In the consolidation workpaper, the amount of the intercompany sale must be eliminated from both sales and cost of goods sold to correctly state the consolidated totals:

E(7) Sales	10,000	
Cost of Goods Sold		10,000
Eliminate intercompany inventory sale.		

Note that this entry does not affect consolidated net income because sales and cost of goods sold both are reduced by the same amount. No elimination of intercompany profit is needed because all the intercompany profit has been realized through resale of the inventory to the external party during the current period.

Resale in Period Following Intercorporate Transfer

When inventory is sold to an affiliate at a profit and the inventory is not resold during the same period, appropriate adjustments are needed to prepare consolidated financial statements in the period of the intercompany sale and in each subsequent period until the inventory is sold to a nonaffiliate. By way of illustration, assume that Peerless Products purchases inventory in 20X1 for $7,000 and sells the inventory during the year to Special Foods for $10,000. Special Foods sells the inventory to Nonaffiliated Corporation for $15,000 on January 2, 20X2, as follows:

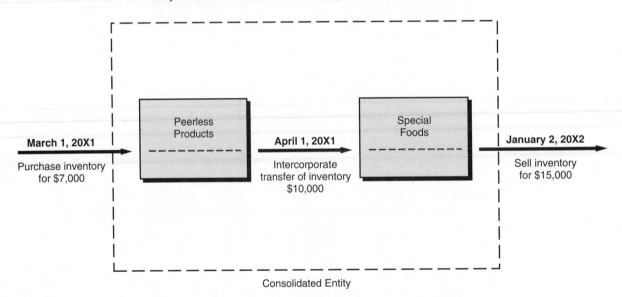

Consolidated Entity

During 20X1, Peerless records the purchase of the inventory and the sale to Special Foods with journal entries (1) through (3), given previously; Special Foods records the purchase of the inventory from Peerless with entry (4). In 20X2, Special Foods records the sale of the inventory to Nonaffiliated with entries (5) and (6), given earlier.

Basic Equity-Method Entries—20X1. Using the basic equity method, Peerless records its share of Special Foods' income and dividends for 20X1 in the normal manner:

(8) Investment in Special Foods Stock	40,000	
Income from Subsidiary		40,000
Record equity-method income:		
$50,000 \times .80$		

(9) Cash	24,000	
Investment in Special Foods Stock		24,000
Record dividends from Special Foods:		
$30,000 \times .80$		

As a result of these entries, the ending balance of the investment account is $256,000 ($240,000 + $40,000 − $24,000).

Consolidation Workpaper—20X1. The consolidation workpaper prepared at the end of 20X1 appears in Figure 7–1. Four elimination entries are included in the workpaper:

E(10) Income from Subsidiary	40,000	
Dividends Declared		24,000
Investment in Special Foods Stock		16,000
Eliminate income from subsidiary.		
E(11) Income to Noncontrolling Interest	10,000	
Dividends Declared		6,000
Noncontrolling Interest		4,000
Assign income to noncontrolling interest:		
$10,000 = $50,000 \times .20$		
E(12) Common Stock—Special Foods	200,000	
Retained Earnings, January 1	100,000	
Investment in Special Foods Stock		240,000
Noncontrolling Interest		60,000
Eliminate beginning investment balance.		
E(13) Sales	10,000	
Cost of Goods Sold		7,000
Inventory		3,000
Eliminate intercompany downstream sale of inventory.		

Only entry E(13) relates to the elimination of unrealized inventory profits; the other entries are the type normally found in the workpaper.

Entry E(10) is based on entries (8) and (9) on Peerless's books and eliminates Peerless's share of Special Foods' income and dividends. This entry also eliminates the change in the investment account for the period and returns the investment account balance in the workpaper to the beginning balance of $240,000.

The noncontrolling interest is not affected by the downstream inventory transfer and is assigned a pro rata portion ($50,000 × .20) of the net income of Special Foods in workpaper entry E(11). This entry also eliminates the noncontrolling stockholders' share of Special Foods' dividends ($30,000 × .20) and establishes the $4,000 increase in the noncontrolling interest for the period due to the excess of Special Foods' net income over its dividends [($50,000 − $30,000) × .20].

Entry E(12) eliminates the beginning balances of Special Foods' stockholders' equity accounts and Peerless's investment account. This entry also establishes the amount of the noncontrolling interest at the beginning of the period. The intercompany inventory sale has no effect on this entry because the entry eliminates balances as of the beginning of the year, while the intercompany transaction occurred during the year.

Entry E(13) is needed to eliminate the effects of the intercompany sale of inventory. The journal entries recorded by Peerless Products and Special Foods in 20X1 on their separate books will result in an overstatement of consolidated gross profit for 20X1 and the consolidated inventory balance at year-end unless the amounts are adjusted in the consolidation workpaper. The amounts resulting from the intercompany

FIGURE 7–1   December 31, 20X1, Consolidation Workpaper, Period of Intercompany Sale; Downstream Inventory Sale, Perpetual Inventory

Item	Peerless Products	Special Foods	Eliminations Debit		Eliminations Credit		Consolidated
Sales	400,000	200,000	(13)	10,000			590,000
Income from Subsidiary	40,000		(10)	40,000			
Credits	440,000	200,000					590,000
Cost of Goods Sold	170,000	115,000			(13)	7,000	278,000
Depreciation and Amortization	50,000	20,000					70,000
Other Expenses	40,000	15,000					55,000
Debits	(260,000)	(150,000)					(403,000)
							187,000
Income to Noncontrolling Interest			(11)	10,000			(10,000)
Net Income, carry forward	180,000	50,000		60,000		7,000	177,000
Retained Earnings, January 1	300,000	100,000	(12)	100,000			300,000
Net Income, from above	180,000	50,000		60,000		7,000	177,000
	480,000	150,000					477,000
Dividends Declared	(60,000)	(30,000)			(10)	24,000	
					(11)	6,000	(60,000)
Retained Earnings, December 31, carry forward	420,000	120,000		160,000		37,000	417,000
Cash	264,000	75,000					339,000
Accounts Receivable	75,000	50,000					125,000
Inventory	100,000	75,000			(13)	3,000	172,000
Land	175,000	40,000					215,000
Buildings and Equipment	800,000	600,000					1,400,000
Investment in Special Foods Stock	256,000				(10)	16,000	
					(12)	240,000	
Debits	1,670,000	840,000					2,251,000
Accumulated Depreciation	250,000	220,000					470,000
Accounts Payable	100,000	100,000					200,000
Bonds Payable	400,000	200,000					600,000
Common Stock	500,000	200,000	(12)	200,000			500,000
Retained Earnings, from above	420,000	120,000		160,000		37,000	417,000
Noncontrolling Interest					(11)	4,000	
					(12)	60,000	64,000
Credits	1,670,000	840,000		360,000		360,000	2,251,000

Elimination entries:

(10) Eliminate income from subsidiary.

(11) Assign income to noncontrolling interest.

(12) Eliminate beginning investment balance.

(13) Eliminate intercompany downstream sale of inventory.

inventory transactions from the separate books of Peerless Products and Special Foods, and the appropriate consolidated amounts, are as follows:

Item	Peerless Products	Special Foods	Unadjusted Totals	Consolidated Amounts
Sales	$10,000	$ -0-	$10,000	$ -0-
Cost of Goods Sold	(7,000)	-0-	(7,000)	-0-
Gross Profit	$ 3,000	$ -0-	$ 3,000	$ -0-
Inventory	$ -0-	$10,000	$10,000	$7,000

Eliminating entry E(13) corrects the unadjusted totals to the appropriate consolidated amounts. Both sales and cost of goods sold taken from the trial balance of Peerless Products are reduced in preparing the consolidated income statement. In doing so, income is reduced by the difference of $3,000 ($10,000 − $7,000). In addition, ending inventory reported on the books of Special Foods is stated at the intercompany exchange price rather than the historical cost to the consolidated entity. Until resold to an external party by Special Foods, the inventory must be reduced by the amount of unrealized intercompany profit each time consolidated statements are prepared.

Consolidated Net Income—20X1. Consolidated net income for 20X1 is shown as $177,000 in the Figure 7–1 workpaper. This amount is verified as follows:

Peerless's separate operating income		$140,000
Less: Unrealized intercompany profit on downstream inventory sale		(3,000)
Peerless's separate realized income		$137,000
Peerless's share of Special Foods' income:		
Special Foods' net income	$50,000	
Peerless's proportionate share	× .80	40,000
Consolidated net income, 20X1		$177,000

Basic Equity-Method Entries—20X2. During 20X2, Special Foods receives $15,000 when it sells to Nonaffiliated Corporation the inventory that it had purchased for $10,000 from Peerless in 20X1. Also, Peerless records its pro rata portion of Special Foods' net income and dividends for 20X2 with the normal basic equity-method entries:

(14)	Investment in Special Foods Stock	60,000	
	Income from Subsidiary		60,000
	Record equity-method income:		
	$75,000 × .80		
(15)	Cash	32,000	
	Investment in Special Foods Stock		32,000
	Record dividends from Special Foods:		
	$40,000 × .80		

Investment Account Balance.   The investment account on Peerless's books appears as follows:

Investment in Special Foods Stock					
	Original cost	240,000			
(8)	20X1 equity accrual		(9)	20X1 dividends	
	($50,000 × .80)	40,000		($30,000 × .80)	24,000
	Balance, 12/31/X1	256,000			
(14)	20X2 equity accrual		(15)	20X2 dividends	
	($75,000 × .80)	60,000		($40,000 × .80)	32,000
	Balance, 12/31/X2	284,000			

Consolidation Workpaper—20X2.   The consolidation workpaper prepared at the end of 20X2 is shown in Figure 7–2. Four elimination entries are needed:

E(16)	Income from Subsidiary	60,000	
	Dividends Declared		32,000
	Investment in Special Foods Stock		28,000
	Eliminate income from subsidiary.		
E(17)	Income to Noncontrolling Interest	15,000	
	Dividends Declared		8,000
	Noncontrolling Interest		7,000
	Assign income to noncontrolling interest:		
	$15,000 = $75,000 × .20		
E(18)	Common Stock—Special Foods	200,000	
	Retained Earnings, January 1	120,000	
	Investment in Special Foods Stock		256,000
	Noncontrolling Interest		64,000
	Eliminate beginning investment balance.		
E(19)	Retained Earnings, January 1	3,000	
	Cost of Goods Sold		3,000
	Eliminate beginning inventory profit.		

Entry E(16) eliminates the effects of basic equity-method entries (14) and (15) recorded by Peerless Products during 20X2. Entry E(17) assigns the noncontrolling shareholders their share of income ($75,000 × .20) and establishes in the workpaper the 20X2 increase in the claim of the noncontrolling shareholders on the net assets of Special Foods. Because the sale is downstream, the amount of income assigned to noncontrolling shareholders and the balance of the noncontrolling interest are not affected by the intercompany profit.

Workpaper entry E(18) eliminates the beginning stockholders' equity balances of Special Foods and Peerless's beginning investment balance. The investment account is credited for 80 percent of Special Foods' book value at the beginning of the period, while the noncontrolling interest is credited with a beginning balance equal to 20 percent of Special Foods' book value.

Entry E(19) is needed to adjust cost of goods sold to the proper consolidated balance and to reduce beginning retained earnings. The unrealized intercompany profit included in Special Foods' beginning inventory was charged to Cost of Goods Sold when Special Foods sold the inventory during the period. Thus, consolidated cost of goods sold will be overstated for 20X2 if it is reported in the consolidated income statement at the unadjusted total from the books of Peerless and Special Foods:

These eliminating entries are the same as those following use of the basic equity method, except for entry E(62). This entry eliminates the parent's dividend income from Special Foods rather than its share of Special Foods' net income.

Consolidation Elimination Entries—20X2. Elimination entries needed in the consolidation workpaper prepared at the end of 20X2 are as follows:

E(66)	Dividend Income	32,000	
	Dividends Declared		32,000
	Eliminate dividend income from subsidiary:		
	$40,000 × .80		
E(67)	Income to Noncontrolling Interest	15,600	
	Dividends Declared		8,000
	Noncontrolling Interest		7,600
	Assign income to noncontrolling interest:		
	$15,600 = ($75,000 + $3,000) × .20		
E(68)	Common Stock—Special Foods	200,000	
	Retained Earnings, January 1	100,000	
	Investment in Special Foods Stock		240,000
	Noncontrolling Interest		60,000
	Eliminate investment balance at date of acquisition.		
E(69)	Retained Earnings, January 1	4,000	
	Noncontrolling Interest		4,000
	Assign undistributed prior earnings of subsidiary to		
	noncontrolling interest: $20,000 × .20		
E(70)	Retained Earnings, January 1	2,400	
	Noncontrolling Interest	600	
	Cost of Goods Sold		3,000
	Eliminate beginning inventory profit.		

Entries E(67) and E(70) are the same as those following use of the basic equity method. Entry E(66) eliminates the dividend income recorded by Peerless in 20X2. Entry E(68) eliminates the balances at the date of combination of Special Foods' stockholders' equity accounts and the investment account. This entry is the same each year. Because this entry does not change, it assigns to the noncontrolling stockholders only their share of Special Foods' book value at the date of combination. Therefore, entry E(69) is needed to assign to the noncontrolling interest a proportionate share of the undistributed earnings of Special Foods from the date of combination to the beginning of the current year.

Questions

Q7–1 Why must inventory transfers to related companies be eliminated in preparing consolidated financial statements?

Q7–2 Why is there need for an eliminating entry when an intercompany inventory transfer is made at cost?

Q7–3 Distinguish between an upstream sale of inventory and a downstream sale. Why is it important to know whether a sale is upstream or downstream?

Q7–4 How do unrealized intercompany profits on a downstream sale of inventory made during the current period affect the computation of consolidated net income?

Q7–5 How do unrealized intercompany profits on an upstream sale of inventory made during the current period affect the computation of consolidated net income?

Q7–6 Will the elimination of unrealized intercompany profits on an upstream sale or on a downstream sale in the current period have a greater effect on income assigned to the noncontrolling interest? Why?

Q7–7   What is the basic eliminating entry needed when inventory is sold to an affiliate at a profit and is resold to an unaffiliated party before the end of the period, if perpetual inventory systems are used by both affiliates?

Q7–8   What is the basic eliminating entry needed when inventory is sold to an affiliate at a profit and is not resold before the end of the period, if perpetual inventory systems are used by both affiliates?

Q7–9   How is the amount to be reported as cost of goods sold by the consolidated entity determined when there have been intercorporate sales during the period?

Q7–10   How is the amount to be reported as consolidated retained earnings determined when there have been intercorporate sales during the period?

Q7–11   How is the amount of consolidated retained earnings assigned to the noncontrolling interest affected by unrealized inventory profits at the end of the year?

Q7–12   How do unrealized intercompany inventory profits from a prior period affect the computation of consolidated net income when the inventory is resold in the current period? Is it important to know if the sale was upstream or downstream? Why, or why not?

Q7–13   How will the elimination of unrealized intercompany inventory profits recorded on the parent's books affect consolidated retained earnings?

Q7–14   How will the elimination of unrealized intercompany inventory profits recorded on the subsidiary's books affect consolidated retained earnings?

Q7–15* Is an inventory sale from one subsidiary to another treated in the same manner as an upstream sale or a downstream sale? Why?

Q7–16* Par Company regularly purchased inventory from Eagle Company. Recently, Par Company purchased a majority of the voting shares of Eagle Company. How should it treat inventory profits recorded by Eagle Company before the day of acquisition? Following the day of acquisition?

Q7–17A What are the basic eliminating entries needed when inventory is sold to an affiliate at a profit and is not resold before the end of the period if periodic inventory systems are used by both affiliates?

Q7–18A What is the basic eliminating entry needed when inventory is sold to an affiliate at a profit and is resold to an unaffiliated party before the end of the period if periodic inventory systems are used by both affiliates?

Q7–19A What is the basic eliminating entry needed under a periodic inventory system when intercompany inventory profits that are unrealized at the beginning of the period are realized during the year?

Cases

C7–1   **Measuring Cost of Goods Sold**

Shortcut Charlie usually manages to develop some simple rule to handle even the most complex situations. In providing for the elimination of the effects of inventory transfers between the parent company and a subsidiary or between subsidiaries, Shortcut started with the following rules:

1. When the buyer continues to hold the inventory at the end of the period, credit cost of goods sold for the amount recorded as cost of goods sold by the company that made the intercompany sale.

2. When the buyer resells the inventory before the end of the period, credit cost of goods sold for the amount recorded as cost of goods sold by the company that made the intercompany sale plus the profit recorded by that company.

3. Debit sales for the total amount credited in rule 1 or 2 above.

One of the new employees is seeking some assistance in understanding how the rules work and why.

---

*Indicates that the item relates to "Additional Considerations."

Required

a. Explain why rule 1 is needed when consolidated statements are prepared.

b. Explain what is missing from rule 1, and prepare an alternative or additional statement for the elimination of unrealized profit when the purchasing affiliate does not resell to an unaffiliated company in the period in which it purchases inventory from an affiliate.

c. Does rule 2 lead to the correct result? Explain your answer.

d. The rules do not provide assistance in determining how much profit was recorded by either of the two companies. Where should the employee look to determine the amount of profit referred to in rule 2?

C7–2 Unrealized Inventory Profits

Morrison Company owns 80 percent of the stock of Bloom Corporation. The companies frequently engage in intercompany inventory transactions.

Required

Name the conditions that would make it possible for each of the following statements to be true. Treat each statement independently.

a. Income assigned to the noncontrolling interest in the consolidated income statement for 20X3 is greater than a pro rata share of the reported net income of Bloom Corporation.

b. Income assigned to the noncontrolling interest in the consolidated income statement for 20X3 is greater than a pro rata share of Bloom's reported net income, but consolidated net income is reduced as a result of the elimination of intercompany inventory transfers.

c. Cost of goods sold reported in the income statement of Morrison is greater than consolidated cost of goods sold for 20X3.

d. Ending inventory is not included in the December 31, 20X3, trial balance of Bloom Corporation.

C7–3 Intercompany Profit Elimination Alternatives

Rockness Corporation purchases much of its inventory from its 90 percent owned subsidiary, Mauch Company. Mauch prices its sales to Rockness to earn a 40 percent gross profit on the sales. During 20X4, Rockness purchases $400,000 of inventory from Mauch and resells all of the inventory to unrelated parties, except for $40,000 left in ending inventory.

In reviewing the preparation of consolidated financial statements for the year, the controller of Rockness Corporation, Liz Weber, notes that all the unrealized intercompany profit remaining in ending inventory is eliminated proportionately against the controlling and noncontrolling interests. This proportionate elimination is reflected in the amounts reported for consolidated net income and the income assigned to the noncontrolling interest. Liz recalls that several alternatives exist when preparing consolidated financial statements for dealing with unrealized intercompany profits on transfers from less-than wholly owned subsidiaries to the parent, but not all are considered currently acceptable. She remembers, for example, that proportionate elimination has been suggested, where only the parent's proportionate share (based on the extent to which the parent shares in the subsidiary's profits) would be eliminated. Also, she has heard that some companies eliminate all of the unrealized intercompany profit against the controlling interest.

Having been impressed previously with your knowledge of accounting theory, Liz asks you to provide her with some additional information about different approaches to the elimination of unrealized intercompany profits on upstream sales.

Required

a. Compute the amount at which Rockness's inventory purchased from Mauch would be reported in the consolidated balance sheet at December 31, 20X4, under each of the following three approaches to the elimination of unrealized intercompany profits:

(1) Proportionate or pro rata (90 percent) elimination.

(2) Full elimination against the controlling interest.

(3) Full elimination, with proportionate allocation against the controlling and noncontrolling interests.

   b. What amount of unrealized intercompany profit would be eliminated from consolidated net income and from the income assigned to the noncontrolling interest for 20X4 under each of the three approaches listed in part *a?*

   c. Provide supporting arguments for the use of each of the three methods listed in part *a,* and indicate which are acceptable in practice based on current authoritative standards.

C7–4   **Eliminating Inventory Transfers**

Ready Building Products has six subsidiaries that sell building materials and supplies to the public and to the parent and other subsidiaries. Because of the invoicing system used by Ready Building Products, it is not possible to keep track of which items have been purchased from related companies and which were bought from outside sources. Due to the nature of products purchased, there are substantially different profit margins on different product groupings.

   a. If no effort is made to eliminate intercompany sales for the period or unrealized profits at year-end, what elements of the financial statements are likely to be misstated?

   b. What type of control system would you recommend to the controller of Ready Building Materials to provide the information needed to make the required eliminating entries?

   c. Would it matter if the buyer and seller used different inventory systems (FIFO, LIFO, or weighted average)? Explain.

   d. Assume you feel the adjustments for unrealized profit would be material. How would you go about determining what amounts must be eliminated at the end of the current period?

C7–5   **Intercompany Profits and Transfers of Inventory**

Many companies transfer inventories from one affiliate to another. Often the companies have integrated operations in which one affiliate provides the raw materials, another manufactures finished products, another distributes the products, and perhaps another sells the products at retail. In other cases, various affiliates may be established for selling the company's products in different geographic locations, especially in different countries. Often tax considerations also have an effect on intercompany transfers.

Required

   a. Are Xerox Corporation's intercompany transfers significant? How does Xerox treat intercompany transfers for consolidation purposes?

   b. How does ExxonMobil Corporation price its products for intercompany transfers? Are these transfers significant? How does ExxonMobil treat intercompany profits for consolidation purposes?

   c. What types of intercompany and intersegment sales does Ford Motor Company have? Are they significant? How are they treated for consolidation?

Exercises

E7–1   **Multiple-Choice Questions on Intercompany Inventory Transfers [AICPA Adapted]**

Select the correct answer for each of the following questions.

   1. Perez Inc. owns 80 percent of Senior Inc. During 20X2, Perez sold goods with a 40 percent gross profit to Senior. Senior sold all of these goods in 20X2. For 20X2 consolidated financial statements, how should the summation of Perez and Senior income statement items be adjusted?

     a. Sales and cost of goods sold should be reduced by the intercompany sales.

     b. Sales and cost of goods sold should be reduced by 80 percent of the intercompany sales.

     c. Net income should be reduced by 80 percent of the gross profit on intercompany sales.

     d. No adjustment is necessary.

2. Parker Corporation owns 80 percent of Smith Inc.'s common stock. During 20X1, Parker sold Smith $250,000 of inventory on the same terms as sales made to third parties. Smith sold all of the inventory purchased from Parker in 20X1. The following information pertains to Smith and Parker's sales for 20X1:

	Parker	Smith
Sales	$1,000,000	$700,000
Cost of Sales	400,000	350,000
Gross Profit	$ 600,000	$350,000

What amount should Parker report as cost of sales in its 20X1 consolidated income statement?

a. $750,000.

b. $680,000.

c. $500,000.

d. $430,000.

Items 3 and 4 are based on the following information:

Nolan owns 100 percent of the capital stock of both Twill Corporation and Webb Corporation. Twill purchases merchandise inventory from Webb at 140 percent of Webb's cost. During 20X0, merchandise that cost Webb $40,000 was sold to Twill. Twill sold all of this merchandise to unrelated customers for $81,200 during 20X0. In preparing combined financial statements for 20X0, Nolan's bookkeeper disregarded the common ownership of Twill and Webb.

3. What amount should be eliminated from cost of goods sold in the combined income statement for 20X0?

a. $56,000.

b. $40,000.

c. $24,000.

d. $16,000.

4. By what amount was unadjusted revenue overstated in the combined income statement for 20X0?

a. $16,000.

b. $40,000.

c. $56,000.

d. $81,200.

5. Clark Company had the following transactions with affiliated parties during 20X2:

• Sales of $60,000 to Dean Inc., with $20,000 gross profit. Dean had $15,000 of this inventory on hand at year-end. Clark owns a 15 percent interest in Dean and does not exert significant influence.

• Purchases of raw materials totaling $240,000 from Kent Corporation, a wholly owned subsidiary. Kent's gross profit on the sale was $48,000. Clark had $60,000 of this inventory remaining on December 31, 20X2.

Before eliminating entries, Clark had consolidated current assets of $320,000. What amount should Clark report in its December 31, 20X2, consolidated balance sheet for current assets?

a. $320,000.

b. $317,000.

c. $308,000.

d. $303,000.

6. Selected data for two subsidiaries of Dunn Corporation taken from the December 31, 20X8, preclosing trial balances are as follows:

	Banks Co. (Debits)	Lamm Co. (Credits)
Shipments to Banks	$ —	$150,000
Shipments from Lamm	200,000	—
Intercompany Inventory Profit on Total Shipments		50,000

Additional data relating to the December 31, 20X8, inventory are as follows:

Inventory acquired by Banks from outside parties	$175,000
Inventory acquired by Lamm from outside parties	200,000
Inventory acquired by Banks from Lamm	60,000

At December 31, 20X8, the inventory reported on the combined balance sheet of the two subsidiaries should be:

  a. $425,000.

  b. $435,000.

  c. $470,000.

  d. $485,000.

E7–2 **Multiple-Choice Questions on the Effects of Inventory Transfers [AICPA Adapted]**
Select the correct answer for each of the following questions.

1. During 20X3, Park Corporation recorded sales of inventory costing $500,000 to Small Company, its wholly owned subsidiary, on the same terms as sales made to third parties. At December 31, 20X3, Small held one-fifth of these goods in its inventory. The following information pertains to Park and Small's sales for 20X3:

	Park	Small
Sales	$2,000,000	$1,400,000
Cost of Sales	800,000	700,000
Gross Profit	$1,200,000	$ 700,000

In its 20X3 consolidated income statement, what amount should Park report as cost of sales?

  a. $1,000,000.

  b. $1,060,000.

  c. $1,260,000.

  d. $1,500,000.

Items 2 through 6 are based on the following:

Selected information from the separate and consolidated balance sheets and income statements of Pard Inc. and its subsidiary, Spin Company, as of December 31, 20X8, and for the year then ended is as follows:

	Pard	Spin	Consolidated
Balance Sheet Accounts			
Accounts Receivable	$ 26,000	$ 19,000	$ 39,000
Inventory	30,000	25,000	52,000
Investment in Spin	67,000	—	—
Patents	—	—	30,000
Minority Interest	—	—	10,000
Stockholders' Equity	154,000	50,000	154,000
Income Statement Accounts			
Revenues	$200,000	$140,000	$308,000
Cost of Goods Sold	150,000	110,000	231,000
Gross Profit	$ 50,000	$ 30,000	$ 77,000
Equity in Earnings of Spin	11,000	—	—
Amortization of Patents	—	—	2,000
Net Income	36,000	20,000	40,000

Additional information

- During 20X8, Pard sold goods to Spin at the same markup on cost that Pard uses for all sales. At December 31, 20X8, Spin had not paid for all of these goods and still held 37.5 percent of them in inventory.

- Pard acquired its interest in Spin on January 2, 20X5. Pard's policy is to amortize patents by the straight-line method.

2. What was the amount of intercompany sales from Pard to Spin during 20X8?
   - *a.* $3,000.
   - *b.* $6,000.
   - *c.* $29,000.
   - *d.* $32,000.

3. At December 31, 20X8, what was the amount of Spin's payable to Pard for intercompany sales?
   - *a.* $3,000.
   - *b.* $6,000.
   - *c.* $29,000.
   - *d.* $32,000.

4. In Pard's consolidated balance sheet, what was the carrying amount of the inventory that Spin purchased from Pard?
   - *a.* $3,000.
   - *b.* $6,000.
   - *c.* $9,000.
   - *d.* $12,000.

5. What is the percent of minority interest ownership of Spin?
   - *a.* 10 percent.
   - *b.* 20 percent.
   - *c.* 25 percent.
   - *d.* 45 percent.

6. Over how many years has Pard chosen to amortize patents?
   - *a.* 15 years.
   - *b.* 19 years.
   - *c.* 23 years.
   - *d.* 40 years.

E7–3   Multiple-Choice Questions—Consolidated Income Statement

Select the correct answer for each of the following questions.

Blue Company purchased 60 percent ownership of Kelly Corporation in 20X1. On May 10, 20X2, Kelly purchased inventory from Blue for $60,000. Kelly sold all of the inventory to an unaffiliated company for $86,000 on November 10, 20X2. Blue Company produced the inventory sold to Kelly for $47,000. The companies had no other transactions during 20X2.

1. What amount of sales will be reported in the 20X2 consolidated income statement?
   a. $51,600.
   b. $60,000.
   c. $86,000.
   d. $146,000.

2. What amount of cost of goods sold will be reported in the 20X2 consolidated income statement?
   a. $36,000.
   b. $47,000.
   c. $60,000.
   d. $107,000.

3. What amount will be reported as consolidated net income for 20X2:
   a. $13,000.
   b. $26,000.
   c. $28,600.
   d. $39,000.

E7–4   Multiple-Choice Questions—Consolidated Balances

Select the correct answer for each of the following questions.

Lorn Corporation purchased inventory from Dresser Corporation for $120,000 on September 20, 20X1, and resold 80 percent of the inventory to unaffiliated companies prior to December 31, 20X1, for $140,000. Dresser Corporation produced the inventory sold to Lorn for $75,000. Lorn owns 70 percent of the voting common stock of Dresser. The companies had no other transactions during 20X1.

1. What amount of sales will be reported in the 20X1 consolidated income statement?
   a. $98,000.
   b. $120,000.
   c. $140,000.
   d. $260,000.

2. What amount of cost of goods sold will be reported in the 20X1 consolidated income statement?
   a. $60,000.
   b. $75,000.
   c. $96,000.
   d. $120,000.
   e. $171,000.

3. What amount of consolidated net income will be reported for 20X1?
   a. $20,000.
   b. $30,800.
   c. $44,000.
   d. $45,000.
   e. $69,200.
   f. $80,000.

4. What inventory balance will be reported by the consolidated entity on December 31, 20X1?

    a. $15,000.

    b. $16,800.

    c. $24,000.

    d. $39,000.

E7–5   **Multiple-Choice Questions—Consolidated Income Statement**

Select the correct answer for each of the following questions.

    Showtime Corporation holds 80 percent of the stock of Movie Productions Inc. During 20X4, Showtime purchased an inventory of snack bar items for $40,000 and resold $30,000 to Movie Productions Inc. for $48,000. Movie Productions Inc. reported sales of $67,000 in 20X4 and had inventory of $16,000 on December 31, 20X4. The companies held no beginning inventory and had no other transactions in 20X4.

1. What amount of cost of goods sold will be reported in the 20X4 consolidated income statement?

    a. $20,000.

    b. $30,000.

    c. $32,000.

    d. $52,000.

    e. $62,000.

2. What amount of net income will be reported in the 20X4 consolidated income statement?

    a. $12,000.

    b. $18,000.

    c. $40,000.

    d. $47,000.

    e. $53,000.

3. What amount of income will be assigned to the noncontrolling interest in the 20X4 consolidated income statement?

    a. $7,000.

    b. $8,000.

    c. $9,400.

    d. $10,200.

    e. $13,400.

E7–6   **Realized Profit on Intercompany Sale**

Nordway Corporation purchased 90 percent of the voting shares of stock of Olman Company in 20X1. During 20X4, Nordway purchased 40,000 Playday doghouses for $24 each and sold 25,000 of the doghouses to Olman for $30 each. Olman sold all of the doghouses to retail establishments prior to December 31, 20X4, for $45 each. Both companies use perpetual inventory systems.

Required

  a. Give the journal entries recorded by Nordway Corporation for the purchase of inventory and resale to Olman Company in 20X4.

  b. Give the journal entries recorded by Olman Company for the purchase of inventory and resale to retail establishments in 20X4.

  c. Give the workpaper eliminating entry or entries needed in preparing consolidated financial statements for 20X4 to remove all effects of the intercompany sale.

E7–7   **Sale of Inventory to Subsidiary**

Nordway Corporation purchased 90 percent of the voting shares of stock of Olman Company in 20X1. During 20X4, Nordway purchased 40,000 Playday doghouses for $24 each and sold 25,000 of the doghouses to Olman for $30 each. Olman sold 18,000 of the doghouses to retail establishments prior to December 31, 20X4, for $45 each. Both companies use perpetual inventory systems.

Required

a. Give all journal entries recorded by Nordway Corporation for the purchase of inventory and resale to Olman Company in 20X4.

b. Give the journal entries recorded by Olman Company for the purchase of inventory and resale to retail establishments in 20X4.

c. Give the workpaper eliminating entry or entries needed in preparing consolidated financial statements for 20X4 to remove the effects of the intercompany sale.

E7–8   **Inventory Transfer between Parent and Subsidiary**

Karlow Corporation owns 60 percent of the voting shares of Draw Company. During 20X3, Karlow produced 25,000 computer desks at a cost of $82 each and sold 10,000 desks to Draw Company for $94 each. Draw Company sold 7,000 of the desks to unaffiliated companies for $130 each prior to December 31, 20X3, and sold the remainder in early 20X4 for $140 each. Both companies use perpetual inventory systems.

Required

a. What amounts of cost of goods sold were recorded by Karlow Corporation and Draw Company in 20X3?

b. What amount of cost of goods sold must be reported in the consolidated income statement for 20X3?

c. Give the workpaper eliminating entry or entries needed in preparing consolidated financial statements at December 31, 20X3, relating to the intercorporate sale of inventory.

d. Give the workpaper eliminating entry or entries needed in preparing consolidated financial statements at December 31, 20X4, relating to the intercorporate sale of inventory.

e. Give the workpaper eliminating entry or entries needed in preparing consolidated financial statements at December 31, 20X4, relating to the intercorporate sale of inventory if Draw Company had produced the computer desks at a cost of $82 each and sold 10,000 to Karlow Corporation for $94 each in 20X3, with Karlow selling 7,000 desks to unaffiliated companies in 20X3 and the remaining 3,000 in 20X4..

E7–9   **Income Statement Effects of Unrealized Profit**

Holiday Bakery owns 60 percent of the stock of Farmco Products Company. During 20X8, Farmco Products produced 100,000 bags of flour, which it sold to Holiday Bakery for $900,000. On December 31, 20X8, Holiday Bakery had 20,000 bags of flour purchased from Farmco Products on hand. Farmco prices its sales at cost plus 50 percent of cost for profit. Holiday Bakery, which purchased all its flour from Farmco Products in 20X8, had no inventory on hand on January 1, 20X8.

    Holiday Bakery reported income from its baking operations of $400,000, and Farmco Products reported net income of $150,000 for 20X8.

Required

a. Compute the amount reported as cost of goods sold in the 20X8 consolidated income statement.

b. Give the workpaper eliminating entry or entries required to remove the effects of the intercompany sale in preparing consolidated statements at the end of 20X8.

c. Compute the amount reported as consolidated net income for 20X8.

E7–10   **Prior-Period Unrealized Inventory Profit**

Holiday Bakery owns 60 percent of the stock of Farmco Products. On January 1, 20X9, inventory reported by Holiday Bakery included 20,000 bags of flour purchased from Farmco Products at $9 per bag. By December 31, 20X9, all the beginning inventory purchased from Farmco Products had been baked into products and sold to customers by Holiday Bakery. There were no transactions between Holiday Bakery and Farmco Products during 20X9.

Both Holiday Bakery and Farmco Products price their sales at cost plus 50 percent markup for profit. Holiday Bakery reported income from its baking operations of $300,000, and Farmco Products reported net income of $250,000 for 20X9.

Required

a. Compute the amount reported as cost of goods sold in the 20X9 consolidated income statement for the flour purchased from Farmco Products in 20X8.

b. Give the eliminating entry or entries required to remove the effects of the unrealized profit in beginning inventory in preparing the consolidation workpaper as of December 31, 20X9.

c. Compute the amount reported as consolidated net income for 20X9.

E7–11   Computation of Consolidated Income Statement Data

Bass Company purchased 60 percent of the voting shares of Cooper Company for $260,000 on January 1, 20X2. Cooper Company reported total stockholders' equity of $400,000 at the time of acquisition. The purchase differential is assigned to patents with an expected economic life of 10 years from the date of combination.

During 20X5, Bass Company purchased inventory for $20,000 and sold the full amount to Cooper Company for $30,000. On December 31, 20X5, Cooper's ending inventory included $6,000 of items purchased from Bass Company. Also in 20X5, Cooper Company purchased inventory for $50,000 and sold the units to Bass Company for $80,000. Bass included $20,000 of its purchase from Cooper in ending inventory on December 31, 20X5.

Summary income statement data for the two companies revealed the following:

	Bass Company	Cooper Company
Sales	$ 400,000	$ 200,000
Income from Subsidiary	25,000	
	$ 425,000	$ 200,000
Cost of Goods Sold	$ 250,000	$ 120,000
Other Expenses	70,000	35,000
Total Expenses	$(320,000)	$(155,000)
Net Income	$ 105,000	$ 45,000

Required

a. Compute the amount to be reported as sales in the 20X5 consolidated income statement.

b. Compute the amount to be reported as cost of goods sold in the 20X5 consolidated income statement.

c. What amount of income will be assigned to the noncontrolling shareholders in the 20X5 consolidated income statement?

d. What amount of consolidated net income will be reported for 20X5?

E7–12   Sale of Inventory at a Loss

The price of high-quality burnwhistles fluctuates substantially from month to month. As a result, it is not uncommon for a company that deals in burnwhistles to report a substantial gain in one period, followed by a substantial loss in the following period. The price of burnwhistles was relatively high during the first three months of 20X8, declined substantially for the next four months, and then recovered nicely by year-end. On February 6, 20X8, Trent Company purchased burnwhistles for $400,000 and sold them to Gord Corporation on July 10, 20X8, for $300,000. Gord held its purchase for several months before selling 60 percent to nonaffiliates for $360,000 in late November. The remaining units were held at year-end and are expected to be sold in early 20X9 for approximately $240,000. Gord Corporation owns 75 percent of the stock of Trent Company.

Required

a. Give the journal entries recorded by Trent and Gord during 20X8 related to the initial purchase, intercorporate sale, and resale of inventory.

b. What amount should be reported as cost of goods sold in the 20X8 consolidated income statement?

c. If Gord reported operating income of $230,000 and Trent reported net income of $80,000, what amount of consolidated net income should be reported by Gord for 20X8?

d. Give the workpaper eliminating entry or entries needed in preparing consolidated financial statements for 20X8 to remove all effects of the intercompany transfer.

E7–13   Intercompany Sales

Hollow Corporation purchased 70 percent of the voting stock of Surg Corporation on May 18, 20X1, at underlying book value. The companies reported the following data with respect to intercompany sales in 20X4 and 20X5:

Year	Purchased by	Purchase Price	Sold to	Sale Price	Unsold at End of Year	Year Sold to Unaffiliated Co.
20X4	Surg Corp.	$120,000	Hollow Corp.	$180,000	$ 45,000	20X5
20X5	Surg Corp.	90,000	Hollow Corp.	135,000	30,000	20X6
20X5	Hollow Corp.	140,000	Surg Corp.	280,000	110,000	20X6

Hollow Corporation reported operating income (excluding income from its investment in Surg Corporation) of $160,000 and $220,000 in 20X4 and 20X5, respectively. Surg Corporation reported net income of $90,000 and $85,000 in 20X4 and 20X5, respectively.

Required

a. Compute consolidated net income for 20X4.

b. Compute the inventory balance reported in the consolidated balance sheet at December 31, 20X5, for the transactions shown above.

c. Compute the amount included in consolidated cost of goods sold for 20X5 relating to the transactions shown above.

d. Compute consolidated net income for 20X5.

E7–14   Consolidated Balance Sheet Workpaper

The December 31, 20X8, balance sheets for Doorst Corporation and its 70 percent owned subsidiary Hingle Company contained the following summarized amounts:

Doorst Corporation and Hingle Company
Balance Sheets
December 31, 20X8

	Doorst Corporation	Hingle Company
Cash and Receivables	$ 98,000	$ 40,000
Inventory	150,000	100,000
Buildings and Equipment (net)	310,000	280,000
Investment in Hingle Company Stock	280,000	
Total Assets	$838,000	$420,000
Accounts Payable	$ 70,000	$ 20,000
Common Stock	200,000	150,000
Retained Earnings	568,000	250,000
Total Liabilities and Equity	$838,000	$420,000

Doorst purchased the shares of Hingle Company at underlying book value on January 1, 20X7. On December 31, 20X8, the balance sheet of Doorst contains inventory items purchased from Hingle for $95,000. The items cost Hingle $55,000 to produce. In addition, Hingle's inventory contains goods it purchased from Doorst for $25,000 that Doorst had produced for $15,000.

Required

a. Prepare all eliminating entries needed to complete a consolidated balance sheet workpaper as of December 31, 20X8.

b. Prepare a consolidated balance sheet workpaper as of December 31, 20X8.

E7–15* **Multiple Transfers between Affiliates**

Klon Corporation owns 70 percent of the stock of Brant Company and 60 percent of the stock of Torkel Company. During 20X8, Klon sold inventory purchased in 20X7 for $100,000 to Brant Company for $150,000. Brant then sold the inventory at its cost of $150,000 to Torkel. Prior to December 31, 20X8, Torkel sold $90,000 of inventory to a nonaffiliate for $120,000 and held $60,000 in inventory at December 31, 20X8.

Required

a. Give the journal entries recorded by Klon, Brant, and Torkel during 20X8 relating to the intercorporate sale and resale of inventory.

b. What amount should be reported in the 20X8 consolidated income statement as cost of goods sold?

c. What amount should be reported in the December 31, 20X8, consolidated balance sheet as inventory?

d. Give the eliminating entry needed at December 31, 20X8, to remove the effects of the inventory transfers.

E7–16A **Inventory Sales under Periodic Inventory System**

Herb Corporation holds 60 percent ownership of Spice Company. Each year, Spice Company purchases large quantities of a gnarl root used in producing health drinks. Spice purchased $150,000 of roots in 20X7 and sold $40,000 of these purchases to Herb Corporation for $60,000. By the end of 20X7, Herb Corporation had resold all but $15,000 of its purchase from Spice. Herb Corporation generated $90,000 on the sale of roots to various health stores during the year. Both Herb Corporation and Spice Company use periodic inventory systems in accounting for inventory.

Required

a. Give the journal entries recorded by Herb Corporation and Spice Company during 20X7 relating to the initial purchase, intercorporate sale, and resale of gnarl roots.

b. Give the workpaper eliminating entries needed as of December 31, 20X7, to remove all effects of the intercompany transfer in preparing the 20X7 consolidated financial statements.

E7–17A **Prior-Period Profits under Periodic Inventory System**

Home Products Corporation sells a broad line of home detergent products. Home Products owns 75 percent of the stock of Level Brothers Soap Company. During 20X8, Level Brothers sold soap products to Home Products for $180,000, which it had produced for $120,000. Home Products sold $150,000 of its purchase from Level Brothers in 20X8 and the remainder in 20X9. In addition, Home Products purchased $240,000 of inventory from Level Brothers in 20X9 and resold $90,000 of the items before year-end. The cost to Level Brothers of producing the items sold to Home Products in 20X9 was $160,000. Both companies use periodic inventory systems.

---

*Indicates that the item relates to "Additional Considerations."

Required

a. Give all workpaper eliminating entries needed for December 31, 20X9, to remove the effects of the intercompany inventory transfers in 20X8 and 20X9.

b. Compute the amount of income assigned to noncontrolling shareholders in the 20X8 and 20X9 consolidated income statements if Level Brothers reported net income of $350,000 for 20X8 and $420,000 in 20X9.

Problems

P7–18   Consolidated Income Statement Data

Sweeny Corporation owns 60 percent of the shares of Bitner Company. Partial 20X2 financial data for the companies and consolidated entity were as follows:

	Sweeny Corporation	Bitner Company	Consolidated Totals
Sales	$550,000	$450,000	$820,000
Cost of Goods Sold	310,000	300,000	420,000
Inventory, Dec. 31	180,000	210,000	375,000

On January 1, 20X2, the inventory of Sweeny Corporation contained items purchased from Bitner Company for $75,000. The cost of the units to Bitner Company was $50,000. All intercorporate sales during 20X2 were made by Bitner Company to Sweeny Corporation.

Required

a. What amount of intercorporate sales occurred in 20X2?

b. How much unrealized intercompany profit existed on January 1, 20X2? On December 31, 20X2?

c. Give the workpaper eliminating entries relating to inventory and cost of goods sold needed to prepare consolidated financial statements for 20X2.

d. If Bitner Company reports net income of $90,000 for 20X2, what amount of income is assigned to the noncontrolling interest in the 20X2 consolidated income statement?

P7–19   Unrealized Profit on Upstream Sales

Carroll Company sells all its output at 25 percent above cost. Pacific Corporation purchases all its inventory from Carroll Company. Selected information on the operations of the companies over the past three years is as follows:

	Carroll Company		Pacific Corporation	
Year	Sales to Pacific Corp.	Net Income	Inventory, Dec. 31	Operating Income
20X2	$200,000	$100,000	$ 70,000	$150,000
20X3	175,000	90,000	105,000	240,000
20X4	225,000	160,000	120,000	300,000

Pacific Corporation purchased 60 percent of the ownership of Carroll on January 1, 20X1, at underlying book value.

Required

Compute consolidated net income and income assigned to the noncontrolling interest for 20X2, 20X3, and 20X4.

P7–20   Net Income of Consolidated Entity

Stem Corporation purchased 70 percent of the voting stock of Crown Corporation on January 1, 20X2, for $465,000. At that date, Crown reported common stock outstanding of $200,000 and retained earnings of $350,000. The purchase differential is assigned to buildings with an expected life of 20 years from the date of combination.

On December 31, 20X4, Stem had $25,000 of unrealized profits on its books from inventory sales to Crown, and Crown had unrealized profit on its books of $40,000 from inventory sales to Stem. All inventory held at December 31, 20X4, was sold during 20X5.

On December 31, 20X5, Stem had $14,000 of unrealized profit on its books from inventory sales to Crown, and Crown had unrealized profit on its books of $55,000 from inventory sales to Stem.

Stem reported income from its separate operations (excluding income on its investment in Crown and amortization of purchase differential) of $118,000 in 20X5, and Crown reported net income of $65,000.

Required

Compute consolidated net income for 20X5.

P7–21   Correction of Eliminating Entries

In preparing the consolidation workpaper for Bolger Corporation and its 60 percent owned subsidiary, Feldman Company, the following eliminating entries were proposed by the bookkeeper for Bolger Corporation:

E(1) Cash	80,000	
Accounts Payable		80,000
To eliminate the unpaid balance for intercorporate inventory sales in 20X5.		
E(2) Cost of Goods Sold	12,000	
Income from Subsidiary		12,000
To eliminate unrealized inventory profits at December 31, 20X5.		
E(3) Income from Subsidiary	140,000	
Sales		140,000
To eliminate intercompany sales for 20X5.		

The bookkeeper for Bolger recently graduated from Oddball University, and while the dollar amounts recorded are correct, he had some confusion in determining which accounts needed adjustment. All of the intercorporate sales in 20X5 were from Feldman to Bolger, and Feldman sells inventory at cost plus 40 percent of cost. Bolger uses the equity method in accounting for its ownership in Feldman.

Required

a. What percentage of the intercompany inventory transfer was resold prior to the end of 20X5?

b. Give the appropriate eliminating entries needed at December 31, 20X5, to prepare consolidated financial statements.

P7–22   Incomplete Data

Keller Corporation acquired 75 percent of the ownership of Tropic Company on January 1, 20X1. The purchase differential paid by Keller is assigned to buildings and equipment and expensed over 10 years. Financial statement data for the two companies and the consolidated entity at December 31, 20X6, are as follows:

Keller Corporation and Tropic Company
Balance Sheet Data
December 31, 20X6

Item	Keller Corporation	Tropic Company	Consolidated Entity
Cash	$ 67,000	$ 45,000	$112,000
Accounts Receivable	?	55,000	145,000
Inventory	125,000	90,000	211,000
Buildings and Equipment	400,000	240,000	670,000
Less: Accumulated Depreciation	(180,000)	(110,000)	(?)
Investment in Tropic Company	?		
Total Assets	$?	$320,000	$?
Accounts Payable	$ 86,000	$ 20,000	$ 89,000
Other Payables	?	8,000	?
Notes Payable	250,000	120,000	370,000
Common Stock	120,000	60,000	120,000
Retained Earnings	180,000	112,000	177,000
Noncontrolling Interest			42,000
Total Liabilities and Equities	$?	$320,000	$?

Keller Corporation and Tropic Company
Income Statement Data
For the Year Ended December 31, 20X6

Item	Keller Corporation	Tropic Company	Consolidated Entity
Sales	$420,000	$260,000	$650,000
Income from Subsidiary	27,000		
Total Income	$447,000	$260,000	$650,000
Cost of Goods Sold	$310,000	$170,000	$445,000
Depreciation Expense	20,000	25,000	48,000
Interest Expense	25,000	9,500	34,500
Other Expenses	22,000	15,500	37,500
Total Expenses	($377,000)	($220,000)	($565,000)
			$ 85,000
Income to Noncontrolling Interest			(9,000)
Net Income	$ 70,000	$ 40,000	$ 76,000

Required

a. What amount of purchase differential was paid by Keller in acquiring its ownership of Tropic?

b. What amount should be reported as accumulated depreciation for the consolidated entity at December 31, 20X6?

c. If Tropic reported retained earnings of $30,000 on January 1, 20X1, what amount did Keller pay to acquire its ownership in Tropic?

d. What balance does Keller report as its investment in Tropic at December 31, 20X6?

e. What amount of intercorporate sales of inventory occurred in 20X6?

f. What amount of unrealized inventory profit exists at December 31, 20X6?

g. Assuming all unrealized profits on intercompany inventory sales at January 1, 20X6, were on Keller's books, were the inventory sales during 20X6 upstream or downstream? How do you know?

h. Give the eliminating entry used in eliminating intercompany inventory sales during 20X6.

i. Assuming all unrealized profits on intercompany inventory sales at January 1, 20X6, were on Keller's books, what was the amount of unrealized profit at January 1, 20X6?

j. What balance in accounts receivable was reported by Keller at December 31, 20X6?

P7–23   Eliminations for Upstream Sales

Clean Air Products owns 80 percent of the stock of Superior Filter Company, which it acquired at underlying book value on August 30, 20X6. Summarized trial balance data for the two companies as of December 31, 20X8, are as follows:

	Clean Air Products		Superior Filter Company	
Cash and Accounts Receivable	$ 145,000		$ 90,000	
Inventory	220,000		110,000	
Buildings and Equipment (net)	270,000		180,000	
Investment in Superior Filter Stock	280,000			
Cost of Goods Sold	175,000		140,000	
Depreciation Expense	30,000		20,000	
Current Liabilities		$ 150,000		$ 30,000
Common Stock		200,000		90,000
Retained Earnings		488,000		220,000
Sales		250,000		200,000
Income from Subsidiary		32,000		
Total	$1,120,000	$1,120,000	$540,000	$540,000

On January 1, 20X8, the inventory held by Clean Air Products contained filters purchased for $60,000 from Superior Filter Company. Superior had produced the filters for $40,000. In 20X8, Superior Filter spent $100,000 to produce additional filters, which it sold to Clean Air for $150,000. By December 31, 20X8, Clean Air had sold all the filters that had been on hand January 1, 20X8, but continued to hold in inventory $45,000 of the 20X8 purchase from Superior Filter.

Required

a. Prepare all eliminating entries needed to complete a consolidation workpaper for 20X8.

b. Compute consolidated net income for 20X8.

c. Compute the balance assigned to the noncontrolling interest in the consolidated balance sheet as of December 31, 20X8.

P7–24   Multiple Inventory Transfers

Ajax Corporation purchased at book value 70 percent of the ownership of Beta Corporation and 90 percent of the ownership of Cole Corporation in 20X5. There are frequent intercompany transfers among the companies. Activity relevant to 20X8 is presented below.

Year	Producer	Production Cost	Buyer	Transfer Price	Unsold at End of Year	Year Sold
20X7	Beta Corporation	$24,000	Ajax Corporation	$30,000	$10,000	20X8
20X7	Cole Corporation	60,000	Beta Corporation	72,000	18,000	20X8
20X8	Ajax Corporation	15,000	Beta Corporation	35,000	7,000	20X9
20X8	Beta Corporation	63,000	Cole Corporation	72,000	12,000	20X9
20X8	Cole Corporation	27,000	Ajax Corporation	45,000	15,000	20X9

For the year ended December 31, 20X8, Ajax Corporation reported $80,000 of income from its separate operations (excluding income from intercorporate investments), Beta Corporation reported net income of $37,500, and Cole Corporation reported net income of $20,000.

Required

a. Compute the amount to be reported as consolidated net income for 20X8.

b. Compute the amount to be reported as inventory in the December 31, 20X8, consolidated balance sheet for the items shown above.

c. Compute the amount to be reported as income assigned to noncontrolling shareholders in the 20X8 consolidated income statement.

P7–25   **Consolidation with Inventory Transfers and Other Comprehensive Income**

On January 1, 20X1, Priority Corporation purchased 90 percent of the common stock of Tall Corporation at underlying book value. Priority uses the equity method in accounting for its investment in Tall. The stockholders' equity section of Tall at January 1, 20X5, contained the following balances:

Common Stock ($5 par)	$ 400,000
Additional Paid-In Capital	200,000
Retained Earnings	790,000
Accumulated Other Comprehensive Income	10,000
Total	$1,400,000

During 20X4, Tall sold goods costing $30,000 to Priority for $45,000, and Priority resold 60 percent prior to year-end. The reminder was sold in 20X5. Also in 20X4, Priority sold inventory items costing $90,000 to Tall for $108,000. Tall resold $60,000 of its purchases in 20X4 and the remaining $48,000 in 20X5.

In 20X5, Priority sold additional inventory costing $30,000 to Tall for $36,000, and Tall resold $24,000 prior to year-end. Tall sold inventory costing $60,000 to Priority in 20X5 for $90,000, and Priority resold $48,000 of its purchase by December 31, 20X5.

Priority reported 20X5 income from its separate operations of $240,000 and paid dividends of $150,000. Tall reported 20X5 net income of $90,000 and comprehensive income of $110,000. Tall reported other comprehensive income of $10,000 in 20X4. In both years, other comprehensive income arose from an increase in the market value of securities classified as available-for-sale. Tall paid dividends of $60,000 in 20X5.

Required

a. Compute the balance in the investment account reported by Priority at December 31, 20X5.

b. Compute the amount of investment income reported by Priority on its investment in Tall for 20X5.

c. Compute the amount of income assigned to noncontrolling shareholders in the 20X5 consolidated income statement.

d. Compute the balance assigned to noncontrolling shareholders in the consolidated balance sheet prepared at December 31, 20X5.

e. Priority and Tall report inventory balances of $120,000 and $100,000, respectively, at December 31, 20X5. What amount should be reported as inventory in the consolidated balance sheet at December 31, 20X5?

f. Compute the amount reported as consolidated net income for 20X5.

g. Prepare the eliminating entries needed to complete a consolidation workpaper as of December 31, 20X5.

20X9 Trial Balance Data

Item	Foster Company Debit	Foster Company Credit	Block Corporation Debit	Block Corporation Credit
Cash	$ 187,000		$ 57,400	
Accounts Receivable	80,000		90,000	
Other Receivables	40,000		10,000	
Inventory	137,000		130,000	
Land	80,000		60,000	
Buildings and Equipment	500,000		250,000	
Investment in Block Corporation Stock	238,500			
Cost of Goods Sold	593,000		270,000	
Depreciation Expense	45,000		15,000	
Other Expenses	95,000		75,000	
Dividends Declared	40,000		20,000	
Accumulated Depreciation		$ 155,000		$ 75,000
Accounts Payable		63,000		35,000
Other Payables		95,000		20,000
Bonds Payable		250,000		200,000
Bond Premium				2,400
Common Stock		210,000		50,000
Additional Paid-In Capital		110,000		
Retained Earnings		248,500		165,000
Sales		815,000		415,000
Other Income		26,000		15,000
Income from Subsidiary		63,000		
Total	$2,035,500	$2,035,500	$977,400	$977,400

On January 1, 20X7, Block Corporation sold equipment to Foster Company for $48,000. The equipment had been purchased for $90,000 on January 1, 20X5, by Block Company and was depreciated on a straight-line basis with an expected life of 10 years and no anticipated scrap value. The total expected life of the equipment is unchanged as a result of the intercompany transfer.

During 20X9, Block Corporation produced inventory for $20,000 and sold it to Foster Company for $30,000. Foster resold 60 percent of the inventory in 20X9. Also in 20X9, Foster sold inventory purchased from Block in 20X8. It had cost Block $60,000 to produce the inventory, and Foster purchased it for $75,000.

Required

a. What amount of cost of goods sold will be reported in the 20X9 consolidated income statement?

b. What inventory balance will be reported in the December 31, 20X9, consolidated balance sheet?

c. What amount of income will be assigned to noncontrolling shareholders in the 20X9 consolidated income statement?

d. What amount will be assigned to noncontrolling interest in the consolidated balance sheet prepared at December 31, 20X9?

e. What amount of retained earnings will be reported in the consolidated balance sheet at December 31, 20X9?

f. Give all eliminating entries required to prepare a three-part consolidated working paper at December 31, 20X9.

P7–33   **Comprehensive Multiple-Choice Problem**

Mega Retail Corporation purchased 80 percent of the voting shares of Dime Store Enterprises on January 1, 20X4, for $227,200. On that date Dime Store Enterprises reported retained earnings of $50,000 and common stock outstanding of $200,000.

    Partial balance sheets and income statements for the companies are available at December 31, 20X6, as follows:

Mega Retail Corporation and Dime Store Enterprises
Balance Sheets
December 31, 20X6

Item	Mega Retail Corporation		Dime Store Enterprises	
Cash		$?		$163,000
Inventory		200,000		200,000
Land		50,000		30,000
Buildings and Equipment	$500,000		$400,000	
Less: Accumulated Depreciation	(250,000)	250,000	(180,000)	220,000
Investment in Smith Company Bonds		106,400		
Investment in Dime Store Stock		?		
Total Assets		$1,080,000		$613,000
Current Liabilities		$ 150,000		$ 80,000
Bonds Payable		400,000	$200,000	
Bond Premium			8,000	208,000
Common Stock		300,000		200,000
Retained Earnings		230,000		125,000
Total Liabilities and Equity		$1,080,000		$613,000

Mega Retail Corporation and Dime Store Enterprises
Income Statements
Year Ended December 31, 20X6

Item	Mega Retail Corporation		Dime Store Enterprises	
Sales		$ 300,000		$200,000
Other Income		34,000		
Income from Subsidiary		?		
		$?		$200,000
Cost of Goods Sold	$220,000		$100,000	
Depreciation and Amortization	50,000		20,000	
Interest Expense	24,000		14,000	
Other Expenses	16,000	(310,000)	26,000	(160,000)
Net Income		$?		$ 40,000

On the date of combination, all Dime Store's assets were carried at book values that were equal to their market values except for buildings, which had a fair value of $30,000 greater than book value. The buildings had an expected 10-year remaining life on that date. At the end of each year, the management of Mega Retail has reviewed the amount attributed to goodwill as a result of its purchase of Dime Store shares and found no evidence of impairment.

Dime Store sells part of its inventory to Mega Retail each year. During 20X5, Dime Store sold goods costing $30,000 to Mega Retail for $35,000. Mega resold 60 percent of the inventory in 20X5 and 40 percent in 20X6. In 20X6, Dime Store sold goods costing $50,000 to Mega Retail for $70,000, and Mega resold 70 percent of the goods during 20X6.

During 20X6, Mega Retail Corporation paid dividends of $20,000, and Dime Store Enterprises paid dividends of $15,000.

Required

Select the correct answer for each of the following questions.

1. What total amount of depreciation and amortization will be reported in the 20X6 consolidated income statement?
   a. $70,000.
   b. $72,400.
   c. $73,000.
   d. $72,720.

2. What amount of inventory will be reported in the consolidated balance sheet as of December 31, 20X6?
   a. $380,000.
   b. $394,000.
   c. $396,000.
   d. $400,000.

3. What amount of cost of goods sold will be reported in the 20X6 consolidated income statement?
   a. $248,000.
   b. $254,000.
   c. $256,000.
   d. $320,000.

4. What was the amount of unamortized purchase differential on January 1, 20X6?
   a. $19,200.
   b. $22,400.
   c. $24,000.
   d. $27,200.
   e. $32,000.

5. What amount of goodwill will be reported in the December 31, 20X6, consolidated balance sheet?
   a. $0.
   b. $3,200.
   c. $22,400.
   d. $24,000.
   e. $27,200.

6. What amount of income will be assigned to the noncontrolling interest in the 20X6 consolidated income statement?
   a. $6,800.
   b. $7,200.
   c. $8,000.
   d. $8,400.

7. What amount will be reported as the noncontrolling shareholders' claim in the consolidated balance sheet as of December 31, 20X6?
   a. $59,000.
   b. $63,800.
   c. $64,200.
   d. $65,000.

8. What is consolidated net income for 20X6?

    a. $50,400.

    b. $52,800.

    c. $56,000.

    d. $57,600.

P7–34   **Consolidated Balance Sheet Workpaper [AICPA Adapted]**

The December 31, 20X6, condensed balance sheets of Pine Corporation. and its 90 percent owned subsidiary, Slim Corporation, are presented in the accompanying worksheet.

Additional information is as follows:

- Pine's investment in Slim was purchased for $1,200,000 cash on January 1, 20X6, and is accounted for by the basic equity method.
- At January 1, 20X6, Slim's retained earnings amounted to $600,000, and its common stock amounted to $200,000.
- Slim declared a $1,000 cash dividend in December 20X6, payable in January 20X7.
- As of December 31, 20X6, Pine had not recorded any portion of Slim's 20X6 net income or dividend declaration.
- Slim borrowed $100,000 from Pine on June 30, 20X6, with the note maturing on June 30, 20X7, at 10 percent interest. Correct accruals have been recorded by both companies.
- During 20X6, Pine sold merchandise to Slim at an aggregate invoice price of $300,000, which included a profit of $60,000. At December 31, 20X6, Slim had not paid Pine for $90,000 of these purchases, and 5 percent of the total merchandise purchased from Pine still remained in Slim's inventory.
- Pine's excess cost over book value of its investment in Slim has appropriately been identified as goodwill. At December 31, 20X6, the management of Pine Corporation reviewed the amount attributed to goodwill and found no evidence of impairment.

Required

Complete the accompanying workpaper for Pine Corporation and its subsidiary, Slim Corporation, at December 31, 20X6.

Pine Corporation and Subsidiary
Consolidated Balance Sheet Workpaper
December 31, 20X6

	Pine Corporation	Slim Corporation	Adjustments and Eliminations Debit	Adjustments and Eliminations Credit	Consolidated
Assets					
Cash	75,000	15,000			
Accounts and Other Current					
Receivables	410,000	120,000			
Merchandise Inventory	920,000	670,000			
Plant and Equipment, Net	1,000,000	400,000			
Investment in Slim	1,200,000				
Totals	3,605,000	1,205,000			
Liabilities and Stockholders' Equity:					
Accounts Payable and Other					
Current Liabilities	140,000	305,000			
Common Stock ($10 par)	500,000	200,000			
Retained Earnings	2,965,000	700,000			
Totals	3,605,000	1,205,000			

P7–35 **Comprehensive Worksheet Problem—Perpetual Inventories**

Randall Corporation acquired 80 percent of the voting shares of Sharp Company on January 1, 20X4, for $280,000 in cash and marketable securities. At the time of acquisition, Sharp Company reported net assets of $300,000. Trial balances for the two companies on December 31, 20X7, are as follows:

	Randall Corporation			Sharp Company	
Item	Debit	Credit		Debit	Credit
Cash	$ 130,300			$ 10,000	
Accounts Receivable	80,000			70,000	
Inventory	170,000			110,000	
Buildings and Equipment	600,000			400,000	
Investment in Sharp Company Stock	304,000				
Cost of Goods Sold	416,000			202,000	
Depreciation and Amortization	30,000			20,000	
Other Expenses	24,000			18,000	
Dividends Declared	50,000			25,000	
Accumulated Depreciation		$ 310,000			$120,000
Accounts Payable		100,000			15,200
Bonds Payable		300,000			100,000
Bond Premium					4,800
Common Stock		200,000			100,000
Additional Paid-In Capital					20,000
Retained Earnings		345,900			215,000
Sales		500,000			250,000
Other Income		20,400			30,000
Income from Subsidiary		28,000			
	$1,804,300	$1,804,300		$855,000	$855,000

Additional Information

1. The purchase differential is appropriately assigned to buildings and equipment that had a remaining 10-year economic life at the date of combination.

2. Randall Corporation and Sharp Company regularly purchase inventory from each other. During 20X6, Sharp sold inventory costing $40,000 to Randall Corporation for $60,000, and Randall resold 60 percent of the inventory in 20X6 and 40 percent in 20X7. Also in 20X6, Randall sold inventory costing $20,000 to Sharp for $26,000. Sharp resold two-thirds of the inventory in 20X6 and one-third in 20X7.

3. During 20X7, Sharp sold inventory costing $30,000 to Randall Corporation for $45,000, and Randall sold items purchased for $9,000 to Sharp for $12,000. Randall resold before the end of the year one-third of the inventory it purchased from Sharp in 20X7. Sharp continues to hold all the units purchased from Randall during 20X7.

4. Randall Corporation sold equipment originally purchased for $75,000 to Sharp for $50,000 on December 31, 20X5. Accumulated depreciation over the 12 years of use before the intercorporate sale was $45,000. The estimated remaining life at the time of transfer was eight years. Straight-line depreciation is used by both companies.

5. Sharp owes Randall $10,000 on account on December 31, 20X7.

Required

a. Prepare the 20X7 journal entries recorded on the books of Randall Corporation related to its investment in Sharp Company if Randall uses the basic equity method.

b. Prepare all eliminating entries needed to complete a consolidation workpaper as of December 31, 20X7.

c. Prepare a three-part consolidation workpaper as of December 31, 20X7.

d. Prepare, in good form, a consolidated income statement, balance sheet, and retained earnings statement for 20X7.

P7–36   **Comprehensive Consolidation Workpaper; Equity Method [AICPA Adapted]**

Fran Corporation acquired all the outstanding $10 par value voting common stock of Brey Inc. on January 1, 20X9, in exchange for 25,000 shares of its $20 par value voting common stock. On December 31, 20X8, Fran's common stock had a closing market price of $30 per share on a national stock exchange. The acquisition was appropriately accounted for as a purchase. Both companies continued to operate as separate business entities maintaining separate accounting records with years ending December 31. Fran accounts for its investment in Brey stock using the equity method without adjusting for unrealized intercompany profits.

On December 31, 20X9, the companies had condensed financial statements as follows:

	Fran Corporation		Brey Inc.	
	Dr	(Cr)	Dr	(Cr)
Income Statement				
Net Sales		$(3,800,000)		$(1,500,000)
Equity in Brey's Income		(181,000)		
Gain on Sale of Warehouse		(30,000)		
Cost of Goods Sold	2,360,000		870,000	
Operating Expenses (Including Depreciation)	1,100,000		440,000	
Net Income		$ (551,000)		$ (190,000)
Retained Earnings Statement				
Balance, 1/1/X9		$ (440,000)		$ (156,000)
Net Income		(551,000)		(190,000)
Dividends Paid			40,000	
Balance, 12/31/X9		$ (991,000)		$ (306,000)
Balance Sheet				
Assets:				
Cash	$ 570,000		$ 150,000	
Accounts Receivable (net)	860,000		350,000	
Inventories	1,060,000		410,000	
Land, Plant, and Equipment	1,320,000		680,000	
Accumulated Depreciation		(370,000)		(210,000)
Investment in Brey	891,000			
Total Assets	$ 4,331,000		$ 1,380,000	
Liabilities and Stockholders' Equity				
Accounts Payable and Accrued Expenses		$(1,340,000)		$ (594,000)
Common Stock		(1,700,000)		(400,000)
Additional Paid-in Capital		(300,000)		(80,000)
Retained Earnings		(991,000)		(306,000)
Total Liabilities and Equity		$(4,331,000)		$(1,380,000)

Additional Information

There were no changes in the Common Stock and Additional Paid-In Capital accounts during 20X9 except the one necessitated by Fran's acquisition of Brey.

At the acquisition date, the fair value of Brey's machinery exceeded its book value by $54,000. The excess cost will be amortized over the estimated average remaining life of six years. The fair values of all of Brey's other assets and liabilities were equal to their book values. At December 31, 20X9, the management of Fran Corporation reviewed the amount attributed to goodwill as a result of its purchase of Brey's common stock and concluded an impairment loss of $35,000 should be recognized in 20X9.

On July 1, 20X9, Fran sold a warehouse facility to Brey for $129,000 cash. At the date of sale, Fran's book values were $33,000 for the land and $66,000 for the undepreciated cost of the building. Based on a real estate appraisal, Brey allocated $43,000 of the purchase price to land and $86,000 to building. Brey is depreciating the building over its estimated five-year remaining useful life by the straight-line method with no salvage value.

During 20X9, Fran purchased merchandise from Brey at an aggregate invoice price of $180,000, which included a 100 percent markup on Brey's cost. At December 31, 20X9, Fran owed Brey $86,000 on these purchases, and $36,000 of this merchandise remained in Fran's inventory.

Required

Develop and complete a consolidation workpaper that would be used to prepare a consolidated income statement and a consolidated retained earnings statement for the year ended December 31, 20X9, and a consolidated balance sheet as of December 31, 20X9. List the accounts in the workpaper in the same order as they are listed in the financial statements provided. Formal consolidated statements are not required. Ignore income tax considerations. Supporting computations should be in good form.

P7–37A **Comprehensive Worksheet Problem—Periodic Inventories**

Randall Corporation acquired 80 percent of the voting shares of Sharp Company on January 1, 20X4, for $280,000 in cash and marketable securities. At the time of acquisition, Sharp Company reported net assets of $300,000. Trial balances for the two companies on December 31, 20X7, are as follows:

Item	Randall Corporation		Sharp Company	
	Debit	*Credit*	*Debit*	*Credit*
Cash	$ 130,300		$ 10,000	
Accounts Receivable	80,000		70,000	
Inventory	150,000		120,000	
Buildings and Equipment	600,000		400,000	
Investment in Sharp Company Stock	304,000			
Purchases	436,000		192,000	
Depreciation and Amortization	30,000		20,000	
Other Expenses	24,000		18,000	
Dividends Declared	50,000		25,000	
Accumulated Depreciation		$ 310,000		$120,000
Accounts Payable		100,000		15,200
Bonds Payable		300,000		100,000
Bond Premium				4,800
Common Stock		200,000		100,000
Additional Paid-In Capital				20,000
Retained Earnings		345,900		215,000
Sales		500,000		250,000
Other Income		20,400		30,000
Income from Subsidiary		28,000		
	$1,804,300	$1,804,300	$855,000	$855,000

Additional Information

1. Both companies use periodic inventory systems. At December 31, 20X7, Sharp Company reported ending inventory of $110,000, and Randall Corporation reported ending inventory of $170,000.

2. The purchase differential is appropriately assigned to buildings and equipment that had a remaining 10-year economic life at the date of combination.

3. Randall Corporation and Sharp Company regularly purchase inventory from each other. During 20X6, Sharp sold inventory costing $40,000 to Randall Corporation for $60,000, and Randall resold 60 percent of the inventory in 20X6 and 40 percent in 20X7. Also in 20X6, Randall sold inventory costing $20,000 to Sharp for $26,000. Sharp resold two-thirds of the inventory in 20X6 and one-third in 20X7.

4. During 20X7, Sharp sold inventory costing $30,000 to Randall Corporation for $45,000, and Randall sold items purchased for $9,000 to Sharp for $12,000. Randall resold before the end of the year one-third of the inventory it purchased from Sharp in 20X7. Sharp continues to hold all the units purchased from Randall during 20X7.

5. Randall Corporation sold equipment originally purchased for $75,000 to Sharp for $50,000 on December 31, 20X5. Accumulated depreciation over the 12 years of use before the intercorporate sale was $45,000. The estimated remaining life at the time of transfer was eight years. Straight-line depreciation is used by both companies.

6. Sharp owes Randall $10,000 on account on December 31, 20X7.

Required

a. Prepare the 20X7 journal entries recorded on the books of Randall Corporation related to its investment in Sharp Company if Randall uses the basic equity method.

b. Prepare all eliminating entries needed to complete a consolidation workpaper as of December 31, 20X7.

c. Prepare a three-part consolidation workpaper as of December 31, 20X7.

d. Prepare, in good form, a consolidated income statement, balance sheet, and retained earnings statement for 20X7.

P7–38B   Fully Adjusted Equity Method
On December 31, 20X7, Randall Corporation recorded the following entry on its books to adjust from the basic equity method to the fully adjusted equity method for its investment in Sharp Company stock:

Retained Earnings	25,900	
Income from Subsidiary	100	
Investment in Sharp Company Stock		26,000

Required

a. Adjust the data reported by Randall Corporation in the trial balance contained in Problem 7–35 for the effects of the adjusting entry presented above.

b. Prepare the journal entries that would have been recorded on the books of Randall Corporation during 20X7 under the fully adjusted equity method.

c. Prepare all eliminating entries needed to complete a consolidation workpaper at December 31, 20X7, assuming Randall has used the fully adjusted equity method.

d. Complete a three-part consolidation workpaper as of December 31, 20X7.

P7–39B   Comprehensive Consolidation Workpaper; Cost Method [AICPA Adapted]
Fran Corporation acquired all the outstanding $10 par value voting common stock of Brey Inc. on January 1, 20X9, in exchange for 25,000 shares of its $20 par value voting common stock. On December 31, 20X8, Fran's common stock had a closing market price of $30 per share on a national stock exchange. The acquisition was appropriately accounted for as a purchase. Both

companies continued to operate as separate business entities maintaining separate accounting records with years ending December 31.

On December 31, 20X9, the companies had condensed financial statements as follows:

	Fran Corporation		Brey Inc.	
	Dr	(Cr)	Dr	(Cr)
Income Statement				
Net Sales		$(3,800,000)		$(1,500,000)
Dividends from Brey		(40,000)		
Gain on Sale of Warehouse		(30,000)		
Cost of Goods Sold	2,360,000		870,000	
Operating Expenses (Including Depreciation)	1,100,000		440,000	
Net Income		$ (410,000)		$ (190,000)
Retained Earnings Statement				
Balance, 1/1/X9		$ (440,000)		$ (156,000)
Net Income		(410,000)		(190,000)
Dividends Paid			40,000	
Balance, 12/31/X9		$ (850,000)		$ (306,000)
Balance Sheet				
Assets:				
Cash	$ 570,000		$ 150,000	
Accounts Receivable (net)	860,000		350,000	
Inventories	1,060,000		410,000	
Land, Plant, and Equipment	1,320,000		680,000	
Accumulated Depreciation		(370,000)		(210,000)
Investment in Brey (at cost)	750,000			
Total Assets	$ 4,190,000		$ 1,380,000	
Liabilities and Stockholders' Equity				
Accounts Payable and Accrued Expenses		$(1,340,000)		$ (594,000)
Common Stock		(1,700,000)		(400,000)
Additional Paid-in Capital		(300,000)		(80,000)
Retained Earnings		(850,000)		(306,000)
Total Liabilities and Equity		$(4,190,000)		$(1,380,000)

Additional Information

There were no changes in the Common Stock and Additional Paid-In Capital accounts during 20X9 except the one necessitated by Fran's acquisition of Brey.

At the acquisition date, the fair value of Brey's machinery exceeded its book value by $54,000. The excess cost will be amortized over the estimated average remaining life of six years. The fair values of all of Brey's other assets and liabilities were equal to their book values. At December 31, 20X9, the management of Fran Corporation reviewed the amount attributed to goodwill as a result of its purchase of Brey's common stock and concluded an impairment loss of $35,000 should be recognized in 20X9.

On July 1, 20X9, Fran sold a warehouse facility to Brey for $129,000 cash. At the date of sale, Fran's book values were $33,000 for the land and $66,000 for the undepreciated cost of the building. Based on a real estate appraisal, Brey allocated $43,000 of the purchase price to land and

$86,000 to building. Brey is depreciating the building over its estimated five-year remaining useful life by the straight-line method with no salvage value.

During 20X9, Fran purchased merchandise from Brey at an aggregate invoice price of $180,000, which included a 100 percent markup on Brey's cost. At December 31, 20X9, Fran owed Brey $86,000 on these purchases, and $36,000 of this merchandise remained in Fran's inventory.

Required

Develop and complete a consolidation workpaper that would be used to prepare a consolidated income statement and a consolidated retained earnings statement for the year ended December 31, 20X9, and a consolidated balance sheet as of December 31, 20X9. Formal consolidated statements are not required. Ignore income tax considerations. Supporting computations should be in good form.

P7–40B   Cost Method

The trial balance data presented in Problem 7–35 can be converted to reflect use of the cost method by inserting the following amounts in place of those presented for Randall Corporation:

Investment in Sharp Company Stock	$280,000
Retained Earnings	329,900
Income from Subsidiary	-0-
Dividend Income	20,000

Required

a. Prepare the journal entries that would have been recorded on the books of Randall Corporation during 20X7 under the cost method.

b. Prepare all eliminating entries needed to complete a consolidation workpaper as of December 31, 20X7, assuming Randall uses the cost method.

c. Complete a three-part consolidation workpaper as of December 31, 20X7.

INTERCOMPANY INDEBTEDNESS

One advantage of having control over other companies is that management has the ability to transfer resources from one legal entity to another as needed by the individual companies. Companies often find it beneficial to lend excess funds to affiliates and to borrow from affiliates when cash shortages arise. The borrower often benefits from lower borrowing rates, less restrictive credit terms, and the informality and lower debt issue costs of intercompany borrowing relative to public debt offerings. The lending affiliate may benefit by being able to invest excess funds in a company about which it has considerable knowledge, perhaps allowing it to earn a given return on the funds invested while incurring less risk than if it invested in unrelated companies. Also, the combined entity may find it advantageous for the parent company or another affiliate to borrow funds for the entire enterprise rather than having each affiliate going directly to the capital markets.

Consolidation Overview

Figure 8–1 illustrates two types of intercorporate debt transfers. A **direct intercompany debt transfer** involves a loan from one affiliate to another without the participation of an unrelated party, as in Figure 8–1a. Examples include a trade receivable/payable arising from an intercompany sale of inventory on credit, and the issuance of a note payable by one affiliate to another in exchange for operating funds.

An **indirect intercompany debt transfer** involves the issuance of debt to an unrelated party and the subsequent purchase of the debt instrument by an affiliate of the issuer. For example, in Figure 8–1b, Special Foods borrows funds by issuing a debt instrument, such as a note or a bond, to Nonaffiliated Corporation. The debt instrument subsequently is purchased from Nonaffiliated Corporation by Special Foods' parent, Peerless Products. Thus, Peerless Products acquires the debt of Special Foods indirectly through Nonaffiliated Corporation.

All account balances arising from intercorporate financing arrangements must be eliminated when consolidated statements are prepared. The consolidated financial statements portray the consolidated entity as a single company. Therefore, in Figure 8–1, transactions that do not cross the boundary of the consolidated entity are not reported in the consolidated financial statements. Although in illustration (a) Special Foods borrows funds from Peerless, the consolidated entity as a whole does not

FIGURE 8–1   **Intercompany Debt Transactions**

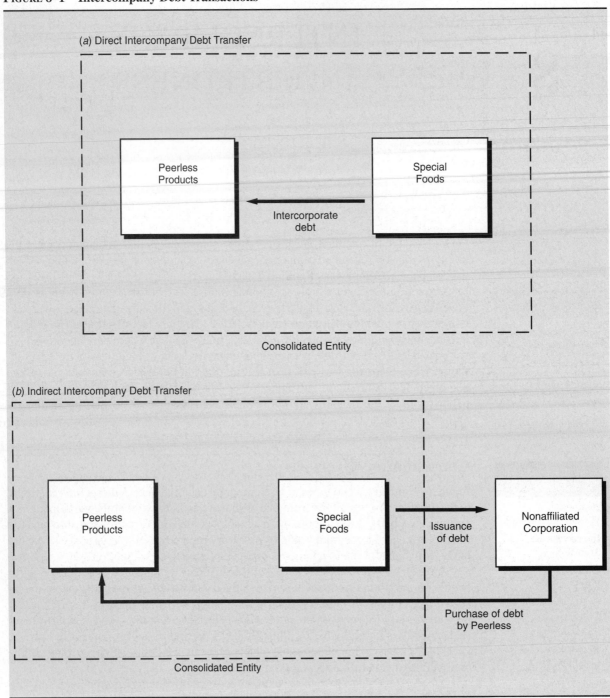

(*a*) Direct Intercompany Debt Transfer

Peerless Products

Special Foods

Intercorporate debt

Consolidated Entity

(*b*) Indirect Intercompany Debt Transfer

Peerless Products

Special Foods

Nonaffiliated Corporation

Issuance of debt

Purchase of debt by Peerless

Consolidated Entity

borrow and the intercompany loan is not reflected in the consolidated financial statements.

In illustration (*b*), Special Foods borrows funds from Nonaffiliated Corporation. Because this transaction is with an unrelated party and crosses the boundary of the consolidated entity, it is reflected in the consolidated financial statements. In effect, the consolidated entity is borrowing from an outside party, and the liability is included in the consolidated balance sheet. When Peerless purchases Special Foods' debt instrument from Nonaffiliated, this transaction also crosses the boundary of the consolidated entity. In effect, the consolidated entity repurchases its debt, and needs to report the purchase as a debt retirement. As with most retirements of debt before maturity, a purchase of an affiliate's bonds usually gives rise to a gain or loss on the retirement; the gain or loss is reported in the consolidated income statement even though it does not appear in the separate income statement of either affiliate.

This chapter discusses the procedures used to prepare consolidated financial statements when intercorporate indebtedness arises from either direct or indirect debt transfers. Although the discussion focuses on bonds, the same concepts and procedures also apply to notes and other types of intercorporate indebtedness.

Bond Sale Directly to an Affiliate

When one company sells bonds directly to an affiliate, all effects of the intercompany indebtedness must be eliminated in preparing consolidated financial statements. A company cannot report an investment in its own bonds or a bond liability to itself. Thus, when the consolidated entity is viewed as a single company, all amounts associated with the intercorporate indebtedness must be eliminated, including the investment in bonds, the bonds payable, any unamortized discount or premium on the bonds, and the interest income and expense on the bonds.

Transfer at Par Value

When a note or bond payable is sold directly to an affiliate at par value, the entries recorded by the investor and the issuer should be mirror images of each other. To illustrate, assume that on January 1, 20X1, Special Foods borrows $100,000 from Peerless Products by issuing to Peerless $100,000 par value, 12 percent, 10-year bonds. This transaction is represented by Figure 8–1*a*. During 20X1, Special Foods records interest expense on the bonds of $12,000 ($100,000 × .12), and Peerless records an equal amount of interest income.

In the preparation of consolidated financial statements for 20X1, two elimination entries are needed in the consolidation workpaper to remove the effects of the intercompany indebtedness:

E(1)	Bonds Payable	100,000	
	Investment in Special Foods Bonds		100,000
	Eliminate intercorporate bond holdings.		
E(2)	Interest Income	12,000	
	Interest Expense		12,000
	Eliminate intercompany interest.		

These entries eliminate from the consolidated statements the bond investment and associated income recorded on Peerless's books and the liability and related interest expense recorded on Special Foods' books. The resulting statements appear as if the indebtedness does not exist, which from a consolidated viewpoint it does not.

Note that these entries have no effect on consolidated net income because they reduce interest income and interest expense by the same amount. Eliminating entries E(1) and E(2) are required at the end of each period for as long as the intercorporate indebtedness continues.

Transfer at a Discount or Premium

When the coupon or nominal interest rate on a bond is different from the yield demanded by those who lend funds, a bond will sell at a discount or premium. In such cases, the amount of bond interest income or expense recorded no longer is equal to the cash interest payments. Instead, interest income and expense amounts are adjusted for the amortization of the discount or premium.

As an illustration of the treatment of intercompany bond transfers at other than par, assume that on January 1, 20X1, Peerless Products purchases $100,000 par value, 12 percent, 10-year bonds from Special Foods for $90,000. Interest on the bonds is payable on January 1 and July 1. The interest expense recognized by Special Foods and the interest income recognized by Peerless each year include straight-line amortization of the discount, as follows:

Cash interest ($100,000 × .12)	$12,000
Amortization of discount ($10,000 ÷ 20 semiannual interest periods) × 2 periods	1,000
Interest expense or income	$13,000

Half these amounts are recognized in each of the two interest payment periods during a year. Although the effective-interest method of amortization usually is required for amortizing discounts and premiums, the straight-line method is acceptable where it does not depart materially from the effective-interest method and where transactions are between parent and subsidiary companies or between subsidiaries of a common parent.

Entries by the Debtor. Special Foods records the issuance of the bonds on January 1 at a discount of $10,000. Interest expense is recognized on July 1, when the first semiannual interest payment is made, and on December 31, when interest is accrued for the second half of the year. The amortization of the bond discount causes interest expense to be greater than the cash interest payment and causes the balance of the discount to decrease. The following entries related to the bonds are recorded by Special Foods during 20X1:

January 1, 20X1		
(3) Cash	90,000	
Discount on Bonds Payable	10,000	
Bonds Payable		100,000
Issue bonds to Peerless Products.		
July 1, 20X1		
(4) Interest Expense	6,500	
Discount on Bonds Payable		500
Cash		6,000
Semiannual payment of interest.		

December 31, 20X1

(5) Interest Expense   6,500
          Discount on Bonds Payable   500
          Interest Payable   6,000
     Accrue interest expense at year-end.

Entries by the Bond Investor. Peerless Products records the purchase of the bonds and the interest income derived from the bonds during 20X1 with the following entries:

January 1, 20X1

(6) Investment in Special Foods Bonds   90,000
          Cash   90,000
     Purchase of bonds from Special Foods.

July 1, 20X1

(7) Cash   6,000
          Investment in Special Foods Bonds   500
          Interest Income   6,500
     Receive interest on bond investment.

December 31, 20X1

(8) Interest Receivable   6,000
     Investment in Special Foods Bonds   500
          Interest Income   6,500
     Accrue interest income at year-end.

The amortization of the discount by Peerless increases interest income to an amount greater than the cash interest payment and causes the balance of the bond investment account to increase.

Elimination Entries at Year-End. The December 31, 20X1, bond-related amounts taken from the books of Peerless Products and Special Foods, and the appropriate consolidated amounts, are as follows:

Item	Peerless Products	Special Foods	Unadjusted Totals	Consolidated Amounts
Bonds Payable	-0-	$(100,000)	$(100,000)	-0-
Discount on Bonds Payable	-0-	9,000	9,000	-0-
Interest Payable	-0-	(6,000)	(6,000)	-0-
Investment in Bonds	$91,000	-0-	91,000	-0-
Interest Receivable	6,000	-0-	6,000	-0-
Interest Expense	-0-	$13,000	$13,000	-0-
Interest Income	$(13,000)	-0-	(13,000)	-0-

All account balances relating to the intercorporate bond holdings must be eliminated in the preparation of consolidated financial statements. Toward that end, the consolidation workpaper prepared on December 31, 20X1, includes the following eliminating entries related to the intercompany bond holdings:

E(9) Bonds Payable   100,000
          Investment in Special Foods Bonds   91,000
          Discount on Bonds Payable   9,000
     Eliminate intercorporate bond holdings.

E(10)	Interest Income	13,000	
	Interest Expense		13,000
	Eliminate intercompany interest.		
E(11)	Interest Payable	6,000	
	Interest Receivable		6,000
	Eliminate intercompany interest receivable/payable.		

Entry E(9) eliminates the bonds payable and associated discount against the investment in bonds. The book value of the bond liability on Special Foods' books and the investment in bonds on Peerless's books will be the same so long as both companies amortize the discount in the same way.

Entry E(10) eliminates the bond interest income recognized by Peerless during 20X1 against the bond interest expense recognized by Special Foods. Because the interest for the second half of 20X1 was accrued and not paid, an intercompany receivable/payable exists at the end of the year. Entry E(11) eliminates the interest receivable against the interest payable.

Consolidation at the end of 20X2 requires elimination entries similar to those at the end of 20X1. Because $1,000 of the discount is amortized each year, the bond investment balance on Peerless's books increases to $92,000 ($90,000 + $1,000 + $1,000). Similarly, the bond discount on Special Foods' books decreases to $8,000, resulting in an effective bond liability of $92,000. The consolidation elimination entries related to the bonds at the end of 20X2 are as follows:

E(12)	Bonds Payable	100,000	
	Investment in Special Foods Bonds		92,000
	Discount on Bonds Payable		8,000
	Eliminate intercorporate bond holdings.		
E(13)	Interest Income	13,000	
	Interest Expense		13,000
	Eliminate intercompany interest.		
E(14)	Interest Payable	6,000	
	Interest Receivable		6,000
	Eliminate intercompany interest receivable/payable.		

Bonds of Affiliate Purchased from a Nonaffiliate

A more complex situation occurs when bonds that were issued to an unrelated party are acquired later by an affiliate of the issuer. From the viewpoint of the consolidated entity, an acquisition of an affiliate's bonds retires the bonds at the time they are purchased. The bonds no longer are held outside the consolidated entity once they are purchased by another company within the consolidated entity, and they must be treated as if repurchased by the debtor. Acquisition of the bonds of an affiliate by another company within the consolidated entity is referred to as *constructive retirement.* Although the bonds actually are not retired, they are treated as if they were retired in preparing consolidated financial statements.

When a constructive retirement occurs, the consolidated income statement for the period reports a gain or loss on debt retirement based on the difference between the carrying value of the bonds on the books of the debtor and the purchase price paid by the affiliate in acquiring the bonds. Neither the bonds payable nor the purchaser's investment in the bonds is reported in the consolidated balance sheet because the bonds no longer are considered outstanding.

Purchase at Book Value

In the event that a company purchases the debt of an affiliate from an unrelated party at a price equal to the liability reported by the debtor, the elimination entries required in preparing the consolidated financial statements are identical to those used in eliminating a direct intercorporate debt transfer. In this case, the total of the bond liability and the related premium or discount reported by the debtor will equal the balance in the investment account shown by the bondholder, and the interest income reported by the bondholder each period will equal the interest expense reported by the debtor. All these amounts need to be eliminated to avoid misstating the accounts in the consolidated financial statements.

Purchase at an Amount Less than Book Value

Continuing movement in the level of interest rates and the volatility of other factors influencing the securities markets make it unlikely that a company's bonds will sell after issuance at a price identical to their book value. When the price paid to acquire the bonds of an affiliate differs from the liability reported by the debtor, a gain or loss is reported in the consolidated income statement in the period of constructive retirement. In addition, the bond interest income and interest expense reported by the two affiliates subsequent to the purchase must be eliminated in preparing consolidated statements. Interest income reported by the investing affiliate and interest expense reported by the debtor are not equal in this case because of the different bond carrying amounts on the books of the two companies. The difference in the bond carrying amounts is reflected in the amortization of the discount or premium and, in turn, causes interest income and expense to differ.

As an example of consolidation following the purchase of an affiliate's bonds at less than book value, assume Peerless Products Corporation purchases 80 percent of the common stock of Special Foods Inc. on December 31, 20X0, for its underlying book value of $240,000. In addition, the following conditions occur:

1. On January 1, 20X1, Special Foods issues 10-year, 12 percent bonds payable with a par value of $100,000; the bonds are issued at 102. The bonds are purchased from Special Foods by Nonaffiliated Corporation.
2. The bonds pay interest on June 30 and December 31.
3. Both Peerless Products and Special Foods amortize bond discount and premium using the straight-line method.
4. On December 31, 20X1, Peerless Products purchases the bonds from Nonaffiliated for $91,000.
5. Special Foods reports net income of $50,000 for 20X1 and $75,000 for 20X2. Special Foods declares dividends of $30,000 in 20X1 and $40,000 in 20X2.
6. Peerless earns $140,000 in 20X1 and $160,000 in 20X2 from its own separate operations. Peerless declares dividends of $60,000 in both 20X1 and 20X2.

The bond transactions of Special Foods and Peerless appear as follows:

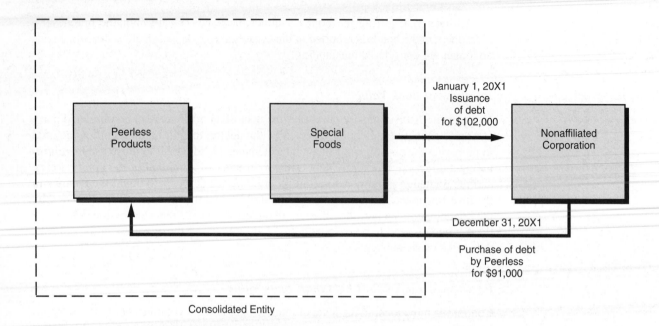

Consolidated Entity

Bond Liability Entries—20X1.   Special Foods records the following entries related to its bonds during 20X1:

January 1, 20X1			
(15)	Cash	102,000	
	Bonds Payable		100,000
	Premium on Bonds Payable		2,000
	Sale of bonds to Nonaffiliated.		

June 30, 20X1			
(16)	Interest Expense	5,900	
	Premium on Bonds Payable	100	
	Cash		6,000
	Semiannual payment of interest:		
	$5,900 = $6,000 − $100		
	$100 = $2,000 ÷ 20 interest periods		
	$6,000 = $100,000 × .12 × 6/12		

December 31, 20X1			
(17)	Interest Expense	5,900	
	Premium on Bonds Payable	100	
	Cash		6,000
	Semiannual payment of interest.		

Entry (15) records the issuance of the bonds to Nonaffiliated Corporation for $102,000. Entries (16) and (17) record the payment of interest and the amortization of the bond premium at each of the two interest payment dates during 20X1. Total interest expense for 20X1 is $11,800 ($5,900 × 2), and the book value of the bonds on December 31, 20X1, is as follows:

Book value of bonds at issuance	$102,000
Amortization of premium, 20X1	(200)
Book value of bonds, December 31, 20X1	$101,800

Bond Investment Entries—20X1. Peerless Products records the purchase of Special Foods' bonds from Nonaffiliated with the following entry:

December 31, 20X1			
(18)	Investment in Special Foods Bonds	91,000	
	Cash		91,000
	Purchase of Special Foods bonds from Nonaffiliated Corporation.		

This entry is the same as if the bonds purchased were those of an unrelated company. The bonds are purchased by Peerless at the very end of the year, after payment of the interest to Nonaffiliated; therefore, Peerless earns no interest on the bonds during 20X1, nor is there any interest accrued on the bonds at the date of purchase.

Computation of Gain on Constructive Retirement of Bonds. From a consolidated viewpoint, the purchase of Special Foods' bonds by Peerless is considered a retirement of the bonds by the consolidated entity. Therefore, in the preparation of consolidated financial statements, a gain or loss must be recognized for the difference between the book value of the bonds on the date of repurchase and the amount paid by the consolidated entity in reacquiring the bonds:

Book value of Special Foods' bonds, December 31, 20X1	$101,800
Price paid by Peerless to purchase bonds	(91,000)
Gain on constructive retirement of bonds	$ 10,800

This gain is included in the consolidated income statement as a gain on the retirement of bonds. Gains and losses on the retirement of debt, if material, are required to be treated as extraordinary by **FASB Statement No. 4,** "Reporting Gains and Losses from Extinguishment of Debt."

Assignment of Gain on Constructive Retirement. Four approaches have been used in practice for assigning the gain or loss on the constructive retirement of the bonds of an affiliate to the shareholders of the participating companies:

1. To the affiliate issuing the bonds.
2. To the affiliate purchasing the bonds.
3. To the parent company.
4. To the issuing and purchasing companies based on the difference between the carrying amounts of the bonds on their books at the date of purchase and the par value of the bonds.

There do not seem to be compelling reasons for choosing one of these methods over the others, and in practice the choice often is based on expediency and lack of materiality. The FASB's approach is to assign the gain or loss to the issuing company. In previous chapters, gains and losses on intercompany transactions were viewed as accruing to the shareholders of the selling affiliate. When this approach is applied in the case of intercorporate debt transactions, gains and losses arising from the intercompany debt transactions are viewed as accruing to the shareholders of the selling or issuing affiliate. In effect, the purchasing affiliate is viewed as acting on behalf of the issuing affiliate by acquiring the bonds.

An important difference exists between the intercompany gains and losses discussed in previous chapters and the gains and losses arising from intercorporate debt transactions. Gains and losses from intercorporate transfers of assets are recognized by the individual affiliates and are eliminated in consolidation. Gains and losses from intercorporate debt transactions are not recognized by the individual affiliates, but must be included in consolidation.

When the subsidiary is the issuing affiliate, the gain or loss on constructive retirement of the bonds is viewed as accruing to the shareholders of the subsidiary. Thus, the gain or loss is apportioned between consolidated net income and the noncontrolling interest based on the relative ownership interests in the common stock. If the parent is the issuing affiliate, the entire gain or loss on the constructive retirement accrues to the controlling interest, and none is apportioned to the noncontrolling interest.

As a result of the interest income and expense entries recorded annually by the companies involved, the constructive gain or loss is recognized over the remaining term of the bond issue; accordingly, the total amount of the unrecognized gain or loss decreases each period and is fully amortized at the time the bond matures. Thus, no permanent gain or loss is assigned to the shareholders of the debtor company.

Basic Equity-Method Entries—20X1.   In addition to recording the bond investment with entry (18), Peerless records the following basic equity-method entries during 20X1 to account for its investment in Special Foods stock:

(19)	Investment in Special Foods Stock	40,000	
	Income from Subsidiary		40,000
	Record equity-method income:		
	$50,000 × .80		
(20)	Cash	24,000	
	Investment in Special Foods Stock		24,000
	Record dividends from Special Foods:		
	$30,000 × .80		

These entries result in a balance of $256,000 in the investment account at the end of 20X1.

Consolidation Workpaper—20X1.   The December 31, 20X1, workpaper to prepare consolidated financial statements for Peerless Products and Special Foods is presented in Figure 8–2. The following eliminating entries are included in the workpaper:

E(21)	Income from Subsidiary	40,000	
	Dividends Declared		24,000
	Investment in Special Foods Stock		16,000
	Eliminate income from subsidiary.		
E(22)	Income to Noncontrolling Interest	12,160	
	Dividends Declared		6,000
	Noncontrolling Interest		6,160
	Assign income to noncontrolling interest:		
	$12,160 = ($50,000 + $10,800) × .20		
E(23)	Common Stock—Special Foods	200,000	
	Retained Earnings, January 1	100,000	
	Investment in Special Foods Stock		240,000
	Noncontrolling Interest		60,000
	Eliminate beginning investment balance.		

FIGURE 8–2 **December 31, 20X1, Consolidation Workpaper; Repurchase of Bonds at Less than Book Value**

Item	Peerless Products	Special Foods	Eliminations Debit		Eliminations Credit		Consolidated
Sales	400,000	200,000					600,000
Income from Subsidiary	40,000		(21)	40,000			
Gain on Bond Retirement					(24)	10,800	10,800
Credits	440,000	200,000					610,800
Cost of Goods Sold	170,000	115,000					285,000
Depreciation and Amortization	50,000	20,000					70,000
Other Expenses	20,000	3,200					23,200
Interest Expense	20,000	11,800					31,800
Debits	(260,000)	(150,000)					(410,000)
							200,800
Income to Noncontrolling Interest			(22)	12,160			(12,160)
Net Income, carry forward	180,000	50,000		52,160		10,800	188,640
Retained Earnings, January 1	300,000	100,000	(23)	100,000			300,000
Net Income, from above	180,000	50,000		52,160		10,800	188,640
	480,000	150,000					488,640
Dividends Declared	(60,000)	(30,000)			(21)	24,000	
					(22)	6,000	(60,000)
Retained Earnings, December 31, carry forward	420,000	120,000		152,160		40,800	428,640
Cash	173,000	76,800					249,800
Accounts Receivable	75,000	50,000					125,000
Inventory	100,000	75,000					175,000
Land	175,000	40,000					215,000
Buildings and Equipment	800,000	600,000					1,400,000
Investment in Special Foods Bonds	91,000				(24)	91,000	
Investment in Special Foods Stock	256,000				(21)	16,000	
					(23)	240,000	
Debits	1,670,000	841,800					2,164,800
Accumulated Depreciation	450,000	320,000					770,000
Accounts Payable	100,000	100,000					200,000
Bonds Payable	200,000	100,000	(24)	100,000			200,000
Premium on Bonds Payable		1,800	(24)	1,800			
Common Stock	500,000	200,000	(23)	200,000			500,000
Retained Earnings, from above	420,000	120,000		152,160		40,800	428,640
Noncontrolling Interest					(22)	6,160	
					(23)	60,000	66,160
Credits	1,670,000	841,800		453,960		453,960	2,164,800

Elimination entries:

(21) Eliminate income from subsidiary.

(22) Assign income to noncontrolling interest.

(23) Eliminate beginning investment balance.

(24) Eliminate intercompany bond holdings.

E(24)	Bonds Payable	100,000	
	Premium on Bonds Payable	1,800	
	Investment in Special Foods Bonds		91,000
	Gain on Bond Retirement		10,800
	Eliminate intercorporate bond holdings.		

Workpaper entry E(21) eliminates the changes in the investment account during 20X1, the parent's share of the subsidiary's net income, and the dividends recognized by Peerless during the year. Income of $12,160 is assigned to the noncontrolling interest in entry E(22), computed as follows:

Net income of Special Foods	$50,000
Gain on constructive retirement of bonds	10,800
Realized net income of Special Foods	$60,800
Noncontrolling stockholders' share	× .20
Noncontrolling interest's share of income	$12,160

The gain on the constructive retirement of the bonds is attributed to the shareholders of the issuing company, Special Foods. Therefore, a proportionate share of the gain ($10,800 × .20) is assigned to the noncontrolling interest along with a proportionate share of Special Foods' reported net income. If Peerless had been the issuing affiliate, all the gain would be included in consolidated net income and none would be allocated to the noncontrolling interest.

Entry E(22) also eliminates the noncontrolling interest's share of Special Foods' dividends declared during 20X1 and recognizes the increase in the noncontrolling interest's claim on the net assets of the subsidiary. Entry E(23) eliminates Peerless's investment account and the stockholders' equity balances of Special Foods at the beginning of the year, and establishes in the workpaper the amount of the noncontrolling interest at the beginning of the year.

The final entry in the workpaper, E(24), eliminates the intercompany bond holdings and recognizes the gain on constructive retirement of the bonds. The appropriate consolidated balances and the amounts recorded on the books of Peerless and Special Foods are as follows:

Item	Peerless Products	Special Foods	Unadjusted Totals	Consolidated Amounts
Bonds Payable	-0-	$(100,000)	$(100,000)	-0-
Premium on Bonds Payable	-0-	(1,800)	(1,800)	-0-
Investment in Bonds	$91,000	-0-	91,000	-0-
Interest Expense	-0-	$ 11,800	$ 11,800	$11,800
Interest Income	-0-	-0-	-0-	-0-
Gain on Bond Retirement	-0-	-0-	-0-	(10,800)

Consolidation Elimination Entries—20X2.   Elimination entries needed in the consolidation workpaper at the end of 20X2 are as follows:

E(66)	Dividend Income	32,000	
	Dividends Declared		32,000
	Eliminate dividend income from subsidiary: $40,000 × .80		
E(67)	Income to Noncontrolling Interest	14,760	
	Dividends Declared		8,000
	Noncontrolling Interest		6,760
	Assign income to noncontrolling interest:		
	$14,760 = ($75,000 − $1,200) × .20		
E(68)	Common Stock—Special Foods	200,000	
	Retained Earnings, January 1	100,000	
	Investment in Special Foods Stock		240,000
	Noncontrolling Interest		60,000
	Eliminate investment balance at date of acquisition.		
E(69)	Retained Earnings, January 1	4,000	
	Noncontrolling Interest		4,000
	Assign undistributed prior earnings of subsidiary to		
	noncontrolling interest: $20,000 × .20		
E(70)	Bonds Payable	100,000	
	Premium on Bonds Payable	1,600	
	Interest Income	13,000	
	Investment in Special Foods Bonds		92,000
	Interest Expense		11,800
	Retained Earnings, January 1		8,640
	Noncontrolling Interest		2,160
	Eliminate intercorporate bond holdings:		
	$1,600 = $2,000 − $200 − $200		
	$13,000 = ($100,000 × .12) + $1,000		
	$92,000 = $91,000 + $1,000		
	$11,800 = ($100,000 × .12) − $200		
	$8,640 = $10,800 × .80		
	$2,160 = $10,800 × .20		

Questions

Q8–1   When is a gain or loss on bond retirement included in the consolidated income statement?

Q8–2   What is meant by a constructive bond retirement in a multicorporate setting? How does a constructive bond retirement differ from an actual bond retirement?

Q8–3   When a bond issue has been placed directly with an affiliate, what account balances will be stated incorrectly in the consolidated statements if the intercompany bond ownership is not eliminated in preparing the consolidation workpaper?

Q8–4   When bonds of an affiliate are purchased from a nonaffiliate during the period, what balances will be stated incorrectly in the consolidated financial statements if the intercompany bond ownership is not eliminated in preparing the consolidation workpaper?

Q8–5   For a multicorporate entity, how is the recognition of gains or losses on bond retirement changed when emphasis is placed on the economic entity rather than the legal entity?

Q8–6   When a parent company sells land to a subsidiary at more than book value, the consolidation eliminating entries at the end of the period include a debit to the gain on the sale of land. When a parent purchases the bonds of a subsidiary from a nonaffiliate at less than book value, the eliminating entries at the end of the period contain a credit to a gain on bond retirement. Why are these two situations not handled in the same manner in the consolidation workpaper?

Q8–7   What is the effect on consolidated net income of eliminating intercompany interest income and interest expense when there has been a direct sale of bonds to an affiliate? Why?

Q8–8   What is the effect on consolidated net income of eliminating intercompany interest income and interest expense when a loss on bond retirement has been reported in a prior year's consolidated financial statements as a result of a constructive retirement of an affiliate's bonds? Why?

Q8–9   If the bonds of an affiliate are purchased from a nonaffiliate at the beginning of the current year, how can the amount of the gain or loss on constructive retirement be computed by looking at the year-end trial balances of the two companies?

Q8–10 When the parent company purchases the bonds of a subsidiary from a nonaffiliate for more than book value, what income statement accounts will be affected in preparing consolidated financial statements? What will be the effect of the purchase upon consolidated net income? Explain.

Q8–11 When a subsidiary purchases the bonds of its parent from a nonaffiliate for less than book value, what will be the effect on consolidated net income?

Q8–12 How is the amount of income assigned to the noncontrolling interest affected by the direct placement of a subsidiary's bonds with the parent company?

Q8–13 How is the amount of income assigned to the noncontrolling interest affected when bonds of the subsidiary are purchased by the parent from an unaffiliated company for less than book value?

Q8–14 How would the relationship between interest income recorded by a subsidiary and interest expense recorded by the parent be expected to change when a direct placement of the parent's bonds with the subsidiary is compared with a constructive retirement in which the subsidiary purchases the bonds of the parent from a nonaffiliate?

Q8–15 A subsidiary purchased bonds of the parent company from a nonaffiliate in the preceding period, and a gain on bond retirement was reported in the consolidated income statement as a result of the purchase. What effect will that event have on the amount of consolidated net income reported in the current period?

Q8–16 A parent company purchased bonds of its subsidiary from a nonaffiliate in the preceding year, and a loss on bond retirement was reported in the consolidated income statement. How will income assigned to the noncontrolling interest be affected in the year following the constructive retirement?

Q8–17 A parent purchases bonds of a subsidiary directly from the subsidiary. The parent later sells the bonds to a nonaffiliate. From a consolidated viewpoint, what occurs when the parent sells the bonds? Is a gain or loss reported in the consolidated income statement when the parent sells the bonds? Why?

Q8–18 Shortly after a parent company purchased its subsidiary's bonds from a nonaffiliate, the subsidiary retired the entire issue. How is the gain or loss on bond retirement that is reported by the subsidiary treated for consolidation purposes?

Q8–19* Describe the consolidation procedures needed to deal with intercorporate leasing arrangements for the following types of leases: (*a*) operating, (*b*) direct financing, and (*c*) sales-type.

Cases

C8–1   **Recognition of Retirement Gains and Losses**
Bradley Corporation sold bonds to Flood Company in 20X2 at 90. At the end of 20X4, Century Corporation purchased the bonds from Flood Company at 105. Bradley Corporation then retired the full bond issue on December 31, 20X7, at 101. Century Corporation holds 80 percent of the voting stock of Bradley Corporation. Neither Century Corporation nor Bradley Corporation owns stock of Flood Company.

---

*Indicates that the item relates to "Additional Considerations."

Required

a. Indicate how each of the three bond transactions should be recorded by the companies involved.

b. Indicate when, if at all, the consolidated entity headed by Century Corporation should recognize a gain or loss on bond retirement and indicate whether a gain or a loss should be recognized.

c. Will income assigned to the noncontrolling shareholders of Bradley Corporation be affected by the bond transactions? If so, in which years?

C8–2   Interest Income and Expense

The controller of Snerd Corporation is experiencing difficulty in explaining the impact of several of the company's intercorporate bond transactions.

Required

a. Snerd receives interest payments in excess of the amount of interest income it records on its investment in Snort bonds. Did Snerd purchase the bonds at par value, at a premium, or at a discount? How can you tell?

b. The 20X3 consolidated income statement reported a gain on the retirement of a subsidiary's bonds. If Snerd purchased the bonds from a nonaffiliate at par value:

   (1) Were the bonds of the subsidiary originally sold at a premium or a discount? How can you tell?

   (2) Will the annual interest payments received by Snerd be greater or less than the interest expense recorded by the subsidiary? Explain.

   (3) How is the difference between the interest income recorded by Snerd and the interest expense recorded by the subsidiary treated in preparing consolidated financial statements at the end of each period?

C8–3   Intercompany Debt

Intercompany debt, both long–term and short–term, arises frequently. In some cases intercorporate borrowings may arise because one affiliate can borrow at a cheaper rate than others, and lending to other affiliates may reduce the overall cost of borrowing. In other cases, intercompany receivables/payables arise because of intercompany sales of goods or services or other types of intercompany transactions.

Required

a. During the first quarter of 1996, Associates First Capital Corporation incurred a $1.75 billion intercompany debt to Ford FSG. How did this debt arise? Although Ford and Associates First Capital were affiliates in 1996, how has their relationship changed?

b. How does Campbell Soup Company finance its foreign operations?

c. What major problem might arise with intercompany debt between a domestic parent and a foreign subsidiary or between subsidiaries in different countries? How has Hershey Foods dealt with this problem?

d. Did the intercompany loans of Hershey Foods arise because of direct loans or because of intercompany sales of goods and services on credit?

Exercises

E8–1   Bond Sale from Parent to Subsidiary

Lamar Corporation owns 60 percent of the voting shares of Humbolt Corporation. On January 1, 20X2, Lamar Corporation sold $150,000 par value 6 percent first mortgage bonds to Humbolt for $156,000. The bonds mature in 10 years and pay interest seminannually on January 1 and July 1.

Required

a. Prepare the journal entries for 20X2 for Humbolt Corporation related to its ownership of Lamar's bonds.

b. Prepare the journal entries for 20X2 for Lamar Corporation related to the bonds.

c. Prepare the workpaper eliminating entries needed on December 31, 20X2, to remove the effects of the intercorporate ownership of bonds.

E8–2   Computation of Transfer Price

Nettle Corporation sold $100,000 par value, 10–year, first mortgage bonds to Timberline Corporation on January 1, 20X5. The bonds, which bear a nominal interest rate of 12 percent, pay interest semiannually on January 1 and July 1. The entry to record interest income by Timberline Corporation on December 31, 20X7, was as follows:

Interest Receivable	6,000	
Interest Income		5,750
Investment in Nettle Corporation Bonds		250

Timberline Corporation owns 65 percent of the voting stock of Nettle Corporation, and consolidated statements are prepared on December 31, 20X7.

Required

a. What was the original purchase price of the bonds to Timberline Corporation?

b. What is the balance in Timberline's bond investment account on December 31, 20X7?

c. Give the workpaper eliminating entry or entries needed to remove the effects of the intercompany ownership of bonds in preparing consolidated financial statements for 20X7.

E8–3   Bond Sale at Discount

Wood Corporation owns 70 percent of the voting shares of Carter Company. On January 1, 20X3, Carter Company sold bonds with a par value of $600,000 at 98. Wood Corporation purchased $400,000 par value of the bonds and the remainder was sold to nonaffiliates. The bonds mature in five years and pay an annual interest rate of 8 percent. Interest is paid semiannually on January 1 and July 1.

Required

a. What amount of interest expense should be reported in the 20X4 consolidated income statement?

b. Give the journal entries recorded by Wood Corporation during 20X4 with regard to its investment in Carter Company bonds.

c. Give all workpaper eliminating entries needed to remove the effects of the intercorporate bond ownership in preparing consolidated financial statements for 20X4.

E8–4   Evaluation of Intercorporate Bond Holdings

Stellar Corporation purchased bonds of its subsidiary from a nonaffiliate during 20X6. Although Stellar purchased the bonds at par value, a loss on bond retirement is reported in the 20X6 consolidated income statement as a result of the purchase.

Required

a. Were the bonds originally sold by the subsidiary at a premium or a discount? Explain.

b. Will the annual interest payments received by Stellar be greater or less than the interest expense recorded by the subsidiary each period? Explain.

c. As a result of the entry recorded at December 31, 20X7, to eliminate the effects of the intercompany bond holding, will consolidated net income be increased or decreased? Explain.

E8–5   Multiple Choice Questions

Select the correct answer for each of the following questions.

1. [AICPA Adapted] Wagner, a holder of a $1,000,000 Palmer Inc. bond, collected the interest due on March 31, 20X8, and then sold the bond to Seal Inc. for $975,000. On that date, Palmer, a 75

percent owner of Seal, had a $1,075,000 carrying amount for this bond. What was the effect of Seal's purchase of Palmer's bond on the retained earnings and minority interest amounts reported in Palmer's March 31, 20X8, consolidated balance sheet?

Retained Earnings	Minority Interest
a. $100,000 increase	No effect
b. $75,000 increase	$25,000 increase
c. No effect	$25,000 increase
d. No effect	$100,000 increase

2. [AICPA Adapted] P Company purchased term bonds at a premium on the open market. These bonds represented 20 percent of the outstanding class of bonds issued at a discount by S Company, P's wholly owned subsidiary. P intends to hold the bonds to maturity. In a consolidated balance sheet, the difference between the bond carrying amounts of the two companies would be:

   a. Included as a decrease to retained earnings.

   b. Included as an increase in retained earnings.

   c. Reported as a deferred debit to be amortized over the remaining life of the bonds.

   d. Reported as a deferred credit to be amortized over the remaining life of the bonds.

This information relates to questions 3–6.

Kruse Corporation holds 60 percent of the voting common shares of Gary's Ice Cream Parlors. On January 1, 20X6, Gary's Ice Cream Parlors purchased $50,000 par value, 10 percent, first mortgage bonds of Kruse Corporation from Cane Corporation for $58,000. Kruse Corporation originally issued the bonds to Cane Corporation on January 1, 20X4, for $53,000. The bonds have a 10-year maturity from the date of issue.

Gary's Ice Cream Parlors reported net income of $20,000 for 20X6, and Kruse Corporation reported income (excluding income from ownership of Gary's Ice Cream Parlors stock) of $40,000.

3. What amount of interest expense is recorded annually by Kruse Corporation?

   a. $4,000.

   b. $4,700.

   c. $5,000.

   d. $10,000.

4. What amount of interest income is recorded by Gary's Ice Cream Parlors for 20X6?

   a. $4,000.

   b. $5,000.

   c. $9,000.

   d. $10,000.

5. What gain or loss on the retirement of bonds should be reported in the 20X6 consolidated income statement?

   a. $2,400 gain.

   b. $5,600 gain.

   c. $5,600 loss.

   d. $8,000 loss.

6. What amount of consolidated net income should be reported for 20X6?

   a. $47,100.

   b. $52,000.

   c. $54,400.

   d. $60,000.

E8–6 **Multiple-Choice Questions**

Parent Company paid a nonaffiliate $95,000 in 20X4 to purchase bonds that are recorded as a liability of $105,000 on the books of Subsidiary Company. Parent Company owns 60 percent of the shares of Subsidiary Company stock. The bonds have five years remaining to maturity from the date of purchase by Parent Company. Subsidiary Company reports net income of $40,000 in 20X4 and $60,000 in 20X5. Parent Company reports income, excluding investment income from Subsidiary Company stock, of $200,000 in both 20X4 and 20X5.

Required

Select the correct answer for each of the following questions.

1. If the bond purchase occurred on December 31, 20X4, what amount of consolidated net income should be reported for 20X4?
    a. $228,800.
    b. $230,000.
    c. $232,000.
    d. $234,000.

2. If the bond purchase occurred on January 1, 20X4, what amount of consolidated net income should be reported for 20X4?
    a. $228,800.
    b. $230,000.
    c. $232,000.
    d. $234,000.

3. What amount of consolidated net income should be reported for 20X5 if the bond purchase occurred on January 1, 20X4?
    a. $234,000.
    b. $234,800.
    c. $237,200.
    d. $238.000.

4. What amount of consolidated net income should be reported for 20X5 if the bond purchase occurred on December 31, 20X4?
    a. $234,000.
    b. $234,800.
    c. $237,200.
    d. $238,000.

5. Suppose the bond liability had been recorded on the books of Parent Company and Subsidiary Company purchased the bonds under the conditions indicated. What amount of consolidated net income would be reported for 20X4 if the purchase occurred on December 31, 20X4?
    a. $228,800.
    b. $230,000.
    c. $232,000.
    d. $234,000.

6. Suppose the bond liability had been recorded on the books of Parent Company and Subsidiary Company purchased the bonds under the conditions indicated. What amount of consolidated net income would be reported for 20X4 if the purchase occurred on January 1, 20X4?
    a. $228,800.
    b. $230,000.
    c. $232,000.
    d. $234,000.

E8–7   **Multiple-Choice Questions**

On January 1, 20X4, Passive Heating Corporation paid $104,000 for $100,000 par value, 9 percent bonds of Solar Energy Corporation. Solar Energy Corporation had issued $300,000 of the 10-year bonds on January 1, 20X2, for $360,000. Passive previously had purchased 80 percent of the common stock of Solar on January 1, 20X1, at underlying book value.

Passive Heating Corporation reported operating income (excluding income from subsidiary) of $50,000, and Solar Energy Corporation reported net income of $30,000 for 20X4.

Required

Select the correct answer for each of the following questions.

1. What amount of interest expense should be included in the 20X4 consolidated income statement?
   a. $14,000.
   b. $18,000.
   c. $21,000.
   d. $27,000.

2. What amount of gain or loss on bond retirement should be included in the 20X4 consolidated income statement?
   a. $4,000 gain.
   b. $4,000 loss.
   c. $12,000 gain.
   d. $16,000 loss.

3. Income assigned to the noncontrolling interest in the 20X4 consolidated income statement should be:
   a. $6,000.
   b. $8,100.
   c. $8,400.
   d. $16,000.

E8–8   **Constructive Retirement at End of Year**

Able Company issued $600,000 of 9 percent first mortgage bonds on January 1, 20X1, at 103. The bonds mature in 20 years and pay interest semiannually on January 1 and July 1. Prime Corporation purchased $400,000 of Able's bonds from the original purchaser on December 31, 20X5, for $397,000. Prime Corporation owns 60 percent of Able's voting common stock.

Required

a. Prepare the workpaper elimination entry or entries needed to remove the effects of the intercorporate bond ownership in preparing consolidated financial statements for 20X5.

b. Prepare the workpaper elimination entry or entries needed to remove the effects of the intercorporate bond ownership in preparing consolidated financial statements for 20X6.

E8–9   **Constructive Retirement at Beginning of Year**

Able Company issued $600,000 of 9 percent first mortgage bonds on January 1, 20X1, at 103. The bonds mature in 20 years and pay interest semiannually on January 1 and July 1. Prime Corporation purchased $400,000 of Able's bonds from the original purchaser on January 1, 20X5, for $396,800. Prime Corporation owns 60 percent of Able's voting common stock.

Required

a. Prepare the workpaper elimination entry or entries needed to remove the effects of the intercorporate bond ownership in preparing consolidated financial statements for 20X5.

b. Prepare the workpaper elimination entry or entries needed to remove the effects of the intercorporate bond ownership in preparing consolidated financial statements for 20X6.

E–10   **Retirement of Bonds Sold at a Discount**

Farley Corporation owns 70 percent of the stock of Snowball Enterprises. On January 1, 20X1, Farley Corporation sold $1,000,000 par value 7 percent, 20-year, first mortgage bonds to Kling Corporation at 97. On January 1, 20X8, Snowball Enterprises purchased $300,000 par value of the Farley Corporation bonds directly from Kling Corporation for $296,880.

Required

Prepare the eliminating entry needed at December 31, 20X8, to remove the effects of the intercorporate bond ownership in preparing consolidated financial statements.

E8–11   **Loss on Constructive Retirement**

Apple Corporation holds 60 percent of the voting shares of Shortway Publishing Company. Apple Corporation issued $500,000 of 10 percent bonds with a 10-year maturity on January 1, 20X2, at 90. On January 1, 20X8, Shortway Publishing Company purchased $100,000 of the Apple Corporation bonds for $108,000. Partial trial balances for the two companies on December 31, 20X8, are as follows:

	Apple Corporation	Shortway Publishing Company
Investment in Shortway Publishing Company Stock	$141,000	
Investment in Apple Corporation Bonds		$106,000
Bonds Payable	500,000	
Discount on Bonds Payable	15,000	
Interest Expense	55,000	
Interest Income		8,000
Interest Payable	25,000	
Interest Receivable		5,000

Required

Prepare the workpaper eliminating entry or entries needed on December 31, 20X8, to remove the effects of the intercorporate bond ownership in preparing consolidated financial statements.

E8–12   **Determining the Amount of Retirement Gain or Loss**

Downlink Corporation is 95 percent owned by Online Enterprises. On January 1, 20X1, Downlink Corporation issued $200,000 of five-year bonds at 115. Annual interest of 12 percent is paid semiannually on January 1 and July 1. Online Enterprises purchased $100,000 of the bonds on August 31, 20X3, at par value. The following balances are taken from the separate 20X3 financial statements of the two companies:

	Online Enterprises	Downlink Corporation
Investment in Downlink Corporation Bonds	$100,000	
Interest Income	4,000	
Interest Receivable	6,000	
Bonds Payable		$200,000
Bond Premium		12,000
Interest Expense		18,000
Interest Payable		12,000

Required

a. Compute the amount of interest expense that should be reported in the consolidated income statement for 20X3.

b. Compute the gain or loss on constructive bond retirement that should be reported in the 20X3 consolidated income statement.

c. Prepare the consolidation workpaper eliminating entry or entries as of December 31, 20X3, to remove the effects of the intercorporate bond ownership.

E8–13   Evaluation of Bond Retirement

Bundle Company issued $500,000 par value 10-year bonds at 104 on January 1, 20X3, which were purchased by Mega Corporation. The coupon rate on the bonds is 11 percent. Interest payments are made semiannually on July 1 and January 1. On July 1, 20X6, Parent Company purchased $200,000 par value of the bonds from Mega Corporation for $192,200. Parent Company owns 70 percent of the voting shares of Bundle Company.

Required

a. What amount of gain or loss will be reported in Bundle's 20X6 income statement on the retirement of bonds?

b. Will a gain or loss be reported in the 20X6 consolidated financial statements for Parent Company for the constructive retirement of bonds? What amount will be reported?

c. How much will the purchase of the bonds by Parent Company change consolidated net income for 20X6?

d. Prepare the workpaper eliminating entry or entries needed to remove the effects of the intercorporate bond ownership in preparing consolidated financial statements at December 31, 20X6.

e. Prepare the workpaper eliminating entry or entries needed to remove the effects of the intercorporate bond ownership in preparing consolidated financial statements at December 31, 20X7.

f. If Bundle Company reports net income of $50,000 for 20X7, what amount of income will be assigned to the noncontrolling interest in the consolidated income statement?

E8–14   Elimination of Intercorporate Bond Holdings

Stang Corporation issued to Bradley Company $400,000 par value, 10-year bonds with a coupon rate of 12 percent on January 1, 20X5, at 105. The bonds pay interest semiannually on July 1 and January 1. On January 1, 20X8, Purple Corporation purchased $100,000 of the bonds from Bradley for $104,900.

Purple Corporation owns 65 percent of the voting common shares of Stang Corporation and prepares consolidated financial statements.

Required

a. Prepare the workpaper eliminating entry or entries needed to remove the effects of the intercorporate bond ownership in preparing consolidated financial statements for 20X8.

b. Assuming Stang Corporation reports net income of $20,000 for 20X8, compute the amount of income assigned to noncontrolling shareholders in the 20X8 consolidated income statement.

c. Prepare the workpaper eliminating entry or entries needed to remove the effects of the intercorporate bond ownership in preparing consolidated financial statements for 20X9.

E8–15*   Intercorporate Leases

Thomas Company owns 95 percent of the common stock of Bradley Financial Corporation, from which Thomas leases some of the assets it uses in its operations. On November 7, 20X8, Thomas entered into an operating lease with Bradley under which Thomas leases several delivery trucks for $38,000 per year; the lease payments are made at the end of each calendar year. Bradley recognizes $21,000 of depreciation per year on the trucks.

On January 2, 20X9, Thomas leased some heavy-duty lifting equipment from Bradley under a 10-year direct financing lease. The terms of the lease call for Thomas to pay $100,000 on signing the lease and to make payments of $59,612 on December 31 of each year. The present value of the 10 end-of-year lease payments of $59,612 each is $400,000. The equipment has an estimated life of 10 years, with no residual value. An interest rate of 8 percent is implicit in the terms of the lease. The equipment had been purchased by Bradley on December 31, 20X8, for $500,000. Both companies use straight-line depreciation.

Required

a. Present all entries recorded by Thomas during 20X9 with respect to (1) the operating lease and (2) the direct financing lease.

b. Present all entries recorded by Bradley during 20X9 with respect to (1) the operating lease and (2) the direct financing lease.

c. Present all eliminating entries regarding the intercompany leases that should appear in the workpaper to prepare a complete set of consolidated financial statements for 20X9.

Problems

P8–16   **Consolidation Workpaper with Sale of Bonds to Subsidiary**
Porter Company purchased 60 percent ownership of Temple Corporation on January 1, 20X1, at underlying book value. On that date, Porter sold $80,000 par value 8 percent five-year bonds directly to Temple for $82,000. The bonds pay interest annually on December 31. Porter uses the basic equity method in accounting for its ownership of Temple. On December 31, 20X2, the trial balances of the two companies are as follows:

Item	Porter Company Debit	Porter Company Credit	Temple Corporation Debit	Temple Corporation Credit
Cash and Accounts Receivable	$ 80,200		$ 40,000	
Inventory	120,000		65,000	
Buildings and Equipment	500,000		300,000	
Investment in Temple Corporation Stock	102,000			
Investment in Porter Company Bonds			81,200	
Cost of Goods Sold	99,800		61,000	
Depreciation Expense	25,000		15,000	
Interest Expense	6,000		14,000	
Dividends Declared	40,000		10,000	
Accumulated Depreciation		$175,000		$ 75,000
Accounts Payable		68,800		41,200
Bonds Payable		80,000		200,000
Bond Premium		1,200		
Common Stock		200,000		100,000
Retained Earnings		230,000		50,000
Sales		200,000		114,000
Interest Income				6,000
Income from Subsidiary		18,000		
	$973,000	$973,000	$586,200	$586,200

Required

a. Record the journal entry or entries for 20X2 on the books of Porter Company related to its investment in Temple Corporation.

b. Record the journal entry or entries for 20X2 on the books of Porter Company related to its bonds payable.

c. Record the journal entry or entries for 20X2 on the books of Temple Corporation related to its investment in Porter Company Bonds.

d. Prepare the elimination entries needed to complete a consolidated workpaper for 20X2.

e. Prepare a three-part consolidated workpaper for 20X2.

P8–17   Consolidation Workpaper with Sale of Bonds to Parent

Mega Corporation purchased 90 percent of the voting common shares of Tarp Company on January 1, 20X2, at underlying book value. Mega also purchased $100,000 of 6 percent five-year bonds directly from Tarp on January 1, 20X2, for $104,000. The bonds pay interest semiannually on July 1 and January 1. Trial balances of the companies as of December 31, 20X4, are as follows:

Item	Mega Corporation Debit	Mega Corporation Credit	Tarp Company Debit	Tarp Company Credit
Cash and Accounts Receivable	$ 22,000		$ 36,600	
Inventory	165,000		75,000	
Buildings and Equipment	400,000		240,000	
Investment in Tarp Company Stock	121,500			
Investment in Tarp Company Bonds	101,600			
Cost of Goods Sold	86,000		79,800	
Depreciation Expense	20,000		15,000	
Interest Expense	16,000		5,200	
Dividends Declared	30,000		20,000	
Accumulated Depreciation		$140,000		$ 80,000
Accounts Payable		92,400		35,000
Bonds Payable		200,000		100,000
Bond Premium				1,600
Common Stock		120,000		80,000
Retained Earnings		242,000		50,000
Sales		140,000		125,000
Interest Income		5,200		
Income from Subsidiary		22,500		
	$962,100	$962,100	$471,600	$471,600

Required

a. Record the journal entry or entries for 20X4 on the books of Mega Corporation related to its investment in Tarp Company common stock.

b. Record the journal entry or entries for 20X4 on the books of Mega Corporation related to its investment in Tarp Company bonds.

c. Record the journal entry or entries for 20X4 on the books of Tarp Company related to its bonds payable.

d. Prepare the elimination entries needed to complete a consolidated workpaper for 20X4.

e. Prepare a three-part consolidated workpaper for 20X4.

P8-18   Direct Sale of Bonds to Parent

On January 1, 20X1, Elm Corporation paid Morton Advertising $122,000 to acquire 70 percent of the stock of Vincent Company. Elm Corporation also paid $45,000 to acquire $50,000 par value 8 percent 10-year bonds directly from Vincent Company on that date. Interest payments are made on January 1 and July 1. The purchase price of the stock was $45,000 above book value and resulted from an increase in the value of depreciable assets held by Vincent. The assets had an estimated remaining economic life of 15 years on January 1, 20X1.

The trial balances for the two companies as of December 31, 20X3, are as follows:

Item	Elm Corporation		Vincent Company	
	Debit	Credit	Debit	Credit
Cash and Accounts Receivable	$ 24,500		$ 46,000	
Inventory	170,000		70,000	
Land, Buildings, and Equipment (net)	320,000		180,000	
Investment in Vincent Bonds	46,500			
Investment in Vincent Stock	155,000			
Discount on Bonds Payable			7,000	
Operating Expenses	198,500		161,000	
Interest Expense	27,000		9,000	
Dividends Declared	60,000		10,000	
Current Liabilities		$ 35,000		$ 33,000
Bonds Payable		300,000		100,000
Common Stock		100,000		50,000
Retained Earnings		244,000		100,000
Sales		300,000		200,000
Interest Income		4,500		
Income from Subsidiary		18,000		
Total	$1,001,500	$1,001,500	$483,000	$483,000

On July 1, 20X2, Vincent Company sold land which it had purchased for $17,000 to Elm Corporation for $25,000. Elm continues to hold the land at December 31, 20X3.

Required

a. Record the journal entries for 20X3 on the books of Elm Corporation related to its investment in Vincent Company's stock and bonds.

b. Record the entries for 20X3 on the books of Vincent Company related to its bond issue.

c. Prepare elimination entries needed to complete a consolidation workpaper for 20X3.

d. Prepare a three-part consolidation workpaper for 20X3.

P8–19   Information Provided in Eliminating Entry

Gross Corporation issued $500,000 par value, 10-year, bonds at 104 on January 1, 20X1, which were purchased by Independent Corporation. On July 1, 20X5, Rupp Corporation purchased $200,000 par value bonds of Gross Corporation from Independent Corporation. The bonds pay interest of 9 percent annually on December 31. In preparing consolidated financial statements for Gross Corporation and Rupp Corporation at December 31, 20X7, the following eliminating entry was required:

Bonds Payable	200,000	
Premium on Bonds Payable	2,400	
Interest Income	18,600	
Investment in Gross Corporation Bonds		198,200
Interest Expense		17,200
Retained Earnings, January 1		4,200
Noncontrolling Interest		1,400

Required

With the information given, answer each of the following questions. Show how your answer was derived.

a. Is Gross Corporation or Rupp Corporation the parent company? How do you know?

b. What percentage of the subsidiary's ownership is held by the parent?

c. What amount did Rupp Corporation pay when it purchased the bonds on July 1, 20X5?

d. Was a gain or a loss on bond retirement included in the 20X5 consolidated income statement? What amount was reported?

e. If 20X7 consolidated net income of $70,000 would have been reported without the above eliminating entry, what amount will actually be reported?

f. Will income to noncontrolling interest reported in 20X7 increase or decrease as a result of the above eliminating entry? By what amount?

g. Prepare the eliminating entry needed to remove the effects of the intercorporate bond ownership in completing a three–part consolidation workpaper at December 31, 20X8.

P8–20 **Prior Retirement of Bonds**

Amazing Corporation purchased $100,000 par value bonds of its subsidiary, Broadway Company, on December 31, 20X5, from Lemon Corporation. The 10-year bonds bear a 9 percent coupon rate and were originally sold by Broadway on January 1, 20X3, to Lemon Corporation. Interest is paid annually on December 31. Amazing Corporation owns 85 percent of the stock of Broadway Company.

In preparing the consolidation workpaper at December 31, 20X6, the Controller of Amazing Corporation prepared the following entry to eliminate the effects of the intercorporate bond ownership:

Bonds Payable	100,000	
Interest Income	8,600	
Retained Earnings, January 1	5,355	
Noncontrolling Interest	945	
Investment in Broadway Company Bonds		102,400
Discount on Bonds Payable		3,000
Interest Expense		9,500

The assistant controller of Amazing Corporation looked at the consolidation workpapers at the end of 20X6 and concluded he requires assistance on the following items.

Required

a. What amount did Amazing Corporation pay when it purchased the bonds of Broadway Company?

b. Prepare the journal entry made by Broadway Company in 20X6 to record its interest expense for the year.

c. Prepare the journal entry made by Amazing Corporation in 20X6 to record its interest income on the Broadway Company bonds which it holds.

d. Prepare the eliminating entry needed to remove the effects of the intercorporate bond ownership in completing a three-part consolidation workpaper at December 31, 20X5.

e. Broadway Company reported net income of $60,000 and $80,000 for 20X5 and 20X6, respectively. Amazing Corporation reported income from its separate operations of $120,000 and $150,000 for 20X5 and 20X6, respectively. What amount of net income was reported for the consolidated entity in each of the two years?

P8–21 Incomplete Data

Ballard Corporation purchased 70 percent of the voting shares of Condor Company on January 1, 20X4, at underlying book value. It also purchased $100,000 par value, 12 percent Condor Company bonds on that date. The bonds had been issued on January 1, 20X1, with a 10-year maturity.

During preparation of the consolidated financial statements for December 31, 20X4, the following eliminating entry was made on the workpaper:

Bonds Payable	100,000	
Bond Premium	6,000	
Loss on Bond Retirement	3,500	
Interest Income	?	
Investment in Condor Company Bonds		109,000
Interest Expense		?

Required

a. What was the price paid by Ballard Corporation to purchase the Condor bonds?

b. What was the carrying amount of the bonds on the books of Condor Company on the date of purchase?

c. If Condor Company reports net income of $30,000 in 20X5, what amount of income should be assigned to the noncontrolling interest in the 20X5 consolidated income statement?

P8–22 Eliminations with Other Comprehensive Income

Andover Corporation acquired 65 percent of the ownership of Chad Company on January 1, 20X6, at underlying book value. Financial statements for the two companies at December 31, 20X8, are as follows:

Andover Corporation and Chad Company
Balance Sheets
December 31, 20X8

Item	Andover Corporation	Chad Company
Cash	$ 36,700	$ 21,000
Accounts Receivable	190,000	40,000
Inventory	140,000	70,000
Buildings and Equipment	450,000	260,000
Less: Accumulated Depreciation	(180,000)	(110,000)
Investment in Other Marketable Securities	70,000	64,000
Investment in Andover Corporation Bonds		67,000
Investment in Chad Company Common Stock	131,300	
Total Assets	$838,000	$412,000
Accounts Payable	$ 90,000	$ 30,000
Other Payables	40,000	20,000
Bonds Payable	300,000	160,000
Common Stock	200,000	80,000
Retained Earnings	173,000	102,000
Accumulated Other Comprehensive Income	35,000	20,000
Total Liabilities and Equities	$838,000	$412,000

Andover Corporation and Chad Company
Income Statements
For the Year Ended December 31, 20X8

Item	Andover Corporation	Chad Company
Sales	$380,000	$216,200
Interest Income		3,800
Income from Subsidiary	26,000	
Total Income	$406,000	$220,000
Cost of Goods Sold	$270,000	$130,000
Depreciation Expense	25,000	25,000
Interest Expense	30,000	13,500
Other Expenses	11,000	11,500
Total Expenses	($336,000)	($180,000)
Net Income	$ 70,000	$ 40,000

Andover Corporation and Chad Company
Statements of Comprehensive Income
For the Year Ended December 31, 20X8

Item	Andover Corporation	Chad Company
Net Income	$70,000	$40,000
Other Comprehensive Income: Unrealized		
Gain on Investments	20,000	14,000
Other Comprehensive Income from Subsidiary	9,100	
Comprehensive Income	$99,100	$54,000

Andover and Chad paid dividends of $45,000 and $28,000, respectively, in 20X8.

On July 1, 20X8, Chad purchased $70,000 of Andover bonds from nonaffiliates for $66,700. The bonds pay 10 percent interest annually on December 31 and were issued on January 1, 20X4, to mature in 10 years. Chad uses straight-line write-off of the bond discount.

Andover purchased inventory costing $60,000 and $96,000 from Chad during 20X7 and 20X8, respectively. Chad prices its products at cost plus a 50 percent markup on cost. Andover held $18,000 of inventory purchased from Chad at December 31, 20X7. These purchases were sold in 20X8, along with $63,000 of inventory purchased from Chad in 20X8.

Both Andover and Chad have investments classified as available-for-sale that have increased in value since acquisition. Securities owned by Andover increased in value $2,000 in 20X7 and $20,000 in 20X8, while those held by Chad increased by $6,000 in 20X7 and $14,000 in 20X8.

Required

a. Prepare the journal entries recorded by Andover during 20X8 for its investment in Chad Company's common stock.

b. Prepare the eliminating entries needed at December 31, 20X8, to complete a consolidation workpaper for Andover and Chad.

P8–23   Balance Sheet Eliminations

Bath Corporation purchased 80 percent of the stock of Stang Brewing Company on January 1, 20X1, at underlying book value. On that date, Stang Brewing Company issued $300,000 par value, 8 percent, 10-year bonds to Sidney Malt Company. Bath Corporation subsequently purchased $100,000 of the bonds from Sidney Malt for $102,000 on January 1, 20X3. Interest is paid semiannually on January 1 and July 1.

Summarized balance sheets for Bath Corporation and Stang Brewing Company as of December 31, 20X4, are as follows:

Bath Corporation
Balance Sheet
December 31, 20X4

Cash and Receivables	$122,500	Accounts Payable	$ 40,000
Inventory	200,000	Bonds Payable	400,000
Buildings and Equipment (net)	320,000	Common Stock	200,000
Investment in Stang Brewing:		Retained Earnings	320,000
Bonds	101,500		
Stock	216,000		
Total Assets	$960,000	Total Liabilities and Owners' Equity	$960,000

Stang Brewing Company
Balance Sheet
December 31, 20X4

Cash and Receivables	$124,000	Accounts Payable	$ 28,000
Inventory	150,000	Bonds Payable	300,000
Buildings and Equipment (net)	360,000	Bond Premium	36,000
		Common Stock	100,000
		Retained Earnings	170,000
Total Assets	$634,000	Total Liabilities and Owners' Equity	$634,000

At December 31, 20X4, Stang Brewing holds $42,000 of inventory purchased from Bath Corporation and Bath holds $26,000 of inventory purchased from Stang Brewing. Stang Brewing and Bath sell at cost plus markups of 30 percent and 40 percent, respectively.

Required

a. Prepare all elimination entries needed on December 31, 20X4, to complete a consolidation balance sheet workpaper.

b. Prepare a consolidated balance sheet workpaper.

c. Prepare a consolidated balance sheet in good form.

P8–24 **Computations Relating to Bond Purchase from Nonaffiliate**

Bliss Perfume Company issued $300,000 of 10 percent bonds on January 1, 20X2, at 110. The bonds mature 10 years from issue and have semiannual interest payments on January 1 and July 1. Parsons Corporation owns 80 percent of the stock of Bliss Perfume Company. On April 1, 20X4, Parsons Corporation purchased $100,000 par value of Bliss Perfume bonds in the securities markets.

Partial trial balances for the two companies on December 31, 20X4, are as follows:

	Parsons Corporation	Bliss Perfume Company
Investment in Bliss Perfume Company Bonds	$105,600	
Interest Income	6,900	
Interest Receivable	5,000	
Bonds Payable		$300,000
Bond Premium		21,000
Interest Expense		27,000
Interest Payable		15,000

Required

a. What was the purchase price of the Bliss Perfume Company bonds to Parsons Corporation?

b. What amount of gain or loss on bond retirement should be reported in the consolidated income statement for 20X4?

c. Prepare the necessary workpaper eliminating entries as of December 31, 20X4, to remove the effects of the intercorporate bond ownership.

P8–25 **Consolidation Procedures [AICPA Adapted]**

Presented below are selected amounts from the separate unconsolidated financial statements of Poe Corporation and its 90 percent owned subsidiary, Shaw Company, at December 31, 20X2. Additional information follows:

	Poe	Shaw
Selected Income Statement Amounts		
Sales	$710,000	$530,000
Cost of Goods Sold	490,000	370,000
Gain on Sale of Equipment	—	21,000
Earnings from Investment in Subsidiary	63,000	—
Interest Expense	—	16,000
Depreciation	25,000	20,000
Selected Balance Sheet Amounts		
Cash	$ 50,000	$ 15,000
Inventories	229,000	150,000
Equipment	440,000	360,000
Accumulated Depreciation	(200,000)	(120,000)
Investment in Shaw Stock	191,000	—
Investment in Bonds	100,000	—
Discount on Bonds	(9,000)	—
Bonds Payable	—	(200,000)
Common Stock	(100,000)	(10,000)
Additional Paid-In Capital	(250,000)	(40,000)
Retained Earnings	(402,000)	(140,000)
Selected Statement of Retained Earnings Amounts		
Beginning Balance, December 31, 20X1	$272,000	$100,000
Net Income	212,000	70,000
Dividends Paid	80,000	30,000

Additional Information

1. On January 2, 20X2, Poe Corporation purchased 90 percent of Shaw Company's outstanding common stock for cash of $155,000. On that date, Shaw's stockholders' equity equaled $150,000, and the fair values of Shaw's assets and liabilities equaled their carrying amounts. Poe has accounted for the acquisition as a purchase. On December 31, 20X2, the management of Poe Corporation reviewed the amount attributed to goodwill as a result of its purchase of Shaw Company common stock and found no evidence of impairment.

2. On September 4, 20X2, Shaw paid cash dividends of $30,000.

3. On December 31, 20X2, Poe recorded its equity in Shaw's earnings.

Required

a. The following represent transactions between Poe and Shaw during 20X2. For each transaction, determine the dollar amount by which consolidated net income (before considering minority interest) will be increased or decreased when the consolidating (eliminating) entries are prepared:

   (1) On January 3, 20X2, Shaw sold equipment with an original cost of $30,000 and a carrying value of $15,000 to Poe for $36,000. The equipment had a remaining life of three years and was depreciated using the straight-line method by both companies.

   (2) During 20X2, Shaw sold merchandise to Poe for $60,000, which included profit of $20,000. At December 31, 20X2, half of this merchandise remained in Poe's inventory.

   (3) On December 31, 20X2, Poe paid $91,000 to purchase 50 percent of the outstanding bonds issued by Shaw. The bonds mature on December 31, 20X8, and were originally issued at

par. The bonds pay interest annually on December 31 of each year, and the interest was paid to the prior investor immediately before Poe's purchase of the bonds.

b. Determine the amount to be reported as goodwill at January 2, 20X2.

c. Choose the amount to be reported in the consolidated financial statements at December 31, 20X2, for each of the financial statement elements (a through l) listed below:

Amount to be reported:

(1) Equal to the sum of the amounts reported on Poe and Shaw's separate unconsolidated financial statements.

(2) Less than the sum of the amounts reported on Poe and Shaw's separate unconsolidated financial statements.

(3) Equal to the amount reported by Poe.

(4) Equal to the amount reported by Shaw.

(5) Eliminated entirely in consolidation.

(6) Shown in the consolidated financial statements but not in the separate statements of either company.

(7) Not reported in the consolidated financial statements or the separate statements of either company.

Financial Statement Element:

a. Cash

b. Equipment

c. Investment in Subsidiary

d. Bonds Payable

e. Minority Interest

f. Common Stock

g. Beginning Retained Earnings

h. Dividends Paid

i. Gain on Retirement of Bonds

j. Cost of Goods Sold

k. Interest Expense

l. Depreciation Expense

P8–26 **Computations following Parent's Acquisition of Subsidiary Bonds**

Mainstream Corporation holds 80 percent of the voting shares of Offenberg Company, acquired on January 1, 20X1, at underlying book value. On January 1, 20X4, Mainstream purchased Offenberg Company bonds with a par value of $40,000. The bonds pay 10 percent interest annually on December 31 and mature on December 31, 20X8. Mainstream uses the basic equity method in accounting for its ownership in Offenberg Company. Partial balance sheet data for the two companies on December 31, 20X5, are as follows:

	Mainstream Corporation	Offenberg Company
Investment in Offenberg Company Stock	$120,000	
Investment in Offenberg Company Bonds	42,400	
Interest Income	3,200	
Bonds Payable		$100,000
Bond Premium		11,250
Interest Expense		6,250
Common Stock	300,000	100,000
Retained Earnings, December 31, 20X5	500,000	50,000

Required

a. Compute the gain or loss on bond retirement reported in the 20X4 consolidated income statement.

b. Prepare the eliminating entry needed to remove the effects of the intercorporate bond ownership in completing the consolidation workpaper for 20X5.

c. What balance should be reported as consolidated retained earnings on December 31, 20X5?

P8–27 Consolidation Workpaper—Year of Retirement

Tyler Manufacturing purchased 60 percent of the ownership of Brown Corporation stock on January 1, 20X1, at underlying book value. Tyler also purchased $50,000 of Brown Corporation bonds at par value on December 31, 20X3. The bonds were sold by Brown Corporation on January 1, 20X1, at 120 and have a stated interest rate of 12 percent. Interest is paid semiannually on June 30 and December 31.

On December 31, 20X1, Brown sold to Tyler for $30,000 a building with a remaining life of 15 years. The building was purchased by Brown 10 years earlier for $40,000 and is being charged to operating expense on a 25-year expected life.

Trial balances for the two companies on December 31, 20X3, are as follows:

Item	Tyler Manufacturing Debit	Tyler Manufacturing Credit	Brown Corporation Debit	Brown Corporation Credit
Cash	$ 68,000		$ 55,000	
Accounts Receivable	100,000		75,000	
Inventory	120,000		110,000	
Investment in Brown Bonds	50,000			
Investment in Brown Stock	102,000			
Depreciable Assets (net)	360,000		210,000	
Interest Expense	20,000		20,000	
Operating Expenses	302,200		150,000	
Dividends Declared	40,000		10,000	
Accounts Payable		$ 94,200		$ 52,000
Bonds Payable		200,000		200,000
Bond Premium				28,000
Common Stock		300,000		100,000
Retained Earnings		150,000		50,000
Sales		400,000		200,000
Income from Subsidiary		18,000		
Total	$1,162,200	$1,162,200	$630,000	$630,000

Required

a. Prepare a consolidation workpaper for 20X3, in good form.

b. Prepare a consolidated balance sheet, income statement, and statement of changes in retained earnings for 20X3.

P8–28   **Consolidation Workpaper—Year after Retirement**

Bennett Corporation owns 60 percent of the stock of Stone Container Company, which it acquired at book value in 20X1. On December 31, 20X3, Bennett Corporation purchased $100,000 par value bonds of Stone Container. The bonds originally were issued by Stone Container Company at par value. The coupon rate on the bonds is 9 percent. Interest is paid semiannually on June 30 and December 31. Trial balances for the two companies on December 31, 20X4, are as follows:

Item	Bennett Corporation		Stone Container Company	
	Debit	Credit	Debit	Credit
Cash	$ 61,600		$ 20,000	
Accounts Receivable	100,000		80,000	
Inventory	120,000		110,000	
Other Assets	340,000		250,000	
Investment in Stone Container Bonds	106,000			
Investment in Stone Container Stock	126,000			
Interest Expense	20,000		18,000	
Other Expenses	368,600		182,000	
Dividends Declared	40,000		10,000	
Accounts Payable		$ 80,000		$ 50,000
Bonds Payable		200,000		200,000
Common Stock		300,000		100,000
Retained Earnings		214,200		70,000
Sales		450,000		250,000
Interest Income		8,000		
Income from Subsidiary		30,000		
Total	$1,282,200	$1,282,200	$670,000	$670,000

All the interest income recognized by Bennett is related to its investment in Stone Container bonds.

Required

a. Prepare a consolidation workpaper for 20X4 in good form.

b. Prepare a consolidated balance sheet, income statement, and retained earnings statement for 20X4.

P8–29   **Intercorporate Transfers of Inventory and Equipment**

Lance Corporation purchased 75 percent of the common stock of Avery Company at underlying book value on January 1, 20X3. Trial balances for Lance Corporation and Avery Company on December 31, 20X7, are as follows:

| | 20X7 Trial Balance Data | | | |
| | Lance Corporation | | Avery Company | |
Item	Debit	Credit	Debit	Credit
Cash	$ 37,900		$ 48,800	
Accounts Receivable	110,000		105,000	
Other Receivables	30,000		15,000	
Inventory	167,000		120,000	
Land	90,000		40,000	
Buildings and Equipment	500,000		250,000	
Investment in Avery Company				
Bonds	78,800			
Stock	183,000			
Cost of Goods Sold	620,000		240,000	
Depreciation Expense	45,000		15,000	
Interest and Other Expenses	35,000		22,000	
Dividends Declared	50,000		24,000	
Accumulated Depreciation		$ 155,000		$ 75,000
Accounts Payable		118,000		35,000
Other Payables		40,000		20,000
Bonds Payable		250,000		200,000
Bond Premium				4,800
Common Stock		250,000		50,000
Additional Paid-In Capital		40,000		
Retained Earnings		291,700		170,000
Sales		750,000		320,000
Interest and Other Income		16,000		5,000
Income from Subsidiary		36,000		
Total	$1,946,700	$1,946,700	$879,800	$879,800

During 20X7, Lance Corporation resold inventory purchased from Avery in 20X6. It cost Avery $44,000 to produce the inventory, and Lance purchased it for $59,000. In 20X7, Lance purchased inventory for $40,000 and sold it to Avery for $60,000. At December 31, 20X7, Avery continued to hold $27,000 of the inventory.

Avery issued $200,000 8 percent 10-year, first mortgage bonds on January 1, 20X4, at 104. Lance Corporation purchased $80,000 of the bonds from one of the original owners for $78,400 on December 31, 20X5. Both companies use straight-line write-off of premiums and discounts. Interest is paid annually on December 31.

Required

a. What amount of cost of goods sold will be reported in the 20X7 consolidated income statement?

b. What inventory balance will be reported in the December 31, 20X7, consolidated balance sheet?

c. Prepare the journal entry to record interest expense for Avery for 20X7.

d. Prepare the journal entry to record interest income for Lance for 20X7.

e. What amount will be assigned to noncontrolling interest in the consolidated balance sheet prepared at December 31, 20X7?

f. Prepare all eliminating entries needed at December 31, 20X7, to complete a three-part consolidated working paper.

g. Prepare a consolidation workpaper for 20X7 in good form.

P8–30 **Intercorporate Bond Holdings and Other Transfers**

On January 1, 20X5, Pond Corporation purchased 75 percent of the stock of Skate Company at underlying book value. The balance sheets for Pond and Skate at January 1, 20X8, and December 31, 20X8, and income statements for 20X8 were reported as follows:

	20X8 Balance Sheets			
	Pond Corporation		Skate Company	
	January 1	*December 31*	*January 1*	*December 31*
Cash	57,600	53,100	10,000	47,000
Accounts Receivable	130,000	176,000	60,000	65,000
Interest and Other Receivables	40,000	45,000	8,000	10,000
Inventory	100,000	140,000	50,000	50,000
Land	50,000	50,000	22,000	22,000
Buildings and Equipment	400,000	400,000	240,000	240,000
Accumulated Depreciation	(150,000)	(185,000)	(70,000)	(94,000)
Investment in Skate Company				
Stock	150,000	165,000		
Bonds	42,800	42,400		
Investment in Tin Co. Bonds	135,000	134,000		
Total Assets	955,400	1,020,500	320,000	340,000
Accounts Payable	60,000	65,000	16,500	11,000
Interest and Other Payables	40,000	45,000	7,000	12,000
Bonds Payable	300,000	300,000	100,000	100,000
Bond Discount			(3,500)	(3,000)
Common Stock	150,000	150,000	30,000	30,000
Additional Paid-In Capital	155,000	155,000	20,000	20,000
Retained Earnings	250,400	305,500	150,000	170,000
Total Liabilities and Equities	955,400	1,020,500	320,000	340,000

	20X8 Income Statements			
	Pond Corporation		Skate Company	
Sales		450,000		250,000
Income from Subsidiary		22,500		
Interest Income		18,500		
Total Revenue		491,000		250,000
Cost of Goods Sold	285,000		136,000	
Other Operating Expenses	50,000		40,000	
Depreciation Expense	35,000		24,000	
Interest Expense	24,000		10,500	
Miscellaneous Expenses	11,900	405,900	9,500	220,000
Net Income		85,100		30,000

Additional Information

1. Pond Corporation sold a building to Skate for $65,000 on December 31, 20X7. The building was purchased by Pond for $125,000 and depreciated on a straight-line basis over 25 years. At the time of sale, Pond reported accumulated depreciation of $75,000 and a remaining life of 10 years.

2. On July 1, 20X6, Skate sold land that it had purchased for $22,000 to Pond for $35,000. Pond is planning to build a new warehouse on the property prior to the end of 20X9.

3. Skate Company issued $100,000 par value, 10-year bonds with a coupon rate of 10 percent on January 1, 20X5, at $95,000. On December 31, 20X7, Pond Corporation purchased $40,000 par value of Skate's bonds for $42,800. Both companies amortize bond premiums and discounts on a straight-line basis. Interest payments are made on July 1 and January 1.

4. Pond and Skate paid dividends of $30,000 and $10,000, respectively, in 20X8.

Required

a. Prepare all eliminating entries needed at December 31, 20X8, to complete a three-part consolidated working paper.

b. Prepare a three-part workpaper for 20X8 in good form.

P8–31   Comprehensive Multiple-Choice Questions

Blackwood Enterprises owns 80 percent of the voting stock of Grange Corporation. Blackwood purchased the shares on January 1, 20X4, for $234,500, at which time Grange reported common stock outstanding of $200,000 and retained earnings of $50,000. The book values of all Grange's assets were equal to their market values, except for buildings with a fair value $30,000 greater than book value at the date of combination. The buildings had an expected 10-year remaining economic life from the date of combination. On December 31, 20X6, the management of Blackwood Enterprises reviewed the amount attributed to goodwill as a result of its purchase of Grange Corporation common stock and concluded an impairment loss of $7,500 should be recorded in 20X6.

The following trial balances were prepared by the companies on December 31, 20X6:

Item	Blackwood Enterprises Debit	Blackwood Enterprises Credit	Grange Corporation Debit	Grange Corporation Credit
Cash	$ 194,220		$183,000	
Inventory	200,000		180,000	
Buildings and Equipment	500,000		400,000	
Investment in Grange Corporation Bonds	106,400			
Investment in Grange Corporation Stock	287,300			
Cost of Goods Sold	220,000		140,000	
Depreciation and Amortization	50,000		30,000	
Interest Expense	24,000		16,000	
Other Expenses	16,000		14,000	
Dividends Declared	20,000		15,000	
Accumulated Depreciation		$ 250,000		$180,000
Current Liabilities		100,000		50,000
Bonds Payable		400,000		200,000
Bond Premium				8,000
Common Stock		300,000		200,000
Retained Earnings		202,400		100,000
Sales		300,000		240,000
Other Income		35,920		
Income from Subsidiary		29,600		
Total	$1,617,920	$1,617,920	$978,000	$978,000

Blackwood purchases much of its inventory from Grange. The inventory held by Blackwood on January 1, 20X6, contained $2,000 of unrealized intercompany profit. During 20X6, Grange sold goods costing $50,000 to Blackwood for $70,000. Blackwood resold 70 percent of the inventory in 20X6 and the remaining 30 percent in 20X7.

On January 1, 20X6, Blackwood Enterprises purchased from Kirkwood Corporation $100,000 par value bonds of Grange Corporation. The bonds had been sold to Kirkwood Corporation on January 1, 20X1, with a 10-year maturity. The coupon rate is 9 percent, and interest is paid annually on December 31.

Required

Select the correct answer for each of the following questions.

1. What should be the total amount of inventory reported in the consolidated balance sheet as of December 31, 20X6?
   a. $360,000.
   b. $374,000.
   c. $375,200.
   d. $380,000.

2. What amount of cost of goods sold should be reported in the 20X6 consolidated income statement?
   a. $288,000.
   b. $294,000.
   c. $296,000.
   d. $360,000.

3. What amount of interest income did Blackwood Enterprises record from its investment in Grange Corporation bonds during 20X6?
   a. $7,400.
   b. $7,720.
   c. $9,000.
   d. $10,600.

4. What amount of interest expense should be reported in the 20X6 consolidated income statement?
   a. $24,000.
   b. $32,000.
   c. $33,000.
   d. $40,000.

5. What is the unamortized balance of the purchase differential as of January 1, 20X6?
   a. $19,200.
   b. $29,700.
   c. $32,100.
   d. $34,500.

6. What amount of depreciation and amortization should be reported in the 20X6 consolidated income statement?
   a. $77,600.
   b. $80,000.
   c. $82,400.
   d. $83,450.

7. What amount of gain or loss on bond retirement should be included in the 20X6 consolidated income statement?

   a. $2,400.

   b. $3,000.

   c. $4,000.

   d. $6,400.

8. What amount of income should be assigned to the noncontrolling interest in the 20X6 consolidated income statement?

   a. $6,720.

   b. $7,200.

   c. $8,000.

   d. $8,400.

9. What amount should be assigned to the noncontrolling interest in the consolidated balance sheet as of December 31, 20X6?

   a. $63,200.

   b. $63,320.

   c. $63,800.

   d. $65,000.

10. What amount of goodwill, if any, should be reported in the consolidated balance sheet as of December 31, 20X6?

    a. $0.

    b. $3,000.

    c. $10,500.

    d. $27,000.

P8–32   Comprehensive Problem: Intercorporate Transfers

Berry Manufacturing Company purchased 90 percent of the outstanding common stock of Bussman Corporation on December 31, 20X5, for $1,150,000. On that date, Bussman reported common stock of $500,000, premium on common stock of $280,000, and retained earnings of $420,000. The fair values of all of Bussman's assets and liabilities were equal to their book values on the date of combination, except for land, which was worth more than its book value. Berry estimated that its 90 percent share of the increase in the value of Bussman's land was $30,000.

On April 1, 20X6, Berry issued at par $200,000 of 10 percent bonds directly to Bussman; interest on the bonds is payable March 31 and September 30. On January 2, 20X7, Berry purchased all of Bussman's outstanding 10-year, 12 percent bonds from an unrelated institutional investor at 98. The bonds originally had been issued on January 2, 20X1, for 101. Interest on the bonds is payable December 31 and June 30.

Since the date it was acquired by Berry Manufacturing, Bussman has sold inventory to Berry on a regular basis. The amount of such intercompany sales totaled $64,000 in 20X6 and $78,000 in 20X7, including a 30 percent gross profit. All the inventory transferred in 20X6 had been resold by December 31, 20X6, except inventory for which Berry paid $15,000 and which was not resold until January 20X7. All the inventory transferred in 20X7 had been resold at December 31, 20X7, except merchandise for which Berry had paid $18,000.

At December 31, 20X7, trial balances for Berry Manufacturing and Bussman Corporation appeared as follows:

	Berry Manufacturing		Bussman Corporation	
Item	*Debit*	*Credit*	*Debit*	*Credit*
Cash	$ 41,500		$ 29,000	
Current Receivables	112,500		85,100	
Inventory	301,000		348,900	
Investment in Bussman Stock	1,249,000			
Investment in Bussman Bonds	985,000			
Investment in Berry Bonds			200,000	
Land	1,231,000		513,000	
Buildings and Equipment	2,750,000		1,835,000	
Cost of Goods Sold	2,009,000		430,000	
Depreciation and Amortization	195,000		85,000	
Other Expenses	643,000		206,000	
Dividends Declared	50,000		40,000	
Accumulated Depreciation		$1,210,000		$ 619,000
Current Payables		98,000		79,000
Bonds Payable		200,000		1,000,000
Premium on Bonds Payable				3,000
Common Stock		1,000,000		500,000
Premium on Common Stock		700,000		280,000
Retained Earnings, January 1		3,033,000		470,000
Sales		3,101,000		790,000
Other Income		135,000		31,000
Income from Subsidiary		90,000		
Total	$9,567,000	$9,567,000	$3,772,000	$3,772,000

As of December 31, 20X7, Bussman had declared but not yet paid its fourth-quarter dividend of $10,000. Both Berry Manufacturing and Bussman use straight-line depreciation and amortization, including the amortization of bond discount and premium. On December 31, 20X7, the management of Berry Manufacturing reviewed the amount attributed to goodwill as a result of its purchase of Bussman Corporation common stock and concluded an impairment loss in the amount of $25,000 occurred during 20X7. Berry Manufacturing uses the basic equity method to account for its investment in Bussman Corporation.

Required

a. Compute the amount of the differential as of January 1, 20X7.

b. Compute the balance of Berry Manufacturing's Investment in Bussman Stock account as of January 1, 20X7.

c. Compute the gain or loss on the constructive retirement of Bussman's bonds that should appear in the 20X7 consolidated income statement.

d. Compute the income that should be assigned to the noncontrolling interest in the 20X7 consolidated income statement.

e. Compute the total noncontrolling interest as of December 31, 20X6.

f. Present all elimination entries that would appear in a three-part consolidation workpaper as of December 31, 20X7.

g. Prepare and complete a three-part workpaper for the preparation of consolidated financial statements for 20X7.

P8–33[*]   **Intercorporate Leases**

Johnson Company owns 75 percent of the voting shares of Hall Leasing Corporation. On January 1, 20X3, Hall Leasing Corporation purchased a fleet of small delivery trucks with an expected economic life of six years and no anticipated residual value. Hall Leasing Corporation leased the trucks to Chech Corporation for two years and on January 1, 20X5, leased the fleet to Johnson Company. The vehicles had a remaining estimated economic life of four years at the time they were leased to Johnson Company. Both Johnson Company and Hall Leasing record depreciation on a straight-line basis.

Required

Give the eliminating entries needed to remove the effects of the intercorporate lease in preparing the consolidated financial statements for 20X5 in each of the following situations:

a. Assume Hall purchased the trucks for $720,000 and leases them to Johnson under an operating lease at an annual rental of $175,000.

b. Assume Hall purchased the trucks for $696,000 and leases them to Johnson for their remaining four-year life under a direct financing lease. An annual payment of $146,400 is made at the end of each year. The lease with Johnson provides approximately a 10 percent return on the unrecovered investment balance.

c. Assume Hall purchased the trucks for $600,000 and leases them to Johnson for their remaining four-year life on a sales-type lease. An annual payment of $146,400 is made at the end of each year. The present value of the lease payments on January 1, 20X5, using a 10 percent discount rate was approximately $464,000.

P8–34A   **Fully Adjusted Equity Method**

On December 31, 20X4, Bennett Corporation recorded the following entry on its books to adjust its investment in Stone Container Company stock from the basic equity method to the fully adjusted equity method:

Retained Earnings	4,200	
Income from Subsidiary		600
Investment in Stone Container Company Stock		3,600

Required

a. Adjust the data reported by Bennett Corporation in the trial balance contained in Problem 8–28 for the effects of the adjusting entry presented above.

b. Prepare the journal entries that would have been recorded on the books of Bennett Corporation during 20X4 under the fully adjusted equity method.

c. Prepare all eliminating entries needed to complete a consolidation workpaper as of December 31, 20X4, assuming Bennett has used the fully adjusted equity method.

d. Complete a three-part consolidation workpaper as of December 31, 20X4.

P8–35A   **Cost Method**

The trial balance data presented in Problem 8–28 can be converted to reflect use of the cost method by inserting the following amounts in place of those presented for Bennett Corporation:

Investment in Stone Container Stock	$ 75,000
Retained Earnings	187,200
Income from Subsidiary	-0-
Dividend Income	6,000

Stone Container Company reported retained earnings of $25,000 on the date Bennett Corporation purchased 60 percent of the stock.

Required

a. Prepare the journal entries that would have been recorded on the books of Bennett Corporation during 20X4 under the cost method.

b. Prepare all eliminating entries needed to complete a consolidation workpaper as of December 31, 20X4, assuming Bennett uses the cost method.

c. Complete a three-part consolidation workpaper as of December 31, 20X4.

CONSOLIDATION OWNERSHIP ISSUES

Only simple ownership situations have been presented in the preceding chapters. In practice, however, relatively complex ownership structures often are found. For example, a subsidiary may have preferred stock outstanding in addition to its common stock, and in some cases a parent may acquire shares of both the common and the preferred stock of a subsidiary. Other times, one or more subsidiaries may acquire stock of the parent or of other related companies. Sometimes the parent's ownership claim on a subsidiary may change through its purchase or sale of subsidiary shares or through stock transactions of the subsidiary.

The discussion in this chapter is intended to provide a basic understanding of some of the consolidation problems arising from complex ownership situations commonly encountered in practice. The following topics are discussed:

1. Subsidiary preferred stock outstanding.
2. Changes in the parent's ownership interest in the subsidiary.
3. Multiple ownership levels.
4. Reciprocal ownership.
5. Subsidiary stock dividends.

Subsidiary Preferred Stock Outstanding

Many companies have more than one type of stock outstanding. Each type of security typically serves a particular function, and each has a different set of rights and features. Preferred stockholders normally have preference over common shareholders with respect to dividends and the distribution of assets in a liquidation. The right to vote usually is withheld from preferred shareholders, so that preferred stock ownership normally does not convey control, regardless of the number of shares owned.

Because preferred shareholders of a subsidiary do have a claim on the net assets of the subsidiary, special attention must be given to that claim in the preparation of consolidated financial statements.

Consolidation with Subsidiary Preferred Stock Outstanding

During preparation of consolidated financial statements, the amount of subsidiary stockholders' equity accruing to preferred shareholders must be determined before dealing with the elimination of the intercorporate common stock ownership. If the parent holds some of the subsidiary's preferred stock, its portion of the preferred stock interest must be eliminated. Any portion of the subsidiary's preferred stock interest not held by the parent is assigned to the noncontrolling interest.

As an illustration of the preparation of consolidated financial statements with subsidiary preferred stock outstanding, recall the following information from the example of Peerless Products Corporation and Special Foods Incorporated used in previous chapters:

1. Peerless Products purchases 80 percent of the common stock of Special Foods on December 31, 20X0, at its book value of $240,000 and accounts for the investment using the basic equity method.
2. Peerless Products earns income from its own operations of $140,000 in 20X1 and declares dividends of $60,000.
3. Special Foods reports net income of $50,000 in 20X1 and declares common dividends of $30,000.

Also assume that on January 1, 20X1, Special Foods issues $100,000 of 12 percent preferred stock at par value, none of which is purchased by Peerless. The regular $12,000 preferred dividend is paid in 20X1.

Allocation of Special Foods' Net Income. Of the total $50,000 of net income reported by Special Foods for 20X1, $12,000 ($100,000 × .12) is assigned to the preferred shareholders as their current dividend. Peerless Products records its share of the remaining amount, computed as follows:

Special Foods' net income, 20X1	$50,000
Less: Preferred dividends ($100,000 × .12)	(12,000)
Special Foods' income accruing to common shareholders	$38,000
Peerless's proportionate share	× .80
Peerless's income from Special Foods	$30,400

Income assigned to the noncontrolling interest for 20X1 is the total of Special Foods' preferred dividends and the noncontrolling common stockholders' 20 percent share of Special Foods' $38,000 of income remaining after preferred dividends are deducted:

Preferred dividends of Special Foods	$12,000
Income assigned to Special Foods' noncontrolling common shareholders ($38,000 × .20)	7,600
Income to noncontrolling interest	$19,600

Consolidation Workpaper.   The workpaper to prepare consolidated financial statements at the end of 20X1 appears in Figure 9–1. The following elimination entries are included in the workpaper:

E(1)	Income from Subsidiary	30,400	
	Dividends Declared—Common		24,000
	Investment in Special Foods Common		6,400
	Eliminate income from subsidiary.		
E(2)	Income to Noncontrolling Interest	19,600	
	Dividends Declared—Preferred		12,000
	Dividends Declared—Common		6,000
	Noncontrolling Interest		1,600
	Assign income to noncontrolling interest.		
E(3)	Common Stock—Special Foods	200,000	
	Retained Earnings, January 1	100,000	
	Investment in Special Foods Common		240,000
	Noncontrolling Interest		60,000
	Eliminate beginning investment in common stock.		
E(4)	Preferred Stock—Special Foods	100,000	
	Noncontrolling Interest		100,000
	Eliminate subsidiary preferred stock.		

In consolidation, the $12,000 preferred dividend is treated as income assigned to the noncontrolling interest. Because none of Special Foods' preferred stock is held by Peerless, all of it is classified as part of the noncontrolling interest.

Subsidiary Preferred Stock Held by Parent

Occasionally a parent company will hold preferred stock of a subsidiary in addition to its investment in the subsidiary's common stock. Because the preferred stock held by the parent is within the consolidated entity, it must be eliminated when consolidated financial statements are prepared. Likewise, any income from the preferred stock recorded by the parent also must be eliminated.

As an illustration of the treatment of subsidiary preferred stock held by the parent, assume that Peerless Products purchases 60 percent of Special Foods' $100,000 par value, 12 percent preferred stock for $60,000 when issued on January 1, 20X1. During 20X1, dividends of $12,000 are declared on the preferred stock. Peerless recognizes $7,200 ($12,000 × .60) of dividend income from its investment in Special Foods' preferred stock, and the remaining $4,800 ($12,000 × .40) is paid to the holders of the other preferred shares.

In consolidation, the total income assigned to the noncontrolling interest includes the portion of the preferred dividend paid on the shares not held by Peerless:

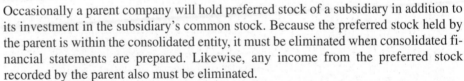

Noncontrolling interest's share of preferred dividends ($12,000 × .40)	$ 4,800
Income assigned to Special Foods' noncontrolling common shareholders ($38,000 × .20)	7,600
Income to noncontrolling interest	$12,400

E(16) Gain on Sale of Investment	3,000	
Additional Paid-In Capital		3,000
Eliminate gain on transaction involving subsidiary stock.		

This entry treats the stock transaction as the issuance of stock by the consolidated entity to the noncontrolling interest.

The consolidation workpaper prepared as of December 31, 20X2, is shown in Figure 9–2. In addition to entry E(16), the workpaper includes the normal entries, to eliminate a 75 percent investment in Special Foods:

E(17) Income from Subsidiary	56,250	
Dividends Declared		30,000
Investment in Special Foods Stock		26,250
Eliminate income from subsidiary:		
$56,250 = $75,000 × .75		
$30,000 = $40,000 × .75		
$26,250 = $56,250 − $30,000		
E(18) Income to Noncontrolling Interest	18,750	
Dividends Declared		10,000
Noncontrolling Interest		8,750
Assign income to noncontrolling interest:		
$18,750 = $75,000 × .25		
$10,000 = $40,000 × .25		
$8,750 = $18,750 − $10,000		
E(19) Common Stock—Special Foods	200,000	
Retained Earnings, January 1	120,000	
Investment in Special Foods Stock		240,000
Noncontrolling Interest		80,000
Eliminate beginning investment in common stock:		
$240,000 = $320,000 × .75		
$80,000 = $320,000 × .25		

Entry E(17) eliminates Peerless's 75 percent share of Special Foods' income and dividends. Entry E(18) assigns income to the noncontrolling stockholders based on their 25 percent ownership interest.

The balance in Peerless's investment account shown in the consolidation workpaper is $266,250. This amount is the result of the following entries in the investment account:

Investment in Special Foods Stock

Original cost	240,000			
20X1 equity accrual			20X1 dividends	
($50,000 × .80)	40,000		($30,000 × .80)	24,000
Balance, 12/31/X1	256,000			
			(15) Sale of 1,000 shares	
			($256,000 × ¹⁄₁₆)	16,000
20X2 equity accrual			20X2 dividends	
($75,000 × .75)	56,250		($40,000 × .75)	30,000
Balance, 12/31/X2	266,250			

FIGURE 9–2   December 31, 20X2, Consolidation Workpaper, Second Year Following Combination; 75 Percent Ownership, Purchased at Book Value

Item	Peerless Products	Special Foods	Eliminations Debit		Eliminations Credit		Consolidated
Sales	450,000	300,000					750,000
Gain on Sale of Investment	3,000		(16)	3,000			
Income from Subsidiary	56,250		(17)	56,250			
Credits	509,250	300,000					750,000
Cost of Goods Sold	180,000	160,000					340,000
Depreciation and Amortization	50,000	20,000					70,000
Other Expenses	60,000	45,000					105,000
Debits	(290,000)	(225,000)					(515,000)
							235,000
Income to Noncontrolling Interest			(18)	18,750			(18,750)
Net Income, carry forward	219,250	75,000		78,000			216,250
Retained Earnings, January 1	420,000	120,000	(19)	120,000			420,000
Net Income, from above	219,250	75,000		78,000			216,250
	639,250	195,000					636,250
Dividends Declared:	(60,000)	(40,000)			(17)	30,000	
					(18)	10,000	(60,000)
Retained Earnings, December 31, carry forward	579,250	155,000		198,000		40,000	576,250
Cash	308,000	85,000					393,000
Accounts Receivable	150,000	80,000					230,000
Inventory	180,000	90,000					270,000
Land	175,000	40,000					215,000
Buildings and Equipment	800,000	600,000					1,400,000
Investment in Special Foods Stock	266,250				(17)	26,250	
					(19)	240,000	
Debits	1,879,250	895,000					2,508,000
Accumulated Depreciation	300,000	240,000					540,000
Accounts Payable	100,000	100,000					200,000
Bonds Payable	400,000	200,000					600,000
Common Stock	500,000	200,000	(19)	200,000			500,000
Additional Paid-In Capital					(16)	3,000	3,000
Retained Earnings, from above	579,250	155,000		198,000		40,000	576,250
Noncontrolling Interest					(18)	8,750	
					(19)	80,000	88,750
Credits	1,879,250	895,000		398,000		398,000	2,508,000

Elimination entries:

(16) Eliminate gain on transaction involving subsidiary stock.

(17) Eliminate income from subsidiary.

(18) Assign income to noncontrolling interest.

(19) Eliminate beginning investment in common stock.

The amount of Peerless's investment eliminated in entry E(19) is the balance at the beginning of 20X2 immediately after Peerless sold the 1,000 shares; this amount is equal to Peerless's 75 percent share of the $320,000 beginning book value of Special Foods. Entries E(17) and E(19) together eliminate the total investment balance reported by Peerless on December 31, 20X2.

The amount assigned to the noncontrolling interest in entry E(19) is 25 percent of Special Foods' beginning book value. The total noncontrolling interest established in entries E(18) and E(19) together is $88,750, equal to 25 percent of Special Foods' $355,000 book value on December 31, 20X2.

Consolidation Subsequent to 20X2. In preparing consolidated financial statements each year after 20X2, a workpaper entry similar to E(16) is needed to reestablish the $3,000 increase in additional paid-in capital. Because the gain recognized by Peerless in 20X2 has been closed to retained earnings, beginning retained earnings must be reduced to eliminate the effects of the gain. The entry that would be included in the consolidation workpaper each year after 20X2 is as follows:

E(20)	Retained Earnings, January 1	3,000	
	Additional Paid-In Capital		3,000
	Eliminate effects of gain on transaction involving subsidiary stock.		

Subsidiary's Sale of Additional Shares to Nonaffiliate

Additional funds are generated for the consolidated enterprise when a subsidiary sells new shares to parties outside the economic entity. A sale of additional shares to an unaffiliated party increases the total shares of the subsidiary outstanding and, consequently, reduces the percentage ownership held by the parent company. At the same time, the dollar amount assigned to the noncontrolling interest in the consolidated financial statements increases. The resulting amounts of the controlling and noncontrolling interests are affected by two factors:

1. The number of shares sold to nonaffiliates.
2. The price at which the shares are sold to nonaffiliates.

Difference between Book Value and Sale Price of Subsidiary Shares. If the sale price of new shares equals the book value of outstanding shares, there is no change in the claim of the existing shareholders. If the stockholders' equity of the subsidiary is viewed as a pie, the overall size of the pie increases. While the parent's share of the pie decreases, the size of the parent's slice remains the same because of the increase in the overall size of the pie. The eliminating entries used in consolidation simply are changed to recognize the increase in the claim of the noncontrolling shareholders and the corresponding increase in the stockholders' equity balances of the subsidiary.

Most sales, however, do not occur at book value. When the sale price and book value are not the same, all common shareholders are assigned a pro rata portion of the difference.

In this situation, the book value of the subsidiary's shares held by the parent changes even though the number remains constant. Both the size of the pie and the size of the parent's share of the pie change; the size of the parent's slice changes because the increase in the size of the pie and the decrease in the parent's share do not exactly offset one another.

The change in book value of the shares held by the parent company can be reported in the consolidated statements in one of two ways under current reporting standards:

1. An adjustment to paid-in capital
2. A gain or loss in the consolidated income statement

While support for both alternatives can be found in the accounting literature, the FASB has recommended that the acquisition of treasury stock or the issuance of additional shares by the subsidiary be treated as transactions in the equity of the consolidated entity with no gain or loss recognized.[3]

From a consolidated viewpoint, the sale of additional shares to unaffiliated parties by a subsidiary and a sale of subsidiary shares by the parent are similar transactions: in both cases the consolidated entity sells shares to the noncontrolling interest. Because the participants in a consolidation are regarded as members of a single economic entity, the sale of subsidiary shares to the noncontrolling interest should be treated in the same way regardless of whether the shares are sold by the parent or the subsidiary. The recognition of a gain or loss on such a transaction seems inappropriate because the sale of stock to unaffiliated parties by the consolidated entity is a capital transaction from a single-entity viewpoint.

Illustration of Sale of Subsidiary Stock to Nonaffiliate.   To examine the sale of additional shares by a subsidiary to a nonaffiliate, assume that Peerless Products acquires an 80 percent interest in Special Foods by purchasing 16,000 shares of Special Foods' $10 par common stock on December 31, 20X0, at book value of $240,000. Special Foods has only common stock outstanding. All other information is the same as that used previously. On January 1, 20X2, Special Foods sells 5,000 additional shares of stock to nonaffiliates for $20 per share, a total of $100,000. After the sale, Special Foods has 25,000 shares outstanding, and Peerless has a 64 percent interest (16,000 ÷ 25,000) in Special Foods.

The January 1, 20X2, sale of additional shares results in the following change in Special Foods' balance sheet:

	Before Sale	*Following Sale*
Common Stock, $10 par value	$200,000	$250,000
Additional Paid-In Capital		50,000
Retained Earnings	120,000	120,000
Total Stockholders' Equity	$320,000	$420,000

The book value of Peerless's investment in Special Foods changes as a result of the sale of additional shares as follows:

	Before Sale	*Following Sale*
Special Foods' total stockholders' equity	$320,000	$420,000
Peerless's proportionate share	× .80	× .64
Book value of Peerless's investment in Special Foods	$256,000	$268,800

[3]Ibid.

dividends of the subsidiary, stock dividends must be eliminated because they are not viewed as dividends of the consolidated entity.

Impact on Subsequent Periods

At the end of 20X1, the stock dividend declaration is closed into the subsidiary's retained earnings and does not separately appear in the financial statements of future periods. The stock dividend results in a common stock balance $50,000 higher and a retained earnings balance $50,000 lower on the books of the subsidiary than if there had been no stock dividend. The investment elimination entry in the consolidation workpaper must reflect these changed balances.

Thus, assume that the appropriate investment elimination entry on December 31, 20X2, is as follows if Special Foods declares no stock dividend:

E(42)	Common Stock—Special Foods	200,000	
	Retained Earnings, January 1	120,000	
	Investment in Special Foods Stock		256,000
	Noncontrolling Interest		64,000
	Eliminate beginning investment balance.		

The following entry would replace entry E(42) in the consolidation workpaper prepared as of December 31, 20X2, if Special Foods had declared the stock dividend during 20X1:

E(43)	Common Stock—Special Foods	250,000	
	Retained Earnings, January 1	70,000	
	Investment in Special Foods Stock		256,000
	Noncontrolling Interest		64,000
	Eliminate beginning investment balance.		

Entry E(43) is identical to entry E(42) except that the elimination of common stock is $50,000 higher and the elimination of retained earnings is $50,000 lower, reflecting the differences in the balances of those accounts due to the stock dividend.

Summary of Key Concepts and Terms

A number of stockholders' equity issues arise in the preparation of consolidated financial statements. When subsidiaries have preferred stock outstanding, any of the preferred stock held by the parent must be eliminated because it is held within the consolidated entity. The remaining preferred stock is treated as part of the noncontrolling interest. In the assessment of the preferred shareholders' claim, consideration must be given to all the features of the preferred stock, including cumulative dividends in arrears, dividend participation features, and retirement premiums.

Transactions involving subsidiary common stock may affect the percentage ownership of the controlling shareholders. Although existing accounting standards permit some degree of diversity in practice, the concept of a single economic entity implies that subsidiary stock transactions should be viewed as transactions of the consolidated entity. Thus, no gains or losses should be reported in the consolidated income statement when a subsidiary issues new shares or purchases treasury stock. For example, a gain or loss recognized by a parent on a sale of subsidiary shares back to the subsidiary should be eliminated in preparing consolidated statements because the transfer is entirely within the consolidated entity.

The organizational structure of some consolidated entities may be more complex than just a parent and one or more subsidiaries. In some cases, subsidiaries hold controlling interests in other companies, thus giving the parent an indirect interest. Consolidation proceeds from the lowest level to the highest in these cases. In a relatively few cases, a subsidiary may own common shares of its parent. Usually those common shares are treated as treasury stock in consolidated financial statements.

Stock dividends declared by a subsidiary result in only minor changes in the eliminations needed to prepare consolidated financial statements. In the year the stock dividend is declared, the stock dividend declaration and the higher balance of the common stock must be eliminated in preparing consolidated statements. In subsequent years, the investment elimination entry reflects the higher amount of the subsidiary's common stock and the lower amount of retained earnings.

Direct ownership	Multilevel ownership
Entity approach	Reciprocal ownership
Indirect control	Treasury stock method

APPENDIX 9A ILLUSTRATION OF CONSOLIDATED NET INCOME COMPUTATION IN A COMPLEX OWNERSHIP SITUATION

As an illustration of the entity approach to computing consolidated net income in a complex ownership situation, assume the following ownership relations between A Company, B Company, and C Company:

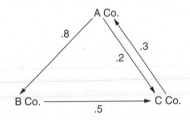

The income accruing to each company is defined as:

A = the net income of A Company on an equity basis
B = the net income of B Company on an equity basis
C = the net income of C Company on an equity basis

If the separate operating incomes of A, B, and C Companies are $122,000, $80,000, and $100,000, respectively, the algebraic equations to determine the appropriate balances are:

$A = \$122,000 + .8B + .2C$
$B = \$80,000 + .5C$
$C = \$100,000 + .3A$

$A = \$122,000 + .8[\$80,000 + .5(\$100,000 + .3A)] + .2(\$100,000 + .3A)$
$\quad = \$122,000 + .8(\$80,000 + \$50,000 + .15A) + \$20,000 + .06A$
$\quad = \$122,000 + \$64,000 + \$40,000 + .12A + \$20,000 + .06A$
$\quad = \$246,000 + .18A$

$.82A = \$246,000$
$A = \$300,000$
$C = \$100,000 + .3(\$300,000)$
$\quad = \$100,000 + \$90,000 = \$190,000$
$B = \$80,000 + .5(\$190,000)$
$\quad = \$80,000 + \$95,000 = \$175,000$

These income figures provide the basis for determining the amount to be reported as consolidated net income and the amount to be assigned to the noncontrolling shareholders of each company. However, none of the computed totals can be reported without adjustment in this case because each company has some portion of its shares held by an affiliate. The income amounts assigned are based on the portion of ownership held by outside shareholders, as follows:

Consolidated net income:		
A's income	$300,000	
Proportion of shares held outside consolidated entity	× .70	
		$210,000
Income to noncontrolling interest:		
B's income	$175,000	
Proportion of shares held by noncontrolling stockholders	× .20	
		35,000
C's income	$190,000	
Proportion of shares held by noncontrolling stockholders	× .30	
		57,000
Total income assigned		$302,000

Consolidated net income in this situation is not the amount of income computed for A Company; rather, it is the computed amount adjusted for the percentage of total shares held outside the consolidated entity itself. The total of the amounts reported as consolidated net income and income assigned to noncontrolling shareholders of the subsidiaries should always equal the sum of the separate operating incomes of the individual companies:

Separate operating income:	
A Company	$122,000
B Company	80,000
C Company	100,000
Total operating income	$302,000

Questions

Q9–1 How does the consolidation process deal with preferred stock of a subsidiary?

Q9–2 What portion of subsidiary preferred stock outstanding is reported as part of the noncontrolling interest in the consolidated balance sheet?

Q9–3 Why are subsidiary preferred dividends that are paid to nonaffiliates normally deducted from earnings in arriving at consolidated net income? When is it not appropriate to deduct subsidiary preferred dividends in computing consolidated net income?

Q9–4 How does a call feature on subsidiary preferred stock affect the claim of the noncontrolling interest reported in the consolidated balance sheet?

Q9–5 Explain how the existence of a subsidiary's preferred shares might affect the amount of goodwill reported following the purchase of the subsidiary.

Q9–6 A parent company sells common shares of one of its subsidiaries to a nonaffiliate for more than their carrying value on the parent's books. How should the sale be reported by the parent company? How should the sale be reported in the consolidated financial statements?

Q9–7   A subsidiary sells additional shares of its common stock to a nonaffiliate at a price that is greater than the previous book value per share. How does the sale benefit the existing shareholders?

Q9–8   A parent company purchases additional common shares of one of its subsidiaries from a nonaffiliate at $10 per share above underlying book value. Explain how this purchase is reflected in the consolidated financial statements for the year.

Q9–9   How are treasury shares held by a subsidiary reported in the consolidated financial statements?

Q9–10   What is indirect ownership? How does one company gain control of another through indirect ownership?

Q9–11   Explain how a reciprocal ownership arrangement between two subsidiaries could lead the parent company to overstate its income if no adjustment is made for the reciprocal relationship.

Q9–12   How will parent company shares held by a subsidiary be reflected in the consolidated balance sheet when the treasury stock method is used?

Q9–13   How does the entity method differ from the treasury stock method in computing consolidated net income when there is reciprocal ownership between the parent and the subsidiary?

Q9–14   Parent Company holds 80 percent ownership of Subsidiary Company, and Subsidiary Company owns 90 percent of the stock of Tiny Corporation. What effect will $100,000 of unrealized intercompany profits on the books of Tiny Corporation on December 31, 20X5, have on the amount of consolidated net income reported for the year?

Q9–15   Snapper Corporation holds 70 percent ownership of Bit Company, and Bit Company holds 60 percent ownership of Slide Company. Should Slide Company be consolidated with Snapper Corporation? Why?

Q9–16   What effect will a subsidiary's 15 percent stock dividend have on the consolidated financial statements?

Q9–17   What effect will a subsidiary's 15 percent stock dividend have on the elimination entries used in preparing a consolidated balance sheet at the end of the year in which the dividend is distributed?

Q9–18   When there are multilevel affiliations, explain why it generally is best to prepare consolidated financial statements by completing the eliminating entries for companies furthest from parent company ownership first and completing the eliminating entries for those owned directly by the parent company last.

Cases

C9–1   Effect of Subsidiary Preferred Stock

Snow Corporation issued common stock with a par value of $100,000 and preferred stock with a par value of $80,000 on January 1, 20X5, when the company was created. Klammer Corporation acquired a controlling interest in Snow Corporation on January 1, 20X6.

Required

What does the controller of Klammer Corporation need to know about the preferred stock in order to determine consolidated net income for 20X6?

C9–2   Sale of Subsidiary Shares

Hardcore Mining Company acquired 88 percent of the common stock of Mountain Trucking Company on January 1, 20X2, at a cost of $30 per share. On December 31, 20X7, when the book value of Mountain Trucking stock was $70 per share, Hardcore sold one-quarter of its investment in Mountain Trucking to Basic Manufacturing Company for $90 per share.

Required

What effect will the sale have on the 20X7 consolidated financial statements of Hardcore mining if (*a*) Basic Manufacturing is an unrelated company; and (*b*) Hardcore Mining holds 60 percent of the voting shares of Basic Manufacturing?

C9–3 **Reciprocal Ownership**

Strong Manufacturing Company holds 94 percent ownership of Thorson Farm Products and 68 percent ownership of Kenwood Distributors. Thorson Farm Products has excess cash at the end of 20X4 and is considering buying shares of its own stock, shares of Strong Manufacturing, or shares of Kenwood Distributors.

Required

If Thorson Farm Products wishes to take the action that will be best for the consolidated entity, what factors will it need to consider in making its decision? How can it maximize consolidated net income?

Exercises

E9–1 **Multiple-Choice Questions on Preferred Stock Ownership**

Blank Corporation prepared the following summarized balance sheet on January 1, 20X1:

Assets	$150,000	Liabilities	$ 20,000
		Preferred Stock	30,000
		Common Stock	40,000
		Retained Earnings	60,000
Total Assets	$150,000	Total Liabilities and Equities	$150,000

Required

Select the correct answer for each of the following questions.

1. If Shepard Company purchases 80 percent of the common shares of Blank Corporation for $90,000, the amount reported as noncontrolling interest in the consolidated balance sheet is:
   a. $20,000.
   b. $26,000.
   c. $30,000.
   d. $50,000.

2. Shepard Company purchases 80 percent of the common shares of Blank Corporation for $90,000 and 70 percent of the preferred shares of Blank Corporation for $21,000. The amount reported as noncontrolling interest in the consolidated balance sheet of Shepard Company is:
   a. $9,000.
   b. $20,000.
   c. $29,000.
   d. $50,000.

3. Shepard Company purchases 80 percent of the common shares of Blank Corporation for $90,000 and 70 percent of the preferred shares of Blank Corporation for $21,000 on January 1, 20X1. If Shepard Company's retained earnings is $150,000 on December 31, 20X0, the consolidated retained earnings reported immediately after the stock purchases is:
   a. $48,000.
   b. $150,000.
   c. $198,000.
   d. $210,000.

4. Shepard Company purchases 80 percent of the common shares of Blank Corporation for $90,000 and 70 percent of the preferred shares of Blank Corporation for $21,000 on January 1, 20X1. Shepard Company has no preferred shares outstanding. The amount of preferred stock reported in the consolidated balance sheet immediately after the stock purchases is:

   a. $0.

   b. $9,000.

   c. $21,000.

   d. $30,000.

E9–2　**Multiple-Choice Questions on Multilevel Ownership**

Musical Corporation purchases 80 percent of the common shares of Dustin Corporation on January 1, 20X2. On January 2, 20X2, Dustin Corporation purchases 60 percent of the common stock of Rustic Corporation. Information on company book values on the date of purchase and operating results for 20X2 is as follows:

Company	Book Value	Purchase Price	20X2 Operating Income
Musical Corporation	$800,000		$100,000
Dustin Corporation	300,000	$240,000	80,000
Rustic Corporation	200,000	120,000	50,000

Required

Select the correct answer for each of the following questions.

1. Consolidated net income for 20X2 is:

   a. $180,000.

   b. $188,000.

   c. $194,000.

   d. $234,000.

2. The amount of 20X2 income assigned to the noncontrolling interest of Rustic Corporation is:

   a. $0.

   b. $20,000.

   c. $30,000.

   d. $50,000.

3. The amount of 20X2 income assigned to the noncontrolling interest of Dustin Corporation is:

   a. $10,000.

   b. $16,000.

   c. $22,000.

   d. $26,000.

4. The amount of income assigned to the noncontrolling interest in the 20X2 consolidated income statement is:

   a. $20,000.

   b. $22,000.

   c. $42,000.

   d. $46,000.

5. Assume that Dustin Corporation pays $160,000, rather than $120,000, to purchase 60 percent of the common stock of Rustic Corporation. If the purchase differential is amortized over 10 years, the effect on 20X2 consolidated net income will be a decrease of:

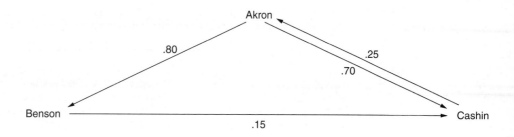

Income from the separate operations of each corporation is as follows:

Akron Inc.	$190,000
Benson Company	170,000
Cashin Inc.	230,000

The following notations relate to items 1 through 4. Ignore all income tax considerations.

A = Akron's consolidated net income; that is, its income plus its share of the consolidated net incomes of Benson and Cashin

B = Benson's consolidated net income; that is, its income plus its share of the consolidated net income of Cashin

C = Cashin's consolidated net income; that is, its income plus its share of the consolidated net income of Akron

Select the correct answer for each of the following questions.

1. The equation, in a set of simultaneous equations, that computes A is:
   a. $A = .75(\$190,000 + .8B + .7C)$.
   b. $A = \$190,000 + .8B + .7C$.
   c. $A = .75(\$190,000) + .8(\$170,000) + .7(\$230,000)$.
   d. $A = .75(\$190,000) + .8B + .7C$.

2. The equation, in a set of simultaneous equations, that computes B is:
   a. $B = \$170,000 + .15C - .75A$.
   b. $B = \$170,000 + .15C$.
   c. $B = .2(\$170,000) + .15(\$230,000)$.
   d. $B = .2(\$170,000) + .15C$.

3. Cashin's noncontrolling interest in consolidated net income is:
   a. $.15(\$230,000)$.
   b. $\$230,000 + .25A$.
   c. $.15(\$230,000) + .25A$.
   d. $.15C$.

4. Benson's noncontrolling interest in consolidated net income is:
   a. $\$25,500$.
   b. $\$30,675$.
   c. $\$34,316$.
   d. $\$45,755$.

524   Chapter 9

P9–20   Subsidiary Stock Dividend

Pound Manufacturing Corporation prepared the following balance sheet as of January 1, 20X8:

Cash	$ 40,000	Accounts Payable	$ 50,000
Accounts Receivable	90,000	Bonds Payable	200,000
Inventory	180,000	Common Stock	100,000
Buildings and Equipment	500,000	Additional Paid-In Capital	70,000
Less: Accumulated Depreciation	(110,000)	Retained Earnings	280,000
Total Assets	$700,000	Total Liabilities and Equities	$700,000

The company is considering a 2 for 1 stock split, a stock dividend of 4,000 shares, or a stock dividend of 1,500 shares on its $10 par value common stock. The current market price per share of Pound Manufacturing stock on January 1, 20X8, is $50. Quick Sales Corporation acquired 68 percent of the common shares of Pound Manufacturing on January 1, 20X4, at underlying book value.

Required

Give the investment elimination entry required to prepare a consolidated balance sheet at the close of business on January 1, 20X8, for each of the alternative transactions under consideration by Pound Manufacturing.

P9–21   Subsidiary Preferred Stock Outstanding

Emerald Corporation purchased 10,500 shares of the common stock and 800 shares of the 8 percent preferred stock of Pert Company on December 31, 20X4, at underlying book value. Pert Company reported the following balance sheet amounts on January 1, 20X5:

Cash	$ 30,000	Accounts Payable	$ 20,000
Accounts Receivable	70,000	Bonds Payable	100,000
Inventory	120,000	Preferred Stock	200,000
Buildings and Equipment	600,000	Common Stock	150,000
Less: Accumulated Depreciation	(150,000)	Retained Earnings	200,000
Total Assets	$670,000	Total Liabilities and Equities	$670,000

The preferred stock of Pert Company is $100 par value, and the common stock is $10 par value. The preferred dividends are cumulative and are two years in arrears on January 1, 20X5. Pert Company reports net income of $34,000 for 20X5 and pays no dividends.

Required

a. Present the workpaper eliminating entries needed to prepare a consolidated balance sheet on January 1, 20X5.
b. Assuming Emerald Corporation reported income from its separate operations of $80,000 in 20X5, compute the amount of consolidated net income and the amount of income to be assigned to noncontrolling shareholders in the 20X5 consolidated income statement.

P9–22   Ownership of Subsidiary Preferred Stock

Presley Pools Inc. purchased 60 percent of the common stock of Jacobs Jacuzzi Company on December 31, 20X6, for $1,800,000. All the excess of the cost of the investment over the book value of the shares acquired was attributable to goodwill. On December 31, 20X7, the management of Presley Pools reviewed the amount attributed to goodwill and concluded an impairment loss of $26,000 should be recognized in 20X7. On January 2, 20X7, Presley purchased 20 percent of the outstanding preferred shares of Jacobs for $42,000.

In its 20X6 annual report, Jacobs reported the following stockholders' equity balances at the end of the year:

Preferred Stock (10 percent, $100 par)	$ 200,000
Premium on Preferred Stock	5,000
Common Stock	500,000
Additional Paid-In Capital—Common	800,000
Retained Earnings	1,650,000
Total Stockholders' Equity	$3,155,000

The preferred stock is cumulative and has a liquidation value equal to its call price of $101 per share. Because of cash flow problems, Jacobs declared no dividends during 20X6, the first time a preferred dividend had been missed. With the improvement in operations during 20X7, Jacobs declared the current stated preferred dividend as well as preferred dividends in arrears; Jacobs also declared a common dividend for 20X7 of $10,000. Jacobs' reported net income for 20X7 was $280,000.

Required

a. Compute the amount of the preferred stockholders' claim on the net assets of Jacobs Jacuzzi on December 31, 20X6.

b. Compute the December 31, 20X6, book value of the Jacobs common shares purchased by Presley.

c. Compute the amount of goodwill associated with Presley's purchase of Jacobs common stock at the date of acquisition.

d. Compute the amount of income that should be assigned to the noncontrolling interest in the 20X7 consolidated income statement.

e. Compute the amount of income from its subsidiary that Presley should have recorded during 20X7 using the basic equity method.

f. Compute the total amount that should be reported as noncontrolling interest in the December 31, 20X7, consolidated balance sheet.

g. Present all elimination entries that should appear in a consolidation workpaper to prepare a complete set of 20X7 consolidated financial statements for Presley Pools and its subsidiary.

P9–23   Consolidation Workpaper with Subsidiary Preferred Stock

Brown Company owns 90 percent of the common stock and 60 percent of the preferred stock of White Corporation, both acquired at underlying book value on January 1, 20X1. Trial balances for the companies on December 31, 20X6, are as follows:

	Brown Company		White Corporation	
	Debit	*Credit*	*Debit*	*Credit*
Cash	$ 58,000		$100,000	
Accounts Receivable	80,000		120,000	
Dividends Receivable	9,000			
Inventory	100,000		200,000	
Buildings and Equipment (net)	360,000		270,000	
Investment in White Corporation:				
Preferred Stock	120,000			
Common Stock	364,500			
Cost of Goods Sold	280,000		170,000	
Depreciation and Amortization	40,000		30,000	
Other Expenses	131,000		20,000	
Dividends Declared:				
Preferred Stock			15,000	
Common Stock	60,000		10,000	
Accounts Payable		$ 100,000		$ 70,000
Bonds Payable		300,000		
Dividends Payable				15,000
Preferred Stock				200,000
Common Stock		200,000		100,000
Retained Earnings		435,000		250,000
Sales		500,000		300,000
Dividend Income		9,000		
Income from Subsidiary		58,500		
Total	$1,602,500	$1,602,500	$935,000	$935,000

White Corporation's preferred shares pay a 7.5 percent annual dividend and are cumulative. Preferred dividends for 20X6 were declared on December 31, 20X6, and are to be paid January 1, 20X7.

Required

a. Prepare the eliminating entries needed to complete a full consolidation workpaper for 20X6.

b. Prepare a consolidation workpaper as of December 31, 20X6.

P9–24   Subsidiary Stock Transactions

Apex Corporation acquired 75 percent of the common stock of Beta Company on May 15, 20X3, at underlying book value. The balance sheet of Beta Company on December 31, 20X6, contained the following amounts:

Cash	$ 55,000	Accounts Payable	$ 30,000
Accounts Receivable	70,000	Bonds Payable	200,000
Inventory	125,000	Common Stock ($10 par)	100,000
Buildings and Equipment	700,000	Additional Paid-In Capital	80,000
Less: Accumulated Depreciation	(220,000)	Retained Earnings	320,000
Total Assets	$730,000	Total Liabilities and Equities	$730,000

The consolidated income statement for 20X1 shows the following amounts:

Consolidated Operating Income	$190,000
Less: Income Tax Expense	(76,000)
Income Available to All Shareholders	$114,000
Less: Income Assigned to Noncontrolling Interest	(6,000)
Consolidated Net Income	$108,000

Income assigned to the noncontrolling interest is computed as follows:

Special Foods' income before tax	$50,000
Income tax expense assigned to Special Foods	(20,000)
Special Foods' net income	$30,000
Noncontrolling stockholders' proportionate share	× .20
Income assigned to noncontrolling interest	$ 6,000

Other allocation bases may be preferred when affiliates have significantly different tax characteristics, such as when only one of the companies qualifies for special tax exemptions or credits.

Tax Effects of Unrealized Intercompany Profit Eliminations

The income tax effects of unrealized intercompany profit eliminations depend on whether the companies within the consolidated entity file a consolidated tax return or separate tax returns.

Unrealized Profits When a Consolidated Return Is Filed. Intercompany transfers are eliminated in computing both consolidated net income and taxable income when a consolidated tax return is filed. Only sales outside the consolidated entity are recognized, both for tax and for financial reporting purposes. Because profits are taxed in the same period they are recognized for financial reporting purposes, no *temporary differences* arise, and no additional tax accruals are needed in preparing the consolidated financial statements.

Unrealized Profits When Separate Returns Are Filed. When the companies within a consolidated entity each file separate income tax returns, they are taxed individually on the profits from intercompany sales. The focus in separate tax returns is on the transactions of the separate companies, and no consideration is given to whether the intercompany profits are realized from a consolidated viewpoint. Thus, the profit from an intercompany sale is taxed when the intercompany transfer occurs, without waiting for confirmation through sale to a nonaffiliate. For consolidated financial reporting purposes, however, unrealized intercompany profits must be eliminated. While the separate company may pay income taxes on the unrealized intercompany profit, the tax expense must be eliminated when the unrealized intercompany profit is eliminated in the preparation of consolidated financial statements. This difference in the timing of the income tax expense recognition results in the recording of *deferred income taxes.*

For example, if Special Foods sells inventory costing $23,000 to Peerless Products for $28,000, and none is resold before year-end, the entry to eliminate the intercorporate transfer when consolidated statements are prepared is:

E(17) Sales	28,000	
Cost of Goods Sold		23,000
Inventory		5,000
Eliminate intercompany upstream sale of inventory.		

Income assigned to the shareholders of Special Foods is reduced by $5,000 as a result of entry E(17). An adjustment to tax expense also is required in preparing consolidated statements if Special Foods files a separate tax return. With a 40 percent corporate income tax rate, eliminating entry E(18) adjusts income tax expense of the consolidated entity downward by $2,000 ($5,000 × .40) to reflect the reduction of reported profits:

E(18) Deferred Tax Asset	2,000	
Income Tax Expense		2,000
Eliminate tax expense on unrealized intercompany profit.		

The debit to the deferred tax asset in entry E(18) reflects the tax effect of a temporary difference between the income reported in the consolidated income statement and that reported in the separate tax returns of the companies within the consolidated entity. Consistent with the treatment accorded other temporary differences, this tax effect normally is carried to the consolidated balance sheet as an asset. If the intercompany profit is expected to be recognized in the consolidated income statement in the next year, the deferred taxes are classified as current.

Unrealized Profit in Separate Tax Return Illustrated.   For purposes of illustrating the treatment of income taxes when Peerless and Special Foods file separate tax returns, assume the following information:

1. Peerless owns 80 percent of the common stock of Special Foods, purchased at book value.
2. During 20X1, Special Foods purchases inventory for $23,000 and sells it to Peerless for $28,000. Peerless continues to hold all the inventory at the end of 20X1.
3. The effective combined federal and state tax rate for both Peerless and Special Foods is 40 percent.

While the trial balance of Special Foods includes $50,000 of income before taxes and tax expense of $20,000 ($50,000 × .40), consolidated net income and income assigned to noncontrolling shareholders are based on realized net income of $27,000, computed as follows:

Special Foods' net income	$30,000
Add back income tax expense	20,000
Special Foods' income before taxes	$50,000
Unrealized profit on upstream sale	(5,000)
Special Foods' realized income before taxes	$45,000
Income taxes on realized income (40%)	(18,000)
Special Foods' realized net income	$27,000
Special Foods' realized net income assigned to:	
Controlling interest ($27,000 × .80)	$21,600
Noncontrolling interest ($27,000 × .20)	5,400
Special Foods' realized net income	$27,000

If Peerless accounts for its investment in Special Foods using the basic equity method, the eliminating entries needed for the preparation of a consolidation work-paper as of December 31, 20X1, are as follows:

E(19)	Income from Subsidiary	24,000	
	Dividends Declared		24,000
	Eliminate income from subsidiary:		
	$30,000 × .80		
E(20)	Income to Noncontrolling Interest	5,400	
	Noncontrolling Interest	600	
	Dividends Declared		6,000
	Assign income to noncontrolling interest:		
	$5,400 = $27,000 × .20		
	$600 = $6,000 − $5,400		
	$6,000 = $30,000 × .20		
E(21)	Common Stock—Special Foods	200,000	
	Retained Earnings, January 1	100,000	
	Investment in Special Foods Stock		240,000
	Noncontrolling Interest		60,000
	Eliminate beginning investment balance.		
E(22)	Sales	28,000	
	Cost of Goods Sold		23,000
	Inventory		5,000
	Eliminate intercompany upstream sale of inventory.		
E(23)	Deferred Tax Asset	2,000	
	Income Tax Expense		2,000
	Eliminate tax expense on unrealized intercompany profit:		
	$5,000 × .40		

Entries E(19), E(20), and E(21) are the normal entries to eliminate the dividends declared and beginning stockholders' equity accounts of the subsidiary, the investment account of the parent, and income from the subsidiary recognized by the parent, and to establish the noncontrolling interest. As can be seen from entry E(19), Special Foods distributed its entire 20X1 reported net income as dividends. Thus, the balance of the investment account remains at the original cost. Because the realized net income of Special Foods ($27,000) was less than dividends paid ($30,000), entry E(20) contains a debit to noncontrolling interest indicating a reduction in the claim of the noncontrolling shareholders during the period. Entries E(22) and E(23) eliminate the effects of the intercompany transaction, establish the tax effects of the temporary difference, and reduce consolidated net income by the unrealized intercompany profit net of taxes.

Another temporary difference normally would be included in the consolidated balance sheet and in the computation of consolidated income tax expense. In addition to temporary differences arising from unrealized profits, there normally are differences between subsidiary net income and dividend distributions. Peerless pays income taxes for the period based on its reported dividends from Special Foods but includes in consolidated net income for financial reporting its proportionate share of Special Foods' realized net income. This difference between the amount of income reported in the consolidated income statement and the amount reported in the tax return is considered a temporary difference, and deferred taxes normally must be recognized on this difference. In this example, Special Foods distributes all its income as dividends, and the only temporary difference relates to the unrealized intercompany profit.

Subsequent Profit Realization When Separate Returns Are Filed.   When unrealized intercompany profits at the end of one period subsequently are recognized in another period, the tax effects of the temporary difference must again be considered.

If income taxes were ignored, eliminating entry E(24) would be used in preparing consolidated statements as of December 31, 20X2, assuming Special Foods had $5,000 of unrealized inventory profit on its books on January 1, 20X2, and the inventory was resold in 20X2:

E(24)	Retained Earnings, January 1	4,000	
	Noncontrolling Interest	1,000	
	Cost of Goods Sold		5,000
	Eliminate beginning inventory profit.		

On the other hand, if the 40 percent tax rate is considered, eliminating entry E(25) is used in place of entry E(24):

E(25)	Retained Earnings, January 1	2,400	
	Noncontrolling Interest	600	
	Income Tax Expense	2,000	
	Cost of Goods Sold		5,000
	Eliminate beginning inventory profit:		
	$2,400 = ($5,000 − $2,000) × .80		
	$600 = ($5,000 − $2,000) × .20		
	$2,000 = $5,000 × .40		

Unrealized profit of $3,000 rather than $5,000 is apportioned between the controlling and noncontrolling shareholders in this case. Tax expense of $2,000 is recognized for financial reporting purposes in 20X2 even though the $5,000 of intercompany profit was reported on Special Foods' separate tax return and the $2,000 of taxes was paid on the profit in 20X1. Entry E(25) recognizes the tax expense in the consolidated income statement in the same year as the income is recognized from a consolidated viewpoint. No workpaper adjustment to the Deferred Tax Asset account is needed at the end of 20X2 because the deferred tax asset was entered only in the consolidation workpaper at the end of 20X1 and not on the books of either company; it does not carry over to 20X2.

MULTINATIONAL ACCOUNTING: FOREIGN CURRENCY TRANSACTIONS AND FINANCIAL INSTRUMENTS

Many companies, large and small, depend on international markets for supplies of goods and for sales of their products and services. Every day the business press carries stories about the effects of export and import activity on the U.S. economy and the large flows of capital among the world's major countries. Also reported are changes in the exchange rates of the major currencies of the world, such as "The dollar weakened today against the yen." This chapter and Chapter 12 discuss the accounting issues associated with companies that operate internationally.

A company operating in international markets is subject to normal business risks such as lack of demand for its products in the foreign marketplace, labor strikes, and transportation delays in getting its products to the foreign customer. In addition, the U.S. entity may incur foreign currency risks whenever it conducts transactions in other currencies. For example, if a U.S. company acquires a machine on credit from a Swiss manufacturer, the Swiss company may require payment in Swiss francs (SFr). This means the U.S. company must eventually use a foreign currency broker or a bank to exchange U.S. dollars for Swiss franc in order to pay for the machine. In the process, the U.S. company may experience foreign currency gains or losses from fluctuations in the value of the U.S. dollar relative to the Swiss franc.

Multinational enterprises (MNEs) often transact in a variety of currencies as a result of their export and import activities. There are approximately 150 different currencies around the world, but most international trade has been settled in seven major currencies that have shown stability and general acceptance over time: the U.S. dollar, the British pound, the Canadian dollar, the French franc, the German mark, the Japanese yen, and the Swiss franc. The International Monetary Fund (IMF) is an organization that provides financial assistance to many countries and promotes international monetary cooperation, currency stability, and trade. Among the 150 members of the IMF are the leaders of the seven major industrial democracies—the United States, Britain, Canada, France, Germany, Italy, and Japan. These seven countries are sometimes referred to as The Group of Seven because of their dominance of the IMF.

A growing international trend is the adoption of the ISO 9000 series of standards by companies engaging in international trade. These standards, adopted by the International Organization for Standardization (ISO) in 1987, specify the degree of conformance to rigorous quality programs in various product design and production processes. Companies undergo a thorough quality control audit during the certification process, and many of these companies see the ISO 9000 series of standards as part of their total quality management programs. The value of the ISO certification in the marketplace is that a company's customers are given additional assurance that the certified company focuses on continuous improvement and has a quality focus in all its processes from the initial stages of production through postsale servicing. Awareness of the ISO 9000 standards is broadening, and some international customers now specify that their company's preferred vendors must have ISO 9000 certification.

Regional groupings will become increasingly important in the future. Three regional blocs, the North American, Western European, and Asian, have seen trade grow rapidly within each bloc while growing more slowly with trading partners outside the blocs. On November 17, 1993, the U.S. Congress approved the North American Free Trade Agreement (NAFTA) that created a free-trade area of Canada, the United States, and Mexico, a market exceeding 360 million people. Over time, the agreement will result in the elimination of tariffs (taxes) on goods shipped between these three countries. The European Economic Area (EEA) encompasses about 355 million people and 18 European nations. Consistent efforts have been made to reduce barriers to trade among the European nations since the original signing of the Treaty of Rome in 1957. The East Asia Economic Group (EAEG) is composed of more than 600 million persons from the Pacific Rim countries. The agreements among the members of the EAEG tend to focus on formalizing trade arrangements in Pacific Asia rather than on standardizing production quality as is the focus of many of the agreements within the European Economic Area.

The European Monetary Union (EMU) is comprised of 15 of the major European countries. Beginning in 1999, and continuing through 2002, a common currency, termed the *euro,* is being introduced into the EMU countries. Over time, it is planned that the "old" currencies such as the French franc, the German mark, and other European currencies will be traded in for the joint European currency. The transition to the common currency is expected to take several years because some citizens in each of the individual countries will likely be unwilling to give up their national currencies.

Currency names and symbols often reflect a country's nationalistic pride and history. For example, the U.S. dollar receives its name from a variation of the German word *Taler,* the name of a silver piece that was first minted in 1518 and became the chief coin of Europe and the new world. Some historians argue that the dollar symbol ($) is derived from a capital letter *U* superimposed over a capital letter *S.* The greenback as we know it today was first printed in 1862, in the midst of the Civil War, and now is issued by the 12 Federal Reserve banks scattered across the United States. The U.S. dollar can be identified in virtually every corner of the world because it has become one of the most widely traded currencies.

The Accounting Issues

Accountants must be able to record and report transactions involving exchanges of U.S. dollars and foreign currencies. ***Foreign currency transactions*** of a U.S. company include sales, purchases, and other transactions giving rise to a transfer of foreign currency or recording receivables or payables which are *denominated*—that is, numerically specified to be settled—in a foreign currency. Because financial statements of virtually all U.S. companies are prepared using the U.S. dollar as the reporting currency, transactions denominated in other currencies must be restated to their U.S. dollar equivalents before they can be recorded in the U.S. company's books and included in its financial statements. This process of restating foreign currency transactions to their U.S. dollar equivalent values is termed *translation.*

In addition, many large U.S. corporations have multinational operations, such as foreign-based subsidiaries or branches. For example, a U.S. auto manufacturer may have manufacturing subsidiaries in Canada, Mexico, Spain, and Great Britain. The foreign subsidiaries prepare their financial statements in the currency of their countries; for example, the Mexican subsidiary reports its operations in pesos. The foreign currency amounts in the financial statements of these subsidiaries have to be translated, that is, restated, into their U.S. dollar equivalents, before they can be consolidated with the financial statements of the U.S. parent company that uses the U.S. dollar as its reporting currency unit.

This chapter presents the accounting procedures for recording and reporting foreign transactions. Chapter 12 presents the procedures for combining or consolidating a foreign entity with a U.S. parent company. **FASB Statement No. 52,** "Foreign Currency Translation" **(FASB 52),** issued in 1981, serves as the primary guide for accounting for accounts receivable and accounts payable foreign currency–denominated transactions that require payment or receipt of foreign currency. **FASB Statement No. 133,** "Accounting for Derivative Instruments and Hedging Activities" **(FASB 133),** issued in 1998, guides the accounting for financial instruments specified as derivatives for the purpose of hedging certain items.

Foreign Currency Exchange Rates

Before 1972, most major currencies were valued on the basis of a gold standard whereby their international values were fixed per ounce of gold. However, in 1972, most countries signed an agreement to permit the values of their currencies to "float" based on the supply and demand for their currencies. The resulting *foreign currency exchange rates* between currencies are established daily by foreign exchange brokers who serve as agents for individuals or countries wishing to deal in foreign currencies. Some countries, such as China, maintain an official fixed rate of currency exchange and have established fixed exchange rates for dividends remitted outside the country. These official rates may be changed at any time, and companies doing business abroad should contact the government of the foreign country to ensure that the companies are in compliance with any currency exchange restrictions.

The Determination of Exchange Rates

A country's currency is much like any other commodity, and exchange rates change because of a number of economic factors affecting the supply of, and demand for, a nation's currency. For example, if a nation is experiencing high levels of inflation, the purchasing power of its currency will decrease. This reduction in the value of a currency is reflected by a decrease in the positioning of that country's currency relative to other nations' currencies. Other factors causing exchange rate fluctuations are a nation's balance of payments, changes in a country's interest rate and investment levels, and the stability and process of governance. For example, if the United States had a higher average interest rate than Great Britain, the international investment community would seek to invest in the United States, thus increasing the demand for U.S. dollars relative to British pounds. The dollar would increase in value relative to the pound because of the increased demand. Exchange rates are determined daily and published in several sources, including *The Wall Street Journal.* Figure 11–1 presents an example of a typical daily business press report for selected foreign exchange rates. The rates illustrated in the table are representative averages of the relationships between the U.S. dollar and the other currencies over the last five years. They are not meant to illustrate current exchange rates. Current exchange rates may be obtained from most business publications and from many metropolitan newspapers.

The business press also notes the European currency unit which is called the "euro" (symbol €). In 2002, the euro becomes the standard currency unit for the members of the European Monetary Union (EMU). The initial EMU members joining together in 1998 include Germany, France, Italy, Spain, Portugal, Finland, Ireland, Belgium, The Netherlands, and Austria. Of special note is that the United Kingdom decided not to immediately join the EMU. The official conversion rate of the local currencies and the euro were established as of January 1, 1999. For example, it was decided that the conversion rate for the German mark would be DM 1.95583 equals 1 euro. Euro bank notes and coins go into circulation in 2002. With such a large monetary conversion, however, it is also expected that several countries will take some time to convert their day-to-day transactions to the euro. Nevertheless, for U.S. companies engaged in international trade with foreign companies located in the EMU countries, the euro will become an accepted currency of international business.

Direct versus Indirect Exchange Rates

As indicated in Figure 11–1, the relative value of one currency to another may be expressed in two different ways: either *directly or indirectly.*

Direct Exchange Rate.   The direct exchange rate is the number of ***local currency units (LCUs)*** needed to acquire one ***foreign currency unit (FCU).*** From the viewpoint of a U.S. entity, the direct exchange rate can be viewed as the dollar cost of one foreign currency unit. The direct exchange rate ratio is expressed as follows, with the LCU, the U.S. dollar, in the numerator:

$$\frac{\text{U.S. dollar equivalent value}}{1 \text{ FCU}}$$

The direct exchange rate is used most often in accounting for foreign operations and transactions because the foreign currency–denominated accounts must be translated to their U.S. dollar equivalent values. For example, if $1.20 can acquire €1 (1 European euro), the direct exchange rate of the dollar versus the European euro is $1.20, as follows:

$$\frac{\$1.20}{€1} = \$1.20$$

Indirect Exchange Rate.   The indirect exchange rate is the reciprocal of the direct exchange rate. From the viewpoint of a U.S. entity, the indirect exchange rate can be viewed as the number of foreign currency units that 1 U.S. dollar can acquire. The ratio to compute the indirect exchange rate is:

$$\frac{1 \text{ FCU}}{\text{U.S. dollar equivalent value}}$$

FIGURE 11–1   Average Foreign Exchange Rates for Selected Major Currencies

Country	Direct Exchange Rate (U.S. Dollar Equivalent)	Indirect Exchange Rate (Currency per U.S. Dollar)
Australia (dollar)	.7700	1.2987
Belgium (franc)	.0306	32.68
Brazil (real)	.9518	1.0506
Britain (pound)	1.6120	.6203
30-day forward	1.6110	.6207
90-day forward	1.6090	.6215
180-day forward	1.6060	.6227
Canada (dollar)	.7340	1.3623
30-day forward	.7360	1.3587
90-day forward	.7390	1.3532
180-day forward	.7430	1.3459
Chile (peso)	.0030	333.33
China (renminbi)	.1201	8.3239
France (franc)	.1850	5.4054
30-day forward	.1851	5.4025
90-day forward	.1855	5.3908
180-day forward	.1852	5.4000
Germany (mark)	.6000	1.6667
30-day forward	.5900	1.6950
90-day forward	.5800	1.7241
180-day forward	.5500	1.8182
Greece (drachma)	.0038	263.85
Hong Kong (dollar)	.1280	7.8125
India (rupee)	.0279	35.88
Ireland (pound)	1.6800	.5952
Israel (shekel)	.2990	3.344
Italy (lira)	.0008	1250.00
Japan (yen)	.0070	142.86
30-day forward	.0071	140.85
90-day forward	.0073	136.99
180-day forward	.0075	133.33
Mexico (peso)	.1289	7.76
Spain (peseta)	.007	142.86
Sweden (krona)	.1350	7.4074
Switzerland (franc)	.7300	1.3698
30-day forward	.7310	1.3680
90-day forward	.7350	1.3605
180-day forward	.7400	1.3514
Taiwan (dollar)	.0370	27.03
EMU (euro)	.9262	1.0796

For the European euro example, the indirect exchange rate is:

$$\frac{€1}{\$1.20} = €0.8333$$

This is also expressed as €0.8333 = $1 to show the number of foreign currency units that may be obtained for 1 U.S. dollar. Note that the direct and indirect rates are inversely related and that both state the same relationship between two currencies. Some slight differences between the two rates may be found in the exchange markets because of brokers' commissions.

Changes in Exchange Rates

A change in an exchange rate is referred to as a *strengthening* or *weakening* of one currency against another. For example, the exchange rate of the U.S. dollar versus the euro changed as follows:

	January 1	July 1	December 31
Direct exchange rate (U.S. dollar equivalent of 1 FCU)	$1.200	$1.100	$1.160
Indirect exchange rate (FCU per 1 U.S. dollar)	€0.8333	€0.9090	€0.862

Strengthening of the U.S. Dollar—Direct Exchange Rate Decreases. Between January 1 and July 1, the direct exchange rate has decreased from $1.20 = €1 to $1.10 = €1, indicating that it takes less U.S. currency ($) to acquire 1 European euro (€). Note that the cost of 1 euro was $1.20 on January 1, but decreased to $1.10 on July 1. This means that the value of the U.S. currency has risen relative to the euro. This is termed a *strengthening* of the dollar versus the euro. Alternatively, looking at the indirect exchange rate, 1 U.S. dollar can acquire .8333 European euros on January 1, but it can acquire more euros, .9090, on July 1. Thus the relative value of the dollar versus the euro is greater on July 1 than on January 1.

Imports from Europe would be less expensive for U.S. consumers on July 1 than on January 1 because of the strengthening of the dollar. For example, assume that a European manufacturer is selling a German-made automobile for €25,000. To determine the U.S. dollar equivalent value of the €25,000 on January 1, the following equation is used:

$$
\begin{array}{ccccc}
\textbf{U.S. dollar} & & \textbf{Foreign currency} & & \textbf{Direct exchange} \\
\textbf{equivalent value} & = & \textbf{units} & \times & \textbf{rate} \\
\$30{,}000 & = & €25{,}000 & \times & \$1.20
\end{array}
$$

Between January 1 and July 1, the direct exchange rate decreased as the dollar strengthened relative to the euro. On July 1, the U.S. dollar equivalent value of the €25,000 is:

$$
\begin{array}{ccccc}
\textbf{U.S. dollar} & & \textbf{Foreign currency} & & \textbf{Direct exchange} \\
\textbf{equivalent value} & = & \textbf{units} & \times & \textbf{rate} \\
\$27{,}500 & = & €25{,}000 & \times & \$1.10
\end{array}
$$

While a strengthening of the dollar is favorable for U.S. companies purchasing goods from another country, it adversely affects U.S. companies selling products in that country. Following a strengthening of the dollar, U.S. exports to Europe would be more expensive for European customers. For example, assume a U.S. manufacturer is selling a U.S.-made machine for $10,000. To determine the foreign currency (euro) equivalent value of the $10,000 on January 1, the following equation is used:

$$
\begin{array}{ccccc}
\textbf{Foreign currency} & & \textbf{U.S. dollar} & & \textbf{Indirect exchange} \\
\textbf{equivalent value} & = & \textbf{units} & \times & \textbf{rate} \\
€8{,}333 & = & \$10{,}000 & \times & €0.8333
\end{array}
$$

On July 1, after a strengthening of the dollar, the machine would cost the European customer €9,090, as follows:

$$
\begin{array}{ccccc}
\textbf{Foreign currency} & & \textbf{U.S. dollar} & & \textbf{Indirect exchange} \\
\textbf{equivalent value} & = & \textbf{units} & \times & \textbf{rate} \\
€9{,}090 & = & \$10{,}000 & \times & €0.9090
\end{array}
$$

FIGURE 11–2   **Relationships between Currencies and Exchange Rates**

	January 1	July 1	December 31
Direct exchange rate ($/€1)	$1.200	$1.100	$1.160
Indirect exchange rate (€/$1)	€0.8333	€0.9090	€0.8620

Between January 1 and July 1:

Direct rate decreases
Dollar strengthens
Euro weakens
Indirect rate increases
Foreign goods imported into U.S. less expensive
U.S.-made exports from U.S. more expensive

Between July 1 and December 31:

Direct rate increases
Dollar weakens
Euro strengthens
Indirect rate decreases

This substantial increase in cost could result in the European customer's deciding not to acquire the machine from the U.S. company. Thus, a U.S. company's international sales can be seriously affected by changes in foreign currency exchange rates.

Weakening of the U.S. Dollar—Direct Exchange Rate Increases. Between July 1 and December 31, the direct exchange rate has increased from $1.10 = €1 to $1.16 = €1, indicating that it now takes more dollars to acquire euros. On July 1, a euro costs $1.10, but on December 31, the relative cost for 1 euro has increased to $1.16. This means that the value of the U.S. currency has dropped relative to the euro. This is termed a *weakening* of the dollar against the euro. Another way to view this change is to note that the indirect exchange rate has decreased, indicating that on December 31, 1 dollar acquires fewer euros than on July 1. On July 1, 1 U.S. dollar can acquire .9090 euros, but on December 31, 1 U.S. dollar can acquire fewer euros, .862, indicating that the relative value of the dollar has dropped between July 1 and December 31.

The relationships between currencies, imports, and exports is summarized in Figure 11–2.

During the latter part of the 1970s, the dollar consistently weakened against other major currencies because of several factors, including the high inflation the United States experienced. This weakening did help the United States' balance of trade, because it reduced the quantity of then-more expensive imports, while making U.S.-made goods less expensive in other countries. In the first half of the 1980s, the dollar consistently strengthened relative to other currencies. Not only was the U.S. economy strong and producing goods more efficiently, but high interest rates attracted large foreign investment in the U.S. capital markets. A stronger dollar added to the foreign trade deficit by making imports less expensive and U.S.-made goods more expensive on the world market. Beginning in 1986 and continuing through the early 1990s, the dollar again weakened relative to the major international currencies. But in the latter 1990s and into the early 2000s, the dollar generally strengthened because of the robustness of the U.S. economy.

These changes in the international value of the dollar affect any consumer acquiring imported goods. A weakening dollar means that imports become more expensive while a strengthening dollar means that imports become less expensive.

Spot Rates versus Current Rates

FASB 52 refers to the use of both spot rates and current rates for measuring foreign operations. The spot rate is the exchange rate for immediate delivery of currencies. The current rate is defined simply as the spot rate on the entity's balance sheet date.

Forward Exchange Rates

A third exchange rate is the rate on future, or forward, exchanges of currencies. Figure 11–1 shows these exchange rates for the major international currencies for 30, 90, and 180 days forward. Active markets in *forward exchange contracts* are maintained for companies wishing to receive, or deliver, major international currencies. The advantage of a forward exchange market is that the U.S. dollar equivalent value of a future receipt or disbursement of foreign currency units may be fixed at the time a contract is made. For example, a U.S. company may have a liability in British pounds due in 30 days. Rather than wait 30 days to buy the pounds and risk having the dollar weaken in value relative to the pound, the company can buy a 30-day forward exchange contract at the forward exchange rate in effect on the contract date. The contract enables the buyer to receive British pounds from an exchange broker 30 days from the contract date at a price fixed now by the contract.

The next section of the chapter presents the accounting for import and export transactions and for forward exchange contracts.

Foreign Currency Transactions

As defined earlier, foreign currency transactions are economic activities denominated in a currency other than the entity's recording currency. These transactions may be:

1. Purchases or sales of goods or services (imports or exports), the prices of which are stated in a foreign currency.
2. Loans payable or receivable in a foreign currency.
3. The purchase or sale of forward exchange contracts.
4. Purchase or sale of foreign currency units.

One of the parties in a foreign exchange transaction must exchange its own currency for another country's currency. The normal business practice is to require settlement of the transaction in the domestic currency of the selling or lending company, but the agreement between the parties may state otherwise.

For financial statement purposes, transactions denominated in a foreign currency must be translated into the currency used by the reporting company. Additionally, at each balance sheet date—interim as well as annual—account balances denominated in a currency other than the entity's reporting currency must be adjusted to reflect changes in exchange rates during the period since the last balance sheet date or since the foreign currency transaction date if it occurred during the period. This adjustment restates the foreign currency–denominated accounts to their U.S. dollar equivalent values as of the balance sheet date. The adjustment in equivalent U.S. dollar values is a *foreign currency transaction gain or loss* for the entity when exchange rates have changed. For example, assume that a U.S. company acquires €5,000 from its bank on January 1, 20X1, for use in future purchases from German companies. The direct exchange rate is $1.20 = €1; thus the company pays the bank $6,000 for the €5,000. The following entry records this exchange of currencies:

January 1, 20X1
(1)	Foreign Currency Units (€)	6,000	
	Cash		6,000

The parenthetical notation (€) is used after the debit account to indicate that the asset is European euros, but for accounting purposes it is recorded and reported in its U.S. dollar equivalent value. This translation to the U.S. equivalent value is required in order to add the value of the foreign currency units to all the company's other accounts that are reported in dollars.

On July 1, 20X1, the exchange rate is $1.100 = €1 as represented in the following time line:

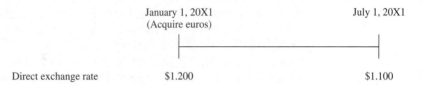

	January 1, 20X1 (Acquire euros)	July 1, 20X1
Direct exchange rate	$1.200	$1.100

By holding the foreign currency units during a time when the dollar strengthens relative to the euro, the company experiences a foreign currency transaction loss, as follows:

Equivalent dollar value of €5.000 on January 1:	
€5.000 × $1.200	$6,000
Equivalent dollar value of €5.000 on July 1:	
€5.000 × $1.100	5,500
Foreign currency transaction loss	$ 500

If the U.S. company prepares financial statements on July 1, the following adjusting entry is required:

July 1, 20X1
(2)	Foreign Currency Transaction Loss	500	
	Foreign Currency Units (€)		500

The foreign currency transaction loss is the result of a foreign currency transaction and is included in this period's income statement, usually as a separate item under "Other Income or Loss." Some accountants use the account title Exchange Loss instead of the longer title Foreign Currency Transaction Loss. In this book, the longer, more descriptive account title is used in order to communicate fully the source of the loss. The Foreign Currency Units account is reported on the balance sheet at a value of $5,500, its equivalent U.S. dollar value on that date.

In the previous examples, the U.S. company used the U.S. dollar as its primary currency for performing its major financial and operating functions, that is, as its *functional currency.* Also, the U.S. company prepared its financial statements in U.S. dollars, its *reporting currency.* Any transactions denominated in currencies other than the U.S. dollar require translation to their equivalent U.S. dollar values. Generally, the majority of cash transactions of a business take place in the *local currency* of the country in which the entity operates. The U.S. dollar is the functional currency for virtually all companies based in the United States. A company operating in Germany might use the European euro as its functional currency. In this chapter, the local currency is assumed to be the entity's functional and reporting currency. The few exceptions to this general case are discussed in Chapter 12.

Illustrations of various types of foreign currency transactions are given in the sections that follow. Note that different exchange rates are used to value selected foreign currency transactions, depending on a number of factors such as management's reason for entering the foreign currency transaction, the nature of the transaction, and the timing of the transaction.

Foreign Currency Import and Export Transactions

Payables and receivables that arise from transactions with foreign-based entities, and that are denominated in a foreign currency, must be measured and recorded by the U.S. entity in the currency used for its accounting records—the U.S. dollar. The relevant exchange rate for settlement of a transaction denominated in a foreign currency is the spot exchange rate on the date of settlement. At the time the transaction is settled, payables or receivables denominated in foreign currency units must be adjusted to their current U.S. dollar equivalent value. If financial statements are prepared before the foreign currency payables or receivables are settled, their account balances must be adjusted to their U.S. dollar equivalent values as of the balance sheet date, using the current rate on the balance sheet date.

An overview of the required accounting for an import or export foreign currency transaction on credit is as follows:

1. *Transaction date.* Record the purchase or sale transaction at the U.S. dollar equivalent value using the spot rate of exchange on this date.
2. *Balance sheet date.* Adjust the payable or receivable to its U.S. dollar equivalent, end-of-period value using the current exchange rate. Recognize any exchange gain or loss for the change in rates between the transaction and balance sheet dates.
3. *Settlement date.* First adjust the foreign currency payable or receivable for any changes in the exchange rate between the balance sheet date (or transaction date if transaction occurs after the balance sheet date) and the settlement date, recording any exchange gain or loss as required. Then record the settlement of the foreign currency payable or receivable.

This adjustment process is required because the FASB adopted what is called the *two-transaction approach,* which views the purchase or sale of an item as a separate transaction from the foreign currency commitment. By adopting the two-transaction approach to foreign currency transactions, the FASB established the general rule that foreign currency exchange gains or losses resulting from the revaluation of assets or liabilities denominated in a foreign currency must be recognized currently in the income statement of the period in which the exchange rate changes. A few exceptions to this general rule are allowed and are discussed later in this chapter.

Illustration of Foreign Purchase Transaction.   Figure 11–3 illustrates the journal entries used to measure and record a purchase of goods from a foreign supplier denominated either in the entity's local currency or in a foreign currency. On the left side of Figure 11–3, the transaction is denominated in U.S. dollars, the recording and

FIGURE 11–3   **Comparative U.S. Company Journal Entries for Foreign Purchase Transaction Denominated in Dollars versus Foreign Currency Units**

If Denominated in U.S. Dollars			If Denominated in Japanese Yen		
			October 1, 20X1 (Date of Purchase)		
Inventory	14,000		Inventory	14,000	
Accounts Payable		14,000	Accounts Payable (¥)		14,000
			$14,000 = ¥2,000,000 × $.0070 spot rate		
			December 31, 20X1 (Balance Sheet Date)		
No entry			Foreign Currency Transaction Loss	2,000	
			Accounts Payable (¥)		2,000
			Adjust payable denominated in foreign currency to current U.S. dollar equivalent and recognize exchange loss:		
			$\$ 16,000 = ¥2,000,000 × \$.0080$ Dec. 31 spot rate		
			$-14,000 = ¥2,000,000 × \$.0070$ Oct. 1 spot rate		
			$\$ \ \ 2,000 = ¥2,000,000 × (\$.0080 - \$.0070)$		
			April 1, 20X2 (Settlement Date)		
			Accounts Payable (¥)	800	
			Foreign Currency Transaction Gain		800
			Adjust payable denominated in foreign currency to current U.S. dollar equivalent and recognize exchange gain:		
			$\$ 15,200 = ¥2,000,000 × \$.0076$ Apr. 1 spot rate		
			$-16,000 = ¥2,000,000 × \$.0080$ Dec. 31 spot rate		
			$\$ \ \ \ \ 800 = ¥2,000,000 × (\$.0076 - \$.0080)$		
			Foreign Currency Units (¥)	15,200	
			Cash		15,200
			Acquire FCU to settle debt:		
			$\$15,200 = ¥2,000,000 × \$.0076$ April 1 spot rate		
Accounts Payable	14,000		Accounts Payable (¥)	15,200	
Cash		14,000	Foreign Currency Units (¥)		15,200

reporting currency of the U.S. company; on the right side, the transaction is denominated in Japanese yen (¥). The U.S. company is subject to a foreign currency transaction gain or loss only if the transaction is denominated in the foreign currency. If the foreign transaction is denominated in U.S. dollars, no special accounting problems exist and no currency rate adjustments are necessary.

The following information describes the case:

1. On October 1, 20X1, Peerless Products, a U.S. company, acquired goods on account from Tokyo Industries, a Japanese company, for $14,000, or 2,000,000 yen.

2. Peerless Products prepared financial statements at its year-end of December 31, 20X1.

3. Settlement of the payable was made on April 1, 20X2.

The direct spot exchange rates of the U.S. dollar equivalent value of 1 yen were as follows:

Date	Direct Exchange Rate
October 1, 20X1 (transaction date)	$.0070
December 31, 20X1 (balance sheet date)	.0080
April 1, 20X2 (settlement date)	.0076

A time line may help to clarify the relationships between the dates and the economic events, as follows:

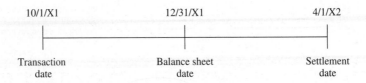

10/1/X1	12/31/X1	4/1/X2
Transaction date	Balance sheet date	Settlement date

Accounts relating to transactions denominated in yen are noted by the parenthetical symbol for the yen (¥) after the account title. As you proceed through the example, you should especially note the assets and liabilities denominated in the foreign currency and the adjustment needed to reflect their current values by use of the U.S. dollar equivalent rate of exchange.

Key Observations from Illustration. If the purchase contract is denominated in dollars, the foreign entity (Tokyo Industries) bears the foreign currency exchange risk. If the transaction is denominated in yen, then the U.S. company (Peerless Products Corporation) is exposed to exchange rate gains and losses. The accounts relating to liabilities denominated in foreign currency units must be valued at the spot rate, with any foreign currency transaction gain or loss recognized in the period's income. The purchase contract includes specification of the denominated currency as agreed upon by the two parties.

On October 1, 20X1, the purchase is recorded on the books of Peerless Products. The U.S. dollar equivalent value of 2,000,000 yen on this date is $14,000 (¥2,000,000 × $.0070).

On December 31, 20X1, the balance sheet date, the payable denominated in foreign currency units must be adjusted to its current U.S. dollar equivalent value. The direct exchange rate has increased since the date of purchase, indicating that the U.S. dollar has weakened relative to the yen. Therefore, on December 31, 20X1, $16,000 is required to acquire 2,000,000 yen (¥2,000,000 × $.0080), whereas, on October 1, 20X1, only $14,000 was required to obtain 2,000,000 yen (¥2,000,000 × $.0070). This increase in the exchange rate requires the recognition of a $2,000 foreign currency transaction loss if the transaction is denominated in yen, the foreign currency unit. No entry is made if the transaction is denominated in U.S. dollars, because Peerless has a liability for $14,000 regardless of the changes in exchange rates.

occurred; that is, the purchase contract is still executory (unrecognized). The company will not have a liability obligation until after delivery of the goods, but it is exposed to changes in currency exchange rates before the transaction date (the date of delivery of the goods).

FASB 133, specified the accounting requirements for the use of forward exchange contracts *hedging identifiable, foreign currency commitments.* The company can separate the commitment into its financial instrument (the obligation to pay yen) and nonfinancial asset (the right to receive inventory) aspects. The forward contract taken out would then be a hedge of the obligation to pay yen (the foreign currency payable). This type of hedge comes under the accounting for fair-value hedges and the forward contract is to be valued at its fair value. **FASB 131** provides for management of an enterprise to select the basis by which the effectiveness of the hedge will be measured. Management may select the forward exchange rate, the spot rate, or the intrinsic value for measuring effectiveness. The examples used in this chapter use the forward rate, which is consistent with the general rule of valuing forward exchange contracts as specified in **FASB 133.** The measure of the change in fair value of the forward contract uses the forward exchange rate for the remainder of the term and then, if interest is significant, the change in the forward rates is discounted to reflect the time value of money. The entries for a hedge of an identifiable foreign currency commitment are presented in the following illustration.

Illustration of Hedging an Identifiable, Unrecognized Foreign Currency Commitment. For purposes of illustration, the import transaction between Peerless Products and Tokyo Industries used throughout this chapter is extended with the following information:

1. On August 1, 20X1, Peerless Products Corporation contracts to purchase special-order goods from Tokyo Industries. The manufacture and delivery of the goods will take place in 60 days (on October 1, 20X1). The contract price is 2,000,000 yen, to be paid by April 1, 20X2, which is 180 days after delivery.
2. On August 1, Peerless Products hedges its foreign currency payable commitment with a forward exchange contract to receive 2,000,000 yen in 240 days (the 60 days until delivery plus 180 days of credit period). The future rate for a 240-day forward contract is $.0073 to 1 yen. The purpose of this 240-day forward exchange contract is twofold. First, for the 60 days from August 1, 20X1, until October 1, 20X1, the forward exchange contract is a hedge of an identifiable foreign currency commitment. For the 180-day period from October 1, 20X1, until April 1, 20X2, the forward exchange contract is a hedge of a foreign currency exposed net liability position.

The relevant exchange rates for this example are as follows:

	U.S. Dollar Equivalent Value of 1 Yen	
Date	*Spot Rate*	*Forward Exchange Rate*
August 1, 20X1	$.0065	$.0073 (240-day)
October 1, 20X1	.0070	.0075 (180-day)

A time line for the transactions follows:

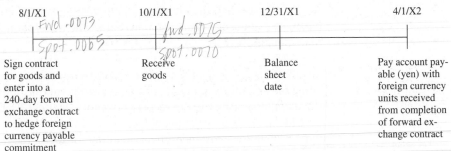

8/1/X1	10/1/X1	12/31/X1	4/1/X2
Sign contract for goods and enter into a 240-day forward exchange contract to hedge foreign currency payable commitment	Receive goods	Balance sheet date	Pay account payable (yen) with foreign currency units received from completion of forward exchange contract

On August 1, 20X1, the company determines the value of the obligation to pay yen for the future accounts payable, using the forward exchange rate. However, the payable is not recorded on August 1, because the exchange transaction has not yet occurred; the payable is maintained in a memorandum account only. The forward exchange contract must be valued at its fair value. At the time the company enters into the forward exchange contract, the contract has no net fair value because the foreign currency receivable equals the dollars payable under the contract. The subsequent changes in the fair value of the forward contract are measured using the forward rate and then, if interest is significant, discounted to reflect the time value of money. For purposes of this illustration, we assume that interest is not significant and that hedge effectiveness is measured with reference to the change in the forward exchange rates.

August 1, 20X1		
(14) Foreign Currency Receivable from Exchange Broker (¥)	14,600	
Dollars Payable to Exchange Broker ($)		14,600
Sign forward exchange contract for receipt of		
2,000,000 yen in 240 days:		
$14,600 = ¥2,000,000 × $.0073 Aug. 1 240-day forward rate		

On October 1, 20X1, the forward exchange contract is revalued to its fair value in accordance with **FASB 133.** The accounts payable in yen are recorded at the time the inventory is received.

October 1, 20X1		
(15) Foreign Currency Receivable from Exchange Broker (¥)	400	
Foreign Currency Transaction Gain		400
Adjust forward contract to fair value, using		
the forward rate at this date, and recognize gain:		
$ 15,000 = ¥2,000,000 × $.0075 Oct. 1 180-day forward rate		
−14,600 = ¥2,000,000 × $.0073 Aug. 1 240-day forward rate		
$ 400 = ¥2,000,000 × ($.0075 − $.0073)		

(16) Foreign Currency Transaction Loss	400	
Firm Commitment		400
To record the loss on the financial instrument aspect		
of the firm commitment:		
$ 15,000 = ¥2,000,000 × $.0075 Oct. 1 180-day forward rate		
−14,600 = ¥2,000,000 × $.0073 Aug. 1 240-day forward rate		
$ 400 = ¥2,000,000 × $($.0075 − $.0073)		

The firm commitment account is a temporary account for the term of the unrecognized firm commitment and, in this example, is shown in the liability section of the balance sheet.

The next entry is to record the receipt of the inventory and the recognition of the acounts payable in yen. Note that the temporary account, Firm Commitment, is closed against the purchase price of the inventory. The accounts payable are valued at the spot exchange rate in accordance with **FASB 52.**

(17)	Inventory	13,600	
	Firm Commitment	400	
	Accounts Payable(¥)		14,000
	Record accounts payable at spot rate and record inventory purchase:		
	$14,000 = ¥2,000,000 × $.0070 Oct. 1 spot rate		

Key Observations from Illustration.   The August 1, 20X1, entry records the signing of the forward exchange contract that is used to hedge the identifiable foreign currency commitment arising from the noncancelable purchase agreement. In entries (15) and (16), the forward contract and the underlying hedged foreign currency payable commitment are both revalued to their current value, and the gain of $400 on the forward contract offsets the loss of $400 on the foreign currency payable commitment. Entry (17) records the accounts payable in yen at the current spot rate and records the inventory net of the $400 that resulted from the recognition of the $400 loss on the financial instrument aspect of the firm commitment in entry (16).

At this point, the company has an exposed net liability position, which is hedged with a forward exchange contract, and the subsequent accounting follows the accounting for an exposed foreign currency liability position as presented in Case 1 previously in the chapter. Figure 11–5 presents a side-by-side comparison of the journal entries for the forward contract and the unrecognized firm commitment, which are valued at the forward exchange rates. The exposed foreign currency denominated account payable is recognized at the time the company receives the inventory and is valued using the spot exchange rate.

Case 3. Speculation in Foreign Currency Markets

An entity may also decide to speculate in foreign currency as with any other commodity. For example, a U.S. company expects that the dollar will strengthen against the Swiss franc; that is, that the direct exchange rate will decrease. In this case, the U.S. company might *speculate with a forward exchange contract* to sell francs for future delivery, expecting to be able to purchase them at a lower price at the time of delivery.

The economic substance of this foreign currency speculation is to expose the investor to foreign exchange risk for which the investor expects to earn a profit. The exchange rate for valuing accounts related to speculative foreign exchange contracts is the forward rate for the remaining term of the forward contract. The gain or loss on a speculative forward contract is computed by determining the difference between the forward exchange rate on the date of contract (or on the date of a previous valuation) and the forward exchange rate available for the remaining term of the contract. The forward exchange rate is used to value the forward contract.

Illustration of Speculation with Forward Contract.   The following example illustrates the accounting for a U.S. company entering into a speculative forward exchange contract in Swiss francs (SFr), a currency in which the company has no receivables, payables, or commitments.

FIGURE 11–5 Comparison of Journal Entries: Hedge of an Unrecognized Firm Commitment

Forward Exchange Contract (Use forward exchange rate)			Hedge of an Unrecognized Firm Commitment (Use forward exchange rate)		

August 1, 20X1. Recognize forward exchange contract valued at forward rate.

(14) Foreign Currency Receivable (¥)	14,600				
Dollars Payable to Exchange Broker		14,600			

October 1, 20X1. Revalue foreign currency receivable and firm commitment hedge using forward rate.

(15) Foreign Currency Receivable (¥)	400		(16) Foreign Currency Transaction Loss	400	
Foreign Currency Transaction Gain		400	Firm Commitment		400

			Economic Hedge of an Exposed Payable (Use spot exchange rate)		

October 1, 20X1. Receive inventory, close firm commitment, and recognize foreign currency accounts payable.

			(17) Inventory	13,600	
			Firm Commitment	400	
			Accounts Payable (¥)		14,000

December 31, 20X1. Revalue forward contract using forward rate, and accounts payable in yen using spot rate.

(7) Foreign Currency Receivable (¥)	400		(8) Foreign Currency Transaction Loss	2,000	
Foreign Currency Transaction Gain		400	Accounts Payable (¥)		2,000

April 1, 20X2. Revalue forward contract at its termination to spot rate, and accounts payable in yen to spot rate.

(9) Foreign Currency Transaction Loss	200		(10) Accounts Payable (¥)	800	
Foreign Currency Receivable. (¥)		200	Foreign Currency Transaction Gain		800

April 1, 20X2. Deliver $14,600 in U.S. dollars to exchange broker, receiving yen. Use yen to settle accounts payable.

(11) Dollars Payable to Exchange Broker	14,600				
Cash		14,600			
(12) Foreign Currency Units (¥)	15,200		(13) Accounts Payable (¥)	15,200	
Foreign Curency Receivable (¥)		15,200	Foreign Currency Units (¥)		15,200

1. On October 1, 20X1, Peerless Products entered into a 180-day forward exchange contract to deliver SFr 4,000 at a forward rate of $.74 = SFr 1, when the spot rate was $.73 = SFr 1. Thus, the forward contract was to deliver SFr 4,000 and receive $2,960 (SFr 4,000 × $.74).

2. On December 31, 20X1, the balance sheet date, the forward rate for a 90-day forward contract was $.78 = SFr 1, and the spot rate for francs was $.75 = SFr 1.

3. On April 1, 20X2, the company acquired SFr 4,000 in the open market and delivered the francs to the broker, receiving the agreed forward contract price of $2,960. At this date, the spot rate was $.77 = SFr 1.

A summary of the direct exchange rates for this illustration is presented below.

	U.S. Dollar Equivalent of 1 Franc	
Date	*Spot Rate*	*Forward Rate*
October 1, 20X1	$.73	$.74 (180-day)
December 31, 20X1	.75	.78 (90-day)
April 1, 20X2	.77	

A time line of the economic events is as follows:

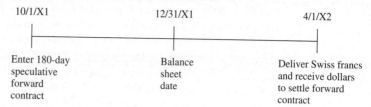

The entries for these transactions are as follows:

October 1, 20X1
(18)   Dollars Receivable from Exchange Broker ($)   2,960
        Foreign Currency Payable to Exchange Broker (SFr)   2,960
      Enter into speculative forward exchange contract:
      $2,960 = SFr 4,000 × $.74, the 180-day forward rate

December 31, 20X1
(19)   Foreign Currency Transaction Loss   160
        Foreign Currency Payable to Exchange Broker (SFr)   160
      Recognize speculation loss on forward contract for
      difference between initial 180-day forward
      rate and forward rate for remaining term
      to maturity of contract of 90 days:
      $160 = SFr 4,000 × ($.78 − $.74)

April 1, 20X2
(20)   Foreign Currency Payable to Exchange Broker (SFr)   40
        Foreign Currency Transaction Gain   40
      Revalue foreign currency payable to spot rate at
      end of term of forward contract:
      $40 = SFr 4,000 × $.78 − $.77)

(21)   Foreign Currency Units (SFr)   3,080
        Cash   3,080
      Acquire foreign currency units (SFr) in
      open market when spot rate is $.77 = SFr1:
      $3,080 = SFr 4,000 × $.77 spot rate

(22)   Foreign Currency Payable to Exchange Broker (SFr)   3,080
        Foreign Currency Units (SFr)   3,080
      Deliver foreign currency units to exchange
      broker in settlement of forward contract:
      $3,080 = SFr 4,000 × $.77 spot rate

(23)   Cash   2,960
        Dollars Receivable from Exchange Broker ($)   2,960
      Receive U.S. dollars from exchange broker as contracted.

Key Observations from Illustration.   The October 1 entry records the forward contract payable of 4,000 Swiss francs to the exchange broker. The payable is denominated in a foreign currency, but must be translated into U.S. dollars used as the reporting currency of Peerless Products. For speculative contracts, the forward exchange contract accounts are valued to fair value by using the forward exchange rate for the remaining term of the contract.

The December 31 entry adjusts the payable denominated in foreign currency to its appropriate balance at the balance sheet date. The payable, Foreign Currency Payable to Exchange Broker, is adjusted for the increase in the forward exchange rate from October 1, 20X1. The foreign currency transaction loss is reported on the income statement, usually under "Other Income (Loss)."

Entry (20), the first April 1 entry, revalues the foreign currency payable to its current U.S. dollar equivalent value using the spot rate of exchange, and recognizes the speculation gain. Entry (21) shows the acquisition of the 4,000 francs in the open market, at the spot rate of $.77 = SFr 1. These francs will be used to settle the foreign currency payable to the exchange broker. The next two entries on this date, entries (22) and (23), recognize the settlement of the forward contract with the delivery of the 4,000 francs to the exchange broker and the receipt of the $2,960 agreed to when the contract was signed on October 1, 20X1. The $40 foreign currency transaction gain is the difference between the value of the foreign currency contract on December 31 using the forward rate and the value of the foreign currency units on April 1 using the spot rate.

Note that the company has speculated and lost, because the dollar actually weakened against the Swiss franc. The net loss on the speculative forward contract was $120, which is the difference between the $160 loss recognized in 20X1 and the $40 gain recognized in 20X2.

Although this example shows a delivery of foreign currency units with a forward exchange contract, a company may also arrange a future contract for the receipt of foreign currency units. In this case, the October 1 entry would be as follows:

October 1, 20X1

(24)	Foreign Currency Receivable from Exchange Broker (SFr)	2,960	
	Dollars Payable to Exchange Broker ($)		2,960
	Sign forward exchange contract for future receipt of foreign currency units:		
	$2,960 = SFr 4,000 × $.74		

The remainder of the accounting is similar to that of a delivery contract, except that the company records an exchange gain on December 31 because it has a receivable denominated in a foreign currency that has now strengthened relative to the dollar.

Foreign Exchange Matrix

The relationships between changes in exchange rates and the resulting exchange gains and losses are summarized in Figure 11–6. For example, if a company has an account receivable denominated in a foreign currency, the exposed net monetary asset position will result in the recognition of an exchange gain if the direct exchange rate increases, but an exchange loss if the exchange rate decreases. If a company offsets an asset denominated in a foreign currency with a liability also denominated in that currency, the company has protected itself from any changes in the exchange rate because any gain is offset by an equal exchange loss.

Additional Considerations

A Note on Measuring Hedge Effectiveness

FASB 133 states that a company must define, at the beginning of each hedging transaction, the method it will use to measure the effectiveness of the hedge. *Effectiveness* means that there will be an approximate offset, within the range of 80 to 125 percent, of the changes in the fair value of the cash flows or changes in fair value to the risk being hedged. Effectiveness must be assessed at least every three months and whenever financial statements or earnings are reported by the company. A company may elect to

(55)	Other Comprehensive Income	500	
	Realized Gain on Sale of Securities		500

                    Reclassify the other comprehensive income on Special
                    Foods stock that was recorded on Dec. 31, 20X1, to
                    earnings because the securities have now been sold.
                    $100 = ($30 − $29) × 100 shares

Finally, it is important to note that **FASB 133** does not permit hedge accounting for hedges of trading securities. **FASB 115** requires that trading securities be marked-to-market with the gain or loss reported in net earnings for the period. Therefore, any gains or losses on financial instruments that are planned to hedge the risks of holding trading securities are always taken to net earnings for the period.

Example of an Interest-Rate Swap to Hedge Variable-Rate Debt: A Cash-Flow Hedge

Assume that on June 30, 20X1, Peerless borrows $5,000,000 of three-year, variable-rate debt with interest payments equal to the six-month U.S.$ LIBOR (London Interbank Offered Rate) for the prior six months. The debt is not prepayable. The company then enters into a three-year interest-rate swap with First Bank to convert the debt's variable rate to a fixed rate. The swap agreement specifies that Peerless will pay interest at a fixed rate of 7.5 percent and receive interest at a variable rate equal to the six-month U.S.$ LIBOR rate, based on the notional amount of $5,000,000. Both the debt and the swap require interest to be paid semiannually on June 30 and December 31. Peerless specifies the swap as a cash-flow hedge.

    The six-month U.S.$ LIBOR rate and the market value of the swap agreement, as determined by a swap broker, are provided below for the first year of the swap agreement:

Date	Six-Month U.S. $ LIBOR Rate	Swap Agreement Fair Value Asset (Liability)
June 30, 20X1	6.0%	$ -0-
December 31, 20X1	7.0%	165,000
June 30, 20X2	5.5%	(70,000)

Note that Peerless must still pay the variable interest to the holders of the $5,000,000 debt. The interest-rate swap is just between Peerless and First Bank. The estimate of the fair value of the swap agreement was obtained from a broker-dealer who deals in interest swap agreements. Note that the value of the swap agreement to Peerless is positive if it is felt that the variable rate will rise to above the fixed rate. But the value of the swap agreement to Peerless is negative if it is felt that the variable rate will remain below the fixed rate. Peerless's payments on the variable-rate debt and the net payments to First Bank on the interest-swap agreement are presented for the initial two semiannual periods:

	Interest Payments	
	December 31, 20X1	*June 30, 20X2*
Variable-rate interest payment	$150,000 *(a)*	$175,000 *(b)*
Interest-rate swap net payment	37,500 *(c)*	12,500
Total cash payment	$187,500 *(d)*	$187,500

(a) $150,000 = $5,000,000 × .06 × 6/12 months
(b) $175,000 = $5,000,000 × .07 × 6/12 months
(c) $37,500 = net payment required to First Bank for difference between variable and fixed interest rates
(d) $187,500 = $5,000,000 × .075 fixed rate × 6/12 months

Peerless will recognize interest expense based on the two factors of the variable rate plus the net payment or receipt from the swap agreement. In essence, Peerless will have an interest expense equal to 7.5 percent of the notional amount of $5,000,000.

The entries to account for the first year of the interest swap are:

June 30, 20X1		
(56) Cash	5,000,000	
Debt Payable		5,000,000
Issue variable-rate debt.		

December 31, 20X1		
(57) Interest Expense	150,000	
Cash		150,000
Pay debt holders semiannual interest at a		
variable rate of 6.0 percent (from *(a)* above).		

(58) Interest Expense	37,500	
Cash		37,500
Payment to First Bank for semiannual net		
settlement of swap agreement (from *(c)* above).		

(59) Swap Agreement	165,000	
Other Comprehensive Income		165,000
Recognize change in fair value of swap agreement		
to other comprehensive income because the swap		
is a cash-flow hedge.		

June 30, 20X2		
(60) Interest Expense	175,000	
Cash		175,000
Pay debtholders semiannual interest at a		
variable rate of 7.0 percent (from *(b)* above).		

(61) Interest Expense	12,500	
Cash		12,500
Payment to First Bank for semiannual net		
settlement of swap agreement		

(62) Other Comprehensive Income	235,000	
Swap Agreement		235,000
Recognize decrease in fair value of swap agreement		
from $165,000 asset to $(70,000) liability to other		
comprehensive income because the swap		
is a cash-flow hedge.		

The swap agreement is reported on the balance sheet at its fair value. The amounts accumulated in other comprehensive income are indirectly recognized in Peerless's earnings as periodic settlements of the payments required under the swap agreement are made, and the fair value of the swap agreement reaches zero at the end of the term of the agreement.

Reporting and Disclosure Requirements: Disclosures about Fair Value of Financial Instruments

FASB Statement No. 107, "Disclosures about Fair Value of Financial Instruments" **(FASB 107),** required disclosure of information pertaining to all financial instruments. This standard is the first to require information with respect to the current fair value of the financial instruments. Estimating fair value is of great practical difficulty, as many financial instruments do not have a readily traded market from which to determine their value. Estimation methods are permitted, but if no estimation can be made, the reasons for the impracticality must be disclosed.

FASB 107 does not permit the fair values of derivatives to be netted or aggregated with nonderivative financial instruments. The required disclosures are as follows:

E11–5 Determining Year-End Account Balances for Import and Export Transactions

Delaney Inc. has several transactions with foreign entities. Each transaction is denominated in the local currency unit of the country in which the foreign entity is located. For each of the following independent cases, determine the December 31, 20X2, year-end balance in the appropriate accounts for the case. Write "NA" for "not applicable" in the space provided below if that account is not relevant to the specific case.

Case 1. On November 12, 20X2, Delaney Company purchased goods from a foreign company at a price of LCU 40,000 when the direct exchange rate was 1 LCU = $.45. The account has not been settled as of December 31, 20X2, when the exchange rate has decreased to 1 LCU = $.40.

Case 2. On November 28, 20X2, Delaney Company sold goods to a foreign entity at a price of LCU 20,000 when the direct exchange rate was 1 LCU = $1.80. The account has not been settled as of December 31, 20X2, when the exchange rate has increased to 1 LCU = $1.90.

Case 3. On December 2, 20X2, Delaney Company purchased goods from a foreign company at a price of LCU 30,000 when the direct exchange rate was 1 LCU = $.80. The account has not been settled as of December 31, 20X2, when the exchange rate has increased to 1 LCU = $.90.

Case 4. On December 12, 20X2, Delaney Company sold goods to a foreign entity at a price of LCU 2,500,000 when the direct exchange rate was 1 LCU = $.003. The account has not been settled as of December 31, 20X2, when the exchange rate has decreased to 1 LCU = $.0025.

Required

Provide the December 31, 20X2, year-end balances on the records of Delaney, Inc., for each of the following applicable items:

	Accounts Receivable	Accounts Payable	Foreign Currency Transaction Exchange Loss	Foreign Currency Transaction Exchange Gain
Case 1	_____	_____	_____	_____
Case 2	_____	_____	_____	_____
Case 3	_____	_____	_____	_____
Case 4	_____	_____	_____	_____

E11–6 Transactions with Foreign Companies

Harris Inc. had the following transactions:

1. On May 1, Harris Inc. purchased parts from a Japanese company for a U.S. dollar equivalent value of $8,400, to be paid on June 20. The exchange rates were:

May 1	1 yen = $.0070
June 20	1 yen = .0075

2. On July 1, Harris Inc. sold products to a French customer for a U.S. dollar equivalent of $10,000, to be received on August 10. The exchange rates were:

July 1	1 franc = $.20
August 10	1 franc = .22

Required

a. Assume the two transactions are denominated in U.S. dollars. Prepare the entries required for the dates of the transactions and their settlement in U.S. dollars.

b. Assume the two transactions are denominated in the applicable local currency units of the foreign entities. Prepare the entries required for the dates of the transactions and their settlement in the local currency units of the Japanese company (yen) and the French customer (franc).

E11–7   Foreign Purchase Transaction

On December 1, 20X1, Rone Imports, a U.S. company, purchased clocks from Switzerland for 15,000 francs (SFr), to be paid on January 15, 20X2. Rone's fiscal year ends on December 31, and Rone's reporting currency is the U.S. dollar. The exchange rates are:

December 1, 20X1	1 SFr = $.70
December 31, 20X1	1 SFr = .66
January 15, 20X2	1 SFr = .68

Required

a. In which currency is the transaction denominated?

b. Prepare journal entries for Rone Imports to record the purchase, the adjustment on December 31, and the settlement.

E11–8   Adjusting Entries for Foreign Currency Balances

Chocolate De-lites imports and exports chocolate delicacies. Some transactions are denominated in U.S. dollars and others in foreign currencies. A summary of accounts receivable and accounts payable on December 31, 20X6, before adjustments for the effects of changes in exchange rates during 20X6, follows:

Accounts receivable:	
In U.S. dollars	$164,000
In 475,000 French francs (FF)	$ 73,600 = 475,000 × = .155
Accounts payable:	
In U.S. dollars	$ 86,000
In 21,000,000 yen (¥)	$175,300 = 21,000,000 × = .0083

 83600

The spot rates on December 31, 20X6, were:

$$FF\ 1 = \$.176 \qquad 83600$$

$$¥\ 1\ = \$.0081 \qquad 170,100$$

take mou US currency to aquire 1 franc

The average exchange rates during the collection and payment period in 20X7 are:

$$\uparrow FF\ 1 = \$.18$$

$$\downarrow ¥\ 1\ = \$.0078$$

Required

a. Prepare the adjusting entries on December 31, 20X6.

b. Record the collection of the accounts receivable in 20X7.

c. Record the payment of the accounts payable in 20X7.

d. What was the foreign currency gain or loss on the accounts receivable transaction denominated in FF for the year ended December 31, 20X6? For the year ended December 31, 20X7? Overall for this transaction?

e. What was the foreign currency gain or loss on the accounts receivable transaction denominated in ¥? For the year ended December 31, 20X6? For the year ended December 31, 20X7? Overall for this transaction?

f. What was the combined foreign currency gain or loss for both transactions? What could Chocolate De-lites have done to reduce the risk associated with the transactions denominated in foreign currencies?

E11–9   Purchase with Forward Exchange Contract

Merit & Family purchased engines from Germany for 30,000 marks on March 10, with payment due on June 8. Also, on March 10, Merit acquired a 90-day forward contract to purchase 30,000 marks at a forward rate of DM 1 = $.58. The forward contract was acquired to hedge Merit & Family's exposed net liability position in marks. The spot rates were:

March 10	DM 1 = $.57
June 8	DM 1 = .60

Required

Prepare journal entries for Merit & Family to record the purchase of the engines, entries associated with the forward contract, and entries for the payment of the foreign currency payable.

E11–10   Purchase with Forward Exchange Contract and Intervening Fiscal Year-End

Pumped Up Company purchased equipment from Switzerland for 140,000 francs on December 16, 20X7, with payment due on February 14, 20X8. On December 16, 20X7, Pumped Up also acquired a 60-day forward contract to purchase francs at a forward rate of SFr 1 = $.67. On December 31, 20X7, the forward rate for an exchange on February 14, 20X8, is SFr 1 = $.695. The spot rates were:

December 16, 20X7	1 SFr = $.68	95 200
December 31, 20X7	1 SFr = .70	
February 14, 20X8	1 SFr = .69	

Required

a. Prepare journal entries for Pumped Up Company to record the purchase of equipment, all entries associated with the forward contract, the adjusting entries on December 31, 20X7, and entries to record the payment on February 14, 20X8.

b. What was the effect on the income statement of the hedged transaction for the year ended December 31, 20X7?

c. What was the overall effect on the income statement of this transaction from December 16, 20X7 to February 14, 20X8?

E11–11   Foreign Currency Transactions [AICPA Adapted]

Select the correct answer for each of the following questions.

1. Dale Inc., a U.S. company, bought machine parts from a German company on March 1, 20X1, for 30,000 marks, when the spot rate for marks was $.4895. Dale's year-end was March 31, when the spot rate was $.4845. On April 20, 20X1, Dale paid the liability with 30,000 marks acquired at a rate of $.4945. Dale's income statements should report a foreign exchange gain or loss for the years ended March 31, 20X1 and 20X2 of:

	20X1	20X2
a.	$0	$0
b.	$0	$150 loss
c.	$150 loss	$0
d.	$150 gain	$300 loss

2. Marvin Company's receivable from a foreign customer is denominated in the customer's local currency. This receivable of 900,000 local currency units (LCU) has been translated into $315,000 on Marvin's December 31, 20X5, balance sheet. On January 15, 20X6, the receivable was collected in full when the exchange rate was 3 LCU to $1. The journal entry Marvin should make to record the collection of this receivable is:

		Debit	Credit
a.	Foreign Currency Units	300,000	
	Accounts Receivable		300,000
b.	Foreign Currency Units	300,000	
	Exchange Loss	15,000	
	Accounts Receivable		315,000
c.	Foreign Currency Units	300,000	
	Deferred Exchange Loss	15,000	
	Accounts Receivable		315,000
d.	Foreign Currency Units	315,000	
	Accounts Receivable		315,000

3. On July 1, 20X1, Black Company lent $120,000 to a foreign supplier, evidenced by an interest-bearing note due on July 1, 20X2. The note is denominated in the currency of the borrower and was equivalent to 840,000 local currency units (LCU) on the loan date. The note principal was appropriately included at $140,000 in the receivables section of Black's December 31, 20X1, balance sheet. The note principal was repaid to Black on the July 1, 20X2, due date when the exchange rate was 8 LCU to $1. In its income statement for the year ended December 31, 20X2, what amount should Black include as a foreign currency transaction gain or loss on the note principal?

   a. $0.

   b. $15,000 loss.

   c. $15,000 gain.

   d. $35,000 loss.

4. If 1 Canadian dollar can be exchanged for 90 cents of United States money, what fraction should be used to compute the indirect quotation of the exchange rate expressed in Canadian dollars?

a. 1.10/1.

b. 1/1.10.

c. 1/.90.

d. .90/1.

5. On July 1, 20X4, Bay Company borrowed 1,680,000 local currency units (LCU) from a foreign lender, evidenced by an interest-bearing note due on July 1, 20X5, which is denominated in the currency of the lender. The U.S. dollar equivalent of the note principal was as follows:

Date	Amount
7/1/X4 (date borrowed)	$210,000
12/31/X4 (Bay's year-end)	240,000
7/1/X5 (date repaid)	280,000

In its income statement for 20X5, what amount should Bay include as a foreign exchange gain or loss on the note principal?

a. $70,000 gain.

b. $70,000 loss.

c. $40,000 gain.

d. $40,000 loss.

6. A sale of goods was denominated in a currency other than the entity's functional currency. The sale resulted in a receivable that was fixed in terms of the amount of foreign currency that would be received. The exchange rate between the functional currency and the currency in which the transaction was denominated changed. The effect of the change should be included as a:

a. Separate component of stockholders' equity whether the change results in a gain or a loss.

b. Separate component of stockholders' equity if the change results in a gain, and as a component of income if the change results in a loss.

c. Component of income if the change results in a gain, and as a separate component of stockholders' equity if the change results in a loss.

d. Component of income whether the change results in a gain or a loss.

7. A December 15, 20X6, purchase of goods was denominated in a currency other than the entity's functional currency. The transaction resulted in a payable that was fixed in terms of the amount of foreign currency, and was paid on the settlement date, January 20, 20X7. The exchange rates between the functional currency and the currency in which the transaction was denominated changed at December 31, 20X6, resulting in a loss that should:

a. Not be reported until January 20, 20X7, the settlement date.

b. Be included as a separate component of stockholders' equity at December 31, 20X6.

c. Be included as a deferred charge at December 31, 20X6.

d. Be included as a component of income from continuing operations for 20X6.

E11–12 **Sale in Foreign Currency**

Marko Company sold spray paint equipment to Spain for 5,000,000 pesetas (P) on October 1, with payment due in six months. The exchange rates were:

October 1, 20X6	1 peseta = $.0068
December 31, 20X6	1 peseta = .0078
April 1, 20X7	1 peseta = .0076

Required

a. Did the dollar strengthen or weaken relative to the peseta during the period from October 1 to December 31? Did it strengthen or weaken between January 1 and April 1 of the next year?

b. Prepare all required journal entries for Marko Company as a result of the sale and settlement of the foreign transaction, assuming its fiscal year ends on December 31.

c. Did Marko Company have an overall net gain or net loss from its foreign currency exposure?

E11–13   Sale with Forward Exchange Contract

Alman Company sold pharmaceuticals to a Swedish company for 200,000 kronor (SKr) on April 20, with settlement to be in 60 days. On the same date, Alman entered into a 60-day forward contract to sell 200,000 kronor at a forward rate of 1 krona = $.167 in order to hedge its exposed foreign currency receivable. The spot rates were:

April 20	SKr 1 = $.170
June 19	SKr 1 = .165

Required

a. Record all necessary entries related to the foreign transaction and the forward contract.

b. Compare the effects on net income of Alman's hedging use of the forward exchange contract versus the effects if Alman had not hedged its foreign currency receivable.

E11–14   Foreign Currency Transactions [AICPA Adapted]

Choose the correct answer for each of the following questions.

1. On November 15, 20X3, Chow Inc., a U.S. company, ordered merchandise FOB shipping point from a German company for 200,000 marks. The merchandise was shipped and invoiced on December 10, 20X3. Chow paid the invoice on January 10, 20X4. The spot rates for marks on the respective dates were:

November 15, 20X3	$.4955
December 10, 20X3	.4875
December 31, 20X3	.4675
January 10, 20X4	.4475

In Chow's December 31, 20X3, income statement, the foreign exchange gain is:

a. $9,600.

b. $8,000.

c. $4,000.

d. $1,600.

2. Stees Corporation had the following foreign currency transactions during 20X2:

   (1) Merchandise was purchased from a foreign supplier on January 20, 20X2, for the U.S. dollar equivalent of $90,000. The invoice was paid on March 20, 20X2, at the U.S. dollar equivalent of $96,000.

   (2) On July 1, 20X2, Stees borrowed the U.S. dollar equivalent of $500,000 evidenced by a note that was payable in the lender's local currency on July 1, 20X4. On December 31,

      20X2, the U.S. dollar equivalents of the principal amount and accrued interest were $520,000 and $26,000, respectively. Interest on the note is 10 percent per annum.

In Stees' 20X2 income statement, what amount should be included as a foreign exchange loss?

a. $0.

b. $6,000.

c. $21,000.

d. $27,000.

3. On September 1, 20X1, Cott Corporation received an order for equipment from a foreign customer for 300,000 local currency units (LCU) when the U.S. dollar equivalent was $96,000. Cott shipped the equipment on October 15, 20X1, and billed the customer for 300,000 LCU when the U.S. dollar equivalent was $100,000. Cott received the customer's remittance in full on November 16, 20X1, and sold the 300,000 LCU for $105,000. In its income statement for the year ended December 31, 20X1, Cott should report a foreign exchange gain of:

a. $0.

b. $4,000.

c. $5,000.

d. $9,000.

4. On April 8, 20X3, Trul Corporation purchased merchandise from an unaffiliated foreign company for 10,000 units of the foreign company's local currency. Trul paid the bill in full on March 1, 20X4, when the spot rate was $.45. The spot rate was $.60 on April 8, 20X3, and was $.55 on December 31, 20X3. For the year ended December 31, 20X4, Trul should report a transaction gain of:

a. $1,500.

b. $1,000.

c. $500.

d. $0.

5. On October 1, 20X5, Stevens Company, a U.S. company, contracted to purchase foreign goods requiring payment in francs one month after their receipt in Stevens' factory. Title to the goods passed on December 15, 20X5. The goods were still in transit on December 31, 20X5. Exchange rates were 1 dollar to 22 francs, 20 francs, and 21 francs on October 1, December 15, and December 31, 20X5, respectively. Stevens should account for the exchange rate fluctuations in 20X5 as

a. A loss included in net income before extraordinary items.

b. A gain included in net income before extraordinary items.

c. An extraordinary gain.

d. An extraordinary loss.

6. On October 2, 20X5, Louis Co., a U.S. company, purchased machinery from Stroup, a German company, with payment due on April 1, 20X6. If Louis's 20X5 operating income included no foreign exchange gain or loss, then the transaction could have

a. Resulted in an extraordinary gain.

b. Been denominated in U.S. dollars.

c. Caused a foreign currency gain to be reported as a contra account against machinery.

d. Caused a foreign currency translation gain to be reported as a separate component of stockholders' equity.

7. Cobb Co. purchased merchandise for 300,000 pounds from a vendor in London on November 30, 20X5. Payment in British pounds was due on January 30, 20X6. The exchange rates to purchase 1 pound were as follows:

	November 30, 20X5	December 31, 20X5
Spot-rate	$1.65	$1.62
30-day rate	1.64	1.59
60-day rate	1.63	1.56

In its December 31, 20X5, income statement, what amount should Cobb report as foreign exchange gain?

a. $12,000.

b. $9,000.

c. $6,000.

d. $0.

E11–15   Sale with Forward Contract and Fiscal Year-End

Jerber Electronics Inc. sold electrical equipment to a Netherlands company for 50,000 guilders (G) on May 14, with collection due in 60 days. On the same day, Jerber Electronics entered into a 60-day forward contract to sell 50,000 guilders at a forward rate of G 1 = $.541. Jerber Electronics' fiscal year ends on June 30. On June 30, the forward rate for an exchange on July 13 is G 1 = $.530. The spot rates were:

May 14	G 1 = $.530
June 30	G 1 = .534
July 13	G 1 = .525

Required

a. Prepare journal entries for Jerber Electronics Inc. to record: (1) the sale of equipment, (2) the forward contract, (3) the adjusting entries on June 30, (4) the July 13 collection of the receivable, and (5) the July settlement of the forward contract.

b. What was the effect on the income statement in the fiscal year ending June 30?

c. What was the overall effect on the income statement from this transaction?

d. What would have been the overall effect on income if the transaction were left unhedged?

E11–16   Hedge of a Purchase (Commitment without and with Time Value of Money Considerations)

On November 1, 20X6, Smith Imports Inc. contracted to purchase teacups from England for 30,000 pounds (£). The teacups were to be delivered on January 30, 20X7, and payment would be due on March 1, 20X7. On November 1, 20X6, Smith Imports entered into a 120-day forward contract to receive 30,000 pounds at a forward rate of £1 = $1.59. The forward contract was acquired to hedge the financial component of the foreign currency commitment.

Additional information and data for the exchange rate is:

1. Assume the company uses the forward rate in measuring the forward exchange contract and for measuring hedge effectiveness.

2. Spot and exchange rates are:

Date	Spot Rate	Forward Rate for March 1, 20X7
November 1, 20X6	£1 = $1.61	£1 = $1.59
December 31, 20X6	£1 = 1.65	£1 = 1.62
January 30, 20X7	£1 = 1.59	£1 = 1.60
March 1, 20X7	£1 = 1.585	

Required

a. What is Smith's net exposure to changes in the exchange rate of pounds for dollars between November 1, 20X6, and March 1, 20X7?

b. Prepare all journal entries from November 1, 20X6, through March 1, 20X7, for the purchase of the subassemblies, the forward exchange contract, and the foreign currency transaction. Assume Smith's fiscal year ends on December 31, 20X6.

Requirement *c.* requires information from Appendix 11A.

c. Assume interest is significant and the time value of money is considered in valuing the forward contract and hedged commitment. Use a 12 percent annual interest rate. Prepare all journal entries from November 1, 20X6, through March 1, 20X7, for the purchase of the subassemblies, the forward exchange contract, and the foreign currency transaction. Assume Smith's fiscal year-ends on December 31, 20X7.

E11–17   Gain or Loss on Speculative Forward Exchange Contract

On December 1, 20X1, Sycamore Company acquired a 90-day speculative forward contract to sell 120,000 German marks (DM) at a forward rate of DM 1 = $.58. The rates are as follows:

Date	Spot Rate	Forward Rate for March 1
December 1, 20X1	DM 1 = $.60	DM 1 = $.58
December 31, 20X1	DM 1 = .59	DM 1 = .56
March 1, 20X2	DM 1 = .57	

Required

a. Prepare a schedule showing the effects of this speculation on 20X1 income before income taxes.

b. Prepare a schedule showing the effects of this speculation on 20X2 income before income taxes.

E11–18   Speculation in a Foreign Currency

Nick Andros of Streamline suggested that the company speculate in foreign currency as a partial hedge against its operations in the cattle market, which fluctuates like a commodity market. On October 1, 20X1, Streamline bought a 180-day forward contract to purchase 50,000,000 yen (¥) at a forward rate of ¥1 = $.0075 when the spot rate was $.0070. Other exchange rates were as follows:

Date	Spot Rate	Forward Rate for March 31, 20X2
December 31, 20X1	$.0073	$.0076
March 31, 20X2	.0072	

Required

a. Prepare all journal entries related to Streamline Company's foreign currency speculation from October 1, 20X1, through March 31, 20X2, assuming the fiscal year ends on December 31, 20X1.

b. Did Streamline Company gain or lose on its purchase of the forward contract? Explain.

E11–19   Forward Exchange Transactions [AICPA Adapted]

Select the correct answer for each of the following questions.

1. The following information applies to Denton Inc.'s sale of 10,000 foreign currency units under a forward contract dated November 1, 20X5, for delivery on January 31, 20X6:

	11/1/X5	12/31/X5
Spot rates	$0.80	$0.83
30-day future rates	0.79	0.82
90-day future rates	0.78	0.81

Denton entered into the forward contract to speculate in the foreign currency. In Denton's income statement for the year ended December 31, 20X5, what amount of loss should be reported from this forward contract?

a. $400.

b. $300.

c. $200.

d. $0.

2. On September 1, 20X5, Johnson Inc. entered into a foreign exchange contract for speculative purposes by purchasing 50,000 deutsche marks for delivery in 60 days. The rates to exchange U.S. dollars for deutsche marks follow:

	9/1/X5	9/30/X5
Spot rate	$.75	$.70
30-day forward rate	.73	.72
60-day forward rate	.74	.73

In its September 30, 20X5, income statement, what amount should Johnson report as foreign exchange loss?

a. $2,500.

b. $1,500.

c. $1,000.

d. $500.

Items 3 through 5 are based on the following:

On December 12, 20X5, Dahl Company entered into three forward exchange contracts, each to purchase 100,000 francs in 90 days. The relevant exchange rates are as follows:

	Spot Rate	Forward Rate for March 12, 20X6
December 12, 20X5	$.88	$.90
December 31, 20X5	.98	.93

3. Dahl entered into the first forward contract to hedge a purchase of inventory in November 20X5, payable in March 20X6. At December 31, 20X5, what amount of foreign currency transaction gain should Dahl include in income from this forward contract?

   a. $0.

   b. $3,000.

   c. $5,000.

   d. $10,000.

4. Dahl entered into the second forward contract to hedge a commitment to purchase equipment being manufactured to Dahl's specifications. At December 31, 20X5, what amount of foreign currency transaction gain should Dahl include in income from this forward contract?

   a. $0.

   b. $3,000.

   c. $5,000.

   d. $10,000.

5. Dahl entered into the third forward contract for speculation. At December 31, 20X5, what amount of foreign currency transaction gain should Dahl include in income from this forward contract?

   a. $0.

   b. $3,000.

   c. $5,000.

   d. $10,000.

Problems

P11–20   **Multiple-Choice Questions on Foreign Currency Transactions**
Jon-Jan Restaurants purchased green rice, a special variety of rice, from China for 100,000 renminbi on November 1, 20X8. Payment is due on January 30, 20X9. On November 1, 20X8, the company also entered into a 90-day forward contract to purchase 100,000 reuminbi. The rates were as follows:

Date	Spot Rate	Forward Rate
November 1, 20X8	$.120	$.126 (90-day)
December 31, 20X8	.124	.129 (30-day)
January 30, 20X9	.127	

Required

Select the correct answer for each of the following questions.

1. The entry on November 1, 20X8, to record the forward contract includes a:
    a. Debit to Foreign Currency Receivable from Exchange Broker, 100,000 renminbi.
    b. Debit to Foreign Currency Receivable from Exchange Broker, $12,600.
    c. Credit to Premium on Forward Contract, $600.
    d. Credit to Dollars Payable to Exchange Broker, $12,600.

2. The entries on December 31, 20X8, include a:
    a. Debit to Financial Expense, $300.
    b. Credit to Foreign Currency Payable to Exchange Broker, $300.
    c. Debit to Foreign Currency Receivable from Exchange Broker, $300.
    d. Debit to Foreign Currency Receivable from Exchange Broker, $12,600.

3. The entries on January 30, 20X9, include a:
    a. Debit to Dollars Payable to Exchange Broker, $12,000.
    b. Credit to Cash, $12,600.
    c. Credit to Premium on Forward Contract, $600.
    d. Credit to Foreign Currency Receivable from Exchange Broker, $12,600.

4. The entries on January 30, 20X9, include a:
    a. Debit to Financial Expense, $400.
    b. Debit to Dollars Payable to Exchange Broker, $12,600.
    c. Credit to Foreign Currency Units (renminbi), $12,600.
    d. Debit to Foreign Currency Payable to Exchange Broker, $12,700.

5. The entries on January 30, 20X9, include a:
    a. Debit to Foreign Currency Units (renminbi), $12,700.
    b. Debit to Dollars Payable to Exchange Broker, $12,700.
    c. Credit to Foreign Currency Transaction Gain, $100.
    d. Credit to Foreign Currency Receivable from Exchange Broker, $12,600.

P11–21   Foreign Sales

Tex Hardware sells many of its products overseas. The following are some selected transactions.

1. Tex sold electronic subassemblies to a firm in France for 120,000 French francs (FF) on June 6, when the exchange rate was FF 1 = $.1750. Collection was made on July 3, when the rate was FF 1 = $.1753.

2. On July 22, Tex sold copper fittings to a company in London for 30,000 pounds (£), with payment due on September 20. Also, on July 22, Tex entered into a 60-day forward contract to sell 30,000 pounds at a forward rate of £1 = $1.630. The spot rates were:

July 22	£1 = $1.580
September 20	£1 = $1.612

3. Tex sold storage devices to a Canadian firm for C$70,000 (Canadian dollars) on October 11, with payment due on November 10. On October 11, Tex entered into a 30-day forward contract to sell Canadian dollars at a forward rate of C$1 = $.730. The spot rates were as follows:

October 11	C$1 = $.7350
November 10	C$1 = $.7320

Required

Prepare journal entries to record Tex Hardware's foreign sales of its products, use of forward contracts, and settlements of the receivables.

P11–22 **Foreign Currency Transactions**

Globe Shipping, a U.S. company, is an importer and exporter. The following are some transactions with foreign companies.

1. Globe Shipping sold blue jeans to a French importer on January 15 for $7,400, when the exchange rate was FF 1 = $.185. Collection, in dollars, was made on March 15, when the exchange rate was $.180.

2. On March 8, Globe Shipping purchased woolen goods from Ireland for 7,000 pounds (IR£). The exchange rate was IR£1 = $1.68 on March 8, but the rate was $1.66 when payment was made on May 1.

3. On May 12, Globe Shipping signed a contract to purchase toys made in Taiwan for 80,000 Taiwan dollars (NT$). The toys were to be delivered 80 days later on August 1, and payment was due on September 9, which was 40 days after delivery. Also, on May 12, Globe Shipping entered into a 120-day forward contract to buy 80,000 Taiwan dollars at a forward rate of NT$1 = $.0376. On August 1, the forward rate for a September 9 exchange is NT $1 = $.0378. The spot rates were as follows:

May 12	NT$1 = $.0370
August 1	NT$1 = .0375
September 9	NT$1 = .0372

4. Globe Shipping sold microcomputers to a German enterprise on June 6 for 150,000 marks. Payment was due in 90 days, on September 4. On July 6, Globe Shipping entered into a 60-day forward contract to sell 150,000 marks at a forward rate of DM 1 = $.580. The spot rates were as follows:

June 6	DM 1 = $.600
July 6	DM 1 = .590
September 4	DM 1 = .585

Required

Prepare all necessary journal entries for Globe Shipping to account for the foreign transactions, including the sales and purchases of inventory, forward contracts, and settlements.

P11–23 **Three Uses of Forward Exchange Contracts without and with Time Value of Money Considerations**

On December 1, 20X1, Micro World, Inc., entered into a 120-day forward contract to purchase 100,000 marks (DM). Micro World's fiscal year ends on December 31. The direct exchange rates were as follows:

Date	Spot Rate	Forward Rate for March 31, 20X2
December 1, 20X1	$.600	$.609
December 31, 20X1	.610	.612
January 30, 20X2	.608	.605
March 31, 20X2	.602	

Required

Prepare all journal entries for Micro World Inc. for the following *independent* situations:

a. The forward contract was to hedge the purchase of furniture for 100,000 marks on December 1, 20X1, with payment due on March 31, 20X2.

b. The forward contract was to hedge the agreement made on December 1, 20X1, to purchase furniture on January 30, with payment due on March 31, 20X2.

c. The forward contract was for speculative purposes only.

Requirement *d* uses the material in Appendix 11A.

d. Assume interest is significant and the time value of money is considered in valuing the forward contract. Use a 12 percent annual interest rate. Prepare all journal entries required if, as in case *a*, the forward contract was to hedge the foreign currency denominated payable from the purchase of furniture for 100,000 marks on December 1, 20X1, with payment due on March 31, 20X2.

P11–24   **Foreign Purchases and Sales Transactions and Hedging**

Part I

Maple Company had the following export and import transactions during 20X5:

1. On March 1, Maple sold goods to a German company for 30,000 marks, receivable on May 30. The spot rates for marks were DM 1 = $.65 on March 1 and DM 1 = $.68 on May 30.

2. On July 1, Maple signed a contract to purchase equipment from a Japanese company for 500,000 yen. The equipment was manufactured in Japan during August and was delivered to Maple on August 30, with payment due in 60 days on October 29. The spot rates for yen were ¥ 1 = $.102 on July 1, ¥1 = $.104 on August 30, and ¥1 = $.106 on October 29. The 60-day forward exchange rate on August 30, 20X5, was ¥1 = $.1055.

3. On November 16, Maple purchased inventory from a London company for 10,000 pounds, payable on January 15, 20X6. The spot rates for pounds were £1 = $1.65 on November 16, £1 = $1.63 on December 31, and £1 = $1.64 on January 15, 20X6. The forward rate on December 31, 20X5, for a January 15, 20X6, exchange was £1 = $1.645.

Required Part I

a. Prepare journal entries to record Maple's import and export transactions during 20X5 and 20X6.

b. What amount of foreign currency transaction gain or loss would Maple report on its income statement for 20X5?

Part II

Assume that Maple hedged all of its export and import transactions during 20X5.

1. On March 1, 20X5, Maple, anticipating a weaker mark on the May 30, 20X5, settlement date, entered into a 90-day forward contract to sell 30,000 marks at a forward exchange rate of DM 1 = $.64.

2. On July 1, 20X5, Maple, anticipating a strengthening of the yen on the October 29, 20X5, settlement date, entered into a 120-day forward contract to purchase 500,000 yen at a forward exchange rate of ¥1 = $.105.

3. On November 16, 20X5, Maple, anticipating a strengthening of the pound on the January 15, 20X6, settlement date, entered into a 60-day forward exchange contract to purchase 10,000 pounds at a forward exchange rate of £1 = $1.67.

Required Part II

a. Prepare journal entries to record Maple's hedging activities during 20X5 and 20X6.

b. What amount of foreign currency transaction gain or loss would Maple report on its income statement for 20X5, combining both Parts I and II of this problem?

c. What amount of foreign currency transaction gain or loss would Maple report on its statement of income for 20X6, combining both Parts I and II of this problem?

P11–25 **Understanding Foreign Currency Transactions**
Dexter Inc. had the following items in its unadjusted and adjusted trial balances at December 31, 20X5:

	Trial Balances	
	Unadjusted	*Adjusted*
Accounts Receivable (denominated in German marks)	$42,000	$41,700
Dollars Receivable from Exchange Broker	40,600	?
Foreign Currency Receivable from Exchange Broker	82,000	81,000
Accounts Payable (denominated in French francs)	80,000	?
Dollars Payable to Exchange Broker	?	?
Foreign Currency Payable to Exchange Broker	40,600	?

Additional Information

1. On December 1, 20X5, Dexter sold goods to a company in Germany for 70,000 German marks. Payment in German marks is due on January 30, 20X6. On the transaction date, Dexter entered into a 60-day forward contract to sell 70,000 German marks on January 30, 20X6. The 30-day forward rate on December 31, 20X5, was DM1 = $.57.

2. On October 2, 20X5, Dexter purchased equipment from a French company for 400,000 French francs, payable on January 30, 20X6. On the transaction date, Dexter entered into a 120-day forward contract to purchase 400,000 French francs on January 30, 20X6. On December 31, 20X5, the spot rate was Fr1 = $.2020.

Required

Using the information contained in the trial balances, answer each of the following questions:

a. What was the indirect exchange rate for German marks on December 1, 20X5? What was the indirect exchange rate on December 31, 20X5?

b. What is the balance in the account Foreign Currency Payable to Exchange Broker in the adjusted trial balance?

c. When Dexter entered into the 60-day forward contract to sell 70,000 German marks, what was the direct exchange rate for the 60-day forward contract?

d. What is the amount of Dollars Receivable from Exchange Broker in the adjusted trial balance?

e. What was the indirect exchange rate for French francs on October 2, 20X5? What was the indirect exchange rate on December 31, 20X5?

f. What is the balance in the account Dollars Payable to Exchange Broker in both the unadjusted and the adjusted trial balance columns?

g. When Dexter entered into the 120-day forward contract to purchase 400,000 French francs, what was the direct exchange rate for the 120-day forward contract?

h. What was the Accounts Payable balance at December 31, 20X5?

P11–26   Matching Key Terms

Match the items in the left-hand column with the descriptions/explanations in the right-hand column.

Items	Descriptions/Explanations
1. Direct exchange rate	A. The exchange rate for immediate delivery of currencies.
2. Indirect exchange rate	
3. Hedging an exposed net asset position	B. Imports and exports whose prices are stated in a foreign currency.
4. Spot rates	C. The primary currency used by a company for performing its major financial and operating functions.
5. Current rates	
6. Foreign currency transaction gain	
7. Foreign currency transaction loss	D. United States companies prepare their financial statements in U.S. dollars.
8. Foreign currency transactions	
9. Hedging an identifiable commitment	E. 1 German mark equals $.65.
10. Functional currency	F. A forward contract is entered into when receivables denominated in French francs exceed payables denominated in that currency.
11. Speculating in a foreign currency	
12. Hedging an exposed net liability position	
13. Settlement date	G. Accounts which are fixed in terms of foreign currency units.
14. Denominated	
15. Reporting currency	H. 1 U.S. dollar equals 99 Japanese yen.
	I. The spot rate on the entity's balance sheet date.
	J. In an export or import transaction, the date that foreign currency units are received or paid, respectively.
	K. A forward contract is entered into when payables denominated in British pounds exceeds receivables denominated in that currency.
	L. Reported when receivables are denominated in German marks and the mark strengthens compared to the U.S. dollar.
	M. A forward contract is entered into on May 1 that hedges an import transaction that will occur on July 1.
	N. A forward contract in which no hedging is intended.
	O. Reported when payables are denominated in Swiss francs and the franc strengthens compared to the U.S. dollar.

P11–27B   Multiple-Choice Questions on Derivatives and Hedging Activities

Select the correct answer for each of the following questions.

reinvest the currency they generate or may distribute funds to their home office or parent company in the form of dividends. Exchange rate changes do not directly affect the U.S. parent company's cash flows. Rather, the rate changes affect the foreign affiliate's net assets (assets minus liabilities), and therefore the U.S. parent company's net investment in the entity.

The second group of foreign affiliates is made up of entities that are an extension of the U.S. company. These affiliates operate in a foreign country but are directly affected by changes in exchange rates because they are dependent on the U.S. economy for sales markets, production components, or financing. For this group, the U.S. dollar is the functional currency. There is a presumption that the effect of exchange rate changes on the foreign affiliate's net assets will directly affect the U.S. parent company's cash flows, so the exchange rate adjustments are reported in the U.S. parent's income.

Translation and remeasurement include different adjustment procedures and may result in significantly different consolidated financial statements. Both methods are illustrated in this chapter.

Translation of Functional Currency Statements into the Reporting Currency of the U.S. Company

Most business entities transact and record business activities in the local currency. Therefore, the local currency of the foreign entity is its functional currency. The translation of the foreign entity's statement into U.S. dollars is a relatively straightforward process.

The FASB felt that the underlying economic relationships presented in the financial statements of the foreign entity should not be distorted or changed during the translation process from the functional currency of the foreign entity into the currency of the U.S. parent. For example, if the foreign entity's functional currency statements report a current ratio of 2:1 and a gross margin of 60 percent of sales, these relationships should pass through the translation process into the reporting currency of the U.S. parent. It is important to be able to evaluate the performance of the foreign entity's management with the same economic measures used to operate the foreign entity. In order to maintain the economic relationships in the functional currency statements, the account balances must be translated by a comparable exchange rate.

The translation is made by using the current exchange rate for *all* assets and liabilities. This rate is the spot rate on the balance sheet date. The income statement items—revenue, expenses, gains, and losses—should be translated at the exchange rate on the dates on which the underlying transactions occurred, although for practical purposes a weighted-average exchange rate for the period may be used for these items with the assumption that revenues and expenses are recognized evenly over the period. However, if a material gain or loss results from a specific event, the exchange rate on the date of the event, rather than the average exchange rate, should be used to translate the results of the transaction.

The stockholders' equity accounts, other than retained earnings, are translated at historical exchange rates. The appropriate historical rate is the rate on the latter of the date the parent company acquired the investment in the foreign entity or the date the subsidiary had the stockholders' equity transaction. This is necessary to complete the elimination of the parent company's investment account against the foreign subsidiary's capital accounts in the consolidation process. The subsidiary's translated retained earnings are carried forward from the previous period with additions for this period's income and deductions for dividends declared during the period. Dividends are translated at the exchange rate on the date of declaration. It is interesting to observe that if the foreign entity has not paid its declared dividend by the end of its fiscal period, it has a dividends payable account that is translated at the current rate. Nevertheless, the dividend deduction from retained earnings is translated using the exchange rate on the date of dividend declaration.

In summary, the translation of the foreign entity's financial statements from its functional currency into the reporting currency of the U.S. company is made as follows:

Translation

Income statement accounts:
   Revenue and expenses   Generally, weighted-average exchange rate
                                 for period covered by statement

Balance sheet accounts:
   Assets and liabilities   Current exchange rate on balance sheet date
   Stockholders' equity   Historical exchange rates

Because a variety of rates are used to translate the foreign entity's individual accounts, the trial balance debits and credits after translation generally are not equal. The balancing item to make the translated trial balance debits equal the credits is called the ***translation adjustment.***

Financial Statement Presentation of Translation Adjustment

The translation adjustment resulting from the translation process is part of the entity's comprehensive income for the period. **FASB Statement No. 130,** "Reporting Comprehensive Income" (**FASB 130**), issued in June 1997, defined comprehensive income to include all changes in equity during a period except those resulting from investments by owners and distributions to owners. The FASB supported the theoretical move to a more "all-inclusive" definition of income. ***Comprehensive income*** includes net income and ***"other comprehensive income"*** items that are part of the changes in the net assets of a business enterprise from nonowner sources (e.g., not additional capital investments and dividends) during a period. **FASB 130** requires the reporting of comprehensive income as part of the primary financial statements of the entity. The major items comprising the other comprehensive items are the changes during the period in foreign currency translation adjustments, unrealized gains or losses on available-for-sale securities, revaluation of cash-flow hedges, and adjustments in the minimum pension liability item.

FASB 130 allows for several alternative presentation formats for comprehensive income. The single-statement, combined income approach first presents the items comprising net income and then has a section presenting the other comprehensive income items. An alternative, two-statement presentation first presents the computation of net income on one statement and then a related statement that begins with net income and reconciles to comprehensive income by reporting the other comprehensive income items separately. A third alternative, used by many companies, is just to present the items comprising other comprehensive income in a schedule of accumulated other comprehensive income in the consolidated statement of shareholders' equity. An entity may present the components of other comprehensive income items net-of-tax or can show the aggregate tax effects related to the total other comprehensive income items as one amount.

Each period's other comprehensive income (OCI) is closed to accumulated other comprehensive income (AOCI), which is displayed separately from other stockholders' equity items (e.g., capital stock, additional paid-in capital, and retained earnings). An appropriate title such as, *"Accumulated Other Comprehensive Income"* is used to describe this stockholders' equity item. The statement of changes in stockholders' equity opens with the accumulated balance of the other comprehensive income items at the beginning of the period, then includes the change in the translation adjustment and the additional other comprehensive income items during the period that were included in the period's comprehensive income, and ends with the accumulated other comprehensive income balance at the end of the period. The accumulated ending balance of the other comprehensive income items is then reported in the entity's balance sheet as part of the stockholders' equity section, usually below retained earnings. The discussion of the disclosure requirements presented later in this chapter demonstrates the financial statements for the Peerless Products example presented in the chapter.

Illustration of Translation and Consolidation of a Foreign Subsidiary

In Chapter 11, the examples illustrated the effects of a dollar that was strengthening against the euro during 20X1. In the examples for the remainder of this chapter, the dollar weakens against the euro during 20X1. Thus, in Chapters 11 and 12, changes in exchange rates in both directions will have been illustrated.

To examine the consolidation of a foreign subsidiary, assume the following facts:

1. On January 1, 20X1, Peerless Products, a U.S. company, purchased 80 percent of the outstanding capital stock of German Company, a firm located in Berlin, Germany, for $54,000, which is $6,000 above book value. (The proof of the differential is shown at the end of the next section of the chapter.) The excess of cost over book value is attributable to a patent amortizable over 10 years. Balance sheet accounts in a trial balance format for both companies immediately *before* the acquisition are presented in Figure 12–2.
2. The local currency for German Company is the euro (€), which is also its functional currency.
3. On October 1, 20X1, the subsidiary declared and paid dividends of €6,250.
4. The subsidiary received $4,200 in a sales transaction with a U.S. company when the exchange rate was $1.20 = €1. The subsidiary still has this foreign currency on December 31, 20X1.
5. Relevant direct spot exchange rates ($/€1) are:

Date	Rate
January 1, 20X1	$1.20
October 1, 20X1	1.36
December 31, 20X1	1.40
20X1 average	1.30

FIGURE 12–2   **Balance Sheet Accounts for the Two Companies on January 1, 20X1 (Immediately before Acquisition of 80 Percent of German Company's Stock by Peerless Products, a U.S. Company)**

	Peerless Products	German Company
Cash	$ 350,000	€2,500
Receivables	75,000	10,000
Inventory	100,000	7,500
Land	175,000	-0-
Plant and Equipment	800,000	50,000
Total Debits	$1,500,000	€70,000
Accumulated Depreciation	$ 400,000	€5,000
Accounts Payable	100,000	2,500
Bonds Payable	200,000	12,500
Common Stock	500,000	40,000
Retained Earnings, 12/31/X0	300,000	10,000
Total Credits	$1,500,000	€70,000

Date-of-Acquisition Translation Workpaper.   Figure 12–3 presents the translation of German Company's trial balance on January 1, 20X1. This illustration assumes that the subsidiary's books and records are maintained in European euros, the subsidiary's functional currency.

The translation of the subsidiary's trial balance from the functional currency (€) into dollars, the reporting currency of the U.S. parent, is made using the ***current rate method.*** The appropriate historical rate used to translate the stockholders' equity accounts depends on the accounting method used to account for the business combination, as follows:

1. *Purchase accounting.* The subsidiary's stockholders' equity accounts are translated using the current rate on the date of the parent company's purchase of the subsidiary's stock.
2. *Pooling accounting.* The subsidiary's stockholders' equity accounts are translated using the exchange rate in effect on the date the subsidiary originally issued its stock. This is consistent with the retroactive restatement required under the pooling of interests method.

The entry made by Peerless Products to record the purchase of 80 percent of German Company's stock is:

January 1, 20X1
(1)   Investment in German Company Stock   54,000
      Cash   54,000
    Purchase of German Company stock.

The differential on January 1, 20X1, the date of acquisition, is computed as follows:

FIGURE 12–3 **Workpaper to Translate Foreign Subsidiary on January 1, 20X1 (Date of Acquisition)**

Functional Currency Is the European Euro

Item	Trial Balance, €	Exchange Rate, $/€	Trial Balance, $
Cash	2,500	1.20	3,000
Receivables	10,000	1.20	12,000
Inventory	7,500	1.20	9,000
Plant and Equipment	50,000	1.20	60,000
Total Debits	70,000		84,000
Accumulated Depreciation	5,000	1.20	6,000
Accounts Payable	2,500	1.20	3,000
Bonds Payable	12,500	1.20	15,000
Common Stock	40,000	1.20	48,000
Retained Earnings	10,000	1.20	12,000
Total Credits	70,000		84,000

Note: $1.20 is direct exchange rate on January 1, 20X1.

1/1/X1 (P)	Investment cost		$54,000
80%	Book value of investment:		
	Common stock	$48,000	
	Retained earnings	12,000	
(G)	Total	$60,000	
	Percent of German Company's stock acquired by Peerless Company	× .80	
	Book value acquired by Peerless Company		(48,000)
	Differential (excess of cost over book value) attributable to patent		$ 6,000

A graphic representation of the acquisition is as follows:

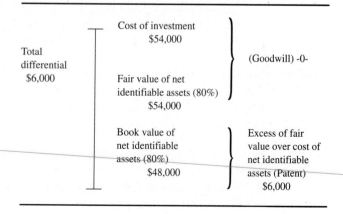

FIGURE 12–4   January 1, 20X1, Workpaper for Consolidated Balance Sheet, Date of Acquisition

80 Percent Purchase at More Than Book Value

	Peerless Products	German Company	Eliminations Debit		Eliminations Credit		Consolidated
Cash	$ 296,000	$ 3,000					$ 299,000
Receivables	75,000	12,000					87,000
Inventory	100,000	9,000					109,000
Land	175,000						175,000
Plant and Equipment	800,000	60,000					860,000
Investment in German Co. Stock	54,000				(2)	54,000	
Differential			(2)	6,000	(3)	6,000	
Patent			(3)	6,000			6,000
Total Debits	$1,500,000	$84,000					$1,536,000
Accumulated Depreciation	400,000	6,000					406,000
Accounts Payable	100,000	3,000					103,000
Bonds Payable	200,000	15,000					215,000
Common Stock	500,000	48,000	(2)	48,000			500,000
Retained Earnings	300,000	12,000	(2)	12,000			300,000
Noncontrolling Interest					(2)	12,000	12,000
Total Credits	$1,500,000	$84,000		72,000		72,000	$1,536,000

Date-of-Acquisition Consolidated Balance Sheet.   The consolidated balance sheet workpaper for Peerless Products and its German subsidiary on January 1, 20X1, is presented in Figure 12–4. The consolidation process is identical to the date-of-acquisition consolidations presented in Chapter 4. The eliminating entries are as follows:

E(2)	Common Stock—German Company	48,000	
	Retained Earnings	12,000	
	Differential	6,000	
	Investment in German Company Stock		54,000
	Noncontrolling Interest		12,000
	Eliminate investment balance:		
	$12,000 = ($48,000 + $12,000) × .20		
E(3)	Patent	6,000	
	Differential		6,000
	Assign differential.		

Subsequent to Date of Acquisition.   The accounting subsequent to the date of acquisition is very similar to the accounting used for domestic subsidiaries. The major differences are due to the effects of changes in the exchange rates of the foreign currency.

Translation of Foreign Subsidiary's Postacquisition Trial Balance.   Figure 12–5 illustrates the translation of German Company's December 31, 20X1, trial balance.

Note the account Foreign Currency Units in the trial balance of the German subsidiary. This account represents the $4,200 of U.S. dollars held by the subsidiary.

FIGURE 12–5   December 31, 20X1, Translation of Foreign Subsidiary's Trial Balance
European Euro Is the Functional Currency

Item	Balance, €	Exchange Rate	Balance, $
Cash	10,750	1.40 ✓	15,050
Foreign Currency Units	3,000	1.40	4,200
Receivables	10,500	1.40 ✓	14,700
Inventory	5,000	1.40	7,000
Plant and Equipment	50,000	1.40	70,000
Cost of Goods Sold	22,500	1.30	29,250
Operating Expenses	14,500	1.30	18,850
Foreign Currency Transaction Loss	500	1.30	650
Dividends Paid	6,250	1.36	8,500
Total Debits	123,000		168,200
Accumulated Depreciation	7,500	1.40 ×E	10,500
Accounts Payable	3,000	1.40	4,200
Bonds Payable	12,500	1.40	17,500
Common Stock	40,000	1.20	48,000
Retained Earnings (1/1)	10,000	(a)	12,000
Sales	50,000	1.30	65,000
Total	123,000		157,200
Accumulated Other Comprehensive Income—Translation Adjustment			11,000
Total Credits			168,200

(a) From the January 1, 20X1, translation workpaper.

Because this account is denominated in a currency other than the subsidiary's reporting currency, German Company made an adjusting journal entry to revalue the account from the amount originally recorded using the exchange rate on the date the company received the currency to that amount's equivalent exchange value at the end of the year.

The subsidiary made the following entry on its books when it received the U.S. dollars:

(4)	Foreign Currency Units ($)	€3,500	
	Sales		€3,500
	Record sales and receipt of 4,200 U.S. dollars at spot exchange rate on date of receipt: €3,500 = $4,200/$1.20 exchange rate		

At the end of the period, the subsidiary adjusted the foreign currency units (the U.S. dollars) to the current exchange rate ($1.40 = € 1) by making the following entry:

(5)	Foreign Currency Transaction Loss	€500	
	Foreign Currency Units ($)		€500
	Adjust account denominated in foreign currency units to current exchange rate:		
	$4,200/$1.40	€3,000	
	Less: Preadjusted balance	(3,500)	
	Foreign currency transaction loss	€ (500)	

The foreign currency transaction loss is a component of the subsidiary's net income, and the Foreign Currency Units account is classified as a current asset on the subsidiary's balance sheet. The subsidiary's net income consists of the following elements:

Sales	€50,000
Cost of Goods Sold	(22,500)
Operating Expenses	(14,500)
Foreign Currency Transaction Loss	(500)
Net Income	€12,500

Because the European euro is the foreign entity's functional currency, the subsidiary's statements must be translated into U.S. dollars using the *current rate method.* The assets and liabilities are translated using the current exchange rate at the balance sheet date ($1.40), the income statement accounts are translated using the average rate for the period ($1.30), and the stockholders' equity accounts are translated using the appropriate historical exchange rates ($1.20 and $1.36). The dividends are translated at the October 1 rate ($1.36), which was the exchange rate at the time the dividends were declared. The example assumes the dividends were paid on October 1, the same day they were declared. If the dividends had not been paid by the end of the year, the liability dividends payable would be translated at the current exchange rate of $1.40 = €1.

One of the analytical features provided by the current rate method is that many of the ratios management uses to manage the foreign subsidiary are the same in U.S. dollars as they are in the foreign currency unit. This relationship is true for the assets and liabilities of the balance sheet and the revenue and expenses of the income statement, because the translation for these accounts uses the same exchange rate—the current rate for the assets and liabilities, the average exchange rate for the income statement accounts. Thus, the scale of these accounts has changed, but not their relative amounts within their respective statements. This relationship is not true when the ratio includes numbers from both the income statement and the balance sheet, or when a stockholders' equity account is included with an asset or liability. The following table illustrates the relative relationships within the financial statements, using the data in Figure 12–5:

	Measured in €	Measured in U.S. Dollars
Current ratio:		
Current assets	€29,250	$40,950
Current liabilities	€ 3,000	$ 4,200
Current ratio	9.75	9.75
Cost of goods sold as a percentage of sales:		
Cost of goods sold	€22,500	$29,250
Sales	€50,000	$65,000
Percent	45%	45%

FIGURE 12–6   **Proof of Translation Adjustment as of December 31, 20X1**
European Euro Is the Functional Currency

Peerless Products and Subsidiary
Proof of Translation Adjustment
Year Ended December 31, 20X1

	€	Translation Rate	$
Net assets at beginning of year	50,000 BOY	1.20	60,000
Adjustment for changes in net assets position during year:			
Net income for year	12,500	1.30	16,250
Dividends paid	(6,250)	1.36	(8,500)
Net assets translated at:			
Rates during year			67,750
Rates at end of year	56,250	1.40	78,750
Change in other comprehensive income—translation adjustment during year (net increase)			11,000
Accumulated other comprehensive income—translation adjustment, 1/1			-0-
Accumulated other comprehensive income—translation adjustment, 12/31 (credit)			11,000

The translation adjustment in Figure 12–5 arises because the investee's assets and liabilities are translated at the current rate, whereas other rates are used for the stockholders' equity and income statement account balances. Although the translation adjustment may be thought of as a balancing item to make the trial balance debits equal the credits, the effects of changes in the exchange rates during the period should be calculated to prove the accuracy of the translation process. This proof for 20X1, the year of acquisition, is provided in Figure 12–6.

The proof begins with determination of the effect of changes in the exchange rate on the beginning investment and on the elements that alter the beginning investment. Note that only events affecting the stockholders' equity accounts will change the net assets investment. In this example, the changes to the investment account occurred from income of €12,500 and dividends of €6,250. There were no changes in the stock outstanding during the year. The beginning net investment is translated using the exchange rate at the beginning of the year. The income and dividends are translated using the exchange rate at the date the transactions occurred. The income was earned evenly over the year; thus the average exchange rate for the period is used to translate income. The ending net assets position is translated using the exchange rate at the end of the year. The cumulative translation adjustment at the beginning of the year is zero in this example because the subsidiary was acquired on January 1, 20X1.

The Accumulated Other Comprehensive Income—Translation Adjustment account has a credit balance because the spot exchange rate at the end of the first period of ownership is higher than the exchange rate at the beginning of the period or the average for the period. If the exchange rate had decreased during the period, the translation adjustment would have a debit balance. Another way of determining if the accumulated translation adjustment has a debit or credit balance is to use balance sheet logic. For example, the subsidiary's translated balance sheet at the beginning of the year would be:

Translated Balance Sheet, 1/1/X1			
Net assets	$60,000	Common stock	$60,000

The translated balance sheet at the end of the year would be:

Translated Balance Sheet, 12/31/X1			
Net assets	$78,750	Common stock	$60,000
		Retained earnings	7,750
		(net income less dividends)	
		Accumulated other	
		comprehensive income—	
		translation adjustment	11,000
Total	$78,750	Total	$78,750

Note that the $11,000 is a credit balance in order to make the balance sheet "balance."

Entries on Parent Company's Books.   Entries on the parent company's books are made to recognize the dollar equivalent values of the parent's share of the subsidiary's income, amortization of the excess of cost over book value, a cumulative translation adjustment for the parent's differential, and the dividends received from the foreign subsidiary. In addition, the parent company must recognize its share of the translation adjustment arising from the translation of the subsidiary's financial statements. The periodic change in the parent company's translation adjustment from the foreign investment is reported as a component of the parent company's other comprehensive income.

The entries Peerless Products makes to account for its investment in German Company are presented below. The dividend was received by Peerless Products on October 1, 20X1, and immediately converted to U.S. dollars, as follows:

October 1, 20X1			
(6) Cash		6,800	
Investment in German Company Stock			6,800
Dividend received from foreign subsidiary:			
€6,250 × .80 × $1.36 exchange rate			
December 31, 20X1			
(7) Investment in German Company Stock		13,000	
Income from Subsidiary			13,000
Equity in net income of foreign subsidiary:			
€12,500 × .80 × $1.30 average exchange rate			
(8) Investment in German Company Stock		8,800	
Other Comprehensive Income—Translation Adjustment			8,800
Parent's share of change in translation adjustment from			
translation of subsidiary's accounts: $11,000 × .80			

If some time passed between the declaration and payment of dividends, the parent company would record dividends receivable from foreign subsidiary on the declaration date. This account would be denominated in a foreign currency and would be adjusted to its current exchange rate on the balance sheet date and on the payment date, just like any other account denominated in a foreign currency. Any foreign transaction gain or loss resulting from the adjustment procedure would be included in the parent's income for the period.

The Differential. The allocation and amortization of the excess of cost over book value require special attention in the translation of a foreign entity's financial statements. The differential does not exist on the books of the foreign subsidiary; it is part of the parent's investment account. However, the translated book value of the foreign subsidiary is a major component of the investment account on the parent's books and is directly related to a foreign-based asset. **FASB 52** requires that the allocation and amortization of the difference between the investment cost and its book value be made in terms of the functional currency of the foreign subsidiary and that these amounts then be translated at the appropriate exchange rates on the workpaper balance sheet date. The periodic amortization affects the income statement and is therefore measured at the average exchange rate used to translate other income statement accounts. On the other hand, the remaining unamortized balance of the differential is reported in the balance sheet and is translated at the current exchange rate used for balance sheet accounts. The effect of this difference in rates is shown in the parent company's translation adjustment as a revision of part of the parent's original investment in the subsidiary.

Peerless products amortizes the patent over a period of 10 years. The patent amortization is presented below.

	European Euros	Translation Rate	U.S. Dollars
Income Statement			
Differential at beginning of year	€5,000	1.20	$6,000
Amortization this period (€5,000/10 years)	(500)	1.30	(650)
Remaining balances	€4,500		$5,350
Balance Sheet			
Remaining balance on			
12/31/X1 translated at year-end exchange rates	€4,500	1.40	$6,300
Difference to other comprehensive income—			
translation adjustment (credit)			$950

Another way of viewing the differential adjustment of $950 is that it adjusts the parent company's differential, which is currently part of the investment account, to the amount necessary to prepare the consolidated balance sheet. In this example, if no differential adjustment is made, the patent on the consolidated balance sheet would be $5,350, which is incorrect. Because the balance sheet must report the patent translated at the end-of-period exchange rate in the amount of $6,300, the differential adjustment is made to properly report the amount in the consolidated balance sheet. Thus, the adjustment may be thought of as an adjustment necessary to obtain the correct amount of the differential to prepare the consolidated balance sheet. Depending on the direction of the changes in the exchange rate, the differential adjustment could be a debit or credit amount. In this case, the differential must be increased from $5,350 to $6,300, necessitating a debit of $950 to the investment account and a corresponding credit to the comprehensive income—translation adjustment account.

Entry (9) below recognizes the amortization of the patent for the period. Entry (10) records the portion of the translation adjustment on the increase in the differential for the investment in the foreign subsidiary.

(9)	Income from Subsidiary	650	
	Investment in German Company Stock		650
	Amortization of patent:		
	$650 = €500 × $1.30 average exchange rate		
(10)	Investment in German Company Stock	950	
	Other Comprehensive Income—Translation Adjustment		950
	Recognize translation adjustment on increase in differential.		

It is important to note that the $950 translation adjustment from the differential is attributed solely to the parent company. Noncontrolling Interest is not assigned any portion of this translation adjustment. This $950 translation adjustment is attributable to the excess of cost paid over the book value of the assets, and therefore is added to the differential, which is a component of the investment in the foreign subsidiary, thereby resulting in a debit to the investment account on the parent company's books.

The December 31, 20X1, balance in the Investment in German Company Stock account is $69,300, as shown in the following T-account. The numbers in parentheses are the corresponding journal entry numbers from the text.

Investment in German Company Stock				
(1) Purchase price	54,000			
		(6)	Dividends	6,800
(7) Equity income	13,000			
(8) Share of subsidiary's				
translation adjustment	8,800			
		(9)	Amortization of	
			differential	650
(10) Translation adjustment				
on differential	950			
Balance, 12/31/X1	69,300			

Note that the $9,750 Other Comprehensive Income—Translation Adjustment account balance in the parent company's books is comprised of its share of the translation adjustment from translating the subsidiary's trial balance ($8,800) plus the parent company's adjustment ($950) due to its differential it paid for the investment.

During the parent company's closing entries process, the following two entries would be included to separately close net income from the subsidiary, and the other comprehensive income arising from its investment in the subsidiary.

(11)	Income from Subsidiary	12,350	
	Retained Earnings		12,350
	To close net income from subsidiary.		
(12)	Other Comprehensive Income—Translation Adjustment	9,750	
	Accumulated Other Comprehensive Income—		
	Translation Adjustment		9,750
	To close other comprehensive income resulting from the		
	investment in the German subsidiary.		

Subsequent Consolidation Workpaper. The consolidation workpaper is prepared after the translation process is completed. The process of consolidation is the same as for a domestic subsidiary, except for two major differences: *(a)* The translation adjustment arising from the translation of the foreign subsidiary's accounts is divided between the parent company and noncontrolling interest, and *(b)* as shown previously, the patent amortization for the period is translated at the income statement rate (average for the period), whereas the ending patent balance is translated at the balance sheet rate (current exchange rate). As shown in entry (10), a translation adjustment must be computed on the differential and assigned as part of the parent company's investment in the foreign subsidiary.

The workpaper is presented in Figure 12–7. The trial balance for German Company is obtained from the translated amounts computed earlier in Figure 12–5. The workpaper entries are presented below in journal entry form. These entries are *not* made on either company's books; they are only in the workpaper elimination columns.

E(13)	Income from Subsidiary	12,350	
	Dividends Declared		6,800
	Investment in German Company Stock		5,550
	Eliminate income from subsidiary:		
	$12,350 = $13,000 equity share - $650 amortization		
E(14)	Income to Noncontrolling Interest	3,250	
	Dividends Declared		1,700
	Noncontrolling Interest		1,550
	Assign net income to noncontrolling interest:		
	$3,250 = $16,250 subsidiary net income × .20		
	$1,700 = $8,500 dividends × .20		
E(15)	Other Comprehensive Income—Translation Adjustment	8,800	
	Investment in German Co. Stock		8,800
	To eliminate the other comprehensive income from the		
	subsidiary that had been recorded by the parent.		
E(16)	Other Comprehensive Income to Noncontrolling Interest	2,200	
	Noncontrolling Interest		2,200
	To assign a proportionate share of the subsidiary's other		
	comprehensive income to the noncontrolling interest.		
E(17)	Common Stock—German Co.	48,000	
	Retained Earnings, January 1, 20X1	12,000	
	Accumulated Other Comprehensive Income, January 1, 20X1	0	
	Differential	6,000	
	Investment in German Co. Stock		54,000
	Noncontrolling Interest		12,000
	Eliminate beginning-of-period investment balance and establish		
	noncontrolling interest's share of beginning equity of subsidiary:		
	$12,000 = ($48,000 + $12,000) × .20		

FIGURE 12–7   December 31, 20X1, Consolidation Workpaper, Prepared after Translation of Foreign Statements

Item	Peerless Products	German Company	Eliminations Debit		Eliminations Credit		Consolidated
Sales	400,000	65,000					465,000
Income from Subsidiary	12,350		(13)	12,350			
Credits	412,350	65,000					465,000
Cost of Goods Sold	170,000	29,250					199,250
Operating Expenses	90,000	18,850	(20)	650			109,500
Foreign Currency Transaction Loss		650					650
Debits	(260,000)	(48,750)					(309,400)
							155,600
Income to Noncontrolling Interest			(14)	3,250			(3,250)
Net Income, carry forward	152,350	16,250		16,250			152,350
Retained Earnings, 1/1	300,000	12,000	(17)	12,000			300,000
Net Income, from above	152,350	16,250		16,250			152,350
	452,350	28,250					452,350
Dividends Declared	(60,000)	(8,500)			(13)	6,800	(60,000)
					(14)	1,700	
Retained Earnings, 12/31	392,350	19,750		28,250		8,500	392,350
Cash	432,800	15,050					447,850
Dollars Held by Sub		4,200					4,200
Receivables	75,000	14,700					89,700
Inventory	100,000	7,000					107,000
Land	175,000						175,000
Plant and Equipment	800,000	70,000					870,000
Investment in German Co. Stock	69,300				(13)	5,550	
					(15)	8,800	
					(17)	54,000	
					(18)	950	
					(19)	6,950	
Differential			(17)	6,000			
			(18)	950			
Patent			(19)	6,950	(20)	650	6,300
Debits	1,652,100	110,950					1,700,050
Accumulated Depreciation	450,000	10,500					460,500
Accounts Payable	100,000	4,200					104,200
Bonds Payable	200,000	17,500					217,500
Common Stock	500,000	48,000	(17)	48,000			500,000
Retained Earnings, from above	392,350	19,750		28,250		8,500	392,350
Accumulated Other Comprehensive Income, from below	9,750	11,000		11,000			9,750
Noncontrolling Interest					(14)	1,550	15,750
					(16)	2,200	
					(17)	12,000	
Credits	1,652,100	110,950		101,150		101,150	1,700,050
Accumulated Other Comp. Income, 1/1	0	0	(17)	0			0
Other Comp. Income—Translation Adj.	9,750	11,000	(15)	8,800			11,950
Other Comprehensive Income to Ncl			(16)	2,200			(2,200)
Accumulated Other Comp. Income, 12/31, (credit) carry up	9,750	11,000		11,000		0	9,750

Key to eliminations:
(13) Eliminate net income from subsidiary.
(14) Assign net income to noncontrolling interest.
(15) Eliminate parent company's share of other comprehensive income from change in translation adjustment.
(16) Assign a proportionate share of the subsidiary's other comprehensive income to the noncontrolling interest.
(17) Eliminate beginning investment account balance and establish differential and noncontrolling interest.
(18) Eliminate translation adjustment to differential.
(19) Assign differential to patent.
(20) Amortize patent.

E(18)	Differential	950	
	Investment in German Co. Stock		950
	Eliminate end-of-period differential adjustment that was recorded in investment account.		
E(19)	Patent	6,950	
	Differential		6,950
	Assign differential, including periodic adjustment of $950, to patent: $6,950 = $6,000 + $950 differential adjustment		
E(20)	Operating Expenses—Amortization of Patent	650	
	Patent		650
	Amortize patent: $650 = €500 × $1.30		

When the equity method is used by the parent company and there are no intercompany revenue transactions, the parent's net income and retained earnings are equal to the consolidated net income and consolidated retained earnings. This makes it possible to verify the amounts reported on the consolidated financial statements.

Noncontrolling interest shares in the $11,000 translation adjustment which was assigned to the subsidiary because the source of this adjustment is the translation of the financial statements of the foreign subsidiary. Total noncontrolling interest in the subsidiary's net assets at year-end can be proved as follows:

Common stock ($48,000 × .20)		$9,600
Retained earnings:		
Beginning retained earnings ($12,000 × .20)	$2,400	
Add: Net income ($16,250 × .20)	3,250	
Less: Dividends ($8,500 × .20)	(1,700)	
Total retained earnings		3,950
Accumulated other comprehensive income—translation adjustment ($11,000 × .20)		2,200
Total noncontrolling interest		$15,750

The $11,000 translation adjustment of the subsidiary as shown in Figure 12–7 is eliminated in entries E(15) and E(16). As a result, the final balance of the accumulated other comprehensive income—translation adjustment reported in the consolidated balance sheet is $9,750, which is carried forward from the parent company's trial balance.

Remeasurement of the Books of Record into the Functional Currency

A second method of restating foreign affiliates' financial statements in U.S. dollars is remeasurement. Although remeasurement is not as commonly used as translation, some situations exist in which the functional currency of the foreign affiliate is not its local currency. Remeasurement is similar to translation in that its goal is to obtain equivalent U.S. dollar values for the foreign affiliate's accounts so they may be combined or consolidated with the U.S. company's statements. The exchange rates used for remeasurement, however, are different from those used for translation, resulting in different dollar values for the foreign affiliate's accounts.

The FASB provided examples of several situations requiring remeasurement:[5]

1. A foreign sales branch or subsidiary of a U.S. manufacturer which primarily takes orders from foreign customers for U.S.-manufactured goods, which bills and collects from foreign customers, and which might have a warehouse to provide for timely delivery of the product to those foreign customers. In substance, this foreign operation may be the same as the export sales department of a U.S. manufacturer.

2. A foreign division, branch, or subsidiary which primarily manufactures a subassembly that is shipped to a U.S. plant for inclusion in a product that is sold to customers located in the U.S. or in different parts of the world.

3. A foreign shipping subsidiary which primarily transports ore from a U.S. company's foreign mines to the United States for processing in a U.S. company's smelting plants.

4. A foreign subsidiary which is primarily a conduit for Eurodollar borrowings to finance operations in the United States.

In most cases, the foreign affiliate may be thought of as a direct production or sales arm of the U.S. company, but it uses the local currency to record and report its operations. In addition, foreign entities located in highly inflationary economies, defined as economies having a cumulative three-year inflation rate exceeding 100 percent, must use the dollar as their functional currency, and their statements are remeasured into U.S. dollars. Many South American countries have experienced hyperinflation, with some countries having annual inflation rates in excess of 100 percent. If the foreign affiliate uses the U.S. dollar as both its functional and its reporting currency, no remeasurement is necessary, because its operations are already reported in U.S. dollars.

The remeasurement process should produce the same end result as if the foreign entity's transactions had been initially recorded in dollars. For this reason, certain transactions and account balances are restated to their U.S. dollar equivalents using a historical exchange rate, the spot exchange rate at the time the transaction originally occurred. The remeasurement process divides the balance sheet into monetary and nonmonetary accounts. Monetary assets and liabilities, such as cash, short-term or long-term receivables, and short-term or long-term payables, have their amounts fixed in terms of the units of currency. These accounts are subject to gains or losses from changes in exchange rates. Nonmonetary assets are accounts such as inventories, and plant and equipment, which are not fixed in relation to monetary units.

The monetary accounts are remeasured using the current exchange rate. The appropriate historical exchange rate is used to remeasure nonmonetary balance sheet account balances and related revenue, expense, gain, and loss account balances. A list of the accounts to be remeasured with the appropriate historical exchange rate is provided in Figure 12–8.[6]

Because of the variety of rates used to remeasure the foreign currency trial balance, the debits and credits of the U.S. dollar equivalent trial balance will probably not

---

[5]The examples were provided in the exposure draft of **FASB 52** but were not included in the final draft of the standard. The FASB did not want the examples to limit remeasurement to those cases in which the U.S. dollar is the functional currency.

[6]*FASB 52,* par. 48.

b. List the first five companies and their country of origin, as listed by IASC in their homepage, that refer to their use of International Accounting Standards in their financial statements. (*Hint:* Look in the "About IASC" section.)

c. Briefly summarize the two most recent accounting standards issued by the IASC.

Exercises

E12–1 **Multiple-Choice Questions on Translation and Remeasurement [AICPA Adapted]**
For each of the seven cases presented below, work the case twice and select the best answer. First assume that the foreign currency is the functional currency; then assume that the U.S. dollar is the functional currency.

1. Certain balance sheet accounts in a foreign subsidiary of Shaw Company on December 31, 20X1, have been restated in United States dollars as follows:

	Restated at	
	Current Rates	*Historical Rates*
Accounts Receivable, Current	$100,000	$110,000
Accounts Receivable, Long-Term	50,000	55,000
Prepaid Insurance	25,000	30,000
Patents	40,000	45,000
Total	$215,000	$240,000

What total should be included in Shaw's balance sheet for December 31, 20X1, for the above items?

a. $215,000.

b. $225,000.

c. $230,000.

d. $240,000.

2. A wholly owned foreign subsidiary of Nick Inc. has certain expense accounts for the year ended December 31, 20X4, stated in local currency units (LCU) as follows:

	LCU
Depreciation of Equipment (related assets were purchased January 1, 20X2)	120,000
Provision for Uncollectible Accounts	80,000
Rent	200,000

The exchange rates at various dates were as follows:

	Dollar Equivalent of 1 LCU
January 1, 20X2	$.50
December 31, 20X4	.40
Average, 20X4	.44

What total dollar amount should be included in Nick's statement of income to reflect the above expenses for the year ended December 31, 20X4?

a. $160,000.

b. $168,000.

c. $176,000.

d. $183,200.

3. Linser Corporation owns a foreign subsidiary with 2,600,000 local currency units (LCU) of property, plant, and equipment before accumulated depreciation on December 31, 20X4. Of this amount, 1,700,000 LCU were acquired in 20X2 when the rate of exchange was 1.5 LCU = $1, and 900,000 LCU were acquired in 20X3 when the rate of exchange was 1.6 LCU = $1. The rate of exchange in effect on December 31, 20X4, was 1.9 LCU = $1. The weighted average of exchange rates that were in effect during 20X4 was 1.8 LCU = $1. Assuming that the property, plant, and equipment are depreciated using the straight-line method over a 10-year period with no salvage value, how much depreciation expense relating to the foreign subsidiary's property, plant, and equipment should be charged in Linser's statement of income for 20X4?

a. $144,444.

b. $162,000.

c. $169,583.

d. $173,333.

4. On January 1, 20X1, Pat Company formed a foreign subsidiary. On February 15, 20X1, Pat's subsidiary purchased 100,000 local currency units (LCU) of inventory. 25,000 LCU of the original inventory purchased on February 15, 20X1, made up the entire inventory on December 31, 20X1. The exchange rates were 2.2 LCU = $1 from January 1, 20X1, to June 30, 20X1, and 2 LCU = $1 from July 1, 20X1, to December 31, 20X1. The December 31, 20X1, inventory balance for Pat's foreign subsidiary should be restated in United States dollars in the amount of:

a. $10,500.

b. $11,364.

c. $11,905.

d. $12,500.

5. At what rates should the following balance sheet accounts in the foreign currency financial statements be restated into United States dollars?

	Equipment	Accumulated Depreciation of Equipment
a.	Current	Current
b.	Current	Average for year
c.	Historical	Current
d.	Historical	Historical

    a. $31,000.

    b. $31,100.

    c. $33,000.

    d. $30,000.

5. Refer to the above information. The receipt of the dividend will result in:

    a. A credit to the investment account for $6,200.

    b. A debit to the income from subsidiary account for $6,600.

    c. A credit to the investment account for $6,600.

    d. A credit to the investment account for $6,500.

6. Refer to the above information. On Bartell's consolidated balance sheet at December 31, 20X5, what amount should be reported for the goodwill acquired on January 1, 20X5?

    a. $37,660.

    b. $37,800.

    c. $41,580.

    d. $39,880.

7. Refer to the above information. In the stockholders' equity section of Bartell's consolidated balance sheet at December 31, 20X5, Bartell should report the translation adjustment as a component of other comprehensive income of:

    a. $12,000.

    b. $15,920.

    c. $13,400.

    d. $8,080.

E12–5   **Translation**

On January 1, 20X1, Popular Creek Corporation organized RoadTime Company as a subsidiary in Switzerland with an initial investment cost of SFr 60,000. RoadTime's December 31, 20X1, trial balance in Swiss francs (SFr) is as follows:

	Debit	Credit
Cash	SFr 7,000	
Accounts Receivable (net)	20,000	
Receivable from Popular Creek	5,000	
Inventory	25,000	
Plant and Equipment	100,000	
Accumulated Depreciation		SFr 10,000
Accounts Payable		12,000
Bonds Payable		50,000
Common Stock		60,000
Sales		150,000
Cost of Goods Sold	70,000	
Depreciation Expense	10,000	
Operating Expense	30,000	
Dividends Paid	15,000	
Total	SFr 282,000	SFr 282,000

Additional Information

1. The receivable from Popular Creek is denominated in Swiss francs. Popular Creek's books show a payable to RoadTime at $4,000.

2. Purchases of inventory goods are made evenly during the year. Items in the ending inventory were purchased November 1.

3. Equipment is depreciated by the straight-line method with a 10-year life and no residual value. A full year's depreciation is taken in the year of acquisition. The equipment was acquired on March 1.

4. The dividends were declared and paid on November 1.

5. Exchange rates were as follows:

January 1	SFr 1 = $.73
March 1	SFr 1 = .74
November 1	SFr 1 = .77
December 31	SFr 1 = .80
20X1 Average	SFr 1 = .75

6. The Swiss franc is the functional currency.

Required

Prepare a schedule translating the December 31, 20X1, trial balance from Swiss francs to dollars.

E12–6   Proof of Translation Adjustment
Refer to the data in exercise 12–5.

Required

a. Prepare a proof of the translation adjustment computed in exercise 12–5.

b. Where is the translation adjustment reported on the consolidated financial statements of Popular Creek Corporation and its foreign subsidiary?

E12–7   Remeasurement
Refer to the data in exercise 12–5, but assume that the dollar is the functional currency for the foreign subsidiary.

Required

Prepare a schedule remeasuring the December 31, 20X1, trial balance from Swiss francs to dollars.

E12–8*   Proof of Remeasurement Gain (Loss)
Refer to the data in exercises 12–5 and 12–7.

Required

a. Prepare a proof of the remeasurement gain or loss computed in exercise 12–7.

b. How should this remeasurement gain or loss be reported on the consolidated financial statements of Popular Creek Corporation and its foreign subsidiary?

E12–9   Translation with Strengthening U.S. Dollar
Refer to the data in exercise 12–5, but now assume that the exchange rates were as follows:

January 1	SFr1 = $.80
March 1	SFr1 = .77
November 1	SFr1 = .74
December 31	SFr1 = .73
20X1 Average	SFr1 = .75

The receivable from Popular Creek Corporation is denominated in Swiss francs. Popular Creek's books show a payable to RoadTime at $3,650.

Assume the Swiss franc is the functional currency.

Required

a. Prepare a schedule translating the December 31, 20X1, trial balance from Swiss francs to dollars.

b. Compare the results of exercise 12–5, in which the dollar is weakening against the Swiss franc during 20X1, with the results in this exercise (E12–9), in which the dollar is strengthening against the Swiss franc during 20X1.

E12–10   Remeasurement with Strengthening U.S. Dollar

Refer to the data in exercise 12–5, but now assume that the exchange rates were as follows:

January 1	SFr1 = $.80
March 1	SFr1 = .77
November 1	SFr1 = .74
December 31	SFr1 = .73
20X1 Average	SFr1 = .75

The receivable from Popular Creek Corporation is denominated in Swiss francs. Popular Creek's books show a payable to RoadTime at $3,650.

Assume the U.S. dollar is the functional currency.

Required

a. Prepare a schedule remeasuring the December 31, 20X1, trial balance from Swiss francs to dollars.

b. Compare the results of exercise 12–7 in which the dollar weakens against the Swiss franc during 20X1 with the results in this exercise (E12–10) in which the dollar strengthened against the Swiss franc during 20X1.

E12–11   Remeasurement and Translation of Cost of Goods Sold

Duff Company is a subsidiary of Rand Corporation and is located in Madrid, Spain, where the currency is the Spanish peseta (P). Data on Duff's inventory and purchases are as follows:

Inventory, January 1, 20X7	P220,000
Purchases during 20X7	P846,000
Inventory, December 31, 20X7	P180,000

The beginning inventory was acquired during the fourth quarter of 20X6, and the ending inventory was acquired during the fourth quarter of 20X7. Purchases were made evenly over the year. Exchange rates were as follows:

Fourth quarter of 20X6	P1 = $0.0070
January 1, 20X7	P1 = $0.0075
Average during 20X7	P1 = $0.0080
Fourth quarter of 20X7	P1 = $0.0082
December 31, 20X7	P1 = $0.0085

Required

a. Show the remeasurement of cost of goods sold for 20X7, assuming the U.S. dollar is the functional currency.

b. Show the translation of cost of goods sold for 20X7, assuming the Spanish peseta is the functional currency.

E12–12   Equity-Method Entries for a Foreign Subsidiary

The Thames Company is located in London, England. The local currency is the British pound (£). On January 1, 20X8, Dek Company purchased an 80 percent interest in Thames Company for $400,000, which resulted in an excess of cost-over-book value of $48,000 due solely to a trademark having a remaining life of 10 years. Dek uses the equity method to account for its investment.

Dek's December 31, 20X8, trial balance has been translated into U.S. dollars, requiring a translation adjustment debit of $6,400. Thames Company's net income translated into U.S. dollars is $60,000. Thames declared and paid a £15,000 dividend on May 1, 20X8.

Relevant exchanges rates are as follows:

January 1, 20X8	£1 = $1.60
Average for 20X8	£1 = $1.63
May 1, 20X8	£1 = $1.64
December 31, 20X8	£1 = $1.65

Required

a. Record the dividend received by Dek Company from The Thames Company.

b. Prepare the entries to record Dek Company's equity in the net income of The Thames Company and the parent's share of the translation adjustment.

c. Show a calculation of the goodwill reported on the consolidated balance sheet of December 31, 20X8, and the translation adjustment from goodwill.

d. Record the amortization of the trademark on Dek's books.

e. Calculate the amount of the translation adjustment reported on the statement of comprehensive income as an element of other comprehensive income.

E12–13   Effects of a Change in the Exchange Rate—Translation and Other Comprehensive Income

The Bentley Company owns a subsidiary in India. The subsidiary's balance sheets for the last two years are presented below, in rupees (R):

	December 31, 20X6	December 31, 20X7
Assets:		
Cash	R 100,000	R 80,000
Receivables	450,000	550,000
Inventory	680,000	720,000
Fixed Assets, net	1,000,000	900,000
Total Assets	R2,230,000	R2,250,000
Equities:		
Current Payables	R 260,000	R 340,000
Long-term Debt	1,250,000	1,100,000
Common Stock	500,000	500,000
Retained Earnings	220,000	310,000
Total Equities	R2,230,000	R2,250,000

The Bentley Company formed the subsidiary on January 1, 20X6, when the exchange rate was 30 rupees for 1 U.S. dollar. On December 31, 20X6, the exchange rate had increased to 35 rupees for 1 U.S. dollar, and on December 31, 20X7, the exchange rate was 40 rupees for 1 U.S. dollar. Income is earned evenly over the year, and no dividends have been declared by the subsidiary during its first two years of existence.

Required

a. Present both the direct and the indirect exchange rate for the rupees for the three dates of: (1) January 1, 20X6, (2) December 31, 20X6, and (3) December 31, 20X7. Has the dollar strengthened or weakened in 20X6, and in 20X7?

b. Prepare the subsidiary's translated balance sheet as of December 31, 20X6, assuming the rupee is the subsidiary's functional currency.

c. Prepare the subsidiary's translated balance sheet as of December 31, 20X7, assuming the rupee is the subsidiary's functional currency.

d. Compute the amount that 20X7's other comprehensive income would include as a result of the translation.

E12–14   Computation of Gain or Loss on Sale of Asset by Foreign Subsidiary
On December 31, 20X2, your company's Mexican subsidiary sold land at a selling price of 3,000,000 pesos. The land had been purchased for 2,000,000 pesos on January 1, 20X1, when the exchange rate was 10 pesos to 1 U.S. dollar. On December 31, 20X1, the exchange rate was 11 pesos to 1 U.S. dollar, and on December 31, 20X2, the exchange rate was 12 pesos to 1 U.S. dollar. Assume the subsidiary had no other assets, and no liabilities, during the two years that it owned the land.

Required

a. Prepare all entries regarding the purchase and sale of the land that would be made on the books of the Mexican subsidiary whose reporting currency is the Mexican peso.

b. Determine the amount of the gain or loss on the transaction that would be reported on the subsidiary's remeasured statement of income in U.S. dollars, assuming the U.S. dollar is the functional currency. Determine the amount of the remeasurement gain or loss that would be reported on the remeasured statement of income in U.S. dollars.

c. Determine the amount of the gain or loss on the transaction that would be reported on the subsidiary's translated statement of income in U.S. dollars, assuming the Mexican peso is the functional currency. Determine the amount of the other comprehensive income that would be reported on the consolidated statement of other comprehensive income for 20X2.

E12–15*   Intercompany Transactions
Hawk Company sold inventory to United Ltd., an English subsidiary. The goods cost Hawk $8,000 and were sold to United for $12,000 on November 27, payable in British pounds. The goods are still on hand at the end of the year on December 31. The British pound (£) is the functional currency of the English subsidiary. The exchange rates were:

November 27	£1 = $1.60
December 31	£1 = 1.70

Required

a. At what dollar amount is the ending inventory shown in the trial balance of the consolidated workpaper?

b. What amount is eliminated for the unrealized intercompany gross profit, and at what amount is the inventory shown on the consolidated balance sheet?

* Indicates that the item relates to "Additional Considerations."

Problems

P12–16   **Parent Company Journal Entries and Translation**
On January 1, 20X1, Par Company purchased all the outstanding stock of North Bay Company, located in Canada, for $120,000. On January 1, 20X1, the direct exchange rate for the Canadian dollar (C$) was C$1 = $.80. The book value of North Bay Company on January 1, 20X1, was C$90,000. The fair value of North Bay's plant and equipment was C$10,000 greater than book value, and the plant and equipment is being depreciated over 10 years, with no salvage value. The remainder of the differential is attributable to a trademark which will be amortized over 10 years.

During 20X1, North Bay Company earned C$20,000 in income and declared and paid C$8,000 in dividends. The dividends were declared and paid in Canadian dollars when the exchange rate was C$1 = $.75. On December 31, 20X1, Par Company continues to hold the Canadian currency received from the dividend. On December 31, 20X1, the direct exchange rate is C$1 = $.70. The average exchange rate during 20X1 was C$1 = $.75. Management has determined that the Canadian dollar is the appropriate functional currency for North Bay Company.

Required

a. Prepare a schedule showing the differential allocation and amortization for 20X1. The schedule should present both Canadian dollars and U.S. dollars.

b. Par Company uses the basic equity method to account for its investment. Provide the entries that Par Company would record in 20X1 for its investment in North Bay Company for the following items:

  (1) Purchase of investment in North Bay Company.

  (2) Equity accrual for Par's share of North Bay's income.

  (3) Recognition of dividend declared and paid by North Bay Company.

  (4) Amortization of differential.

  (5) Recognition of translation adjustment on differential.

c. Prepare a schedule showing the proof of the translation adjustment for North Bay Company as a result of the translation of the subsidiary's accounts from Canadian dollars to U.S. dollars. Then provide the entry that Par Company would record for its share of the translation adjustment resulting from the translation of the subsidiary's accounts.

d. Provide the entry required by Par Company to restate the C$8,000 in the Foreign Currency Units account into its year-end U.S. dollar equivalent value.

 P12–17   **Translation, Journal Entries, Consolidated Comprehensive Income, and Stockholders' Equity**
On January 1, 20X5, Taft Company acquired all of the outstanding stock of Bordeaux Inc., a French company at a cost of $151,200. The net assets of Bordeaux on the date of acquisition were 700,000 francs. On January 1, 20X5, the book and fair values of the French subsidiary's identifiable assets and liabilities approximated their fair values except for property, plant, and equipment and patents acquired. The fair value of Bordeaux's property, plant, and equipment exceeded its book value by $18,000. The remaining useful life of Bordeaux's equipment at January 1, 20X5 was 10 years. The remainder of the differential was attributable to a patent having an estimated useful life of 5 years. Bordeaux's trial balance on December 31, 20X5, in francs, is presented below:

	Debits	Credits
Cash	FF 150,000	
Accounts Receivable (net)	200,000	
Inventory	270,000	
Property, Plant, and Equipment	600,000	
Accumulated Depreciation		FF 150,000

Accounts Payable		90,000
Notes Payable		190,000
Common Stock		450,000
Retained Earnings		250,000
Sales		690,000
Cost of Goods Sold	410,000	
Operating Expenses	100,000	
Depreciation Expense	600 50,000	200
Dividends Paid	40,000	
Total	FF1,820,000	FF1,820,000

Additional Information

1. Bordeaux uses the FIFO method for its inventory. The beginning inventory was acquired on December 31, 20X4, and its ending inventory was acquired on December 15, 20X5. Purchases of FF420,000 were made evenly throughout 20X5.

2. Bordeaux acquired all of its property, plant, and equipment on July 1, 20X3, and uses straight-line depreciation.

3. Bordeaux's sales were made evenly throughout 20X5, and its operating expenses were incurred evenly throughout 20X5.

4. The dividends were declared and paid on July 1, 20X5.

5. Taft Company's income from its own operations was $275,000 for 20X5, and its total stockholders' equity on January 1, 20X5, was $3,500,000. Taft declared $100,000 of dividends during 20X5.

6. Exchange rates were as follows:

July 1, 20X3	FF1 = $.15
December 30, 20X4	FF1 = $.18
January 1, 20X5	FF1 = $.18
July 1, 20X5	FF1 = $.19
December 15, 20X5	FF1 = $.205 E1
December 31, 20X5	FF1 = $.21
Average for 20X5	FF1 = $.20 *purch*

all own
assets: EOY

Required

a. Prepare a schedule translating the trial balance from French francs into U.S. dollars. Assume the franc is the functional currency.

b. Assume that Taft uses the basic equity method. Record all journal entries that relate to its investment in the French subsidiary during 20X5. Provide the necessary documentation and support for the amounts in the journal entries, including a schedule of the translation adjustment related to the differential.

c. Prepare a schedule which determines Taft's consolidated comprehensive income for 20X5.

d. Compute Taft's total consolidated stockholders' equity at December 31, 20X5.

P12–18 **Remeasurement, Journal Entries, Consolidated Net Income, and Stockholders' Equity**
Refer to the information contained in problem 12–17. Assume the U.S. dollar is the functional currency, not the franc.

Required

a. Prepare a schedule remeasuring the trial balance from French francs into U.S. dollars.

b. Assume that Taft uses the basic equity method. Record all journal entries that relate to its investment in the French subsidiary during 20X5. Provide the necessary documentation and support for the amounts in the journal entries.

c. Prepare a schedule that determines Taft's consolidated net income for 20X5.

d. Compute Taft's total consolidated stockholders' equity at December 31, 20X5.

P12–19   Proof of Translation Adjustment
Refer to the information presented in problem 12–17, and to your answer to part *a* of problem 12–17.

Required

Prepare a schedule providing a proof of the translation adjustment.

P12–20*   Remeasurement Gain or Loss
Refer to the information given in problem 12–17, and your answer to part *a* of problem 12–18.

Required

Prepare a schedule providing a proof of the remeasurement gain or loss. For this part of the problem, assume that the French subsidiary had the following monetary assets and liabilities at January 1, 20X5:

Monetary Assets	
Cash	FF 10,000
Accounts Receivable (net)	140,000

Monetary Liabilities	
Accounts Payable	FF 70,000
Notes Payable	140,000

On January 1, 20X5, the French subsidiary has a net monetary liability position of FF60,000.

P12–21   Translation and Calculation of Translation Adjustment
On January 1, 20X4, Alum Corporation acquired Franco Company, a French subsidiary, by purchasing all the common stock at book value. Franco's trial balances on January 1, 20X4, and December 31, 20X4, expressed in French francs (FF), are as follows:

	January 1, 20X4		December 31, 20X4	
	Debit	*Credit*	*Debit*	*Credit*
Cash	FF 62,000		FF 57,700	
Accounts Receivable (net)	83,900		82,000	
Inventories	95,000		95,000	
Prepaid Insurance	5,600		2,400	
Plant and Equipment	250,000		350,000	
Accumulated Depreciation		FF 67,500		FF 100,000
Intangible Assets	42,000		30,000	
Accounts Payable		20,000		24,000

Income Taxes Payable	30,000		27,000
Interest Payable	1,000		1,100
Notes Payable	20,000		20,000
Bonds Payable	120,000		120,000
Common Stock	80,000		80,000
Additional Paid-In Capital	150,000		150,000
Retained Earnings	50,000		50,000
Sales			500,000
Cost of Goods Sold		230,000	
Insurance Expense		3,200	
Depreciation Expense		32,500	
Amortization Expense		12,000	
Operating Expense		152,300	
Dividends Paid		25,000	
Total	FF 538,500	FF 538,500	FF1,072,100	FF1,072,100

Additional Information

1. Franco uses FIFO inventory valuation. Purchases were made uniformly during 20X4. Ending inventory for 20X4 is comprised of units purchased when the exchange rate was $.25.

2. The insurance premium for a two-year policy was paid on October 1, 20X3.

3. Plant and equipment were acquired as follows:

Date	Cost
January 1, 20X1	FF 200,000
July 10, 20X2	50,000
April 7, 20X4	100,000

4. Plant and equipment are depreciated using the straight-line method and a 10-year life with no residual value. A full month's depreciation is taken in the month of acquisition.

5. The intangible assets are patents acquired on July 10, 20X2, at a cost of FF 60,000. The estimated life is five years.

6. The common stock was issued on January 1, 20X1.

7. Dividends of FF 10,000 were declared and paid on April 7. On October 9, FF 15,000 of dividends were declared and paid.

8. Exchange rates were as follows:

January 1, 20X1	FF 1 = $.45
July 10, 20X2	FF 1 = .40
October 1, 20X3	FF 1 = .34
January 1, 20X4	FF 1 = .30
April 7, 20X4	FF 1 = .28
October 9, 20X4	FF 1 = .23
December 31, 20X4	FF 1 = .20
20X4 average	FF 1 = .25

Required

a. Prepare a schedule translating the December 31, 20X4, trial balance of Franco Company from francs to dollars.

b. Prepare a schedule calculating the translation adjustment as of the end of 20X4. The net assets on January 1, 20X4, were FF 280,000.

P12–22*　Remeasurement and Proof of Remeasurement Gain or Loss

Refer to the information in problem 12–21. Assume that the dollar is the functional currency.

Required

a. Prepare a schedule remeasuring the December 31, 20X4, trial balance of Franco Company from francs to dollars.

b. Prepare a schedule providing a proof of the remeasurement gain or loss.

P12–23　Translation

Alamo Inc. purchased 80 percent of the outstanding stock of Western Ranching Company, a company located in Australia, on January 1, 20X3. The purchase price was A$200,000, and A$40,000 of the differential was allocated to plant and equipment which is amortized over a 10-year period. The remainder of the differential was attributable to a patent. Alamo, Inc., amortizes the patent over 10 years. Western Ranching Company's trial balance on December 31, 20X3, in Australian dollars (A$) is as follows:

	Debit	Credit
Cash	A$ 44,100	
Accounts Receivable (net)	72,000	
Inventory	86,000	
Plant and Equipment	240,000	
Accumulated Depreciation		A$ 60,000
Accounts Payable		53,800
Payable to Alamo, Inc.		10,800
Interest Payable		3,000
12% Bonds Payable		100,000
Premium on Bonds		5,700
Common Stock		90,000
Retained Earnings		40,000
Sales		579,000
Cost of Goods Sold	330,000	
Depreciation Expense	24,000	
Operating Expenses	131,500	
Interest Expense	5,700	
Dividends Paid	9,000	
Total	A$942,300	A$942,300

Additional Information

1. Western Ranching Company uses average cost for cost of goods sold. Inventory increased by A$20,000 during the year. Purchases were made uniformly during 20X3. The ending inventory was acquired at the average exchange rate for the year.

2. Plant and equipment were acquired as follows:

Date	Cost
January, 20X1	A$180,000
January 1, 20X3	60,000

3. Plant and equipment are depreciated using the straight-line method, a 10-year life, and no residual value.

4. The payable to Alamo Inc. is in Australian dollars. Alamo's books show a receivable from Western Ranching Company of $6,480.

5. The 10-year bonds were issued on July 1, 20X3, for A$106,000. The premium is amortized on a straight-line basis. The interest is paid on April 1 and October 1.

6. The dividends were declared and paid on April 1.

7. Exchange rates were as follows:

January, 20X1	A$1 = $.93
August, 20X1	A$1 = $.88
January 1, 20X3	A$1 = $.70
April 1, 20X3	A$1 = $.67
July 1, 20X3	A$1 = $.64
December 31, 20X3	A$1 = $.60
20X3 average	A$1 = $.65

Required

a. Prepare a schedule translating the December 31, 20X3, trial balance of Western Ranching Company from Australian dollars to U.S. dollars.

b. Prepare a schedule providing a proof of the translation adjustment.

P12–24   Parent Company Journal Entries and Translation
Refer to the information given in problem 12–23 for Alamo and its subsidiary, Western Ranching. Assume that the Australian dollar (A$) is the functional currency and that Alamo uses the basic equity method for accounting for its investment in Western Ranching Company.

Required

Prepare the entries that would be recorded by Alamo Inc. in 20X3 for its investment in Western Ranching. Your entries should include the following:

(1) Record the initial investment on January 1, 20X3.

(2) Record the dividend received by the parent company.

(3) Recognize the parent company's share of the equity income of the subsidiary.

(4) Record the amortizations of the differential.

(5) Recognize the translation adjustment required by the parent from the adjustment of the differential.

(6) Recognize the parent company's share of the translation adjustment resulting from the translation of the subsidiary's accounts.

Provide the necessary documentation and support for the amounts recorded in the journal entries, including a schedule of the translation adjustment related to the differential.

P12–25   Consolidation Workpaper after Translation

Refer to the information given in problems 12–23 and 12–24 for Alamo and its subsidiary, Western Ranching. Assume that the Australian dollar (A$) is the functional currency and that Alamo uses the basic equity method for accounting for its investment in Western Ranching Company. A December 31, 20X3, trial balance for Alamo Inc. is presented below. Use this trial balance for completing this problem.

Item	*Debit*	*Credit*
Cash	$ 38,000	
Accounts Receivable (net)	140,000	
Receivable from Western Ranching	6,480	
Inventory	128,000	
Plant and Equipment	500,000	
Investment in Western Ranching	152,064	
Cost of Goods Sold	600,000	
Depreciation Expense	28,000	
Operating Expenses	204,000	
Interest Expense	2,000	
Dividends Declared	50,000	
Translation Adjustment	22,528	
Accumulated Depreciation		$ 90,000
Accounts Payable		60,000
Interest Payable		2,000
Common Stock		500,000
Retained Earnings, January 1, 20X3		179,656
Sales		1,000,000
Income from Subsidiary		39,416
Total	$1,871,072	$1,871,072

Required

a. Prepare a set of eliminating entries, in general journal form, for the entries required to prepare a comprehensive (including other comprehensive income) consolidation workpaper as of December 31, 20X3.

b. Prepare a comprehensive consolidation workpaper as of December 31, 20X3.

P12–26*   Remeasurement

Refer to the information in problem 12–23. Assume the U.S. dollar is the functional currency.

Required

a. Prepare a schedule remeasuring the December 31, 20X3, trial balance of Western Ranching Company from Australian dollars to U.S. dollars.

b. Prepare a schedule providing a proof of the remeasurement gain or loss. The subsidiary's net monetary liability position on January 1, 20X3, was A$80,000.

P12–27   Parent Company Journal Entries and Remeasurement

Refer to the information given in problems 12–23 and 12–26* for Alamo and its subsidiary, Western Ranching. Assume that the U.S. dollar is the functional currency and that Alamo uses the basic equity method for accounting for its investment in Western Ranching Company.

Required

Prepare the entries that would be recorded by Alamo Inc. in 20X3 for its investment in Western Ranching. Your entries should include the following:

(1) Record the initial investment on January 1, 20X3.

(2) Record the dividend received by the parent company.

(3) Recognize the parent company's share of the equity income from the subsidiary.

(4) Record the amortizations of the differential.

Provide the necessary documentation and support for the amounts recorded in the journal entries.

P12–28*   **Consolidation Workpaper after Remeasurement**

Refer to the information given in problems 12–23 and 12–27 for Alamo and its subsidiary, Western Ranching. Assume that the U.S. dollar is the functional currency and that Alamo uses the basic equity method for accounting for its investment in Western Ranching Company. A December 31, 20X3, trial balance for Alamo Inc. is presented below. Use this remeasured trial balance for completing this problem.

Item	Debit	Credit
Cash	$ 38,000	
Accounts Receivable (net)	140,000	
Receivable from Western Ranching	6,480	
Inventory	128,000	
Plant and Equipment	500,000	
Investment in Western Ranching	178,544	
Cost of Goods Sold	600,000	
Depreciation Expense	28,000	
Operating Expenses	204,000	
Interest Expense	2,000	
Dividends Declared	50,000	
Accumulated Depreciation		$ 90,000
Accounts Payable		60,000
Interest Payable		2,000
Common Stock		500,000
Retained Earnings, January 1, 20X3		179,656
Sales		1,000,000
Income from Subsidiary		43,368
Total	$1,875,024	$1,875,024

Required

a. Prepare a set of eliminating entries, in general journal form, for the entries required to prepare a three-part consolidation workpaper as of December 31, 20X3.

b. Prepare a three-part consolidation workpaper as of December 31, 20X3.

P12–29   **Foreign Currency Remeasurement [AICPA Adapted]**

On January 1, 20X1, the Kiner Company formed a foreign subsidiary that issued all its currently outstanding common stock on that date. Selected accounts from the balance sheets, all of which are shown in local currency units, are as follows:

	December 31	
	20X2	*20X1*
Accounts Receivable (net of allowance for uncollectible accounts of 2,200 LCU on December 31, 20X2, and 2,000 LCU on December 31, 20X1)	40,000	35,000
Inventories, at cost	80,000	75,000
Property, Plant, and Equipment (net of allowance for accumulated depreciation of 31,000 LCU on December 31, 20X2, and 14,000 LCU on December 31, 20X1)	163,000	150,000
Long-Term Debt	100,000	120,000
Common Stock, authorized 10,000 shares, par value 10 LCU per share; issued and outstanding, 5,000 shares on December 31, 20X2, and December 31, 20X1	50,000	50,000

Additional Information

1. Exchange rates are as follows:

January 1, 20X1–July 31, 20X1	2 LCU = $1
August 1, 20X1–October 31, 20X1	1.8 LCU = $1
November 1, 20X1–June 30, 20X2	1.7 LCU = $1
July 1, 20X2–December 31, 20X2	1.5 LCU = $1
Average monthly rate for 20X1	1.9 LCU = $1
Average monthly rate for 20X2	1.6 LCU = $1

2. An analysis of the accounts receivable balance is as follows:

	20X2	*20X1*
Accounts Receivable:		
Balance at beginning of year	37,000	
Sales (36,000 LCU per month in 20X2 and 31,000 LCU per month in 20X1)	432,000	372,000
Collections	(423,600)	(334,000)
Write-offs (May 20X2 and December 20X1)	(3,200)	(1,000)
Balance at end of year	42,200	37,000

	20X2	*20X1*
Allowance for Uncollectible Accounts:		
Balance at beginning of year	2,000	
Provision for uncollectible accounts	3,400	3,000
Write-offs (May 20X2 and December 20X1)	(3,200)	(1,000)
Balance at end of year	2,200	2,000

are included in the segment's profit or loss that is used by the chief operating decision maker. Also, only those assets that are included in the measure of the segment's assets that is used by the chief operating decision maker shall be reported for that segment. Thus, again the FASB is striving to align the segments' external financial disclosures with the internal reporting used by the company's management to make resource allocations and other decisions regarding the operating segments.

Information about Operating Segments

Many entities are diversified across several lines of business. Each line may be subject to unique competitive factors and may react differently to changes in the economic environment. For example, a large company such as Johnson & Johnson operates in several major lines: consumer, pharmaceutical, and professional. Its products include disposable contact lenses, baby products, surgical products, antibody therapies, and cold and flu medications. A conglomerate may operate in several consumer markets, each with different characteristics. In addition, a company is exposed to different risks in each of the markets in which it acquires its factors of production. Consolidated statements present all these heterogeneous factors in a single-entity context. The purpose of segment reporting is to allow financial statement users to look behind the consolidated totals to the individual components that constitute the entity.

Defining Reportable Segments

The process of determining separately ***reportable operating segments***, that is, segments for which separate supplemental disclosures must be made, is based on management's specification of its operating segments that are used internally for evaluating the enterprise's financial position and operating performance.

Ten Percent Quantitative Thresholds.   The FASB specified three ***10 percent significance rules*** to determine which of the operating segments shall have separately reported information. The separate disclosures are required for segments meeting at least one of the following tests:[5]

1. Its reported revenue, including both sales to external customers and intersegment sales or transfers, is 10 percent or more of the combined revenue, internal and external, of all operating segments.
2. The absolute amount of its reported profit or loss is 10 percent or more of the greater, in absolute amount, of (*a*) the combined reported profit of all operating segments that did not report a loss or (*b*) the combined reported loss of all operating segments that did report a loss.
3. Its assets are 10 percent or more of the combined assets of all operating segments.

Note that the revenue test includes intersegment sales or transfers. The FASB felt that the full impact of a particular segment on the entire enterprise should be

---

[5]*FASB 131*, par. 18.

measured. Also, the FASB felt that the definition of an operating segment should include components of an enterprise that sell primarily or exclusively to other components of the enterprise. Information about these "vertically integrated" operations provide insight into the production and operations of the enterprise.

FASB 131 states that the segment disclosure should include the reportable segments' measures of profit or loss. Thus, the report shall be the same as used for internal decision-making purposes. Some companies may allocate operating expenses arising from shared facilities such as a common warehouse. Other companies may allocate items such as interest costs, income taxes, or income from equity investments to specific segments. Whatever is used for internal decision-making purposes to measure the operating segment's profit or loss shall be reported in the external disclosure.

Although an enterprise is required to report the assets of the separately reportable operating segments, **FASB 131** also allows companies to report their segments' liabilities if the company feels the fuller disclosure would be meaningful. The assets to be reported are those used by the chief operating decision maker in making decisions about the segment and might include intangible assets such as goodwill or other intangibles. If commonly used assets are allocated to the segments, then these should be included in the reported amounts. The assets might also include financing items such as investments in equity securities or intersegment loans. The key point is that the revenues, profit or loss, and assets should be reported on the same basis as used for internal decision-making purposes.

If the total external revenue of the separately reportable operating segments is less than 75 percent of the total consolidated revenue, then management must select and disclose information about additional operating segments until at least 75 percent of consolidated revenue is included in reportable segments. The choice of which additional operating segments to report is left to management.

Information about the operating segments that are not separately reportable is combined and disclosed in an "All Other" category. The sources of the revenue in the All Other category must be described, but the level of disclosure for this category is significantly less than for the separately reportable segments. Again note that the corporate headquarters (or corporate administration) is not typically included as an operating segment of an enterprise.

Illustration of 10 Percent Tests.   Figure 13–1 represents the consolidated financial statements for Peerless Products Corporation and Special Foods Inc. Information for the example is as follows:

1. Peerless owns 80 percent of Special Foods' common stock. Special Foods reports a profit of $50,000 for 20X1 and pays dividends of $30,000. The December 31, 20X1, balances in Special Foods' stockholders' equity accounts total $300,000, of which the noncontrolling interest is 20 percent.
2. Peerless acquires 40 percent of Barclay Company stock on January 1, 20X1, for a cost of $160,000, which is equal to the book value of the stock on that date. The equity method is used to account for this investment. Barclay Company earns $80,000 in profit during 20X1 and pays $20,000 in dividends. This investment is managed by the corporate office and is not assigned to any operating segment.

Segment disclosure provides a breakdown of the consolidated totals into their constituent parts. The items that appear in the consolidated statements and must be

Extraordinary items should be disclosed separately and included in the determination of net income for the interim period in which they occur. In determining materiality, extraordinary items should be related to the estimated income for the full fiscal year. Effects of disposals of a segment of a business and unusual and infrequently occurring transactions and events that are material with respect to the operating results of the interim period . . . should be reported separately. . . . Extraordinary items, gains or losses from disposal of a segment of a business, and unusual or infrequently occurring items should not be prorated over the balance of the fiscal year. [15]

Contingencies or other major uncertainties that could affect the company must also be disclosed on the same basis as that used in the annual report. This disclosure is required to provide information on items that might affect the fairness of the interim report. The procedures for measuring and reporting contingencies in both interim and annual reports are presented in **FASB Statement No. 5,** "Accounting for Contingencies" (**FASB 5**).

Accounting Changes in Interim Periods

Accounting for changes in accounting principles or estimates should be presented in interim reports in the same manner as in annual reports. **APB 20** provides the guidelines for treatments of changes in annual reports. Changes in estimates are handled currently and prospectively, that is, from the change date forward in time, because estimates are a normal part of the accounting process.

Changes in accounting principles present additional problems because of the different methods used to present various types of changes. The alternatives are (1) cumulative effect changes, such as a change in depreciation method, (2) retroactive adjustment changes, such as a change *from* the LIFO method of inventory pricing, and (3) special exceptions, such as a change *to* the LIFO inventory method. **FASB Statement No. 3,** "Reporting Accounting Changes in Interim Financial Statements" (**FASB 3**), embraces the general recommendation that accounting changes, if made, should be made during the first interim period of a fiscal year.

Cumulative Effect Accounting Changes

Consistent with the view that all accounting changes should be made effective as of the beginning of the fiscal period, the cumulative effect of the accounting change on retained earnings is computed at the beginning of the fiscal year and reported in the first interim period's income statement. If a cumulative-effect type of change is made during an interim period subsequent to the first one, the prior interim reports of the current fiscal year must be restated as if the change had been made effective as of the first day of the fiscal year. The effect of this provision is to make all changes effective as of the beginning of the fiscal period and to use the new accounting method to present all the interim reports for the fiscal year. Pro forma earnings per share figures are required to allow comparison with prior years' interim income statements.

Retroactive-Type Accounting Changes

If a change in accounting principle requires the restatement of prior years' financial statements, it also requires the restatement of previously issued interim financial statements in the same manner as for the annual statements. For example, if a company

---
[15]*APB 28,* par. 21.

acquires a subsidiary in the third quarter and consolidates it on a pooling of interests basis, the first two quarters' interim reports, as well as the previous years' interims, should be restated to reflect the pooling.

Adoption of LIFO

In the case of the adoption of LIFO, neither the cumulative effect nor the necessary pro forma information is usually available on an annual basis. However, for interim reporting purposes, the change to LIFO should be made effective as of the first interim period of the fiscal year of the change. If the change is actually made in a later interim period, such as the third quarter of the year, the previously issued interim reports must be restated as if the LIFO inventory method had been adopted as of the beginning of the fiscal year.

Summary of Key Concepts and Terms

Segment disclosures about the specific industries of an entity and foreign areas in which an entity operates provide information about the different risks and profitability of each of the individual components that the entity comprises. These additional disclosures are useful in assessing past performance and prospects of future performance. A critical issue is the definition of a segment. The FASB allows management the flexibility it needs to disaggregate its operations but imposes several significance tests to determine which segments are separately reportable.

Interim reports must be issued by publicly held corporations so users of the information can assess corporate performance and make predictions about results for the annual fiscal period. The major issues are the measurement and disclosure problems of breaking down the annual reporting period into smaller parts. The FASB selected the integral theory of interim reporting, which views an interim period as an integral part of an annual period. Many of the technical problems revolve around cost of goods sold and income taxes. Estimates based on expected annual results are allowed when determining both of these costs. Even with the estimation and measurement problems, interim reports are primary disclosure vehicles that are quickly and carefully evaluated by investors and other users of financial statements.

Discrete theory of interim reporting	Management approach
Enterprisewide disclosure	Reportable operating segments
Integral theory of interim reporting	75 percent consolidated revenue test
Interim income tax	10 percent significance rules
Interim reports	

Questions

Q13–1 How might information on a company's operations in different industries be helpful to investors?

Q13–2 What is the relationship between the FASB's requirements for segment-based disclosures and a company's profit centers?

Q13–3 What are the three 10 percent significance tests used to determine reportable segments under **FASB 131?** Give the numerator and denominator for each of the tests.

Q13–4 Specifically, what items are in the determination of a segment's profit or loss?

Q13–5 A company has 10 industry segments, of which the largest five account for 80 percent of the combined revenues of the company. What considerations are important in determining the number of segments that are separately reportable? How are the remaining segments reported?

Q13–6 Only two materiality tests are used to determine separately reportable foreign operations. What are these two tests? Why isn't the third test, the profit or loss test, used to assess foreign operations?

Q13–7 What information must be disclosed about a company's major customers? Are the names of customers disclosed?

Q13–8 How can interim reports be used by investors to identify a company's seasonal trends?

Q13–9 Distinguish between the discrete and integral views of interim reporting. Which view is used in **APB Opinion No. 28?**

Q13–10 How is revenue recognized on an interim basis?

Q13–11 Describe the basic rules for computing cost of goods sold and inventory on an interim basis. In what circumstances are estimates permitted to determine costs?

Q13–12 How does the application of the lower-of-cost-or-market valuation method for inventories differ between interim statements and annual statements?

Q13–13 How might the accounting for an advertising campaign expenditure of $200,000 in the first quarter of a company's fiscal year differ between the integral theory and the discrete theory of interim reporting?

Q13–14 Describe the process of updating the estimate of the effective tax rate in the second quarter of a company's fiscal year.

Q13–15 How is the tax benefit of an interim period's operating loss treated if the future realizability of the tax benefit is *not* assured beyond a reasonable doubt?

Q13–16 How are extraordinary items reported on an interim basis?

Q13–17 The Allied Company made a change in depreciation accounting during the third quarter of its fiscal year. This change is a cumulative-effect type of accounting change. Describe the effect of this accounting change on prior interim reports and on the third quarter's interim report.

Cases

C13–1 **Segment Disclosures [CMA Adapted]**

Chemax Inc. manufactures a wide variety of pharmaceuticals, medical instruments, and other related medical supplies. Eighteen months ago the company developed and began to market a new product line of antihistamine drugs under various trade names. Sales and profitability of this product line during the current fiscal year greatly exceeded management's expectations. The new product line will account for 10 percent of the company's total sales and 12 percent of the company's operating income for the fiscal year ending June 30, 20X0. Management believes sales and profits will be significant for several years.

Chemax is concerned that its market share and competitive position may suffer if it discloses the volume and profitability of its new product line in its annual financial statements. Management is not sure how **FASB 131** applies in this case.

Required

a. What is the purpose of requiring segment information in financial statements?

b. Identify and explain the factors that should be considered when attempting to decide how products should be grouped to determine a single business segment.

c. What options, if any, does Chemax Inc. have with the disclosure of its new antihistamine product line? Explain your answer.

C13–2 **Matching Revenue and Expenses for Interim Periods**

Periodic reporting adds complexity to accounting by requiring estimates, accruals, deferrals, and allocations. Interim reporting creates even greater difficulties in matching revenue and expenses.

Required

a. Explain how revenue, product costs, gains, and losses should be recognized for interim periods.

b. Explain how determination of cost of goods sold and inventory differs for interim period reports versus annual reports.

c. Explain the treatment of period costs at interim dates.

d. Explain the treatment of the following items for interim financial statements:

(1) Long-term contracts

(2) Advertising

(3) Seasonal revenue

(4) Flood loss

(5) Annual major repairs and maintenance to plant and equipment during the last two weeks in December

C13–3   Segment Disclosures in the Financial Statements [CMA Adapted]

Bennett Inc. is a publicly held corporation whose diversified operations have been separated into five industry segments. Bennett is in the process of preparing its annual financial statements for the year ended December 31, 20X5. The following information has been collected for the preparation of the segment reports required by **FASB 131.**

Bennett Inc.
Selected Data
For the Year Ended December 31, 20X5
(in thousands)

Item	Power Tools	Fastening Systems	Household Products	Plumbing Products	Security Systems
Sales to Unaffiliated Customers	$32,000	$ 4,500	$ 4,800	$3,000	$2,000
Intersegment Sales	10,000	5,500	200	1,000	—
Total Revenue	42,000	10,000	5,000	4,000	2,000
Cost of Goods Sold	30,000	8,000	4,500	3,100	1,700
Operating Profit	4,500	1,000	(600)	700	(100)
Net Income	2,600	800	(750)	(100)	(200)
Identifiable Assets	50,000	23,000	17,000	6,000	4,000

Required

a. Determine which of the operating segments are reportable segments for Bennett Inc. Your determination should include all required tests and the results of those tests for each of the five segments of Bennett.

b. The reportable segments determined above must represent a substantial portion of Bennett Inc.'s total operations when taken together. Describe how to determine whether a substantial portion of Bennett's operations are explained by its segment information.

C13–4   Determining Industry and Geographic Segments

A major producer of cereal breakfast foods had been reporting in its annual reports just one dominant product line (cereals) in only the U.S. domestic geographic area. The company had no other separately reportable segments. For several years, the U.S. company had a Canadian subsidiary that produced a variety of pasta. In 20X5, one brand of pasta, "Healthcare," suddenly became very popular with the health-conscious public in both the United States and Canada, and the Canadian subsidiary more than tripled its sales and profits within the year.

The management of the U.S. parent company did not want to disclose to its competitors how profitable the Canadian subsidiary was because the company wanted to maintain its strong economic position without more competition.

You have been able to determine the following (in millions):

	Cereal Products	*Pasta Products*
Net sales	$3,885	$834
Operating profit	445	151
Identifiable assets	1,565	147

All cereal product operations are located in the United States, and all pasta product operations are located in Canada. The Standard Industrial Classification (SIC) number for cereal products is 2043, and is 2098 for the Canadian subsidiary's pasta products. (The Standard Industrial Classification Index is prepared by the U.S. Office of Management and Budget and is used widely to define a company's major industrial groups.)

Required

a. Why would management be reluctant to disclose information about very successful—and very unsuccessful—operations in the segmental disclosure footnote in the annual report?

b. Present both theoretical and applied arguments for including the pasta products segment with the cereal products segment as one internal operating segment, thus not requiring separate disclosure under **FASB 131.** How does the fact that the pasta products have suddenly become popular affect the disclosure requirements under **FASB 131?**

c. Present the requirements under **FASB 131** for reporting the cereal products and pasta products by geographic area. Must the Canadian operations be disclosed separately in a geographic disclosure footnote?

C13–5 **Research Related to Segment Reporting**

The manager you work for has asked you to perform some research to determine what types of information public companies are providing on their Internet home pages. The public company you work for is considering establishing their own home page. In particular the manager wants you to note how these companies describe their products and services on the home page. After researching the home pages, the manager wants you to review the company's Form 10–K by using the Electronic Data Gathering, Analysis, and Retrieval Database (EDGAR). While looking at the Form 10–K, the manager wants you to observe how the companies describe the segments of their business. For example, are the segments as described in the Form 10–K similar to the products and services mentioned on the same company's home page?

Required

a. Using an Internet search engine find a home page of a *public* company. (*Hint:* A helpful search term is "Company Home Pages.") Then write two paragraphs summarizing what you find on the company's home page discussing the following:

(1) What type of information is provided related to the company's products or services?

(2) What other information is listed on the home page?

b. Using the EDGAR database, locate the most recent Form 10–K for the company you selected. (Note: The Electronic Data Gathering, Analysis, and Retrieval Database [EDGAR] collects and maintains the forms that are required to be filed by public companies to the U.S. Securities and Exchange Commission [SEC].) (*Hint:* The Internet URL for the EDGAR Database is http://www.sec.gov/edgarhp.htm.)

(1) Review the Form 10–K and locate the segment disclosure information. If your company does have segment disclosure information, print this information.

(2) Write two paragraphs summarizing what you find in the company's Form 10–K regarding segment disclosures. Include the following information:

(a) Describe the company's segments as displayed in the 10–K. Discuss on what basis the segments are presented.

(b) Discuss which segment(s) has (have) the highest revenues, is (are) the most profitable, and has (have) the most assets.

C13–6

Research Related to Interim Reporting

The company you work for is considering going public. Your current position is within the external financial reporting group. The manager you work for wants you to review some public company quarterly reports, Form 10–Qs, to see what type of information is disclosed. The manager does not want you to perform technical research to determine what the exact reporting requirements are for the Form 10–Q. Rather the manager wants you to understand generally what information other companies seem to be supplying in their Form 10–Qs.

Required

a. Determine the name of two public companies you would like to use in your review of Form 10–Qs. (*Hint:* There are a variety of ways to determine the public companies you want to research. For example, you could use an Internet search engine to find a home page of a *public* company. A helpful search term is "Company Home Pages." Another method would be to simply select public companies you already know of or you find through the use of a newspaper or periodical.)

b. Using the EDGAR database, locate the most recent Form 10–Qs for the two companies you selected. (*Hint:* The Internet URL for the EDGAR Database is http://www.sec.gov/edgarhp.htm.) In addition, for one of these companies locate the Form 10–Q for the same period in the prior year. Prepare a one- to two-page summary after performing the following analysis:

(1) Take one company's recent Form 10–Q, and write a brief summary of the contents of the Form 10–Q. Discuss how the Form 10–Q information compares with the information you know is included in a Form 10–K.

(2) Review the same company's Form 10–Q from the previous year, and provide a discussion of the similarities and differences you notice in the Form 10–Qs for different time periods.

(3) Review the other company's Form 10–Q from the current year, and provide a discussion of the similarities and differences you notice in the Form 10–Qs for different companies.

Exercises

E13–1 **Reportable Segments**

Amalgamated Products has seven operating segments. Data on the segments are as follows:

Segments	Revenues	Segment Profit (Loss)	Segment Assets
Electronics	$ 42,000	$ (8,600)	$ 73,000
Bicycles	105,000	30,400	207,000
Sporting Goods	53,000	(4,900)	68,000
Home Appliances	147,000	23,000	232,000
Gas and Oil Equipment	186,000	11,700	315,000
Glassware	64,000	(19,100)	96,000
Hardware	178,000	38,600	194,000
Total	$775,000	$71,100	$1,185,000

Included in the $105,000 revenue of the Bicycles segment are sales of $25,000 made to the Sporting Goods segment.

Required

a. Indicate which segments are reportable.

b. Do the reportable segments include a sufficient portion of total revenue? Explain.

E13–2   **Multiple-Choice Questions on Segment Reporting [AICPA Adapted]**
Select the correct answer for each of the following questions.

1. Barbee Corporation discloses supplementary operating segment information for its two reportable segments. Data for 20X5 are available as follows:

	Segment E	Segment W
Sales	$750,000	$250,000
Traceable operating expenses	325,000	130,000

   Additional 20X5 expenses are as follows:

Indirect operating expenses	$120,000

   Appropriately selected common operating expenses are allocated to segments based on the ratio of each segment's sales to total sales. The 20X5 operating profit for Segment E was:

   a. $260,000.

   b. $335,000.

   c. $395,000.

   d. $425,000.

2. The viewpoint used to determine segmental disclosures in annual reports is called the:

   a. Segment approach.

   b. Portfolio approach.

   c. Economic entity approach.

   d. Management approach.

3. Dutko Company has three lines of business, each of which is a significant industry segment. Company sales aggregated $1,800,000 in 20X6, of which Segment 3 contributed 60 percent. Traceable costs were $600,000 for Segment 3 from a total of $1,200,000 for the company as a whole. In addition, $350,000 of common costs are allocated in the ratio of a segment's income before common costs to the total income before common costs. For Segment 3 Dutko should report a 20X6 segment profit of:

   a. $200,000.

   b. $270,000.

   c. $280,000.

   d. $480,000.

   e. None of the above.

4. The Stein Company is a diversified company that discloses supplemental financial information on its industry segments. The following information is available for 20X2:

	Sales	Traceable Costs	Allocable Costs
Segment A	$400,000	$225,000	
Segment B	300,000	240,000	
Segment C	200,000	135,000	
Totals	$900,000	$600,000	$150,000

Allocable costs are assigned based on the ratio of a segment's income before allocable costs to total income before allocable costs. This is an appropriate method of allocation. The segment profit for Segment B for 20X2 is:

a. $0.

b. $10,000.

c. $30,000.

d. $50,000.

e. None of the above.

5. Selected data for a segment of a business enterprise are to be reported separately in accordance with **FASB 131** when the revenue of the segment exceeds 10 percent of the:

a. Combined net income of all segments reporting profits.

b. Total revenue obtained in transactions with outsiders.

c. Total revenue of all the enterprise's industry segments.

d. Total combined revenue of all segments reporting profits.

6. Kimber Company operates in four different industries, each of which is appropriately regarded as a reportable segment. Total sales for 20X2 for all segments combined were $1,000,000. Sales for Segment 2 were $400,000, and the traceable costs were $150,000. Total common costs for all the segments combined were $500,000. Kimber allocates common costs based on the ratio of a segment's sales to total sales, an appropriate method of allocation. The segment profit to be reported for Segment 2 for 20X2 is:

a. $50,000.

b. $125,000.

c. $200,000.

d. $250,000.

e. None of the above.

7. The following information pertains to Reding Corporation for the year ended December 31, 20X6.

Sales to unaffiliated customers	$2,000,000
Intersegment sales of products similar to those sold to unaffiliated customers	600,000

All of Reding's segments are engaged solely in manufacturing operations. Reding has a reportable segment if that segment's revenue exceeds:

a. $264,000.

b. $260,000.

c. $204,000.

d. $200,000.

8. Snow Corporation's revenue for the year ended December 31, 20X2, was as follows:

Consolidated revenue per income statement	$1,200,000
Intersegment sales	180,000
Intersegment transfers	60,000
Combined revenue of all industry segments	$1,440,000

Snow has a reportable operating segment if that segment's revenue exceeds:

a. $6,000.

b. $24,000.

c. $120,000.

d. $144,000.

9. Porter Corporation is engaged solely in manufacturing operations. The following data (consistent with prior years' data) pertain to the industries in which operations were conducted for the year ended December 31, 20X5:

Industry Segment	Total Revenue	Segment Profit	Assets at 12/31/X5
A	$10,000,000	$1,750,000	$20,000,000
B	8,000,000	1,400,000	17,500,000
C	6,000,000	1,200,000	12,500,000
D	3,000,000	550,000	7,500,000
E	4,250,000	675,000	7,000,000
F	1,500,000	225,000	3,000,000
Totals	$32,750,000	$5,800,000	$67,500,000

In its segment information for 20X5, how many reportable segments does Porter have?

a. Three.

b. Four.

c. Five.

d. Six.

10. Boecker is a multidivisional corporation which has both intersegment sales and sales to unaffiliated customers. Boecker should report segment financial information for each segment meeting which of the following criteria?

a. Segment profit or loss is 10 percent or more of consolidated profit or loss.

b. Segment profit or loss is 10 percent or more of combined profit or loss of all company segments.

c. Segment revenue is 10 percent or more of combined revenue of all company segments.

d. Segment revenue is 10 percent or more of consolidated revenue.

Use the following information to answer questions 11 and 12.

Ward Corporation, a publicly owned corporation, is subject to the requirements for segment reporting. In its income statement for the year ending December 31, 20X5, Ward reported revenues of $50,000,000, operating expenses of $47,000,000, and net income of $3,000,000. Operating expenses included payroll costs of $15,000,000. Ward's combined assets of all industry segments at December 31, 20X5, were $40,000,000.

11. In its 20X5 financial statements, Ward should disclose major customer data if sales to any single customer amount to at least:

    a. $300,000.

    b. $1,500,000.

    c. $4,000,000.

    d. $5,000,000.

12. In its 20X5 financial statements, Ward should disclose foreign revenues in a specific country if revenues from foreign operations in that country are at least:

    a. $5,000,000.

    b. $4,700,000.

    c. $4,000,000.

    d. $1,500,000.

E13–3   Multiple-Choice Questions on Interim Reporting [AICPA Adapted]

Select the correct answer for each of the following questions.

1. In considering interim financial reporting, how did the Accounting Principles Board conclude that such reporting should be viewed?

    a. As a "special" type of reporting that need not follow generally accepted accounting principles.

    b. As useful only if activity is evenly spread throughout the year so that estimates are unnecessary.

    c. As reporting for a basic accounting period.

    d. As reporting for an integral part of an annual period.

2. Which of the following is an inherent difficulty in determining the results of operations on an interim basis?

    a. Cost of sales reflects only the amount of product expense allocable to revenue recognized as of the interim date.

    b. Depreciation on an interim basis is a partial estimate of the actual annual amount.

    c. Costs expensed in one interim period may benefit other periods.

    d. Revenue from long-term construction contracts accounted for by the percentage-of-completion method is based on annual completion, and interim estimates may be incorrect.

3. Which of the following reporting practices is permissible for interim financial reporting?

    a. Use of the gross profit method for interim inventory pricing.

    b. Use of the direct costing method for determining manufacturing inventories.

    c. Deferral of unplanned variances under a standard cost system until year-end.

    d. Deferral of nontemporary inventory market declines until year-end.

4. On January 1, 20X2, Harris Inc. paid property taxes on its plant for the calendar year 20X2, amounting to $40,000. In March 20X2, Harris made annual major repairs to its machinery amounting to $120,000. These repairs will benefit the entire calendar year's operations. How should these expenses be reflected in Harris's quarterly income statements?

| | **Three Months Ended** | | | |
	March 31, 20X2	June 30, 20X2	September 30, 20X2	December 31, 20X2
a.	$ 22,000	$46,000	$46,000	$46,000
b.	40,000	40,000	40,000	40,000
c.	70,000	30,000	30,000	30,000
d.	160,000	-0-	-0-	-0-

5. An inventory loss from market decline of $420,000 occurred for the Wenger Company in April 20X2. The company recorded this loss in April 20X2 after its March 31, 20X2, quarterly report

was issued. None of this loss was recovered by the end of the year. How should this loss be reflected in Wenger's quarterly income statements?

Three Months Ended

	March 31, 20X2	June 30, 20X2	September 30, 20X2	December 31, 20X2
a.	$ -0-	$ -0-	$ -0-	$420,000
b.	-0-	140,000	140,000	140,000
c.	-0-	420,000	-0-	-0-
d.	105,000	105,000	105,000	105,000

6. A company that uses the last-in, first-out (LIFO) method of inventory costing finds, at an interim reporting date, that there has been a partial liquidation of the base-period inventory level. The decline is considered temporary, and the base inventory will be replaced before year-end. The amount shown as inventory on the interim reporting date should:

   a. Not give effect to the LIFO liquidation, and cost of sales for the interim reporting period should include the expected cost of replacement of the liquidated LIFO base.

   b. Be shown at the actual level, and cost of sales for the interim reporting period should reflect the decrease in LIFO base-period inventory level.

   c. Not give effect to the LIFO liquidations, and cost of sales for the interim reporting period should reflect the decrease in LIFO base-period inventory level.

   d. Be shown at the actual level, and the decrease in inventory level should not be reflected in the cost of sales for the interim reporting period.

7. During the second quarter of 20X5, Camerton Company sold a piece of equipment at a $12,000 gain. What portion of the gain should Camerton report in its income statement for the second quarter of 20X5?

   a. $12,000.

   b. $6,000.

   c. $4,000.

   d. $0.

8. On March 15, 20X1, Burge Company paid property taxes of $180,000 on its factory building for calendar year 20X1. On April 1, 20X1, Burge made $300,000 in unanticipated repairs to its plant equipment. The repairs will benefit operations for the remainder of the calendar year. What total amount of these expenses should be included in Burge's quarterly income statement for the three months ended June 30, 20X1?

   a. $75,000.

   b. $145,000.

   c. $195,000.

   d. $345,000.

9. The SRB Company had an inventory loss from a market price decline which occurred in the first quarter. The loss was not expected to be restored in the fiscal year. However, in the third quarter the inventory had a market price recovery that exceeded the first-quarter decline. For interim financial reporting, the dollar amount of net inventory should:

   a. Decrease in the first quarter by the amount of the market price decline and increase in the third quarter by the amount of the market price recovery.

   b. Decrease in the first quarter by the amount of the market price decline and increase in the third quarter by the amount of the decrease in the first quarter.

   c. Not be affected in the first quarter and increase in the third quarter by the amount of the market price recovery that exceeded the amount of the market price decline.

   d. Not be affected in either the first quarter or the third quarter.

10. For external reporting purposes, it is appropriate to use estimated gross profit rates to determine the cost of goods sold for:

	Interim Financial Reporting	Year-End Financial Reporting
a.	Yes	Yes
b.	Yes	No
c.	No	Yes
d.	No	No

11. On June 30, 20X5, Park Corporation incurred a $100,000 net loss from disposal of a business segment. Also, on June 30, 20X5, Park paid $40,000 for property taxes assessed for the calendar year 20X5. What amount of the foregoing items should be included in the determination of Park's net income or loss for the six-month interim period ended June 30, 20X5?

  a. $140,000.

  b. $120,000.

  c. $90,000.

  d. $70,000.

E13–4 Temporary LIFO Liquidation

During June, Kissick Hardware, which uses a perpetual inventory system, sold 920 units from its LIFO-base inventory, which had originally cost $12 per unit. The replacement cost is expected to be $21 per unit. Kissick is reducing inventory levels, and expects to replace only 640 of these units by December 31, the end of the fiscal year.

Required

a. Prepare the entry in June to record the sale of the 920 units.

b. Prepare the entry for the replacement of the 640 units in August at an actual cost of $19.80 per unit.

E13–5 Inventory Write-Down and Recovery

Comeback Company, a calendar-year entity, had 9,000 medical instruments in its beginning inventory for 20X2. On December 31, 20X1, the instruments had been adjusted down to $10.20 per unit, which was the lower of average cost or market, from an actual average cost of $10.55 per unit. No additional units were purchased during 20X2. The following additional information is provided for 20X2:

Quarter	Date	Inventory (units)	Replacement Cost
1	March 31, 20X2	8,000	$10.10
2	June 30, 20X2	7,500	10.35
3	September 30, 20X2	6,000	9.90
4	December 31, 20X2	4,000	10.00

Required

Determine the cost of goods sold for each quarter, and verify the total cost of goods sold by computing annual cost of goods sold on a lower-of-cost-or-market basis.

E13–6 Multiple-Choice Questions on Income Taxes at Interim Dates [AICPA Adapted]

Select the correct answer for each of the following questions.

1. According to **APB Opinion No. 28,** "Interim Financial Reporting," income tax expense in an income statement for the first interim period of an enterprise's fiscal year should be computed by:

  a. Applying the estimated income tax rate for the full fiscal year to the pretax accounting income for the interim period.

  b. Applying the estimated income tax rate for the full fiscal year to the taxable income for the interim period.

  c. Applying the statutory income tax rate to the pretax accounting income for the interim period.

  d. Applying the statutory income tax rate to the taxable income for the interim period.

2. Neil Company, which has a fiscal year ending January 31, had the following pretax accounting income and estimated effective annual income tax rates for the first three quarters of the year ended January 31, 20X2:

Quarter	Pretax Accounting Income	Estimated Effective Annual Income Tax Rate at End of Quarter, %
First	$60,000	40
Second	70,000	40
Third	40,000	45

  Neil's income tax expenses in its interim income statement for the third quarter are:

  a. $18,000.

  b. $24,500.

  c. $25,500.

  d. $76,500.

  e. None of the above.

3. Beckett Corporation expects to sustain an operating loss of $100,000 for the full year ending December 31, 20X3. Beckett operates entirely in one jurisdiction, where the tax rate is 40 percent. Anticipated tax credits for 20X3 total $10,000. No permanent differences are expected. Realization of the full tax benefit of the expected operating loss and realization of anticipated tax credits are assured beyond any reasonable doubt because they will be carried back. For the first quarter ended March 31, 20X3, Beckett reported an operating loss of $20,000. How much of a tax benefit should Beckett report for the interim period ended March 31, 20X3?

  a. $0.

  b. $8,000.

  c. $10,000.

  d. $12,500.

  e. None of the above.

4. The computation of a company's third-quarter provision for income taxes should be based on earnings:

  a. For the quarter at an expected annual effective income tax rate.

  b. For the quarter at the statutory rate.

  c. To date at an expected annual effective income tax rate less prior quarters' provisions.

  d. To date at the statutory rate less prior quarters' provisions.

5. During the first quarter of 20X5, Stahl Company had income before taxes of $200,000, and its effective income tax rate was 15 percent. Stahl's 20X4 effective annual income tax rate was 30 percent, but Stahl expects its 20X5 effective annual income tax rate to be 25 percent. In its first-quarter interim income statement, what amount of income tax expense should Stahl report?

  a. $0.

  b. $30,000.

  c. $50,000.

  d. $60,000.

E13–7   Significant Foreign Operations

Information about the domestic and foreign operations of Radon Inc. is as follows:

	Geographic Area					
	United States	*Britain*	*Brazil*	*Israel*	*Australia*	*Total*
Sales to unaffiliated customers	$364,000	$252,000	$72,000	$58,000	$47,000	$ 793,000
Interarea sales between affiliates	38,000	19,000	6,000			63,000
Total revenue	$402,000	$271,000	$78,000	$58,000	$47,000	$ 856,000
Profit	34,500	22,500	11,300	3,200	4,500	76,000
Long-lived assets	509,000	439,000	93,000	66,000	75,000	1,182,000

Required

Prepare schedules showing appropriate tests to determine which countries are material, using a 10 percent materiality threshold.

E13–8   Major Customers

Sales by Knight Inc. to major customers are as follows:

Customer	*Sales*	*Reporting Segment*
State of Illinois	$2,700,000	Computer hardware
Cook County, Illinois	3,500,000	Computer software
U.S. Treasury Department	3,900,000	Service contract
U.S. Department of Defense	2,200,000	Service contract
Bank of England	4,650,000	Computer software
Philips NV	2,850,000	Computer hardware
Honda	5,400,000	Computer hardware

Required

If worldwide sales total $43,000,000 for the year, which of Knight's customers should be disclosed as major customers?

E13–9   Estimated Annual Tax Rates

World Inc. estimates total federal and state tax rates to be 50 percent. World's first-quarter earnings are $300,000 and expected annual earnings are $1,500,000. For the year, premiums for life insurance on officers will be $60,000, and dividend exclusions are expected to be $80,000. A business tax credit of $20,000 should be available.

Required

a. Estimate World Inc.'s effective combined federal and state tax rate for the year.

b. Prepare the entry to record the tax provision for the first quarter.

1. *Public Utility Holding Company Act of 1935.* This act prohibits artificial pyramids of capital in public utilities and allows the Commission to restructure those "holding companies" whose only purpose is to concentrate the stock voting power in a few individuals.

2. *Trust Indenture Act of 1939.* This act requires a trustee to be appointed for sales of bonds, debentures, and other debt securities of public corporations, thus bringing in a bonded expert to administer the debt.

3. *Investment Company Act of 1940.* This act controls companies such as mutual funds that invest funds for the public. These companies must be audited annually, with the auditor reporting directly to the SEC.

4. *Investment Advisors Act of 1940.* This act requires complete disclosure of information about investment advisers including their backgrounds, business affiliations, and bases for compensation.

5. *Securities Investor Protection Act of 1970.* This act created the Securities Investor Protection Corporation (SIPC), an entity responsible for insuring investors from possible losses if an investment house enters bankruptcy. A small fee is added to the cost of each stock trade to cover the costs of the SIPC.

6. *Foreign Corrupt Practices Act of 1977.* This act amended the 1934 Securities Exchange Act. It requires accurate and fair recording of financial activities and requires management to maintain an adequate system of internal control.

7. *Federal Bankruptcy Acts.* The SEC provides assistance to the courts when a publicly held company declares bankruptcy. The primary concern of the SEC in these cases is the protection of security holders.

The Regulatory Structure

Many people beginning a study of the regulatory structure of the SEC are overwhelmed by the myriad of regulations, acts, guides, and releases the SEC uses to perform its tasks. It is easier to understand how the SEC operates after obtaining a basic understanding of these public documents and the nature of the SEC's pronouncements. Figure 14–2, which will be referenced throughout the chapter, presents an overview of this regulatory structure.

The Securities Act of 1933 and the Securities Exchange Act of 1934 are broken down into rules, regulations, forms, guides, and releases. The rules generally provide specific definitions for complying with the acts. The regulations establish compliance requirements; for example, the regulations of the 1933 act detail specific reporting requirements for special cases such as small companies. The forms specify the format of the reports to be made under each of the acts. The guides provide specified additional disclosure requirements for selected industries such as oil and gas, and banks. The releases are used for amendments or adoptions of new requirements under the acts.

Two major regulations, **Regulation S-X** and **Regulation S-K,** govern the preparation of financial statements and associated disclosures made in reports to the SEC. Specifically, Regulation S-X presents the rules for preparing financial statements, footnotes, and the auditor's report. Regulation S-K covers all the nonfinancial items, such as management's discussion and analysis of the company's operations and present financial position.

The SEC needed some reporting vehicle to inform accountants about changes made in disclosure requirements, regulatory changes in the auditor-client relationship,

FIGURE 14–2   The Regulatory Structure

Item	Contents
Securities Act of 1933	Statute regulating initial registration and sale of securities.
Securities Act rules	Basic definitions of Securities Act terms such as *offers, distribution, participation,* and *accredited investor.*
Securities Act regulations	Detailed requirements of registration. At the present time there are six regulations (Regulations A, B, C, D, E, F), of which two (A and D) specify exemptions from registration requirements for small or private stock offerings.
Securities Act forms	Content of registration forms. The most frequently used forms are Form 1–A for small offerings of securities and Forms S–1, S–2, and S–3, which are general registration forms.
Securities Act industry guides	Specifications of additional disclosures required in registration statements of companies in special industries such as oil and gas, banking, and real estate.
Securities Act releases (SRs)	Announcements amending or adopting new rules, guides, forms, or policies under the 1933 act. Approximately 6,000 releases have been published. These are noted with a prefix; for example, for release number 6,000, Release 33-6000.
Securities Exchange Act of 1934	Regulation of security trading and requirements for periodic reports by publicly held companies.
Exchange Act rules	Specific reporting requirements of over-the-counter securities, special reports required by stockholders who own 5 percent or more of a company's outstanding stock, and prohibition of manipulative and deceptive devices or contrivances.
Exchange Act forms	Specification of the content of periodic reports. The most commonly used forms are Form 10–K (annual report), Form 10– Q (quarterly report), and Form 8–K (current events report).
Exchange Act industry guides	Additional periodic reporting requirements of companies in specialized industries such as electric and gas utilities, oil and gas, and banking.
Securities Exchange Act releases (SRs)	Announcements of amendments or adoptions of new rules, guides, forms, or policy statements pertaining to the 1934 act. More than 15,000 have been issued, identified with a prefix; for example, for number 15,000, Release 34-15000.
Regulation S-X (Reg. S-X)	Articles specifying the form and content of financial disclosures: financial statements, schedules, footnotes, reports of accountants, and pro forma disclosures.
Regulation S-K (Reg. S-K)	Articles specifying disclosure rules of nonfinancial items to be included in registration statements, annual reports, and proxy statements. Major items are description of business, management's discussion and analysis, disagreements with accountants, and required information about new stock issues.
Financial Reporting Releases (FRRs)	Amendments to Securities Act, additional disclosure requirements, and other current issues regarding accounting and auditing principles and standards. Financial Reporting Release No. 1 is a codification of the accounting and auditing materials in the 307 Accounting Series Releases published between 1933 and 1982.
Accounting and Auditing Enforcement Releases (AAERs)	Announcements of enforcement actions involving accountants practicing before the SEC. Includes discussion of the findings and opinions (including sanctions against the accountants involved) of enforcement hearings held by the Commission. *AAER No. 1* is a codification of all enforcement topics previously included in the Accounting Series Releases.
Staff Accounting Bulletins (SABs)	New or revised administrative practices and interpretations used by the Commission's staff in reviewing financial statements.

and the results of enforcement actions taken against participants in the financial disclosure or securities trading process. Before 1982, the Commission used Accounting Series Releases (ASRs) for this purpose and had issued 307 ASRs covering a wide range of topics. In 1982, these ASRs were classified as covering either financial accounting topics or enforcement actions and codified into a more organized reporting format.

The ***Financial Reporting Releases (FRRs)*** disclose amendments or adoptions of new rules that affect preparers of financial statements and other disclosures. The ***Accounting and Auditing Enforcement Releases (AAERs)*** present the results of enforcement actions taken against accountants or other participants in the filing process. Most of these actions result from the filing of a false or misleading statement. The ***Staff Accounting Bulletins (SABs)*** allow the Commission's staff to make announcements on technical issues with which it is concerned as a result of reviews of SEC filings. The SABs are not formal actions of the Commission; nevertheless, most preparers do follow these bulletins because they represent the views of the staff that will be reviewing their companies' filings.

A recent example of a Staff Accounting Bulletin is SAB No. 101, "Revenue Recognition in Financial Statements," issued in 1999. SAB No. 101 focused on the several revenue recognition procedures the SEC Staff found inconsistently applied by registrants. One special item was the discussion of revenue recognition by the "New Economy" Internet firms. These companies focus on revenue growth, and many do not report any positive income. Analysts and stock-market investors gauge these companies based on their revenue growth. For example, Company A, an Internet company, may offer another company's products (Company T) on Company A's Web site. Customers place their orders and provide a credit card number to the Internet site. Company A then forwards the order to Company T, which ships the goods to the customer. The goods normally cost $200, for which Company A receives $20 for its facilitating of the sale. The question is: Can Company A record the entire gross sale of $200 and a cost of goods sold of $180 to report its profit of $20, or should Company A record just the net $20 sales commission as its revenue. SAB No. 101 states that the revenue should be reported on the net basis, not the gross basis which the SEC staff believes inflates both the reported revenue and cost of goods sold. The SEC staff believed Company A did not take title to the goods, did not incur the risks and rewards of ownership of the goods, and was only an agent or broker for Company T for which it received a commission or fee.

Integrated Disclosure System

In 1980, the SEC undertook a project to reduce the duplicative disclosures companies were required to make for the annual report and in each additional filing with the SEC; that is, the Commission sought to integrate all the disclosures. For this ***integrated disclosure system*** the Commission adopted a standard financial reporting package for the annual report and then provided that "incorporation by reference" could be made from the annual report to other SEC reports by citing the appropriate annual report page number on which the required information appears. In addition, the Commission adopted a ***basic information package (BIP),*** which includes the most important information investors and others need in order to assess a company's financial risk.

The five classes of information constituting the BIP are presented in Figure 14–3 and are as follows.

1. *Market price of and dividends on common equity and related security matters.* This part of the package provides investors with dividend information, including any restrictions on the company's ability to pay future dividends.

2. *Selected financial data.* Companies are required to provide five-year trend data on summary statistics representing the company's ability to earn income and service its debt. Many companies provide more than the minimum required, often disclosing 7 to 10 years of summary data.

FIGURE 14–3 Basic Information Package (BIP)

1. Market price of and dividends on common equity and related security matters:
   a. Markets in which stock is traded
   b. Quarterly common stock price for the last two years
   c. Approximate number of common stockholders
   d. Frequency and amount of dividends during the last two years
   e. Any restrictions on the issuer's present or future ability to pay dividends

2. Selected financial data:
   a. Net sales or operating revenue
   b. Income (loss) from continuing operations
   c. Income (loss) from continuing operations per share
   d. Total assets
   e. Long-term obligations, including capital leases and redeemable preferred stock

3. Management's discussion and analysis of financial condition and results of operations (MDA):
   a. Discussion of liquidity, capital resources, and results of operations
   b. Discussion of any known matters that materially affect or are expected to affect the company's financial condition and results of operations
   c. Discussion of causes for material changes in line items of financial statements for all years presented
   d. Discussion of the impact of inflation and changing prices on the company's sales and income from continuing operations

4. Audited financial statements and supplementary data not covered by the auditors' report:
   a. Income statements and statements of cash flows for the last three years
   b. Balance sheets for the last two years
   c. Required footnotes, including condensed interim data and inflation disclosures

5. Other information:
   a. Brief description of business
   b. Major operating developments such as bankruptcies or major dispositions or acquisitions of assets
   c. Industry and foreign segment information
   d. Description of major properties currently owned
   e. Description of major active legal proceedings
   f. Information about management: backgrounds, remuneration, and major transactions between members of management and the company
   g. Selected industry-specific disclosures for insurance, banking, and other regulated industries

3. *Management's discussion and analysis of financial condition and results of operations.* **Management discussion and analysis (MDA)** provides analysis of the company's financial condition and changes in financial condition. The focus is on discussion of the company's present and future prospects for liquidity, capital resources, and changes in operations. Management must disclose unused lines of credit and capital budgeting plans and must perform a line-by-line analysis of the causes of changes in the financial statements presented. Financial analysts are extremely interested in management's assessment of the company's present and expected financial position. This disclosure is one of the most important in the annual report.

4. *Audited financial statements and supplementary data.* The company must provide audited statements, including three years of income statements and statements of cash flows so investors may determine trends, and the last two years' balance sheets. In addition, all required footnotes must accompany the financial statements.

5. *Other information.* This category includes a brief description of the business, details relating to operations and management, and disclosures required of special industries such as insurance and banking.

1977. The report typically contains four paragraphs: (1) a statement that management is responsible for the statements, (2) a discussion of the company's internal control environment, (3) a discussion of the board of directors audit committee, and (4) any other information, such as the adoption of a set of ethical standards. The number of companies issuing this report has increased each year since its advent in 1977, and this report is likely to be included in most annual reports in the future.

Pro Forma Disclosures

Pro forma disclosures are essentially "what-if" financial presentations often taking the form of summarized financial statements. Pro forma statements are used to show the effects of major transactions that occur after the end of the fiscal period, or that have occurred during the year and are not fully reflected in the company's historical cost financial statements. The SEC requires these to be presented whenever the company has made a significant business combination or disposition, a corporate reorganization, an unusual asset exchange, or a restructuring of existing indebtedness. A pro forma condensed income statement presented in the footnotes shows the impact of the transaction on the company's income from continuing operations, thereby helping investors to focus on the specific effects of the major transaction. The pro forma balance sheet includes all the adjustments reflecting the full impact of the transaction. Investors therefore have (1) the historical cost primary financial statements, which report these items as discontinued operations or as a cumulative effect accounting change, and (2) the pro forma statements, which restate the company's financial condition to include these items.

Additional Considerations

The following section contains special topics that can enhance your understanding of the impact the SEC has had on auditing practices and on accounting firms.

Influence on the Practice of Auditing

The SEC has consistently taken the lead in requiring the independence of the auditor from the client company and in defining the parameters of the audit function. The SEC insists on strict independence of the auditor as the best protection of the public investors' need for full and fair disclosure of a company's financial position and performance. Many of the present auditing standards are results of actions taken by the Commission. In addition to its registration review process, the SEC's Division of Enforcement has actively investigated instances of possible false or misleading statements that may have been caused by the failure of generally accepted auditing standards (GAAS). For example, although fraud detection is not one of the primary goals of an audit, the Commission has consistently examined major litigation involving management frauds, including notorious cases such as McKesson-Robbins, Equity Funding, Penn Central, and Stirling Homex, and has repeatedly questioned if the auditing standards applied in each of these cases were adequate and why the fraud was not uncovered earlier. Although auditors cannot be the "police officers" of business, it is apparent that the SEC will continue to insist that auditors use every possible device to explore situations in which management fraud is suspected.

AICPA's Division of Firms

In 1977, the American Institute of Certified Public Accountants (AICPA) divided its member CPA firms into two groups: the SEC Practice Section and the Private Companies Section. In the *AICPA's division of firms,* only those auditing firms belonging to the SEC Practice Section are permitted to practice before the Commission by auditing publicly traded companies and providing SEC-related services. Each CPA firm elects the section to which it wishes to belong. Firms in the SEC Practice Section have a number of quality review standards to which its members must subscribe. These firms are subject to peer reviews, in which one auditing firm is selected to review another auditing firm's client workpapers and audit procedures. In addition, each firm in the SEC Practice Section must maintain continuing education programs for its professional staff and partners, and the primary partner on an SEC client company must be rotated periodically to ensure "fresh looks" at the client over evenly spaced intervals. The SEC Practice Section is aided by a public oversight board that establishes policies for the section.

The Private Companies Section is made up of auditing firms that do not provide SEC-related services. A different set of quality standards that includes a requirement for continuing education is imposed on these firms.

The division of auditing firms has received both positive and negative responses from accountants. On one hand, many accountants support independence and continued review to assure top-quality services for publicly traded companies. On the other hand, some accountants disagree with the intrusion on the auditor-client relationship, especially the requirement to rotate partners on SEC clients. Dividing auditing firms into two groups has had some favorable outcomes by requiring comprehensive continuing education programs and by providing a mechanism for an auditing firm offering SEC services to undergo an extensive self-evaluation. The benefits seem to outweigh the costs.

Summary of Key Concepts and Terms

Since its creation in 1934, the SEC has played a significant role in the development of financial disclosures necessary for investor confidence in the capital formation process. The Commission has consistently worked for full and fair disclosure of information it considers necessary so investors can assess the risk and returns of companies wishing to offer their securities to the public. The SEC has taken the leadership in a myriad of reporting issues, predominantly in reporting liquidity and solvency measures, and a management narrative of the company's performance.

Although the SEC has the statutory responsibility to develop and maintain accounting principles used for financial reporting, it has permitted the rule-making bodies of the accounting profession to take the initiative in establishing accounting principles and reporting standards. The cooperation has worked with varying success over the years. The SEC has shown its willingness and capacity to assume the lead in those areas in which it feels the private sector is not moving rapidly enough. It is expected that this arrangement will continue in the future.

AICPA's division of firms	Financial Reporting Releases (FRRs)
Accounting and Auditing Enforcement Releases (AAERs)	Foreign Corrupt Practices Act of 1977 (FCPA)
Audit committees	Insider trading rules
Basic information package (BIP)	Integrated disclosure system
Comment letter	Management discussion and analysis (MDA)

Periodic reporting forms: Form 10-K, Form   Regulation S-K
  10-Q, Form 8-K   Regulation S-X

Preliminary prospectus   Shelf registration

Pro forma disclosures   Staff Accounting Bulletins (SABs)

Proxy statements

Registration statements: Form S-1, Form S-2,
  Form S-3

Questions

Q14–1   What is the basis of the SEC's legal authority to regulate accounting principles?

Q14–2   Which securities act—the 1933 or 1934 act—regulates the initial registration of securities? Which regulates the periodic reporting of publicly traded companies?

Q14–3   Which division of the SEC receives the registration statements of companies wishing to make public offerings of securities? Which division investigates individuals or firms that may be in violation of a security act?

Q14–4   Which law requires that companies maintain accurate accounting records and an adequate system of internal control? What is meant by an "adequate system of internal control"?

Q14–5   What does Regulation S-X cover? What is included in Regulation S-K?

Q14–6   What are the objectives of the integrated disclosure system?

Q14–7   Present the five major items included in the basic information package.

Q14–8   What types of public offerings of securities are exempted from the comprehensive registration requirements of the SEC?

Q14–9   When can a company use a Form S-1 registration form? In what circumstances must the company use a Form S-3 registration form?

Q14–10   Define the following terms, which are part of the SEC terminology: *(a)* customary review, *(b)* comment letter, *(c)* red herring prospectus, *(d)* shelf registration.

Q14–11   What is included in Form 10-K? When must a 10-K be filed with the SEC?

Q14–12   Must interim reports submitted to the SEC be audited? What is the role of the public accountant in the preparation of Form 10-Q?

Q14–13   What types of items are reported on Form 8-K?

Q14–14   What is a proxy? What must be included in the proxy material submitted to security holders?

Q14–15   Describe Parts I and II of the Foreign Corrupt Practices Act. What is the impact of this act on companies and public accountants?

Q14–16   What types of information must be disclosed in the management discussion and analysis?

Q14–17*   What role has the SEC played in defining the relationship between public accountants (external, independent auditor) and publicly traded companies?

Cases

C14–1   **Objectives of Securities Acts [CMA Adapted]**

During the late 1920s, approximately 55 percent of all personal savings in the United States were used to purchase securities. Public confidence in the business community was extremely high as stock values doubled and tripled in short periods of time. The road to wealth was believed to be through the stock market, and everyone who was able participated. Thus, the public was severely

---

*Indicates that the item relates to "Additional Considerations."

affected when the Dow Jones Industrial Average fell 89 percent between 1929 and 1933. The public outcry arising from this decline in stock prices motivated the passage of major federal laws regulating the securities industry.

Required

a. Describe the investment practices of the 1920s that contributed to the erosion of the stock market.

b. Explain the basic objectives of each of the following:

   (1) Securities Act of 1933.

   (2) Securities Exchange Act of 1934.

c. More recent legislation has resulted from abuses in the securities industry. Explain the provisions of the Foreign Corrupt Practices Act of 1977.

C14–2   Roles of SEC and FASB [CMA Adapted]

The development of accounting theory and practice has been influenced directly and indirectly by many organizations and institutions. Two of the most important institutions have been the Financial Accounting Standards Board (FASB) and the Securities and Exchange Commission (SEC).

The FASB is an independent body that was established in 1972. The FASB is composed of seven persons who represent public accounting and fields other than public accounting.

The SEC is a governmental regulatory agency that was created in 1934 to administer the Securities Act of 1933 and the Securities Exchange Act of 1934. These acts and the creation of the SEC resulted from the widespread collapse of business and the securities markets in the early 1930s.

Required

a. What official role does the SEC have in the development of financial accounting theory and practice?

b. What is the interrelationship between the FASB and the SEC with respect to the development and establishment of financial accounting theory and practice?

C14–3   SEC Organization and Responsibilities [CMA Adapted]

The U.S. Securities and Exchange Commission (SEC) was created in 1934 and consists of five commissioners and a staff of approximately 1,900. The SEC professional staff is organized into five divisions and several principal offices. The primary objectives of the SEC are to support fair securities markets and to foster enlightened shareholder participation in major corporate decisions. The SEC has a significant presence in financial markets and corporation-shareholder relations and has the authority to exert significant influence on entities whose actions lie within the scope of its authority. The SEC chair has identified enforcement cases and full disclosure filings as major activities of the SEC.

Required

a. The SEC must have some "license" to exercise power. Explain where the SEC receives its authority.

b. Discuss in general terms the major ways in which the SEC:

   (1) Supports fair securities markets

   (2) Fosters enlightened shareholder participation in major corporate decisions

c. Describe the means by which the SEC attempts to assure the material accuracy and completeness of registrants' financial disclosure filings.

C14–4   Proxy Solicitations [CMA Adapted]

The Securities and Exchange Commission has the authority to regulate proxy solicitations. This authority is derived from the Securities and Exchange Act of 1934 and is closely tied to the disclosure objective of this act. Regulations established by the SEC require corporations to mail a proxy statement to each shareholder shortly before the annual shareholder meeting.

Required

a. Explain the purpose of proxy statements.

b. Identify four types of events or actions for which proxy statements normally are solicited.

c. Identify the conditions that must be met in order to have a dissident shareholder proposal included in a proxy statement.

C14–5   Registration Process [CMA Adapted]

Bandex Inc. has been in business for 15 years. The company has compiled a record of steady but not spectacular growth. Bandex's engineers have recently perfected a product that has an application in the small computer market. Initial orders have exceeded the company's capacity and the decision has been made to expand.

Bandex has financed past growth from internally generated funds, and since the initial stock offering 15 years ago, no further shares have been sold. Bandex's finance committee has been discussing methods of financing the proposed expansion. Both short-term and long-term notes were ruled out because of high interest rates. Mel Greene, the chief financial officer, said, "It boils down to either bonds, preferred stock, or additional common stock." Alice Dexter, a consultant employed to help in the financing decision, stated, "Regardless of your choice, you will have to file a registration statement with the SEC."

Bob Schultz, Bandex's chief accountant for the past five years, stated, "I've coordinated the filing of all the periodic reports required by the SEC—10-Ks, 10-Qs, and 8-Ks. I see no reason I can't prepare a registration statement also."

Required

a. Identify the circumstances under which a firm must file a registration statement with the Securities and Exchange Commission (SEC).

b. Explain the objectives of the registration process required by the Securities Act of 1933.

c. Identify and explain the SEC publications Bob Schultz would use to guide him in preparing the registration statement.

C14–6   Form 10-K [CMA Adapted]

The Jerford Company is a well-known manufacturing company with several wholly owned subsidiaries. The company's stock is traded on the New York Stock Exchange, and the company files all appropriate reports with the Securities and Exchange Commission. Jerford Company's financial statements are audited by a public accounting firm.

Part A. Jerford Company's annual report to stockholders for the year ended December 31, 20X4, contained the following phrase in boldface type: **"The Company's 10-K is available upon written request."**

Required

a. What is Form 10-K, who requires that the form be completed, and why is the phrase "The Company's 10-K is available upon written request" shown in the annual report?

b. What information not normally included in the company's annual report could be ascertained from the 10-K?

c. Indicate three items of financial information that are often included in annual reports that are not required for the 10-K.

Part B. Jerford Company changed independent auditors during 20X4. Consequently, the financial statements were certified by a different public accounting firm in 20X4 than in 20X3:

Required

What information is Jerford Company responsible for filing with the SEC with respect to this change in auditors? Explain your answer completely.

C14–7   Form 8-K [CMA Adapted]

The purpose of the Securities Act of 1933 is to regulate the initial offering of a firm's securities by ensuring that investors are given full and fair disclosure of all pertinent information about the firm. The Securities Exchange Act of 1934 was passed to regulate the trading of securities on secondary markets and to eliminate abuses in the trading of securities after their initial distribution. To accomplish these objectives, the 1934 act created the Securities and Exchange Commission. Under the auspices of the SEC, public companies must not only register their securities but must also periodically prepare and file Forms 8-K, 10-K, and 10-Q.

Required

a. With regard to Form 8-K, discuss:

(1) The purpose of the report

(2) The timing of the report

(3) The format of the report

(4) The role of financial statements in the filing of the report

b. Identify five circumstances under which the Securities and Exchange Commission requires the filing of Form 8-K.

c. Discuss how the filing of Form 8-K fosters the purpose of the SEC.

d. Does the SEC pass judgment on securities based on information contained in periodic reports? Explain your answer.

C14–8   Audit Committees [CMA Adapted]

An early event leading to the establishment of audit committees as a regular subcommittee of boards of directors occurred in 1940 as part of the consent decree relative to the McKesson-Robbins scandal. An audit committee composed of outside directors was required as part of the consent decree. (A consent decree is the formal statement issued in an enforcement action when a person agrees to terms of a disciplinary nature without admitting to the allegations in the complaint.)

Since June 1978, the New York Stock Exchange (NYSE) has required all domestic listed members to establish and maintain an audit committee composed solely of directors independent of management. The SEC has advised audit committees, boards of directors, and managements about factors which should be considered in determining whether to engage their independent accountants to perform nonaudit services.

Despite the increasing interest in audit committees and the official actions taken as described above, no specific role, duties, or liabilities have been established for them by the SEC, the NYSE, or any of the accounting organizations. Nevertheless, a commonly accepted set of duties and expectations has developed for the conduct and performance of audit committees.

Required

a. Explain the role the audit committee generally assumes with respect to the annual audit conducted by the company's external auditors.

b. Identify duties other than those associated with the annual audit which might be assigned to the audit committee by the board of directors.

c. Discuss the relationship which should exist between the audit committee and a company's internal audit staff.

d. Explain why board members appointed to serve on the audit committee should be outside (independent of management) board members.

C14–9   Research Related to the SEC

The company that employs you is a U.S. publicly traded corporation that manufactures chemicals. You are in the external financial reporting department, and your position requires that you keep current on all the new accounting requirements. While you realize that Staff Accounting Bulletins (SABs) are not formal actions of the SEC, periodically you like to review the new SABs to see if any are relevant to your company.

Today you decided to perform some research and ascertain if there have been any new SABs issued. In addition, your boss, the manager in charge of the department, recently mentioned something to you about the SEC's Division of Enforcement. You do not know a lot about this particular division; however, because you will be doing some SEC research today anyway, you have decided you will find out more about the SEC's Division of Enforcement.

Required

a. Prepare a one-page memo summarizing a recent SAB.

b. Research the SEC's Division of Enforcement. Answer or perform the following:

    (1) What year was the division formed?

    (2) Discuss various actions the division may take.

    (3) Prepare a one-paragraph summary of a recent litigation proceeding.

    (4) Prepare a one-paragraph summary of a recent administrative proceeding.

C14–10   **Research Related to the EDGAR Database**

Currently, you are an experienced senior working at a public accounting firm. For the upcoming busy season you received a new client, a publicly traded corporation. The manager on this client is someone you have not worked with before. You hope to impress this manager because you hear that she strongly supports those seniors who work for her if she considers them to be excellent employees. At the end of this busy season you will be up for promotion to manager and would like her support.

Next week you have an internal planning meeting with the manger. Today you will be working in the office, and you have decided to devote the day to performing some background reading to become acquainted with this client. When you get to the office today you learn that the manager is at a client location and unreachable. Since you will not be able to get any background information on your client from her today, you decide you will get information alternatively using the Internet.

Required

a. Select a company from the EDGAR database with a name beginning with the first letter of your last name. The company selected will be your new client as discussed above. (*Hint:* It may be helpful to determine the company through use of *The Wall Street Journal* or other business periodical.)

b. Prepare a one- or two-paragraph summary listing the types of reports made to the SEC by your client over the last year. Include a brief description of the contents of each of these reports. Select one of the reports and print the first page of that report.

Exercises

E14–1   **Organization Structure and Regulatory Authority of the SEC [CMA Adapted]**

Select the correct answer for each of the following questions.

1. Two interesting and important topics concerning the SEC are the role the Commission plays in the development of accounting principles and the impact it has had and will continue to have on the accounting profession and business in general. Which of the following statements about the SEC's authority on accounting practice is false?

    a. The SEC has the statutory authority to regulate and to prescribe the form and content of financial statements and other reports it receives.

    b. Regulation S-X of the SEC is the principal source of the form and content of financial statements to be included in registration statements and financial reports filed with the Commission.

    c. The SEC has little if any authority over disclosures in corporate annual reports mailed to shareholders with proxy solicitations. The type of information disclosed and the format to be used are left to the discretion of management.

    d. If the Commission disagrees with some presentation in the registrant's financial statements but the principles used by the registrant have substantial authoritative support, the SEC often will accept footnotes to the statements in lieu of correcting the statements to the SEC view, provided the SEC has not previously expressed its opinion on the matter in published material.

2. The Securities and Exchange Commission was established in 1934 to help regulate the U.S. securities market. Which of the following statements is true about the SEC?

    a. The SEC prohibits the sale of speculative securities.

    b. The SEC regulates only securities offered for public sale.

    c. Registration with the SEC guarantees the accuracy of the registrant's prospectus.

    d. The SEC's initial influences and authority have diminished in recent years as the stock exchanges have become more organized and better able to police themselves.

    e. The SEC's powers are broad with respect to enforcement of its reporting requirements as established in the 1933 and 1934 acts but narrow with respect to new reporting requirements because these require confirmation by Congress.

3. The Securities and Exchange Commission is organized into several divisions and principal offices. The organization unit that reviews registration statements, annual reports, and proxy statements that are filed with the Commission is:

    a. The Office of the Chief Accountant.

    b. The Division of Corporation Finance.

    c. The Division of Enforcement.

    d. The Division of Market Regulation.

    e. The Office of the Comptroller.

4. Regulation S-X:

    a. Specifies the information that can be incorporated by reference from the annual report into the registration statement filed with the SEC.

    b. Specifies the regulation and reporting requirements of proxy solicitations.

    c. Provides the basis for generally accepted accounting principles.

    d. Specifies the general form and content requirements of financial statements filed with the SEC.

    e. Provides explanations and clarifications of changes in accounting or auditing procedures used in reports filed with the SEC.

5. The Securities Exchange Act of 1934 specifies the types of companies that must report periodically to the SEC. Which one of the following types of companies is not required to report to the SEC under this act?

    a. Banks subject to the Federal Reserve Board.

    b. Companies whose securities are listed on the National Securities Exchange.

    c. Companies whose securities are traded over the counter, if those companies have total assets in excess of $1 million and 500 or more stockholders.

    d. Companies whose securities are traded over the counter that voluntarily elect to comply with the reporting requirements even though they have total assets less than $1 million and less than 500 stockholders.

    e. Companies with more than 300 stockholders of a class of securities that is registered under the Securities Act of 1933.

6. Which of the following is not a purpose of the Securities Exchange Act of 1934?

    a. To establish federal regulation over securities exchanges and markets.

    b. To prevent unfair practices on securities exchanges and markets.

    c. To discourage and prevent the use of credit in financing excessive speculation in securities.

The following schedule presents the key concepts in Case 1:

	Prior Capital	New Partner's Tangible Investment	New Partner's Proportion of Partnership's Book Value (25%)	Total Resulting Capital	New Partner's Share of Total Resulting Capital (25%)
Case 1:					
New partner's investment equals proportionate book value	$30,000	$10,000	$10,000		
No revaluations, bonus, or goodwill				$40,000	$10,000

Case 2. New Partner's Investment Greater than Proportion of the Partnership's Book Value.

In some cases a new partner may invest more in an existing partnership than his or her proportionate share of the partnership's book value. This means that the partner perceives some value in the partnership that is not reflected on the books of account.

For example, Cha invests $11,000 for a one-fourth capital interest in the ABC Partnership. The first step is to compare the new partner's investment with the new partner's proportionate book value, as follows:

Investment in partnership	$11,000
New partner's proportionate book value:	
($30,000 + $11,000) × .25	(10,250)
Difference (investment > book value)	$ 750

Cha has invested $11,000 for an interest with a book value of $10,250, thus paying an excess of $750 over the present book value.

Generally, an excess of investment over the respective book value of the partnership interest indicates that the partnership's prior net assets are undervalued or that the partnership has some unrecorded goodwill. Three alternative accounting treatments exist in this case:

1. *Revalue assets upward.* Under this alternative:
   a. Asset book values are increased to their market values.
   b. The prior partners' capital accounts are increased for their respective shares of the increase in the book values of the assets.
   c. Total resulting capital of the partnership is the prior capital balances plus the amount of asset revaluation plus the new partner's investment.
2. *Record unrecognized goodwill.* With this method:
   a. Unrecognized goodwill is recorded.

b. The prior partners' capital accounts are increased for their respective shares of the goodwill.

c. Total resulting capital of the partnership is the prior capital balances plus the goodwill recognized plus the new partner's investment.

3. *Use bonus method.* Essentially, the bonus method is a transfer of capital balances among the partners. This method is used when the partners do not wish to record adjustments in asset accounts and do not want to recognize goodwill. Under this method:

a. The prior partners' capital accounts are increased for their respective shares of the bonus paid by the new partner.

b. Total resulting capital of the partnership is the prior capital balances plus the new partner's investment.

Any one of the three alternatives may be used by the partnership. The decision is usually a result of negotiations between the prior partners and the prospective partner. The revaluation of assets or recognition of goodwill is criticized by some accountants because it results in a marked departure from the historical cost principle and differs from the accepted accounting principles in **APB Opinion No. 17,** "Intangible Assets" (**APB 17**), which prohibits corporations from recognizing goodwill that has not been acquired by purchase. Accountants who support the recognition of goodwill point out that whenever a new partner is admitted to the partnership, the old partnership is legally dissolved and a new partnership entity is formed. Therefore the basis of valuation for new entities is the fair value of the assets acquired by the newly formed entity. Consequently, assets should be recorded at their fair values and should include previously unrecognized goodwill. Finally, accountants who use the goodwill or asset revaluation methods argue that the goal of partnership accounting is to state fairly the relative capital equities of the partners, and this may require different accounting procedures from those used in corporate entities.

The accountant's function is to ensure that any estimates used in the valuation process are based on the best evidence available. Subjective valuations that could impair the fairness of the presentations made in the partnership's financial statements should be avoided or minimized.

Illustration of Revaluation of Assets Approach.   Assume that Cha paid a $750 excess ($11,000 − $10,250) over her proportionate book value because the partnership owns land with a book value of $4,000 but a recent appraisal indicates the land has a market value of $7,000. The prior partners decide to use the admission of the new partner to recognize the increase in value of the land and to assign this increase to the capital accounts of the prior partners. The increase in land value is allocated to the partners' capital accounts in the profit and loss ratio that existed during the time of the increase. Alt's capital is increased by $1,800 (60 percent of the $3,000 increase), and Blue's capital is increased by $1,200 (40 percent of the $3,000). The partnership makes the following entry for the revaluation of the land:

(11) Land	3,000	
Alt, Capital		1,800
Blue, Capital		1,200
Revalue partnership land to market value.		

The $11,000 investment by Cha brings the partnership's total resulting capital to $44,000, as follows:

Prior capital of AB Partnership	$30,000
Revaluation of land to market value	3,000
Cha's investment	11,000
Total resulting capital of ABC Partnership	$44,000

Cha is acquiring a one-fourth interest in the total resulting capital of the ABC Partnership. Cha's capital credit, after revaluing the land, is calculated as follows:

$$\text{New partner's share of total resulting capital} = (\$30,000 + \$3,000 + \$11,000) \times .25 = \$11,000$$

The entry to record the admission of Cha into the partnership is:

(12)	Cash	11,000	
	Cha, Capital		11,000
	Admission of Cha for one-fourth capital interest in ABC Partnership.		

When the land is eventually sold, Cha will participate in the gain or loss calculated on the basis of the new $7,000 book value, which is the land's market value at the time of her admission into the partnership. The entire increase in the value of the land before the admission of Cha belongs to the prior partners.

Illustration of Goodwill Recognition. An entering partner may be paying an excess because of unrecognized goodwill, indicated by high profitability of the partnership. Some partnerships use the change in membership as an opportunity to record unrecognized goodwill that has been created by the prior partners. Recording unrecognized goodwill is allowed for partnership accounting because of the need to establish appropriate capital equity among the partners. As noted earlier, this is an exception to the general rule established in **APB 17,** but the information needs of the partners and specific purposes of the partnership's financial statements justify the exception.

Generally, the amount of goodwill is determined by negotiations between the prior and prospective partners and is based on estimates of future earnings. For example, the prior and new partners may agree that, due to the efforts of the prior partners, the partnership has superior earnings potential and that $3,000 of goodwill should be recorded to recognize this fact. The new partner's negotiated investment cost will be based partly on the earnings potential of the partnership. Alternatively, goodwill may be estimated from the amount of the new partner's investment. For example, in this case, Cha is investing $11,000 for a one-fourth interest; therefore, she must feel the total resulting partnership capital is $44,000 ($11,000 × 4). The estimated goodwill is $3,000 as follows:

Step 1:
25% of estimated total resulting capital $11,000
Estimated total resulting capital ($11,000 ÷ .25) $44,000

Step 2:
Estimated total resulting capital $44,000
Total net assets not including goodwill
  ($30,000 prior plus $11,000 invested by Cha)   (41,000)
Estimated goodwill $ 3,000

Another way of viewing the creation of goodwill at the time of the admission of a new partner is to use a T-account form for the partnership's balance sheet. Any additional net assets, such as recognizing goodwill, must be balanced with additional capital, as follows:

		Balance Sheet		
Prior to admission of new partner Cha	Net assets	$30,000	Partners' capital	$30,000
New partner's cash investment	Cash	11,000	New tangibile capital	11,000
Captial prior to recognizing goodwill		$41,000		$41,000
Estimated new goodwill	Goodwill	3,000	Capital from goodwill	3,000
Total resulting capital	Net assets	$44,000	Total resulting capital	$44,000

Once the new ABC partnership's total resulting capital is estimated ($44,000), the new goodwill ($3,000) is the balance sheet balancing difference between the tangible capital ($41,000), which includes the new partner's cash investment, and the estimated total resulting capital of the ABC partnership ($44,000).

The unrecorded goodwill is recorded, and the prior partners' capital accounts are credited for the increase in assets. The adjustments to the capital accounts are in the profit and loss ratio that existed during the periods the goodwill was developed. Alt's capital is increased by 60 percent of the goodwill, and Blue's by 40 percent. The entries to record goodwill and the admission of Cha are as follows:

(13)   Goodwill   3,000
            Alt, Capital   1,800
            Blue, Capital   1,200
        Recognize unrecorded goodwill.

(14)   Cash   11,000
            Cha, Capital   11,000
        Admission of Cha to partnership for a one-fourth
        capital interest: $44,000 × .25

Another reason for recording goodwill is that the new partner may want her capital balance to equal the amount of investment made. The investment is based on the market value of the partnership, and for this equality to occur, the partnership must restate its prior net assets to their fair values.

It is important to note that the $11,000 credit to Cha's capital account is one-fourth of the total resulting capital of ABC Partnership of $44,000 as follows:

$$\frac{\text{New partner's share of}}{\text{total resulting capital}} = (\$30,000 + \$3,000 + \$11,000) \times .25 = \$11,000$$

In futur̶e̶ ̶̶ oodwill will be amortized against partnership earnings before net in̶ ̶ the partners. Consequently, Cha's future profit distribution will ̶ 'll recognized at the time of her admission into the partnership.

d. Some partnerships are averse to recognizing asset oodwill when a new partner is admitted. Instead, they rtner's investment as a bonus to the existing partners nces properly at the time of the admission of the new cess paid by Cha is a bonus allocated to the prior ratio of 60 percent to Alt and 40 percent to Blue. The e ABC Partnership consists of $30,000 prior capital of Alt 1,000 investment of Cha. No additional capital is recognized by s. The value of the capital credit acquired by the new partner is cal-

$$\frac{\text{New partner's share of}}{\text{total resulting capital}} = (\$30,000 + \$11,000) \times .25 = \$10,250$$

The entry to record the admission of Cha under the bonus method is as follows:

(15)	Cash	11,000	
	Alt, Capital		450
	Blue, Capital		300
	Cha, Capital		10,250
	Admission of Cha with bonus to Alt and Blue.		

Cha may dislike the bonus method because her capital balance is $750 less than her investment in the partnership. This is one of the disadvantages of the bonus method.

A comparison of the goodwill and bonus methods shows that the differences between the two methods are reconciled in future periods by the write-off of goodwill. If no future changes are made in the membership of the partnership, the profit and loss percentages remain the same, and the goodwill of $3,000 recognized in the second alternative is written off, the partners' capital balances will be the same as with the bonus method. Apart from any other future changes in the partners' capital accounts, the comparison is as follows:

	Partner			
	Alt	*Blue*	*Cha*	*Total*
Profit percentage	45%	30%	25%	100%
Capital balance under goodwill method at time of Cha's admission	$21,800	$11,200	$11,000	$44,000
Goodwill of $3,000 written off	(1,350)	(900)	(750)	(3,000)
Capital balance after write-off	$20,450	$10,300	$10,250	$41,000
Capital balance under bonus method	$20,450	$10,300	$10,250	$41,000

Again, the capital balances after the goodwill is written off are equal to the capital balances under the bonus method only if the profit and loss ratio remains constant during the period of goodwill write-off. However, if the ratio changes because of changes in partnership members or changes in the profit agreement, then the goodwill and bonus methods will result in different capital balances for each of the partners. In effect, the goodwill method adjusts the capital balances by writing off the goodwill over time, whereas the bonus method makes the capital adjustments at the time the new partner is admitted.

The following schedule presents the key concepts for Case 2:

	Prior Capital	New Partner's Tangible Investment	New Partner's Proportion of Partnership's Book Value (25%)	Total Resulting Capital	New Partner's Share of Total Resulting Capital (25%)
Case 2:					
New partner's investment greater than proportionate book value	$30,000	$11,000	$10,250		
1. Revalue assets by increasing land $3,000				$44,000	$11,000
2. Recognize $3,000 goodwill for prior partners				$44,000	$11,000
3. Bonus of $750 to prior partners				$41,000	$10,250

Case 3. New Partner's Investment Less than Proportion of the Partnership's Book Value.

It is possible that a new partner may pay less than his or her proportionate share of the partnership's book value. For example, Cha invests $8,000 for a one-fourth capital interest in the ABC Partnership. The first step is to compare the new partner's investment with the new partner's proportionate book value, as follows:

Investment in partnership	$ 8,000
New partner's proportionate book value: ($30,000 + $8,000) × .25	(9,500)
Difference (investment < book value)	$(1,500)

The fact that Cha's investment is less than the book value of a one-fourth interest in the partnership indicates that the partnership has overvalued assets or the prior partners recognize that Cha is contributing additional value in the form of expertise or skills she possesses which are needed by the partnership. In this case, Cha is investing $8,000 in cash and an additional amount that may be viewed as goodwill.

As with Case 2, in which the investment is greater than the book value acquired, there are three alternative approaches when the investment is less than the book value acquired. The three approaches are as follows:

1. *Revalue assets downward.* Under this alternative:
   a. Asset book values are decreased to recognize the reduction in their values.
   b. The prior partners' capital accounts are decreased for their respective shares of the decrease in the values of the assets.
   c. Total resulting capital of the partnership is the prior capital balances less the amount of the asset valuation write-down plus the new partner's investment.
2. *Recognize goodwill brought in by the new partner.* In this approach:
   a. Goodwill or other intangible benefits brought in by the new partner are recorded and also included in the new partner's capital account.
   b. The prior partners' capital accounts remain unchanged.
   c. Total resulting capital of the partnership is the prior capital balances plus the new goodwill brought in plus the new partner's tangible investment.
3. *Use bonus method.* Under the bonus method:
   a. The new partner is assigned a bonus from the prior partners' capital accounts, which are decreased for their respective shares of the bonus paid to the new partner.
   b. Total resulting capital of the partnership is the prior capital balances plus the new partner's investment.

Illustration of Revaluation of Assets Approach. Assume that the reason Cha paid only $8,000 for a one-fourth interest in the partnership is that inventory currently recorded at a book value of $14,000 has a fair market value of only $8,000 because of the obsolescence of several items. The partners agree to write down the inventory to its fair value before admission of the new partner. The write-down is allocated to the prior partners in the profit and loss ratio that existed during the period of the inventory decline: 60 percent to Alt and 40 percent to Blue. The write-down is recorded as follows:

(16)	Alt, Capital	3,600	
	Blue, Capital	2,400	
	Inventory		6,000
	Revalue inventory to market.		

Note that the total capital of the partnership has now been reduced from $30,000 to $24,000 as a result of the $6,000 write-down. The value of Cha's share of total resulting capital of the ABC Partnership, *after the write-down,* is calculated as follows:

$$\text{New partner's share of total resulting capital} = (\$24{,}000 + \$8{,}000) \times .25 = \$8{,}000$$

The entry to record the admission of Cha as a partner in the ABC Partnership is:

(17)	Cash	8,000	
	Cha, Capital		8,000
	Admission of Cha to partnership.		

Cha's recorded capital credit is equal to her investment because the total partnership capital of $32,000 ($24,000 + $8,000) now represents the fair value of the partnership.

Illustration of Recording Goodwill for New Partner. The prior partners may offer Cha a one-fourth capital interest in the ABC Partnership for an investment of $8,000 because Cha has essential business experience, skills, customer contacts, reputation, or other ingredients of goodwill that she will bring into the partnership. The amount of goodwill brought in by the new partner is usually determined through negotiations between the prior partners and the prospective partner. For example, Alt, Blue, and Cha may agree that Cha's abilities will generate excess earnings for the resulting ABC Partnership. They agree that Cha should be given $2,000 of goodwill recognition at the time she joins the partnership in recognition of her anticipated excess contribution to the future earnings of the partnership. The negotiated goodwill is recognized and is added to her tangible investment to determine the amount of capital credit.

Alternatively, the amount of goodwill brought in by the new partner may be estimated from the amount of the total capital being retained by the prior partners. In this case, the prior partners are retaining a 75 percent interest in the partnership and allowing the new partner a 25 percent capital interest. The dollar amount of the prior partners' 75 percent interest is $30,000. Cha's investment of $8,000 plus goodwill makes up the remaining 25 percent. The amount of goodwill brought into the partnership by Cha is determined as follows:

Step 1:	
75% of estimated total resulting capital	$30,000
Estimated total resulting capital	
($30,000 ÷ .75)	$40,000
Step 2:	
Estimated total resulting capital	$40,000
Total net assets not including goodwill	
($30,000 + $8,000)	(38,000)
Estimated goodwill	$ 2,000

Note that the estimate of goodwill for the new partner is made using the information from the prior partners' interests. Earlier, in Case 2, the estimate of goodwill to the prior partners was made using the information from the new partner's investment. The reason for this difference is that the best available information should be used for the estimates of goodwill. If the new partner's goodwill is being estimated, it is not logical to use the new partner's tangible investment to estimate the total investment made by the new partner, including goodwill. That is circular reasoning which involves using a number to estimate itself. Furthermore, when goodwill is being assigned to the prior partners, it is not logical to use the existing capital of the prior partners to estimate their goodwill. A useful mnemonic to remember how to estimate goodwill is to use the opposite partners' information for the estimate:

Use new partner to estimate goodwill to prior partners; use prior partners to estimate goodwill to new partner.

The entry to record the admission of Cha into the ABC Partnership is:

(18)	Cash	8,000	
	Goodwill	2,000	
	Cha, Capital		10,000
	Admission of Cha to partnership.		

Note that the total resulting capital of the ABC Partnership is now $40,000, with Alt and Blue together having a 75 percent interest and Cha having a 25 percent interest.

Illustration of Bonus Method. The admission of Cha as a new partner with a one-fourth interest in the ABC Partnership for an investment of only $8,000 may be accounted for by recognizing a bonus given to Cha from the prior partners. The bonus of $1,500 is the difference between the new partner's $9,500 book value and her $8,000 investment. The prior partners' capital accounts are reduced by $1,500 in their profit and loss ratio of 60 percent for Alt and 40 percent for Blue, and Cha's capital account is credited for $9,500, as follows:

(19)	Cash	8,000	
	Alt, Capital	900	
	Blue, Capital	600	
	Cha, Capital		9,500
	Admission of Cha to partnership.		

Note that the amount of the capital credit assigned to the new partner is her share of the total resulting capital, as follows:

$$\text{New partner's share of total resulting capital} = (\$30,000 + \$8,000) \times .25 = \$9,500$$

The following schedule presents the key concepts for Case 3:

	Prior Capital	New Partner's Tangible Investment	New Partner's Proportion of Partnership's Book Value (25%)	Total Resulting Capital	New Partner's Share of Total Resulting Capital (25%)
Case 3: New partner's investment less than proportionate book value	$30,000	$8,000	$9,500		
1. Revalue assets by decreasing inventory by $6,000.				$32,000	$ 8,000
2. Recognize goodwill of $2,000 for new partner.				$40,000	$10,000
3. Bonus of $1,500 to new partner.				$38,000	$ 9,500

Summary and Comparison of Accounting for Investment of New Partner. Figure 15–2 presents the entries made in each of the three cases discussed above. In addition, the capital balances of each of the three partners immediately after the admission of Cha are presented to the right of the journal entries.

Summarizing the alternative methods of accounting for the investment of a new partner:

Case 1. **New partner's investment *equals* his or her proportion of the partnership's book value.**

1. The new partner's capital credit is equal to his or her investment.
2. No goodwill or bonus is recognized in this case.

FIGURE 15–2   **Summary of Accounting for Investment of New Partner: Journal Entries and Capital Balances after Admission of New Partner**

Case 1: New partner's investment equals proportionate book value. Cha invests $10,000 cash for one-fourth capital interest.

Cash	10,000		Alt	$20,000
Cha, Capital		10,000	Blue	10,000
			Cha	10,000
			Total	$40,000

Case 2: New partner's investment greater than proportionate book value. Cha invests $11,000 cash for one-fourth capital interest.

(a) Revalue assets:

Land	3,000		Alt	$21,800
Alt, Capital		1,800	Blue	11,200
Blue, Capital		1,200	Cha	11,000
Cash	11,000		Total	$44,000
Cha, Capital		11,000		

(b) Recognize goodwill for prior partners:

Goodwill	3,000		Alt	$21,800
Alt, Capital		1,800	Blue	11,200
Blue, Capital		1,200	Cha	11,000
Cash	11,000		Total	$44,000
Cha, Capital		11,000		

(c) Bonus to prior partners:

Cash	11,000		Alt	$20,450
Alt, Capital		450	Blue	10,300
Blue, Capital		300	Cha	10,250
Cha, Capital		10,250	Total	$41,000

Case 3: New partner's investment less than proportionate book value. Cha invests $8,000 cash for a one-fourth capital interest.

(a) Revalue assets:

Alt, Capital	3,600		Alt	$16,400
Blue, Capital	2,400		Blue	7,600
Inventory		6,000	Cha	8,000
Cash	8,000		Total	$32,000
Cha, Capital		8,000		

(b) Recognize goodwill for new partner:

Cash	8,000		Alt	$20,000
Goodwill	2,000		Blue	10,000
Cha, Capital		10,000	Cha	10,000
			Total	$40,000

(c) Bonus to new partner:

Cash	8,000		Alt	$19,100
Alt, Capital	900		Blue	9,400
Blue, Capital	600		Cha	9,500
Cha, Capital		9,500	Total	$38,000

Case 2. **New partner's investment is** *greater than* **his or her proportion of the partnership's book value.**

1. The revaluation of an asset or recognition of goodwill increases the total resulting capital of the partnership. The increase is allocated to the prior partners in their profit and loss ratio.

2. After recognition of the asset revaluation or unrecorded goodwill, the new partner's capital credit is equal to his or her investment and to his or her percentage of the total resulting capital.

3. Under the bonus method, the total resulting capital of the partnership is the sum of the prior partnership's capital plus the investment by the new partner. The capital credit recorded for the new partner is less than the investment but is equal to his or her percentage of the resulting partnership capital.

Case 3. **New partner's investment is** *less than* **his or her proportion of the partnership's book value.**

1. Under the revaluation of assets approach, the write-down of the assets reduces the prior partners' capital in their profit and loss ratio. The new partner's capital is then credited for the amount of the investment.

2. Under the goodwill method, goodwill is assigned to the new partner, and the total resulting capital of the partnership is increased. The new partner's capital is credited for his or her percentage interest in the total resulting capital of the partnership.

3. The bonus method results in a transfer of capital from the prior partners to the new partner. The total resulting capital of the new partnership is equal to the prior capital plus the investment of the new partner. The new partner's capital credit is greater than the investment made but is equal to his or her percentage of the total resulting capital.

Determining a New Partner's Investment Cost

In the previous sections, the amount of the new partner's contribution has been provided. In some instances, accountants are asked to determine the amount of cash investment the new partner should be asked to contribute. The basic principles of partnership accounting provide the means to solve this question. For example, let us continue the basic example from the chapter, for which partners Alt and Blue wish to admit Cha as a new partner. The prior partnership capital was $30,000 and the partners wish to invite Cha into the partnership for a one-fourth interest.

Assume that the prior partners, Alt and Blue, agree that the assets of the partnership should be revalued up by $3,000 to recognize the increase in value of the land held by the partnership. The question is how much Cha, the new partner, should be asked to invest for her one-fourth interest.

When determining the new partner's investment cost, it is important to note the total resulting capital of the partnership and the percentage of ownership interest retained by the prior partners. In this example, the prior partners retain a three-fourths' interest in the resulting partnership, for which their 75 percent capital interest is $33,000, the $30,000 of prior capital plus the $3,000 from the revaluation of the land, as follows:

75% of total resulting capital	$33,000
Total resulting capital (100%)	$44,000
Less prior partners' capital	(33,000)
Cash contribution required of new partner	$11,000

Note that this is simply another way of evaluating the admission process as was discussed in the asset revaluation illustration under Case 2.

In some cases, the amount of bonus may be determined prior to the determination of the cash contribution required from the new partner. For example, assume that Alt and Blue agree to give Cha a bonus of $1,500 for joining the partnership. The following schedule determines the amount of cash investment required of Cha, the new partner:

Prior capital of Alt and Blue	$30,000
Less bonus given to Cha upon admission	(1,500)
Capital retained by Alt and Blue	$28,500
75% of the total resulting capital	$28,500
Total resulting capital	
($28,500 ÷ .75)	$38,000
Less prior partners' capital	(28,500)
Capital credit required of new partner	$ 9,500
Less bonus to new partner from prior partners	(1,500)
Cash contribution required of new partner	$ 8,000

This second example is another way of viewing the bonus to new partner method under Case 3 as presented earlier. The key is to determine the amount of capital that will be retained by the prior partners for their percentage share in the total resulting capital of the partnership after admitting the new partner. The new partner's cash contribution can be computed simply by determining the amount of the capital credit that will be assigned to him or her and then recognizing any bonuses that will be used to align the capital balances.

Retirement of a Partner from the Partnership

When a partner retires or withdraws from a partnership, the partnership is dissolved but the remaining partners may wish to continue operating the business. The articles of copartnership should specify the procedures to be followed by the partnership to ensure that the agreement of the partners is carried out. The primary accounting issue is the proper measurement of the retiring partner's capital account. This sometimes requires a determination of the fair value of the partnership at the time the partner retires, including the computation of partnership income since the end of the last fiscal period.

Most partnerships have covenants in their partnership agreements to guide the process of accounting for retirement of a partner. For example, in some large public accounting firms, retiring partners receive only the book value of their capital accounts, not the fair value. Other partnerships may require that the partnership's net assets be appraised and that the retiring partner receive the proportionate share of the fair value of the business.

The retiring partner is still personally liable for any partnership debts accumulated before the withdrawal date, but is not responsible for any partnership debts incurred after the retirement date. Therefore, it is especially important to determine all liabilities that exist on the retirement date.

Some partnerships have an audit performed whenever a change in partners is made. This audit establishes the accuracy of the book values of the assets and liabilities. On occasion, accounting errors are found during an audit. Errors should be corrected and the partners' capital accounts adjusted based on the profit and loss ratio that existed in the period in which the errors were made. For example, if an audit disclosed that three years ago depreciation expense was charged for $4,000 less than it should have been, the error is corrected with a prior period adjustment, and the partners' capital accounts are charged with their respective shares of the adjustment based on their profit and loss ratio of three years ago.

Generally, the existing partners buy out the retiring partner either by making a direct acquisition or by having the partnership acquire the retiring partner's interest. If the present partners directly acquire the retiring partner's interest, then the only entry on the partnership's books is to record the reclassification of capital among the partners. If the partnership acquires the retiring partner's interest, then the partnership must record the reduction of total partnership capital and the corresponding reduction of assets paid to the retiring partner. For example, assume that Alt retires from the ABC Partnership when his capital account has a balance of $55,000, after recording all increases in the net assets of the partnership including income earned up to the date of the retirement. The entry made by the ABC Partnership is:

(20)	Alt, Capital	55,000
	Cash	55,000
	Retirement of Alt.	

If the partnership is unable to pay the total of $55,000 to Alt at the time of retirement, it must recognize a liability for the remaining portion.

Often, a partnership pays a "retirement premium" for a retiring partner. The premium is usually treated as a bonus from the other partners, allocated in the remaining profit and loss ratio. For example, if the ABC Partnership agrees to pay Alt $65,000 at the time of retirement, the bonus of $10,000 ($65,000 paid less $55,000 capital balance) reduces the capital accounts of Blue and Cha in their profit ratio. Blue has a 30 percent interest, and Cha has a 25 percent interest in the net income of the ABC Partnership. The sum of their respective shares is 55 percent (30 percent + 25 percent), and their relative profit percentages, rounded to the nearest percentage, are 55 percent for Blue and 45 percent for Cha, computed as follows:

	Prior Profit Percentage	Remaining Profit Percentage
Alt	45	0
Blue	30	55 (30/55)
Cha	25	45 (25/55)
Total	100	100

The entry to record the retirement of Alt is:

(21)	Alt, Capital	55,000	
	Blue, Capital	5,500	
	Cha, Capital	4,500	
	Cash		65,000
	Retirement of Alt.		

The $10,000 bonus paid to Alt is allocated to Blue and Cha in their respective profit ratios. Blue is charged for 55 percent, and Cha is charged for the remaining 45 percent.

Sometimes partners wish to leave a partnership badly enough to accept less than their current capital balances upon retirement. In that case, a bonus may be assigned to the remaining partners. For example, Alt agrees to accept $50,000 cash upon retirement even though his capital balance is $55,000. The $5,000 remaining balance is distributed as a bonus to Blue and Cha in their respective profit and loss ratio.

Occasionally, a partnership uses the retirement of a partner and dissolution of the old partnership to record unrecognized goodwill. In this case, the partnership may record the retiring partner's share only, or it may impute the entire amount of goodwill based on the retiring partner's profit percentage. If total goodwill is imputed, the remaining partners also receive their respective shares of the total goodwill recognized. Many accountants criticize recording goodwill on the retirement of a partner on the same theoretical grounds as they criticize recording unrecognized goodwill on the admission of a new partner. Nevertheless, partnership accounting allows the recognition of goodwill at dissolution.

For example, if a $10,000 premium is paid to Alt and only Alt's share of unrecognized goodwill is to be recorded, the partnership makes the following entries at the time of Alt's retirement:

(22)	Goodwill	10,000	
	Alt, Capital		10,000
	Recognize Alt's share of goodwill.		
(23)	Alt, Capital	65,000	
	Cash		65,000
	Retirement of Alt.		

Summary of Key Concepts and Terms

Accounting for partnerships recognizes the unique aspects of this form of business organization. Profits must be distributed to partners in accordance with the partnership agreement or, in the absence of agreement, in accordance with the Uniform Partnership Act. The partnership is a separate accounting entity but not a separate legal or tax entity. For financial accounting purposes, noncash capital investments are recorded at their fair values at the time of the contribution to the partnership.

A partnership is legally dissolved when a new partner is admitted to the partnership or when a present partner retires. From a legal viewpoint, a new partnership is formed after each change in membership. From a practical point of view, however, the business often continues to operate. Some partnerships use the dissolution as an opportunity to revalue assets or to recognize unrecorded goodwill, thus adjusting their capital accounts for changes in the values of the net assets of the partnership. Others adhere more closely to the historical cost method of accounting and use the bonus method of realigning capital accounts for changes in the relative equity positions of the partners when membership changes. A variety of alternative methods are allowed for partnership accounting. The key is to find accounting policies that meet the needs of the partners and partnership. Flexibility is provided in partnership accounting to meet those needs.

c. How would your answer to Required part *a* change if all of the provisions of the income distribution plan were the same except that the salaries were $30,000 to Apple and $35,000 to Jack?

E15–5   Matching Partnership Terms with Their Descriptions

Required

Match the descriptions of terms on the left with the terms on the right. A term may be used once, more than once, or not at all.

Descriptions of Terms	Terms
1. Occurs when the new partner's investment exceeds the new partner's capital credit.	A. General partner
2. A partner who cannot actively participate in the management of the partnership.	B. Note payable to a partner
3. How partnership profits and losses are allocated when there is nothing stated in the partnership agreement.	C. Neither bonus nor goodwill recognized
4. Occurs when the new partner's investment equals the new partner's capital credit and there is no change in the old partners' capital balances.	D. Drawing account
5. This cost is not deducted to determine the partnership's net income for the period.	E. Limited partner
6. A partner who actively participates in the management of the partnership and who is personally liable for the debts of the partnership.	F. Bonus to old partners
7. Occurs when the new partner's capital credit exceeds the new partner's investment and there is no change in the old partners' capital balances.	G. Interest on capital accounts
8. This account is increased when a partner takes assets out of the partnership in anticipation of partnership net income.	H. Partnership income or loss shared equally
9. This account is increased for the fair value of noncash assets invested by a partner.	I. New partner's goodwill recognized
10 This represents a related-party transaction that must be disclosed in the notes to the financial statements.	J. Old partners' goodwill recognized
11. Occurs when the new partner's investment equals the new partner's capital credit and there is an increase in the old partners' capital balances.	K. Articles of Copartnership
12. Occurs when the new partner's capital credit exceeds the new partner's investment and there is a decrease in the old partners' capital balances.	L. Bonus to new partner
13. When a new partner is admitted to the partnership, an intangible asset is recognized that results in increases in the old partners' capital balances.	M. Capital account
14. This account is closed to the capital account at year-end.	
15. Interest expense on this payable is deducted to determine the net income of the partnership.	

E15–6   Admission of a Partner

In the GMP partnership, the capital balances of Mary, Gene, and Pat, who share income in the ratio of 6:3:1. are:

Mary	$240,000
Gene	120,000
Pat	40,000

Required

a. If no goodwill or bonus is recorded, how much must Elan invest for a one-third interest?

b. Prepare journal entries for the admission of Elan if she invests $80,000 for a one-fifth interest, and goodwill is recorded.

c. Prepare journal entries for the admission of Elan if she invests $200,000 for a 20 percent interest, and total capital will be $600,000.

E15–7   Admission of a Partner

Jeff and Kristie, partners in the J & K partnership, have capital balances of $100,000 and $40,000 and share income in a ratio of 4:1, respectively. Brad is to be admitted into the partnership with a 20 percent interest in the business.

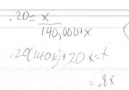

Required

Record the admission of Brad for each of the following independent situations:

a. Brad invests $60,000, and goodwill is to be recorded.

b. Brad invests $60,000. Total capital is to be $200,000.

c. Brad purchases the 20 percent interest by paying Jeff $22,000 and Kristie $11,000. Brad is assigned 20 percent of each of Jeff's and Kristie's capital accounts.

d. Brad invests $32,000. Total capital is to be $172,000.

e. Brad invests $32,000, and goodwill is to be recorded.

E15–8   Multiple-Choice Questions on the Admission of a Partner

Select the correct answer for each of the following questions.

The following balance sheet is for the partnership of Alex, Betty, and Claire, and relates to questions 1 and 2:

Cash	$ 20,000
Other Assets	180,000
	$200,000
Liabilities	$ 50,000
Alex, Capital (40%)	37,000
Betty, Capital (40%)	65,000
Claire, Capital (20%)	48,000
Total Liabilities and Capital	$200,000

(*Note:* Figures shown parenthetically reflect agreed profit and loss sharing percentages.)

1. If the assets are fairly valued on the above balance sheet and the partnership wishes to admit Denise as a new one-sixth-interest partner without recording goodwill or bonus, Denise should contribute cash or other assets of:

  a. $40,000.

  b. $36,000.

  c. $33,333.

  d. $30,000.

2. If assets on the initial balance sheet are fairly valued, Alex and Betty consent and Denise pays Claire $51,000 for her interest; the revised capital balances of the partners would be:

  a. Alex, $38,000; Betty, $66,500; Denise, $51,000.

  b. Alex, $38,500; Betty, $66,500; Denise, $48,000.

  c. Alex, $37,000; Betty, $65,000; Denise, $51,000.

  d. Alex, $37,000; Betty, $65,000; Denise, $48,000.

3. On December 31, 20X4, Alan and Dave are partners with capital balances of $80,000 and $40,000, and they share profit and losses in the ratio of 2:1, respectively. On this date Scott invests $36,000 cash for a one-fifth interest in the capital and profit of the new partnership. The partners agree that the implied partnership goodwill is to be recorded simultaneously with the admission of Scott. The total implied goodwill of the firm is:

   a. $4,800.
   b. $6,000.
   c. $24,000.
   d. $30,000.

4. Boris and Richard are partners who share profits and losses in the ratio of 6:4, respectively. On May 1, 20X9, their respective capital accounts were as follows:

Boris	$60,000
Richard	50,000

   On that date, Lisa was admitted as a partner with a one-third interest in capital and profits for an investment of $40,000. The new partnership began with a total capital of $150,000. Immediately after Lisa's admission, Boris's capital should be:

   a. $50,000.
   b. $54,000.
   c. $56,667.
   d. $60,000.

5. At December 31, Rod and Sheri are partners with capital balances of $40,000 and $20,000, and they share profits and losses in the ratio of 2:1, respectively. On this date Pete invests $17,000 in cash for a one-fifth interest in the capital and profit of the new partnership. Assuming that the bonus method is used, how much should be credited to Pete's capital account on December 31?

   a. $12,000.
   b. $15,000.
   c. $15,400.
   d. $17,000.

6. The capital accounts of the partnership of Ella, Nick, and Brandon are presented below with their respective profit and loss ratios:

Ella	$139,000	(.500)
Nick	209,000	(.333)
Brandon	96,000	(.167)

   Tony was admitted to the partnership when he purchased directly, for $132,000, a proportionate interest from Ella and Nick in the net assets and profits of the partnership. As a result, Tony acquired a one-fifth interest in the net assets and profits of the firm. Assuming implied goodwill is not to be recorded, what is the combined gain realized by Ella and Nick upon the sale of a portion of their interests in the partnership to Tony?

   a. $0.
   b. $43,200.
   c. $62,400.
   d. $82,000.

7. Fred and Ralph are partners who share profits and losses in the ratio of 7:3, respectively. Their respective capital accounts are as follows:

| Fred | $35,000 |
| Ralph | 30,000 |

They agreed to admit Lute as a partner with a one-third interest in the capital and profits and losses, upon an investment of $25,000. The new partnership will begin with a total capital of $90,000. Immediately after Lute's admission, what are the capital balances of Fred, Ralph, and Lute, respectively?

a. $30,000, $30,000, $30,000.
b. $31,500, $28,500, $30,000.
c. $31,667, $28,333, $30,000.
d. $35,000, $30,000, $25,000.

8. If A is the total capital of a partnership before the admission of a new partner, B is the total capital of the partnership after the investment of a new partner, C is the amount of the new partner's investment, and D is the amount of capital credit to the new partner, then there is:

a. A bonus to the new partner if $B = A + C$ and $D < C$.
b. Goodwill to the old partners if $B > (A + C)$ and $D = C$.
c. Neither bonus nor goodwill if $B = A - C$ and $D > C$.
d. Goodwill to the new partner if $B > (A + C)$ and $D < C$.

E15–9   Withdrawal of a Partner

In the LMK partnership, Luis's capital is $40,000, Marty's is $50,000, and Karl's is $30,000. They share income in a 4:1:1 ratio, respectively. Karl is retiring from the partnership.

Required

Prepare journal entries to record Karl's withdrawal according to each of the following independent assumptions:

a. Karl is paid $38,000, and no goodwill is recorded.
b. Karl is paid $42,000, and only his share of the goodwill is recorded.
c. Karl is paid $35,000, and all implied goodwill is recorded.

E15–10   Retirement of a Partner

On January 1, 20X1, Eddy decides to retire from the partnership of Cobb, Davis, and Eddy, who share profits and losses in the ratio of 3:2:1 respectively. The following condensed balance sheets present the account balances immediately before and, for six independent cases, after Eddy's retirement.

Accounts	Balances prior to Eddy's Retirement	Case 1	Case 2	Case 3	Case 4	Case 5	Case 6
Assets:							
Cash	$ 90,000	$ 10,000	$ 16,000	$ 25,000	$ 16,000	$ 50,000	$ 90,000
Other Assets	200,000	200,000	200,000	200,000	200,000	220,000	200,000
Goodwill	10,000	10,000	14,000	10,000	34,000	10,000	10,000
Total Assets	$300,000	$220,000	$230,000	$235,000	$250,000	$280,000	$300,000
Liabilities and Capital:							
Liabilities	$ 60,000	$ 60,000	$ 60,000	$ 60,000	$ 60,000	$ 60,000	$ 60,000
Cobb, Capital	80,000	74,000	80,000	83,000	92,000	110,000	80,000
Davis, Capital	90,000	86,000	90,000	92,000	98,000	110,000	160,000
Eddy, Capital	70,000	-0-	-0-	-0-	-0-	-0-	-0-
Total Liabilities and Capital	$300,000	$220,000	$230,000	$235,000	$250,000	$280,000	$300,000

Required

Prepare the necessary journal entries to record Eddy's retirement from the partnership for each of the six independent cases.

Problems

P15–11 **Admission of a Partner**

Debra and Merina sell electronic equipment and supplies through their partnership. They wish to expand their computer lines and decide to admit Wayne to the partnership. Debra's capital is $200,000, Merina's capital is $160,000, and they share income in a ratio of 3:2, respectively.

Required

Record the admission of Wayne for each of the following independent situations:

a. Wayne directly purchases half of Merina's investment in the partnership for $90,000.

b. Wayne invests the amount needed to give him a one-third interest in the capital of the partnership if no goodwill or bonus is recorded.

c. Wayne invests $110,000 for a one-fourth interest. Goodwill is to be recorded.

d. Debra and Merina agree that some of the inventory is obsolete. The inventory account is decreased before Wayne is admitted. Wayne invests $100,000 for a one-fourth interest.

e. Wayne directly purchases a one-fourth interest by paying Debra $80,000 and Merina $60,000. The land account is increased before Wayne is admitted.

f. Wayne invests $80,000 for a one-fifth interest in the total capital of $440,000.

g. Wayne invests $100,000 for a one-fifth interest. Goodwill is to be recorded.

P15–12 **Division of Income**

C. Eastwood, A. North, and M. West are manufacturers' representatives in the architecture business. Their capital accounts in the ENW partnership for 20X1 were as follows:

C. Eastwood, Capital				A. North, Capital				M. West, Capital			
9/1	8,000	1/1	30,000	3/1	9,000	1/1	40,000	8/1	12,000	1/1	50,000
		5/1	6,000			7/1	5,000			4/1	7,000
						9/1	4,000			6/1	3,000

Required

For each of the following independent income-sharing agreements, prepare an income distribution schedule.

a. Salaries are $15,000 to Eastwood, $20,000 to North, and $18,000 to West. Eastwood receives a bonus of 5 percent of net income after deducting his bonus. Interest is 10 percent of ending capital balances. Any remainder is divided by Eastwood, North, and West in a 3:3:4 ratio. Net income was $78,960.

b. Interest is 10 percent of weighted-average capital balances. Salaries are $24,000 to Eastwood, $21,000 to North, and $25,000 to West. North receives a bonus of 10 percent of net income after deducting the bonus and her salary. Any remainder is divided equally. Net income was $68,080.

c. West receives a bonus of 20 percent of net income after deducting the bonus and the salaries. Salaries are $21,000 to Eastwood, $18,000 to North, and $15,000 to West. Interest is 10 percent of beginning capital balances. Any remainder is divided by Eastwood, North, and West in an 8:7:5 ratio. Net income was $92,940.

P15–13   **Determining a New Partner's Investment Cost**

The following condensed balance sheet is presented for the partnership of Der, Egan, and Oprins, who share profits and losses in the ratio of 4:3:3, respectively.

Cash	$ 40,000	Accounts Payable	$150,000
Other Assets	710,000	Der, Capital	260,000
		Egan, Capital	180,000
		Oprins, Capital	160,000
Total Assets	$750,000	Total Liabilities and Capital	$750,000

Assume that the partnership decides to admit Snider as a new partner with a one-fourth interest.

Required

For each of the following independent cases, determine the amount that Snider must contribute in cash or other assets.

a. No goodwill or bonus is to be recorded.

b. Goodwill of $30,000 is to be recorded and allocated to the prior partners.

c. A bonus of $24,000 is to be paid by Snider and allocated to the prior partners.

d. The prior partners, Der, Egan, and Oprins, agree to give Snider $10,000 of goodwill upon admission into the partnership.

e. Other assets are revalued for an increase of $20,000, and goodwill of $40,000 is recognized and allocated to the prior partners at the time of the admission of Snider.

f. The partners agree that total resulting capital should be $820,000 and no goodwill should be recognized.

g. Other assets are revalued down by $20,000 and a bonus of $40,000 is paid to Snider at the time of admission.

P15–14   **Division of Income**

The Champion Play Company is a partnership that sells sporting goods. The partnership agreement provides for 10 percent interest on invested capital, salaries of $24,000 to Luc and $28,000 to Dennis and a bonus for Luc. The 20X3 capital accounts were as follows:

	Luc, Capital				Dennis, Capital		
8/1	15,000	1/1	50,000	7/1	10,000	1/1	70,000
		4/1	5,000			9/1	22,500

Required

For each of the following independent situations, prepare an income distribution schedule.

a. Interest is based on weighted-average capital balances. The bonus is 5 percent and is calculated on net income after deducting the bonus. In 20X3, net income was $64,260. Any remainder is divided between Luc and Dennis in a 3:2 ratio, respectively.

b. Interest is based on ending capital balances after deducting salaries, which the partners normally withdraw during the year. The bonus is 8 percent and is calculated on net income after deducting the bonus and salaries. Net income was $108,700. Any remainder is divided equally.

c. Interest is based on beginning capital balances. The bonus is 12.5 percent and is calculated on net income after deducting the bonus. Net income was $76,950. Any remainder is divided between Luc and Dennis in a 4:2 ratio, respectively.

The following describes this case.

1. The partners' net worth statements on May 1, 20X5, are as follows:

	Alt	Blue	Cha
Personal assets	$150,000	$12,000	$42,000
Personal liabilities	(86,000)	(16,000)	(14,000)
Net worth (deficit)	$ 64,000	$ (4,000)	$28,000

Blue is personally insolvent; Alt and Cha are personally solvent.

2. The terms of the note between Cha and the partnership state that the interest on the loan payable to Cha stops accruing at the point the partnership ceases operating as a going concern. This date is determined to be May 1, 20X5.

3. The noncash assets are sold as follows:

Date	Book Value	Proceeds	Loss
5/15/X5	$55,000	$45,000	$10,000
6/15/X5	30,000	15,000	15,000
7/15/X5	5,000	5,000	

4. The outside creditors are paid $40,000 on May 20.

5. The partners agree to maintain a $10,000 cash reserve during the liquidation process to pay for any liquidation expenses.

6. The partners agree to distribute the available cash at the end of each month; that is, installment liquidations will be made on May 31 and June 30. The final cash distributions to partners will be made on July 31, 20X5, the end of the liquidation process.

Figure 16–4 presents the statement of partnership realization and liquidation for the installment liquidation of the ABC Partnership.

Transactions during May 20X5.   The events during May 20X5 result in a distribution of $5,000 to the partners. The procedure to arrive at this amount is as follows:

1. The sale of $55,000 of assets results in a loss of $10,000, which is distributed to the three partners in their profit and loss sharing ratio.

2. Payments of $40,000 are made to outside creditors for the known liabilities.

3. Available cash is distributed to the partners on May 31, 20X5.

To determine the safe payment of cash to be distributed to partners, the accountant must make some assumptions about the future liquidation of the remaining assets. Assuming the worst possible situation, the remaining $35,000 of assets will result in a total loss. Before making a cash distribution to the partners, the accountant prepares a *schedule of safe payments to partners* using the worst-case assumptions. Figure 16–5 presents the schedule of safe payments to partners as of May 31, 20X5.

FIGURE 16–4 Installment Liquidation Workpaper

ABC Partnership
Statement of Partnership Realization and Liquidation
Lump-Sum Liquidation

	Cash	Noncash Assets	Liabilities	Cha Loan	Capital Balance Alt, 40%	Blue, 40%	Cha, 20%
Preliquidation balances, May 1	10,000	90,000	(40,000)	(4,000)	(34,000)	(10,000)	(12,000)
May 20X5:							
Sale of assets and distribution of $10,000 loss	45,000	(55,000)			4,000	4,000	2,000
	55,000	35,000	(40,000)	(4,000)	(30,000)	(6,000)	(10,000)
Payment to outside creditors	(40,000)		40,000				
	15,000	35,000	–0–	(4,000)	(30,000)	(6,000)	(10,000)
Payment to partners (Schedule 1, Figure 16–5)	(5,000)			1,000	4,000		
	10,000	35,000	–0–	(3,000)	(26,000)	(6,000)	(10,000)
June 20X5:							
Sale of assets and distribution of $15,000 loss	15,000	(30,000)			6,000	6,000	3,000
	25,000	5,000	–0–	(3,000)	(20,000)	–0–	(7,000)
Payment to partners (Schedule 2, Figure 16–5)	(15,000)			3,000	10,000		2,000
	10,000	5,000	–0–	–0–	(10,000)	–0–	(5,000)
July 20X5:							
Sale of assets at book value	5,000	(5,000)					
	15,000	–0–	–0–	–0–	(10,000)	–0–	(5,000)
Payment of $7,500 in liquidation costs	(7,500)				3,000	3,000	1,500
	7,500	–0–	–0–	–0–	(7,000)	3,000	(3,500)
Distribution of deficit of insolvent partner:						(3,000)	
40/60 × $3,000					2,000		
20/60 × $3,000							1,000
	7,500	–0–	–0–	–0–	(5,000)	–0–	(2,500)
Payment to partners	(7,500)				5,000		2,500
Postliquidation balances, July 31	–0–	–0–	–0–	–0–	–0–	–0–	–0–

Note: Parentheses indicate credit amount.

The schedule begins with the partners' capital and loan balances as of May 31. The potential right of offset is applied fully in this worst-case plan to fully reflect the loss-bearing capability of Cha. This is not an actual offset, but rather is for worst-case planning only. If the loan had continued to be interest-bearing during liquidation, interest would continue to accrue and would be recorded on the statement of realization and liquidation until the loan was extinguished or utilized for offset against an actual deficit. Therefore, under this worst-case set of assumptions as of May 31, 20X5, Cha's May 31 loan balance of $4,000 is combined with her $10,000 capital balance because the loan payable could be used, if necessary, to eliminate a deficit in her capital account resulting from losses during the liquidation process. The partners agreed to withhold $10,000 for possible liquidation expenses. In addition, the noncash assets have a remaining balance of $35,000 on May 31. A worst-case assumption is a complete loss

FIGURE 16–5 Schedule of Safe Payment to Partners for an Installment Liquidation

ABC Partnership
Schedule of Safe Payment to Partners

	Partner		
	Alt, *40%*	*Blue,* *40%*	*Cha,* *20%*
Schedule 1, May 31, 20X5			
Computation of distribution of cash available on May 31, 20X5:			
Capital and loan balances, May 31, before cash distribution	(30,000)	(6,000)	(14,000)
Assume full loss of $35,000 on remaining noncash assets and $10,000 in possible future liquidation expenses	18,000	18,000	9,000
	(12,000)	12,000	(5,000)
Assume Blue's potential deficit must be absorbed by Alt and Cha:		(12,000)	
40/60 × $12,000	8,000		
20/60 × $12,000			4,000
Safe payment to partners, May 31	(4,000)	–0–	(1,000)
Schedule 2, June 30, 20X5			
Computation of distribution of cash available on June 30, 20X5:			
Capital and loan balances, June 30	(20,000)	–0–	(10,000)
Assume full loss of $5,000 on remaining noncash assets and $10,000 in possible future liquidation expenses	6,000	6,000	3,000
	(14,000)	6,000	(7,000)
Assume Blue's potential deficit must be absorbed by Alt and Cha:		(6,000)	
40/60 × $6,000	4,000		
20/60 × $6,000			2,000
Safe payment to partners, June 30	(10,000)	–0–	(5,000)

Note: Parentheses indicate credit amount.

on the noncash assets and $10,000 of liquidation expenses, totaling $45,000 of charges to be distributed to the partners' capital accounts. The capital accounts of Alt, Blue, and Cha would be charged for $18,000, $18,000, and $9,000, respectively, for their shares of the $45,000. These assumptions result in a pro forma deficit in Blue's capital account. This is not an actual deficit that must be remedied! It is merely the result of applying the worst-case assumptions.

Continuing such worst-case planning, the accountant assumes that Blue is insolvent (which happens to be true in this example) and distributes the pro forma deficit in Blue's capital account to Alt and Cha in their profit and loss sharing ratio of 40:60 to Alt and 20:60 to Cha. The resulting credit balances indicate the amount of cash that may be safely distributed to the partners. The May 31 cash distribution is shown in Figure 16–4. The available cash of $5,000 is distributed to Alt and Cha, with the $1,000 paid to Cha reducing the loan payable because loan arrangements have a higher priority in liquidation than capital amounts. The ending balances should satisfy the equality of assets and equities of the accounting equation. If the equality has been destroyed, an error has occurred that must be corrected before proceeding further. As of May 31, after the installment distribution, the accounting equation is:

$$\text{Assets} - \text{Liabilities} = \text{Owners' equity}$$
$$\$45,000 - \$3,000 = \$42,000$$

Transactions during June 20X5. Figure 16–4 continues with transactions for June 20X5, as follows:

1. Noncash assets of $30,000 are sold on June 15 for a loss of $15,000. The loss is distributed to the partners in their profit and loss sharing ratio, resulting in a zero capital balance for Blue.
2. On June 30, 20X5, available cash is distributed as an installment payment to the partners.

The schedule of safe payments to partners as of June 30, 20X5, in Figure 16–5 shows how the amounts of distribution are calculated. A worst-case plan assumes that the remaining noncash assets of $5,000 must be written off as a loss and that the $10,000 cash in reserve will be completely used for liquidation expenses. This pro forma loss of $15,000 is allocated to the partners in their profit and loss sharing ratio, which creates a $6,000 deficit in Blue's capital account. Continuing the worst-case scenario, it is assumed Blue will not eliminate this debit balance. Therefore, the $6,000 potential deficit is allocated to Alt and Cha in their resulting profit and loss sharing ratio of 40:60 to Alt and 20:60 to Cha. The resulting credit balances in the partners' capital accounts show the amount of cash that can be distributed safely. Only $15,000 of the available cash is distributed to Alt and Cha on June 30, as shown in Figure 16–4. Of the $5,000 paid to Cha, $3,000 repays the loan payable. The remaining $2,000 reduces Cha's capital account.

Transactions during July 20X5. The last part of Figure 16–4 shows the completion of the liquidation transactions during July 20X5:

1. The remaining assets are sold at their book values.
2. Actual liquidation costs of $7,500 are paid and allocated to the partners in their profit and loss sharing ratio, creating a deficit of $3,000 in Blue's capital account. The remaining $2,500 of the $10,000 reserved for the expenses is released for distribution to the partners.
3. Because Blue is personally insolvent and cannot contribute to the partnership, the $3,000 deficit is distributed to Alt and Cha in their profit and loss sharing ratio. Note that this is an actual deficit, not a pro forma deficit.
4. The $7,500 of remaining cash is paid to Alt and Cha to the extent of their capital balances. After this last distribution, all account balances are zero, indicating the completion of the liquidation process.

Cash Distribution Plan

At the beginning of the liquidation process, it is common for accountants to prepare a *cash distribution plan,* which gives the partners an idea of the installment cash payments each will receive as cash becomes available to the partnership. The actual installment distributions are determined using the statement of realization and liquidation, supplemented with the schedule of safe payments to partners as presented in the last section of the chapter. The cash distribution plan is a pro forma projection of the application of cash as it becomes available.

Loss Absorption Power. A basic concept of the cash distribution plan at the beginning of the liquidation process is *loss absorption power* (**LAP**). An individual partner's LAP is defined as the maximum loss that can be realized by the partnership before that partner's capital and loan account balances are extinguished. For planning purposes, the potential rule of offset is applied fully and loan accounts become available for capital deficits. Thus loan accounts are fully offset against the capital accounts before a partner's LAP is computed. This offset is just for planning purposes; any actual offsets will be performed as necessary during the liquidation process. The loss absorption power is a function of two elements, as follows:

$$LAP = \frac{\text{Partner's capital and loan account balances}}{\text{Partner's profit and loss share}}$$

For example, Alt has a capital account credit balance of $34,000 and a 40 percent share in the profits and losses of ABC Partnership. Alt's LAP is

$$LAP = \frac{\$34,000}{.40} = \$85,000$$

This means that $85,000 in losses on disposing of noncash assets or from additional liquidation expenses would eliminate the credit balance in Alt's capital account, as follows:

$$\$85,000 \times .40 = \$34,000$$

Illustration of Cash Distribution Plan. The following illustration is based on the ABC Partnership example. A trial balance of the balance sheet accounts of the ABC Partnership on May 1, 20X5, the day the partners decide to liquidate the business, is presented below.

ABC Partnership
Trial Balance
May 1, 20X5

Cash	$ 10,000	
Noncash Assets	90,000	
Liabilities		$ 40,000
Loan Payable to Partner Cha		4,000
Alt, Capital (40%)		34,000
Blue, Capital (40%)		10,000
Cha, Capital (20%)		12,000
Total	$100,000	$100,000

The partners ask for a cash distribution plan as of May 1, 20X5, to determine the distributions of cash as it becomes available during the liquidation process. Such a plan always provides for payment to the outside creditors before any distributions may be made to the partners. Figure 16–6 presents the cash distribution plan as of May 1, the beginning date of the liquidation process.

The important observations from this illustration are as follows:

1 The cash distribution plan does not distinguish between partners' capital and loan accounts. Because of the potential right of offset, the balances of such

FIGURE 16–6   Cash Distribution Plan for Liquidating Partnership

ABC Partnership
Cash Distribution Plan
May 1, 20X5

	Loss Absorption Power			Capital and Loan Accounts		
	Alt	*Blue*	*Cha*	*Alt*	*Blue*	*Cha*
Profit and loss sharing percentages				40%	40%	20%
Preliquidation capital and loan account balances, May 1, 20X5				(34,000)	(10,000)	(16,000)
Loss absorption power (LAP) (Capital and loan accounts ÷ profit and loss ratio)	(85,000)	(25,000)	(80,000)			
Decrease highest LAP to next-highest LAP: Decrease Alt by $5,000 (cash distribution: $5,000 × .40 = $2,000)	5,000			2,000		
	(80,000)	(25,000)	(80,000)	(32,000)	(10,000)	(16,000)
Decrease LAPs to next-highest level: Decrease Alt by $55,000 (cash distribution: $55,000 × .40 = $22,000)	55,000			22,000		
Decrease Cha by $55,000 (cash distribution: $55,000 × .20 = $11,000)			55,000			11,000
	(25,000)	(25,000)	(25,000)	(10,000)	(10,000)	(5,000)
Decrease LAPs by distributing cash in profit and loss sharing percentages	40%	40%	20%			

Summary of Cash Distribution Plan

Step 1: First $40,000 to outside creditors						
Step 2: Next $10,000 to liquidation expenses						
Step 3: Next $2,000 to Alt				2,000		
Step 4: Next $33,000 to Alt and Cha in their respective profit and loss ratios				22,000		11,000
Step 5: Any additional distributions in the partners' profit and loss ratio				40%	40%	20%

Note: Parentheses indicates credit amount.

accounts are combined for purposes of the cash distribution plan. Cha's beginning amount of $16,000 in Figure 16–6 is the sum of the $4,000 loan and the May 1 capital balance of $12,000.

2. The loss absorption power of each partner is computed as the partner's preliquidation capital and loan balances divided by that partner's profit and loss sharing percentage. Alt has the highest LAP ($85,000), Cha has the next highest ($80,000), and Blue has the lowest ($25,000). Each partner's LAP is the amount of loss that would completely eliminate his or her net capital credit balance. Alt is the least vulnerable to a loss, and Blue is the most vulnerable.

3. The least vulnerable partner will be the first to receive any cash distributions after payment of creditors. Alt will be the only partner to receive cash until his LAP is decreased to the level of the next highest partner, Cha. To decrease

Bell is demanding that the loan to her be paid before any cash is distributed to Alexander. Alexander feels the available cash should be paid to him until his capital account is reduced to $40,000, the same as Bell's. Alexander will then pay the loan receivable to the partnership with the cash received. You have been asked to reconcile the argument.

Required

How would you advise in this case?

C16–3   Incorporation of a Partnership

After successfully operating a partnership for several years, the partners have proposed to incorporate the business and admit another investor. The original partners will purchase at par an amount of preferred stock equal to the book values of their capital interests in the partnership and common stock for the amount of the market value, including unrecognized goodwill, of the business that exceeds their book value. The new investor will make an investment, at a 5 percent premium over par value, in both preferred and common stock equal to one-third of the total number of shares purchased by the original partners. The corporation will acquire all the partnership's assets, assume the liabilities, and employ the original partners and the new investor.

Required

a. Discuss the differences in accounts used and in valuations that would be expected in comparing the balance sheets of the proposed corporation and that of the partnership.

b. Discuss the differences that would be expected in a comparison of the income statements of the proposed corporation and that of the partnership.

C16–4   Sharing Losses during Liquidation

Hiller, Luna, and Welsh are attempting to form a partnership to operate a travel agency. They have agreed to share profits in a ratio of 4:3:2, but cannot agree on the terms of the partnership agreement relating to possible liquidation. Hiller feels that it is best not to get into any arguments about potential liquidation at this time because the partnership will be a success and it is not necessary to think negatively at this point in time. Luna feels that in the event of liquidation, any losses should be shared equally because each of the partners would have worked equally for the success, or lack thereof, of the partnership. Welsh feels that any losses during liquidation should be distributed in the ratio of capital balances at the beginning of any liquidation because then the losses will be distributed based on a capital ability to bear the losses.

You have been asked to help resolve the differences and to prepare a memo to the three individuals including the following items.

Required

a. Specify the procedures for allocating losses among partners that is stated in the Uniform Partnership Act of 1914 that would be used if no partnership agreement terms are agreed upon regarding liquidation. (You may wish to obtain a copy of the Uniform Partnership Act for this requirement.)

b. Critically assess each of the partner's viewpoints, discussing the pros and cons of each position.

c. Specify another option for allocating potential liquidation losses that is not included in the positions currently taken by the three individuals. Critically assess the pros and cons of your alternative.

Exercises

E16–1   Multiple-Choice Questions on Partnership Liquidations

Select the correct answer for each of the following questions.

Questions 1, 2, and 3 are based on the following information:

The balance sheet for the partnership of Joan, Charles, and Thomas, whose shares of profits and losses are 40, 50, and 10 percent, is as follows:

Cash	$ 50,000	Accounts Payable	$150,000
Inventory	360,000	Joan, Capital	160,000
		Charles, Capital	45,000
		Thomas, Capital	55,000
Total Assets	$410,000	Total Liabilities and Equities	$410,000

1. If the inventory is sold for $300,000, how much should Joan receive upon liquidation of the partnership?
   a. $48,000.
   b. $100,000.
   c. $136,000.
   d. $160,000.

2. If the inventory is sold for $180,000, how much should Thomas receive upon liquidation of the partnership?
   a. $28,000.
   b. $32,500.
   c. $37,000.
   d. $55,000.

3. The partnership will be liquidated in installments. As cash becomes available, it will be distributed to the partners. If inventory costing $200,000 is sold for $140,000, how much cash should be distributed to each partner at this time?

	Joan	Charles	Thomas
a.	$56,000	$70,000	$14,000
b.	$16,000	$20,000	$ 4,000
c.	$32,000	$ 0	$ 8,000
d.	$20,000	$ 0	$20,000

4. In accounting for the liquidation of a partnership, cash payments to partners after all nonpartner creditors' claims have been satisfied, but before the final cash distribution, should be according to:
   a. The partners' relative profit and loss sharing ratios.
   b. The final balances in partner capital accounts.
   c. The partners' relative share of the gain or loss on liquidations.
   d. Safe payments computations.

5. After all noncash assets have been converted into cash in the liquidation of the Adam and Kay partnership, the ledger contains the following account balances:

	Debit	Credit
Cash	$47,000	
Accounts Payable		$32,000
Loan Payable to Adam		15,000
Adam, Capital	7,000	
Kay, Capital		7,000

Available cash should be distributed with $32,000 going to accounts payable and:

a. $15,000 to the loan payable to Adam.

b. $7,500 each to Adam and Kay.

c. $8,000 to Adam and $7,000 to Kay.

d. $7,000 to Adam and $8,000 to Kay.

Questions 6 and 7 are based on the following information.

F, A, S, and B are partners sharing profits and losses equally. The partnership is insolvent and is to be liquidated. The status of the partnership and each partner is as follows:

	Partnership Capital Balance	Personal Assets (exclusive of partnership interest)	Personal Liabilities (exclusive of partnership interest)
F	$(15,000)	$100,000	$40,000
A	(10,000)	30,000	60,000
S	20,000^a	80,000	5,000
B	30,000^a	1,000	28,000
Total	$ 25,000^a		

^{a}Deficit

6. The partnership creditors:

a. Must first seek recovery against S because she is personally solvent and has a negative capital balance.

b. Will *not* be paid in full regardless of how they proceed legally because the partnership assets are less than the partnership liabilities.

c. Will have to share A's interest in the partnership on a pro rata basis with A's personal creditors.

d. Have first claim to the partnership assets before any partner's personal creditors have rights to the partnership assets.

7. The partnership creditors may obtain recovery of their claims:

a. In the amount of $6,250 from each partner.

b. From the personal assets of either F or A.

c. From the personal assets of either S or B.

d. From the personal assets of either F or S for all or some of their claims.

E16–2 Multiple-Choice Questions on Partnership Liquidation [AICPA Adapted]
Select the correct answer for each of the following questions.

1. On January 1, 20X7, the partners of Casey, Dithers, and Edwards, who share profits and losses in the ratio of 5:3:2, respectively, decided to liquidate their partnership. On this date the partnership condensed balance sheet was as follows:

Assets		Liabilities and Capital	
Cash	$ 50,000	Liabilities	$ 60,000
Other Assets	250,000	Casey, Capital	80,000
		Dithers, Capital	90,000
		Edwards, Capital	70,000
Total	$300,000	Total	$300,000

On January 15, 20X7, the first cash sale of other assets with a carrying amount of $150,000 realized $120,000. Safe installment payments to the partners were made the same date. How much cash should be distributed to each partner?

	Casey	Dithers	Edwards
a.	$15,000	$51,000	$44,000
b.	$40,000	$45,000	$35,000
c.	$55,000	$33,000	$22,000
d.	$60,000	$36,000	$24,000

2. In a partnership liquidation, the final cash distribution to the partners should be made in accordance with the:
   a. Partners' profit and loss sharing ratio.
   b. Balances of the partners' loan and capital accounts.
   c. Ratio of the capital contributions by the partners.
   d. Ratio of capital contributions less withdrawals by the partners.

The following balance sheet is for the partnership of Art, Blythe, and Cooper and relates to questions 3 through 5:

Assets		Liabilities and Capital	
Cash	$ 20,000	Liabilities	$ 50,000
Other Assets	180,000	Art, Capital (40%)	37,000
		Blythe, Capital (40%)	65,000
		Cooper, Capital (20%)	48,000
Total	$200,000	Total	$200,000

Figures shown parenthetically reflect agreed profit and loss sharing percentages.

3. If the firm, as shown on the original balance sheet, is dissolved and liquidated by selling assets in installments, and if the first sale of noncash assets having a book value of $90,000 realizes $50,000 and all cash available after settlement with creditors is distributed, the respective partners would receive (to the nearest dollar):

	Art	Blythe	Cooper
a.	$8,000	$ 8,000	$ 4,000
b.	$6,667	$ 6,667	$ 6,666
c.	$ 0	$13,333	$ 6,667
d.	$ 0	$ 3,000	$17,000

4. If the facts are as in question 3 except that $3,000 cash is to be withheld, the respective partners would then receive (to the nearest dollar):

	Art	Blythe	Cooper
a.	$6,800	$ 6,800	$ 3,400
b.	$5,667	$ 5,667	$ 5,666
c.	$ 0	$11,333	$ 5,667
d.	$ 0	$ 1,000	$16,000

5. If each partner properly received some cash in the distribution after the second sale, if the cash to be distributed amounts to $12,000 from the third sale, and if unsold assets with an $8,000 book value remain, ignoring questions 3 and 4, the respective partners would receive:

a. $93,300.

b. $93,500.

c. $94,100.

d. $98,900.

10. Personal financial statements should report an investment in life insurance at the:

a. Face amount of the policy less the amount of premiums paid.

b. Cash value of the policy less the amount of any loans against it.

c. Cash value of the policy less the amount of premiums paid.

d. Face amount of the policy less the amount of any loans against it.

11. Mrs. Taft owns a $150,000 insurance policy on her husband's life. The cash value of the policy is $125,000, and there is a $50,000 loan against the policy. In the Tafts' personal statement of financial condition at December 31, 20X3, what amount should be shown as an investment in life insurance?

a. $150,000.

b. $125,000.

c. $100,000.

d. $ 75,000.

E16–13A   Personal Financial Statements

Leonard and Michelle have asked you to prepare their statement of changes in net worth for the year ended August 31, 20X3. They have prepared the following comparative statement of financial condition based upon estimated current values as required by **SOP 82-1:**

Leonard and Michelle
Statement of Financial Condition
August 31, 20X3 and 20X2

Assets		20X3		20X2
Cash		$ 3,600		$ 6,700
Marketable securities		4,900		16,300
Residence		94,800		87,500
Personal effects		10,000		10,000
Cash surrender value of life insurance		3,200		5,600
Investment in farm business:				
Farm land	$42,000		$32,100	
Farm equipment	22,400		9,000	
Note payable on farm equipment	(10,000)		–0–	
Net investment in farm		54,400		41,100
Total assets		$170,900		$167,200
Liabilities and Net Worth				
Credit card		$ 2,400		$ 1,500
Income taxes payable		11,400		12,400
Mortgage payable on residence		71,000		76,000
Estimated income taxes on the difference between the estimated current values of assets and liabilities and their tax bases		19,700		16,500
Net worth		66,400		60,800
Total liabilities and net worth		$170,900		$167,200

Additional Information

1. Leonard and Michelle's total salaries during the fiscal year ended August 31, 20X3, were $44,300; farm income was $6,700; personal expenditures were $43,500, interest and dividends received were $1,400.

2. Marketable securities that were purchased in 20X1 at a cost of $11,000 and having a current market value of $11,000 on August 31, 20X2, were sold on March 1, 20X3, for $10,700. No additional marketable securities were purchased or sold during the fiscal year.

3. The values of the residence and farm land are based upon year-end appraisals.

4. On August 31, 20X3, Leonard purchased a used combine at a cost of $14,000. A down payment of $4,000 was made, and a five-year, 10 percent note payable was signed for the $10,000 balance owed. No other farm equipment was purchased or sold during the fiscal year.

5. The cash surrender value of the life insurance policy increased during the fiscal year by $1,600. However, Leonard borrowed $4,000 against the policy on September 1, 20X2. Interest at 15 percent for the first year of this loan was paid when due on August 31, 20X3.

6. Federal income taxes of $12,400 were paid during the 20X3 fiscal year.

7. Total mortgage payments made during the year were $9,000, which included payments of principal and interest.

Required

Using the comparative statement of financial condition and additional information provided, prepare the statement of changes in net worth for the year ended August 31, 20X3. (*Hint:* It will be helpful to use T-accounts to determine several realized and unrealized amounts. An analysis of the cash, personal effects, and credit card accounts should not be required to properly complete the statement.)

Problems

P16–14   Lump-Sum Liquidation

The Carlos, Dan, and Gail (CDG) Partnership has decided to liquidate as of December 1, 20X6. A balance sheet as of December 1, 20X6, appears below:

CDG Partnership
Balance Sheet
At December 1, 20X6

Assets

Cash		$ 25,000
Accounts Receivable (net)		75,000
Inventories		100,000
Property, Plant, and Equipment (net)		300,000
Total Assets		$500,000

Liabilities and Capital

Liabilities		
Accounts Payable		$240,000
Loan Payable to Dan		30,000
Total Liabilities		$270,000
Capital:		
Carlos, Capital	$120,000	
Dan, Capital	50,000	
Gail, Capital	60,000	
Total Capital		230,000
Total Liabilities and Capital		$500,000

Additional Information

1. The personal assets (excluding partnership capital and loan interests) and personal liabilities of each partner as of December 1, 20X6, are presented below:

	Carlos	Dan	Gail
Personal assets	$250,000	$300,000	$350,000
Personal liabilities	(230,000)	(240,000)	(325,000)
Personal net worth	$ 20,000	$ 60,000	$ 25,000

2. Carlos, Dan, and Gail share profits and losses in the ratio 20:40:40, respectively.
3. According to the partnership agreement, interest does not accrue on partners' loan balances during the liquidation process.
4. All of the noncash assets were sold on December 10, 20X6, for $260,000.

Required

a. Prepare a statement of realization and liquidation for the CDG Partnership on December 10, 20X6.

b. Prepare a schedule showing how the partners' personal assets are to be distributed according to the provisions of the Uniform Partnership Act.

P16–15 Installment Liquidation

The trial balance of the NOT Partnership on April 30, 20X1, is presented below. The profit and loss percentages are shown in the trial balance:

	Debit	Credit
Cash	$ 15,000	
Accounts Receivable (net)	85,000	
Inventory	82,000	
Plant Assets (net)	120,000	
Accounts Payable		$ 90,000
Otter, Loan		15,000
Nate, Capital (60%)		80,000
Otter, Capital (20%)		57,000
Trin, Capital (20%)		60,000
Total	$302,000	$302,000

The partnership is being liquidated. Liquidation activities are as follows:

	May	June	July
Accounts receivable collected	$40,000	$28,000	$ 13,000
Noncash assets sold:			
Book value	44,000	35,000	123,000
Selling price	50,000	30,000	80,000
Accounts payable paid	65,000	25,000	
Liquidation expenses:			
Paid during month	3,500	3,000	2,500
Anticipated for remainder of liquidation process	6,000	4,000	

Cash is distributed at the end of each month, and the liquidation is completed by July 31, 20X1. No interest accrues on Otter's loan during the liquidation.

Required

Prepare a statement of partnership realization and liquidation for the NOT Partnership with schedules of safe payments to partners.

P16–16   Installment Liquidation [AICPA Adapted]

On January 1, 20X1, the partners of Able, Black, and Ciou, who share profits and losses in the ratio of 5:3:2, respectively, decide to liquidate their partnership. The partnership trial balance at this date is as follows:

	Debit	Credit
Cash	$ 18,000	
Accounts Receivable	66,000	
Inventory	52,000	
Machinery and Equipment (net)	189,000	
Able, Loan	30,000	
Accounts Payable		$ 53,000
Black, Loan		20,000
Able, Capital		118,000
Black, Capital		90,000
Ciou, Capital		74,000
Total	$355,000	$355,000

The partners plan a program of piecemeal conversion of assets in order to minimize liquidation losses. All available cash, less an amount retained to provide for future expenses, is to be distributed to the partners at the end of each month. No interest accrues on partners' loans during liquidation. A summary of the liquidation transactions is as follows:

January 20X1:

1. $51,000 was collected on accounts receivable; the balance is uncollectible.
2. $38,000 was received for the entire inventory.
3. $2,000 liquidation expenses were paid.
4. $50,000 was paid to outside creditors, after offset of a $3,000 credit memorandum received on January 11, 20X1.
5. $10,000 cash was retained in the business at the end of the month for potential unrecorded liabilities and anticipated expenses.

February 20X1:

6. $4,000 liquidation expenses were paid.
7. $6,000 cash was retained in the business at the end of the month for potential unrecorded liabilities and anticipated expenses.

March 20X1:

8. $146,000 was received on sale of all items of machinery and equipment.
9. $5,000 liquidation expenses were paid.
10. The $30,000 loan from Able is approved by the partners for offset against his capital account.
11. No cash was retained in the business.

Required

Prepare a statement of partnership liquidation for the partnership with schedules of safe payments to partners.

P16–17 **Cash Distribution Plan**

The partnership of Fox, Gold, and Hare has asked you to assist it in winding up the affairs of the business. You compile the following information.

1. The trial balance of the partnership on June 30, 20X1, is:

	Debit	Credit
Cash	$ 6,000	
Accounts Receivable (net)	22,000	
Inventory	14,000	
Plant and Equipment (net)	99,000	
Loan to Fox	12,000	
Loan to Hare	7,500	
Accounts Payable		$ 17,000
Fox, Capital		67,000
Gold, Capital		45,000
Hare, Capital		31,500
Total	$160,500	$160,500

2. The partners share profits and losses as follows: Fox, 50 percent; Gold, 30 percent; and Hare, 20 percent.

3. The partners are considering an offer of $100,000 for the accounts receivable, inventory, and plant and equipment as of June 30. The $100,000 will be paid to creditors and the partners in installments, the number and amounts of which are to be negotiated.

Required

Prepare a cash distribution plan as of June 30, 20X1, showing how much cash each partner will receive if the offer to sell the assets is accepted.

P16–18 **Installment Liquidation**

Refer to the facts in Problem 16–17. The partners have decided to liquidate their partnership by installments instead of accepting the offer of $100,000. Cash is distributed to the partners at the end of each month. No interest on partners' loans accrues during liquidation. A summary of the liquidation transactions follows:

July:

   $16,500 collected on accounts receivable; balance is uncollectible.

   $10,000 received for the entire inventory.

   $1,000 liquidation expense paid.

   $17,000 paid to outside creditors.

   $8,000 cash retained in the business at the end of the month.

August:

   $1,500 in liquidation expenses paid.

   As part payment of his capital, Hare accepted an item of special equipment that he developed which had a book value of $4,000. The partners agreed that a value of $10,000 should be placed on this item for liquidation purposes.

   $2,500 in cash retained in the business at the end of the month.

September:

$75,000 received on sale of remaining plant and equipment.

The partners agree to allow the offset of the loans to Fox and Hare against their capital accounts.

$1,000 liquidation expenses paid. No cash retained in the business.

Required

Prepare a statement of partnership realization and liquidation with supporting schedules of safe payments to partners.

P16–19   Cash Distribution Plan

The Jackson, Jensen, and Johnson (JJJ) Partnership has decided to liquidate its operations as of December 31, 20X6. A balance sheet prepared at that date is presented as follows:

JJJ Partnership
Balance Sheet
At December 31, 20X6

Assets		
Cash		$ 45,000
Accounts Receivable (net)		75,000
Inventories		100,000
Plant, Property, and Equipment (net)		180,000
Total Assets		$400,000
Liabilities and Capital		
Liabilities:		
Accounts Payable		$195,000
Loan Payable to Johnson		25,000
Total Liabilities		$220,000
Capital:		
Jackson, Capital	$70,000	
Jensen, Capital	90,000	
Johnson, Capital	20,000	
Total Capital		180,000
Total Liabilities and Capital		$400,000

Required

a. The JJJ Partnership wishes to know how cash will be distributed as it becomes available. Therefore, it wants you to prepare a cash distribution plan. Jackson, Jensen, and Johnson share profits and losses in the ratio 20:30:50, respectively. The partnership does not expect to incur any liquidation expenses.

b. The partners also want to know how much cash would have to be received from the sale of the noncash assets in order for Johnson to receive $25,000 of cash from the liquidation. Prepare a schedule that discloses this amount. Assume that the partnership agreement states that interest does not accrue on loans from partners during the liquidation process.

P16–20   **Installment Liquidation**

The KGB Partnership decided to liquidate the partnership as of June 30, 20X5. The balance sheet of the partnership as of this date is presented as follows:

KGB Partnership
Balance Sheet
At June 30, 20X5

Assets

Cash	$ 50,000
Accounts Receivable (net)	95,000
Inventories	75,000
Property, Plant, and Equipment (net)	500,000
Total Assets	$720,000

Liabilities and Partners' Capitals

Liabilities:

Accounts Payable	$405,000
Loan Payable to G	50,000
Total Liabilities	$455,000

Partners' Capitals:

K, Capital	$100,000
G, Capital	90,000
B, Capital	75,000
Total Capital	$265,000
Total Liabilities and Capital	$720,000

Additional Information

1. According to the partnership agreement, interest on notes payable to partners does not accrue during the liquidation of the partnership.

2. The personal assets (excluding partnership loan and capital interests) and personal liabilities of each partner as of June 30, 20X5, are presented below:

	K	G	B
Personal assets	$250,000	$450,000	$300,000
Personal liabilities	(270,000)	(420,000)	(240,000)
Personal net worth	$ (20,000)	$ 30,000	$ 60,000

The KGB Partnership was liquidated during the months of July, August, and September. The assets sold and the amounts realized are presented below:

Month	Assets Sold	Carrying Amount	Amount Realized
July:	Inventories	$ 50,000	$ 45,000
	Accounts receivable (net)	60,000	40,000
	Property, plant, and equipment	400,000	305,000
August:	Inventories	$ 25,000	$ 18,000
	Accounts receivable (net)	10,000	4,000
September:	Accounts receivable (net)	$ 25,000	$ 10,000
	Property, plant, and equipment	100,000	45,000

Required

Prepare a statement of partnership realization and liquidation for the KGB Partnership for the three-month period ended September 30, 20X5. K, G, and B share profits and losses in the ratio 50:30:20, respectively. The partners wish to distribute available cash at the end of each month, after reserving $10,000 of cash at the end of July and August to meet unexpected liquidation expenses. Actual liquidation expenses incurred and paid each month amounted to $2,500. Support each cash distribution to the partners with a schedule of safe installment payments.

P16–21   Cash Distribution Plan

Refer to the information contained in Problem 16–20. Assume the following amounts of cash were received during the months of July, August, and September from the sale of the noncash assets of the KGB Partnership:

July	$390,000
August	22,000
September	55,000

The partnership wishes to keep $10,000 of cash on hand at the end of July and August to pay for unexpected liquidation expenses.

Liquidation expenses of $2,500 were paid at the end of July, August, and September.

Required

a. Prepare a statement, as of June 30, 20X5, showing how cash will be distributed among partners as it becomes available.

b. Prepare schedules showing how cash is distributed at the end of July, August, and September, 20X5.

P16–22 **Matching**

Match the terms on the left with the descriptions on the right. A description may be used only once.

Terms	*Descriptions of Terms*
1. Dissolution	A. The sale of the partnership assets, payment of the partnership creditors, and the distribution of any remaining assets to partners.
2. Right of offset	
3. A partner's loss absorption power	B. Allocated to other partners in their profit and loss sharing ratio if the partner is personally insolvent.
4. Liquidation	C. A schedule which shows how cash is to be distributed as it becomes available during liquidation process.
5. Marshaling of assets	
6. Claims of a partner's personal creditors	D. These have priority over the claims of partnership creditors to the personal assets of a partner.
7. Claims of the partnership creditors	E. This is computed by dividing the sum of a partner's capital and loan balances by that partner's profit and loss sharing ratio.
8. Statement of partnership realization and liquidation	F. A partnership's assets and liabilities are revalued to their market values.
9. Installment liquidation	G. A change in the legal relationship between partners.
10. Cash distribution plan	H. The end of the normal business function of the partnership.
11. Incorporation of a partnership	I. The order of creditors' rights against the partnership's assets and the personal assets of each partner.
12. Partner's deficit in capital	J. The personal assets of Partner L may be used to satisfy these after the personal creditors of Partner L are satisfied.
13. Lump-sum liquidation	K. A deficit in Partner D's capital account is reduced to zero because the partnership has a loan payable to Partner D.
14. Safe payments to partners	L. A liquidation in which all assets are converted into cash over a short time period, enabling all creditors to be paid, with any remaining cash being distributed according to the partner's capital balance.
	M. These cash payments to partners are computed on the assumption that all noncash assets will be sold for nothing.
	N. This presents, in workpaper form, the effects of the liquidation process on the balance sheet accounts of the partnership.
	O. A liquidation in which cash is periodically distributed to partners during the liquidation process.

P16–23 **Partnership Agreement Issues [AICPA Adapted]**

A partnership involves an association between two or more persons to carry on a business as co-owners for profit. Items 1 through 10 relate to partnership agreements.

Required

The statement of facts for parts A and B are followed by numbered sentences that state legal conclusions relating to those facts. Determine whether each legal conclusion is correct.

Part A

Adams, Webster, and Coke were partners in the construction business. Coke decided to retire and found Black, who agreed to purchase his interest. Black was willing to pay Coke $20,000 and promised to assume Coke's share of all firm obligations.

1. Unless the partners agree to admit Black as a partner, he could not become a member of the firm.

2. The retirement of Coke would cause a dissolution of the firm.

3. The firm creditors are third-party beneficiaries of Black's promise to Coke.

4. Coke would be released from all liability for firm debts if his interest were purchased by Black and Black promised to pay Coke's share of firm debts.

5. If the other partners refused to accept Black as a partner, Coke could retire, thereby causing a dissolution.

Part B

Carson, Crocket, and Kitt were partners in the importing business. They needed additional capital to expand and located an investor named White, who agreed to purchase a one-quarter interest in the partnership by contributing $50,000 in capital to the partnership. At the time White became a partner, there were several large creditors who had previously loaned money to the partnership. The partnership subsequently failed, and the creditors are attempting to assert personal liability against White.

6. White is personally liable on all firm debts contracted subsequent to his entry into the firm.

7. Creditors of the first partnership automatically become creditors of the new partnership continuing the business.

8. Creditors of the old firm which existed prior to White's entry can assert rights against his capital contribution.

9. White has personal liability for firm debts existing prior to his entry into the firm.

10. White must remain in the partnership for at least one year to be subject to personal liability.

GOVERNMENTAL ENTITIES: INTRODUCTION AND GENERAL FUND ACCOUNTING

In the early 2000s, the combined annual spending of federal, state, and local governments exceeded $2.5 trillion. This is the equivalent of more than $9,000 for each person in the United States, or almost $30,000 per family. Governmental purchases of goods and services constitute approximately 20 percent of the total gross national product of the United States.[1]

The first part of this chapter presents an introduction to the accounting and reporting requirements for state and local governmental units. The major concepts of governmental accounting are discussed and illustrated first. The last part of this chapter presents a comprehensive illustration of accounting for the general fund of a city. The comprehensive illustration reviews and integrates the concepts presented in the first part of the chapter. Chapter 18 continues the comprehensive illustration to complete the discussion on state and local governmental accounting and reporting.

Each of the 50 states follows relatively uniform accounting standards; however, some states have unique statutory provisions for selected items. Local governments are political subdivisions of state government. The 80,000 local governmental units in the United States are classified as (1) general-purpose local governments, such as counties, cities, towns, villages, and townships; (2) special-purpose local governments, such as soil conservation districts; and (3) authorities and agencies, such as the New York Port Authority and local housing authorities. Authorities and agencies differ from other governmental units because they typically do not have taxing power and may sell only revenue bonds, not general obligation bonds.

Governmental entities have operating objectives different from those of commercial entities; therefore, governmental accounting is different from accounting for commercial enterprises. The major differences between governmental and for-profit entities are as follows:

1. Governmental and accounting must recognize that governmental units collect resources and make expenditures to fulfill societal needs. Society expects governmental units to develop and maintain an infrastructure of highways, streets, and sewer and sanitation systems, as well as to provide public protection, recreation, and cultural services.

---

[1] Annual reports of the national income and product accounts, including aggregate revenues and expenditures of governmental entities, are presented in the *Survey of Current Business,* published periodically by the U.S. Department of Commerce.

2. Except for some proprietary activities such as utilities, governmental entities do not have a general profit motive. Police and fire departments do not have a profit motive; instead these units must be evaluated on their abilities to provide for society's needs.

3. Governmental operations have legal authorization for their existence, conduct revenue raising through the power of taxation, and have mandated expenditures they must make to provide their services. The governmental accounting system must make it possible to determine and demonstrate compliance with finance-related legal and contractual provisions. Governmental units are subject to extensive regulatory oversight through laws, grant restrictions, bond indentures, and a variety of other legal constraints.

4. Governmental entities use comprehensive budgetary accounting, which serves as a significant control mechanism and provides the basis for comparing actual operations against budgeted amounts. The budget is a legally established statutory control vehicle.

5. The primary emphasis in governmental fund accounting is to measure and report on management's stewardship of the financial resources committed to the objectives of the governmental unit. Accountability for the flow of financial resources is a chief objective of governmental accounting. The managers of the governmental unit must be able to show they are in compliance with the many legal regulations governing its operations.

6. Governmental entities typically are required to establish separate funds to carry out their various missions. Each fund is an independent accounting and fiscal entity and is responsible for using its own resources to accomplish its specific responsibilities.

7. Many fund entities do not record fixed assets or long-term debt in their funds. These fund entities record the purchase of assets such as equipment and buildings as expenditures of the period. A separate record of the fixed assets and long-term debt is maintained within the governmental unit.

Expendability of Resources versus Capital Maintenance Objectives

The major differences between commercial and governmental accounting are due to the objectives of the entities. In commercial enterprises, the emphasis is on the measurement of the flow of all economic resources of the firm. The accrual basis of accounting is used to match the revenues and expenses during a period with the objective of measuring profitability. The company's balance sheet contains both current and noncurrent assets and liabilities, and the change in retained earnings reflects the company's ability to maintain its capital investment.

In contrast, the major focus for many of the operations within the governmental funds of a governmental entity is the flow of current financial resources available to provide services to the public. The emphasis is on the expendability of the resources to accomplish the objectives and purposes of the governmental entity. Operating authorization is initiated by a budget that is passed by the legislative governing body. Managers of governmental units must be very careful to ensure that resources are expended in full and complete compliance with the legal and financial restrictions placed upon the governmental entity. The focus on expendability affects many of the accounting and financial reporting standards of governmental entities.

History of Governmental Accounting

Before 1984, the development of accounting principles for local governmental units was directed by the Municipal Finance Officers Association (MFOA). In 1934, the National Committee on Municipal Accounting, a committee of the MFOA, published the first statement on local governmental accounting. The report was entitled *A Tentative Outline—Principles of Municipal Accounting.* In 1968, the National Committee on Governmental Accounting, the successor committee, published *Governmental Accounting, Auditing, and Financial Reporting (GAAFR).* Some governmental accountants call it the "blue book," after the color of its cover. The GAAFR is periodically updated to include the most recent governmental financial reporting standards.

In 1974, the American Institute of Certified Public Accountants published an industry audit guide, *Audits of State and Local Governmental Units,* in which it stated that "except as modified in this guide, they [GAAFR] constitute generally accepted accounting principles."[2] In March 1979, the National Council on Governmental Accounting (NCGA) issued its **Statement No. 1,** "Governmental Accounting and Financial Reporting Principles" (**NCGA 1**), which established a set of accounting principles for governmental reporting.

In 1984, the Financial Accounting Foundation created a companion group to the Financial Accounting Standards Board. The Governmental Accounting Standards Board (GASB) is now responsible for maintaining and developing accounting and reporting standards for state and local governmental entities. In **GASB Statement No. 1,** "Authoritative Status of NCGA Pronouncements and AICPA Industry Audit Guide" (**GASB 1**), released in July 1984, the GASB stated that all NCGA statements and interpretations issued and in effect on that date were accepted as generally accepted accounting principles for governmental accounting. In 1985, the GASB published a codification of the existing GAAP for state and local governments entitled *Codification of Governmental Accounting and Financial Reporting Standards.* The first section of the codification is virtually identical to **NCGA 1** as amended by subsequent NCGA statements. Section 2 presents the financial reporting issues for governmental entities. Sections 3 and 4 present specific balance sheet and operating statement topics. The GASB continues to publish updated codifications periodically. The codification is an authoritative source for accounting and financial reporting principles for governmental units.

Accounting for governmental units is given the general description of fund accounting to distinguish it from accounting for commercial entities. This chapter presents an overview of fund accounting and illustrates accounting in the general fund, typically the most important part of most governmental units. Chapter 18 presents the accounting for the remaining funds of a governmental entity and the financial statements required of government units.

Definitions and Types of Funds

Fund accounting must recognize the unique aspects of governmental operations. Governmental units must provide a large range of services, such as fire and police protection, water and sewerage, legal courts, and construction of public buildings and

---

[2]*Committee on Governmental Accounting and Auditing,* "Audits of State and Local Governmental Units," American Institute of Certified Public Accountants (New York), 1974, pp. 8–9.

other facilities. In addition, governmental units receive their resources from many different sources and must make expenditures in accordance with legal restrictions.

The operations of a governmental unit must also be broken down into periodic reporting intervals of fiscal years because the management of these public operations may change as a result of elections or new appointments. Thus, governmental accounting must recognize the many different purposes, the different sources of revenue, the mandated expenditures, and the fiscal periodicity of the governmental unit. To accomplish the objectives of the governmental unit, the unit establishes a variety of **funds** as fiscal and accounting entities of the governmental unit. The second principle of governmental accounting presented in the GASB's *Codification of Governmental Accounting and Financial Reporting Standards* states:

> Governmental accounting systems should be organized and operated on a fund basis. A fund is defined as a fiscal and accounting entity with a self-balancing set of accounts recording cash and other financial resources, together with all related liabilities and residual equities or balances, and changes therein, which are segregated for the purpose of carrying on specific activities or attaining certain objectives in accordance with special regulations, restrictions, or limitations.[3]

Different funds are established for the specific functions that a government must provide. Most funds obtain resources from taxes on property, income, or commercial sales; they may also obtain resources as grants from other governmental agencies, from fines or licenses, and from charges for services. Each fund must make its expenditures in accordance with its specified purposes. For example, a fund established for fire protection cannot be used to provide school buses for the local school. The fire department may make expenditures only directly related to its function of providing fire protection.

Each fund has its own asset and liability accounts, and its own revenue and expenditures accounts. The term *expenditures* refers to the outflow of resources in funds providing governmental services. Separate fund-based financial statements must be prepared for each fiscal period. In this manner, governing bodies or other interested parties may assess the financial performance of the funds in the fulfillment of the specific purposes for which they were established.

Types of Funds

Governmental accounting systems are established on a fund basis in three major categories: governmental, proprietary, and fiduciary. Figure 17–1 presents an overview of each of the funds and provides a brief description of the types of activities accounted for in each fund.

Governmental Funds.   Five ***governmental funds*** are used to provide basic governmental services to the public. These are: (1) general fund, (2) special revenue funds, (3) capital projects funds, (4) debt service funds, and (5) permanent funds (see Figure 17–1). The number of governmental funds maintained by the governmental entity is based on the legal and operating requirements of the governmental entity. Only one general fund will be created by each governmental entity, but more than one of each of the other types of governmental funds may be created based on the specific needs of the entity. For example, some governmental entities establish a separate capital projects fund for each major capital project.

---

[3]Governmental Accounting Standards Board, *Codification of Governmental Accounting and Financial Reporting Standards,* updates published frequently, Section 1100–102.

FIGURE 17–1   Fund Structure

Governmental Funds

1. General fund

Accounts for all financial resources except for those required to be accounted for in another fund. Includes transactions for general governmental services provided by the executive, legislative, and judicial operations of the governmental entity.

2. Special revenue funds

Accounts for the proceeds of revenue sources that are legally restricted for specified purposes. Includes resources and expenditures for operations such as public libraries when a separate tax is levied for their support.

3. Capital projects funds

Accounts for financial resources for the acquisition or construction of major capital projects that benefit many citizens, such as parks and municipal buildings. This fund is in existence only during the acquisition or construction of the facilities and is closed once the project is completed.

4. Debt service funds

Accounts for the accumulation of resources for, and the payment of, general long-term debt principal and interest. This fund is used for servicing the long-term debt of the government.

5. Permanent funds

Accounts for resources that are legally restricted such that only earnings, but not principal, may be used in support of governmental programs.

Proprietary Funds

6. Enterprise funds

Accounts for operations of governmental units that charge for services provided to the general public. Includes those activities financed in a manner similar to private business enterprises where the intent of the governing body is to recover the costs of providing goods or services to the general public on a continuing basis through user charges. Also includes those operations that the governing body intends to operate at a profit. Examples include sports arenas, municipal electric utilities, and municipal bus companies.

7. Internal service funds

Accounts for the financing of goods or services provided by one department or agency to other departments or agencies of the governmental unit. The services are usually provided on a cost-reimbursement basis and are offered only to other governmental agencies, not the general public. Examples are municipal motor vehicle pools, city print shops, and central purchasing operations.

Fiduciary Funds and Similar Component Units

8. Pension (and other employee benefit) trust funds

Accounts for resources required to be held in trust for the members and beneficiaries of pension plans, other post-employment benefit plans, or other employee benefit plans.

9. Investment trust funds

Accounts for the external portion of investment pools reported by the sponsoring government.

10. Private-purpose trust funds

Accounts for all other trust arrangements under which the fund's resources are to be used to benefit specific individuals, private organizations, or other governments, as specified in the trust agreement.

11. Agency funds

Accounts for assets held by a governmental unit in an agency capacity for employees or for other governmental units. An example is the city employees' payroll withholding for health insurance premiums.

Proprietary Funds.   Some activities of a governmental unit, such as operation of a public swimming pool or operation of a municipal water system, are similar to those of commercial enterprises. The objective of the governmental unit is to recover its costs in these operations through a system of user charges. The two *proprietary funds* typically used by governmental entities are: (6) enterprise funds and (7) internal service funds (see Figure 17–1). Accounting and reporting for a proprietary fund is similar to accounting for a commercial operation. The balance sheet of each proprietary fund reports all assets, including long-term capital assets, and reports all liabilities, including long-term liabilities. A complete discussion of proprietary funds is presented in Chapter 18.

Fiduciary Funds.   Four *fiduciary funds* are provided for a governmental unit. Three are trust funds that account for financial resources maintained in trust by the government. These three are: (8) pension and other employee benefit trust funds, (9) investment trust funds, and (10) private-purpose trust funds. And the fourth fiduciary fund, (11) agency funds, is used to account for resources held by the government solely in a custodial capacity (see Figure 17–1). Note that the permanent fund, which is a governmental fund, includes resources that are legally restricted, such that the principal must be maintained by the governmental entity and only the earnings from the fund's resources may be used to benefit the government's programs for all of its citizens. But the private-purpose trust funds include trusts under which the principal may or may not be expendable, but for which the trust agreement specifies the principal, if expendable, and the earnings, may be used only for the benefit of specific individuals, organizations, or other governments. A discussion of trust and agency funds is presented in Chapter 18.

Before 1987, many governmental units used a separate governmental fund, the *special assessments fund,* to record the construction and financing of public improvements deemed to benefit a limited group of people. These public improvements, such as sewerage additions, streetlights in a specific neighborhood, or new sidewalks or streets in a specific area, are paid for over time by a special tax assessment on the properties that benefited from the improvement. However, in January 1987 the GASB issued **Statement No. 6,** "Accounting and Financial Reporting for Special Assessments" **(GASB 6),** which requires that these activities be recorded in other governmental funds if the governmental unit is obligated in any manner on the debt issued to finance the construction. In most cases, the governmental unit will provide some type of general governmental commitment on the debt issue. Thus, the capital projects fund is typically used to account for the construction phase of these capital improvements. In those very few cases in which the governmental unit has absolutely no commitment on the debt issue, the debt is not shown as part of the governmental unit.

Financial Reporting of Governmental Entities

The financial statements of a governmental entity include the primary governmental unit, such as a state government, a general-purpose local government, or a special-purpose local government that has a separately elected governing body, and its component units for which the primary governmental unit has financial accountability. This is defined as the *reporting entity.* A governmental unit may have a variety of boards, commissions, authorities, or other component units under its control. **GASB Statement No. 14,** "The Financial Reporting Entity" **(GASB 14),** issued in 1991, states that financial accountability exists for these component units if the primary government unit appoints a majority of an organization's governing body and

(*a*) is able to impose its will on the organization, or

(*b*) possesses a financial benefit or assumes a financial burden for the organization.

The governmental reporting model for governmental units is specified in **GASB Statement 34,** "Basic Financial Statements—and Management's Discussion and Analysis—for State and Local Governments" **(GASB 34),** which was issued in 1999. Figure 17–2 presents the reporting model for general-purpose governmental units such as states, counties, or municipalities, as specified in **GASB 34.** Note that there are actually two levels of disclosure. The foundation for the financial reports will be the fund

---

FIGURE 17–2   The Government Reporting Model

1. Management's Discussion and Analysis (MD&A) (Required Supplementary Information)
2. Government-wide Financial Statements
   a. Statement of Net Assets
   b. Statement of Activities
3. Fund Financial Statements
   a. Governmental Funds
      1. Balance Sheet
      2. Statement of Revenues, Expenditures, and Changes in Fund Balance
   b. Proprietary Funds
      1. Statement of Net Assets (or Balance Sheet)
      2. Statement of Revenues, Expenses, and Changes in Fund Net Assets
      3. Statement of Cash Flows
   c. Fiduciary Funds
      1. Statement of Fiduciary Net Assets
      2. Statement of Changes in Fiduciary Net Assets
4. Notes to the Financial Statements
5. Required Supplementary Information (RSI)
   a. Budgetary Comparison Schedules
   b. Information About Infrastructure Assets

---

financial statements because governments will continue to use fund-based accounting to record transactions in the funds. This is due to the necessity to meet the legal requirements established for each fund. After preparing the fund financial statements, the government unit will prepare reconciliation schedules to go from the fund financial statements to the government-wide financial statements. Chapter 17, and the first part of Chapter 18, focuses on the fund financial statements. After completing the discussion of each of the fund types in Chapter 18, the government-wide financial statements are presented.

GASB 34 specified various required implementation dates for the new government reporting model based on total annual revenues as of the first fiscal year ending after June 15, 1999. Governments with total revenues of $100 million or more must adopt **GASB 34** beginning with fiscal years ending after June 15, 2002. Those governments with total revenues of $10 million or more, but less than $100 million, must adopt the new reporting model beginning with fiscal years ending after June 15, 2003. And those governments with total revenues below $10 million must apply **GASB 34** beginning with the fiscal year ending after June 15, 2004. However, early adoption is encouraged for **GASB 34.**

Fund Financial Statements: Governmental Funds

The financial reporting of the governmental funds and enterprise funds should separately report the major funds, not all funds. The general fund will always be specified as a major fund and will be presented in its own column. The other governmental or enterprise funds are considered major when both of the following criteria are met: *(a)* total assets, liabilities, revenues, or expenditures/expenses of that individual governmental or enterprise fund are at least 10 percent of the governmental or enterprise category, and *(b)* total assets, liabilities, revenues, or expenditures/expenses of the individual governmental or enterprise fund are at least 5 percent of the total for all governmental and enterprise funds combined. The government unit has the availability of classifying any specific fund as major, even if it does not meet the two criteria, if the government feels that separately reporting that fund will be useful to users of the financial statements. The nonmajor funds are aggregated and reported in a single column.

Two financial statements are required for governmental funds: *(a)* balance sheet, and *(b)* statement of revenues, expenditures, and changes in fund balance. The balance sheet for the governmental funds will report the assets, liabilities, and fund balances for each major fund, with the nonmajor funds aggregated. The focus of the balance sheet of the governmental funds is on the dollars available to be expended to fulfill the fund's objectives. Long-term, capital assets of the government, such as buildings, equipment, and so forth, and general long-term liabilities are not reported within the fund financial statements. However, the long-term capital assets and general long-term debt of the governmental entity are reported in the government-wide financial statements, as is illustrated in Chapter 18.

The format of the balance sheet for the governmental funds is:

Balance Sheet Information for Governmental Funds

Assets (listed)		$X,XXX
Total assets		$X,XXX
Liabilities and fund balances:		
Liabilities (listed)		$XXX
Fund balances:		
Reserved	$ X	
Unreserved	XX	XX
Total liabilities and fund balances		$X,XXX

Short term-debt, however, such as from vouchers payable or tax anticipation notes payable, are included in the governmental funds. Tax anticipation notes are a common short-term financing instrument of many governmental units and represent loans obtained using future taxes as collateral for the notes. Most states restrict these borrowings to those taxes that have been levied but not yet collected. These notes payable are paid from the first tax collections of the tax levy to which the notes are related. The account Fund Balance replaces the stockholders' equity section found on commercial operations balance sheets, because no common stock exists, and the general public is the theoretical owner of the fund. Fund Balance reports the difference between the assets and liabilities of the fund and is divided between Unreserved, which is the amount that may still be expended, and Reserved, which is the amount that is restricted from being expended. The various types of restricted reserves are presented later in this chapter.

Each of the major governmental funds must also prepare a statement of revenues, expenditures, and changes in fund balance. This is the primary operating statement of the fund and replaces the combined income statement and statement of retained earnings of a commercial enterprise. The statement of revenues, expenditures, and changes in fund balance has four major sections:

1. *Operating section.* The top section includes the revenues less expenditures for the period, with the difference shown as the excess (or deficiency) of revenues over expenditures.

2. *Other financing sources or uses.* This section includes nonrevenue items such as bond proceeds and interfund transfers.

3. *Special and extraordinary items.* This section presents extraordinary items that are both unusual and infrequent. Special items are transactions or events within the control of management that are either unusual or infrequent in occurrence. Note that the debt refundings of governmental debt are shown in the other financing sources and uses and are not extraordinary items for governmental accounting.

4. *Fund balance.* The bottom section presents both the beginning and the ending fund balance.

This major operating statement is referenced often during the discussion on governmental reporting. An understanding of its basic format, which follows, is important.

Statement of Revenues, Expenditures, and Changes in Fund Balance	
Revenues	$X,XXX
Expenditures	XXX
Excess of Revenues over Expenditures	$ XX
Other Financing Sources or Uses	X
Special Items	X
Net Change in Fund Balance	$ XX
Fund Balance—Beginning	XXX
Fund Balance—Ending	$ XXX

Measurement Focus and Basis of Accounting (MFBA)

The *basis of accounting* refers to the timing of recognizing a transaction for financial reporting purposes. For example, the cash basis recognizes revenue or expenditures when cash is received or paid. The accrual basis recognizes revenue or expenditures when the transaction or event takes place. The *modified accrual basis* is a hybrid system that includes some aspects of accrual accounting and some aspects of cash-basis accounting. The modified accrual basis is used in funds that have a flow of *current financial resources measurement focus*. This measurement focus is on the flow of current financial resources and the proper expendability of the resources for designated purposes and determination of the available resources remaining to be expended. Expenditures recognized under the modified accrual basis are the amounts that would normally be liquidated with expendable available financial resources. The five governmental funds have this focus.

The accrual basis method is used in funds that have a flow of *economic resources measurement focus*. This measurement focus is concerned with all economic resources available to a fund during a particular time period, thereby allowing for a comparison of revenues and expenses and a focus on maintenance of capital. The proprietary funds and fiduciary funds have this focus.

In addition, as is presented in Chapter 18, the government-wide financial statements are based on the accrual basis method. This necessitates a reconciliation schedule for those items that are accounted for under the modified accrual basis for governmental fund accounting to obtain the accrual basis amount that is reported on the government-wide financials. The reconciliation schedule is discussed in more detail in Chapter 18.

Basis of Accounting—Governmental Funds

The current financial resources measurement focus and the modified accrual basis of accounting are used for the governmental funds financial statements. The modified accrual basis is applied as follows:

1. *Revenue* is recorded in the accounting period in which it is both measurable and available to finance expenditures made during the current fiscal period.
2. *Expenditures* are recognized in the period in which the liabilities are both measurable and incurred, and are payable out of current financial resources.

Measurable means that the amount of the revenue or expenditure can be objectively determined. *Available* means due or past due and receivable within the current period, and collected within the current period or expected to be collected soon enough thereafter to be used to pay liabilities of the current period. The definition of "soon enough thereafter" has been stated for property taxes as a period of not more than 60 days after the end of the current fiscal period.

Recognition of Revenue.   When using the accrual method of accounting, revenues are recognized from exchange transactions (sales of goods or services) and from nonexchange transactions in which the government gives or receives value without directly receiving or giving equal value in exchange. In **GASB Statement 33,** "Accounting and Financial Reporting for Nonexchange Transactions" **(GASB 33),** issued in 1998, the GASB classified nonexchange transactions into four categories. **GASB 33** was written from the viewpoint of the accrual basis, and modifications are required to this statement when using the modified accrual basis of accounting. How revenues are recognized depends upon the category. The four categories are discussed below.

1. *Derived tax revenues,* resulting from assessments on exchange transactions. Examples are income taxes and sales taxes. For accrual accounting, governments should recognize the asset when the tax is imposed or when the resources are received, whichever comes first. Revenues would be recognized in the period in which the assets are recognized, provided the nonexchange transaction has occurred. Revenues received in advance would be deferred until the period of the exchange. Under the modified accrual system, an additional requirement is that the revenues are available to finance expenditures in the current period.

2. *Imposed nonexchange revenues,* resulting from assessments on nongovernmental entities, including individuals. Examples include property taxes and fines. The asset should be recognized in the period in which an enforceable legal claim to the resources arises or when the resources are received, whichever comes first. For property taxes, this is typically the lien date. Again, under the modified accrual system, an additional requirement is that the revenues are available to finance expenditures in the current period, although the 60-day rule applies to property taxes. That is, if the property taxes will be collected within 60 days after the end of the current period, they may be considered available this period. Resources received prior to the period in which they can be recognized as revenue should be reported as deferred revenues.

The next two categories have additional eligibility requirements that are often imposed by the providers of financial resources. These eligibility requirements must be met before the transaction can be completed; that is, before the receiving government unit can recognize an asset and the associated revenue. The four types of eligibility requirements are typically: *(a)* required characteristics of the recipient as specified by the provider of the financial resources, such as the receiving entity must be a school district, *(b)* time requirements for expending the resources; for example, the resources must all be expended within a specific fiscal period, *(c)* reimbursements for only costs determined to be allowable and incurred in conformity with a program's requirements, and *(d)* contingencies in which the recipient has met all the actions required by the provider. If all of the eligibility requirements imposed by the provider have been met by the recipient, then the provider should recognize the liability (or decrease in assets) and expense, and the recipient should recognize the receivable (or increase in assets) and revenue at the time the eligibility requirements have been met. The two categories are:

3. *Government-mandated nonexchange transactions,* resulting from when one government unit provides resources to a government unit at another level and requires the recipient to use the resources for a specific purpose. An example of this type is federal programs that state or local governments are required to perform.

4. *Voluntary nonexchange transactions,* resulting from legislative or contractual agreements, other than exchanges. Examples include certain grants and private donations.

GASB Statement No. 36, "Recipient Reporting for Certain Shared Nonexchange Revenues" **(GASB 36),** issued in 2000, amended **GASB 33** for government-mandated and voluntary nonexchange situations in which a providing government provides part of its own derived tax units to recipients. Typically, the providing government provides the recipients with a periodic report of the amount of shared revenues the recipients should anticipate. **GASB 36** states that if the notification from the providing government is not available in a timely manner, the recipient governments should use a reasonable estimate of the amount to be accrued and not wait until the actual receipt of the cash resources.

The following examples present the accounting, under the modified accrual basis of accounting, as used in preparing the governmental funds financial statements.

1. *Property taxes.* Property taxes are recorded as revenue when the taxes are levied and the resources are available to the governmental unit. The receivable is recorded and revenue is accrued for those taxes applicable to and collectible within the current fiscal period, or within a short time after the end of the fiscal period. Generally, taxes are billed in the period of the levy. A *levy* gives the governmental entity the legal right to collect property taxes and to attach a legally enforceable lien against any property on which taxes are not paid. For example, a city council approves a budget, which then becomes the legal basis for imposing a property tax levy. The city clerk then files the budget with the appropriate property tax–collecting agent such as the county treasurer's office, which determines the necessary tax rate and sends out the tax bills. The levy is for a specific year and for the dollar amount determined by multiplying the assessed valuation of the property by the tax rate. The property owner pays the tax, which is then forwarded by the county treasurer to the city for expenditure.

NCGA Interpretation No. 3, "Revenue Recognition-Property Taxes" **(NCGA 3),** specifies that property taxes must be collectible within a maximum of 60 days after the end of the current fiscal period to be recognized as revenue in the current period. Taxes collectible 60 days after the current period ends are deferred and accounted for as next period's revenue.

Some governmental entities bill property owners in advance of the fiscal year to which the revenue is to be applied. If property taxes receivable are not available for current expenditures, or if they are collected in advance of the year for which they are levied, they are recorded as a credit in a deferred revenue account such as Deferred Revenue-Property Tax. The deferred amounts are reclassified as revenue in the period the taxes become available for current expenditure.

Revenue from another governmental unit or tax-exempt entity in lieu of taxes, such as a payment by a university to a city for police and fire protection, should be accrued and recorded as revenue when it becomes billable.

Revenue from property taxes should be recorded net of any uncollectibles or abatements. The Property Taxes Receivable account is debited for the full amount of the taxes levied, with estimated uncollectibles recorded separately in an allowance account reported as a contra account to the receivable.

2. *Interest on investments and delinquent taxes.* Interest on investments or delinquent property taxes is accrued in the period in which the interest is earned and available to finance expenditures in the period. The governmental funds may temporarily invest available cash in interest-generating financial instruments such as certificates of deposit and federal or state securities. Governmental entities should carefully determine the credit risks and market risks of possible investments in order to minimize their potential loss. Governmental funds report their own current and long-term financial investments, and any accrued interest receivable, as assets of the funds.

3. *Income taxes and sales taxes.* These derived tax revenues are recognized as revenue under the modified accrual basis of accounting in the period in which the tax is imposed, or when the resources are received, whichever comes first. And, these taxes must be available to finance expenditures made during the current fiscal period before recognition as revenue for the period. Income tax revenue should be reported net of any anticipated refunds to taxpayers. Sales taxes collected by another governmental unit (e.g., the state government) but not yet distributed should be accrued prior to receipt by the governmental unit to which they will be distributed (e.g., a city) if the taxes are both measurable and available for expenditure. Measurability in this case is based on an estimate of the sales taxes to be received, and availability is based on the ability of the governing entity (the city) to obtain current resources through credit by using future sales tax collections as collateral for the loan.

4. *Miscellaneous revenue.* Miscellaneous revenues such as license fees, fines, parking meter revenue, and charges for services are generally recorded when the cash is received because these cannot be predicted accurately.

5. *Grants, entitlements, and shared revenue.* These are resources received from other governmental units. *Grants* are contributions from another governmental unit to be used for a specified purpose, activity, or facility. *Entitlements* are payments local governments are entitled to receive as determined by the federal government. *Shared revenue* is from revenue such as taxes on the retail sale of gasoline collected by the state. This revenue is levied by one governmental unit but shared with others on some predetermined basis. Grants are recognized as revenue in the period in which all eligibility requirements have been met. This may be at the point the grant is authorized, but, in practice, some governmental units wait until the cash is received because the grant may be withdrawn by the grantor. Some grants are made to reimburse a governmental unit for expenditures made in accordance with legal requirements. The revenue from

such grants should be recognized only when the expenditure is made and all other eligibility requirements have been met.

Proceeds from the sale of bonds are not revenue! These proceeds are reported as other financing sources on the statement of revenues, expenditures, and changes in fund balance. Although bond sales do increase the resources available for expenditure, bonds must be repaid, whereas revenue of the governmental unit does not need to be repaid.

Recognition of Expenditures.   Under the modified accrual basis of accounting, expenditures are recorded in the period in which the related liability is both measurable and incurred. Specific examples are as follows:

1. Costs for personal services, such as wages and salaries, are generally recorded in the period paid because they are normal, recurring expenditures of a governmental unit.
2. Goods and services obtained from outside the governmental entity are recorded as expenditures in the period in which they are received.
3. Capital outlays for equipment, buildings, and other long-term facilities are recorded as expenditures in the period of acquisition.
4. Interest on long-term debt is recorded in the period in which it is legally payable.

Basis of Accounting—Proprietary Funds

The two major proprietary funds are the internal service fund and the enterprise fund. Proprietary funds are established for governmental operations that have a management focus of income determination and capital maintenance; therefore, the accrual method is used to account for these funds in the same manner as for profit-seeking corporate entities. Proprietary funds record their own long-term assets, and depreciation is recognized on these assets. Long-term debt is recorded and interest is accrued as it is for commercial operations.

Basis of Accounting—Fiduciary Funds

The accrual basis of accounting is used for all fiduciary funds. Agency funds are those for which the governing unit is the temporary custodian of these resources. Agency funds have only assets and liabilities; no fund equity, revenue, or expenditures are used. An example of an agency fund is a county's billing and collecting taxes on behalf of other governmental entities, such as a city and a school district. After collection is completed on the "tax roll," the county properly distributes the taxes in accordance with each governmental entity's approved levy.

For fiduciary trust funds, the economic resources measurement focus and the accrual basis of accounting is used. Note that the fiduciary trust funds include those funds in which both the principal and income may be used for the benefit of specific individuals, organizations, or other governments, in accordance with the terms under which the trust fund was established. Agency and trust funds are discussed in depth in Chapter 18.

Budgetary Aspects of Governmental Operations

Budgets are used in governmental accounting to assist in management control and to provide the legal authority to levy taxes, collect revenue, and make expenditures in accordance with the budget. Budgets establish the objectives and priorities of governing units.

For state governments, budgets are proposed by governors and debated by the legislative bodies. After passage, the budget usually becomes part of the fiscal period's state law. For local governments, the mayor or the major administrator may propose the budget. Public hearings and discussions of the budget are then held by governing boards such as the city council, county board, or township board prior to the adoption of the final budget.

A governmental unit may have several types of budgets, including the following:

1. *Operating budgets.* Operating budgets specify expected revenue from the various sources provided by law. The operating budget includes expected expenditures for various line items, such as payrolls of employees, supplies, and goods and services to be obtained from outside the governing unit. Operating budgets are used in the general fund, special revenue funds, and sometimes the debt service funds.
2. *Capital budgets.* A capital budget is prepared to provide information about proposed construction projects such as new buildings or street projects. Capital budgets are used in the capital projects funds.

Although budgets may be prepared for proprietary funds, these budgets do not serve as a primary control vehicle. Budgets in the proprietary funds are advisory in much the same way budgets are used in commercial entities.

Recording the Operating Budget

Budgets are such an important control vehicle that those governmental funds with legally adopted annual operating budgets should enter their budgets into the formal accounting records. Capital budgets are not normally entered into the formal accounting records. Recording the operating budgets permits better management control and facilitates a year-end comparison of budgeted and actual amounts. This comparison is part of the required supplementary information for the government reporting model for the funds that must have operating budgets. A budget to actual comparison provides an assessment of management's stewardship of the governmental entity and allows citizens and others to determine if the governmental entity remained within its operating budgetary limits.

To help understand the process of accounting for operating budgets, this text uses the technique illustrated in the *Governmental Accounting, Auditing, and Financial Reporting* (GAAFR),[4] in which the budgetary accounts are identified with all capital letters. Capitalization of the budgetary accounts clearly separates the budgetary nominal accounts from the operating accounts of the governmental unit. Although budgetary accounts are not capitalized in actual practice, this convention is helpful in learning the following material.

---

[4]*Governmental Accounting, Auditing and Financial Reporting,* Governmental Finance Officers Association (Chicago), updated periodically.

The recording of the operating budget for the general fund is shown with the following example. Assume that at January 1, 20X1, the first day of the new fiscal period, the city council of Barb City approves the operating budget for the general fund, providing for $900,000 in revenue and $850,000 in expenditures. Approval of the budget provides the legal authority to levy the local property taxes and to appropriate resources for the expenditures. The term *appropriation* is the legal description of the authority to expend resources. The entry made in the general fund's accounting records on this date is as follows:

January 1, 20X1
(1)	ESTIMATED REVENUES CONTROL	900,000	
	APPROPRIATIONS CONTROL		850,000
	BUDGETARY FUND BALANCE UNRESERVED		50,000
	Record general fund budget for year.		

Note the word CONTROL used as part of the account titles. In governmental accounting, control accounts often are used in the major journals, with subsidiary accounts recording the detail behind each control account. This method is similar to a commercial entity's using a control account for its accounts receivable and then using subsidiary ledgers for the specific customer transactions. Throughout this chapter, the control account level is illustrated in order to focus on the major issues. In practice, detailed accounting is maintained for each separate classification of revenue and appropriation, either in the major journal or in a subsidiary ledger. The AICPA uses both control-level accounts and budgetary accounts on the Uniform CPA Examination, although it does not capitalize the letters of the budgetary accounts used in the exam.

The ESTIMATED REVENUES CONTROL account is an *anticipatory asset;* that is, the governmental unit anticipates receiving resources from the revenue sources listed in the budget. The APPROPRIATIONS CONTROL account is an *anticipatory liability;* that is, the governmental unit anticipates incurring expenditures and liabilities for the budgeted amount. The excess of estimated revenues over anticipated expenditures is the budget surplus and is recorded to BUDGETARY FUND BALANCE UNRESERVED. Some approved budgets have budget deficits in which expected expenditures exceed anticipated revenue. These budgets are recorded with a debit to BUDGETARY FUND BALANCE UNRESERVED.

Recording the budget in the governmental entity's books makes the budget a formal accounting control mechanism for the fiscal period. In addition, having the budget in the accounting records provides the necessary information for the budgetary comparison schedules that are part of the required supplementary information (RSI) footnotes required by the government reporting model in **GASB 34.** At the end of the year, after the appropriate financial statements have been prepared, all the budgetary accounts are closed.

Accounting for Expenditures

The governmental funds use a variety of controls over expenditures to ensure that each expenditure is made in accordance with any legal restrictions on the fund.

The Expenditure Process

The expenditure process in governmental accounting comprises the following sequential steps: appropriation, encumbrance, expenditure, and disbursement.

Step 1. Appropriation. The budget provides the appropriating authority to make future expenditures. Operating budgets are prepared for the general, special revenue, and often the debt service funds. The capital projects fund prepares capital budgets.

The appropriation was recorded in the budget entry made previously in entry (1) for the general fund of Barb City. Recall that a total of $850,000 in anticipated expenditures was approved in the budget.

Step 2. Encumbrance. An *encumbrance* is a reservation of part of the budgetary appropriation and is recognized at the time an order is placed for goods or services. Encumbrances are a unique element of governmental accounting. Their purpose is to ensure that the expenditures within a period do not exceed the budgeted appropriations. The appropriation level was established by the approved budget and sets the legal maximum that may be expended for each budgeted item. The managers of the governmental unit must be sure that they do not exceed this budgetary authority. Thus, encumbrances provide a control system and safeguard for governmental unit administrators.

When an order is placed for goods or services to be received from outside the governmental unit, the budgeted appropriation is encumbered for the estimated cost of the order. Encumbrances are of greatest use when an order is placed and a period of time expires before delivery. Payroll costs, immaterial costs, and costs for goods acquired from within the governmental entity typically are not encumbered because these are normal and recurring and the managers of the governmental unit are able to predict these costs based on past experiences and other administrative controls, such as employment agreements.

A sensible approach should be used with an encumbrance system. For example, it is not necessary to establish an individual encumbrance when an employee orders a pad of paper. Rather, a blanket purchase order with a maximum dollar amount, for example, a total of $500, should be prepared and encumbered, and then it can serve as the control for small, routine supply purchases. Encumbrances provide the unit administrators with an important accounting control to fulfill their responsibilities to manage within an approved budget.

To illustrate encumbrance accounting, assume that on August 1, 20X1, Barb City completed a purchase order (PO) for goods from an outside vendor that are estimated to cost $15,000. The entry to record this application of part of the budgeted appropriation authority for the period is as follows:

August 1, 20X1		
(2) ENCUMBRANCES	15,000	
BUDGETARY FUND BALANCE RESERVED		
FOR ENCUMBRANCES		15,000
Record order for goods estimated to cost $15,000.		

Note that the ENCUMBRANCES account is a budgetary account that is reserving part of the appropriation authority of the budget. For detailed accounting, governmental entities often maintain a subsidiary ledger including accounts for specific types of encumbrances to correspond to each specific type of appropriation. For purposes of this illustration, the single title ENCUMBRANCES is used to indicate a control-level account to focus attention on the major aspects of governmental accounting. It is important to note that the BUDGETARY FUND BALANCE RESERVED FOR ENCUMBRANCES is a *reservation (or restriction) of the budgetary fund balance* and not an actual liability.

Step 3. Expenditure.   An *expenditure* and a corresponding liability are recorded when the governmental entity receives the goods or services ordered in step 2 above. When the goods are received, the encumbrance entry is reversed for the amount encumbered and the expenditure is recorded for the actual cost to the governmental entity. Although the actual cost is typically very close to the encumbered amount, some differences may exist because of partially completed orders, less expensive replacements, or unforeseen costs. Assume that the goods are received on September 20, 20X1, at an actual cost of $14,000. The entries to reverse the encumbrance for the goods and to record the actual expenditures are as follows:

September 20, 20X1
(3)	BUDGETARY FUND BALANCE RESERVED FOR		
	ENCUMBRANCES	15,000	
	ENCUMBRANCES		15,000
	Reverse encumbrances for goods received.		
(4)	Expenditures	14,000	
	Vouchers Payable		14,000
	Receive goods at cost of $14,000		

At any time, the remaining appropriating authority available to the fund managers can be determined by the following equation:

$$\text{Appropriating authority remaining available} = \text{APPROPRIATIONS} - (\text{ENCUMBRANCES} + \text{Expenditures})$$

Step 4. Disbursement.   A *disbursement* is the payment of cash for expenditures. Disbursements usually must be approved by the governing board or council as an additional level of control over expenditures.

Virtually all governmental entities use a comprehensive voucher system to control cash outflows. The governing board receives a schedule of vouchers to be approved for payment by vote of the board. This is usually one of the early agenda items in any board or council meeting as a vote is taken to "pay all bills." Checks are then written and delivered to the supplier of the goods. If the Barb City council approved the voucher at its October 8 meeting and a check was prepared in the amount of $14,000 and mailed on October 15, 20X1, the following entry would record the disbursement:

October 15, 20X1
(5)	Vouchers Payable	14,000	
	Cash		14,000
	Payment of voucher for goods received.		

Classification of Expenditure Transactions and Accounts

Governmental accounting places many controls over expenditures, and much of the financial reporting focuses on the various aspects of an expenditure. Expenditures should be classified by fund, function (or program), organizational unit, activity, character, and principal classes of objects. Figure 17–3 describes the major expenditure classifications.

Many governmental units have a comprehensive chart of accounts, with specific coding digits, that provide the basis for classifying each expenditure. For example, an

FIGURE 17–3 | **Major Expenditure Classifications for Governmental Funds**

Classification	Description
Fund	The fund is identified to show the specific source of the expenditure. For example, the general fund would be noted for expenditures from that fund.
Character	Character classifications are based primarily on the period the expenditures are anticipated to benefit. Four major character classifications are current, capital outlay, debt service, and intergovernmental.
Function (or program)	Functions are group-related activities directed at accomplishing a major service or regulatory responsibility. Standard classifications of function include general governmental; public safety; highway and streets; sanitation; health and welfare; culture and recreation; and education.
Organizational unit	Classifying by organization unit maintains accountability by each unit director. The organization unit is determined by the governmental unit's organization chart. For example, public safety could be broken down into police, fire, corrections, protective inspection (such as plumbing and electrical code inspections), and other protection (such as flood control, traffic engineering, and examination of licensed occupations).
Activity	Activities within a function are recorded to maintain a record of the efficiency of each activity. For example, the police function could be broken down into the following activities: police administration, crime control and investigation, traffic control, police training, support service (such as communication services and ambulance services), special detail services, and police station and building maintenance. Each of these activities could be broken down further, if desired.
Object class	Object class is a grouping of types of items purchased or services obtained. For example, operating expenditures include personal services, purchased and contractual services, and commodities. Each of these objects could be further broken down, depending on the information needs of the governing entity. For example, purchased services could include utility services, cleaning services (such as custodial, lawn care, and snow plowing), repair and maintenance services, rentals, construction services, and other purchased services, such as insurance or printing.

expenditure journal entry might specify the expenditure account to be charged as number 421.23-110. The chart of accounts shows that the 421.23 account is for public safety: police—crime control and investigation—patrol, as follows:

420. Public safety
    421. Police
        421.2   Crime control and investigation
            421.23   Patrol

The -110 suffix indicates that this expenditure is for personal services in the form of salaries and wages for regular employees. It is not unusual for some accounting systems to have 11- to 14-digit accounts classifying each individual transaction. The level of specificity in the chart of accounts depends upon the information needs of the particular governing entity. Classifying information with such specificity allows the governing entity to maintain complete database control over the expenditure information which it can use at any time in aggregate or relational analysis. For the examples in this chapter, only the expenditure control level is presented; in practice, a complete specification of the expenditure is made.

Outstanding Encumbrances at the End of the Fiscal Period

In the Barb City example given previously, the goods were received within the same fiscal period in which they were ordered. But what happens if the goods are ordered in one fiscal year and received in the next year? In this case, the encumbrance is not reversed before the end of the fiscal period.

Accounting for these outstanding encumbrances depends on the policy of the governmental unit. The government may allow outstanding encumbrances to lapse; that is, the governmental unit is not required to honor these encumbrances carried over to the new year, and the new year's budget must rebudget them. In virtually all cases, the encumbrances will be rebudgeted and honored; however, this policy specifically recognizes the legal authority of the new governing board to determine its own expenditures. A second method is to carry over the encumbrances as nonlapsing spending authority. This method recognizes the practical aspects of encumbrances outstanding at the end of a fiscal period. Either method may be used in governmental accounting.

To illustrate the differences between the lapsing and nonlapsing methods of accounting for encumbrances, assume the following:

1. On August 1, 20X1, $15,000 of goods are ordered and an appropriate entry is made to record the encumbrance.
2. The goods have not yet been received on December 31, 20X1, the end of the fiscal period.
3. The goods are received on February 1, 20X2, at an actual cost of $14,000.

Figure 17–4 presents a comparison of the journal entries that would be required under each of the two methods of accounting for unfilled encumbrances at year-end.

Outstanding Encumbrances Lapse at Year-End. The closing entries on December 31, 20X1, close the remaining budgetary encumbrances and establish a reserve of the actual fund balance on the December 31, 20X1, balance sheet. Although the 1994 GAAFR recommends that a reserve for lapsing encumbrances be reported on the balance sheet, the GASB codification allows the alternative of just footnote disclosure of lapsing open orders at year-end that are expected to be honored in the next fiscal period. If just footnote disclosure is used, the governmental unit would not have the second closing entry which establishes the reserve of the actual fund balance on the balance sheet.

At the beginning of 20X2, the new governing board must decide if it will honor the outstanding encumbrances by including them in the 20X2 budgeted appropriations. If the governing board decides to honor the outstanding purchase orders, an entry is made on January 1, 20X2, to establish budgetary control over the expenditure. A "fresh start" new spending authority is established, and the sequence of entries continues as if this is a new order and purchase completed during 20X2.

If the new governing board decides not to honor outstanding encumbrances, then the following entry is made on January 1, 20X2, to record the cancellation of the open encumbrance:

January 1, 20X2
(6) Fund Balance Reserved for Encumbrances	15,000	
Unreserved Fund Balance		15,000

Eliminate reserve for outstanding encumbrances not being renewed.

FIGURE 17–4   Comparison of Accounting for Lapsing and Nonlapsing Encumbrances at Year-End

Item	Outstanding Encumbrances Lapse at Year-End			Outstanding Encumbrances Do Not Lapse at Year-End		
December 31, 20X1:						
Close remaining budgetary encumbrances	BUDGETARY FUND BALANCE RESERVED FOR ENCUMBRANCES	15,000		BUDGETARY FUND BALANCE RESERVED FOR ENCUMBRANCES	15,000	
	ENCUMBRANCES		15,000	ENCUMBRANCES		15,000
Reserve actual fund balance for outstanding encumbrances at end of 20X1 expected to be honored in 20X1.	Unreserved Fund Balance	15,000		Unreserved Fund Balance	15,000	
	Fund Balance Reserved for Encumbrances		15,000	Fund Balance Reserved for Encumbrances		15,000
January 2, 20X2:						
Reverse prior year encumbrance reserve	Fund Balance Reserved for Encumbrances	15,000				
	Unreserved Fund Balance		15,000			
Establish budgetary control over encumbrances renewed from prior period	ENCUMBRANCES	15,000				
	BUDGETARY FUND BALANCE RESERVED FOR ENCUMBRANCES		15,000			
Reclassify reserve from prior year				Fund Balance Reserved for Encumbrances	15,000	
				Fund Balance Reserved for Encumbrances—20X1		15,000
February 1, 20X2:						
Receive goods and remove budgetary reserve for encumbrances	BUDGETARY FUND BALANCE RESERVED FOR ENCUMBRANCES	15,000				
	ENCUMBRANCES		15,000			
Record actual expenditure for goods received	Expenditures	14,000		Expenditures—20X1	14,000	
	Vouchers Payable		14,000	Vouchers Payable		14,000
December 31, 20X2:						
Close expenditures account	Unreserved Fund Balance	14,000		Fund Balance Reserved for Encumbrances—20X1	15,000	
	Expenditures		14,000	Expenditures—20X1		14,000
				Unreserved Fund Balance		1,000

If the governmental unit used only footnote disclosure for open encumbrances at the end of 20X1, then no entry would be required. The governmental unit would simply cancel the order with the external vendor.

Outstanding Encumbrances at Year-End Are Nonlapsing.   Some governing units carry over the appropriations authority from prior periods as nonlapsing encumbrances. In this case, the budget for the second fiscal period does *not* show these carryovers. Some governmental accountants feel this method is realistic for many situations in which orders placed with outside vendors cannot easily be canceled.

The 20X2 year-end closing entries presented in Figure 17–4 show the required reservation of the actual fund balance. Note that these are the same two entries as under the lapsing method with balance sheet recognition of the reserve of the fund balance. The differences between the two methods become apparent during the second fiscal period. Under the nonlapsing method, it is important to identify separately expenditures made from spending authority carried over from prior periods. Typically this is done in a reclassification entry on the first day of the second fiscal period, which dates the Fund Balance Reserved for Encumbrances. No budgetary entry is made in the second year because the appropriation authority comes from the first year's budget. When the goods are received, the expenditures account is also dated to indicate that the expenditure authority emanated from 20X1.

At the end of 20X2, the Expenditures—20X1 account is closed directly to the Fund Balance Reserved for Encumbrances—20X1. Note that the $1,000 difference between the actual cost of $14,000 and the reserved amount of $15,000 is closed to Unreserved Fund Balance because the actual cost is less than the amount encumbered from the prior year's appropriation authority. If the actual cost is greater than the reserve, then the difference must be approved as part of the appropriation authority for 20X2.

Key Observation from the Illustration. Regardless of the specific method of accounting for unlapsed encumbrances, it is important to note that in this case the statement of revenues, expenditures, and changes in fund balance will report no expenditures in 20X1, and $14,000 of expenditures in 20X2. The method of accounting for open encumbrances at year-end is based on the governmental unit's budgetary policy, and both methods are found in practice. The comprehensive example presented later in this chapter uses the lapsing method because of its widespread use.

Expenditures for Inventory

Most governmental units maintain a small amount of inventory in office supplies. A first issue is to determine which of two methods should be followed to account for the expenditure of inventories. The first method recognizes the entire expenditure for inventory in the period the supplies are acquired. This is called the *purchase* method. The second method is the *consumption* method and recognizes expenditures for only the amount of inventory used in the period. The specific method to follow depends on the policy of the governing unit and how inventory expenditures are included in the budget.

A second issue is whether or not inventory should be shown as an asset on the balance sheet of the governmental funds. Inventory is not an expendable asset; that is, it may not be spent as the governing entity wishes. **NCGA 1** states that inventory should be shown on the balance sheets for governmental funds if the amount of inventory is material. Immaterial inventories need not be shown on the balance sheet. If the inventory is material, it is presented as an asset on the balance sheet; an amount equal to the inventory also should be shown as a reservation of the fund balance, indicating that that amount is no longer expendable.

Figure 17–5 presents the entries to account for inventories under both the purchase method and the consumption method. The illustration assumes that Barb City acquires $2,000 of inventory on November 1, 20X1, having held no inventory previously. On December 31, 20X1, the end of Barb City's fiscal year, a physical count shows $1,400 still in stock. During 20X2, $900 of this inventory is used, resulting in a $500 remaining balance of supplies on December 31, 20X2.

FIGURE 17–5   Comparison of Accounting for Inventories—Purchase versus Consumption Method

Item	Purchase Method of Accounting		Consumption Method of Accounting	
November 1, 20X1:				
Record acquisition of $2,000 of inventory.	Expenditures	2,000	Expenditures	2,000
	Vouchers Payable	2,000	Vouchers Payable	2,000
December 31, 20X1:				
Recognize ending inventory of $1,400.	Inventory of Supplies	1,400	Inventory of Supplies	1,400
	Fund Balance Reserved		Expenditures	1,400
	for Inventories	1,400		
			Unreserved Fund Balance	1,400
			Fund Balance Reserved	
			for Inventories	1,400
December 31, 20X2:				
Record remaining inventory of $500, with $900 of supplies having been consumed during 20X2.	Fund Balance Reserved		Expenditures	900
	for Inventories	900	Inventory of Supplies	900
	Inventory of Supplies	900		
			Fund Balance Reserved	
			for Inventories	900
			Unreserved Fund Balance	900

Purchase Method of Accounting for Inventories. Under the purchase method, the entire amount of inventory acquired is charged to Expenditures in the period acquired. On December 31, 20X1, the end of the fiscal year, an adjusting entry is made to recognize the $1,400 remaining inventory as an asset and to restrict the fund balance for the nonexpendable portion applicable to inventories.

The expenditure of $2,000 is closed into Unreserved Fund Balance for 20X1 in a closing entry made at the end of the fiscal year. The December 31, 20X1, balance sheet includes the inventory of supplies as an asset in the amount of $1,400, and Fund Balance Reserved for Inventories is shown as a fund balance reserve for $1,400. The 20X1 operating statement shows a $2,000 expenditure for supplies.

At the end of 20X2, an adjusting entry is made to recognize the use of the $900 of supplies of the $1,400 remaining from the 20X1 purchase. This entry reduces the reservation of the fund balance and decreases inventory. At the end of 20X2, Inventory of Supplies is $500, and Fund Balance Reserved for Inventories is $500, for the remaining unused supplies.

In summary, the expenditure of $2,000 is recognized in the period in which the supplies are purchased. No expenditures are recognized in subsequent periods, although some of the supplies are used in those periods.

Consumption Method of Accounting for Inventories. Under the consumption method, expenditures for a period are reported just for the amount consumed. In this case, the budget for the period should be based on the expected amount of use so the budgeted and actual amounts compared at the end of the year are on the same basis.

A net expenditure of $600 ($2,000 − $1,400) for supplies used is reported in 20X1, the year the supplies were acquired. With $500 of inventory remaining at the end of 20X2, an expenditure of $900 is reported in the 20X2 operating statement, to show the amount of supplies consumed during 20X2. The consumption method relates the expenditures with the use of the inventory.

A comparison of selected account balances under the purchase method and consumption method shows the different amounts that are reported under these two methods:

	Purchase Method	*Consumption Method*
20X1:		
Expenditures	$2,000	$ 600
Inventory of Supplies	1,400	1,400
20X2:		
Expenditures	0	900
Inventory of Supplies	500	500

Note that the choice of methods has no effect on the balance sheet amounts; the only effect is on the period in which the expenditures for inventory are reported.

Both inventory methods are used in practice. The method to be used by a specific governmental unit depends on its budgeting policy. If the governmental unit includes all inventory acquisitions in its appropriations for the period, the purchase method should be used. If the governmental unit includes just the expected amount of inventory to be used during a period in that period's appropriations, the consumption method should be used.

Accounting for Fixed Assets

Governmental entities may acquire equipment that has an economic life of more than one year. Accounting for this acquisition depends on which fund expends the resources for the acquisition. The governmental funds are concerned with the expendability and control over available resources, and account for the acquisitions of equipment as expenditures. In the governmental funds, the entire amount of the cost of the acquisition of equipment and other capital assets is recognized as an expenditure in the year the asset is acquired. No capital assets are recorded in the general fund; they are treated as expenditures of the period.

The proprietary funds are concerned with capital maintenance and account for acquisitions of capital assets in the same manner as used in commercial entities. Thus, the accounting for the purchase of a capital asset is different in the five governmental funds from that used in the proprietary funds.

For example, assume that Barb City acquires a truck. The acquisition is made from the resources of, and accounted for in, the general fund. The encumbrance is $12,000, but the actual cost is $12,500 because of minor modifications required by the city.

The general fund makes the following entries to account for the acquisition of the truck:

(7)	ENCUMBRANCES	12,000	
	BUDGETARY FUND BALANCE RESERVED		
	FOR ENCUMBRANCES		12,000
	Order truck at estimated cost of $12,000.		
(8)	BUDGETARY FUND BALANCE RESERVED		
	FOR ENCUMBRANCES	12,000	
	ENCUMBRANCES		12,000
	Cancel reserve for truck received.		

(9) Expenditures	12,500	
Vouchers Payable		12,500
Receive truck at actual cost of $12,500.		

The truck is not recorded as an asset in the general fund; it is an expenditure in this fund. A schedule of the acquisition of capital assets, acquired by any fund, should be maintained, but that record is only for the government-wide financial statements which do report the assets of a government unit.

Long-Term Debt and Capital Leases

Commercial, profit-seeking businesses recognize long-term debt and capital leases as noncurrent liabilities. The debt or capital lease is entered into to earn income, and the liability is recognized under the flow of all economic resources measurement model. However, accounting for long-term liabilities in governmental funds is directly affected by the flow of current financial resources measurement focus model.

The governmental funds, which include the general fund, record the proceeds from a bond issue as a debit to Cash and a credit to Bond Issue Proceeds, an other financing source. Bond issue proceeds are not revenue because the bonds must be repaid. Other financing sources are shown in the middle section of the statement of revenues, expenditures, and other changes in fund balances. Bonds are not reported on the governmental funds' balance sheets but rather are reported only on the government-wide financial statements.

Capital leases are accounted for similar to long-term debt. If a proprietary fund (e.g., internal service or enterprise fund) enters in a capital lease, the lease is accounted for similarly to the methods used by commercial, profit-seeking entities, with the recording of an asset and a lease liability. However, if a governmental fund (e.g., general fund) enters into a capital lease, the capital lease is accounted for similarly to a bond.

Investments

Some governmental entities maintain investments in stock or bond securities. The purpose of these investments typically is to obtain an investment return on available resources. **GASB Statement No. 31**, "Accounting and Financial Reporting for Certain Investments and for External Investment Pools" (**GASB 31**), established a general rule of fair market valuation for certain investments held by a governmental entity. The following investments are to be valued at fair value, if determinable, in the asset section of the balance sheet for the governmental entity: (1) investments in debt securities; (2) investments in equity securities (other than those accounted for under the equity method as provided for in **APB 18**), including option contracts, stock warrants, and stock rights; (3) investments in open-end mutual funds; (4) investment pools in which a governmental entity combines with other investors; and (5) interest-earning investment contracts in which the value is affected by market (interest rate) changes. The periodic changes in the fair value of investments should be recognized as an element of investment income in the operating statement (or other statement of activities) of the governmental entity and reported along with any realized gains or losses resulting from investments.

Interfund Activities

A basic concept in governmental accounting is that each fund is a separate entity and has separate sources of resources, sometimes including the power to levy and collect

FIGURE 17–6   Interfund Transactions and Transfers

Item	Entry in General Fund		Entry in Other Fund	
1. Interfund loan			INTERNAL SERVICE FUND:	
	Due from Internal Service Fund	4,000	Cash	4,000
	Cash	4,000	Due to General Fund	4,000
	Cash	4,000	Due to General Fund	4,000
	Due from Internal Service Fund	4,000	Cash	4,000
2. Interfund service			INTERNAL SERVICE FUND:	
provided and	Expenditures	100	Due from General Fund	100
used	Due to Internal Service Fund	100	Charge for Services	100
	Due to Internal Service Fund	100	Cash	100
	Cash	100	Due from General Fund	100
3. Interfund transfer			CAPITAL PROJECTS FUND:	
	Other Financing Uses—		Cash	10,000
	Transfer Out to Capital		Other Financing	
	Projects Fund	10,000	Sources—Transfer In	
	Cash	10,000	from General Fund	10,000
4. Interfund			CAPITAL PROJECTS FUND:	
reimbursement	Cash	3,000	Expenditures	3,000
	Expenditures	3,000	Cash	3,000

taxes. The revenues of each fund must then be expended in accordance with the budget and restrictions established by law. Because a single governmental entity has a number of separate funds, it sometimes becomes necessary to transfer resources from one fund to another. ***Interfund activities*** are resource flows between fund entities. In a consolidated financial statement for a commercial entity, intercompany transactions are eliminated in order to report only the effect of transactions with external entities. Governmental accounting, on the other hand, requires the separate maintenance and reporting of interfund items. The governing body must approve any interfund transfers and transactions in order to provide a public record and to prevent distortion of fund uses. Many governmental entities include interfund activities anticipated during a fiscal year in the operating budgets for the year. Budgetary entries for interfund activities are illustrated in the comprehensive example of Sol City presented later in this chapter. Interfund transfers must be accounted for carefully to ensure that the legal and budgetary restrictions are followed and that resources intended for one fund are not used in another.

GASB 34 established four types of interfund activities, as follows: (1) interfund loans, (2) interfund services provided and used, (3) interfund transfers, and (4) interfund reimbursements. The four interfund items are discussed below and illustrated in Figure 17–6.

(1) Interfund Loans

State law may allow lending or borrowing activities between funds. The loans must be repaid, usually within one year or before the end of the fiscal period. Loans and advances are not shown on a fund's statement of revenues, expenditures, and changes in fund balance; however, all outstanding loans or advances must be shown on the balance sheet as payables or receivables. Interest usually is not charged on interfund financing arrangements. If interest is charged, it is accounted for in the funds in the same manner as other interest income or expense.

Some governmental entities distinguish between short-term and long-term financing arrangements by using the term "Advances to (or from)" to denote a long-term agreement and "Due to (or from)" for a short-term agreement.

The illustration of an interfund financing transaction in Figure 17–6 assumes Barb City's general fund loans the internal service fund $4,000 for two months. The general fund reports a receivable for the amount of the loan until the loan is repaid.

(2) Interfund Services Provided and Used

These interfund activities are transactions that would be treated as revenue, expenditures, or expenses if they involved parties external to the governmental unit. These interfund activities are still reported as revenue, expenditures, or expenses but are different because they are entirely within the governmental unit. These interfund activities are often normal and recurring items, usually involving at least one proprietary fund. Three examples are as follows:

1. The general fund purchases goods or services from an internal service or enterprise fund.
2. Payments are made to the general fund from the enterprise fund for fire and police protection.
3. A transfer of resources from the general fund to the pension trust fund to pay for the city's cost of pension benefits for its employees. This is a cost associated with employee services provided to the city and is therefore an expenditure of the general fund.

Usually these transfers involve the recognition of a receivable or payable because of the time lag between the purchase of the services and the disbursement of funds. A "Due to (or from)" account is used for short-term interfund receivables and payables rather than a formal Vouchers Payable account.

The illustration of this type of interfund activity in Figure 17–6 assumes that the general fund of Barb City uses an auto from the city motor pool. The motor pool operates as an internal service fund. The general fund is billed $100 based on mileage and pays the bill 30 days later.

(3) Interfund Transfers

The general fund often transfers resources into another fund to be used by the receiving fund for its own operations; occasionally, the general fund receives resources from other such. These interfund transfers are not expected to be repaid. Such transfers are not fund revenues or expenditures but are instead called "interfund transfers." These transfers are classified under "Other Financing Sources or Uses" in the operating financial statements of the funds. The reason that the receiving fund does not recognize these transfers as revenue is that the issuing fund has already properly recognized these resources as revenue. Thus, the recording of these transfers as other financing sources eliminates the possibility of double-counting the same resources as revenue in two different funds of the combined governmental entity. Examples include:

1. A transfer of resources, such as cash or other assets, is made from the general fund to an enterprise fund or internal service fund that has an operating deficit that must be eliminated.

2. A transfer of resources from the general fund to a capital projects fund is made to help finance new construction.
3. A transfer of resources from the general fund to the debt service fund is made to pay principal and interest.

The illustration of an interfund transfer in Figure 17–6 assumes that the general fund of Barb City agrees to provide $10,000 to the capital projects fund toward the construction of a new library. The Transfer Out account in the general fund is closed to its Unreserved Fund Balance at the end of the fiscal period. The capital projects fund also closes its Transfer In account at the end of the fiscal period to its Unreserved Fund Balance. These interfund transfers are not expected to be repaid.

(4) Interfund Reimbursements

A reimbursement transaction is for the reimbursement of a fund's expenditure or expense which was initially made from the fund, but which is properly chargeable to another fund. These initial payments are sometimes made either because of improper classification to the wrong fund, or for expediency within the governmental entity. The reimbursement from one fund to another is recorded as a reduction of the expenditure in the fund initially recording the expenditure and a recording of the expenditure in the proper fund for the appropriate amount. Two examples are as follows:

1. An expenditure properly chargeable to the special revenue fund is initially recorded and paid by the general fund, and the general fund subsequently is reimbursed by the special revenue fund.
2. The general fund records and pays for an expenditure to provide preliminary architectural work on the planning for a new sports arena. The general fund is later reimbursed from the sports arena enterprise fund.

The illustration of a reimbursement in Figure 17–6 assumes that the general fund of Barb City recorded a $3,000 expenditure for a bill from outside consultants that is later discovered to be properly chargeable to the capital projects fund. Upon notification, the capital projects fund reimbursed the general fund and properly recorded the expenditure in its fund.

Overview of Accounting and Financial Reporting for the General Fund

Figure 17–7 presents an overview of the accounting for the general fund, including accounting for the interfund activities on the general fund's operating statement, the statement of revenues, expenditures, and changes in fund balance. Note that the interfund loans are reported only on the fund's balance sheet.

Comprehensive Illustration of Accounting for the General Fund

The following example illustrates the accounting for the general fund of Sol City for the January 1, 20X2, to December 31, 20X2, fiscal year. The entries are presented by topic, not necessarily in chronological order. The balance sheet for the general fund as of December 31, 20X1, presented in Figure 17–8, represents the opening balances for fiscal 20X2.

FIGURE 17–7   Overview of General Fund

Item	Description
Measurement focus	Flow of current financial resources—expendability.
Accounting basis	Modified accrual.
Budgetary basis	Operating budget.
Financial statements	1. Balance sheet.
	2. Statement of revenues, expenditures, and changes in fund balance.
Balance Sheet:	
Current assets	Includes current financial resources such as cash, certificates of deposit, and property taxes receivable accrued and allowance for uncollectible taxes estimated.
	Material inventories reported.
Long-term productive assets (buildings, etc.)	Fixed assets not reported in general fund.
Current liabilities	Vouchers payable is primary current liability. Interfund loans also included as liabilities (or assets).
Long-term debt	Governmental unit long-term debt not reported in general fund.
Fund balance	Unreserved fund balance and reservations of fund balance, e.g., encumbrances and inventories.
Statement of Revenues, Expenditures, and Changes in Fund Balance:	
Revenue	Recorded when measurable and available under the modified accrual method of accounting. Interfund services provided and used also included in revenues (or expenditures).
Expenditures	Recognized in period when measurable and fund liability arises.
Other financing sources and uses	Includes bond issue proceeds and interfund transfers.
Changes in fund balance	Reconciles changes in fund balance during period, including changes in reservations of fund balance.

Adoption of the Budget

The city council adopts the budget for fiscal 20X2 as presented in Figure 17–9. Charles Alt, an alderman of Sol City, voted in favor of adopting the budget. The budget summarizes the four major functions of the city: general government, streets and highways, public safety (fire and police), and sanitation. In the complete budget used by the city council, the expenditures in each of the four functions are broken down into the following categories: personal services, supplies, other services and charges, and capital outlay. The public safety budget includes a budgeted capital outlay of $50,000 for a new fire truck.

Among the city's accounting policies are the following:

1. *Consumption method for inventories.* The city budgets supplies inventory on the consumption method, including only the costs of expected inventory use during the year.
2. *Lapsing method of accounting for encumbrances.* The city uses the lapsing method for accounting for any encumbrances outstanding at the end of fiscal periods. The APPROPRIATIONS CONTROL for fiscal 20X2 includes a

FIGURE 17–11 **General Fund Balance Sheet Information at the End of the Fiscal Period**

Sol City General Fund Balance Sheet Information December 31, 20X2		
Assets:		
Cash		$102,000
Property Taxes Receivable—Delinquent	$ 90,000	
Less: Allowance for Uncollectibles—Delinquent	(5,000)	85,000
Due from Enterprise Fund		3,000
Inventory of Supplies		17,000
Total Assets		$207,000
Liabilities and Fund Balance:		
Vouchers Payable		$ 55,000
Fund Balance:		
Reserved for Encumbrances	$ 15,000	
Reserved for Inventories	17,000	
Unreserved	120,000	152,000
Total Liabilities and Fund Balance		$207,000

FIGURE 17–12 **General Fund Statement of Revenues, Expenditures, and Changes in Fund Balance Information for Fiscal 20X2**

Sol City Statement of Revenues, Expenditures, and Changes in Fund Balance Information General Fund For the Year Ended December 31, 20X2		
Revenues:		
Property Taxes	$781,000	
Grants	33,000	
Sales Taxes	32,000	
Miscellaneous	18,000	
Total Revenues		$864,000
Expenditures:		
General Government	$206,000	
Streets and Highways	71,000	
Public Safety	335,000	
Sanitation	141,000	
Capital Outlay:		
Public Safety	58,000	
Total Expenditures		$811,000
Excess of Revenues Over Expenditures		$ 53,000
Other Financing Sources (Uses):		
Transfer Out to Capital Projects Fund	$ (20,000)	
Transfer Out to Internal Service Fund	(10,000)	
Total Other Financing Sources (Uses)		(30,000)
Net Change in Fund Balances		$ 23,000
Fund Balance, January 1		129,000
Fund Balance, December 31		$152,000

not break down the expenditures by function (general government, streets and highways, public safety, and sanitation), this breakdown is done in the actual governmental accounting process, so each expenditure can be classified by both function and object (personal services, supplies, and other services and charges). The amounts presented in the expenditures section in Figure 17–12 are the assumed amounts from a comprehensive accounting system. Total expenditures do reconcile to the expenditures recorded in the Sol City Illustration.

The statement of revenues, expenditures, and changes in fund balance reconciles to the total fund balances, including both reserved and unreserved. Furthermore, note that in this example, there were no extraordinary items or special items that were reported by Sol City. Special items would include significant transactions or other events that were within the control of management, but that were either unusual in nature or infrequent in occurrence. An example of a special item could be a one-time sale of some city parkland. If the city did have a special item or extraordinary item, it would be reported below the other financing sources (uses) line.

Summary of Key Concepts and Terms

Accounting for state and local governmental units requires the use of fund accounting to recognize properly the variety of services and objectives of the governmental unit. Funds are separate fiscal and accounting entities established to segregate, control, and account for resource flows. Three types of funds are used by governmental units: governmental funds, of which the general fund is usually the most important; proprietary funds; and fiduciary funds. The basis of accounting for each fund depends on the fund's objective. The current resources measurement focus and the modified accrual basis of accounting are used for the governmental fund financial statements. The economic resources measurement focus and accrual basis of accounting are used for the government-wide statements, the proprietary fund statements, and the fiduciary fund statements.

Under the modified accrual basis, revenue is recognized when it is both measurable and available for financing expenditures of the period. A major source of revenue is property tax levies, but other sources may include sales taxes; grants from other governmental units; and fines, licenses, or permits. Expenditures are recognized in the period in which the related liability is both measurable and incurred. The expenditure process usually begins with a budget, which establishes the spending authority for the fund. Encumbrances are used for purchases outside the governmental entity to recognize the use of a portion of the spending authority for the period and to avoid overspending the expenditure authority. Encumbrances outstanding at the end of a fiscal period are reported as a reserve of the fund balance and may be accounted for as lapsing or nonlapsing. Another type of fund balance reserve is a reserve for inventories, which is used if the amount of inventory is material.

The general fund is responsible for offering many of the usual services of governmental units. Fire and police protection, the local government's administrative and legislative functions, and many other basic governmental services are administered through the general fund. The general fund will provide balance sheet information and statement of revenues, expenditures and changes in fund balances information to the governmental funds financial statements.

The government reporting model, as established by **GASB 34,** specifies that both fund financial statements, and government-wide financial statements, must be presented for most governmental units. Some funds, such as the general fund, use the modified accrual basis of accounting to recognize revenue and expenditure transactions. Furthermore, no long-term capital assets, or general long-term debt, are recorded in the general fund. However, a reconciliation schedule will be required to go from the fund financial statements to the government-wide financial statements. The government-wide financial statements use the accrual basis of accounting and report all capital assets and all long-term debt. Government-wide financial statements are presented in Chapter 18 after the conclusion of discussion on the remaining funds.

Interfund activities must be evaluated carefully to ensure that the legal and budgetary controls of the governmental unit are not violated. Four types of interfund activities exist: (1) interfund loans, (2) interfund services provided and used, (3) interfund transfers, and (4) interfund reimbursements. Outstanding interfund loans are presented as receivables or payables on the fund's balance sheet information. Interfund services provided and used are reported as part of the revenues and expenditures on the operating statements. Interfund transfers are reported separately in the other financing sources (uses) section of the operating statement. And interfund reimbursements are not reported on the fund's financial statements.

Appropriation	Fiduciary funds
Basis of accounting	Funds
Budgets	Governmental funds
Current financial resources measurement focus	Interfund activities
	Modified accrual basis
Disbursement	Proprietary funds
Economic resources measurement focus	Reporting entity
Encumbrance	Reservation of the budgetary fund balance
Expenditure	

Questions

Q17–1 What is a fund? How does a fund receive resources?

Q17–2 What are the 11 funds generally used by local and state governments? Briefly state the purpose of each fund.

Q17–3 Compare the modified accrual basis with the accrual accounting basis.

Q17–4 Which of the two, the modified accrual basis or the accrual basis, is used for funds for which expendability is the concern? Why?

Q17–5 When are property taxes recognized as revenue in the general fund?

Q17–6 How are taxpayer-assessed income and sales taxes recognized in the general fund? Why?

Q17–7 What is meant by "budgetary accounting"? Explain the accounting for expected revenue and anticipated expenditures.

Q17–8 Are all expenditures encumbered?

Q17–9 Why do some governmental units not report small amounts of inventories of supplies in their balance sheets?

Q17–10 What are the main differences between the lapsing and nonlapsing methods of accounting for encumbrances outstanding at the end of the fiscal year? What are the differences in accounting between the lapsing and nonlapsing methods when accounting for the actual expenditure in the subsequent year?

Q17–11 When is the expenditure for inventories recognized under the purchase method? Under the consumption method?

Q17–12 Explain the difference between an interfund services provided and used and an interfund transfer. Give examples of each.

Q17–13 Where is an interfund transfer reported on the general fund's financial statements?

Q17–14 The general fund agrees to lend the enterprise fund $2,000 for three months. How is this interfund loan reported on the financial statements of the general fund?

Q17–15 Explain how an expenditure may be classified by (1) function, (2) activity, and (3) object within the financial statements of a governmental unit.

Cases

C17–1   **Budget Theory**

Governmental accounting gives substantial recognition to budgets, with budgets being recorded in the accounts of the governmental unit.

Required

a. What is the purpose of a governmental accounting system, and why is the budget recorded in the accounts of a governmental unit? Include in your discussion the purpose and significance of appropriations.

b. Describe when and how (1) a governmental unit records its budget and (2) closes out the budgetary accounts.

C17–2   **Municipal versus Financial Accounting**

William Bates is executive vice president of Mavis Industries Inc., a publicly held industrial corporation. Bates has just been elected to the city council of Gotham City. Before assuming office as a city councilman, he asks you to explain the major differences that exist in accounting and financial reporting for a large city when compared with a large industrial corporation.

Required

a. Describe the major differences that exist in the purpose of accounting and financial reporting and in the type of financial reports of a large city when compared with a large industrial corporation.

b. Why are inventories often ignored in accounting for local governmental units? Explain.

Exercises

E17–1   **Multiple-Choice Questions on the General Fund [AICPA Adapted]**

Select the correct answer for each of the following questions.

1. One of the differences between accounting for a governmental (not-for-profit) unit and a commercial (for-profit) enterprise is that a governmental unit should:
   a. *Not* record depreciation expense in any of its funds.
   b. Always establish and maintain complete self-balancing accounts for each fund.
   c. Use only the cash basis of accounting.
   d. Use only the modified accrual basis of accounting.

2. Belle Valley incurred $100,000 of salaries and wages for the month ended March 31, 20X2. How should this be recorded on that date?

	Debit	Credit
a. Expenditures—Salaries and Wages	100,000	
Vouchers Payable		100,000
b. Salaries and Wages Expense	100,000	
Vouchers Payable		100,000
c. Encumbrances—Salaries and Wages	100,000	
Vouchers Payable		100,000
d. Fund Balance	100,000	
Vouchers Payable		100,000

8. Encumbrances outstanding at year-end in a state's general fund should be reported as a:
   a. Liability in the general fund.
   b. Fund balance designation in the general fund.
   c. Fund balance reserve in the general fund.
   d. Liability in the general long-term debt account group.

9. Interperiod equity is an objective of financial reporting for governmental entities. According to the Governmental Accounting Standards Board, is interperiod equity fundamental to public administration, and is it a component of accountability?

	Fundamental to Public Administration	*Component of Accountability*
a.	Yes	Yes
b.	No	No
c.	Yes	No
d.	No	Yes

10. Which of the following statements is correct regarding comparability of governmental financial reports?
    a. Comparability is not relevant in governmental financial reporting.
    b. Differences between financial reports should be due to substantive differences in underlying transactions or the governmental structure.
    c. Selection of different alternatives in accounting procedures or practices account for the differences between financial reports.
    d. Similarly designated governments perform the same functions.

E17–5 **Encumbrances at Year-End**

Fargo ordered new office equipment for $12,500 on April 20, 20X1. The office equipment had not been received by June 30, 20X1, the end of Fargo's fiscal year.

Required

a. Assume that outstanding encumbrances lapse at year-end.
   (1) Prepare the entries required on June 30, 20X1.
   (2) Assuming that the city council accepts outstanding encumbrances in its budget for the next fiscal period (20X2), prepare entries on July 1, 20X1.
   (3) Prepare entries on July 24, 20X1, when the equipment was received with an invoice for $12,750.

b. Assume that outstanding encumbrances are nonlapsing.
   (1) Prepare the entries required on June 30, 20X1.
   (2) Prepare the entry required on July 1, 20X1, to identify the expenditure with 20X1.
   (3) Prepare the entry on July 24, 20X1, when the equipment was received with an invoice for $12,750.
   (4) Prepare the closing entry on June 30, 20X2, assuming the expenditure is netted against 20X2 expenditures.

E17–6 **Accounting for Inventories of Office Supplies**

Georgetown purchased supplies on August 8, 20X2, for $3,600. At the end of the fiscal year on September 30, the inventory of supplies was $2,800.

Required

a. Assume that Georgetown uses the consumption method of accounting for inventories.
   (1) Prepare the entry for the purchase on August 8, 20X2.
   (2) Prepare the entries required on September 30, 20X2, including the closing of the Expenditures account.

(3) Assuming the supplies were used during 20X3, prepare the entries on September 30, 20X3.

b. Assume that Georgetown uses the purchase method of accounting for inventories.

(1) Prepare the entry for the purchase on August 8, 20X2.

(2) Prepare the entries required on September 30, 20X2, including the closing of the Expenditures account.

(3) Assuming the supplies were used during 20X3, prepare the entry on September 30, 20X3.

E17–7   Accounting for Prepayments and Capital Assets

Required

Prepare journal entries for the Iron City general fund for the following, including any adjusting and closing entries on December 31, 20X1:

1. Acquired a three-year fire insurance policy for $5,400 on September 1, 20X1.

2. Ordered new furniture for the city council meeting room on September 17, 20X1, at an estimated cost of $15,600. The furniture was delivered on October 1, the actual cost was $15,200, the estimated life of the furniture is 10 years, with no residual value.

3. Acquired supplies on November 4, 20X1, for $1,800. Iron City uses the consumption method of accounting. Supplies on hand on December 31 were $1,120.

E17–8   Computation of Revenues Reported on the Statement of Revenues, Expenditures, and Changes in Fund Balance for the General Fund

Gilbert City had the following transactions involving resouce inflows into its general fund for the year ended June 30, 20X8:

1. The general fund levied $2,000,000 of property taxes in July 20X7. The city estimated that 2 percent of the levy would be uncollectible and that $100,000 of the levy would be collected after August 31, 20X8.

2. On April 1, 20X8, the general fund received $50,000 repayment of an advance made to internal service fund. Interest on the advance of $1,500 was also received.

3. During the year ended June 30, 20X8, the general fund received $1,800,000 of the property taxes levied in statement (1).

4. The general fund received a $250,000 grant from the state to acquire computer equipment. During March 20X8, the general fund acquired computer equipment using $235,000 of the grant.

5. During the year ended June 30, 20X8, the general fund received $125,000 from the state as its portion of the sales tax. At June 30, 20X8, the state owed the general fund an additional $25,000 of sales taxes. The general fund does not expect to have the $25,000 available until early August 20X8.

6. In July 20X7, the general fund borrowed $800,000 from a local bank using the property tax levy as collateral. The loan was repaid in September 20X7, with the proceeds of property tax collections.

7. In February 20X8, a terminated debt service fund transferred $30,000 to the general fund. The $30,000 represented excess resources left in the debt service fund after a general long-term debt obligation had been paid in full.

8. On July 1, 20X7, the general fund estimated that it would receive $75,000 from the sale of liquor licenses during the fiscal year ended June 30, 20X8. For the year ended June 30, 20X8, $66,000 was received from the sale of liquor licenses.

9. The general fund received $15,000 in October 20X7, from one of the city's special revenue funds. The amount received represented a reimbursement for an expenditure of the special revenue fund that was paid by the city's general fund.

10. In July 20X7, the general fund collected $80,000 of delinquent property taxes. These property taxes were classified as delinquent on June 30, 20X7. In the entry to record the property tax

levy in July 20X6, the general fund estimated that it would collect all property tax revenues by July 31, 20X7.

Required

Prepare a schedule showing the amount of revenue that should be reported by Gilbert's general fund on the statement of revenues, expenditures, and changes in fund balance for the year ended June 30, 20X8.

E17–9 **Computation of Expenditures Reported on the Statement of Revenues, Expenditures, and Changes in Fund Balance for the General Fund**

Benson City had the following transactions involving resource outflows involving its general fund for the year ended June 30, 20X8:

1. During March 20X8, the general fund transferred $150,000 to a capital projects fund to help pay for the construction of a new police station.
2. During August 20X7, the general fund ordered computer equipment at an estimated cost of $200,000. The equipment was received in September 20X7, and an invoice for $202,000 was paid.
3. In November 20X7, the city authorized the establishment of an internal service fund for the maintenance of city owned vehicles. The general fund was authorized to transfer $500,000 to the internal service fund in late November. Of this amount, $200,000 will be repaid by the internal service fund in two years with interest at 6 percent, while the remaining $300,000 represents a permanent transfer to the internal service fund.
4. In May 20X8, the general fund made a $15,000 payment to one of the city's special revenue funds. The amount paid represented a reimbursement to the special revenue fund for expending $15,000 of its resources on behalf of the general fund.
5. During the year ended June 30, 20X8, the general fund received bills from the city's water department totaling $12,000. Of this amount, the general fund paid all but $500 by June 30, 20X8.
6. During the year ended June 30, 20X8, the general fund acquired supplies costing $35,000 and paid the salaries and wages of its employees totaling $900,000. The general fund uses the purchase method of accounting for its supplies. At June 30, 20X8, unused supplies in the general fund amounted to $5,000.
7. At June 30, 20X8, outstanding encumbrances for goods ordered in the general fund amounted to $25,000. Outstanding encumbrances do not lapse at the end of the fiscal year.
8. On March 15, 20X8, the general fund repaid a loan to a local bank. The amount paid was $265,000, of which $250,000 represented the principal borrowed. The general fund borrowed the money in July 20X7, and used collections of the property tax levy to repay the loan.
9. For the year ended June 30, 20X8, the general fund transferred $95,000 to the city's pension trust fund. The amount transferred represented the employer's contribution to the pension trust on behalf of the employees of the general fund.
10. During May 20X8, the general fund decided to lease several copying machines instead of purchasing them. The lease arrangement was properly accounted for as an operating lease. By June 30, 20X8, the general fund had made lease payments of $10,000 to the owner of the machines.

Required

Prepare a schedule showing the amount of expenditures that should be reported by Benson's general fund on the statement of revenues, expenditures, and changes in fund balance for the year ended June 30, 20X8.

E17–10   Closing Entries and Balance Sheet

The preclosing trial balance at December 31, 20X1, for the general fund of Lone Wolf is given below.

	Debit	Credit
Cash	$ 90,000	
Property Taxes Receivable—Delinquent	100,000	
Allowance for Uncollectibles—Delinquent		$ 7,200
Due from Other Funds	14,600	
Vouchers Payable		65,000
Due to Other Funds		8,400
Unreserved Fund Balance		119,000
Property Tax Revenue		1,130,000
Miscellaneous Revenue		40,000
Expenditures	1,140,000	
Other Financing Use—Transfers Out	25,000	
Estimated Revenues Control	1,200,000	
Appropriations Control		1,145,000
Estimated Other Financing Use—Transfers Out		25,000
Encumbrances	32,000	
Budgetary Fund Balance Reserved for Encumbrances		32,000
Budgetary Fund Balance Unreserved		30,000
Total	$2,601,600	$2,601,600

Lone Wolf uses the purchase method of accounting for inventories and the lapsing method of accounting for encumbrances.

Required

a. Prepare the closing entries for the general fund.

b. Prepare a general fund only balance sheet at December 31, 20X1.

E17–11   Statement of Revenues, Expenditures, and Changes in Fund Balance

Refer to the preclosing trial balance in exercise 17–10. Assume the balances on December 31, 20X0, were as follows:

Fund Balance Reserved for Encumbrances	$28,000
Unreserved Fund Balance	91,000

Required

Prepare a general fund only statement of revenues, expenditures, and changes in fund balance for fiscal 20X1.

E17–12   Matching Questions Involving Interfund Transactions and Transfers in the General Fund

The general fund of Mattville had several interfund activities during the fiscal year ended June 30, 20X9. These interfund activities are described below on the left. A list of the types of interfund activities that occur in state and local governmental accounting is provided on the right. For each general fund transaction/transfer, select a letter from the list on the right that best describes the interfund activity.

General Fund Transactions and Transfers	Type of Interfund Transactions and Transfers
1. Received bills from an internal service fund for using city-owned vehicles.	A. Interfund loan
	B. Interfund service provided and used
2. Transferred cash to start an enterprise fund. The enterprise fund does not have to return the cash back to the general fund.	C. Interfund transfer
	D. Interfund reimbursement
3. Received cash from a special revenue fund that was discontinued.	
4. Transferred cash to a capital projects fund to help construct a building.	
5. Transferred cash to a debt service fund to pay interest and principal of general long-term debt.	
6. Transferred cash to the pension trust fund representing the employer's contribution towards the pension of general fund employees.	
7. Transferred resources to an enterprise fund. It is expected that these resources will be repaid with interest.	
8. Transferred cash to a special revenue fund. The special revenue fund incurred and paid expenditures on behalf of the general fund.	
9. Received cash from an internal service fund. The cash received represented repayment of an advance made during the previous year.	
10. Received bills from an enterprise fund for using public parking facilities.	

Problems

P17–13 **General Fund Entries [AICPA Adapted]**
The following information was abstracted from the accounts of the general fund of the City of Noble after the books had been closed for the fiscal year ended June 30, 20X2.

	Postclosing Trial Balance, June 30, 20X1	Transactions July 1, 20X1–June 30, 20X2		Postclosing Trial Balance, June 30, 20X2
		Debit	Credit	
Cash	$700,000	$1,820,000	$1,852,000	$668,000
Taxes Receivable	40,000	1,870,000	1,828,000	82,000
Total	$740,000			$750,000
Allowance for Uncollectible Taxes	$ 8,000	8,000	10,000	$ 10,000
Vouchers Payable	132,000	1,852,000	1,840,000	120,000
Fund Balance:				
Reserve for Encumbrances			70,000	70,000
Unreserved	600,000	70,000	20,000	550,000
Total	$740,000			$750,000

Additional Information

The budget for the fiscal year ended June 30, 20X2, provided for estimated revenue of $2,000,000 and appropriations of $1,940,000. Encumbrances of $1,070,000 were made during the year.

Required

Prepare proper journal entries to record the budgeted and actual transactions for the fiscal year ended June 30, 20X2. Include closing entries.

P17–14   General Fund Entries

The following selected events occurred in the general fund of the Village of Sleepy Hollow during the fiscal year ended June 30, 20X6:

1. The operating budget included the following resource inflows and outflows:

Estimated revenues:	
Property taxes	$ 800,000
Sales taxes	100,000
Licenses and permits	25,000
Estimated transfer in from special revenue fund	75,000
Total	$1,000,000
Appropriations:	
General government	$ 610,000
Public safety	200,000
Sanitation	150,000
Estimated transfer out to internal service fund	25,000
Total	$ 985,000

2. Sleepy Hollow uses the lapsing method of accounting for encumbrances. The appropriations included encumbrances of $18,000 related to the year ended June 30, 20X5.
3. The property tax levy was $816,000, and estimated uncollectibles were $16,000.
4. Property taxes of $805,000 were collected. The estimated uncollectibles balance was decreased to $6,000, and the remaining receivables and allowance were reclassified to delinquent at year-end.
5. Received $102,000 of sales tax revenue from the state and $24,000 from licenses and permits.
6. Received transfer in of $70,000 from a special revenue fund. Made a $25,000 transfer out to establish an internal service fund. For both of these transactions, record the interfund receivable/payable before recording the cash transfer.
7. Ordered computer equipment costing $50,000. Received computer equipment and paid the actual cost of $50,500 two weeks after receipt of the equipment.
8. Made a loan to an enterprise fund for $20,000 on January 1, 20X6. The loan was repaid with interest at 6 percent on June 30, 20X6.
9. Used the services of the central motor pool and was billed $500. The bill was paid within one week of its receipt by the general fund.

Required

Prepare journal entries for the general fund to record these transactions involving the Village of Sleepy Hollow for the year ended June 30, 20X6.

P17–15 **General Fund Entries [AICPA Adapted]**

The trial balances shown below were taken from the accounts of the Omega City general fund before the books had been closed for the fiscal year ended June 30, 20X2:

	Trial Balance July 1, 20X1	Trial Balance June 30, 20X2
Cash	$400,000	$ 700,000
Taxes Receivable	150,000	170,000
Allowance for Uncollectible Taxes	(40,000)	(70,000)
Estimated Revenues Control	—	3,000,000
Expenditures	—	2,900,000
Encumbrances	—	91,000
Total	$510,000	$6,791,000
Vouchers Payable	$ 80,000	$408,000
Due to Other Funds	210,000	142,000
Fund Balance Reserved for Encumbrances	60,000	—
Unreserved Fund Balance	160,000	220,000
Revenue from Taxes	—	2,800,000
Miscellaneous Revenues	—	130,000
Appropriations Control	—	2,980,000
Budgetary Fund Balance Reserved for Encumbrances	—	91,000
Budgetary Fund Balance Unreserved	—	20,000
Total	$510,000	$6,791,000

Additional Information

1. The estimated taxes receivable for the year ended June 30, 20X2, were $2,870,000, and the taxes collected during the year totaled $2,810,000. Miscellaneous revenue of $130,000 was also collected during the year.

2. Encumbrances in the amount of $2,700,000 were recorded. In addition, the $60,000 of lapsed encumbrances from the 20X1 fiscal year was renewed.

3. During the year, the general fund was billed $142,000 for services performed on its behalf by other city funds (debit Expenditures).

4. An analysis of the transactions in the Vouchers Payable account for the year ended June 30, 20X2, is as follows:

	Debit (Credit)
Current expenditures (liquidating all encumbrances to date except for renewed 20X1 commitment)	$(2,700,000)
Expenditures applicable to previous year	(58,000)
Vouchers for payments to other funds	(210,000)
Cash payments during year	2,640,000
Net change	$ (328,000)

5. On May 10, 20X2, encumbrances were recorded for the purchase of next year's supplies at an estimated cost of $91,000.

Required

On the basis of the data presented, reconstruct the original detailed journal entries that were required to record all transactions for the fiscal year ended June 30, 20X2, including the recording of the current year's budget. Do not prepare closing entries for June 30, 20X2.

P17–16   General Fund Closing Entries and Statements

The unadjusted trial balance for the general fund of Quincy on June 30, 20X2, is given below:

	Debit	Credit
Cash	$ 100,000	
Property Taxes Receivable—Delinquent	108,000	
Allowance for Uncollectibles—Delinquent		$ 8,400
Due from Data Processing Fund	10,000	
Estimated Revenues Control	1,450,000	
Other Financing Use—Transfers Out	50,000	
Encumbrances	23,000	
Expenditures	1,385,000	
Vouchers Payable		44,000
Due to Printing Service Fund		2,600
Property Tax Revenue		1,390,000
Grant Revenue		40,000
Miscellaneous Revenue		32,000
Appropriations Control		1,400,000
Estimated Other Financing Use—Transfers Out		50,000
Budgetary Fund Balance Reserved for Encumbrances		23,000
Unreserved Fund Balance		136,000
Total	$3,126,000	$3,126,000

Additional Information

1. Quincy uses the lapsing method for outstanding encumbrances. Fund Balance Reserved for Encumbrances on June 30, 20X1, was $28,300. The encumbrances were renewed.

2. Unreserved Fund Balance, June 30, 20X1, was $107,700.

3. Quincy uses the consumption method of accounting for inventories. There were no supplies on hand on June 30, 20X1. Supplies on hand on June 30, 20X2, cost $8,000.

Required

a. Prepare adjusting and closing entries for the general fund.

b. Prepare a balance sheet for the general fund as of June 30, 20X2.

c. Prepare a statement of revenues, expenditures, and changes in fund balance for fiscal 20X2, for the general fund.

P17–17   General Fund Closing Entries and Statements

The balance sheet of the general fund of Ruby Valley on June 30, 20X1, follows:

Ruby Valley
Balance Sheet—General Fund
June 30, 20X1

Assets

Cash		$103,000
Property Taxes Receivable—Delinquent	$ 80,000	
Less: Allowance for Uncollectibles—Delinquent	(8,000)	72,000
Inventory of Supplies		11,000
Total Assets		$186,000

Liabilities and Fund Balance

Vouchers Payable		$ 42,000
Fund Balance:		
Reserve for Encumbrances	$ 18,000	
Reserve for Inventories	11,000	
Unreserved	115,000	144,000
Total Liabilities and Fund Balance		$186,000

Budget and transaction information for fiscal 20X2 is as follows:

1. Estimated revenue:

Property taxes	$1,280,500 ✓
Grants	100,000
Miscellaneous	40,000 1,420,000

   The property tax levy was $1,300,000, of which uncollectible taxes were estimated at ✓ 1½ percent.

2. Appropriations were $1,356,000 and estimated transfers out to internal service fund, $25,000. Ruby Valley uses the nonlapsing method to account for encumbrances. The appropriations included $50,000 for a new elevator.

3. Cash receipts were as follows:

Property taxes—delinquent	$ 69,000
Property taxes—current	1,245,000
Grants from the state	90,000
Miscellaneous revenue	46,000
Transfer from capital projects fund	30,000

   The remaining property taxes from fiscal 20X1 were written off, and those remaining from 20X2 were reclassified. The allowance for uncollectibles for 20X2 was reduced to $7,500.

4. The general fund issued purchase orders totaling $1,336,000, of which $120,000 were outstanding at year-end. Actual expenditures were $1,240,000, including $20,000 for 20X1

encumbrances, $27,000 for supplies, and $45,000 for a new elevator. Vouchers paid totaled $1,227,000. The supplies on hand June 30, 20X2, were $6,700. Ruby Valley uses the consumption method to account for inventories.

5. Other cash payments and transfers were as follows:

Other financing use—Transfer out	$25,000
Loan to the computer center	20,000

Required

a. Prepare entries to summarize the general fund budget and transactions for fiscal 20X2.

b. Prepare an unadjusted trial balance.

c. Prepare adjusting and closing entries for the general fund.

d. Prepare a balance sheet for the general fund as of June 30, 20X2.

e. Prepare a statement of revenues, expenditures, and changes in fund balance for fiscal 20X2, for the general fund.

P17–18   General Fund Entries and Statements

The postclosing trial balance of the general fund of the town of Pine Ridge on December 31, 20X1, is as follows:

	Debit	Credit
Cash	$111,000	
Property Taxes Receivable—Delinquent	90,000	
Allowance for Uncollectibles—Delinquent		$ 9,000
Vouchers Payable		31,000
Fund Balance Reserved for Encumbrances		21,000
Unreserved Fund Balance		140,000
Total	$201,000	$201,000

Additional Information Related to 20X2

1. Estimated revenue: property taxes, $1,584,000 from a tax levy of $1,600,000 of which 1 percent was estimated uncollectible; sales taxes, $250,000; and miscellaneous, $43,000. Appropriations totaled $1,840,000; and estimated transfers out $37,000. Appropriations included outstanding purchase orders from 20X1 of $21,000. Pine Ridge uses the lapsing method for outstanding encumbrances.

2. Cash receipts: property taxes, $1,590,000, including $83,000 from 20X1; sales taxes, $284,000; licenses and fees, $39,000; and a loan from the motor pool, $10,000. The remaining property taxes from 20X1 were written off, and those remaining from 20X2 were reclassified.

3. Orders were issued for $1,800,000 in addition to the acceptance of the $21,000 outstanding purchase orders from 20X1. A total of $48,000 of purchase orders still was outstanding at the end of 20X2. Actual expenditures were $1,788,000, including $42,000 for office furniture. Vouchers paid totaled $1,793,000.

4. Other cash payments and transfers were as follows:

Loan to central stores	$13,000
Transfer out	37,000

Required

a. Prepare entries to summarize the general fund budget and transactions for 20X2.

b. Prepare a preclosing trial balance.

c. Prepare closing entries for the general fund.

d. Prepare a balance sheet for the general fund as of December 31, 20X2.

e. Prepare a statement of revenues, expenditures, and changes in fund balance for 20X2 for the general fund.

P17–19   General Fund Entries

The following financial activities affecting Johnson City's general fund took place during the year ended June 30, 20X1. The following budget was adopted:

Estimated revenue:	
Property taxes	$4,500,000
Licenses and permits	300,000
Fines	200,000
Total	$5,000,000
Appropriations:	
General government	$1,500,000
Police services	1,200,000
Fire department services	900,000
Public works services	800,000
Acquisition of fire engines	400,000
Total	$4,800,000

Additional Information Related to 20X1

1. Property tax bills totaling $4,650,000 were mailed. It was estimated that $300,000 of this amount would be delinquent and $150,000 would be uncollectible.

2. Property taxes totaling $3,900,000 were collected. The $150,000 previously estimated to be uncollectible remained unchanged, but $750,000 was reclassified as delinquent. It is estimated that the delinquent taxes will be collected soon enough after June 30, 20X1, to make them available to finance obligations incurred during the year ended June 30, 20X1. There was no balance of uncollected taxes on July 1, 20X0.

3. Tax anticipation notes in the face amount of $300,000 were issued.

4. Other cash collections were as follows:

Licenses and permits	$270,000
Fines	200,000
Sale of public works equipment	
(original cost, $75,000)	15,000
Total	$485,000

5. The following purchase orders were executed:

	Total	Outstanding on June 30, 20X1
General governmental	$1,050,000	$ 60,000
Police services	300,000	30,000
Fire department services	150,000	15,000
Public works services	250,000	10,000
Fire engines	400,000	-0-
Total	$2,150,000	$115,000

6. No encumbrances were outstanding on June 30, 20X0.

7. The following vouchers were approved:

General governmental	$1,440,000
Police services	1,155,000
Fire department services	870,000
Public works services	700,000
Fire engines	400,000
Total	$4,565,000

8. Vouchers totaling $4,600,000 were paid.

Required

Prepare journal entries to record the foregoing financial activities in the general fund, assuming separate appropriation and expenditure accounts are maintained for each function of the city. Ignore interest accruals.

P17–20   General Fund Entries [AICPA Adapted]

The general fund trial balance of the city of Prescott for December 31, 20X2, was as follows:

	Debit	Credit
Cash	$ 62,000	
Taxes Receivable—Delinquent	46,000	
Estimated Uncollectible Taxes—Delinquent		$ 8,000
Stores Inventory—Program Operations	18,000	
Vouchers Payable		28,000
Fund Balance Reserved for Stores Inventory		18,000
Fund Balance Reserved for Encumbrances		12,000
Unreserved Fund Balance		60,000
Total	$126,000	$126,000

Collectible delinquent taxes are expected to be collected within 60 days after the end of the year. Prescott uses the purchases method to account for stores inventory and the nonlapsing method to account for encumbrances outstanding from a prior year. The following data pertain to 20X3 general fund operations:

1. Budget adopted:

Revenue and other financing sources:	
Taxes	$220,000
Fines, forfeits, and penalties	80,000
Miscellaneous revenue	100,000
Share of bond issue proceeds	200,000
Total	$600,000
Expenditures and other financing uses:	
Program operations	$300,000
General administration	120,000
Stores—program operations	60,000
Capital outlay	80,000
Transfer out to capital projects fund	20,000
Total	$580,000

2. Taxes were assessed at an amount that would result in revenue of $220,800, after deduction of 4 percent of the tax levy as uncollectible.

3. Orders placed but not received:

Program operations	$176,000
General administration	80,000
Capital outlay	60,000
Total	$316,000

4. The city council designated $20,000 of the unreserved fund balance for possible future appropriation for capital outlay.

5. Cash collections and transfer:

Delinquent taxes	$ 38,000
Current taxes	226,000
Refund of overpayment of invoice for purchase of equipment	4,000
Fines, forfeits, and penalties	88,000
Miscellaneous revenue	90,000
Share of bond issue proceeds	200,000
Transfer in of remaining fund balance of a discontinued fund	18,000
Total	$664,000

6. The allowance for uncollectible taxes—current was reduced to $3,000. The remaining $8,000 of taxes receivable—delinquent were written off against the allowance for uncollectible taxes—delinquent.

7. Eliminated encumbrances for items received:

	Estimated	Actual
Prior year—program operations	$ 12,000	$ 12,000
Program operations	144,000	154,000
General administration	84,000	80,000
Capital outlay	62,000	62,000
Total	$302,000	$308,000

8. Additional vouchers:

Program operations	$188,000
General administration	38,000
Capital outlay	18,000
Transfer out to capital projects	20,000
Total	$264,000

9. Mr. Harris, a taxpayer, overpaid his 20X3 taxes by $2,000. He applied for a $2,000 credit against his 20X4 taxes. The city council granted his request.

10. Vouchers paid totaled $580,000.

11. Stores inventory on December 31, 20X3, amounted to $12,000.

Required

Prepare journal entries to record the effects of the presented data, assuming Prescott maintains separate appropriation and expenditure accounts for each function of the city.

P17–21 **General Fund Entries and Balance Sheet**

The Village of Margaret reported the following balance sheet at June 30, 20X5:

Village of Margaret
Balance Sheet—General Fund
June 30, 20X5

Assets		
Cash		$35,000
Property Taxes Receivable—Delinquent	$22,000	
Less: Allowance for Uncollectible Taxes—Delinquent	(7,000)	15,000
Due from Enterprise Fund		10,000
Inventory of Supplies		5,000
Total Assets		$65,000

Liabilities and Fund Balance

Vouchers Payable		$27,000
Due to Internal Service Fund		8,000
Total Liabilities		$35,000
Fund Balance:		
Reserve for Encumbrances	$16,000	
Reserve for Inventories	5,000	
Unreserved	9,000	30,000
Total Liabilities and Fund Balance		$65,000

Budget and transaction information for the fiscal year ended June 30, 20X6, are presented below.

1. The city council of Margaret passed the following operating budget for fiscal 20X6:

Budgeted revenues:	
Property taxes	$211,200
State grants	50,000
Sales tax	18,800
Fines, licenses, and permits	9,500
Interest from loan to enterprise fund	500
Estimated transfer in from capital capital projects fund	20,000
Total	$310,000
Appropriations:	
General government	$150,000
Public safety	75,000
Streets and Sanitation	60,000
Estimated transfer out to debt service fund	15,000
Total	$300,000

2. Margaret uses the lapsing method of accounting for encumbrances. Appropriations for fiscal 20X6 include $16,000 for encumbrances related to fiscal 20X5.
3. The property tax levy was $220,000 of which 4 percent was estimated to be uncollectible.
4. Cash was received from the following sources during fiscal 20X6:

Property taxes—delinquent	$ 15,000
Property taxes—current	198,000
State grants	50,000
Sales taxes	17,500
Fines, permits, licenses	11,000
Transfer in from capital projects funds	18,000
Loan collected from enterprise fund, including $500 of interest	10,500

The remaining property taxes from fiscal 20X5 were written off, and those remaining from fiscal 20X6 were reclassified to delinquent. The allowance for uncollectible taxes was reduced to $6,000.

5. Margaret ordered $65,000 of goods during the year, including the $16,000 of goods for which the encumbrances lapsed at the end of fiscal 20X5. All goods ordered during fiscal 20X6 were received by June 30, 20X6, except for an $8,000 order that was placed on June 15, 20X6. The actual cost of the goods acquired was $58,000. All but $8,500 of the invoices were paid at June 30, 20X6.

6. Expenditures incurred during fiscal 20X6 that were not encumbered amounted to $215,000. All but $12,000 of these expenditures were paid during fiscal 20X6.

7. On July 12, 20X5, Margaret transferred $8,000 to the internal service fund to pay for services that were billed and recorded during June of 20X5. In addition, all of the vouchers payable at June 30, 20X5, were paid during July 20X5.

8. On February 24, 20X6, Margaret recorded the transfer out to the debt service fund. Margaret transferred the cash from the general fund to the debt service fund on March 1, 20X6.

9. Margaret uses the purchase method when it acquires supplies. At June 30, 20X6, Margaret had $7,500 of supplies that were not used.

Required

a. Prepare entries to summarize the general fund budget and the transactions for fiscal 20X6, including adjusting and closing entries.

b. Prepare a balance sheet at June 30, 20X6.

P17–22   Matching Governmental Terms with Descriptions

Match the terms on the left with the descriptions on the right. A description may be used once or not at all.

Terms	*Descriptions of Terms*
1. Proprietary funds	A. Trust and agency funds.
2. Modified accrual method	B. The fiscal and accounting entities of a government.
3. Estimated revenues	C. The basis of accounting used by proprietary funds.
4. Appropriations	D. An example of this transaction occurs when the general fund uses the services of an internal service fund.
5. Encumbrances	
6. Expenditures	E. Expenditures for inventories represent the amount of inventories consumed during the period.
7. Budgetary fund balance unreserved	
8. Consumption method for supplies inventories	F. General, special revenue, debt service, capital projects funds, and permanent funds.
9. Nonlapsing encumbrances	G. Legal authority to make expenditures.
10. Interfund services provided or used	H. Budgeted resource inflows.
11. Governmental funds	I. Revenues are recognized when they are both measurable and available to finance expenditures made during the current period.
12. Interfund transfers	
13. Fiduciary funds	
14. Funds	J. Internal service and enterprise funds.
15. Government-wide financials	K. Expenditures for inventories represent the amount of inventories acquired during the current period.
16. Accrual method	L. Reports government unit's infrastructure assets.
	M. Recorded when the general fund orders goods and services.
	N. Appropriation authority carries over to the next fiscal year for these orders.
	O. Appropriation authority does not carry over to the next fiscal year for these orders.
	P. This type of transaction occurs when the general fund makes a cash transfer to establish an internal service fund.
	Q. This account is debited in the general fund when an invoice is received for computer equipment.
	R. The account that would indicate a budget surplus or deficit in the general fund.

P17–23 **Identification of Governmental Accounting Terms**

For each number statement below, write the terms(s) that is (are) described in the statement.

1. This is the set of financial statements that present the government unit's infrastructure assets and long-term debt.

2. At the present time, this body has the authority to prescribe generally accepted accounting principles for state and local governmental entities.

3. This is a fiscal and an accounting entity with a self-balancing set of accounts recording cash and other financial resources, together with all related liabilities and residual equities or balances, and changes therein, that are segregated for the purpose of carrying on specific activities or attaining certain objectives in accordance with special regulations, restrictions, or limitations.

4. This type of interfund activity is accounted for as an expenditure or revenue.

5. These are the proprietary funds.

6. These are assets of the governmental unit and include roads, municipal buildings, sewer systems, sidewalks, and so forth.

7. These are the fiduciary funds.

8. This basis is used in funds that have a flow of financial resources measurement focus.

9. This is the measurement focus of government-wide financials.

10. This gives the governmental entity the legal right to collect property taxes.

11. These are the governmental funds.

12. This is subtracted from property taxes receivable—current to get the revenue from property taxes for the year.

13. This account is credited in the budget entry for the general fund if expected resource inflows exceed expected resource outflows.

14. This account is debited when the general fund records a purchase order for goods or services.

15. This method of accounting for supplies inventories in the general fund reports expenditures for supplies for only the amount used during the year.

16. This account is debited in the general fund when an transfer out is made to another fund.

17. This account is debited in the general fund when it records a billing from another fund for services that were provided to the general fund.

18. This is reported on the general fund balance sheet when assets exceed liabilities and reserved fund balance.

19. This account is debited in the general fund when fixed assets are acquired. Assume a purchase order to acquire the fixed assets was not recorded.

20. This is the legal term that allows the general fund to make expenditures.

21. Under this method of accounting for encumbrances outstanding at year-end, expenditures are dated in the following year when the orders are received.

P17–24 **Questions on General Fund Entries [AICPA Adapted]**

The Dekalb City Council approved and adopted its budget for 20X2. The budget contained the following amounts:

Estimated revenues	$700,000
Appropriations	660,000
Authorized transfer out to the Library debt service fund	30,000

During 20X2, various transactions and events occurred that affected the general fund.

Required

For items 1 through 39, select whether the item should be debited (D), should be credited (C), or is not affected (N).

Items 1 through 5 involve recording the adopted budget in the general fund.

1. Estimated Revenues.
2. Budgetary Fund Balance.
3. Appropriations.
4. Estimated Transfers Out.
5. Expenditures.

Items 6 through 10 involve recording the 20X2 property tax levy in the general fund. It was estimated that $5,000 would be uncollectible.

6. Property Tax Receivable.
7. Bad Debts Expense.
8. Allowance for Uncollectibles—Current.
9. Revenues.
10. Estimated Revenues.

Items 11 through 15 involve recording, in the general fund, encumbrances at the time purchase orders are issued.

11. Encumbrances.
12. Budgetary Fund Balance—Reserved for Encumbrances.
13. Expenditures.
14. Vouchers Payable.
15. Purchases.

Items 16 through 20 involve recording, in the general fund, expenditures which had been previously encumbered in the current year.

16. Encumbrances.
17. Budgetary Fund Balance—Reserved for Encumbrances.
18. Expenditures.
19. Vouchers Payable.
20. Purchases.

Items 21 through 25 involve recording, in the general fund, the transfer out of $30,000 made to the library debt service fund. (No previous entries were made regarding this transaction.)

21. Interfund Services Provided and Used.
22. Due from Library Debt Service Fund.
23. Cash.
24. Other Financing Uses—Transfers Out.
25. Encumbrances.

Items 26 through 35 involve recording, in the general fund, the closing entries (other than encumbrances) for 20X2.

26. Estimated Revenues.
27. Budgetary Fund Balance.
28. Appropriations.
29. Estimated Transfers Out.
30. Expenditures.

FIGURE 18–2 Overview of Accounting and Financial Reporting for Governments

(handwritten annotations: "Gov accg", "exemplify commercial accg")

	Governmental Type Funds					Proprietary Funds		Fiduciary Funds		Government-wide Financials
	General Fund	Special Revenue Fund	Capital Projects Funds	Debt Service Funds	Permanent Funds	Enterprise Funds	Internal Service Funds	Trust Funds	Agency Funds	
Basis of accounting	Modified accrual	Modified accrual	Modified accrual	Modified accrual	Modified accrual	Accrual	Accrual	Accrual	Accrual	Accrual
Budgetary basis recorded: (Budgetary accounts are typically used when a legally adopted annual operating budget is passed.)	Operating budget often recorded	Operating budget often recorded	Capital budget usually not recorded	Not required	Not required	No	No	No		
Long-term productive assets (buildings, equipment, etc.) reported	No	No	No	No	No	Yes	Yes	Yes	No	Yes
Long-term debt reported	No	No	No	No	No	Yes	Yes	Yes	No	Yes
Encumbrance recorded	Yes	Yes	Possibly	Possibly	Possibly	No	No	No	No	
Financial statements:										
Balance sheet	X	X	X	X	X					
Statement of net assets						X	X			X
Statement of revenues, expenditures and changes in fund balance	X	X	X	X	X					
Statement of revenues, expenses, and changes in fund net assets						X	X			
Statement of activities										X
Statement of cash flows						X	X			
Statement of fiduciary net assets								X	X	
Statement of changes in fiduciary net assets								X	X	

FIGURE 18–3 Worksheet for Statement of Net Assets for Governmental Funds

Handwritten margin notes: to be a major fund: → Must pass in 1 of four categories — (A) (L) (R) (Ex); = other categories

	Governmental Funds					Total Governmental Funds	Enterprise Fund	Total Governmental And Enterprise
	General	Special Revenue	Capital Projects	Debt Service	Permanent			
Assets								
Current								
Cash	102,000	15,000	16,000	2,000	13,000			
Property Taxes (net of allowances)	85,000	1,000		3,000				
Due From Enterprise Fund	3,000							
Inventory of Supplies	17,000							
Noncurrent								
Investment in Government Bonds					90,000			
Total Assets	207,000	16,000	16,000	5,000	103,000	347,000	140,000	487,000
Major Fund Test:								
Percent of Total Governmental		4.61%	4.61%	1.44%	29.68%			
Percent of Governmental Plus Enterprise		3.29%	3.29%	1.03%	21.15%		28.75%	
Major Fund Test (Yes or No)	Yes	No	No	No	Yes		Yes	
Liabilities and Fund Balances								
Vouchers Payable	55,000	3,000						
Contract Payable—Retainage			10,000					
Total Liabilities	55,000	3,000	10,000	0	0	68,000	112,000	180,000
Major Fund Test:								
Percent of Total Governmental		4.41%	14.71%	0.00%	0.00%			
Percent of Governmental Plus Enterprise		1.67%	5.56%	0.00%	0.00%		62.22%	
Major Fund Test (Yes or No)	Yes	No	Yes	No	No		Yes	
Fund Balances								
Reserved for:								
Encumbrances	15,000	6,000						
Inventories	17,000							
Debt Service				5,000				
Permanent Fund					100,000			
Unreserved, reported in:								
General Fund	120,000							
Special Revenue Fund		7,000						
Capital Projects Fund			6,000					
Debt Service Fund								
Permanent Fund					3,000			
Total Fund Balances	152,000	13,000	6,000	5,000	103,000	279,000		
Total Liabilities and Fund Balances	207,000	16,000	16,000	5,000	103,000	347,000		

FIGURE 18–4 Worksheet for the Statement of Revenues, Expenditures, and Changes in Fund Balances for the Governmental Funds

		Governmental Funds						
	General	Special Revenue	Capital Projects	Debt Service	Permanent	Total Governmental Funds	Enterprise Fund	Total Governmental And Enterprise
Revenues								
Property Taxes	781,000			33,000				
Sales Taxes	32,000	62,000						
Grants	33,000		10,000					
Miscellaneous	18,000				8,000			
Total Revenues	864,000	62,000	10,000	33,000	8,000	977,000	40,000	1,017,000
Major Fund Test:								
Percent of Total Governmental		6.35%	1.02%	3.38%	0.82%		3.93%	
Percent of Governmental and Enterprise		6.10%	0.98%	3.24%	0.79%		3.93%	
Major Fund Test (Yes or No)	Yes	No	No	No	No		No	
Expenditures								
Current								
General Government	206,000							
Street and Highways	71,000							
Public Safety	335,000							
Sanitation	141,000							
Culture and Recreation		49,000			5,000			
Miscellaneous								
Debt Service								
Principal Retirement				20,000				
Interest Charges				10,000				
Capital Outlay	58,000		124,000					
Total Expenditures	811,000	49,000	124,000	30,000	5,000	1,019,000	38,000	1,057,000
Major Fund Test:								
Percent of Total Governmental		4.81%	12.17%	2.94%	0.49%		3.74%	
Percent of Governmental and Enterprise		4.64%	11.73%	2.84%	0.47%		3.74%	
Major Fund Test (Yes or No)	Yes	No	Yes	No	No		No	
Excess (deficiency) of Revenues over Expenditures	53,000	13,000	(114,000)	3,000	3,000	(42,000)		
Other Financing Sources (Uses)								
Proceeds of Bond Issue			102,000					
Transfers In			20,000	2,000				
Transfers Out	(30,000)		(2,000)					
Total Other Financing Sources and Uses	(30,000)	0	120,000	2,000	0	92,000		
Special Item								
Contribution					100,000	100,000		
Net Change in Fund Balances	23,000	13,000	6,000	5,000	103,000	150,000		
Fund Balances—Beginning	129,000	0	0	0	0	129,000		
Fund Balances—Ending	152,000	13,000	6,000	5,000	103,000	279,000		

statement of revenues, expenditures, and changes in fund balance. The amounts for the general fund are taken from the information in Chapter 17. The amounts for the other funds will be developed throughout this chapter. These two worksheets are used throughout the discussion on the governmental funds and are the basis for preparing the governmental funds' financial statements that will be presented later in the chapter. The worksheets also include a major funds test that will be discussed later in the chapter. Thus, the two worksheets will be developed through the following discussions in this chapter.

Special Revenue Funds

Current governmental resources may be restricted for specific purposes, such as construction of the state highway system, maintenance of public parks, or operation of the public school system, city libraries, and museums. The necessary revenue often comes from special tax levies or federal or state governmental grants. Some minor revenue may be earned through user charges, but these charges are usually not sufficient to fully fund the service. *Special revenue funds* are used to account for such restricted resources. The governmental entity usually has a separate special revenue fund for each different activity of this type. Thus, a city may have several special revenue funds.

Accounting for special revenue funds is the same as for the general fund. The modified accrual basis of accounting is used, no fixed assets or depreciation are recorded in a special revenue fund, the operating budget is typically recorded in the accounts, and no long-term debt is recorded in a special revenue fund.

Special revenue fund accounting is not illustrated in the chapter because the principles for the special revenue fund are the same as those for the general fund as covered in Chapter 17. For purposes of the governmental funds statements, assume that $62,000 of property taxes were collected for the special revenue fund and that $49,000 was expended for the designated culture and recreation purposes for which the special revenue fund was established. The focus of this chapter is on the unique or interesting aspects of governmental accounting and financial reporting. Figure 18–3 presents the assumed numbers for the special revenue fund's statement of net assets, and Figure 18–4 presents the revenues ($62,000) and expenditures ($49,000) assumed for the special revenue fund.

Capital Projects Funds

Capital projects funds account for the acquisition or construction of major capital facilities or improvements that benefit the public. Examples are the construction of libraries, civic centers, fire stations, courthouses, bridges, major streets, and city municipal buildings. A separate capital projects fund is created at the time the project is approved and ceases at the completion of the project. Each project or group of related projects usually is accounted for in a separate capital projects fund.

Accounting for capital projects funds is similar to accounting for the general fund. The modified accrual basis of accounting is used, no fixed assets or depreciation are recorded in the capital projects funds, and no long-term debt is recorded in these funds. Capital projects funds, however, typically do not have annual operating budgets. A capital budget is prepared as a basis for selling bonds to finance a project, and the capital budget is the control mechanism for the length of the project. The capital budget for the project may, or may not, be formally recorded in the accounts. Theoretically, encumbrances are part of the budgetary system and encumbrances should flow from the appropriating authority of the budget. However, encumbrances may be recorded even if the capital project budget is not recorded. Encumbrances maintain an ongoing accounting record of the expenditure commitments that have been made on a project. The reserve for encumbrances reported on the periodic balance sheet for the capital projects fund can be determined from the information in the recorded budgetary encumbrance accounts.

The capital projects fund records capital outlays as expenditures. Thus, no fixed assets are recorded in this fund. A record of the construction in progress, however, may be maintained in memorandum format.

Illustration of Transactions

On January 1, 20X2, Sol City establishes a capital projects fund to account for a capital addition to the municipal courthouse. The expected cost of the addition is $120,000. A $100,000, 10 percent general obligation bond issue is sold at 102, for total proceeds of $102,000. The bond is a five-year serial bond with equal amounts of $20,000 to be paid each year, until the debt is extinguished. The bond proceeds are not revenue to the capital projects fund; they are reported in the other financing sources section of the statement of revenues, expenditures, and changes in fund balance. Sol City chose not to formally enter the project budget into the accounts, but does use an encumbrance system for control over project expenditures.

The capital projects fund is not entitled to the $2,000 premium on the sale of bonds. This premium is transferred as a transfer out to the debt service fund immediately upon receipt. The debt service fund records the receipt of the transfer as an transfer in [see entry (15) later in this chapter]. The premium is viewed as an adjustment of the interest rate, not as a part of the funds expendable by the capital projects fund. If bonds are sold at a discount, either the amount expended for the improvement must be decreased or the general fund must make up the difference to par.

In addition, a federal grant for $10,000 is received as financial support for part of the capital addition, and the capital projects fund receives an interfund transfer in of $20,000 from the city's general fund. Recall that an interfund transfer is an interfund transaction in which resources are moved from one fund, usually from the general fund, to another fund to be used for the operations of the receiving fund. The general fund records this transfer of $20,000 as an interfund transfer out [see entry (34) in Chapter 17]. The following entries are recorded for the 20X2 fiscal year.

Capital Projects Revenue and Bond Proceeds.   The sale of the bonds and receipt of the federal grant and operating transfer in are recorded as follows:

(1)	Cash	102,000	
	Other Financing Sources—Bond Issue Proceeds		102,000
	Issue $100,000 of bonds at 102.		
(2)	Other Financing Use—Transfer Out to Debt Service Fund	2,000	
	Cash		2,000
	Forward bond premium to debt service fund.		
(3)	Cash	10,000	
	Revenue—Federal Grant		10,000
	Receive federal grant to be applied to courthouse addition.		
(4)	Due from General Fund	20,000	
	Other Financing Source—Transfer in from General Fund		20,000
	Establish receivable for interfund transfer in from general fund.		

[handwritten margin notes:] dont get to keep the prem (if thiv is one)   Record premium

(5) Cash	20,000	
Due from General Fund		20,000

Receive transferred resources from general fund.

Entry (3) recognizes the $10,000 grant from the federal government as revenue at the time the grant is received. Some grants from the federal government are termed "expenditure-driven" grants, for which revenue can be recognized only as expenditures are incurred in conformity with the grant agreement. For these expenditure-driven grants, the local governmental unit credits a deferred revenue, instead of revenue, at the time of receipt of the grant, and then recognizes the revenue from the grant as approved expenditures are made.

Capital Projects Fund Expenditures.   The following encumbrances, expenditures, and disbursements are recorded in 20X2.

(6) ENCUMBRANCES	110,000	
BUDGETARY FUND BALANCE RESERVED		
FOR ENCUMBRANCES		110,000

Issue construction contract for $110,000.

(7) BUDGETARY FUND BALANCE RESERVED		
FOR ENCUMBRANCES	110,000	
ENCUMBRANCES		110,000

Project is completed and reverse reserve for encumbrances.

(8) Expenditures	118,000	
Contract Payable		108,000
Contract Payable—Retained Percentage		10,000

Actual construction cost of courthouse addition is $118,000. Additional cost is approved. Contract terms include retained percentage of $10,000 until full and final acceptance of project.

(9) Expenditures	6,000	
Vouchers Payable		6,000

Additional items for courthouse addition.

(10) Vouchers Payable	6,000	
Contract Payable	108,000	
Cash		114,000

Pay current portion of construction contract and vouchers.

In entry (8), Contract Payable is credited for $108,000 for the current portion due, and Contract Payable—Retained Percentage is credited for $10,000. In entry (10), the $108,000 current portion of the contract liability is paid in full. A normal practice of governmental units is to have a retained percentage of the total amount due under a construction contract held back to ensure that the contractor fully completes the project to the satisfaction of the governmental unit. For example, a city may stipulate that 10 percent of the total contract price is retained until the project is fully completed and accepted. This retainage payable is released and paid upon final acceptance of the project by the governmental unit.

Closing Entries in the Capital Projects Fund.   The nominal accounts are closed with the following entries:

(11) Revenue—Federal Grant	10,000	
Unreserved Fund Balance	114,000	
Expenditures		124,000

Close operating accounts of revenue and expenditures.

(12)	Other Financing Sources—Bond Issue Proceeds	102,000	
	Unreserved Fund Balance		102,000
	Close other financing sources.		
(13)	Other Financing Source—Transfer In from General Fund	20,000	
	Other Financing Use—Transfer Out to Debt Service Fund		2,000
	Unreserved Fund Balance		18,000
	Close interfund transfers.		

No encumbrances are outstanding as of the end of the fiscal year. At this point, the Unreserved Fund Balance account has a credit balance of $6,000. Upon completion and final approval of a capital project, the remaining fund balance is transferred either to the general fund or to the debt service fund, depending on the policy of the governmental unit. The transfer is a transfer out for the capital projects fund and a transfer in for the receiving fund because it involves the one-time transfer of the remaining resources in the capital projects fund. In the example above, Sol City decided that the fund should remain open through the first part of the next fiscal year in case any minor modifications of the new courthouse addition are required. If no further modifications are required, and the courthouse addition project is officially accepted, the $10,000 in the Contract Payable—Retained Percentage account is paid to the contractor. Any remaining resources in the capital projects fund are then transferred and the capital projects fund is closed.

Financial Statement Information for the Capital Projects Fund

The financial statement information for the capital projects funds is presented in Figure 18–3 for the balance sheet, and in Figure 18–4 for the statement of revenues, expenditures, and changes in fund balances. The Sol City capital projects fund was created on January 1, 20X2, the date the capital addition was approved and the serial bonds were sold. Figure 18–3 shows that the only asset remaining in this fund on December 31, 20X2, is $16,000 of cash, which includes the $10,000 for the contract payable-retainage. Figure 18–4 for the capital projects fund column presents the $102,000 of proceeds from the bond issue which is reported among other financing sources, with a reduction for the transfer of the $2,000 premium to the debt service fund, and the transfer in of $20,000, netting out the large excess of expenditures over revenue in the amount of $114,000. The statement of revenues, expenditures, and changes in fund balance reconciles to the $6,000 fund balance at the end of the fiscal period.

Debt Service Funds

Debt service funds account for the accumulation and use of resources for the payment of general long-term debt principal and interest. A government may have several types of general long-term debt obligations, as follows:

1. *Serial bonds.* The most common form of debt issued by governments is in the form of serial bonds. The bonds are repaid in installments over the life of the debt. A serial bond is called "regular" if the installments are equal, "irregular" if they are not equal.

2. *Term bonds.* This form of debt is less frequent now than in the past. The entire principal of the debt is due at the maturity date.

3. *Special assessment bonds.* Special assessment bonds are secured by tax liens on the property located within the special assessment tax district. The governmental unit may also become obligated in some manner to assume the payment of the debt in the event of default by the property owners. Special assessment bonds may be used to

finance capital projects, or to acquire other assets, such as ambulances or fire engines, necessary to operate the governmental unit. Special assessment bonds sold to acquire enterprise fund assets, however, should be accounted for within the enterprise fund. The special assessment feature simply states the source of financing and means of repayment.

4. *Notes and warrants.* These consist of debt typically issued for one or two years. These debts are usually secured by specific tax revenue, which may be used only to repay the debt. Property tax anticipation warrants are an example.

5. *Capital leases.* Governmental units must record capital leases in accordance with generally accepted accounting principles. These leases then become long-term liabilities of the governmental unit.

Some governmental units service long-term debt directly from the general fund, thereby eliminating the need for a debt service fund as a separate fiscal, accounting, and reporting entity. However, if a governmental entity has several long-term general obligations outstanding, it may be required by bond indentures or other regulations to establish a separate debt service fund for each obligation to account for the proper servicing of that debt.

The accounting and financial reporting for debt service funds are the same as for the general fund. The modified accrual basis of accounting is used, and only that portion of the long-term debt that has matured and is currently payable is recorded in the debt service funds.

Interest payable on long-term debt is not accrued; interest is recognized as a liability only when it comes due and payable. The "when due" recognition of interest matches the debt service expenditures with the resources accumulated to repay the debt. This approach prevents an understatement of the debt service fund balance. For example, if interest is accrued before it is actually due, the fund balance may show a deficit because of the excess of liabilities over assets. The function of the debt service fund is to accumulate resources to pay debt principal and interest as they become due. Thus, the when-due recognition of interest is consistent with the fund's objectives.

Illustration of Transactions

Sol City establishes a debt service fund to service the $100,000, five-year, 10 percent serial bond issued on January 1, 20X2, to finance the capital project courthouse addition. The bond initially sold at a premium of $2,000. The resources to pay the bond principal and interest as they become due will be obtained from a property tax levy specifically for debt service.

Adoption of Debt Service Fund Budget.   Debt service funds are not required to adopt annual operating budgets because the fund's expenditures are generally mandated by bond agreements and an operating budget may be viewed as unnecessarily redundant. Nevertheless, there is no restriction against having an operating budget for the debt service fund as part of a comprehensive budgeting system for a governmental entity, as illustrated here.

The annual operating budget for the debt service fund is adopted at the time the fund is created to service the serial bonds sold for the courthouse addition. Appropriations of $30,000 are budgeted to pay $20,000 of maturing principal and $10,000 of interest for the year. Sol City budgets all expected interfund transactions, and the anticipated interfund transfer in of the $2,000 premium on the serial bonds sold is part of the entry to record the budget:

(14)	ESTIMATED REVENUES CONTROL	30,000	
	ESTIMATED OTHER FINANCING SOURCE—TRANSFER IN	2,000	
	APPROPRIATIONS CONTROL		30,000
	BUDGETARY FUND BALANCE		2,000
	Adopt budget for 20X2.		

The budgetary accounts ESTIMATED REVENUES CONTROL and APPROPRIATIONS CONTROL are used to account for servicing serial bonds.

Debt Service Fund Revenue and Other Financing Sources.   The debt service fund obtains revenue from a specified property tax levy in this example. The bond premium received from the capital projects fund is recognized as a transfer in. Note that the capital projects fund records this transfer as an interfund transfer out [see entry (2) earlier in this chapter]. The entries to record the receipt of the bond premium and the levy and collection of taxes are as follows:

(15)	Cash	2,000	
	Other Financing Source—Transfer in from Capital Projects fund		2,000
	Receive bond premium from capital projects fund.		
(16)	Property Taxes Receivable	35,000	
	Allowance for Uncollectible Taxes		5,000
	Revenue—Property Tax		30,000
	Levy property taxes and provide for allowance		
	for uncollectible taxes.		
(17)	Cash	30,000	
	Property Taxes Receivable		30,000
	Receive portion of property taxes.		
(18)	Property Taxes Receivable—Delinquent	5,000	
	Allowance for Uncollectible Taxes	5,000	
	Property Taxes Receivable		5,000
	Revenue—Property Tax		3,000
	Allowance for Uncollectible Taxes—Delinquent		2,000
	Reclassify remaining property taxes as delinquent and reduce allowance for uncollectible taxes from $5,000 to $2,000.		

Debt Service Fund Expenditures.   The primary expenditures of the debt service fund are for the first annual payment of principal and for interest on the serial bonds payable. An encumbrance system is typically not used for matured principal and interest because the debt agreement serves as the expenditure control mechanism:

(19)	Expenditures—Principal	20,000	
	Matured Bonds Payable		20,000
	Recognize matured portion of serial bond:		
	$100,000 ÷ 5 years		
(20)	Expenditures—Interest	10,000	
	Matured Interest Payable		10,000
	Recognize interest due this period:		
	$100,000 × .10 × 1 year		
(21)	Matured Bonds Payable	20,000	
	Matured Interest Payable	10,000	
	Cash		30,000
	Pay first year's installment plus interest on bond.		

Closing Entries in the Debt Service Fund.   The nominal accounts are closed as follows:

(22)	APPROPRIATIONS CONTROL	30,000	
	BUDGETARY FUND BALANCE	2,000	
	ESTIMATED REVENUES CONTROL		30,000
	ESTIMATED OTHER FINANCING SOURCE—		
	TRANSFER IN		2,000
	Close budgetary accounts.		
(23)	Revenue—Property Tax	33,000	
	Expenditures—Principal		20,000
	Expenditures—Interest		10,000
	Fund Balance—Reserved for Debt Service		3,000
	Close operating revenue and expenditures.		
(24)	Other Financing Source—Transfer In from Capital Projects Fund	2,000	
	Fund Balance—Reserved for Debt Service		2,000
	Close interfund transfer.		

If the debt service fund services term bonds, a different budgetary account system is used. The following budgetary entry would be made for term bonds for the periods prior to the maturity date:

REQUIRED CONTRIBUTIONS	XXX	
REQUIRED EARNINGS	X	
BUDGETARY FUND BALANCE		XXX

The budgetary amounts are determined based on a computation of the contributions needed each period to be invested, earning a given return to accumulate to the amount required for the payment of the bonds. The debt service fund may then receive resources from the general fund or from a tax levy, which it would invest until the term bonds became due. In the period the term bonds reach maturity, the debt service fund pays the matured principal and interest from its available resources. The debt service fund may make temporary investments of excess cash in order to maximize the return from its resources. These investments are reported as an asset of the debt service fund. Most temporary investments are made in low-risk U.S. Treasury securities or in certificates of deposit from larger banks. Interest income is accrued as earned. The investments are valued in accordance with **GASB Statement No. 31,** "Accounting for Financial Reporting for Certain Investments and for External Investment Pools" (**GASB 31**). The general valuation standard in **GASB 31** is fair value for most investments made by a governmental entity. However, an exception is allowed for governmental entities, other than external investment pools, so that market investments may be reported at amortized cost, provided the investment has a remaining maturity of one year or less from the date of purchase. Unrealized gains or losses on investments are combined with realized gains or losses and are reported on the governmental entity's operating statements as net investment income or loss.

Financial Statement Information for the Debt Service Fund

The financial statement information of the debt service fund is presented in Figure 18–3 for the governmental funds balance sheet, and in Figure 18–4 for the governmental funds statement of revenues, expenditures, and changes in fund balance.

Permanent Funds

Permanent funds are in the governmental funds group and are established in those cases in which the fund principal must be preserved but that the income from these permanent funds is required to be used for the benefit of the government's programs or its general citizenry. The modified accrual basis of accounting is used to measure income. The financial reports for the permanent funds are the same as for all other governmental funds.

Illustration of Transactions

On January 1, 20X2, Sol City receives a $100,000 bequest from a long-term resident of the city. The will stipulates that the $100,000 is to be invested and the income is to be used to provide for maintenance and improvement of the city park. Note that a private-purpose fund, which would be a fiduciary fund, is one in which the government is required to use the principal or earnings for the benefit of specific individuals, private organizations, or other designated governments, as stated in the trust agreement. But this bequest is for the benefit of the general citizenry and is established as a permanent fund which is a governmental fund. The entries in this permanent fund during 20X2 are as follows:

(25)	Cash	100,000	
	Contributions		100,000
	Accept permanent fund resources.		

This contribution will be reported separately after other financing sources and uses at the bottom of the statement of revenues, expenditures, and changes in fund balance.

Investment and Interest. The fund's resources are used to acquire $100,000 face value, high-grade, 8 percent governmental securities at 90 to yield an effective interest rate of 10 percent. Interest income is accrued under the modified accrual method which means that the revenue recognition may be for only that amount of interest that is both measurable and available to finance expenditures made during the current fiscal period. Therefore, only the $8,000 of accrued interest receivable is available for expenditures this period, and the discount amortization would not be shown in the modified accrual basis financial statements. The interest is accrued and then collected within 20X2.

(26)	Investment in Bonds	90,000	
	Cash		90,000
	Acquire $100,000 par value government securities at 90.		
(27)	Accrued Interest Receivable	8,000	
	Interest Revenue		8,000
	Accrue interest:		
	$8,000 = $100,000 × .08, nominal (coupon) rate		
(28)	Cash	8,000	
	Accrued Interest Receivable		8,000
	Collect accrued interest on securities.		

Any capital gain or loss on the sale of investments is normally an adjustment of the fund principal. Capital gains or losses are typically not part of the expendable income.

Expenditures. The permanent trust fund expends $5,000 during the period for maintenance of the city park and recognizes the following entry:

(29)	Expenditures	5,000	
	Cash		5,000
	Expenditures made for maintenance of the city park.		

FIGURE 18–5   Governmental Funds Balance Sheet

Sol City
Balance Sheet
Governmental Funds
December 31, 20X2

	General	Capital Projects	Permanent	Other Governmental Funds	Total Governmental Funds
Assets					
Current					
Cash	$102,000	$16,000	$ 13,000	$17,000	$148,000
Property Taxes (net of allowances)	85,000			4,000	89,000
Due from Enterprise Fund	3,000				3,000
Inventory of Supplies	17,000				17,000
Noncurrent					
Investment in Government Bonds			90,000		90,000
Total Assets	$207,000	$16,000	$103,000	$21,000	$347,000
Liabilities and Fund Balances					
Vouchers Payable	55,000			3,000	$ 58,000
Contract Payable—Retainage		$10,000			10,000
Total Liabilities	$ 55,000	$10,000		$ 3,000	$ 68,000
Fund Balances					
Reserved for:					
Encumbrances	$ 15,000			$ 6,000	$ 21,000
Inventories	17,000				17,000
Debt Service				5,000	5,000
Permanent Fund			$100,000		100,000
Unreserved, reported in:					
General Fund	120,000				120,000
Special Revenue Fund				7,000	7,000
Capital Projects Fund		$ 6,000			6,000
Permanent Fund			3,000		3,000
Total Fund Balances	$152,000	$ 6,000	$103,000	$18,000	$279,000
Total Liabilities and Fund Balances	$207,000	$16,000	$103,000	$21,000	$347,000

The balance sheet information for the permanent trust fund as of December 31, 20X2, is presented in Figure 18–3. The information for the statement of revenues, expenditures, and changes in fund balance for the permanent fund is presented in Figure 18–4. Note that the $100,000 contribution is not part of operations but rather is reported at the bottom of the operating statement.

Governmental Funds Financial Statements

GASB 34 requires two financial statements for the governmental funds. The first is the governmental funds balance sheet presented in Figure 18–5, and the second is the governmental statement of revenues, expenditures, and changes in fund balance presented in Figure 18–6. The worksheets in Figures 18–3 and 18–4 are the basis for preparing these two statements. But the fund financial statements for the governmental funds

FIGURE 18–6 Governmental Funds Statement of Revenues, Expenditures, and Changes in Fund Balances

Sol City
Statement of Revenues, Expenditures, and Changes in Fund Balances
Governmental Funds
For the Year Ended December 31, 20X2

	General	Capital Projects	Permanent	Other Governmental Funds	Total Governmental Funds
Revenues					
Property Taxes	$781,000			$95,000	$ 876,000
Sales Taxes	32,000				32,000
Grants	33,000	$ 10,000			43,000
Miscellaneous	18,000		$ 8,000		26,000
Total Revenues	$864,000	$ 10,000	$ 8,000	$95,000	$ 977,000
Expenditures					
Current					
General Government	$206,000				$ 206,000
Street and Highways	71,000				71,000
Public Safety	335,000				335,000
Sanitation	141,000				141,000
Culture and Recreation			$ 5,000	$49,000	54,000
Debt Service					
Principal Retirement				20,000	20,000
Interest Charges				10,000	10,000
Capital Outlay	$ 58,000	$ 124,000			182,000
Total Expenditures	$811,000	$ 124,000	$ 5,000	$79,000	$1,019,000
Excess (deficiency) of Revenues over Expenditures	$ 53,000	$(114,000)	$ 3,000	$16,000	(42,000)
Other Financing Sources (Uses)					
Proceeds of Bond Issue		$ 102,000			$ 102,000
Transfers In		20,000		$ 2,000	22,000
Transfers Out	$ (30,000)	(2,000)			(32,000)
Total Other Financing Sources and Uses	$ (30,000)	$ 120,000	0	$ 2,000	$ 92,000
Contributions, Special Items and Extraordinary Items:					
Contribution			$100,000		$ 100,000
Net Change in Fund Balances	$ 23,000	$ 6,000	$103,000	$18,000	$ 150,000
Fund Balances—Beginning	129,000	0	0	0	129,000
Fund Balances—Ending	$152,000	$ 6,000	$103,000	$18,000	$ 279,000

separately report only major governmental funds, not necessarily individually each of the five governmental funds. Some of the governmental funds may not be considered major funds and these nonmajor funds are aggregated and reported in a single column as other governmental funds. **GASB 34** specifies the general fund as always a major fund. In addition, **GASB 34** established criteria that also encompass the enterprise funds. To determine which of the other governmental or enterprise funds are major, **GASB 34** specifies the following criteria must be met:

— one —

1. Total assets, liabilities, revenues, or expenditures/expenses of that individual governmental or enterprise fund are at least 10 percent or more of the governmental or enterprise category. — one —

2. Total assets, liabilities, revenues, or expenditures/expenses of the individual governmental or enterprise fund are at least 5 percent of the total for all governmental and enterprise funds combines.

These major funds tests are presented in Figure 18–3 (immediately below assets and below liabilities) and Figure 18–4 (immediately below revenues and below expenditures). To prepare the tests, information is also required for the enterprise fund. The underlying transactions for the enterprise fund are presented in the next section of this chapter. The information for the total assets, liabilities, revenues, and expenses of the enterprise fund is taken from the enterprise fund's financial statement information. For right now, the information for the enterprise fund is presented solely to discuss the major funds tests.

For example, the total assets of the five governmental funds is $347,000. After adding the $140,000 of total assets from the enterprise fund, the total assets for the combined governmental and enterprise funds is $487,000. Then the percentages of total assets in each fund to the total assets in the governmental fund, and the total assets in each fund to the combined total in the governmental and enterprise funds is computed. These tests are computed for assets, for liabilities, for revenues, and for expenditures/expenses. Any individual governmental fund that meets both of the criteria for a major fund on any of the four items of financial information (assets, liabilities, revenues, or expenditures) must be separately disclosed in the governmental funds financial statements. Note that the major fund criteria require meeting both of the percentage tests for at least one of the four financial statement items. Nonmajor funds are then aggregated and reported in one column. However, management of the governmental unit may elect to provide separate disclosure on any nonmajor fund that it feels is important for user of the financial statements to fully understand.

The general fund is always considered a major fund; therefore, no percentages need to be computed for the general fund. The results of the tests for major funds for the remaining governmental funds concludes that the following governmental funds are major: (1) capital projects fund (for expenditures), and (2) permanent fund (for assets). The capital projects fund and permanent fund are reported separately in the governmental funds balance sheet in Figure 18–5 and the governmental funds statement of revenues, expenditures, and changes in fund balances in Figure 18–6. The reporting for the enterprise fund is discussed later in this chapter. Note that the special revenue and debt service funds are aggregated into another governmental funds column. And **GASB 34** requires that a total for all governmental funds be provided. In addition, **GASB 34** requires a reconciliation schedule to convert from the modified accrual basis of accounting used for the governmental funds, to the accrual basis of accounting used for reporting the two government-wide financial statements. This reconciliation schedule is presented later in the chapter within the discussion of preparing the government-wide financial statements for the entire government entity.

Enterprise Funds

Governments sometimes offer goods or services for sale to the public. The amounts charged to customers are intended to recover all or most of the cost of these goods or services. For example, a city may operate electric, gas, and water utilities; transportation systems such as buses, trains, and subways; airports; sports arenas; parking lots and garages; and public housing. Such operations are accounted for in ***enterprise funds.*** Enterprise funds differ from special revenue funds in that the costs of enterprise fund activities are recovered by user charges. Therefore, the primary difference between establishing a special revenue fund and an enterprise fund is the source of revenue.

Enterprise funds are proprietary funds, and the basis of accounting is the same as for commercial entities. The accrual method is used to measure revenue and expenses. Proprietary funds report fixed assets, which are depreciated, and long-term debt, if issued, and they focus on income determination and capital maintenance. The financial statements for a proprietary funds are very similar to those for commercial entities: the statement of net assets (balance sheet), the statement of revenues, expenses, and changes in fund net assets (income statement), and the statement of cash flows.

Budgeting in the proprietary funds also has the same role as in commercial entities. A budget may be prepared for management planning purposes; however, the budget is normally not entered into the accounts.

Illustration of Transactions

Sol City has a municipal water utility that it operates as an enterprise fund. The trial balance of the water utility as of January 1, 20X2, the first day of the 20X2 fiscal year, is presented here:

Sol City
Trial Balance for Water Utility Enterprise Fund
January 1, 20X2

Cash	$ 9,000	
Machinery and Equipment	94,000	
Buildings	40,000	
Accumulated Depreciation—Machinery and Equipment		$ 15,000
Accumulated Depreciation—Buildings		2,000
Bonds Payable, 5%		100,000
Net Assets		26,000
Totals	$143,000	$143,000

One difference between balance sheet accounts for commercial entities and for proprietary funds is the lack of a stockholders' equity section in governmental accounting. The general public is the theoretical owner of all governmental assets. Furthermore, no stock certificates are issued; therefore, a Net Assets section is used instead of Common Stock and Additional Paid-In Capital. Other interesting differences are the large relative amounts of fixed assets and long-term debt. This is because enterprise funds typically require large investments in productive assets in order to provide the necessary level of service to the public, and these investments are usually financed by long-term revenue bonds.

The water utility sells its product to the residents of Sol City based on a user charge. In addition to water revenue, the water utility receives a $3,000 short-term interfund loan from the general fund and obtains its office supplies from the city's centralized purchasing operation, which is accounted for as an internal service fund. During the year, the water utility acquires a new pump costing $6,000.

Enterprise Fund Revenues. The water utility provides service during the period and bills its customers for the amount of water used. These transactions are recorded as follows:

(30)	Accounts Receivable	40,000	
	Revenue—Water Sales		40,000
	Bill customers for water used as indicated by meter readings.		
(31)	Cash	32,000	
	Accounts Receivable		32,000
	Collect portion of accounts receivable.		

Capital Asset Acquisition. The water utility acquires a new pump during the year.

(32)	Equipment	6,000	
	Vouchers Payable		6,000
	Receive new pump for wellhouse.		
(33)	Vouchers Payable	6,000	
	Cash		6,000
	Pay voucher for new pump.		

Interfund Activities. Several interfund transactions occur during the year. First, in an interfund financing transaction, the water utility receives $3,000 from the general fund as a short-term loan to be repaid within 90 days. The general fund records this as a short-term receivable, Due from Enterprise Fund [see entry (39) in Chapter 17]. Second, the utility acquires its office supplies from the internal service fund in an interfund services provided and used transaction. The internal service fund reports this as a revenue transaction [see entry (47) later in this chapter]:

(34)	Cash	3,000	
	Due to General Fund		3,000
	Recognize payable for loan from general fund.		
(35)	General Operating Expenses	3,000	
	Due to Internal Service Fund		3,000
	Receive office supplies from centralized purchasing department at a cost of $3,000.		
(36)	Due to Internal Service Fund	2,000	
	Cash		2,000
	Approve payment of $2,000 to centralized purchasing department for supplies received.		

Enterprise Fund Expenses. The water utility fund incurs $9,000 of operating expenses during the period. In addition, several adjusting journal entries are required at the end of the fiscal year to recognize additional expenses. Note that these adjusting entries are similar to those of a commercial entity:

(37)	General Operating Expenses	9,000	
	Vouchers Payable		9,000
	Incur operating expenses during year.		
(38)	Vouchers Payable	6,000	
	Cash		6,000
	Pay approved vouchers for operating expenses.		
(39)	Bad Debt Expense	3,000	
	Allowance for Uncollectibles		3,000
	Provide for expected uncollectible accounts.		

(40)	Depreciation Expense	18,000	
	Accumulated Depreciation—Buildings		3,000
	Accumulated Depreciation—Machinery and Equipment		15,000
	Recognize depreciation expense for year.		
(41)	Interest Expense	5,000	
	Accrued Interest Payable		5,000
	Accrue interest on bond payable: $100,000 × .05 × 1 year		

Closing Entries in the Enterprise Fund.   The nominal accounts are closed, and the period's profit or loss is determined as follows:

(42)	Revenue—Water Sales	40,000	
	General Operating Expenses		12,000
	Bad Debt Expense		3,000
	Depreciation Expense		18,000
	Interest Expense		5,000
	Profit and Loss Summary		2,000
	Close nominal accounts into profit and loss summary.		
(43)	Profit and Loss Summary	2,000	
	Net Assets		2,000
	Close profit and loss summary into net assets.		

Financial Statements for the Proprietary Funds

Three financial statements are required for the proprietary funds. If a governmental entity has more than one enterprise fund, each of the enterprise funds must be individually assessed to determine if it is a major fund. In the case of Sol City, it has only one enterprise fund. Figure 18–7 presents the statement of net assets for the enterprise proprietary fund and also for the internal service proprietary fund that will be discussed in the next section of this chapter. Figure 18–8 presents the statement of revenues, expenses, and changes in fund net assets for the two proprietary funds of Sol City. And Figure 18–9 presents the statement of cash flows for the two proprietary funds.

The statement of net assets in Figure 18–7 is similar to that required for commercial entities. Proprietary funds report their own fixed assets, investments, and long-term liabilities. Note that the net assets section is divided into the amount invested in capital assets, net of the related debt, and unrestricted assets. The statement of revenues, expenses, and changes in fund net assets is similar to the income statement for commercial entities. A separation of operating and nonoperating revenues and expenses is made to provide greater information value regarding the operations of the proprietary funds. Contributions and transfers in or out are reported below the income (loss) line in the statement of revenues, expenses, and changes in fund net assets. Contributions would include any capital asset transfers from a governmental fund to a proprietary fund. For example, the general fund may transfer equipment to an enterprise fund. Note that the governmental funds describe the interfund transfers as other financing sources or uses, but the proprietary funds use only the terms transfer in or transfer out to describe these nonoperating interfund transactions.

The statement of cash flows for enterprise funds is specified by **GASB Statement No. 9,** "Reporting Cash Flows of Proprietary and Nonexpendable Trust Funds and Governmental Entities that Use Proprietary Fund Accounting" (**GASB 9**). This standard provides a format that differs somewhat from the three-section format of the statement of cash flows for commercial entities. Because of the large number of capital asset acquisition and financing transactions in proprietary funds, the GASB specified four sections of the statement of cash flows, as follows:

FIGURE 18–7   Proprietary Funds Statements of Net Assets

	Enterprise Fund	Internal Service Fund
Sol City		
Statement of Net Assets		
Proprietary Funds		
December 31, 20X2		
Assets		
Current Assets:		
Cash	$ 30,000	$ 4,000
Accounts Receivable (net)	5,000	
Due from Other Funds		1,000
Inventory of Supplies		6,000
Total Current Assets	$ 35,000	$11,000
Noncurrent Assets:		
Capital Assets:		
Machinery and Equipment	100,000	3,000
Less Accumulated Depreciation	(30,000)	(1,000)
Buildings	40,000	
Less Accumulated Depreciation	(5,000)	
Total Noncurrent Assets	$105,000	$ 2,000
Total Assets	$140,000	$13,000
Liabilities		
Current Liabilities:		
Vouchers Payable	3,000	6,000
Accrued Interest Payable	5,000	
Due to Other Funds	4,000	
Total Current Liabilities	12,000	$ 6,000
Noncurrent Liabilities:		
Bonds Payable, 5%	100,000	
Total Liabilities	$112,000	$ 6,000
Net Assets		
Invested in Capital Assets, Net of Related Debt	5,000	2,000
Unrestricted	23,000	5,000
Total Net Assets	$ 28,000	$ 7,000

1. *Cash flows from operating activities.* This first section includes all transactions from providing services and delivering goods. **GASB 34** requires the use of the direct method of computing cash flows from operating activities. It includes cash flows from interfund operating transactions and reimbursements from other funds.

2. *Cash flows from noncapital financing activities.* This second section includes activities such as borrowing or repaying money for purposes other than to acquire, construct, or improve capital assets. It includes cash for financing activities received from, or paid to, other funds except that which is specifically specified for capital asset use.

3. *Cash flows from capital and related financing activities.* This third section includes all activities clearly related to, or attributable to, the acquisition, disposition, construction, or improvement of capital assets. This section also includes the interest paid on borrowings for capital assets.

FIGURE 18–12   Government-wide Statement of Net Assets

Sol City
Statement of Net Assets
December 20X2

	Primary Government			
	Governmental Activities	*Business-type Activities*	*Total*	*Component Unit*
Assets				
Cash and Cash Equivalents	$ 152,000	$ 30,000	$ 182,000	$ 3,000
Receivables, Net	89,000	5,000	94,000	
Internal Balances	4,000	(4,000)	0	
Inventories	23,000		23,000	1,000
Investment in Government Bonds	91,000		91,000	
Capital Assets:				
Land and Infrastructure	3,000,000			
Other Depreciable Assets, Net	1,202,000	105,000	1,307,000	870,000
Total Assets	$4,561,000	$136,000	$4,697,000	$874,000
Liabilities				
Vouchers Payable	$ 64,000	$ 3,000	$ 67,000	
Accrued Interest Payable		5,000	5,000	
Contract Payable-Retainage	10,000		10,000	
Noncurrent Liabilities:				
Due in More Than 1 Year	80,000	100,000	180,000	$120,000
Total Liabilities	$ 154,000	$108,000	$ 262,000	$120,000
Net Assets				
Invested in Capital Assets, Net of Related Debt	$4,122,000	$ 5,000	$4,127,000	$750,000
Restricted for:				
Debt Service	5,000		5,000	
Permanent Funds	100,000		100,000	
Unrestricted	180,000	23,000	203,000	4,000
Total Net Assets	$4,407,000	$ 28,000	$4,435,000	$754,000

notes are not balancing — just 3 categories.

a. Budgetary Comparison Schedules (Figure 18–16)
b. Information About Infrastructure Assets

The fund-based financial statements were discussed previously in the chapter. The following discussion centers on the government-wide financials and the required supplementary information.

Government-wide Financial Statements

The **government-wide financial statements** include the *(a)* statement of net assets, and *(b)* statement of activities. **GASB 34** requires that government-wide financial statements be prepared on the economic resources measurement focus with the accrual basis of accounting.

Statement of Net Assets.   Figure 18–12 presents the statement of net assets for Sol City. Some important points regarding this statement of net assets are:

FIGURE 18–13 **Government-wide Statement of Activities**

Functions/Programs	Expenses	Program Revenues			Net (Expenses) Revenue and Changes in Net Assets			
		Charges for Services	Operating Grants and Contributions	Capital Grants and Contributions	Primary Government Governmental Activities	Primary Government Business-type Activities	Total	Component Unit
Primary Government								
Governmental Activities:								
General Government	$212,000	$ 4,000	$23,000	$20,000	$ (165,000)		$ (165,000)	
Street and Highways	71,000				(71,000)		(71,000)	
Public Safety	335,000				(335,000)		(335,000)	
Sanitation	141,000				(141,000)		(141,000)	
Culture and Recreation	54,000				(54,000)		(54,000)	
Depreciation of Capital Assets	120,000				(120,000)		(120,000)	
Interest on Long-term Debt	10,000				(10,000)		(10,000)	
Total Government Activities	$943,000				$ (896,000)		$ (896,000)	
Business-type Activities:								
Water	$ 38,000	$40,000				$ 2,000	$ 2,000	
Total Business-type Activities	$ 38,000	$40,000				$ 2,000	$ 2,000	
Total Primary Government	$981,000	$44,000	$23,000	$20,000		$ 2,000	$ (894,000)	
Component Unit								
Library	$ 6,000	0						$ (6,000)
Total Component Unit	$ 6,000	0						$ (6,000)
General Revenues:								
Taxes:								
Property Taxes, Levied for General Purposes					$ 781,000			
Property Taxes, Levied for Special Purposes					62,000			
Property Taxes, Levied for Debt Service					33,000			
Sales Taxes					32,000			
Investment Earnings					9,000			
Miscellaneous Revenues					18,000			
Contribution					100,000			12,000
Transfers Between Governmental and Business-type Funds					0			
Total General Revenues, Special Items and Transfers					$1,035,000	2,000	$1,035,000	
Change in Net Assets					139,000	26,000	141,000	6,000
Net Assets—Beginning					$4,268,000	28,000	$4,294,000	$748,000
Net Assets—Ending					$4,407,000		$4,435,000	$754,000

1. The format of the statement is Assets − Liabilities = Net Assets. This focuses attention on the net assets of the government entity.

2. The columns used are for the governmental activities and business-type activities of the primary government, with the component unit, the city library, discretely presented in its own column. Note that **GASB 34** requires that the internal service fund be reported as part of the governmental activities. The business-type activities present the enterprise funds. Any major enterprise funds would be presented in their own columns under the Business-type Activities heading. Fiduciary funds are not reported on the statement of net assets.

3. Assets include all types of assets of the government entity, including infrastructure such as roads, sewers, and so on. These capital assets are not reported in the governmental funds that record costs of capital assets as expenditures of the period. However, **GASB 34** requires that all capital assets be reported on the government-wide financial statements. Furthermore, these assets will be depreciated and the depreciation will be reported on the statement of activities. Note that Sol City distinguishes between its infrastructure net assets and its buildings and equipment. The asset, Internal Balances, represents interfund receivable/payables between the governmental activities (the enterprise funds). These would cancel out each other for the total column.

4. Net assets are separated into three categories: *(a)* invested in capital assets, net of related debt, *(b)* restricted by external requirements of creditors, grantors, contributors, or other government entities, and any restrictions imposed by law, and *(c)* unrestricted. Note that restricted and unrestricted do not mean the same things as reserved and unreserved as used for the fund-based financial statements.

Statement of Activities. The statement of activities for Sol City is presented in Figure 18–13. Important observations regarding this statement of activities are:

1. The full accrual basis of accounting is used to measure revenues and expenses for the government-wide statements. A reconciliation between the modified accrual basis of accounting for the governmental funds and the accrual basis of the government-wide statements is required.

2. The format of the statement of activities is based on the functions or programs of the government entity. Program revenues are categorized by type, and the net expenses (revenues) is shown separately for each of the governmental and business-type activities. The internal service fund is blended into the governmental activities. The enterprise funds are presented in the business-type activities column. Fiduciary funds are not reported on the statement of activities. Again note that the component unit, the city library, is discretely presented in its own column.

3. The expenses include depreciation of the capital assets, including any infrastructure assets. However, the expenses would not include any expenditures in the governmental funds that were made for long-term, capital assets. For government-wide statements, these expenditures must be included as increases to long-term capital assets on the balance sheet.

4. General revenues are reported separately on the bottom of the statement. These are revenues that are not directly tied to any specific program. **GASB 34** requires that contributions to permanent endowments, special items, and extraordinary items be reported in this section for the government-wide statements. Special items are events within the control of management that are either unusual in nature or infrequent in occurrence. Sol City has no special or extraordinary items, and the only contribution to a permanent endowment was the $100,000 contribution received by the permanent

b/c accrual v. modified accrual

FIGURE 18–14　　**Reconciliation Schedule for the Statement of Net Assets**

Sol City Reconciliation of the Balance Sheet of Governmental Funds to the Statement of Net Assets December 31, 20X2	
Fund balances reported in the governmental funds	$ 279,000
Amounts reported for the governmental activities in the statement of net assets are different because:	
Capital assets used in governmental activities are not financial resources and therefore are not reported in the governmental funds.	
($4,202,000-$2,000 internal service assets included below)	4,200,000
Internal service funds are used by management to charge the costs of certain activities, such as centralized purchasing and storage functions to individual funds. The assets and liabilities of the internal service fund are included in governmental activities in the statement of net assets.	7,000
Long-term liabilities, including bonds payable, are not due and payable in the current period and therefore are not reported in the funds.	(80,000)
Interest on bonds in the permanent fund is recognized in that fund under the modified accrual basis, but must be adjusted to the accrual basis for the government-wide financial statements.	1,000
Net assets of governmental activities	$4,407,000

fund. Note that the ending net assets reported in this statement articulates with the ending net assets presented on the statement of net assets.

Reconciliation Schedules

GASB 34 requires that two *reconciliation schedules* be presented to reconcile the net change in the total amounts reported on the governmental funds statements with the amounts reported on the government-wide statements. These reconciliation schedules may be presented as part of the governmental funds statements or in a separate footnote of the financial report.

　　The first reconciliation schedule, the reconciliation between the net reported for the governmental funds to the net assets for the government-wide financials, is presented in Figure 18–14. This statement describes the adjustments necessary to move from the modified accrual method that was used in the governmental funds to the accrual basis that was used for the government-wide statements. For example, the infrastructure and capital assets are not reported in the government funds statement of net assets but must be added to obtain the net assets presented in the government-wide statements. Furthermore, the government-wide statements include the accounts of the internal service funds that were not part of the governmental funds statements.

　　The second reconciliation schedule, the reconciliation between the net change in fund balances reported in the governmental funds statements to the change in net assets reported in the government-wide financials, is presented in Figure 18–15. For example, interest revenue on the investment in bonds in the permanent fund was presented in that fund under the modified accrual basis for the amount of $8,000. However, under the accrual basis, the interest revenue would be computed based on the effective interest rate, with amortization of the discount, in the amount of $9,000. ($90,000 × .10) The difference of $1,000 is an adjustment both to the change in net assets, and to the net assets.

FIGURE 18–15   **Reconciliation Schedule for the Statement of Revenues, Expenditures, and Changes in Fund Balances**

(handwritten margin note: Bonds shown @ book value)

(handwritten margin note: ∆ from cash to accrual)

Sol City **Reconciliation of the Statement of Revenues, Expenditures, and Changes** **in Fund Balances of Governmental Funds to the** **Statement of Activities** **For the Year Ended December 31, 20X2**	
Net change in fund balances—governmental funds	$150,000
Governmental funds report capital outlays as expenditures. However, in the statement of activities, the costs of those assets is capitalized and depreciated over their estimated useful lives. This is the amount by which capital outlays in the governmental funds ($182,000) exceeded depreciation of the governmental assets ($119,000).	63,000
Bond proceeds provide current financial resources for the governmental funds. However, the issuance of debt increases long-term liabilities in the statement of net assets. Repayment of debt principal is an expenditure in the governmental funds, but the repayment reduces the long-term liabilities in the statement of net assets. This is the amount by which bond proceeds ($102,000) exceeded the net repayments of principal ($20,000).	(82,000)
Revenues in the statement of activities are recorded on the accrual basis. Interest revenue in the governmental funds is recorded on the modified accrual basis. This is the amount that accrual interest exceeded the interest recognized in the permanent funds.	1,000
Internal service funds are used by management to charge the costs of certain services, such as a centralized purchasing function, to individual funds. The net revenue (expense) of the internal service funds is reported with governmental activities.	7,000
Change in net assets of governmental activities	$139,000

Budgetary Comparison Schedule

GASB 34 requires that a ***budgetary comparison schedule*** be presented as required supplementary information for the general fund and for each special revenue fund that has a legally adopted annual budget. This schedule will be presented in the footnotes of the annual report. The budgetary comparison schedule for Sol City's general fund is presented in Figure 18–16.

Important observations regarding the budgetary comparison schedule are:

1. **GASB 34** requires that both the original budget and the final budget be presented. The original budget is the first budget for the fiscal period adopted by the government entity. Through the year, many government entities will modify the original budget because of new events or changes in expectations. These changes must go through the legislative process of the government, such as the city council.

2. The budgetary comparison schedule should be presented on the same format, with the same terminology and classifications, as the original budget.

3. A separate column for the variance between the final budget and the actual amounts is encouraged, but not required. It is presented here to provide a complete presentation of the possible disclosures of a governmental entity.

Other Required Supplementary Information (RSI)

GASB 34 also specified additional ***required supplementary information (RSI)*** in addition to that already discussed in the chapter.

FIGURE 18–16   Budgetary Comparison Schedule

may be different b/c of an approved amendment.

Sol City
Budgetary Comparison Schedule
General Fund
For the Year Ended December 31, 20X2

	Budgeted Amounts		Actual Amounts (Budgetary Basis)	Variance with Final Budget Positive (Negative)
	Original	*Final*		
Budgetary fund balance, January 1	$129,000	$129,000	$129,000	$ 0
Resources (inflows):				
Property taxes	775,000	775,000	781,000	6,000
Grants	55,000	55,000	33,000	(22,000)
Sales taxes	25,000	25,000	32,000	7,000
Miscellaneous	20,000	20,000	18,000	(2,000)
Amounts available for appropriation	$875,000	$875,000	$864,000	$(11,000)
Charges to appropriations (outflows):				
General government	$200,000	$200,000	$206,000	$ (6,000)
Streets and highways	75,000	75,000	71,000	4,000
Public safety	400,000	400,000	393,000	7,000
Sanitation	150,000	150,000	141,000	9,000
Nondepartmental:				
Transfers out to other funds	30,000	30,000	30,000	0
Total charges to appropriations	$855,000	$855,000	$841,000	$ 14,000
Budgetary fund balance, December 31	$149,000	$149,000	$152,000	$ 3,000

Management's Discussion and Analysis. The Management's Discussion and Analysis (MDA) is presented before the financial statements and will provide an analytical overview of the government's financial activities. The MDA will discuss current year operations and financial position and then compare it with the prior year's results. The purpose of this RSI item is to provide users of the financial statements with an objective discussion of whether the government's financial position has improved or deteriorated during the year.

Information about Infrastructure Assets and the Modified Approach.   A government does not have to depreciate its major network infrastructure assets, such as roads or sewer systems (termed eligible infrastructure assets), if it meets the following two requirements: *(a)* the government manages its eligible infrastructure assets by maintaining an up-to-date inventory of these assets, periodically performs condition assessments of these assets, and each year estimates the annual amount required to maintain and preserve the eligible infrastructure assets at the condition level established and disclosed by the government, and *(b)* the government documents that the eligible infrastructure assets are being preserved approximately at or above the condition level established and disclosed by the government. If a government entity does not depreciate its eligible infrastructure assets, then all expenditures made for those assets, other than for additions and improvements, are expensed in the period incurred. Additions and improvements are capitalized to noncurrent assets. This alternative is termed the modified approach for accounting for eligible infrastructure assets and the footnote disclosures must indicate for which infrastructure assets the modified approach is being used, the conditions of those assets, and the maintenance expenditures incurred during the period.

Certain Financial Statement Note Disclosures

A number of footnote disclosures are required in government unit financial statements, as specified in various governmental accounting and reporting standards. As a result of a focused project on the effectiveness and usefulness of note disclosures, in June 2001 the GASB issued **GASB Statement No. 38**, "Certain Financial Statement Note Disclosures" **(GASB 38)**. **GASB 38** now requires the footnote disclosures to include the following:

1. In the summary of significant accounting policies, provide descriptions of the activities accounted for in the major funds, internal service fund type, and fiduciary fund types. This change is a result of **GASB 34**'s focus on major funds rather than all funds.

2. Delete the requirement to disclose the accounting policy for encumbrances in the summary of significant accounting policies (i.e., the lapsing or nonlapsing method).

3. Disclose the period of availability used for recording revenues in governmental funds.

4. Debt service requirements to maturity, separately identifying principal and interest for each of the subsequent five years and in five-year increments thereafter, and changes in variable-rate debt. In addition, governments should disclose the future minimum payments for each of the five succeeding years for capital and noncancelable operating leases.

5. Provide a schedule of changes in short-term debt during the year along with the purposes for which the debt was issued.

6. Add the disclosure of actions taken to address any significant violations of finance-related legal or contractual provisions to the footnote describing these significant violations.

7. Disclose detail of the payable and receivable funds for interfund balances, and the purposes of the interfund transfers. In addition disclosure should be made regarding the amounts of interfund transfers during the period, and a description and amount of significant transfers that are not expected to occur on a routine basis.

8. Provide details of the components of accounts payable so that the financial statement users can understand the timeliness and payment priorities of payables.

9. Provide details about significant individual accounts when their nature is obscured by aggregation. For example, more disclosure could be made for receivables that contain a myriad of different credit risks or liquidity attributes.

Other Financial Report Items

Governments may choose to provide additional information beyond that required as discussed previously. For example, some government entities present comprehensive annual financial reports (CAFRs), which include additional statistical information about the sources of revenues, the property tax levies, and property values, demographic statistics, and other miscellaneous statistics that management of the government unit feels will aid users of the financial report. Some government units may additionally disclose financial statements for individual funds, or combined by fund type. And, some governments may go beyond the required footnote disclosures and provide additional schedules and information. As with commercial enterprises, it really is up to the management of the government entity to determine how much additional disclosure it wishes to provide in its annual report.

Interim Reporting

Governmental units generally are not required to publish interim reports, although many prepare monthly or quarterly reports to determine the current progress of compliance with legal and budgetary limitations and to plan for changes in events or developments that were not foreseen when the annual budget was prepared. Interim reports are a valuable internal management control instrument; they typically are not made available to the general public.

Auditing Governmental Entities

Most governmental units are audited annually because of state or federal requirements or because long-term creditors demand audited statements as part of the debt agreements. The audit of a governmental unit is different from the audit of a commercial entity. The auditor not only must express an opinion on the fairness of the audited entity's financial statements in conformity with applicable accounting principles but must also assess the audited entity's compliance with legal or contractual provisions of state law, debt covenants, terms of grants from other governmental entities, and other restrictions on the governmental unit.

The Single Audit Act of 1984 is a federal law specifying the audit requirements for all state and local governments receiving federal financial assistance. The audit act requires auditors to determine *(a)* if the financial statements fairly present the government's financial condition, *(b)* if the governmental unit has an internal control system to provide reasonable assurance that it is managing federal financial assistance programs in compliance with applicable laws and regulations, and *(c)* if the governmental unit has complied with laws and regulations that may have a material effect on each federal program. The auditors not only issue the standard audit report, but also must issue special reports on items *(b)* and *(c)* above. The Single Audit Act does not apply to all governmental units receiving federal financial assistance. Governmental units receiving more than $100,000 in any one year must fully comply; units receiving between $25,000 and $100,000 in any one year may elect the single audit covering all three items or may have an audit examination on just items *(b)* and *(c)*. Governmental units receiving less than $25,000 in any one year are exempt from the provisions of the act.

Additional Considerations

Accounting for Pension Trust Funds

Many states, and some local governments, now have public employee retirement systems (PERSs), which either supplement or replace federal Social Security. Some PERSs are created for employees of specific governments, such as all municipal employees, while some are for employees within certain functional fields, such as teachers, firefighters, or police officers. Employees included in a PERS usually contribute a percentage of their salaries, and the employer also makes a contribution. The advantage of a PERS to a local governmental unit is that the required employer contribution is typically less than that required by the FICA, thereby saving the government and the

  a. Special revenue.

  b. Capital projects.

  c. Internal service.

  d. General.

E18–4 **Multiple-Choice Questions on Various Funds**

Use the information below to answer questions 1 and 2:

  On August 1, 20X6, the City of Rockhaven received $1,000,000 from a prominent citizen to establish a private-purpose trust fund. The donor stipulated that the cash be permanently invested and that the earnings from the investments be spent to support local artists. During the year ended June 30, 20X7, $50,000 of dividends were received from stock investments and $35,000 of interest was earned from bond investments. At June 30, $5,000 of the interest earned was not yet received. During the year ended June 30, 20X7, $75,000 was spent by the trust fund to support local artists.

 1. For the year ended June 30, 20X7, the trust fund should report operating revenues of:

  a. $80,000.

  b. $50,000.

  c. $85,000.

  d. $35,000.

 2. For the year ended June 30, 20X7, the trust fund should report the $75,000 spent to support local artists as a(n):

  a. Expense.

  b. Contra contribution.

  c. Transfer out.

  d. Direct deduction from fund balance.

 3. Which of the following statements is (are) correct about agency funds?

  I. Agency funds should report revenues only when they are both measurable and available.

  II. Agency funds are reported on the proprietary funds' statement of cash flows.

   a. I only.

   b. II only.

   c. I and II.

   d. Neither I nor II.

Use the following information to answer questions 4 through 8.

On July 2, 20X6, the village of Westbury established an internal service fund to service the data processing needs of the other departments of the village. The internal service fund received a transfer of $600,000 from the general fund and a $100,000 long-term advance from the water utility enterprise fund in order to acquire computer equipment. During July of 20X6, computer equipment costing $650,000 was acquired. The following events occurred during the year ended June 30, 20X7:

Charges for services to other departments for data processing services rendered	$100,000
Operating expenses (exclusive of depreciation expense)	45,000
Depreciation expense	40,000
Interest expense on the advance	5,000

At June 30, 20X7, all but $7,000 of the billings were collected, and all the operating expenses and interest expense were paid, except for $3,000 of operating expenses.

 4. For the year ended June 30, 20X7, what was the income of Westbury's internal service fund?

  a. $13,000.

  b. $6,000.

    c. $3,000.

    d. $10,000.

5. At June 30, 20X7, what amount would appear on the internal service fund balance sheet as total assets?

    a. $700,000.

    b. $710,000.

    c. $713,000.

    d. $708,000.

6. Assume the mayor's office and the police department were billed $55,000 for data processing work during the year ended June 30, 20X7. What account should be debited in the general fund to record these billings?

    a. Other Financing Use—Transfers out

    b. Expenditures.

    c. Due to internal service fund.

    d. Operating expenses.

7. Assume that the water utility, an enterprise fund, was billed $25,000 for data processing work during the year ended June 30, 20X7. What account should be debited in the enterprise fund to record these billings?

    a. Operating expenses.

    b. Other Financing Use—Transfers out.

    c. Expenditures.

    d. Due to internal service fund.

8. Assume that the income for Westbury's internal service fund was $10,000 for the year ended June 30, 20X7. What net assets should be reported on the internal service fund's statement of net assets at June 30, 20X7?

    a. $713,000.

    b. $610,000.

    c. $710,000.

    d. $613,000.

E18–5   **Multiple-Choice Questions on Various Funds [AICPA Adapted]**

1. A state government has the following activities:

    I. State-operated lottery $12,000,000

    II. State-operated hospital   3,000,000

    Which of these activities should be accounted for in an enterprise fund?

    a. Neither I nor II.

    b. II only.

    c. I only.

    d. Both I and II.

2. Financing for the renovation of Taft City's municipal park, begun and completed during 20X5, came from the following sources:

Grant from state government	$400,000
Proceeds from general obligation bond issue	500,000
Transfer In from Taft's general fund	100,000

In its operating statement for the year ended December 31, 20X5, Taft should report these amounts as:

	Revenues	*Other Financing Sources*
a.	$1,000,000	$ 0
b.	$ 900,000	$ 100,000
c.	$ 400,000	$ 600,000
d.	$ 0	$1,000,000

3. Bret City is accumulating financial resources that are legally restricted to payments of general obligation debt principal and interest maturing in future years. At December 31, 20X5, $5,000,000 has been accumulated for principal payments and $300,000 has been accumulated for interest payments. These restricted funds should be accounted for in the:

	Debt Service Fund	*General Fund*
a.	$ 0	$5,300,000
b.	$ 300,000	$5,000,000
c.	$5,000,000	$ 300,000
d.	$5,300,000	$ 0

4. The billings for transportation services provided to other governmental units are recorded by the internal service fund as:
   a. Other Financing Source—Transfers in.
   b. Operating revenues.
   c. Interfund reimbursements.
   d. Advances to other funds.

5. Wilbur City should prepare a statement of cash flows for which of the following funds?

	Wilbur City Hall Capital Projects Fund	*Wilbur Water Enterprise Fund*
a.	No	Yes
b.	No	No
c.	Yes	No
d.	Yes	Yes

6. Pearl County received proceeds from various towns and cities for capital projects financed by Pearl's long-term debt. A special tax was assessed by each local government, and a portion of the tax was restricted to repay the long-term debt of Pearl's capital projects. Pearl should account for the restricted portion of the special tax in which of the following funds?
   a. Special revenue fund.
   b. Debt service fund.
   c. Capital projects fund.
   d. Permanent Trust fund.

E18–6   Capital Projects Fund Entries

York established a capital projects fund for the construction of a walkway over Kish Avenue from the courthouse to the parking garage. The estimated cost is $300,000. The county commission agreed to provide a $100,000 grant. A 9 percent, $200,000 bond issue was sold at 102.5. The York City Council awarded a construction contract for $275,000 on March 1, 20X1. The walkway was completed on November 10, 20X1, and the actual cost was $282,000. The city council approved payment of the extra cost. The walkway was carpeted at a cost of $7,400. On December 15, 20X1, the city council gave the final approval of payment for the walkway. The fund balance was transferred to the debt service fund.

Required

Prepare entries for the capital projects fund to record the following:

a. Receipt of the county grant, sale of the bonds, and transfer of the bond premium.

b. Issue of the construction contract, actual cost, carpeting, and payment.

c. Closing of the nominal accounts.

d. Transfer of the balance to the debt service fund.

E18–7   Debt Service Fund Entries and Statement

York established a debt service fund to account for the proceeds of the bonds issued to finance the walkway (see exercise 18–6). The 9 percent, $200,000 bond issue was sold at 102.5 on January 1, 20X1. It is a 10-year serial bond issue. The resources to pay the interest and annual principal will be from a property tax levy.

Additional Information

1. The operating budget for 20X1 included estimated revenue of $38,000 and appropriations of $20,000 for principal and $18,000 for interest and an estimated transfer in of $5,000 from the capital projects fund.

2. The property tax levy was for $40,000, and an allowance for uncollectibles of $4,000 was established. Collections totaled $36,000. The remaining taxes were reclassified as delinquent, and the allowance was reduced to $1,000. The bond premium was received from the capital projects funds.

3. The current portion of the serial bonds and the interest due this year were recorded and paid. Other expenses charged to the debt service fund totaled $1,800, and $1,500 was paid.

4. A transfer in of $10,600 was received from the capital project fund.

5. The nominal accounts were closed.

Required

a. Prepare entries for the debt service fund for 20X1.

b. Prepare a statement of revenues, expenditures, and changes in fund balance for 20X1 for the debt service fund.

E18–8   Enterprise Fund Entries and Statements

Augusta has a municipal water and gas utility district (MUD). The trial balance on January 1, 20X1, was as follows:

	Debit	Credit
Cash	$ 92,000	
Accounts Receivable	25,000	
Inventory of Supplies	8,000	
Land	120,000	
Plant and Equipment	480,000	
Accumulated Depreciation		$ 80,000
Vouchers Payable		15,000
Bonds Payable, 6%		500,000
Net Assets		130,000
Total	$725,000	$725,000

Additional Information for 20X1

1. Charges to customers for water and gas were $420,000; collections were $432,000.

2. A loan of $30,000 for two years was received from the general fund.

3. The water and gas lines were extended to a new development at a cost of $75,000. The contractor was paid.

4. Supplies were acquired from central stores (internal service fund) for $12,400. Operating expenses were $328,000, and interest expense was $30,000. Payment was made for the interest and the payable to central stores, and $325,000 of the vouchers were paid.

5. Adjusting entries were as follows: Bad Debt Expense, $6,300; Depreciation Expense, $32,000; Supplies expense, $15,200.

Required

a. Prepare entries for the MUD enterprise fund for 20X1, and prepare closing entries.

b. Prepare a statement of net assets for the fund for December 31, 20X1.

c. Prepare a statement of revenues, expenses, and changes in fund net assets for 20X1. Assume that the $500,000 of the 6% bonds are related to the net capital assets of land, and plant and equipment

d. Prepare a statement of cash flows for 20X1.

E18–9   Interfund Transfers and Transactions

During 20X8, the following transfers and transactions between funds took place in the city of Matthew.

1. A transfer of $12,000 was made on March 1 from the general fund to establish a building maintenance internal service fund. Matthew uses transfer accounts to account for this type of transfer.

2. On April 1, the general fund made an $8,000 six-month loan to the building maintenance service fund.

3. On April 15, $2,400 was transferred from the general fund to the debt service fund to pay interest.

4. On May 5, the Matthew transportation service fund billed the general fund $825, for April services.

Required

a. Prepare journal entries for the general fund and the other fund involved that should be recorded at the time of each transfer or transaction.

b. For each transfer or transaction, prepare the appropriate closing entries for the general fund and the other fund for the year ended June 30, 20X8.

E18–10   Internal Service Fund Entries and Statements

The Bellevue City printing shop had the following trial balance on January 1, 20X2:

	Debit	Credit
Cash	$ 24,600	
Due from Other Funds	15,600	
Inventory of Supplies	9,800	
Furniture and Equipment	260,000	
Accumulated Depreciation		$ 50,000
Vouchers Payable		12,000
Net Assets		248,000
Total	$310,000	$310,000

Additional Information for 20X2

1. During 20X2, the printing shop acquired supplies for $96,000, furniture for $1,500, and a copier for $3,200.

2. Printing jobs billed to other funds amounted to $292,000; cash received from other funds, $287,300; costs of printing jobs, $204,000, including $84,000 of supplies; operating expenses, $38,000, including $8,400 of supplies; depreciation expense, $23,000; and vouchers paid, $243,000.

Required

a. Prepare entries for the printing shop for 20X2, including closing entries.

b. Prepare a statement of net assets for the fund on December 31, 20X2.

c. Prepare a statement of revenues, expenses, and changes in fund net assets for 20X2.

d. Prepare a statement of cash flows for 20X2.

E18–11   True/False Questions

1. The budgetary comparison schedule in the government-wide financial statements requires only the final budget for the period and the actual amounts for the period.

2. The accrual basis of accounting is used in the government-wide financial statements.

3. A component unit of a primary government is a unit that is related to the primary government but is not financially accountable to the primary government.

4. The statement of net assets in the government-wide financial statements requires the net assets to be segregated by the following: reserved net assets (for items such as encumbrances and inventories), and unreserved net assets.

5. A major governmental fund that must be separately disclosed in the government-wide financial statements would be a fund that comprised 5 percent of the total of the governmental funds.

6. Permanent governmental funds account for resources that has a principal that must be maintained, and its earnings are available for any government program that benefits all citizens.

7. The government unit's infrastructure and other fixed assets are reported on the government-wide statement of net assets.

8. The internal service fund is a proprietary fund and is not, therefore, shown in the governmental activities column of the government-wide statement of net assets.

9. In the reconciliation schedule for the statement of net assets, to reconcile from the net assets reported in the governmental funds to the net assets of governmental activities, capital assets used in governmental activities would be added.

10. In the reconciliation schedule for the statement of revenues, expenditures, and changes in fund balances, to reconcile from the net change in fund balances—governmental funds to the change in net assets of governmental activities, bond proceeds would be added back.

11. In the government-wide statement of activities, transfers between governmental and business-type funds must be reported as part of the change in net assets.

12. In the government-wide statement of activities, depreciation of fixed assets would equal the amount of the expenditures for assets made in the governmental funds.

13. The Management's Discussion and Analysis is a recommended voluntary disclosure in the government-wide financial statements.

14. The government-wide statement of net assets includes the fiduciary funds of the government unit.

15. The format of the government-wide statement of activities is based on the programs of the government entity rather than the type of revenues of the government entity.

Problems

P18–12 Capital Projects Fund Entries and Balance Sheet [AICPA Adapted]
The following information pertains to Elizabeth Township's construction and financing of a new administration center:

Estimated Cost of Project	$9,000,000
Project Financing:	
State Entitlement Grant	3,000,000
General Obligation Bonds:	
Face Amount	6,000,000
Stated Interest Rate	6%
Issue Date	December 1, 20X6
Maturity Date	10 years into the future

During Elizabeth's year ended June 30, 20X7, the following events occurred that affected the capital projects fund established to account for this project:

July 1, 20X6:	The capital projects fund borrowed $300,000 from the general fund for preliminary expenses.
July 9, 20X6:	Received an invoice for engineering and planning costs of $200,000 from Dunn Associates. The invoice was paid on July 16.
December 1, 20X6:	The bonds were sold at 101. Total proceeds were retained by the capital projects fund.
December 1, 20X6:	The entitlement grant was formally approved by the state.
April 30, 20X7:	A $7,000,000 contract was executed with Craft Construction Company, the general contractors, for the major portion of the project. The contract provides that Elizabeth will withhold 4% of all billings pending satisfactory completion of the project.
May 9, 20X7:	$1,000,000 of the state grant was received.
June 10, 20X7:	The $300,000 borrowed from the general fund was repaid.
June 30, 20X7:	Progress billing of $1,200,000 was received from Craft.

Elizabeth uses encumbrance accounting for budgetary control. Unencumbered appropriations lapse at the end of the year.

Required

a. Prepare journal entries in the administration center capital projects fund to record the foregoing transactions.

b. Prepare the June 30, 20X7 closing entries for the administration center capital projects fund.

c. Prepare the administration center capital projects fund balance sheet at June 30, 20X7.

P18–13 Adjusting Entries for General Fund [AICPA Adapted]
On June 30, 20X2, the end of the fiscal year, the Wadsworth Park District prepared the following trial balance for the general fund:

	Debit	Credit
Cash	$ 47,250	
Taxes Receivable—Current	31,800	
Allowance for Uncollectibles—Current		$ 1,800
Temporary Investments	11,300	
Inventory of Supplies	11,450	
Buildings	1,300,000	
Estimated Revenues Control	1,007,000	
Appropriations Control		1,000,000
Revenue—State Grants		300,000
Bonds Payable		1,000,000
Vouchers Payable		10,200
Expenditures	848,200	
Debt Service from Current Funds	130,000	
Capital Outlays (Equipment)	22,000	
Revenue—Taxes		1,008,200
Unreserved Fund Balance		81,800
Budgetary Fund Balance Unreserved		7,000
Total	$3,409,000	$3,409,000

An examination of the records disclosed the following information:

1. The recorded estimate of losses for the current year taxes receivable was considered to be adequate.

2. The local government unit gave the park district 20 acres of land to be used for a new community park. The unrecorded estimated value of the land was $50,000. In addition, a state grant of $300,000 was received, and the full amount was used in payment of contracts pertaining to the construction of the park buildings. Purchases of playground equipment costing $22,000 were paid from general funds.

3. Five years ago, a 4 percent, 10-year sinking fund bond issue in the amount of $1,000,000 for constructing park buildings was sold; it is still outstanding. Interest on the issue is payable at maturity. Budgetary requirements of a contribution of $130,000 to the debt service fund were met. Of this amount, $100,000 represents the fifth equal contribution for principal repayment.

4. Outstanding purchase orders not recorded in the accounts at year-end totaled $2,800.

5. A physical inventory of supplies at year-end revealed $6,500 of the supplies on hand.

6. Except where indicated to the contrary, all recordings were made in the general fund.

Required
Prepare the adjusting entries to correct the general fund records.

P18–14   Adjusting Entries for General Fund [AICPA Adapted]
You have been engaged to examine the financial statements of Fairfield for the year ended June 30, 20X2. You discover that all transactions were recorded in the general fund. The general fund trial balance as of June 30, 20X2 was:

c. Record the journal entry that was made in the general fund during 20X8 to record the transfer out.

d. On the general fund balance sheet at December 31, 20X8, what amount would be reported for unreserved fund balance?

e. Assume that the water utility billed the general fund $2,000 for using water during 20X8. What journal entry would be recorded in the general fund to record the billing? What journal entry would be recorded in the water utility to record the billing?

f. Record the journal entries that were made in the water utility for the sale of the revenue bonds and for the transfer from the general fund.

g. In the government-wide financial statements, what amount should be reported for general long-term debt bonds payable at December 31, 20X8?

h. In the government-wide financial statements, what amount should be reported for the increase in fixed assets at December 31, 20X8, as a result of the capital projects fund's transactions?

i. In the capital projects fund, what was the amount of the total encumbrances recorded during 20X8?

j. In the capital projects fund, what was the unreserved fund balance at December 31, 20X8?

k. How much was the state capital grant for the civic center?

l. What was the completed cost of the civic center?

m. What journal entry would be made by the general fund to record the transfer of $27,000 from the capital project fund in 20X9?

P18–21 Matching Questions Involving Various Funds

The numbered items listed on the left consist of a variety of transactions that occur in a municipality. The lettered items on the right consist of various ways of recording the transactions. Select the appropriate recording for each transaction. Some transactions have more than one correct answer. Some responses under Recording of Transactions may be used once, more than once, or not at all.

Transactions	*Recording of Transactions*
1. Term bond proceeds of $100,000 were received by the capital projects fund.	A. Debit expenditures in the general fund
	B. Debit general operating expenses in the general fund
2. Equipment costing $50,000 was acquired by the water utility, an enterprise fund.	C. Debit equipment in the enterprise fund
3. Land with a fair value of $500,000 was donated to the city to be used as a municipal park.	D. Debit equipment in the general fund
4. Central stores, an internal service fund, received a transfer in of $750,000 from the general fund.	E. Debit building in the capital projects fund
	F. Debit general operating expenses in the enterprise fund
5. General obligation serial bonds of $250,000 matured and were paid by the debt service fund.	G. Debit expenditures in the capital projects fund
6. Expenditures of $5,000,000 were incurred by the capital projects fund to construct a new city hall annex. The project was started and completed within the fiscal year.	H. Credit building in the capital projects fund
	I. Debit expenditures in the debt service fund
	J. Credit revenue in the private-purpose trust fund
7. The water utility, an enterprise fund, billed the mayor's office $200 for water usage.	K. Credit revenue in the capital projects fund
8. The mayor's office received the billing in number 7.	L. Credit other financing sources in the capital projects fund
9. The tax agency fund received $250,000 of tax revenues that are to be distributed to the school districts within the municipality.	M. Credit transfers in in the internal services fund
	N. Debit revenue in the agency fund
10. Salaries and wages of $25,000 incurred by the water utility enterprise fund.	O. Credit due to other governmental units in the agency fund
	P. Credit revenue in the agency fund
	Q. Credit revenue in the enterprise fund
	R. Reported only on the government-wide financial statements

P18–22   Questions on Fund Transactions [AICPA Adapted]

The following information relates to Dane City during its fiscal year ended December 31, 20X2:

1. On October 31, 20X2, to finance the construction of a city hall annex, Dane issued 8 percent, 10-year general obligation bonds at their face value of $600,000. Construction expenditures during the period equaled $364,000.

2. Dane reported $109,000 from hotel room taxes, restricted for tourist promotion, in a special revenue fund. The fund paid $81,000 for general promotions and $22,000 for a motor vehicle.

3. 20X2 general fund revenues of $104,500 were transferred to a debt service fund and used to repay $100,000 of 9 percent, 15-year term bonds, and to pay $4,500 of interest. The bonds were used to acquire a citizens' center.

4. At December 31, 20X2, as a consequence of past services, city firefighters had accumulated entitlements to compensated absences at $86,000. General fund resources available at December 31, 20X2, are expected to be used to settle $17,000 of this amount, and $69,000 is expected to be paid out of future general fund resources.

5. At December 31, 20X2, Dane was responsible for $83,000 of outstanding general fund encumbrances, including the $8,000 for supplies indicated below.

6. Dane uses the purchases method to account for supplies. The following information relates to supplies:

Inventory—1/1/X2	$ 39,000
—12/31/X2	42,000
Encumbrances outstanding—1/1/X2	6,000
—12/31/X2	8,000
Purchase orders during 20X2	190,000
Amount credited to vouchers payable during 20X2	181,000

Required

For items 1 through 10, determine the amounts based solely on the preceding information.

1. What is the amount of 20X2 general fund transfers out?

2. How much should be reported in 20X2 general fund liabilities from entitlements for compensated absences?

3. What is the 20X2 reserved amount of the general fund balance?

4. What is the 20X2 capital projects fund balance?

5. What is the 20X2 fund balance on the special revenue fund for tourist promotion?

6. What is the amount of 20X2 debt service fund expenditures?

7. What amount should be included in the government-wide financial statements for the cost of long-term assets acquired in 20X2?

8. What amount stemming from the 20X2 transactions and events decreased the long-term debt liabilities reported in the government-wide financial statements?

9. Using the purchases method, what is the amount of 20X2 supplies expenditures?

10. What was the total amount of 20X2 supplies encumbrances?

P18–23   Matching Questions Involving the Statement of Cash Flows for a Proprietary Fund

The numbered items on the left consist of a variety of transactions that occurred in the water utility enterprise fund of Jefferson City for the year ended June 30, 20X9. Items A, B, C, and D on the right consist of the four categories of cash flows that are reported on the statement of cash flows for proprietary funds. Item E is for transactions that are not reported on the statement of cash flows. Assume the direct method is used for disclosing cash flows from operating activities. For each transaction, select the letter that represents where that transaction should be disclosed on the statement of cash flows, or state that the item would not be reported on the statement of cash flows.

Transactions	*Categories of Disclosure*
1. Receiver $5,000,000 from revenue bonds to be used for construction of water treatment plant.	A. Operating activities
2. Paid $500,000 of salaries to employees of the water utility.	B. Noncapital financing activities
	C. Capital and related financing activities
3. Received $1,000,000 state grant restricted for construction of water treatment plant.	D. Investing activities
4. Collected $2,500,000 of accounts receivable from households for use of city water.	E. Not reported on the statement of cash flows
5. Depreciation expense for the year amounted to $300,000.	
6. Received $75,000 state grant restricted to the maintenance of fixed assets.	
7. Paid $250,000 of interest on the revenue bonds issued in number 1.	
8. Borrowed $125,000 from a local bank on revenue anticipation notes payable.	
9. Paid $5,000 of interest on the notes payable in number 8.	
10. Spent $1,200,000 of the revenue bonds for construction of the water treatment plant.	
11. Paid $5,000 fire insurance premium on June 30, 20X9, for next year's insurance coverage.	
12. Uncollected accounts receivable amounted to $135,000 on June 31, 20X9.	
13. Acquired $250,000 of state bonds as an investment of idle funds.	
14. Received $7,500 of interest on the state bonds in number 13.	
15. Received a $375,000 contribution from the City's general fund to be used for the construction of water treatment plant.	

P18–24 **Matching Questions Involving the Statement of Revenues, Expenditures, and Changes in Fund Balance for a Capital Projects Fund and a Debt Service Fund**

The numbered items on the left consist of a variety of transactions and events that occurred in the capital projects and debt service funds of Walton City for the year ended June 30, 20X9. Items A, B, and C on the right consist of three categories that are reported of the statement of revenues, expenditures, and changes in fund balance for capital projects and debt service funds. Item D is for transactions that are not reported on the statement of revenues, expenditures, and changes in fund balance for either debt service or capital projects funds. For each transaction, select the letter that represents where that transaction should be reported on the statement of revenues, expenditures, and changes in fund balance, or state that the item would not be reported of the statement.

Transactions/Events	*Categories of Disclosure*

1. The capital projects fund received the proceeds of general obligation bonds to be used for construction of a new courthouse.

    A. Revenues

2. The capital projects fund accepted the lowest bid for the construction of the courthouse.

    B. Expenditures

    C. Other financing sources and uses

3. The capital projects fund received resources from the city's general fund to be used in the construction of the courthouse.

    D. Not reported on the statement of revenues, expenditures, and changes in fund balance

4. The bonds in number 1 were sold at a premium. The capital projects fund transferred the premium to the debt service fund. For this question, indicate how this transaction should be reported by the capital projects fund.

5. During the year ended June 30, 20X9, courthouse construction was completed.

6. In addition to the resources provided by the general obligation bonds and the general fund, the capital projects fund also received a state grant that was used to construct the courthouse.

7. The general fund of the city transferred a portion of the property tax collections to the debt service fund to be used to pay the principal and interest of the general obligation bonds issued in number 1.

8. The debt service fund acquired investments with a part of the resources provided by the general fund.

9. Interest was earned on the investments acquired in number 8.

10. The debt service fund received the bond premium from the capital projects fund.

11. The debt service fund paid semiannual interest on the general obligation bonds on March 1, 20X9.

12. The debt service fund used a local bank to be its fiscal agent with regard to the record-keeping activities related to the general obligation bonds issued in number 1. The bank charged a fee for this service.

13. As of June 30, 20X9, unmatured interest for four months was due on the general obligation bonds issued in number 1. Resources to pay this interest will be transferred to the debt service fund in the next fiscal year.

P18–25   Question on Fund Transactions [AICPA Adapted]

Items 1 through 10 in the left-hand column represent various transactions pertaining to a municipality that uses encumbrance accounting. Items 11 through 20, also listed in the left-hand column, represent the funds and accounts used by the municipality. To the right of these items is a list of possible accounting and reporting methods.

Required

  a. For each of the municipality's transactions (items 1 through 10), select the appropriate recording of the transaction. A method of recording the transactions may be selected once, more than once, or not at all.

  b. For each of the municipality's funds, accounts, and other items (items 11 to 20), select the appropriate method of accounting and reporting. An accounting and reporting method may be selected once, more than once, or not at all.

Transactions	Recording of Transactions
1. General obligation bonds were issued at par.	A. Credit Appropriations Control
2. Approved purchase orders were issued for supplies.	B. Credit Budgetary Fund Balance—Unreserved
3. The above-mentioned supplies were received and the related invoices were approved.	C. Credit Expenditures Control
	D. Credit Deferred Revenues
4. General fund salaries and wages were incurred.	E. Credit Interfund Revenues
5. The internal service fund had interfund billings.	F. Credit Tax Anticipation Notes Payable
6. Revenues were earned from a previously awarded grant.	G. Credit Other Financing Sources
	H. Credit Other Financing Uses
7. Property taxes were collected in advance.	I. Debit Appropriations Control
8. Appropriations were recorded on adoption of the budget.	J. Debit Deferred Revenues
	K. Debit Encumbrances Control
9. Short-term financing was received from a bank, secured by the city's taxing power.	L. Debit Expenditures Control
10. There was an excess of estimated inflows over estimated outflows.	

Funds and Accounts	Accounting and Reporting
11. Enterprise fund fixed assets.	A. Accounted for in a fiduciary fund
12. Capital projects fund.	B. Accounted for in a proprietary fund
13. Permanent fund.	C. Accounts for permanent endowments that can be used for government programs
14. Infrastructure fixed assets.	
15. Enterprise fund cash.	D. Reported as an other financing use
16. General fund.	E. Accounted for in a special assessment fund
17. Agency fund cash.	F. Accounts for major construction activities
18. Transfer out from the general fund to the internal service fund.	G. Accounts for property tax revenues
	H. Accounts for payment of interest and principal on tax-supported debt
19. Special revenue fund. (is a major fund)	I. Accounts for revenues from earmarked sources to finance designated activities
20. Debt service fund. (is a major fund)	
	J. Reported in government-wide statements

P18–26 **Question on Fund Transactions [AICPA Adapted]**

The following events affected the financial statement of Jey City during 20X2:

Budgetary Activities

1. Total general fund estimated revenues $8,000,000
2. Total general fund estimated expenditures $7,500,000
3. Planned construction of a courthouse improvement expected to cost $1,500,000 and to be financed in the following manner: $250,000 from the general fund, $450,000 from state entitlements, and $800,000 from the proceeds of 20-year, 8 percent bonds dated and expected to be issued at par on June 30, 20X2. Interest on the bonds is payable annually on July 1, together with one-twentieth of the bond principal from general fund revenues of the payment period.
4. A budgeted general fund payment of $180,000 to subsidize operations of a solid waste landfill enterprise fund.

Actual results included the following:

5. Jey recorded property tax revenues of $5,000,000 and a related allowance for uncollectibles—current of $60,000. On December 31, 20X2, the remaining $56,000 balance of the allowance for uncollectibles—current was closed, and an adjusted allowance for uncollectibles—delinquent was recorded equal to the property tax receivables balance of $38,000.

6. A police car with an original cost of $25,000 was sold for $7,000.

7. Office equipment to be used by the city's fire department was acquired through a capital lease. The lease required 10 equal payments of $10,000 beginning with the July 1, 20X2, acquisition date. Using a 6 percent discount rate, the 10 payments had a present value of $78,000 at the acquisition date.

8. The courthouse was approved and financed as budgeted except for a $27,000 cost overrun that was paid for by the general fund. Jey plans to transfer cash to the debt service fund during 20X3 to service the interest and principal payments called for in the bonds.

9. Information related to the solid waste landfill at December 31, 20X2:

Capacity	1,000,000 cubic yards
Usage prior to 20X2	500,000 cubic yards
Usage in 20X2	40,000 cubic yards
Estimated total life	20 years
Closure costs incurred to date	$300,000
Estimated future costs of closure and postclosure care	$1,700,000
Expense for closure and postclosure care recognized prior to 20X2	$973,000

Required

For items 1 through 10, describe the amounts based solely on the preceding information.

1. What was the net effect of the budgetary activities on the general fund balance at January 1, 20X2?

2. What was the total amount of transfers out included in the general fund's budgetary accounts at January 1, 20X2?

3. What amount of interest payable related to the 20-year bonds should be reported by the general fund at December 31, 20X2?

4. What lease payment amount should be included in 20X2 general fund expenditures?

5. What amount was collected from 20X2 property taxes in 20X2?

6. What was the total amount of the capital project fund's 20X2 revenues?

7. What amount should be reported as long-term liabilities in the governmental activities column of the government-wide financial statements at December 31, 20X2?

8. What total change in the balance of long-term assets, before depreciation, should be reported in the governmental activities column of the government-wide financial statements at December 31, 20X2?

9. What 20X2 closure and postclosure care expenses should be reported in the solid waste landfill enterprise fund?

10. What should be the December 31, 20X2, closure and postclosure care liability reported in the solid waste landfill enterprise fund?

NOT-FOR-PROFIT ENTITIES

This chapter presents the accounting and financial reporting principles used by both governmental (public) and nongovernmental (private) colleges and universities, by health care providers such as hospitals and nursing homes, voluntary health and welfare organizations such as the Red Cross and United Way, and other not-for-profit organizations such as professional or fraternal associations.

The accounting and financial reporting for governmental, nonprofit entities is controlled by the GASB. Accounting and financial reporting for nongovernmental, nonprofit entities is controlled by the FASB. Thus, it is important to determine the role the government has in the organization.

Special-Purpose Government Entities

Chapters 17 and 18 presented the accounting and financial reporting standards for general-purpose governments such as states, counties, and municipalities. However, a number of governments are *special-purpose governments,* which are legally separate entities. These may be component units of a general-purpose government or may be stand-alone governments, apart from a general-purpose government. Special-purpose governments include governmental entities such as cemetery districts, levee districts, park districts, tollway authorities, and school districts. Some of these special-purpose government entities may be engaged in governmental activities that generally are financed through taxes, intergovernmental revenues, and other nonexchange revenues. These activities are usually reported in governmental or internal service funds. Some of these entities are engaged in business-type activities that are financed by fees charged for goods or services. These activities are usually reported in enterprise funds. **GASB 33** establishes specific reporting requirements for each of the following types of special-purpose governments:

1. Engaged in more than one governmental program or that have both governmental and business-type activities: These governmental entities must provide both fund financial statements and government-wide financial statements as presented in Chapters 17 and 18.

2. Engaged in a single governmental program (such as cemetery districts or drainage districts): These governmental entities may present a simplified set

of government-wide and fund-based financial statements, often combining these two statements.

3. Engaged in only business-type activities: These governmental entities must present only the financial statements required for enterprise funds. Many public universities and public hospitals will be included in this category.

4. Engaged in only fiduciary-type activities: These governmental entities are not required to present the government-wide financials but will provide only the financial statements required for fiduciary funds. This category includes special-purpose governments responsible for managing pension funds.

Regardless of the category of special-purpose government entity, all governments must include in their financial reports the Management Discussion and Analysis, the footnotes, and any required supplementary information.

Financial Reporting for Private, Not-for-Profit Entities

Private, not-for-profit entities follow the accounting and reporting standards established by the FASB. Several FASB standards and statements are particularly relevant for private, not-for-profit entities.

Private, not-for-profit entities must report their net assets in accordance with **Financial Accounting Concepts Statement No. 6,** "Elements of Financial Statements" **(FAC 6). FAC 6** specifies three mutually exclusive groups of net assets: unrestricted net assets, temporarily restricted net assets, and permanently restricted net assets. To be restricted, there must be an externally imposed restriction by contract, agreement, or other external requirement. Temporarily restricted net assets are restricted for time or purpose. A time restriction means that the assets will not be available for use until after a specific time, or a future event, has occurred. A purpose restriction means that the resources may be used only for specified purposes. Permanently restricted net assets include permanently restricted contributions for endowments and plant or museum collections that are intended to be maintained permanently.

Temporarily restricted resources are usually restricted by time, by purpose, or specifically to be used to acquire plant assets. These resources are accounted for in the temporarily restricted net asset class until the restriction is met. For example, if C. Alt donated $40,000 to a not-for-profit organization to be used specifically for a research program, the following entry would be made in the temporarily restricted class of net assets:

(1)	Cash	40,000	
	Contributions		40,000

Then, when the research program expenditures were made in the unrestricted net asset class, the following reclassification entry would be made in the temporarily restricted net asset class to record the completion of the specific use restriction and the transfer of the resources to the unrestricted net asset class.

(2)	Reclassification—Satisfaction of Program Restriction	40,000	
	Cash		40,000

The following entries would be made in the unrestricted net asset class.

(3)	Cash	40,000	
	Reclassification— Satisfaction of Program Restriction		40,000
(4)	Expenses—Research Program	40,000	
	Cash		40,000

Note that a reclassification entry is made for both the temporarily restricted net asset class and the unrestricted net asset class.

Important FASB Standards for Not-for-Profit Entities.   The FASB has issued five standards that have direct applicability to private, not-for-profit entities: **FASB 93,** which guides depreciation; **FASB 116,** which guides accounting for contributions; **FASB 117,** which establishes financial display requirements; **FASB 124,** which establishes the accounting for investments; and **FASB 136,** which guides the accounting for transfers of assets to a not-for-profit organization that raises or holds contributions for others.

   FASB Statement No. 93, "Recognition of Depreciation by Not-for-Profit Organizations" (**FASB 93**), requires that private not-for-profit entities must show depreciation. Depreciation must be recognized on long-lived tangible assets, other than works of art or historical treasures that have cultural, aesthetic, or historical value that is worth preserving perpetually and whose holders have the ability to preserve that value and are so doing. The depreciation is reported as an expenditure of the fund that uses the tangible long-lived assets during the period. **FASB 93** requires disclosure of the following items: (1) depreciation for the period, (2) the balance of the major classes of depreciable assets, (3) the accumulated depreciation at the balance sheet due, and (4) the method used to compute depreciation for the major classes of depreciable assets.

   FASB Statement No. 116, "Accounting for Contributions Received and Contributions Made" (**FASB 116**), establishes the guidelines for private not-for-profit entities to account for contributions. Contributions can be of cash, other assets, or a promise to give (a pledge). The general rule is that contributions received are measured at their fair value and are recognized as revenues or gains in the period received. The contributions are reported as unrestricted support or, if there are donor-imposed restrictions, as restricted support. A private not-for-profit entity does not need to recognize contributions of works of art, historical treasures, and similar assets if the donated items are added to collections that (1) are held for public exhibition, education, or research; (2) are protected, cared for, and preserved; and (3) has an organizational policy in existence that proceeds from the sales of collection items are to be used to acquire other items for collections.

   Contributions of services are recognized as a revenue, with an equivalent amount recorded as an expenditure, if the services received (1) create or enhance nonfinancial assets or (2) require specialized skills, are provided by individuals possessing those skills, and would typically need to be purchased if not provided by donation. Examples of contributed services would be specialized skills provided by accountants, architects, doctors, teachers, and other professionals. Some religious-based colleges record revenue, with an offsetting amount to an expenditure, for the fair value of contributed lay teaching services. This recognition is made to report the full cost of the teaching mission of these private colleges.

   FASB Statement No. 124, "Accounting for Certain Investments Held by Not-for-Profit Organizations" (**FASB 124**), will be discussed before **FASB 117**, which is presented in the next paragraph. **FASB 124** extended to not-for-profit organizations the basic standard of fair value for investments that was presented in **FASB 115** on investments. **FASB 124** specifies that fair value should be the measurement basis for investments in all debt securities and in equity securities that have readily determinable fair values (other than those equity securities that are accounted for under the equity method in accordance with **APB 18**). Note that **FASB 124** requires that debt securities should be valued at fair value. Investment income for the period would include interest or dividends and also the changes in fair value. Changes in fair value of investments in temporarily restricted or permanently restricted net assets should be recognized in accordance with donor restrictions as to the income. Otherwise, investment income would be reported as a change in unrestricted net assets.

FASB Statement No. 117, "Financial Statements of Not-for-Profit Organizations" (**FASB 117**), specifies the financial display standards for private not-for-profit entities. The three major financial statements are (1) a statement of financial position, (2) a statement of activities, and (3) a statement of cash flows. The unique features of the statement of financial position and statement of activities for not-for-profit organizations will be presented in greater detail in the following discussions. While some flexibility exists in the presentation of financial statements under **FASB 117,** a major feature of the statement of financial position is the combined presentation of all assets and equities in a single, simplified statement. In addition, the net assets are separated into those that are (1) unrestricted, (2) temporarily restricted, and (3) permanently restricted.

FASB Statement No. 136, "Transfers of Assets to a Not-for-Profit Organization or Charitable Trust that Raises or Holds Contributions for Others" (**FASB 136**), issued in 1999, establishes the accounting for contributions made to foundations or other similar organizations that raise resources for not-for-profit entities. **FASB 136** defines three parties to the typical contribution process. The *donor* is the initial provider of the resources. The *recipient organization* received the assets from the donor. And the *beneficiary* is the entity that eventually receives the assets through the recipient organization, as specified by the donor.

Many colleges and universities have a foundation that is responsible for raising financial support from alumni and other donors. Typically, these foundations are institutionally related to the college or university and uses its assets for the benefit of the college or university. In most cases, at the time of the contribution of assets from the donor to the foundation (the recipient organizations), the foundation will record an increase in assets and a contribution revenue for the fair value of the donation. Usually these assets are temporarily restricted until the foundation transfers them to the college or university. When the foundation does transfer the assets to the university (the beneficiary), the foundation records an expense and a decrease in its assets. For the college or university accounting, it normally has an interest in the net assets of the foundation and, at the time of the donation to the foundation, the college or university will recognize the change in its interest in the university foundation, usually as a temporarily restricted net asset, unless the donor specified a permanent restriction on the donation. Then, when the college or university actually receives the assets, it increases the specific assets received and decreases its interest in the net assets of the foundation. The contribution revenue was already recognized by the institutionally related foundation at the time the foundation received the donation.

Some recipient organizations, such as United Way, do fundraising that will benefit a number of not-for-profit organizations. Donors may direct the specific recipient of their gifts, or the donor may give to United Way without a restriction as to where the gift should be used. In those cases in which the donor specifies the beneficiary, then United Way would recognize an increase in its assets and record a liability to the specified beneficiary. The organization specified by the donor would record an increase in its net assets, usually as a receivable, and record contribution revenue at the time of the donation. When United Way transferred the assets to the specified beneficiaries, United Way would decrease its liabilities and its assets. For those donations that are unrestricted, and for which United Way may determine the best uses of the resources, United Way would record an increase in its assets and record the unrestricted gifts as contribution revenue. Then, when the assets are distributed, United Way would record the expense and the decrease in its assets, and the beneficiary would record contribution revenue for the fair value of the assets transferred.

Therefore, the key issues are the relationship between the recipient organization and the beneficiary, and whether or not the donor placed any use restrictions on the donation. If the donor does not specify a beneficiary, and the recipient organizations and beneficiary are not institutionally related, then the beneficiary cannot recognize an increase in its net assets until it actually receives the assets and would record contribution revenue at that time. But if the donor does specify a beneficiary, or the recipient organizations and the beneficiary are institutionally related, then the beneficiary recognizes the fair value of the donation at the time it is made to the recipient organization. Finally, in the case of nonfinancial assets such as artwork, the recipient organizations may choose whether or not to record the fair value of these nonfinancial assets in its books. However, all financial assets must be recorded at their fair values.

Colleges and Universities

There are more than 3,000 colleges and universities in the United States. Some offer two-year programs, some offer four-year programs, and others offer a wide selection of both undergraduate and graduate programs. Public and private institutions provide a large variety of liberal arts, science, and professional programs for our society. Public colleges and universities receive a significant portion of their operating resources from state governments. Private not-for-profit colleges and universities receive most of their resources from tuition and fees.

Special Conventions of Revenue and Expenditure Recognition

Colleges and universities have several conventions of recognizing revenue and expenditures. These are as follows:

1. *Tuition and fee remissions/waivers and uncollectible accounts.* Tuition and fees are important revenue sources for colleges and universities. In college and university accounting, the full amount of the standard rate for tuition and fees is recognized as revenue. The university first recognizes revenue at the standard rate of tuition and fees. The accounting for university-sponsored scholarships, fellowships, tuition and fee remissions or waivers, depends on the whether or not the recipient provides any services to the university. For example, if a student receives a university-sponsored scholarship that does not require any employment-type of work to be given to the university, then the university accounts for this as a deduction from revenue (i.e., reduces revenue). On the other hand, if the student must provide employment-type work to the university, then the university accounts for the scholarship as an expenditure. Another example is the tuition remission (reduction) that is often given to graduate students who accept teaching assistantships. The university records revenue for the graduate student's tuition at the standard rate and then records the tuition remission as an expense of the year in which the graduate student is a teaching assistant.

Uncollectible accounts are recorded as expenditures, similar to bad debts expense for commercial entities. An estimate of uncollectible accounts receivable is usually made and recorded as an expenditure. The allowance for uncollectibles is credited. As specific accounts receivable are determined to be uncollectible, the allowance is debited and the specific receivable is credited.

2. *Tuition and fee reimbursements for withdrawals from coursework.* Students withdrawing from classes after the beginning of the class term may be able to collect a reimbursement or return of some of the tuition and fees paid at the beginning of the term. Colleges and universities account for these reimbursements of tuition and fees as a reduction of revenue. When the check to the student is approved, the university debits revenue from tuition and fee reimbursements and credits cash or accounts payable.

3. *Academic terms that span two fiscal periods.* Some academic terms may begin in one fiscal year of the university and be completed in another. This is often true for summer school sessions. For example, many universities end their fiscal years on June 30 of each year. Colleges and universities account for the tuition and fees collected for a term of instruction as revenue in the fiscal year in which the term is predominantly conducted, along with all expenditures incurred to finance that term. For example, if tuition and fees are collected at the beginning of summer school, which takes place predominantly in the next fiscal period, the university records the collection as a debit to cash and a credit to deferred revenue. The deferred revenue and any deferred expenditures are then recognized as revenue and expenditures of the next fiscal period.

Transfers and Board-Designated Funds

As with governmental accounting, colleges and universities may have a variety of interfund transfers. The terms *mandatory transfer* and *nonmandatory transfer,* however, are unique to college and university accounting and reporting. The 1974 edition of CUBA provides a definition and explanation of these transfers, as summarized in the following:

> *Mandatory transfers* are transfers out of the current funds group to other funds resulting from binding legal agreements on financing or renewals and replacements of educational plant, and from grant agreements with agencies of the federal government, donors, or other organizations requiring matching gifts and grants from the governing board to the loan fund or other funds.
>
> *Nonmandatory transfers* are discretionary transfers specified by the governing board for a variety of purposes such as new additions to plant, increases in loan funds, payments on debt principal, and repairs and replacements of plant. Nonmandatory transfers may also be made from the loan, endowment, or annuity funds to the current funds.

Mandatory and nonmandatory transfers are reported separately in the financial statements of the current funds similarly to transfers in or out for governmental funds. Of course, a transfer out of one fund of the college or university must be accounted for as a transfer in to another fund.

The governing board may designate unrestricted current fund resources for specific purposes in future periods. These *board-designated funds* are internal designations similar to appropriations of retained earnings for a commercial entity. The governing board may impose or remove a designation at its own volition. For example, it might designate $50,000 of future expenditures in the unrestricted current fund for development of a foreign student counseling office. Such designations are usually reported in the footnotes to the financial statements, but they may be shown as allocations of part of the fund balance in the unrestricted current fund balance sheet.

Public Colleges and Universities.   The accounting and reporting for public colleges and universities is specified by the GASB. **GASB Statement No. 35,** "Basic Financial Statements—and Management's Discussion and Analysis—for Public Colleges and Universities" **(GASB 35),** issued in 1999, requires that these institutions follow the standards for governmental entities as specified in **GASB 34.** Most public institutions will be special-purpose government entities, engaged in only business-type activities. This is because most public colleges and universities do not have their own taxing authority. However, some community colleges do have their own taxing authority, and these would then be special-purpose government entities engaged in both governmental and business-type activities. The accounting and financial reporting standards in **GASB 34** are covered intensively in Chapters 17 and 18.

Private Colleges and Universities. The FASB specifies the accounting and financial reporting standards for private colleges and universities. Although many private colleges and universities are not-for-profit entities, some private colleges are profit-seeking, such as the University of Phoenix. Accounting for profit-seeking educational entities is similar to accounting for any commercial entity and is not covered in this chapter.

The three financial statements required for private, not-for-profit colleges and universities are: (1) statement of financial position, (2) a statement of activities, and (3) a statement of cash flows. While private colleges and universities are free to select any account structure that best serves its management and financial reporting needs, some choose to use fund accounting similar to that of governmental entities. Fund accounting creates an accounting discipline and provides an accounting vehicle to track revenues and expenses related to specific programs.

The statement of financial position for Sol City University, a private, not-for-profit college, is presented in Figure 19–1. This statement presents all the assets and equities in a single statement. Note that the net assets are separated into three categories: (1) unrestricted, (2) temporarily restricted, and (3) permanently restricted. The unrestricted category includes all assets, including property, plant, and equipment, whose use is not restricted by the provider or donor. Temporarily restricted assets include those that have been designated by the donor for specific use or for use in subsequent periods. Term endowments, funds donated for support of special activities, and those donated for unrestricted (or other) use in future periods are included as temporarily restricted net assets. Permanently restricted assets typically will include only the principal balance of permanent endowments.

The statement of activities presented in Figure 19–2 presents separately the revenues and expenses of the unrestricted, temporarily restricted, and permanently restricted net asset categories. It also shows the transfer of assets between the three categories of net assets during the period. For example, contributions received in 20X1 and available for use in 20X2 are shown as a transfer from temporarily restricted to unrestricted net assets in the statement of activities for 20X2. Auxiliary enterprises include activities such as a student union bookstore, cafeterias, and residence halls.

The statement of cash flows is presented in Figure 19–3 is similar so that used for commercial entities. Either the direct or indirect method may be used to compute cash flows from operating activities. Activities in the restricted funds are noted separately from those in the unrestricted funds. Note that the statement begins with the change in net assets for all funds, but reconciles to the cash at the end of the year.

Health Care Providers

The health care environment is currently undergoing a revolution. Rapidly growing costs of providing medical care are forcing hospitals to merge at an increasing rate in order to consolidate the types of services offered. The cost of new technology is also requiring health care providers to reevaluate their missions to the communities they serve.

FIGURE 19–1   Statement of Financial Position for a Private College

Sol City College
Statement of Financial Position
June 30, 20X2 and 20X1

	20X2	20X1
Cash	$ 579,000	$ 514,000
Investments, at fair value	10,763,000	9,536,000
Deposits with trustees	125,000	122,000
Accounts receivable	161,000	182,000
Less: Allowance for uncollectibles	(13,000)	(14,000)
Loans to students, faculty, and staff	275,000	190,000
Inventories	45,000	40,000
Prepaid expenses	14,000	10,000
Property, plant, and equipment (net)	20,330,000	19,970,000
Total Assets	$32,279,000	$30,550,000
Accounts payable	$ 70,000	$ 53,000
Accrued liabilities	10,000	8,000
Students' deposits	15,000	18,000
Deferred credits	15,000	10,000
Annuities payable	1,080,000	1,155,000
Notes payable	50,000	—
Bonds payable	1,300,000	1,200,000
Mortgage payable	200,000	100,000
Deposits held in custody	55,000	45,000
Total Liabilities	$ 2,795,000	$ 2,589,000
Net Assets:		
Unrestricted	$20,221,000	$20,294,000
Temporarily restricted by donors	5,363,000	4,307,000
Permanently restricted by donors	3,900,000	3,360,000
Total Net Assets	$29,484,000	$27,961,000
Total Liabilities and Net Assets	$32,279,000	$30,550,000

Although the major focus of this section of this chapter is on hospitals, the accounting and financial reporting guidelines for hospitals are the same as those used by all health care providers included within the scope of the AICPA's audit and accounting guide for Health Care Organizations.[1] The audit and accounting guide applies to the following health care entities:

1. Clinics, medical group practices, individual practice associations, individual practitioners, emergency care facilities, laboratories, surgery centers, and other ambulatory care organizations.
2. Continuing-care retirement communities (CCRCs).
3. Health maintenance organizations (HMOs) and similar prepaid health care plans.

---

[1]The AICPA periodically revises its audit and accounting guides for specialized industries. The 1996 Audit and Accounting Guide for Health Care Organizations, which includes hospitals, revises and supersedes the earlier audit guides for hospitals.

FIGURE 19–2 Statement of Activities for a Private College

Sol City College
Statement of Activities
For the Year Ended June 30, 20X2

	Unrestricted	Temporarily Restricted	Permanently Restricted	Total
Revenues, gains, and other support:				
Tuition and fees	$ 1,290,000			$ 1,290,000
Government appropriations	650,000	$ 40,000		690,000
Government grants and contracts	20,000	300,000		320,000
Contributions	425,000	1,063,000	$ 495,000	1,983,000
Auxiliary enterprises	1,100,000			1,100,000
Investment income	265,000	139,000	15,000	419,000
Gain on investments		69,000	25,000	94,000
Net assets transferred or released from restriction:				
Program use restriction	601,000	(601,000)		
Transferred to restricted funds	(101,000)	101,000		
Expired term endowment	50,000	(50,000)		
Transferred to endowment		(5,000)	5,000	
Total revenue, gains, and other support	$ 4,300,000	$1,056,000	$ 540,000	$ 5,896,000
Expenses and other deductions:				
Instruction	$ 1,725,000			$ 1,725,000
Research	250,000			250,000
Public service	77,000			77,000
Academic support	125,000			125,000
Student services	100,000			100,000
Scholarships and fellowships	95,000			95,000
Institutional support	275,000			275,000
Operation and maintenance	110,000			110,000
Depreciation expense	500,000			500,000
Interest expense	106,000			106,000
Auxiliary enterprises	915,000			915,000
Other operating costs	95,000			95,000
Total expenses	$ 4,373,000	–0–	–0–	$ 4,373,000
Change in net assets	$ (73,000)	$1,056,000	$ 540,000	$ 1,523,000
Net assets at beginning of year	20,294,000	4,307,000	3,360,000	27,961,000
Net assets at end of year	$20,221,000	$5,363,000	$3,900,000	$29,484,000

4. Home health agencies.

5. Hospitals.

6. Nursing homes that provide skilled, intermediate, and less intensive levels of health care.

7. Drug and alcohol rehabilitation centers and other rehabilitation facilities.[2]

The AICPA audit guide serves as an important authoritative source in selecting accounting and financial reporting procedures for health care providers. The hospital financial statements illustrated in this chapter incorporate the disclosure standards of

[2]AICPA Audit and Accounting Guide for Health Care Organizations, 1996, p.vii.

FIGURE 19–3   Statement of Cash Flows for a Private College

Sol City College
Statement of Cash Flows
For the Year Ended June 30, 20X2

Cash flows from Operating Activities			
Change in Net Assets			$1,523,000
Adjustments to Reconcile Changes in Net Assets to Net Cash Provided by Operating Activities:			
Depreciation		$ 500,000	
Increase in Deposits with Trustees		(3,000)	
Decrease in Accounts Receivable		20,000	
Increase in Loans to Students, Faculty, and Staff		(85,000)	
Increase in Inventories		(5,000)	
Increase in Prepaid Expenses		(4,000)	
Increase in Accounts Payable		17,000	
Increase in Accrued Liabilities		2,000	
Decrease in Students' Deposits		(3,000)	
Increase in Deferred Credits		5,000	
Restricted Contributions and Investment Income			
Contributions, Grants, and Investment Income in Permanently Restricted Funds	$(1,611,000)		
Contributions, Grants, and Investment Income in Temporarily Restricted Funds	(535,000)		
Total Restricted Contributions and Investment Income		(2,146,000)	
Total Adjustments		$(1,702,000)	(1,702,000)
Net Cash Provided by Operating Activities			$ (179,000)
Cash Flows from Investing Activities			
Acquisition of Property, Plant, and Equipment		(920,000)	
Sale of Used Equipment		60,000	
Net Acquisition of Investments		(65,000)	
Flows Related to Restricted Items:			
Net Acquisition of Temporarily Restricted Investments	$ (112,000)		
Net Acquisition of Permanently Restricted Investments	(1,050,000)		
Net Cash Flow Related to Restricted Items		(1,162,000)	
Net Cash Provided by Investing Activities			(2,087,000)
Cash Flows from Financing Activities			
Decrease in Annuities Payable		$ (75,000)	
Increase in Notes Payable		50,000	
Increase in Bonds Payable		100,000	
Increase in Mortgage Payable		100,000	
Increase in Deposits Held in Custody		10,000	
Flows Related to Restricted Items:			
Contributions, Grants, and Investment Income in Temporarily Restricted Funds	$ 1,611,000		
Contributions, Grants, and Investment Income in Permanently Restricted Funds	535,000		
Cash Flows Related to Restricted Items		$ 2,146,000	
Net Cash Provided by Financing Activities			2,331,000
Net Change in Cash			$ 65,000
Cash at the Beginning of the Year			514,000
Cash at the End of the Year			$ 579,000

FASB 117, as presented and amplified in the AICPA's 1996 Audit and Accounting Guide for Health Care Organizations.

Hospitals may be classified as profit-seeking or as not-for-profit entities. Some hospitals now operate as investor-owned, profit-oriented chains. These investor-owned hospitals seek additional financial resources through sales of stocks and issuance of large amounts of debt. Profit-seeking hospitals provide the same types of financial reports as commercial entities, whereas not-for-profit hospitals use a format somewhat closer to other nonprofit organizations in presenting their financial results. Not-for-profit hospitals are often affiliated with a university, a religious group, or a civic association. Not-for-profit hospitals are discussed in this chapter because of the large number of these hospitals and because of their special accounting and financial reporting issues.

Hospital Accounting

Two professional associations, the American Hospital Association (AHA) and the Hospital Financial Management Association (HFMA), are active in developing and improving hospital management, accounting, and financial reporting. Publications of both organizations can be useful to individuals seeking additional information on hospital accounting and reporting practices.

In this chapter, it is assumed that the hospital is a separate, not-for-profit reporting entity, and is not a component unit of any other governmental or private organization. In the cases in which a hospital is operated by a governmental entity, such as a city, the GASB's *Codification of Governmental Accounting and Financial Reporting Standards* states that the hospital's accounts should be reported as a discrete enterprise fund, as a component unit of the city, using the accounting guidelines in the AICPA's hospital audit and accounting guide.[3]

Hospital Fund Structure.   Although not required to do so, many hospitals have used a fund accounting structure for accounting purposes. In general, operating activities have been carried on in the general fund, and a series of restricted funds have been used to account for assets whose use has been restricted by the donor. The presentation of financial statement information under **FASB 117** requires a distinction between those net assets which are unrestricted, temporarily restricted, and permanently restricted. The discussion of accounting and financial reporting for hospitals that follows assumes that unrestricted assets are accounted for in the general fund and that one or more separate funds are used to account for temporarily restricted and permanently restricted assets.

All transactions involving the use of unrestricted assets are recorded in the general fund. As such, the general fund is the primary operating fund of the hospital. Assets that were restricted as to the period of use or that must be used for particular purposes are accounted for in restricted funds until the restriction is satisfied. At the time the restriction is satisfied, the assets are transferred (reclassified) from the restricted fund to the general (unrestricted) fund. Any expenses that are incurred in satisfying the restrictions are reported as expenses in the general fund.

Restricted funds account for assets received from donors or other third parties who have imposed certain restrictions on their use. The restricted funds are often termed

---

[3]*Codification of Governmental Accounting and Financial Reporting Standards,* Governmental Accounting Standards Board, updates issued frequently, Section *H.50.101.*

FIGURE 19–4   Overview of Hospital Accounting and Reporting

| | | Fund Groups | | | |
| | | | Restricted | | |
	General	Specific Purpose	Time Restricted	Plant Replacement and Expansion	Endowment
Accounting basis	Accrual	Contributions, transfers, and other changes are recorded directly in the fund. Resources are held until transferred to general fund for expenditures.			
Distinguishing features		Resources restricted for specific operating purposes.	Resources not available until date specified by donor.	Resources restricted for additions to plant assets.	Principal must be preserved.
Financial statements		Balance Sheet			
		Statement of Operations			
		Statement of Changes in Net Assets			
		Statement of Cash Flows			

"holding" funds because they must hold the restricted assets and transfer expendable resources to the general funds for expenditure. Figure 19–4 presents an overview of the fund structure and financial reporting for hospitals.

General Fund.   The *general fund* accounts for the resources received and expended in the primary health care mission of the hospital. The basis of accounting is the accrual method in order to measure fully all expenses of providing services during the period. Depreciation is included in the operating expenses. Fixed assets are included in the fund, on the theory that the governing board may use these assets in any manner desired.

The governing board may establish *board-designated resources* within the general fund. For example, the board may designate resources for the expansion of the hospital, for retirement of debt, or for other purposes. While funds designated in this manner are considered to be part of the unrestricted funds, this designation provides information on the intended use of the resources.

Donor Restricted Funds.   All *restricted funds* account for resources whose use is restricted by the donor. For financial reporting purposes, a distinction is made between temporarily and permanently restricted funds. The major *temporarily restricted* funds are (1) specific-purpose funds, (2) time restricted funds, and (3) plant replacement and expansion funds. *Permanently restricted* funds are assets that are to be held into perpetuity and generally are included in an endowment fund. Hospitals may also have restricted loan funds and annuity and life income funds; however, few hospitals use these funds and they are not discussed in this chapter.

Specific-purpose funds are restricted for *specific operating purposes.* For example, a donor may specify that a donation of $25,000 may be used only for maternity care. The donation is held in the specific-purpose fund until the maternity expenditure is approved in the general fund, at which time the specific-purpose fund transfers the resources to the general fund.

Time-restricted funds account for assets received or that have been pledged by donors for use in future periods. The donor's restriction is satisfied by the passage of time. A pledge received in 20X1 to contribute a stated amount in 20X2 to be used for unrestricted purposes would be included in the time restricted fund in the balance sheet prepared at December 31, 20X1.

Plant replacement and expansion restricted funds account for contributions to be used only for additions to fixed assets. When the general fund approves or makes the appropriate expenditures for the fixed assets, the plant replacement and expansion fund transfers the resources to the general fund.

Endowment funds account for resources when the principal must be preserved. The income from these resources is usually available for either a restricted or a general purpose. Endowments may be either permanent or term. Term endowments are for limited time periods, for example, 5 or 10 years, or until a specific event occurs, such as the death of the donor. After the term expires, the principal of the fund is used by the governing board in accordance with the gift agreement.

Financial Statements for a Hospital

Hospitals issue four basic financial statements: (1) the balance sheet, (2) the statement of operations, (3) the statement of changes in net assets, and (4) the statement of cash flows. Comparative data for prior fiscal periods are normally presented within each statement. Each of the four statements is demonstrated in the comprehensive illustration presented later in this chapter.

Balance Sheet.   The balance sheet presents the total assets, liabilities, and net assets of the organization as a whole.

Receivables.   Receivables may include amounts due from patients, third-party payors, other insurers of health care, pledges or grants, and interfund transactions. Receivables should be reported at the anticipated realizable amount. Thus, the realizable amounts may include reductions due to contractual agreements with third-party payors, or provider practices, such as allowing courtesy discounts to medical staff members and employees. An allowance for uncollectibles is recognized for estimated bad debts. Charity care are cases in which health care services are provided, but the patient has demonstrated, in accordance with the hospital's established criteria, an inability to pay. In these cases, charity care does not qualify for recognition as either receivables or revenue in the hospital's financial statements. The determination of a charity care case may not be able to be made at the time the patient is admitted, but at some point the hospital must be able to determine that the person does meet the necessary qualifications for charity care before reducing the amount owed. Receivables from pledges of future contributions are reported in the period the pledge is made, net of an allowance for uncollectible amounts.

Investments.   Investments are initially recorded at cost if purchased, or at fair value at the date of receipt if received as a gift. Subsequently, for investor-owned, *profit-seeking hospitals,* equity and debt securities are reported in accordance with **FASB Statement No. 115,** "Accounting for Certain Investments in Debt and Equity Securities."

FASB 115 establishes three portfolios of investments: trading securities, available-for-sale securities, and hold-to-maturity debt securities. The accounting and reporting of the investment differs according to the category. For *nonprofit hospitals,* equity securities with readily determinable fair values and all investments in debt securities are measured at fair value, in accordance with **FASB Statement No. 124,** "Accounting for Certain Investments Held by Not-for Profit Organizations." The Health Care Organizations audit and accounting guide states that the investment return (including realized and unrealized gains and losses) not restricted by donors should be classified as changes in unrestricted net assets in the hospital's statement of operations. The investment return from trading securities is included above the performance indicator line (Excess of Revenues, Gains, and Other Support Over Expenses) reflecting operations, while the investment return from other than trading securities is reported in the statement of operations below the performance indicator line. Investment returns that are restricted by donors or by law are reported as changes in net assets in the appropriate restricted funds. *For governmental health care entities,* **GASB Statement No. 31,** "Accounting and Financial Reporting for Certain Investments and for External Investment Pools," specifies the general rule of fair value accounting for investments.

For these three types of hospitals, investments in stock accounted for under the equity method are reported in accordance with **APB Statement No. 18,** "The Equity Method of Accounting for Investments in Common Stock." Some hospitals receive income from trusts that donors have established with fiduciaries, such as banks. If the hospital does not own the trust or its investments, then the independent trusts are not an asset of the hospital and are not reported on the hospital's balance sheet. Footnote disclosure may be made of major independent endowment or trust agreements that benefit the hospital.

Plant Assets.   Property, plant, and equipment is reported, together with any accumulated depreciation. Depreciation is recorded in the general fund because the use of assets is part of the cost of providing medical services. The assets are reported in the general fund because they are available for use in any manner deemed necessary by the governing board.

Assets Whose Use Is Limited.   Separate disclosure should be made for assets that have restrictions placed on their use by the donor or that have been designated by the board of directors for special use. Such funds may come from a variety of sources. For example, grant monies received for cancer research would be reported as funds restricted for specific purposes and classified as temporarily restricted until used in support of research. Funds contributed to assist in constructing a new children's wing of the hospital would be reported as restricted for plant replacement and expansion and classified as temporarily restricted until used in construction. Funds received for permanent investment in the principal of an endowment fund would be reported as permanently restricted. Only those funds whose use is restricted by the donor are classified as restricted; thus, assets set aside for identified purposes by the governing board and over which the board retains control would not be classified restricted. They would be regarded as *assets whose use is limited,* however.

Long-Term Debt.   The hospital must also account for its long-term debt and pay the principal and interest as it becomes due. The debt is shown in the balance sheet. This differs from most governmental entities in which a separate debt service fund is established to service debt.

Net Assets.　The net assets held by the hospital are segregated between those which are (1) *unrestricted* and available for use at the discretion of hospital staff and board of directors, (2) *temporarily restricted* and available for use when specific events established by the donor are satisfied, and (3) *permanently restricted* in use by the donor.

Statement of Operations.　For hospitals, the results of their operations are reported in a statement of operations. This statement is also often termed "the statement of activities." This statement includes the revenues, expenses, gains and losses, and other transactions affecting the unrestricted net assets during the period. Gains and losses from transactions that are peripheral or ancillary to the provision of health services are reported separately from net patient service revenue. The statement of operations must report a *performance indicator,* which reports the results of the hospital's operating activities for the period. This performance indicator should include both operating income (loss) for the period and other income available for current operations. An example of other income is investment income (both realized and unrealized holding gains) on trading securities. **FASB 117** requires that net assets released from restrictions for use in operations be included before the performance indicator line on the statement of activities. This is because the transfer of net assets from the restricted group of assets for use in the operations of the entity in the unrestricted group of net assets can then be matched with the expenses incurred to fulfill the operating restriction. The title of the performance indicator should be descriptive such as the "Excess of Revenues, Gains, and Other Support Over Expenses." Some hospitals may report an intermediate computation for operating income as an element of their performance indicator.

Other changes in the unrestricted net assets during the period should be reported after the performance indicator. These other changes would include unrealized gains or losses from other than trading securities, and transfers from restricted net assets of resources that are used for the purchase of property and equipment. Note that the statement of operations must separately report those items related to the acquisitions of property or equipment from those related to operating activities.

A separate, third statement, entitled the statement of changes in net assets, is used to report items affecting the temporarily restricted and permanently restricted net assets. This third statement is covered in this chapter following discussion of the statement of operations.

Net Patient Service Revenue.　Net patient service revenue represents the revenue of the hospital from inpatient and outpatient care excluding charity care and contractual adjustments. Net patient service revenue represents the billings for services provided and the earning capacity of the hospital. Many hospitals are required to perform a certain amount of charity care for which no revenue is recognized. The charity cases are imposed by terms of certain federal medical care grant programs. Charity care helps ensure that indigent persons living in the region served by the hospital may obtain adequate medical services. When charity care is provided, no revenue is recognized, but disclosure of the estimated amount of charity care is presented in the footnotes to the financial statements.

Contractual Adjustments.　Contractual adjustments constitute a major deduction from gross patient service revenue. Contractual adjustments result from the involvement of third-party payors in the medical reimbursement process. Insurance companies or government units (especially the federal government) reimburse less than the full standard rate for medical services provided to patients covered by insurance or government-provided services such as medicare. These third-party payors may stipulate limits on the amount of costs they will pay. A hospital may have a standard rate for a specific service but may contract with the third-party payor to accept a lower amount for that service. For example, medicare establishes specific reimbursement rates for various services, termed a "diagnosis-related group" (DRG). The hospital makes a contractual adjustment from its normal service charge, and this adjustment is a deduction from gross patient service revenue.

Income from Ancillary Programs.   Income from ancillary programs represents the income earned from nonpatient sources such as television rentals, cafeteria sales, sales in gift shops operated by the hospital, parking fees, and tuition on educational programs provided by the hospital. The income reported typically represents the net earnings from such operations rather than the gross receipts.

Interfund Transfers.   It is not appropriate to hold assets in a restricted fund when the requirements specified by the donor have been satisfied. For example, when contributions received to purchase plant and equipment are used to purchase new assets, or when contributions received for use in educational programs are used for that purpose, the funds should be transferred from the restricted fund to the unrestricted fund. For financial reporting purposes, this transfer between funds is reported as "net assets released" in the statement of operations and is shown as an addition to unrestricted funds. If the interfund transfer to the unrestricted fund is to be used for operations, then the unrestricted fund reports it above the operating performance indicator line in the statement of operations. If the interfund transfer to the unrestricted fund is to be used for acquiring long-term assets, then the unrestricted fund reports it below the performance indicator line in the statement of operations.

General Fund Expenses.   The major expenses in the general fund are for nursing services, other professional services, depreciation, bad debts, and the general and administrative costs of the hospital. These costs are recognized on the accrual basis of accounting, similar to commercial entities. Hospitals that self-insure for malpractice costs should recognize an expense and a liability for malpractice costs in the period during which the incidents that give rise to the claims occur, if it is probable that liabilities have been incurred and the amounts of the losses can be reasonably estimated. Any expenses related to fund-raising should be classified separately. Patients pay physicians directly for their medical services.

Donations.   Hospitals often receive a wide variety of services from volunteers. For example, retired physicians or pharmacists may voluntarily work part-time in their professional roles. In addition, the hospital may receive donations of supplies or equipment. The rules on accounting for donations and contributions to hospitals are as follows:

1. *Donated services.* Because it is often difficult to place a value on donated services, their values are usually not recorded. However, if the following conditions exist, the estimated value of the donated services is reported as an expense and a corresponding amount is reported as contributions. **FASB 116** specifies that a contribution of services should be recognized if the services received (*a*) create or enhance nonfinancial assets or (*b*) require specialized

**FIGURE 19–7   Statement of Changes in Net Assets for a
Not-for-Profit Hospital**

Sol City Community Hospital
Statement of Changes in Net Assets
For the Year Ended December 31, 20X2

Unrestricted net assets:	
Excess of revenues over expenses	$ 100,000
Net unrealized gains on other than trading securities	15,000
Net assets released from equipment acquisition restrictions	225,000
Increase in unrestricted net assets	$ 340,000
Temporarily restricted net assets:	
Contributions	$ 200,000
Investment gains	73,000
Net assets released from:	
Program use restrictions	(180,000)
Equipment acquisition restrictions	(225,000)
Passage of time	(12,000)
Decrease in temporarily restricted net assets	$ (144,000)
Permanently restricted net assets:	
Contributions	$ 415,000
Increase in permanently restricted net assets	$ 415,000
Increase in net assets	$ 611,000
Net assets at beginning of year	3,055,000
Net assets at end of year	$3,666,000

probable and reasonably estimated. Cash payments are made for $2,125,000 of the total operating expenses, and the remainder is consumption of prepaid assets, allowance for uncollectibles, depreciation, and increases in liabilities. The hospital receives donated services valued at $10,000, which are recognized in entry (9):

(8)	Nursing Services Expense	800,000	
	Other Professional Services Expense	620,000	
	General Services Expense	700,000	
	Fiscal Services Expense	100,000	
	Administrative Services Expense	80,000	
	Medical Malpractice Costs	30,000	
	Bad Debts Expense	60,000	
	Depreciation Expense	200,000	
	Cash		2,125,000
	Allowance for Uncollectibles		60,000
	Inventories		90,000
	Prepaid Expenses		5,000
	Accumulated Depreciation		200,000
	Accounts Payable		50,000
	Accrued Expenses		30,000
	Estimated Medical Malpractice Costs Payable		30,000
	Record operating expenses.		
(9)	Other Professional Services Expense	10,000	
	Donated Services-Revenue		10,000
	Receive donated services.		

FIGURE 19–8   Statement of Cash Flows for a Not-for-Profit Hospital (Indirect Method)

Sol City Community Hospital
Statement of Cash Flows
For the Year Ended December 31, 20X2

Cash flows from operating activities:		
Change in net assets		$ 611,000
Adjustments to reconcile changes in net assets to net		
cash provided by operating activities:		
Depreciation	$ 200,000	
Net unrealized gains on other than trading securities	(15,000)	
Contribution of property, plant, and equipment	(25,000)	
Gain on disposal of equipment	(5,000)	
Increase in advances from third parties	35,000	
Increase in malpractice costs	30,000	
Increase in accrued expenses	5,000	
Decrease in accounts payable	(40,000)	
Increase in receivables, net	(50,000)	
Decrease in pledges receivable-current	12,000	
Decrease in prepaid expenses	5,000	
Decrease in inventories	10,000	
Restricted contributions and investment income:		
Contribution for permanent endowment	$(415,000)	
Contributions restricted for plant acquisition	(60,000)	
Investment income restricted for plant acquisition	(7,000)	
Investment income on board-designated investments	(10,000)	
Total restricted contributions and investment income	(492,000)	
Total adjustments		(330,000)
Net cash provided by operating activities		$ 281,000
Cash flows from investing activities:		
Sale of used hospital assets		$ 55,000
Sale of investments		50,000
Acquisition of plant, property, and equipment		(250,000)
Flows related to restricted items:		
Purchase of investments in endowment and plant replacement funds	$(522,000)	
Remainder of contributions to endowment fund restricted to investing	(15,000)	
Remainder of contributions to plant fund restricted to plant purchases	(50,000)	
Cash transferred from plant fund for plant expansion	200,000	
Investment income-board designated-restricted for plant assets	(10,000)	
Total investing flows related to restricted items		(397,000)
Net cash used by investing activities		(542,000)
Cash flows from financing activities:		
Paid notes payable		(5,000)
Paid current portion of long-term debt		(60,000)
Proceeds from restricted contributions and investment income:		
Contributions restricted for permanent endowment	$ 415,000	
Contributions restricted for acquiring fixed assets	172,000	
Investment income-board designated	10,000	
Total restricted proceeds		597,000
Net cash provided by financing activities		$ 532,000
Net increase in cash		$ 271,000
Cash at the beginning of year		14,000
Cash at the end of year		$ 285,000

Entry (9) records the fair value of donated services both as a debit for the operating expense and as a credit for operating revenue. Therefore, donated services do not affect the bottom line of the hospital's statement of revenue and expenses, but they do affect the amounts shown for the expenses and revenue sections of the statement.

Contribution Revenue. During 20X2, Sol City Community Hospital received unrestricted cash gifts in the amount of $63,000 and donated medicines and medical supplies with a market value of $30,000:

(10)	Cash	63,000	
	Contributions—Unrestricted		63,000
	Unrestricted contributions received.		
(11)	Inventory	30,000	
	Contributions—Unrestricted		30,000
	Donated supplies received.		

Other Revenues and Gains. Also during 20X2, income of $10,000 was earned in the unrestricted fund on resources designated by the governing board for purposes of future plant expansion. In addition, a gain of $5,000 was realized on the sale of equipment:

(12)	Board Designated Funds for Expansion of Facilities—Cash	10,000	
	Investment Income—Board Designated Funds		10,000
	Earnings on resources reserved by hospital's governing board for purchase of fixed assets.		
(13)	Cash	55,000	
	Accumulated Depreciation	50,000	
	Property, Plant, and Equipment		100,000
	Gain on Disposal of Equipment		5,000
	Sale of hospital equipment. The cash will be used in the operations of the hospital.		

Net Assets Released from Restriction. Assets were released for unrestricted use from a variety of sources in 20X2, as follows:

Amount	From Restricted Fund	Description
$120,000	Specific-Purpose Fund	Resources for education and research
60,000	Specific-Purpose Fund	Income from endowment investment
200,000	Plant Expansion and Replacement	Resources to acquire equipment
25,000	Plant Expansion and Replacement	Donated assets placed into use
12,000	Time-Restricted Fund	Collection of pledges receivable

Entries to record these transactions are presented here:

(14)	Cash	120,000	
	Net Assets Released from Program Use Restrictions		120,000
	Record payment for reimbursement of operating expenditures made in accordance with restricted gift.		
(15)	Cash	60,000	
	Net Assets Released from Program Use Restrictions		60,000
	Deposit in general fund of interest earnings from investments of endowment fund.		

(16)	Cash	200,000	
	Net Assets Released from Equipment Acquisition Restriction		200,000
	Transfer from temporarily restricted plant replacement and expansion fund for use in acquiring plant assets.		
(17)	Property, Plant, and Equipment	25,000	
	Net Assets Released from Equipment Acquisition Restriction		25,000
	Transfer from temporarily restricted plant replacement and expansion fund of donated assets placed in service.		
(18)	Cash	12,000	
	Net Assets Released from Passage of Time		12,000
	Transfer from temporarily restricted funds restricted for use in 20X2.		

Each of the transfers from temporarily restricted funds will involve one or more journal entries in those funds. These amounts are not included among 20X2 contributions in the unrestricted fund because they were recorded as contributions at the time of receipt in the temporarily restricted or permanently restricted funds. The transfer of donated equipment initially is recorded in the temporarily restricted plant fund until the hospital begins using the asset. At the time the assets are placed in service, the value of the donated equipment is transferred to the unrestricted fund.

Other Transactions in the General Fund. The remaining transactions during the 20X2 fiscal year affect only the balance sheet accounts. Transactions affecting only the asset accounts include collecting receivables, acquiring inventory, selling an investment, and purchasing additional physical plant assets, as follows:

(19)	Cash	2,250,000	
	Allowance for Uncollectibles	50,000	
	Accounts Receivable		2,300,000
	Collect some receivables and write off $50,000 as uncollectible.		
(20)	Inventories	50,000	
	Cash		50,000
	Acquire inventories.		
(21)	Cash	50,000	
	Investments		50,000
	Sell investment at cost.		
(22)	Property, Plant, and Equipment	250,000	
	Cash		250,000
	Purchase new plant with cash of $50,000 from sale of investments and $200,000 from transfer in from temporarily restricted plant replacement and expansion fund.		

Transactions affecting the current liability accounts include paying current liabilities and recording the receipt of cash in advance of billings from third parties. The hospital reclassified the portion of the long-term mortgage that is currently due. The hospital also revalued, to fair value, the general fund's other-than-trading securities. The entries for these events are as follows:

(23)	Notes Payable to Bank	5,000	
	Current Portion of Long-Term Debt	60,000	
	Accounts Payable	90,000	
	Accrued Expenses	25,000	
	Cash		180,000
	Pay liabilities outstanding at beginning of period.		

(24)	Cash	35,000	
	Advances from Third Parties		35,000
	Increase in cash received from third parties for deposits in advance of service billings.		

(25)	Mortgage Payable	50,000	
	Current Portion of Long-Term Debt		50,000
	Reclassify current portion of long-term debt.		

(26)	Investments (Other than Trading)	15,000	
	Unrealized Holding Gain on Other than Trading Securities		15,000
	Revalue other than trade securities to fair value and recognize holding gain.		

Closing entries, required for all nominal accounts, are not presented because the focus is on other aspects of hospital accounting and because the closing process for hospitals is the same as for any other accounting entity. As presented in Figure 19–7, the statement of changes in net assets includes a reconciliation of net assets between the beginning of the year and the year-end.

The statement of cash flows (Figure 19–8) is a required statement. Either the direct or the indirect method may be used to display net cash flows from operations. Under the direct method, the specific inflows and outflows from operations are presented. Under the indirect method, the statement begins with the change in net assets as presented on the statement of changes in net assets. It then presents the adjustments necessary to reconcile the net amount shown on the statement of changes in net assets with the cash flow that is provided by operating activities. Figure 19–8 presents the indirect method because of its popularity and wide use by hospitals. The statement of cash flows is similar to that required of commercial, profit-seeking entities. The three categories of operating activities, investing activities, and financing activities are the same as for commercial entities. There is an important feature, however, for the statement of cash flows for a nonprofit hospital. A nonprofit hospital's cash flow statement reconciles to the change in cash and cash equivalents that is reported as a current asset on the hospital's balance sheet. This cash amount does not include the cash balances in the restricted accounts not available for operations (the plant fund and the endowment fund in the Sol City Community Hospital example). The Audit and Accounting Guide for Health Care Organizations states that, "Cash and claims to cash that *(a)* are restricted as to withdrawal or use for other than current operations, *(b)* are designated for expenditure in the acquisition or construction of noncurrent assets, *(c)* are required to be segregated for the liquidation of long-term debts, or *(d)* are required by a donor-imposed restriction that limits their use to long-term purposes are reported separately and are excluded from current assets.[5] For example, Sol City Community Hospital received a cash contribution to the endowment fund in the amount of $415,000 in transaction (40) (presented later in this chapter). The $415,000 must first be subtracted from the change in net assets in the operating section of the statement of cash flows because the endowment fund does not constitute operating activities.

[5]*AICPA Audit and Accounting Guides for Health Care Organizations,* 1996, p. 47, Section 3.01.

The $415,000 is reported as an increase in financing activities on the statement of cash flows. Of the $415,000 received, $400,000 was used to acquire investments [transaction (41) presented later in this chapter] and this amount is included as an investing activity on the statement of cash flows. The $15,000 of contributions not used to acquire investments in 20X2 are reported on the statement of cash flows as an investing activity, "Remainder of contributions to endowment fund restricted to investing." This is because the amount of financing resources from the restricted endowment fund must equal the amount of investing resources from that restricted fund. Thus, the statement of cash flows reconciles only to the change in cash shown as a current asset on the hospital's balance sheet.

In addition to the primary financial statements for the present fiscal period, with comparatives for the prior period, hospitals are required to present extensive footnotes similar to those of a commercial entity. A specific footnote disclosure is required to report the estimated value of charity care services provided by the hospital during the period.

Temporarily Restricted Funds

Sol City Community Hospital has three funds used to account for temporarily restricted funds. The specific-purpose fund is used for contributions designated for a particular use by the donor other than plant replacement and expansion. The time-restricted fund is used to account for contributions pledged or received in advance that will be available for unrestricted use in the future. The plant replacement and expansion fund is for contributions to be used in acquiring additional land, buildings, and equipment.

Specific-Purpose Fund.   The specific-purpose fund is used to account for contributions received for which a specific use has been designated by the donor. For the most part, such contributions support particular operating activities of the hospital, such as educational or research programs, or provide a particular type of service to patients. The specific-purpose fund does not make expenditures; it holds the restricted resources until the general fund satisfies the terms of the restriction, usually by making the appropriate operating expenditure or by having the restricted expenditure approved by the governing board, whereupon the resources are transferred from the specific-purpose fund to the general fund to pay for the operating expenditure.

The specific-purpose restricted fund typically invests its cash and receives interest or dividends from its investments. A variety of investment transactions can affect the fund balance. Nevertheless, the specific fund is only a holding fund for temporarily restricted resources until they are released for use by the hospital.

The following entries record the transactions in Sol City Community Hospital's specific-purpose fund during the 20X2 fiscal year and are reflected in the statement of financial position in Figure 19–5 and the statement of changes in net assets in Figure 19–7.

Additions to Specific-Purpose Fund.   The specific-purpose fund receives $6,000 of interest income from its investment of funds from a restricted gift to support the hospital's research activity. Restricted gifts of $115,000 are received in response to a community fund-raising effort. The restricted gifts are allocated based on the donors' specifications. In addition, endowment fund earnings in the amount of $60,000 were deposited directly in the temporarily restricted fund:

(27)	Cash	6,000	
	Investment Income—Research		6,000
	Interest on investment of research gift resources.		
(28)	Cash	115,000	
	Contributions—Education		60,000
	Contributions—Research		55,000
	Receive restricted gifts.		
(29)	Cash	60,000	
	Investment Income—Endowment Earnings		60,000
	Earnings of endowment fund deposited in		
	temporarily restricted funds until released		
	for unrestricted use.		

Entry (29) assumes the policy of Sol City Community Hospital is to deposit earnings of the permanently restricted fund in the temporarily restricted fund until clearance is given to use the funds for unrestricted purposes. As a result, the earnings are reported as investment income of the temporarily restricted fund. This procedure provides assurance that the income earned on the endowment will be used for the intended purpose. An alternative approach would be to transfer the earnings from the permanently restricted funds directly to the general fund and include the earnings as unrestricted earnings of the general fund.

Deductions from Specific-Purpose Fund. The specific-purpose fund is notified that the general fund fulfilled the terms of agreements for specific restricted grants totaling $120,000. In addition to the $120,000, the specific-purpose fund also transferred $60,000 from endowment income to the general fund.

(30)	Net Assets Released from Program Use		
	Restriction—Education	61,000	
	Net Assets Released from Program Use		
	Restriction—Research	59,000	
	Net Assets Released from Program Use		
	Restriction—Endowment Income	60,000	
	Cash		180,000
	Funds released from temporary restriction.		

This interfund transaction was also recorded in the general fund [see entries (14) and (15) earlier in the chapter].

Time-Restricted Fund. Under **FASB 116,** procedures for recording contributions were changed. Earlier recognition of contribution revenue generally is now required for most not-for-profit organizations, including hospitals. Because of the critical nature of contributions to the operations of voluntary health and welfare organizations, a thorough treatment of this topic is included later in the chapter as part of the discussion of voluntary health and welfare organizations. For purposes of illustration in the hospital setting, it is assumed that in 20X1 the hospital received pledges for $12,000 to be collected in 20X2. During 20X2, the $12,000 in pledges was collected and immediately transferred to the general fund for unrestricted use [see entry (18) earlier in the chapter].

(31)	Cash	12,000	
	Pledges Receivable		12,000
	Collection of prior period pledge.		
(32)	Net Assets Released from Time Restrictions	12,000	
	Cash		12,000
	Funds released from time restrictions.		

Plant Replacement and Expansion Fund.   The plant replacement and expansion fund, sometimes called the "plant fund," is used to account for restricted resources given to the hospital to be used only for additions or major modifications to the physical plant. This fund is used as a holding fund until the expenditures for plant assets are approved in the general fund by the governing board. The resources are then transferred to the general fund.

A primary source of resources for the plant replacement and expansion fund is from fund-raising efforts in the communities served by the hospital. Hospitals often ask potential donors to sign pledges specifying a giving level for a period of time, for example, $100 per month for the next 12 months. The pledges become receivables of the fund, and typically require a substantial allowance for uncollectibles. The fund records contribution revenue at the time the pledge is received.

The entries recorded in Sol City Community Hospital's plant replacement and expansion fund during 20X2 are presented below and are reflected in the statement of financial position in Figure 19–5.

Additions to Plant Fund.   Increases in the plant replacement and expansion fund during the period are a donation of equipment with a fair value of $25,000 that is recorded in the restricted plant fund until the equipment is placed into service; a donation of $60,000 for use to acquire additional equipment; and the receipt of $7,000 of interest on the plant fund's investments restricted to the purchase of plant. Entries to record these events are presented here:

(33)	Property, Plant, and Equipment	25,000	
	Contributions—Plant		25,000
	Receive donated equipment with fair value of $25,000.		
(34)	Cash	60,000	
	Contributions—Plant		60,000
	Receive restricted gifts for use to acquire equipment.		
(35)	Cash	7,000	
	Investment Income—Plant		7,000
	Receive interest on fund's investments.		

Deductions from Plant Fund.   Deductions from the plant fund during the year are two interfund transfers to the general fund. The first is the transfer of $25,000 of donated equipment that is placed into service, and the second is the transfer of $200,000 to the general fund for expenditures for fixed assets. These two interfund transfers are also recorded in the general fund [see entries (16) and (17) earlier in the chapter]:

(36)	Net Assets Released—Plant Acquisition	25,000	
	Property, Plant, and Equipment		25,000
	Transfer donated equipment to general fund at time of placement into service.		
(37)	Net Assets Released—Plant Acquisition	200,000	
	Cash		200,000
	Transfer cash to general fund for use in acquiring plant assets.		

Other Transactions in Plant Funds.   Other transactions affecting only the asset or liability accounts of the plant funds are a collection of pledges made by individual donors during the last capital fund-raising drive, and the acquisition of additional investments in the fund. Entries for these transactions are presented here:

(38)	Cash	105,000	
	Pledges Receivable		105,000
	Collect pledges receivable.		

(39)	Investments	122,000	
	Cash		122,000
	Increase investments.		

Endowment Fund. The hospital has an endowment fund to account for resources for which the principal must be maintained in perpetuity. The income from the investments in the endowment fund is recorded in the funds to which it applies. If the investment income is restricted, it is recorded in the appropriate restricted fund.

The statement of financial position in Figure 19–5 and the statement of changes in net assets in Figure 19–7 include the entries in Sol City Community Hospital's endowment fund for 20X2.

Additions to Endowment Fund. The endowment fund earns $60,000 interest and dividends from its permanent investments that are deposited directly in the temporarily restricted fund. In addition, a total of $415,000 in new permanent endowments is received and $400,000 is used to acquire additional investments:

(40)	Cash	415,000	
	Contributions—Permanent Endowment		415,000
	Receive additional endowments.		

(41)	Investments	400,000	
	Cash		400,000
	Acquire additional investments.		

Summary of Hospital Accounting and Financial Reporting

The major operating activities of a hospital take place in the general fund. The restricted funds are holding funds that transfer resources to the general fund for expenditures upon satisfaction of their respective restrictions. The accrual basis of accounting is used in the general fund to fully measure the revenue and costs of providing health care. Patient services revenue is reported at gross amounts measured at standard billing rates. A deduction for contractual adjustments is then made to arrive at net patient services revenue. Other revenue is recognized for ongoing nonpatient services, such as cafeteria sales and television rentals, and donated supplies and medicines. Charity care services are presented only in the footnotes; no revenue is recognized for them. Operating expenses in the general fund include depreciation, bad debts, and the value of recognized donated services that are in support of the basic services of the hospital. Not all donated services are recognized. Donated property and equipment is typically recorded in a restricted fund, such as plant fund, until placed into service, at which time it is transferred to the general fund. Donated assets are recorded at their fair market values at the date of gift.

The financial statements of a hospital are (1) the balance sheet, (2) the statement of operations, (3) the statement of changes in net assets, and (4) the statement of cash flows.

Voluntary Health and Welfare Organizations

Voluntary health and welfare organizations (VHWOs) provide a variety of social services. Examples of such organizations are the United Way, the American Heart

Association, the March of Dimes, the American Cancer Society, the Red Cross, and the Salvation Army. These organizations solicit funds from the community at large and typically provide their services for no fee, or they may charge a nominal fee to those with the ability to pay.

As in the case of hospitals, accounting and financial reporting principles for VHWOs have undergone major change with the publication of **FASB 116** and **FASB 117.** A variety of sources may be used in gaining additional information on VHWOs as well. The *AICPA Audit Guide for Not-for-Profit Organizations* requires the use of generally accepted accounting principles for VHWOs.[6] VHWOs are typically audited, and the audited reports made available to contributors and to others interested in knowing about the financial condition of the organization and how the resources are being used. The federal government normally provides tax-exempt status to these organizations. Another source for accounting and reporting guidelines for VHWOs is the *Standards of Accounting and Financial Reporting for Voluntary Health and Welfare Organizations,* published by the combined group of the National Health Council, the National Assembly of National Voluntary Health and Social Welfare Organizations, and the United Way of America.[7] The standards book represents an effort to incorporate accounting and financial reporting standards, and the actual experiences of the largest VHWOs in the United States.

Accounting for a VHWO

The accrual basis of accounting is required for VHWOs in order to measure fully the resources available to the organization. Depreciation is reported as an operating expense each period because the omission of depreciation would result in an understatement of the costs of providing the organization's services. Therefore, accounting for VHWOs is similar to other not-for-profit organizations, except for special financial statements that report on the important aspects of VHWOs. An overview of the accounting and financial reporting principles for a VHWO is presented in this section.

Even though not required to do so, VHWOs have been free to use fund accounting in their accounting and reporting processes. In the past, the typical VHWO has been portrayed as using a fund structure with a (1) current unrestricted fund; (2) current restricted fund; (3) land, building, and equipment fund; and (4) an endowment fund. Many VHWOs are considerably smaller in size and scope of activity than hospitals and may find it convenient to convert from the traditional fund structure to a single accounting entity or a fund structure that distinguishes between unrestricted, temporarily restricted, and permanently restricted assets. The journal entries for Voluntary Health and Welfare Service presented in this section assume a single fund or accounting entity is used. Where appropriate, designations have been added to the journal entry captions to show which of the three classes of assets (unrestricted, temporarily restricted, or permanently restricted) is affected. Thus, the entries could be used equally well if separate funds were established for each of the three asset classifications. Journal entries are presented in the following discussion for only a portion of the transactions of Voluntary Health and Welfare Service in 20X2.

---

[6]The AICPA's 1996 *Audit and Accounting Guide for Not-for-Profit Organizations* revises and supersedes earlier audit guides for VHWOs.

[7]*Standards of Accounting and Financial Reporting for Voluntary Health and Welfare Organizations*, 3d ed., National Health Council, Inc. (Washington D.C.), 1988.

Financial Statements for a VHWO

A VHWO must provide the following financial statements: (1) a statement of financial position, (2) a statement of activities, (3) a statement of cash flows, and (4) a statement of functional expenses.

The financial statements are designed primarily for those who are interested in the organizations as "outsiders," not members of management. These include contributors, beneficiaries of services, creditors and potential creditors, and related organizations. A clear distinction should be maintained between restricted resources and those resources available for expenditure for the organization's major missions. As outlined in **FASB Concepts Statement No. 6,** "Elements of Financial Statements," (**FAC 6**), net assets of not-for-profit organizations are divided into three mutually exclusive classes: permanently restricted net assets, temporarily restricted net assets, and unrestricted net assets. Restricted resources are subject to externally imposed constraints, not internal or board-designated decisions that may be changed by the governing board of the VHWO. In addition, readers of the general-purpose financial statements should be able to clearly evaluate management's performance in accomplishing the objectives of the VHWO.

Statement of Financial Position for a VHWO.   Figure 19–9 presents a statement of financial position for a VHWO. The format used is similar to that used in the hospital illustration. Although not required by existing standards, the assets and liabilities are segregated into current and noncurrent classifications. The net asset section of the statement of financial position for VHWOs must be segregated into unrestricted, temporarily restricted, and permanently restricted, as illustrated. Major balance sheet accounts are as follows.

Pledges from Donors.   The current unrestricted fund includes net ***pledges receivable*** of $78,400 in 20X2. The accrual basis of accounting recognizes the receivable and associated revenue at the time the pledge is received and becomes legally enforceable. Of course, an adequate allowance for uncollectibles must be recognized. Pledges or other contributions applicable to future periods should be reported as revenue "Contributions—Temporarily Restricted." Further accuracy could be attained by identifying the temporary restriction as "Contributions—Temporarily Restricted—Time Restrictions."

The following illustrates the entries used in accounting for a portion of the pledges received by Voluntary Health and Welfare Organization in 20X2. Pledges of $100,000 are received. Of this total, $5,000 is to be received in the current period but is to be held for use for unrestricted purposes in the following period. Experience shows that 20 percent of pledges are uncollectible for this organization. An allowance for uncollectibles is recognized in the amount of $20,000. Note that both the current and deferred pledges are reported at their gross amounts and that provisions for estimated uncollectibles are recorded.

(42)	Pledges Receivable—Unrestricted	95,000	
	Pledges Receivable—Temporarily Restricted	5,000	
	Contributions—Unrestricted		95,000
	Contributions—Temporarily Restricted		5,000
	Receive pledges and recognize receivables.		
(43)	Contributions—Unrestricted	19,000	
	Contributions—Restricted	1,000	
	Allowance for Uncollectible Pledges—Unrestricted		19,000
	Allowance for Uncollectible Pledges—Restricted		1,000
	Provide for estimated uncollectible pledges.		

FIGURE 19–9   **Statement of Financial Position for a Voluntary Health and Welfare Organization**

Voluntary Health and Welfare Service
Statement of Financial Position
December 31, 20X2 and 20X1

	20X2	20X1
Assets		
Current:		
Cash	$ 68,000	$ 47,600
Short-term investments	39,000	48,000
Accounts receivable	1,200	1,000
Inventories	6,400	8,300
Net pledges receivable	78,400	61,600
Prepaid expenses	8,000	7,200
Total current assets	$201,000	$173,700
Cash restricted for long-term use	1,000	–0–
Long-term investments	383,000	351,900
Property, plant, and equipment	125,500	121,600
Total assets	$710,500	$647,200
Liabilities and Net Assets		
Current:		
Accounts payable	$ 16,100	$ 12,400
Accrued expenses	$ 4,800	$ 4,300
Total current liabilities	$ 20,900	$ 16,700
Noncurrent:		
Mortgage payable	$ 21,000	$ 23,000
Capital leases	8,000	7,000
Total liabilities	$ 49,900	$ 46,700
Net assets:		
Unrestricted	$498,200	$437,800
Temporarily restricted by donors	22,900	24,100
Permanently restricted by donors	139,500	138,600
Total net assets	$660,600	$600,500
Total liabilities and net assets	$710,500	$647,200

Note that the Contributions accounts are reduced for the estimated amount of uncollectible pledges. **FASB 116** states that unconditional promises to give that are expected to be collected in less than one year may be measured at net realizable value (net settlement value).[8] Pledged contributions expected to be collected in the future beyond one year should be valued at their present value of the estimated future cash flows. Subsequent increases in the present value of the future cash flows due to the reduction of the present value discount are accounted for as contribution income in the appropriate fund for which the pledge was received. If there is a decrease in the future estimated cash flows resulting from greater concerns about the collectibility of the pledge

---

[8]**FASB 116,** par. 21.

receivable, then **FASB 116** states that the decrease should be reported as an expense (loss) in the period the expectation changes. A point of note is that for temporarily restricted funds and for permanently restricted funds, any decreases in contributions because of changes in future expectations of collectibility should be reported as losses in those funds. The allowance for uncollectibles contra account is used, however, to retain account-based information on the gross amount of the pledges receivable.

All $5,000 of the funds pledged for use the following year and $85,000 of unrestricted pledges are collected in the current period, requiring an adjustment to both unrestricted and temporarily restricted contribution revenue. Temporarily restricted contribution revenue is increased by $1,000 to the full $5,000 received, and $9,000 is added to unrestricted contribution revenue due to collections of $85,000 in pledges versus the initial estimate of $76,000 ($95,000 × .80). Of the remaining balance, $3,000 is written off as uncollectible, and the remainder is carried over to the following period:

(44)	Cash—Unrestricted	85,000	
	Cash—Temporarily Restricted	5,000	
	Allowance for Uncollectible Pledges—Unrestricted	9,000	
	Allowance for Uncollectible Pledges—Restricted	1,000	
	Pledges Receivable—Unrestricted		85,000
	Pledges Receivable—Temporarily Restricted		5,000
	Contribution Revenue—Unrestricted		9,000
	Contribution Revenue—Temporarily Restricted		1,000
	Collect pledges including $10,000 above initial estimate of collectibility.		
(45)	Allowance for Uncollectible Pledges	3,000	
	Pledges Receivable—Unrestricted		3,000
	Write off uncollectible pledges.		

In the following period when the $5,000 is available for unrestricted use, the balance is reclassified as unrestricted:

(46)	Cash—Unrestricted	5,000	
	Reclassification of Contributions to Unrestricted		5,000
	Reclassify time restricted funds to unrestricted.		
(47)	Reclassification of Contributions from Temporarily Restricted	5,000	
	Cash—Temporarily Restricted		5,000
	Reclassify time restricted funds from temporarily restricted.		

FASB 116 also prescribes appropriate treatment for pledges that are to be received over a longer period of time. In general, contribution revenue is recognized at the present value of future cash receipts. As is the normal practice in utilizing present value procedures in the corporate sector, the present value is used to record contributions that are to be received in the following accounting periods. For example, if a donor agrees to contribute $10,000 per year at the end of each of the next five years, the stream of the payments is discounted at an appropriate rate (e.g., 8 percent) and the present value is recognized at the time the pledge is received:

(48)	Pledges Receivable—Temporarily Restricted	39,927	
	Contributions—Temporarily Restricted		39,927
	Receipt of pledge.		

At the end of the first year when the first payment of $10,000 is received, that amount is reclassified from temporarily restricted to unrestricted, and the increase in present value of the contributions receivable is recognized as an increase in temporarily restricted contributions and contributions receivable:

(49)	Cash—Unrestricted	10,000	
	Reclassification of Contributions to Unrestricted		10,000
	Reclassify time restricted funds to unrestricted.		
(50)	Reclassification of Contributions from Temporarily Restricted	10,000	
	Pledges Receivable—Temporarily Restricted		10,000
	Reclassify time restricted funds from temporarily restricted.		
(51)	Pledges Receivable—Temporarily Restricted	3,194	
	Contributions—Temporarily Restricted		3,194
	Increase in the present value of contributions receivable.		

Investments.   Investments may be purchased or donated to the organization. Purchased investments should be recorded at cost. Securities donated to the organization should be recorded at their fair market values at the dates of the gifts. Subsequently, equity investments (other than **APB 18** equity investments) and all investments in bonds are reported at market value. Appreciation gains (or reductions in value) are separately identified as unrealized gains (losses) in the organization's statement of activity in accordance with **FASB 124**. Transfers of investments from one portfolio to another should be made at market value, with any gains or losses in valuation recorded.

Investment earnings should be reported as unrestricted, temporarily restricted, or permanently restricted, depending on how they are to be used. Income from unrestricted funds and gains and losses on investment transactions of unrestricted funds should always be reported as unrestricted. The income earned on investments classified as temporarily or permanently restricted also should be reported as unrestricted income if it is available for unrestricted use. When the earnings from temporarily or permanently restricted assets also are restricted by the donor, investment income should be reported in the appropriate restricted category.

Transaction gains and losses on investments of restricted assets typically are reported in the statement of activities as a gain or loss in the appropriate restricted asset category. If available for unrestricted use, an entry would be made in the unrestricted fund to show the availability as unrestricted. Gains and losses on investments of permanent endowments typically are considered principal transactions and added to, or deducted from, the principal balance and subjected to the same restrictions as the original principal.

Land, Buildings, and Equipment.   Land, buildings, and equipment, depreciation expense, and the accumulated depreciation on the fixed assets generally are reported as unrestricted unless restricted by the donor. The basis of fixed assets is cost, and donated assets are recorded at their fair market values at the dates of the gifts. Donations of fixed assets that will be sold by the organization in the near future are equivalent to other contributions, and should be separately reported as unrestricted assets until sold. For example, assume the VHWO receives land as a donation. The VHWO plans to sell the land and use the proceeds from the sale in supporting the entity's program services. The land should be recorded at fair value as an unrestricted asset and reported as land held for resale, until sold.

A VHWO may use any one of the methods of depreciation available to commercial entities. Not-for-profit entities are not required to depreciate assets such as works of art or other historically valuable assets in instances in which the not-for-profit entity has made a commitment to preserve the value of the art or historically valuable asset, and has shown the capacity to do so.

Liabilities.   Liabilities are recorded in the normal manner under the accrual model. In most situations, liabilities will be reported as part of the unrestricted net assets. For example, in Figure 19–9, the mortgage payment made by Voluntary Health and Welfare Service in 20X2 was recorded as a $2,000 debit to Mortgage Payable and a $2,000 credit to Cash—Unrestricted. In this illustration, property, plant, and equipment is classified as an unrestricted asset. In some cases, mortgage payments on assets classified as restricted are made from unrestricted funds. The following entries would be needed in the latter case:

(52)	Reclassification to Restricted Assets	2,000	
	Cash—Unrestricted		2,000
	Mortgage payment made from unrestricted assets.		
(53)	Mortgage Payable—Restricted Assets	2,000	
	Reclassification from Unrestricted Assets		2,000
	Reduction of carrying value of mortgage.		

Net Assets.   Separate disclosure should be provided for the amounts of net assets designated as unrestricted, temporarily restricted, and permanently restricted. The governing board of the VHWO also may show its intent to use unrestricted resources for specific needs in the future by creating one or more board-designated captions. For example, the $498,200 of unrestricted net assets at December 31, 20X2, shown in Figure 19–9 could be divided between board-designated and undesignated. Board-designated purposes might be for purchases of new equipment, research, construction of new facilities, or other asset acquisitions. While the statement of financial position could reflect the designation of resources, the governing board may change these at any time.

Statement of Activities.   Figure 19–10 presents the major operating statement for VHWOs, the statement of activities. The overall structure of the statement of activities for voluntary health and welfare organizations and other not-for-profit entities should be very similar as a result of **FASB 117.** As with other types of nonprofit entities, a number of organizations have issued standards relating to VHWOs. Both the National Health Council's "black book" of standards for VHWOs and the AICPA's Audit Guide for Not-for-Profit Organizations contain recommendations for accounting for VHWOs. Several of the unique aspects of VHWOs are discussed next.

Public Support.   Historically, a distinction was made in the sources of funding received by VHWOs. Nonprofit organizations generally provide services to those who cannot afford to pay for the benefits received or support programs for which little compensation is received. For VHWOs, the primary source of funds is likely to be contributions from individuals or organizations who do not derive any direct benefit from the VHWO for their gifts. The magnitude of funds received and the diversity of contributors is important in evaluating the effectiveness of VHWOs. Four sources of resources included in the 20X2 statement of activities for Voluntary Health and Welfare Service in Figure 19–10 are considered to fall in the category of support. They include contributions, legacies and bequests, collections through affiliates (other organizations in the same community or with similar goals), and contributions received from the federated (national or regional) organization's fund-raising efforts.

FIGURE 19–10   **Statement of Activities for a Voluntary Health and Welfare Organization**

	Unrestricted	Temporarily Restricted	Permanently Restricted	Total
Voluntary Health and Welfare Service				
Statement of Activities				
For the Year Ended December 31, 20X2				
Revenues, gains, and other support:				
Contributions	$627,000	$ 42,300	$ 9,900	$679,200
Legacies and bequests	15,000			15,000
Collections through affiliates	2,800			2,800
Allocated from federated fund-raising effort	45,300			45,300
Memberships	6,100			6,100
Program fees	700			700
Sale of materials	200			200
Investment income	36,400	500		36,900
Gain on investments	12,000		1,000	13,000
Donated services	3,000			3,000
Net assets released from restriction:				
Program use restrictions	25,000	(25,000)		
Passage of time	8,100	(8,100)		
Equipment acquisition	10,900	(10,900)		
Endowment transfers	10,000		(10,000)	
Total revenues, gains and other support	$802,500	$ (1,200)	$ 900	$802,200
Program services and operating costs:				
Research	$274,300			$274,300
Public health education	92,000			92,000
Professional training	106,000			106,000
Community services	98,600			98,600
Management and general	91,700			91,700
Fund-raising	64,500			64,500
Payments to national offices	15,000			15,000
Total expenses	$742,100	$ -0-	$ -0-	$742,100
Change in net assets	$ 60,400	$ (1,200)	$ 900	$ 60,100
Net assets at beginning of year	437,800	24,100	138,600	600,500
Net assets at end of year	$498,200	$ 22,900	$139,500	$660,600

A recent change has occurred in accounting for support received from special events. In the past, the costs of providing the event were deducted from the total proceeds generated and the net amount was reported as support. Under the guidelines of **FASB 117,** total proceeds from a sponsored event such as a dance gala or marathon are reported as support from special events and the costs of sponsoring the event are reported as fund-raising costs. Even though many of the necessary items are contributed for such activities, the costs of sponsoring an event may be rather substantial. The frequency of such events undoubtedly was a factor in the change in the tax laws that now requires nonprofit organizations sponsoring a special event to provide participants with a statement detailing the portion of the cost of a ticket or other contribution that may be treated as a charitable contribution for tax purposes.

Revenues. Funds received in exchange for services provided or other activities are classified as revenues. Although the majority of a VHWO's resources are obtained from public support, funds also are received from memberships, fees charged to program participants, sales of supplies and services, and investment income.

Gains. Investments and other assets may be sold from time to time and the difference between the sale price and the carrying value is included in the statement of activities as a gain or loss. Much of the time, gains received from sales of investments is reinvested in anticipation of future earnings; nevertheless, all gains and losses should be included in the statement of activities for the period.

Donated Materials and Services. A VHWO often relies heavily on ***donated materials and services.*** Donated materials should be recorded at fair value when received. If the donated materials are used in one of the VHWO's program services, then the recorded value of the materials should be reported as an expense in the period used. If the donated materials simply pass through the VHWO to its charitable beneficiaries, then the VHWO is acting as an agent, and the materials would not then be recorded as a contribution or an expense.

Donated services are an essential part of a VHWO. Because of the difficulty of valuing these services, they often are not recorded as contributions. However, if donated services are significant, they should be recognized by the VHWO if the services (1) create or enhance nonfinancial assets or (2) require specialized skills, are provided by individuals possessing those skills, and would typically need to be purchased if not provided by donation.[9] If these conditions are satisfied, the value of donated services should be reported as part of the public support and also as an expense in the period in which the services are provided. As an example of donated services, assume that a CPA donates audit services with an estimated value of $3,000. The VHWO makes the following entry in the current unrestricted fund to recognize the donated services:

```
(50)  Expenses—Supporting Services                    3,000
         Support—Donated Services                              3,000
      CPA donates audit.
```

Expenses. The statement of activities should contain information about the major costs of providing services to the public, fund-raising, and general and administrative costs in order to provide contributors and others with information that is useful in assessing the effectiveness of the VHWO. Those costs of providing goods and services to beneficiaries, customers, or members in fulfilling the primary mission of the VHWO are referred to as program service costs. For VHWOs, the statement of activities normally should include the total costs of providing each of the major classes of program services. As shown in Figure 19–10, the primary activities for the Voluntary Health and Welfare Service are research, public health education, professional training, and community services. A detailed breakdown of these costs is presented in the statement of functional expenses required of all VHWO organizations. The statement of functional expenses (presented later in this chapter) provides information on the amount of salary expense, telephone, travel, supplies, and other costs incurred in providing each of the major programs.

Information also is presented in the statement of activities on the costs of other activities needed to operate effectively but which may not be directly assignable to a

---

[9]**FASB 116,** par. 9.

particular program. These costs generally are reported either as management and general administrative costs or as fund-raising costs. Management and general activities include the costs of maintaining the general headquarters, record-keeping, business management, and other management and administrative activities not directly assignable to program services or fund-raising activities. Fund-raising activities include the costs of special mailings, compiling potential donor lists, conducting campaigns through contacts with foundations and governmental agencies, and other similar costs. In those organizations where membership contributions are an important source of funds, separate disclosure should be made of the costs of soliciting members and providing special benefits to those who are members.

Depreciation costs for 20X2 included in the statement of activities in Figure 19–10 totaled $9,500. An allocation is made to each of the program services and supporting services, based on square footage used or some other reasonable basis. For example, an allocation of the $9,500 of depreciation, based on square footage occupied, to each of the program and supporting services is recorded with the following entry:

(55)	Research—Depreciation	4,300	
	Public Health—Depreciation	1,000	
	Professional Training—Depreciation	2,000	
	Community Services—Depreciation	1,200	
	Management and General—Depreciation	500	
	Fund-Raising—Depreciation	500	
	Accumulated Depreciation		9,500
	Record depreciation for 20X2.		

Costs of Informational Materials that Include a Fund-Raising Appeal. Not-for-profit entities often prepare informational materials that include a direct or indirect message soliciting funds. The issue is how to record the cost of these materials. Should these costs be a program expense or a fund-raising expense? Many VHWOs prefer to classify such costs as program rather than fund-raising to highlight the fulfillment of the basic service mission of the VHWO. Users of the general-purpose financial statements are concerned with the amounts that VHWO organizations spend to solicit contributions, as opposed to the amounts spent for program services. If a not-for-profit entity cannot show that a program or management function has been conducted in conjunction with the appeal for funds, then the entire cost of the informational materials or activities should be reported as a fund-raising expense. However, if it can be demonstrated that a bona fide program or management function has been conducted in conjunction with the appeal for funds, then the ***costs of informational materials*** are allocated between programs and fund-raising. Evidence of a bona fide program intent in a brochure would be an appeal designed to motivate its audience to action other than providing financial support to the organization. An informational content of a brochure might include a description of the symptoms of a disease and the actions an individual should take if one or more of the symptoms occur. Thus, the content of the message and the intended audience are significant factors.

Statement of Cash Flows. The third required financial statement for VHWOs is the statement of cash flows, as presented in Figure 19–11. The format of this statement is similar to that for hospitals as discussed earlier in the chapter. Note that under the indirect approach, the statement begins with the change in net assets and reconciles to the net change in cash during the period.

FIGURE 19–11   **Statement of Cash Flows for a Voluntary Health and Welfare Organization**

Voluntary Health and Welfare Service
Statement of Cash Flows
For the Year Ended December 31, 20X2

Change in net assets		$60,100
Adjustments to reconcile changes in net assets to net cash provided by operating activities:		
Depreciation	$ 9,500	
Gain on sale of investments	(13,000)	
Decrease in short-term investments	9,000	
Increase in accounts receivable	(200)	
Increase in contributions receivable (net)	(16,800)	
Decrease in inventories	1,900	
Increase in prepaid expenses	(800)	
Increase in accounts payable	3,700	
Increase in accrued expenses	500	
Contributions restricted for equipment acquisition	(10,900)	
Endowment contributions restricted for acquisition of investments	(9,900)	(27,000)
Net cash provided by operating activities		$33,100
Cash flows from investing activities:		
Purchase of property, plant, and equipment	$(13,400)	
Proceeds from sale of investments	40,000	
Purchase of investments	(59,100)	
Investment gain restricted to purchase of investments	(1,000)	
Net cash used by investing activities		(33,500)
Cash flows from financing activities:		
Mortgage payments	$ (2,000)	
Capital lease agreements	1,000	
Contributions restricted to acquiring fixed assets	10,900	
Endowment gain restricted to acquiring investments	1,000	
Contributions restricted for permanent endowment	9,900	
Net cash used in financing activities		20,800
Net increase in cash		$20,400
Cash at the beginning of year		47,600
Cash at the end of year		$68,000

Statement of Functional Expenses.   The fourth statement required of all VHWOs is the *statement of functional expenses.* This statement details the items reported in the expenses section of the statement of activities in Figure 19–10. Figure 19–12 is a standard format for the statement of functional expenses. The expense categories are presented across the columns. The rows are the specific nature of the items comprising these expense categories from the various funds.

The statement of functional expenses includes depreciation of $9,500 for the year, allocated among the various programs and supporting services. Total expenses of $742,100 in Figure 19–10 are analyzed and reconciled on the statement of functional expenses in Figure 19–12.

FIGURE 19–12 Statement of Functional Expenses for a Voluntary Health and Welfare Organization

Voluntary Health and Welfare Service
Statement of Functional Expenses
Year Ended December 31, 20X2
(with comparative totals for 20X1)

	Program Services					Supporting Services			Total Program and Supporting Services Expenses	
	Research	Public Health Education	Professional Training	Community Services	Total	Management and General	Fund-Raising	Total	20X2	20X1
Salaries	49,000	58,200	51,100	53,800	212,100	66,100	34,100	100,200	312,300	347,000
Employee benefits	2,800	2,900	2,900	2,900	11,500	4,100	1,000	5,100	16,600	16,800
Payroll taxes, etc.	2,400	3,100	2,600	2,900	11,000	3,600	1,800	5,400	16,400	15,500
Total salaries and related expenses	54,200	64,200	56,600	59,600	234,600	73,800	36,900	100,700	345,300	379,300
Professional fees	200	1,000	5,200	1,600	8,000	3,000	1,500	4,500	12,500	12,000
Supplies	400	600	1,000	1,000	3,000	2,100	3,000	5,100	8,100	7,900
Telephone	400	1,400	1,200	4,300	7,300	2,500	7,200	9,700	17,000	16,800
Bad debts and other	400	3,200	900	2,800	7,300	2,600	6,000	8,600	15,900	14,300
Occupancy	1,000	3,400	6,000	9,000	19,400	3,000	1,000	4,000	23,400	20,500
Rental of equipment	200	800	3,400	400	4,800	600	100	700	5,500	4,800
Printing and publications	600	11,200	6,500	1,400	19,700	900	7,400	8,300	28,000	23,000
Travel	1,600	2,000	10,800	4,200	18,600	1,100	200	1,300	19,900	21,500
Conferences and meetings	800	1,800	10,500	1,600	14,700	1,400	600	2,000	16,700	16,300
Awards and grants	209,300	1,200	600	10,300	221,400				221,400	157,500
Postage and shipping	900	200	1,300	1,200	3,600	200	100	300	3,900	4,200
Total expenses before depreciation	270,000	91,000	104,000	97,400	562,400	91,200	64,000	155,200	717,600	678,100
Depreciation of buildings and equipment	4,300	1,000	2,000	1,200	8,500	500	500	1,000	9,500	6,500
Total functional expenses	274,300	92,000	106,000	98,600	570,900	91,700	64,500	156,200	727,100	684,600
Payments to national office									15,000	12,000
Total expenses									742,100	696,600

Summary of Accounting and Financial Reporting for VHWOs

The accounting and financial reporting requirements for VHWOs are specified in **FASB 116, FASB 117,** and the *AICPA Audit Guide for Not-for-Profit Organizations.* The accrual basis of accounting is used. Primary activities of the VHWO are reported in the unrestricted asset class. Resources restricted by the donor for specific operating purposes or future periods are reported as temporarily restricted assets. Those assets contributed by the donor with permanent restrictions are reported as permanently restricted assets.

A VHWO provides four financial statements: (1) statement of financial position, (2) statement of activities, (3) cash flow statement, and (4) statement of functional expenses. The statement of functional expenses is required of all VHWOs as a means of providing an analysis of all expenses for the organization, including depreciation. Expenses are broken down into types, such as salaries, supplies, and travel, and are summarized by individual program services and individual supporting services.

Other Not-for-Profit Entities

There are many types of not-for-profit entities in addition to hospitals and voluntary health and welfare organizations. Our society depends heavily on such organizations for religious, educational, social, and recreational needs. Examples of other not-for-profit organizations (ONPOs) include the following:

Cemetery organizations	Private and community foundations
Civic organizations	Private elementary and secondary schools
Fraternal organizations	Professional associations
Labor unions	Public broadcasting stations
Libraries	Religious organizations
Museums	Research and scientific organizations
Other cultural institutions	Social and country clubs
Performing arts organizations	Trade associations
Political parties	Zoological and botanical societies

Accounting for ONPOs

The issuance of **FASB 116** and **FASB 117** has done much to bring the financial reporting standards of hospitals, voluntary health and welfare organizations, and other not-for-profit organizations into agreement. In addition to the two FASB statements, the *AICPA Audit Guide for Not-for-Profit Organizations* also provides guidance for accounting and financial reporting standards for ONPOs.

ONPOs vary significantly in size and scope of operations. While accrual accounting is required for all ONPOs, some small organizations operate on a cash basis during the year and convert to an accrual basis at year-end. Other ONPOs have thousands or even millions of members and hold assets worth substantial sums of money. From the viewpoint of asset management and control procedures such organizations may be virtually identical to a large business entity. The fact that they are not in business to earn profits from selling goods and services continues to distinguish some aspects of financial reporting for ONPOs from that of business entities, however.

FIGURE 19–13   Statement of Financial Position for an Other Not-for-Profit Organization

Ellwood Historical Society
Statement of Financial Position
June 30, 20X2 and 20X1

	20X2	20X1
Cash	$ 32,000	$ 16,800
Accounts receivable	17,500	1,500
Contributions receivable	48,000	30,000
Inventories	3,000	1,000
Prepaid expenses	6,500	6,500
Cash restricted for long-term investments	2,000	-0-
Long-term investments (at fair value)	184,000	87,000
Property, plant, and equipment (net)	242,000	246,000
Total Assets	$535,000	$388,800
Accounts payable	$ 28,000	$ 28,000
Mortgage payable	178,000	187,000
Net Assets:		
Unrestricted	179,000	130,800
Temporarily restricted by donors	48,000	43,000
Permanently restricted by donors	102,000	-0-
Total liabilities and net assets	$535,000	$388,800

In the past, it has been assumed fund accounting would be used by ONPOs in a manner similar to accounting for VHWOs. With the adoption of **FASB 116** and **FASB 117,** it is likely the procedures used by ONPOs and VHWOs will move away from the traditional funds used and account for all transactions in a single entity or by establishing separate accounts for unrestricted, temporarily restricted, and permanently restricted assets.

Financial Statements of ONPOs

The principal purpose of the financial statements of an ONPO is to explain how the available resources have been used to carry out the organization's activities. Therefore, the statements should disclose the nature and source of the resources acquired, any restrictions on the resources, and the principal programs and their costs; they should also provide information on the organization's ability to continue to carry out its objectives. An ONPO must provide the following financial statements: (1) a statement of financial position, (2) a statement of activities, and (3) a statement of cash flows. While the statement of functional expenses is not required of ONPOs, it may be appropriate to prepare a statement providing information on expenses by function for each major program when an ONPO is involved in a broad range of activities or it carries on activities that are very distinct from one another.

Statement of Financial Position for an ONPO.   Figure 19–13 presents a balance sheet for a nonprofit organization that renovates and preserves historical buildings in Sol City. The name of the organization is the Ellwood Historical Society. The society has its own governing board and is not associated with a government. The illustrated balance sheet is a very simple one in light of the well-defined mission of the organization.

Land, Buildings, and Equipment.   Land, buildings, and equipment owned by the ONPO and used in its activities generally are recorded at historical cost and depreciated in the normal manner. Operating assets that are donated should be recorded at fair market value at the date of contribution. Unless use of the asset is restricted by the donor, land, buildings, and equipment should be included in unrestricted net assets reported on the balance sheet.

Inexhaustible Collections.   Libraries, museums, art galleries, and similar entities often have collections of works of art or other historical treasures that are held for public viewing or for research. While some organizations recognize such works of art or other historical treasures as assets, most do not. Moreover, when individual works of art or historical treasures are recorded, the Financial Accounting Standards Board in **FASB 93** concluded not-for-profit organizations are not required to record depreciation.[10] Specific rules for disclosure of the costs of items purchased and funds generated from the sale of such items are presented in **FASB 116.**[11]

Statement of Activities.   A statement of activities for the historical society, presented in Figure 19–14, reports the support, revenue, expenses, transfers, and changes in fund balance during the fiscal period.

The format for the statement of activities is comparable to the statement of activities for a VHWO. For the Ellwood Historical Society, contributions are the primary source of support. However, both membership dues and admissions provide a greater source of revenue than in the voluntary health and welfare setting. Memberships often provide free admission or admission at reduced rates in the case of a museum, art gallery, or library. Thus, memberships and admissions may be interrelated in these organizations. Other types of organizations may have very different sources of funds and major expense categories. The financial statement captions and presentation should be adjusted to focus on these attributes in such cases.

As with VHWOs, depreciation charges for the period have been apportioned to the primary programmatic activities of the ONPO and reported as expenses in the unrestricted assets section of the statement of activities. Disclosure should be made of the depreciation charges for the period and the balance of accumulated depreciation in the financial statements or footnotes to the financial statements of the ONPO to assist financial statement readers in assessing the operating effectiveness and financial position of the ONPO.

Assets released from restriction during the period are shown as reclassifications in the statement of activities. Thus, a contribution of $21,000 for research on Civil War activities would be included in the $78,000 reported as temporarily restricted contributions in Figure 19–14. If $19,500 of the contribution is spent during 20X2, that amount would be part of the $62,600 reclassified from temporarily restricted to unrestricted assets (net assets released from program use restrictions) in 20X2. The $19,500 expense incurred in conducting the research would be included in the $24,200 total reported as research expense in 20X2.

---

[10]**Financial Accounting Standards Board Statement No. 93**, "Recognition of Depreciation by Not-for-Profit Organizations," August 1987, para. 6.

[11]Ibid., para. 26.

FIGURE 19–14 Statement of Activities for an Other Not-for-Profit Organization (ONPO)

Ellwood Historical Society
Statement of Activities
For the Year Ended June 30, 20X2

	Unrestricted	Temporarily Restricted	Permanently Restricted	Total
Revenues, gains, and other support:				
Contributions	$130,000	$ 78,000	$100,000	$308,000
Donated services	3,000			3,000
Membership dues	16,000			16,000
Admissions	12,000			12,000
Investment income	12,200	2,600	12,000	26,800
Gain on investments	5,000			5,000
Net assets released from restriction:				
Program use restrictions	62,600	(62,600)		
Equipment acquisition	13,000	(13,000)		
Endowment transfers	10,000		(10,000)	
Total revenues, gains, and other support	$263,800	$ 5,000	$102,000	$370,800
Program services and support:				
Community education	$139,400			$139,400
Research	24,200			24,200
Auxiliary activities	19,000			19,000
General and administrative	20,000			20,000
Fund-raising	13,000			13,000
Total expenses	$215,600	$ -0-	$ -0-	$215,600
Change in net assets	$ 48,200	$ 5,000	$102,000	$155,200
Net assets at beginning of year	130,800	43,000	-0-	173,800
Net assets at end of year	$179,000	$ 48,000	$102,000	$329,000

Statement of Cash Flows. Figure 19–15 presents the statement of cash flows for the illustrated historical society. The statement of cash flows begins with the net change in assets for the combined entity taken from the statement of activities. Adjustments are made for noncash revenues and expenses and changes in account balances to arrive at cash provided by operating activities. Net cash flows from investing activities and financing activities are added (deducted) in arriving at the net increase (decrease) in cash for the period. The net cash flow for the period is added to the beginning cash balance in unrestricted assets to arrive at the balance at the end of the period.

Summary of Accounting and Financial Reporting for ONPOs

Accounting for ONPOs is similar to accounting for VHWOs. The accrual basis of accounting is used for financial reporting purposes. A statement of financial position, a statement of activities, and a statement of cash flows are required for financial reporting purposes. When a large number of programs or a number of very different types of programs are part of the operations of an ONPO, it may be desirable to prepare a statement of expenses by functional area or major program as well. As a result of **FASB 116** and **FASB 117,** the reporting requirements of ONPOs are substantially the same as VHWOs.

Q19–8 Where is a gain on the sale of hospital properties recorded by a hospital? How is the gain reported in the hospital's financial statements?

Q19–9 Is depreciation accounted for by a hospital? Why or why not?

Q19–10 What is the basis of accounting for the unrestricted assets of a VHWO? What is the basis for the restricted assets?

Q19–11 Where are fixed assets recorded for a VHWO? Is depreciation recorded for a VHWO?

Q19–12 An individual contributes $10,000 to a VHWO for restricted use in a public health education service. How does the VHWO account for this contribution? How does it account for the expenditure of the $10,000?

Q19–13 Explain the accounting for pledges from donors to a VHWO.

Q19–14 Why do VHWOs not report all pledges received in the period in the unrestricted assets section of the statement of activities? Identify that which is not included.

Q19–15 How do VHWOs account for donated services?

Q19–16 Describe the statement of functional expenses. What organizations must prepare this statement?

Q19–17 An alumna of a sorority donates $12,000 to the sorority for restricted use in a community service activity of the sorority. How is the contribution accounted for by this ONPO? How is the expenditure of the $12,000 accounted for?

Q19–18 Are donated services received by an ONPO accounted for in the same manner as donated services received by hospitals? Why or why not?

Q19–19 What is the market value unit method of accounting for investments?

Q19–20 Should a rotary club, an ONPO, report depreciation expense? Why or why not?

Q19–21 Describe the statement of activities for an ONPO. Compare it with the statement of activities for a VHWO.

Q19–22 Give two examples of contributions to an ONPO that would be reported as temporarily restricted and two that would be reported as permanently restricted.

Cases

C19–1 **Accounting for Donations**

Hospitals, voluntary health and welfare organizations, and other not-for-profit organizations often rely heavily on donations of volunteers' time and donations of equipment, supplies, or other assets.

Required

a. Specify the criteria to be used to determine the accounting for donated services to (1) hospitals, (2) voluntary health and welfare organizations, and (3) other not-for-profit organizations. Discuss the reasons for any differences in the accounting criteria used.

b. How are donations of capital assets, such as equipment, accounted for by hospitals? Is depreciation recorded on these donations? Why or why not?

c. How are cash contributions accounted for by (1) hospitals, (2) voluntary health and welfare organizations, and (3) other not-for-profit organizations?

C19–2 **Public Support to an Other Not-for-Profit Organization**

L. Dawnes has just been elected treasurer of the local professional association of registered nurses. The association provides public health messages for the community as well as services for members. She is now preparing financial statements for the year and comes to you for advice on accounting for the proceeds from a major fund drive that occurred during the year. The nursing association received $25,000 in unrestricted donations and $15,000 in restricted donations that are restricted to public health advertisements. A total of $6,000 has been incurred for public health advertising since the restricted donations were received.

The former treasurer accounted for the $40,000 of donations as revenue in the unrestricted fund. L. Dawnes feels this may not be correct because it does not disclose the restricted nature of the donations for the public health messages.

Required

a. Discuss the accounting and financial statement disclosure to be used to account for the $25,000 of unrestricted donations to the professional association.

b. How should the $15,000 of restricted contributions have been accounted for at the time of the donation? How should they have been reported on this year's financial statements?

Exercises

E19–1 **Multiple-Choice Questions on Colleges and Universities [AICPA Adapted]**
Select the correct answer for each of the following questions.

1. For the summer session of 20X2, Pacific University assessed its students $1,700,000 (net of refunds), covering tuition and fees for educational and general purposes. However, only $1,500,000 was expected to be realized, because scholarships totaling $150,000 were granted to students, and tuition remissions of $50,000 were allowed to faculty members' children attending Pacific. What amount should Pacific include as revenues from student tuition and fees?
   a. $1,500,000.
   b. $1,550,000.
   c. $1,650,000.
   d. $1,700,000.

2. Tuition remissions for graduate student teaching assistantships should be classified by a university as:

	Revenue	Expenditures
a.	No	No
b.	No	Yes
c.	Yes	Yes
d.	Yes	No

3. For the fall semester of 20X1, Dover University assessed its students $2,300,000 for tuition and fees. The net amount realized was only $2,100,000 because of the following revenue reductions:

Refunds occasioned by class cancellations and student withdrawals	$50,000
Tuition remissions granted to faculty members' families	10,000
Scholarships and fellowships	140,000

How much should Dover report for the period for revenue from tuition and fees?
   a. $2,100,000.
   b. $2,150,000.
   c. $2,250,000.
   d. $2,300,000.

Items 4 through 6 are based on the following information pertaining to Global University, a private institution, as of June 30, 20X1, and for the year then ended:

   Unrestricted net assets comprised $7,500,000 of assets and $4,500,000 of liabilities (including deferred revenues of $150,000). Among the receipts recorded during the year were unrestricted gifts of $550,000 and restricted grants totaling $330,000, of which $220,000 was expended during the year for current operations and $110,000 remained unexpended at the close of the year.

Volunteers from the surrounding communities regularly contribute their services to Global and are paid nominal amounts to cover their travel costs. During the year, the total amount paid to these volunteers aggregated $18,000. The gross value of services performed by them, determined by reference to equivalent wages available in that area for similar services, amounted to $200,000. Global University normally purchases the types of contributed services and the university feels the contributed services enhance its assets.

4. At June 30, 20X1, Global's unrestricted net asset balance was:
   a. $7,500,000.
   b. $3,150,000.
   c. $3,000,000.
   d. $2,850,000.

5. For the year ended June 30, 20X1, what amount should be included in Global's revenue for the unrestricted gifts and restricted grants?
   a. $550,000.
   b. $660,000.
   c. $770,000.
   d. $880,000.

6. For the year ended June 30, 20X1, what amount should Global record as expenditures for the volunteers' services?
   a. $218,000.
   b. $200,000.
   c. $18,000.
   d. $0.

E19–2   Multiple-Choice Questions on Hospital Accounting [AICPA Adapted]
Select the correct answer for each of the following questions.

Questions 1 through 3 are based on the following data:

Under Dodge Hospital's established rate structure, the hospital would have earned patient service revenue of $5,000,000 for the year ended December 31, 20X3. However, Dodge did not expect to collect this amount because of contractual adjustments of $500,000 to third-party payors. In May 20X3, Dodge purchased bandages from Hunt Supply Company at a cost of $1,000. However, Hunt notified Dodge that the invoice was being canceled and that the bandages were being donated to Dodge. On December 31, 20X3, Dodge had board-designated assets consisting of $40,000 in cash and investments of $700,000.

1. For the year ended December 31, 20X3, how much should Dodge report as net patient service revenue?
   a. $4,500,000.
   b. $5,000,000.
   c. $5,500,000.
   d. $5,740,000.

2. For the year ended December 31, 20X3, Dodge should record the donation of bandages as:
   a. A $1,000 reduction in operating expenses.
   b. A decrease in net assets released from restrictions.
   c. An increase in unrestricted revenue, gains, and other support.
   d. A memorandum entry only.

3. How much of Dodge's board-designated assets should be included in unrestricted net assets?
   a. $0.
   b. $40,000.

   c. $700,000.

   d. $740,000.

4. Donated medicines that normally would be purchased by a hospital should be recorded at fair value and should be credited directly to:

   a. Unrestricted revenue.

   b. Expense of medicines.

   c. Fund balance.

   d. Deferred revenue.

5. Which of the following would normally be included as revenue of a not-for-profit hospital?

   a. Unrestricted interest income from an endowment fund.

   b. An unrestricted gift.

   c. Tuition received from an educational program.

   d. All of the above.

6. An unrestricted gift pledge from an annual contributor to a not-for-profit hospital made in December 20X1 and paid in March 20X2 would generally be credited to:

   a. Contribution revenue in 20X1.

   b. Contribution revenue in 20X2.

   c. Other income in 20X1.

   d. Other income in 20X2.

7. An organization of high school seniors assists patients at Lake Hospital. These students are volunteers and perform services that the hospital would not otherwise provide, such as wheeling patients in the park and reading to patients. Lake has no employer-employee relationship with these volunteers, who donated 5,000 hours of service to Lake in 20X2. At the minimum wage, these services would amount to $18,750, while it is estimated that the fair value of these services was $25,000. In Lake's 20X2 statement of operations, what amount should be reported as donated services?

   a. $25,000.

   b. $18,750.

   c. $6,250.

   d. $0.

8. Which of the following would be included in the unrestricted funds of a not-for-profit hospital?

   a. Permanent endowments.

   b. Term endowments.

   c. Board-designated funds originating from previously accumulated income.

   d. Funds designated by the donor for plant expansion and replacement funds.

9. During the year ended December 31, 20X1, Greenacre Hospital received the following donations stated at their respective fair values:

Essential specialized employee-type services from members of a religious group	$100,000
Medical supplies from an association of physicians. These supplies were restricted for indigent care and were used for such purpose in 20X1.	30,000

How much total revenue from donations should Greenacre report its 20X1?

   a. $0.

   b. $30,000.

   c. $100,000.

   d. $130,000.

10. Johnson Hospital's property, plant, and equipment (net of depreciation) consists of the following:

Land	$ 500,000
Buildings	10,000,000
Movable equipment	2,000,000

What amount should be reported as restricted assets?

a. $0.

b. $2,000,000.

c. $10,500,000.

d. $12,500,000.

11. Depreciation should be recognized in the financial statements of:

a. Proprietary (for-profit) hospitals only.

b. Both proprietary and not-for-profit hospitals.

c. Both proprietary and not-for-profit hospitals, only when they are affiliated with a college or university.

d. All hospitals, as a memorandum entry not affecting the statement of revenue and expenses.

12. On March 1, 20X1, J. Rowe established a $100,000 endowment fund, the income from which is to be paid to Central Hospital for general operating purposes. Central does not control the fund's principal. Rowe appointed Sycamore National Bank as trustee of this fund. What journal entry is required by Central to record the establishment of the endowment?

	Debit	Credit
a. Cash	$100,000	
Nonexpendable endowment fund		$100,000
b. Cash	100,000	
Endowment fund balance		100,000
c. Nonexpendable endowment fund	100,000	
Endowment fund balance		100,000
d. Memorandum entry only	—	—

E19–3 **Entries for a Hospital's Unrestricted (General) Fund**

The following are transactions and events of the general fund of Sycamore Hospital, a not-for-profit entity, for the 20X6 fiscal year ending December 31, 20X6.

1. A total of $6,200,000 in patient services was provided.

2. Operating expenses total $5,940,000, as follows:

Nursing services	$2,070,000
Other professional expenses	1,250,000
Fiscal services	225,000
General services	1,510,000
Bad debts	125,000
Administration	260,000
Depreciation	500,000

Accounts credited for operating expenses other than depreciation:

Cash	$4,785,000
Allowance for Uncollectibles	125,000
Accounts Payable	210,000
Inventories	240,000
Donated Services	80,000

3. Contractual adjustments of $220,000 are allowed as deductions from gross patient revenue.

4. A transfer of $180,000 is received from specific-purpose funds. This transfer is for payment of approved operating costs in accordance with the terms of the restricted gift.

5. A transfer of $200,000 is received from the temporarily restricted plant fund to fund the purchase of new equipment for the hospital.

6. Sycamore Hospital receives $155,000 of unrestricted gifts.

7. Accounts receivable are collected except for $75,000 written off.

8. A valuation of the other than trading securities investment portfolio of the general fund reports an increase in the market value from the beginning of the period of $70,000.

Required

a. Prepare journal entries in the general fund for each of the transactions and events.

b. Prepare the statement of operations for the general, unrestricted fund of Sycamore Hospital.

E19–4   **Entries for Other Hospital Funds**

The following are selected transactions of the specific-purpose fund, the plant fund, and the endowment fund of Toddville Hospital, a not-for-profit entity:

1. The endowment fund received new permanent endowments totaling $150,000 and new term endowments totaling $120,000.

2. The plant replacement and expansion fund received pledges of $1,500,000 for the new wing. Uncollectibles were estimated at 10 percent.

3. The specific-purpose fund received gifts of $50,000 for research and $30,000 for education.

4. Interest and dividends received on investments were:

Endowment fund (permanent)	$100,000
Plant fund	45,000
Specific-purpose fund (research)	31,000

5. The specific-purpose fund was notified that the general fund fulfilled the agreements related to restricted gifts as follows:

Research	$55,000
Education	32,000

Cash of $70,000 was transferred to the general fund, with the balance to be sent later.

6. Investments made:

Endowment fund	$270,000
Plant fund	160,000
Specific-purpose fund	75,000

Required

Prepare journal entries for the transactions in the specific-purpose fund, plant fund, and endowment fund, as appropriate.

E19–5 **Multiple-Choice Questions on Voluntary Health and Welfare Organization Accounting [AICPA Adapted]**

Select the correct answer for each of the following questions.

1. Which basis of accounting should a voluntary health and welfare organization use?
   a. Cash basis for all funds.
   b. Modified accrual basis for all funds.
   c. Accrual basis for all funds.
   d. Accrual basis for some funds and modified accrual basis for other funds.

Questions 2 and 3 are based on the following data:

Town Service Center is a voluntary welfare organization funded by contributions from the general public. During 20X6, unrestricted pledges of $800,000 were received, half of which were payable in 20X6, with the other half payable in 20X7 for use in 20X7. It was estimated that 10 percent of these pledges would be uncollectible. In addition, Helen Ladd, a social worker on Town's permanent staff, earning $30,000 annually for a normal workload of 1,500 hours, contributed an additional 600 hours of her time to Town at no charge.

2. How much should Town report as unrestricted contribution revenue for 20X6 with respect to the pledges?
   a. $0.
   b. $360,000.
   c. $720,000.
   d. $800,000.

3. How much should Town record in 20X6 for contributed service expenses?
   a. $0.
   b. $1,200.
   c. $10,000.
   d. $12,000.

4. A voluntary health and welfare organization received a pledge in 20X1 from a donor specifying that the amount pledged be used in 20X3. The donor paid the pledge in cash in 20X2. The pledge should be accounted for as:
   a. Contribution revenue in 20X3.
   b. Contribution revenue in 20X2.
   c. Contribution revenue in 20X1.
   d. Contribution revenue in the period in which the funds are spent.

5. Turner Fund, a voluntary welfare organization funded by contributions from the general public, received unrestricted pledges of $300,000 during 20X4. It was estimated that 10 percent of these pledges would be uncollectible. By the end of 20X4, $240,000 of the pledges had been collected. It was expected that $35,000 more would be collected in 20X5 and that the balance of $25,000 would be written off as uncollectible. What amount should Turner include as contribution revenue in 20X4?

    a. $300,000.

    b. $275,000.

    c. $270,000.

    d. $240,000.

Items 6 through 9 are based on the following:

On January 1, 20X2, State Center Health Agency, a voluntary health and welfare organization, received a bequest of a $200,000 certificate of deposit maturing on December 31, 20X6. The contributor's only stipulations were that the certificate be held to maturity and the interest revenue received annually be used to purchase books for the children to read in the preschool program run by the agency. Interest revenue each of the years was $9,000, and the full $9,000 was spent for books each year. When the certificate was redeemed, the board of trustees adopted a formal resolution designating $150,000 of the proceeds for future purchase of playground equipment for the preschool program.

6. What should be reported by the temporarily restricted fund in the 20X2 statement of activities?

    a. Legacies and bequests of $200,000.

    b. Investment income of $9,000.

    c. Transfers to unrestricted fund of $9,000.

    d. All of the above.

7. What amounts should be reported in the 20X2 statement of activities for the unrestricted fund?

    a. Legacies and bequests of $200,000.

    b. Investment income of $9,000.

    c. Transfers from the restricted fund of $9,000.

    d. Contributions of $209,000.

8. What should be reported in the 20X6 statement of activities for the unrestricted fund?

    a. Transfers from restricted fund of $209,000.

    b. Board-designated funds $150,000.

    c. Playground equipment $150,000.

    d. Transfers to plant and equipment fund $150,000.

9. What should be reported in the December 31, 20X6, statement of financial position for the unrestricted fund?

    a. Liability for purchase of playground equipment $150,000.

    b. Due to plant and equipment fund $150,000.

    c. Board-designated funds $150,000.

    d. Temporarily restricted funds $200,000.

E19–6   **Entries for Voluntary Health and Welfare Organizations**

The following are the 20X2 transactions of the Midwest Heart Association, which has the following funds and fund balances on January 1, 20X2:

Unrestricted net assets	$281,000
Temporarily restricted net assets	87,000
Permanently restricted net assets	219,000

1. Unrestricted pledges total $700,000, of which $150,000 are for 20X3. Uncollectible pledges are estimated at 8 percent.

2. Restricted use grants total $150,000.

3. A total of $520,000 of current pledges are collected, and $30,000 of remaining uncollected current pledges are written off.

4. Office equipment is purchased for $15,000.

5. Unrestricted funds are used to pay the $3,000 mortgage payment due on the buildings.

6. Interest and dividends received are $27,200 on unrestricted investments and $5,400 on temporarily restricted investments. An endowment investment with a recorded value of $5,000 is sold for $6,000, resulting in a realized transaction gain of $1,000.

7. Depreciation is recorded and allocated as follows:

Community services	$12,000
Public health education	7,000
Research	10,000
Fund-raising	15,000
General and administrative	9,000

8. Other operating costs of the unrestricted current fund are:

Community services	$250,600
Public health education	100,000
Research	81,000
Fund-raising	39,000
General and administrative	61,000

9. Clerical services donated during the fund drive total $2,400. These are not part of the expenses reported in item 8. It has been determined that these donated services should be recorded.

Required

a. Prepare journal entries for the transactions in 20X2.

b. Prepare a statement of activities for 20X2.

E19–7 **Determination of Contribution Revenue**

Atwater Health Services, a voluntary health and welfare organization, has provided support for low-income families in the town of Atwater for approximately 20 years. In 20X6, Atwater Health Services conducted a major funding campaign to help replace facilities that are no longer adequate and to generate operating and endowment funds.

The community of Atwater ran a number of special events and the chamber of commerce made the fund-raising campaign a major activity for 20X6. In 20X6, the following gifts and pledges were received:

1. The family of I. B. Plentiful donated a lot adjacent to the current building for future use as a playground and parking lot. The family had purchased the lot for $22,000 several years ago. It had a current value of $42,000 at the date contributed.

2. A number of new pledges were received and many were partially or fully paid in 20X6. The following information was compiled:

Unrestricted pledges for use in 20X6	$120,000
Unrestricted pledges for use in 20X7	70,000
Pledges to support screening tests for children's hearing abilities	90,000
Pledge to assist in construction of addition to building; donor agrees to make eight annual payments of $50,000 each	400,000
	$680,000

3. Also during 20X6, $45,000 was spent in providing vision tests for grade school children. A total of $38,000 of funds collected in 20X4 and 20X5 for this purpose were used to help pay for the costs of providing the tests free of charge to all children in the community.

Required

a. Prepare the journal entries for 20X6 for the above activities, including receipt of the first installment on the pledge for building construction, which was received at the end of 20X6. Atwater currently earns an 8 percent return on its investments. The present value of the seven future payments of $50,000 is $260,318.

b. Prepare the journal entry or entries recorded at the end of 20X7 upon receipt of the second payment on the pledge for building construction.

E19–8 **Multiple-Choice Questions on Other Nonprofit Organizations [AICPA Adapted]**
Select the correct answer for each of the following questions.

1. On January 2, 20X2, a nonprofit botanical society received a gift of an exhaustible fixed asset with an estimated useful life of 10 years and no salvage value. The donor's cost of this asset was $20,000, and its fair market value at the date of the gift was $30,000. What amount of depreciation of this asset should the society recognize in its 20X2 financial statements?
   a. $3,000.
   b. $2,500.
   c. $2,000.
   d. $0.

2. In 20X1, a nonprofit trade association enrolled five new member companies, each of which was obligated to pay nonrefundable initiation fees of $1,000. These fees were receivable by the association in 20X1. Three of the new members paid the initiation fees in 20X1, and the other two new members paid their initiation fees in 20X2. Annual dues (excluding initiation fees) received by the association from all of its members have always covered the organization's costs of services provided to its members. It can be reasonably expected that future dues will cover all costs of the organization's future services to members. Average membership duration is 10 years because of mergers, attrition, and economic factors. What amount of initiation fees from these five new members should the association recognize as revenue in 20X1?
   a. $5,000.
   b. $3,000.
   c. $500.
   d. $0.

3. Roberts Foundation received a nonexpendable endowment of $500,000 in 20X3 from Multi Enterprises. The endowment assets were invested in publicly traded securities. Multi did not specify how gains and losses from dispositions of endowment assets were to be treated. No restrictions were placed on the use of dividends received and interest earned on fund resources. In 20X4, Roberts realized gains of $50,000 on sales of fund investments, and

received total interest and dividends of $40,000 on fund securities. The amount of these capital gains, interest, and dividends available for expenditure by Roberts's unrestricted current fund is:

   a. $0.
   b. $40,000.
   c. $50,000.
   d. $90,000.

4. In July 20X2, Ross donated $200,000 cash to a church with the stipulation that the revenue generated from this gift be paid to him during his lifetime. The conditions of this donation are that after Ross dies, the principal may be used by the church for any purpose voted on by the church elders. The church received interest of $16,000 on the $200,000 for the year ended June 30, 20X3, and the interest was remitted to Ross. In the church's June 30, 20X3, annual financial statements:

   a. $200,000 should be reported as temporarily restricted net assets in the balance sheet.
   b. $184,000 should be reported as revenue in the activity statement.
   c. $216,000 should be reported as revenue in the activity statement.
   d. Both *a* and *c*.

5. The following expenditures were among those incurred by a nonprofit botanical society during 20X4:

Printing of annual report	$15,000
Unsolicited merchandise sent to encourage contributions	35,000

   What amount should be classified as fund-raising costs in the society's activity statement?
   a. $0.
   b. $5,000.
   c. $35,000.
   d. $40,000.

6. Trees Forever, a community foundation, incurred $5,000 in expenses during 20X3 putting on its annual talent fund-raising show. In the statement of activities of Trees Forever, the $5,000 should be reported as:

   a. A contra asset account.
   b. A contra revenue account.
   c. A reduction of fund-raising costs.
   d. As part of fund-raising costs.

7. In 20X3, the board of trustees of Burr Foundation designated $100,000 from its current funds for college scholarships. Also in 20X3, the foundation received a bequest of $200,000 from an estate of a benefactor who specified that the bequest was to be used for hiring teachers to tutor handicapped students. What amount should be accounted for as temporarily restricted funds?

   a. $0.
   b. $100,000.
   c. $200,000.
   d. $300,000.

Items 8 through 10 are based on the following information:

United Together, a labor union, had the following receipts and expenses for the year ended December 31, 20X2:

Receipts:	
Per capita dues	$680,000
Initiation fees	90,000
Sales of organizational supplies	60,000
Nonexpendable gift restricted by donor for loan purposes for 10 years	30,000
Nonexpendable gift restricted by donor for loan purposes in perpetuity	25,000
Expenses:	
Labor negotiations	500,000
Fund-raising	100,000
Membership development	50,000
Administrative and general	200,000

Additional Information

The union's constitution provides that 10 percent of the per capita dues are designated for the strike insurance fund to be distributed for strike relief at the discretion of the union's executive board.

8. In United Together's statement of activities for the year ended December 31, 20X2, what amount should be reported under the classification of revenue from unrestricted funds?

    a. $740,000.

    b. $762,000.

    c. $770,000.

    d. $830,000.

9. In United Together's statement of activities for the year ended December 31, 20X2, what amount should be reported under the classification of program services?

    a. $500,000.

    b. $550,000.

    c. $600,000.

    d. $850,000.

10. In United Together's statement of activities for the year ended December 31, 20X2, what amounts should be reported under the classifications of temporarily and permanently restricted net assets?

    a. $0 and $55,000, respectively.

    b. $55,000 and $0, respectively.

    c. $30,000 and $25,000, respectively.

    d. $25,000 and $30,000, respectively.

E19–9 **Statement of Activities for an Other Nonprofit Organization**

The following is a list of selected account balances in the unrestricted operating fund for the Pleasant School:

	Debit	Credit
Unrestricted net assets, July 1, 20X1		$ 420,000
Tuition and Fees		1,200,000
Contributions		165,000
Auxiliary Activities Revenue		40,000
Investment Income		32,000
Other Revenue		38,000
Instruction	$1,050,000	
Auxiliary Activities Expenses	37,000	
Administration	250,000	
Fund-Raising	28,000	
Transfer from temporarily restricted assets		130,000
Transfer from permanently restricted assets		12,000

Required

Prepare a statement of activities for the unrestricted operating fund of the Pleasant School for the year ended June 30, 20X2.

Problems

P19–10 **Financial Statements for a Private College**

Friendly College is a small, privately supported liberal arts college. The college uses a fund structure; however, it prepares its financial statements in conformance with **FASB 117.**

Partial balance sheet information as of June 30, 20X2, is given as follows:

Unrestricted items:		
Cash	$210,000	
Accounts Receivable (student tuition and fees, less allowance for doubtful accounts of $9,000)	341,000	
State Appropriation Receivable	75,000	
Accounts Payable		$ 45,000
Deferred Revenue		66,000
Unrestricted Net Assets		515,000
Restricted items:		
Cash	$ 7,000	
Investments	60,000	
Restricted Net Assets		$ 67,000

The following transactions occurred during the fiscal year ended June 30, 20X3:

1. On July 7, 20X2, a gift of $100,000 was received from an alumnus. The alumnus requested that half the gift be restricted to the purchase of books for the university library and the remainder be used for the establishment of an endowed scholarship fund. The alumnus further requested that the income generated by the scholarship fund be used annually to award a scholarship to a qualified disadvantaged student. On July 20, 20X2, the board of trustees resolved that the funds of the newly established scholarship endowment fund would be invested in savings certificates. On July 21, 20X2, the savings certificates were purchased.

2. Revenue from student tuition and fees applicable to the year ended June 30, 20X3, amounted to $1,900,000. Of this amount, $66,000 was collected in the prior year, and $1,686,000 was collected during the year ended June 30, 20X3. In addition, on June 30, 20X3, the university had received cash of $158,000 representing deferred revenue fees for the session beginning July 1, 20X3.

3. During the year ended June 30, 20X3, the university had collected $349,000 of the outstanding accounts receivable at the beginning of the year. The balance was determined to be uncollectible and was written off against the allowance account. On June 30, 20X3, the allowance account was increased by $3,000.

4. During the year, interest charges of $6,000 were earned and collected on late student fee payments.

5. During the year the state appropriation was received. An additional unrestricted appropriation of $50,000 was made by the state but had not been paid to the university as of June 30, 20X3.

6. An unrestricted gift of $25,000 cash was received from alumni of the university.

7. During the year, restricted investments of $21,000 were sold for $26,000. Investment income amounting to $1,900 was received.

8. During the year unrestricted operating expenses of $1,777,000 were recorded. On June 30, 20X3, $59,000 of these expenses remained unpaid.

9. Restricted current funds of $13,000 were spent for authorized purposes during the year.

10. The accounts payable on June 30, 20X2, were paid during the year.

11. During the year, $7,000 interest was earned and received on the savings certificates purchased in accordance with the board of trustees' resolutions, as discussed in transaction 1.

Required

a. Prepare a comparative balance sheet for Friendly College as of June 30, 20X2, and June 30, 20X3.

b. Prepare a statement of activities for Friendly College for the year ended June 30, 20X3.

P19–11   **Balance Sheet for a Hospital**

Brookdale Hospital hired an inexperienced controller early in 20X4. Near the end of 20X4, the board of directors decided to put on a major fund-raising campaign. They wished to have the December 31, 20X4, statement of financial position for Brookdale fully conform with current generally accepted principles for hospitals. The trial balance prepared by the controller at December 31, 20X4, is as follows:

	Debit	Credit
Cash	$ 100,000	
Contributions receivable	185,000	
Investment in short-term marketable securities	200,000	
Investment in long-term marketable securities	300,000	
Interest receivable	15,000	
Accounts receivable	55,000	
Inventory	35,000	
Land	120,000	
Buildings and equipment	750,000	
Allowance for depreciation		$ 260,000
Accounts payable		40,000
Mortgage payable		320,000
Fund balance		1,140,000
Total	$1,760,000	$1,760,000

Additional Information

1. Contributions receivable at December 31, 20X4, consist of the following:

For unrestricted use	$ 40,000
For use in cancer research	10,000
For purchase of equipment	20,000
For endowment principal	30,000
Total	$100,000

2. Short-term investments at year-end consist of $150,000 of unrestricted funds and $50,000 of funds designated for future cancer research. All of the long-term investments are held in the endowment fund.

3. Land is carried at its current market value of $120,000. The original owner purchased the land for $70,000, and at the time of donation to the hospital the land had an appraised value of $95,000.

4. Buildings were purchased 11 years ago for $600,000 and have an estimated useful life of 30 years. Equipment costing $150,000 was purchased seven years ago and has an expected life of 10 years.

5. The board of directors voted on December 29, 20X4, to set aside $100,000 of unrestricted funds invested in short-term investments for use in developing a drug rehabilitation center.

Required

Prepare in good form a balance sheet for Brookdale Hospital at December 31, 20X4.

P19–12 Entries and Statement of Activities for an Other Nonprofit Organization [AICPA Adapted]

A group of civic-minded merchants in Eldora organized the "Committee of 100" for the purpose of establishing the Community Sports Club, a nonprofit sports organization for local youth. Each of the committee's 100 members contributed $1,000 toward the club's capital and, in turn, received a participation certificate. In addition, each participant agreed to pay dues of $200 a year for the club's operations. All dues have been collected in full by the end of each fiscal year ending March 31. Members who have discontinued their participation have been replaced by an equal number of new members through transfer of the participation certificates from the former members to the new ones. Following is the club's trial balance for April 1, 20X2:

	Debit	Credit
Cash	$ 9,000	
Investments (at market, equal to cost)	58,000	
Inventories	5,000	
Land	10,000	
Building	164,000	
Accumulated Depreciation—Building		$130,000
Furniture and Equipment	54,000	
Accumulated Depreciation—Furniture and Equipment		46,000
Accounts Payable		12,000
Participation Certificates (100 at $1,000 each)		100,000
Cumulative Excess of Revenue over Expenses		12,000
Total	$300,000	$300,000

Transactions for the year ended March 31, 20X3, were as follows:

Collections from participants for dues	$20,000
Snack bar and soda fountain sales	28,000
Interest and dividends received	6,000
Additions to voucher register:	
House expenses	17,000
Snack bar and soda fountain	26,000
General and administrative	11,000
Vouchers paid	55,000
Assessments for capital improvements not yet incurred (assessed on March 20, 20X3; none collected by March 31, 20X3; deemed 100% collectible during year ending March 31, 20X4)	10,000
Unrestricted bequest received	5,000

Adjustment Data

1. Investments are valued at market, which amounted to $65,000 on March 31, 20X3. There were no investment transactions during the year.

2. Depreciation for year:

Building	$4,000
Furniture and equipment	8,000

3. Allocation of depreciation:

House expenses	$9,000
Snack bar and soda fountain	2,000
General and administrative	1,000

4. Actual physical inventory on March 31, 20X3, was $1,000 and pertains to the snack bar and soda fountain.

Required

a. Record the transactions and adjustments in journal entry form for the year ended March 31, 20X3. Omit explanations.

b. Prepare the appropriate all-inclusive statement of activities for the year ended March 31, 20X3.

P19–13 **Balance Sheet and Entries for a Hospital [AICPA Adapted]**
You have been hired to provide accounting assistance to Grace Hospital. The December 31, 20X1, balance sheet was prepared by a bookkeeper who thought hospitals reported funds as follows:

Grace Hospital
Balance Sheet
As of December 31, 20X1

General Fund

Assets			Liabilities and Fund Balances		
Cash		$ 20,000	Accounts Payable		$ 16,000
Accounts Receivable	$ 37,000		Accrued Expenses		6,000
Less: Allowance for Uncollectible Accounts	(7,000)	30,000	Total Liabilities		$ 22,000
Inventory of Supplies		14,000	Fund Balance		42,000
Total		$ 64,000	Total		$ 64,000

Plant Fund

Assets			Liabilities and Fund Balances		
Cash		$ 53,800	Mortgage Bonds Payable		$ 150,000
Investments		71,200	Fund Balance:		
Land		400,000	Investment in Plant		$2,021,000
Buildings	$1,750,000		Reserved for Plant Improvement		
Less: Accumulated Depreciation	(430,000)	1,320,000	and Replacement		220,000
Equipment	$ 680,000				$2,241,000
Less: Accumulated Depreciation	(134,000)	546,000			
Total		$2,391,000	Total		$2,391,000

continued

Endowment Fund

Assets			Liabilities and Fund Balances	
Cash	$	6,000	Fund Balance	$ 266,000
Investments		260,000		
Total	$	266,000	Total	$ 266,000

During 20X2, the following transactions occurred:

1. Gross charges for patient services, all charged to Accounts Receivable, were as follows:

Room and board charges	$780,000
Charges for other professional services	321,000

2. Deductions from gross earnings were as follows:

Contractual adjustments	$15,000

3. The general fund paid $18,000 to retire mortgage bonds payable with an equivalent fair value.

4. During the year, the general fund received general contributions of $50,000 and income from endowment fund investments of $6,500. The general fund has been designated to receive income earned on endowment fund investments.

5. New equipment costing $26,000 was acquired from general fund resources. The plant replacement and expansion fund reimbursed the general fund for the $26,000. An X-ray machine which originally cost $24,000 and which had an undepreciated cost of $2,400 was sold for $500.

6. Vouchers totaling $1,191,000 were issued for the following items:

Administrative service expense	$120,000
Fiscal service expense	95,000
General service expense	225,000
Nursing service expense	520,000
Other professional service expense	165,000
Supplies	60,000
Expenses accrued as of December 31, 20X1	6,000

7. The provision for uncollectible accounts is increased by $30,000. Collections on accounts receivable totaled $985,000. Accounts written off as uncollectible amounted to $11,000.

8. Cash payments on vouchers payable during the year were $825,000.

9. Supplies of $37,000 were issued to nursing services.

10. On December 31, 20X2, accrued interest income on plant fund investments was $800.

11. Depreciation of buildings and equipment was as follows:

Buildings	$44,000	
Equipment	73,000	

12. On December 31, 20X2, an accrual of $6,100 was made for fiscal service expense on mortgage bonds.

Required

a. Restate the balance sheet of Grace Hospital as of December 31, 20X1, to reflect the fact that hospitals do not have an investment in plant funds. (*Hint:* The $53,800 cash and $71,200 investments belong to temporarily restricted funds for plant replacement, and the other assets reported in the plant fund are properly included as part of unrestricted net assets.)

b. Prepare journal entries to record the transactions for 20X2 in the general fund, the plant replacement and expansion fund, and the endowment fund. Assume that the plant fund balances have been transferred to the appropriate funds as indicated in part *a* of this problem. Omit explanations.

P19–14 **Entries and Statements for General Fund of a Hospital**

The postclosing trial balance of the general fund of Serene Hospital, a not-for-profit entity, on December 31, 20X1, was as follows:

	Debit	Credit
Cash	$ 125,000	
Accounts Receivable	400,000	
Allowance for Uncollectibles		$ 50,000
Due from Specific-Purpose Fund	40,000	
Inventories	95,000	
Prepaid Expenses	20,000	
Investments	900,000	
Property, Plant, and Equipment	6,100,000	
Accumulated Depreciation		1,500,000
Accounts Payable		150,000
Accrued Expenses		55,000
Deferred Revenue—Reimbursement		75,000
Bonds Payable		3,000,000
Unrestricted Fund Balance		2,850,000
Total	$7,680,000	$7,680,000

During 20X2 the following transactions occurred:

1. The value of patient services provided was $6,160,000.

2. Contractual adjustments of $330,000 from patients' bills were approved.

3. Operating expenses totaled $5,600,000, as follows:

Nursing services	$1,800,000
Other professional services	1,200,000
Fiscal services	250,000
General services	1,550,000
Bad debts	120,000
Administration	280,000
Depreciation	400,000

Accounts credited for operating expenses other than depreciation:

Cash	$4,580,000
Allowance for Uncollectibles	120,000
Accounts Payable	170,000
Accrued Expenses	35,000
Inventories	195,000
Prepaid Expenses	30,000
Donated Services	70,000

4. Received $75,000 cash from specific-purpose fund for partial reimbursement of $100,000 for operating expenditures made in accordance with a restricted gift. The receivable increased by the remaining $25,000 to an ending balance of $65,000.

5. Payments for inventories were $176,000 and for prepaid expenses were $24,000.

6. Received $85,000 income from endowment fund investments.

7. Sold an X-ray machine that had cost $30,000 and had accumulated depreciation of $20,000 for $17,000.

8. Collected $5,800,000 receivables and wrote off $132,000.

9. Acquired investments amounting to $60,000.

10. Income from board-designated investments was $72,000.

11. Paid the beginning balance in Accounts Payable and Accrued Expenses.

12. Deferred Revenue—Reimbursement increased $20,000.

13. Received $140,000 from the plant replacement and expansion fund for use in acquiring fixed assets.

14. Net receipts from the cafeteria and gift shop were $63,000.

Required

a. Prepare journal entries to record the transactions for the general fund. Omit explanations.

b. Prepare comparative balance sheets for only the general fund for 20X2 and 20X1.

c. Prepare a statement of operations for the unrestricted, general fund for 20X2.

d. Prepare a statement of cash flows for 20X2.

P19–15 Statements for Current Funds of a Voluntary Health and Welfare Organization [AICPA Adapted]
Following are the adjusted current funds trial balances of Community Association for Handicapped Children, a voluntary health and welfare organization, on June 30, 20X4:

Community Association for Handicapped Children
Adjusted Current Funds Trial Balances
June 30, 20X4

	Unrestricted		Restricted	
	Debit	*Credit*	*Debit*	*Credit*
Cash	$ 40,000		$ 9,000	
Bequest Receivable			5,000	
Pledges Receivable	12,000			
Accrued Interest Receivable	1,000			
Investments (at market)	100,000			
Accounts Payable and Accrued Expenses		$ 50,000		$ 1,000
Deferred Revenue		2,000		
Allowance for Uncollectible Pledges		3,000		
Fund Balances, July 1, 20X3:				
Designated		12,000		
Undesignated		26,000		
Restricted				3,000
Transfers of Expired Endowment Fund Principal		20,000		
Contributions		300,000		15,000
Membership Dues		25,000		
Program Service Fees		30,000		
Investment Income		10,000		
Deaf Children's Program Expenses	120,000			
Blind Children's Program Expenses	150,000			
Management and General Services	45,000		4,000	
Fund-Raising Services	8,000		1,000	
Provision for Uncollectible Pledges	2,000			
Total	$478,000	$478,000	$19,000	$19,000

Required

a. Prepare a statement of activities, for the year ended June 30, 20X4.

b. Prepare a statement of financial position as of June 30, 20X4.

P19–16   Workpaper for Transactions of a Voluntary Health and Welfare Organization

Helping Hand, a voluntary health and welfare organization, provides a variety of services in the local community. The following transactions occurred in the fiscal year ending June 30, 20X7:

1. The following pledges were received:

Unrestricted	$400,000
To provide free medical services	150,000
Future building project	180,000
Endowment fund principal	250,000

2. The following amounts were collected:

Unrestricted pledges	$280,000
Building project pledges	90,000
Contributions for unrestricted use in 20X8	35,000

3. The following unrestricted revenues were received:

Memberships and dues	$30,000
Interest and dividends	18,000
Bequests	47,000
Madrigal dinner	85,000

4. Expenses incurred during the year were:

Cost of madrigal dinner	$ 52,000
Direct payments for medical services	141,000
Information packets distributed	44,000
General administration	69,000
Training volunteer help	12,000

5. Equipment costing $40,000 was purchased. Depreciation on buildings and equipment for the year was allocated as follows:

Medical services program	$6,000
Community information services	4,000
General administration	3,000
Fund-raising	2,000

6. Vouchers totaling $275,000 were paid during the year.

Required

Prepare a workpaper with the column headings presented below. Record the journal entries (without explanation) for the preceding transactions in the proper asset groups.

Helping Hand
Journal Entry Workpaper

	Unrestricted		Temporarily Restricted		Permanently Restricted	
Account Name	Debit	Credit	Debit	Credit	Debit	Credit

P19–17 **Comparative Journal Entries for a Government Entity and a Voluntary Health and Welfare Organization [AICPA Adapted]**

Listed below are four independent transactions or events that relate to a local government and to a voluntary health and welfare organization:

1. A disbursement of $25,000 was made from the general fund unrestricted assets for the cash purchase of new equipment.
2. An unrestricted cash gift of $100,000 was received from a donor.
3. Investments in common stocks with a total carrying value of $50,000, exclusive of any allowance, were sold by an endowment fund for $55,000, before any dividends were earned on these stocks. There are no restrictions on the gain.
4. General obligation bonds payable with a face amount of $1,000,000 were sold at par, with the proceeds required to be used solely for construction of a new building. This building was completed at a total cost of $1,000,000, and the total amount of bond issue proceeds was disbursed toward this cost. Disregard interest capitalization.

Required

   a. For each of these transactions or events, prepare journal entries, without explanations, specifying the affected funds and showing how these transactions or events should be recorded by a local government whose debt is serviced by general tax revenue.

   b. For each of these transactions or events, prepare journal entries, without explanations, specifying the affected funds and showing how these transactions or events should be recorded by a voluntary health and welfare organization.

P19–18   **Effects of Transactions on a Hospital's Financial Statements [AICPA Adapted]**

DeKalb Hospital, a large not-for-profit organization, has adopted an accounting policy that does not imply a time restriction on gifts of long-lived assets.

For each of the six items presented, select the best answer from the following list:

    A   Increase in unrestricted revenues, gains, and other support.
    B   Decrease in an expense.
    C   Increase in temporarily restricted net assets.
    D   Increase in permanently restricted net assets.
    E   No required reportable event.

   1. DeKalb's board designates $1,000,000 to purchase investments whose income will be used for capital improvements.

   2. Income from investments in item 1, which was not previously accrued, is received.

   3. A benefactor provided funds for building expansion.

   4. The funds in item 3 are used to purchase a building in the fiscal period following the period in which the funds were received.

   5. An accounting firm prepared DeKalb's annual financial statements without charge to DeKalb.

   6. DeKalb received investments subject to the donor's requirement that investment income be used to pay for outpatient services.

P19–19   **Balance Sheet for a Hospital**

The following information is contained in the funds that are used to account for the transactions of the Hospital of Havencrest, which is operated by a religious organization. The balances in the accounts are as of June 30, 20X8, the end of the hospital's fiscal year.

	General Fund	Specific Purpose Fund	Plant Replacement and Expansion Fund	Endowment Fund
Cash	$ 30,000	$32,000	$140,000	$ 20,000
Accounts Receivable	25,000			
Allowance for Uncollectibles	(5,000)			
Inventories	50,000			
Prepaid Expenses	10,000			
Long-Term Investments	100,000		60,000	500,000
Property, Plant, and Equipment	300,000			
Accumulated Depreciation	(140,000)			
Accounts Payable	45,000			
Accrued Expenses	17,000			
Deferred Revenue	11,000			
Current Portion—Long-Term Debt	24,000			
Mortgage Payable	125,000			

Additional Information
The $32,000 in the specific-purpose fund is restricted for research activities to be conducted by the hospital.

Required
Prepare a balance sheet for Havencrest at June 30, 20X8.

P19–20 **Matching of Transactions to Effects on Statement of Changes in Net Assets for a Hospital**
Match the transactions on the left with the effects of the transactions on the statement of changes in net assets of a private, not-for-profit hospital.

Transactions	*Effects of Transactions on Statement of Changes in Net Assets*
1. Billed patients for services rendered.	A. Increases unrestricted net assets
2. A gain was realized from the sale of securities that are permanently invested.	B. Decreases unrestricted net assets
3. Depreciation expense was recorded for the year.	C. Increases temporarily restricted net assets
4. The governing board designated assets for plant expansion.	D. Decreases temporarily restricted net assets
5. Received contributions restricted for research activities.	E. Increases permanently restricted net assets
6. Received contributions restricted for equipment acquisition.	F. Decreases permanently restricted net assets
7. Acquired equipment with all of the contributions received in item 6.	G. Transaction does not affect the statement of changes in net assets
8. Endowment income was earned. The donor placed no restrictions on the investment earnings.	
9. Expended 50 percent of the contributions restricted for research in item 5.	
10. Received cash contribution from donor who stipulated the contribution be permanently invested.	
11. Acquired investments with cash received in item 10.	
12. Received tuition revenue from hospital nursing program and cash from sales of goods in the hospital gift shop.	

P19–21 **Matching of Transactions to Effects on Statement of Activities for a Voluntary Health and Welfare Organization**
Match the transactions on the left with the effects of the transactions on the statement of activities for a voluntary health and welfare organization. A transaction may have more than one effect.

Transactions	Effects of Transactions on Statement of Activities
1. Received cash contributions restricted by donors for research.	A. Increases unrestricted net assets
2. Incurred fund-raising costs.	B. Decreases unrestricted net assets
3. Depreciation expense for the year was recorded.	C. Increases temporarily restricted net assets
4. The governing board designated assets for plant expansion.	D. Decreases temporarily restricted net assets
5. A gain was realized from the sale of securities that were permanently invested.	E. Increases permanently restricted net assets
6. Endowment income was earned. The donor specified that the income be used for community service.	F. Decreases permanently restricted net assets
7. Received a multiyear pledge, with cash being received this year and for the next four years. Donors did not place any use restrictions on how the pledges were to be spent.	G. Transaction is not reported on the statement of activities
8. Income was earned from investments of assets that the board designated in item 4.	
9. Received pledges from donors who placed no time or use restrictions on how the pledges were to be spent.	
10. Received cash contributions restricted by donors for equipment.	
11. Acquired equipment with all of the contributions received in item 10.	
12. Expended 75 percent of the contributions received in item 1 for research.	

P19-22 **Net Asset Identification for Transactions Involving a Private University**

Buckwall University (BU), a private university, had the following transactions during the year ended June 30, 20X8:

1. Assessed students $2,000,000 for tuition for the winter semester, starting in January 20X8.
2. Received $1,000,000 from the federal government to be distributed to qualified students as loans and grants.
3. Depreciation expense of $200,000 was recognized on university buildings and equipment for the fiscal year.
4. Received $1,500,000 in alumni contributions restricted to the construction of a new library building. Construction of the library is expected to begin in September 20X8.
5. The contributions received in item 4 above were invested in equity securities that had a market value of $1,650,000 on June 30, 20X8.
6. Received $75,000 of investment revenue from investments in a term endowment. The donor stipulated that the investment revenue be used to fund scholarships for qualified entering freshmen.
7. During the year ended June 30, 20X8, $60,000 of the investment revenue in item 6 was used to fund scholarships.

8. The governing board of BU designated $250,000 of cash to be used for refurbishing the steam tunnels used for heating the university during the winter.

9. Received a contribution of artwork from an alumnus with a fair value of $3,750,000. The donor has stipulated that the artwork be preserved, that it not be sold, and that it be on public view in the university museum. The university has a policy of recording donations of works of art and historical treasures.

10. The governing board of BU acquired debt securities at a cost of $400,000 during the year. The governing board has designated that these investments be kept intact for the next five years and that interest revenue from the securities be used for funding summer research grants to faculty of BU.

11. During the year ended June 30, 20X8, interest revenue from the debt securities in item 10 amounted to $18,000, of which $12,000 was used for research grants.

Required

For each of the numbered transactions, indicate the net asset class affected by the transaction for the year ended June 30, 20X8. The three net asset classes are (1) unrestricted, (2) temporarily restricted, and (3) permanently restricted. Your answer should also specify the dollar amount and whether the asset class increased or decreased.

P19-23 **Questions on Voluntary Health and Welfare Organization [AICPA Adapted]**

Items 1 through 6 represent various transactions pertaining to Crest Haven, a voluntary health and welfare organizations, for the year ended December 31, 20X2. The information presented also includes a listing of how transactions could affect the statement of activities (List A effects) and the statement of cash flows (List B effects). Crest Haven follows both **FASB 116** and **117.**

Transactions

1. Pledges of $500,000 were made by various donors for the acquisition of new equipment. The equipment will be acquired in 20X3.

2. Dividends and interest of $40,000 were received from endowment investments. The donors have stipulated that the earnings from endowment investments be used for research in 20X3.

3. Cash donations of $350,000 were received from donors who did not stipulate how the donations were to be used.

4. Investments of $250,000 were acquired from cash donated in 20X0 by a donor who stipulated that the cash donation be invested permanently.

5. Depreciation expense of $75,000 was recorded for 20X2.

6. Receipt of $300,000 of the amount pledged in transaction 1 above.

Required

Indicate how each transaction should be reported by Crest Haven on (1) the statement of activities and (2) the statement of cash flows prepared for the year ended December 31, 20X2. Crest Haven reports separate columns for changes in unrestricted, temporarily restricted, and permanently restricted net assets on its statement of activities. In addition, Crest Haven uses the direct method of reporting its cash flows from operation activities. List A effects, or List B effects, may be used once, more than once, or not at all.

Example

Cash paid to employees and suppliers: List A = D   List B = I

Statement of Activities *List A Effects*	*Statement of Cash Flows* *List B Effects*
A. Increases unrestricted net assets	H. Increases cash flows from operating activities
B. Increases temporarily restricted net assets	I. Decreases cash flows from operating activities
C. Increases permanently restricted net assets	J. Increases cash flows from investing activities
D. Decreases unrestricted net assets	K. Decreases cash flows from investing activities
E. Decreases temporarily restricted net assets	L. Increases cash flows from financing activities
F. Decreases permanently restricted net assets	M. Decreases cash flows from financing activities
G. Transaction not reported on the statement of activities	N. Transaction not reported on the statement of cash flows

P19-24   Questions on Transactions of Not-for-Profit Organizations [AICPA Adapted]

This problem consists of three parts concerning nongovernmental not-for-profit organizations. Part A consists of three items, Part B consists of six items, and Part C consists of eight times.

Part A.

Community Service Inc. is a nongovernmental not-for-profit voluntary health and welfare calendar-year organization that began operations on January 1, 20X0. It performs voluntary services and derives its revenue from the general public. Community Service Inc. implies a time restriction on all promises to contribute cash in future periods. However, no such policy exists with respect to gifts of long-lived assets.

Selected transactions occurred during Community Service's 20X1 calendar year.

a. Unrestricted written promises to contribute cash—20X0 and 20X1:

20X0 promises (collected in 20X1)	$22,000
20X1 promises (collected in 20X1)	$95,000
20X1 promises (uncollected)	$28,000

b. Written promises to contribute cash restricted to use for community college scholarships—20X0 and 20X1:

20X0 promises (collected and expended in 20X1)	$10,000
20X1 promises (collected and expended in 20X1)	$20,000
20X1 promises (uncollected)	$12,000

c. Written promise to contribute $25,000 if matching funds are raised for the capital campaign during 20X1:

Cash received in 20X1 from contributor as good-faith advance	$25,000
Matching funds received in 20X1)	-0-

d. Cash received in 20X0 with donor's only stipulation that a bus be purchased:

Expenditure of full amount of donation on July 1, 20X1	$37,000

Required

Items 1 through 3 represent the 20X1 amounts that Community Service reported for selected financial statement elements in its December 31, 20X1, statement of financial position, and 20X1 statement of activities. For each item, indicate whether the amount was overstated, understated, or correctly stated. Select your answer from the list below. An answer may be selected once, more than once, or not at all.

List

O Overstated

U Understated

C Correctly stated

Carrying value of the loan:		
Principal	$30,000	
Accrued interest	3,000	
Carrying value		$33,000
Present value of total future cash flows:		
Estimated total future cash flows	$23,000	
Present value factor for 10%, 1 year	×.90909	
Present value of future cash flows		20,909
Creditor loss on impaired loan		$12,091

The entries Creditor Company makes to recognize the impaired loan receivable are as follows:

December 31, 20X5

(1)	Bad Debt Expense	12,091	
	Valuation Allowance for Impaired Loans		12,091
(2)	Impaired Notes Receivable	30,000	
	Notes Receivable		30,000

Entry (1) revalues the carrying value of the loan principal and interest down to its present value of $20,909. The company could have debited an Allowance for Uncollectibles if an adequate provision had already been made. Entry (2) is the entry to reclassify the notes from the current loan portfolio to the impaired loan portfolio. The December 31, 20X5, balance sheet reports the impaired loan in the asset section as follows:

Impaired Note Receivable, including accrued interest of $3,000	$33,000	
Less: Valuation Allowance for Impaired Loan	−12,091	
Present Value of Impaired Loans		$20,909

It is important to note that Peerless Products Corporation will not make any entries for the impaired loan. Indeed, it is very doubtful that Peerless will even know that Creditor Company has revalued its note.

On December 31, 20X6, the end of the next year, Creditor Company will recognize interest revenue using the effective interest method, as follows:

(3)	Accrued Interest Receivable ($30,000 × .10)	3,000	
	Valuation Allowance for Impaired Loans		909
	Interest Revenue ($20,909 PV × .10)		2,091

Note that the balance in the valuation allowance account is now $13,000 ($12,091 plus $909). The final entry recognizes the collection of the note. If Creditor Company actually receives only the $23,000 it had estimated, the entry is as follows:

(4a)	Cash	23,000	
	Valuation Allowance for Impaired Loans	13,000	
	Impaired Notes Receivable		30,000
	Accrued Interest Receivable		6,000

If Creditor Company receives the full amount of the original principal ($30,000) plus the two years of accrued interest receivable ($6,000 = $3,000 per year × 2), then the following entry is made to record the collection, and eliminate the balance in the valuation allowance account against either the bad debts expense or the allowance for uncollectibles, depending on what account was used in entry (1) above to recognize the impairment:

(4b)	Cash	36,000	
	Valuation Allowance for Impaired Loans	13,000	
	Impaired Notes Receivable		30,000
	Accrued Interest Receivable		6,000
	Bad Debts Expense (or Allowance for Uncollectibles)		13,000

The key points from **FASB 114** are that the creditor must recognize an impairment when it becomes probable that the creditor will be unable to collect all amounts due according to the contractual terms of the loan agreement. The maturity value of the original loan is preserved in the accounts by using a contra-valuation allowance account to decrease the impaired loan to its impaired value. Impairment should be measured using the present value of the estimated total future cash flows from the loan, discounted at the original effective interest rate of the impaired loan. Alternatively, if the creditor expects to foreclose on collateralized property, then the fair value of the collateral should be used to determine the value of the impaired loan. The debtor does not record any reductions in the value of the note receivable on its books because there has not been any legal agreement for reducing the basis of the loan. The impairment on the creditor's books is based on the best estimates of future collections, and any changes in circumstances affecting the creditor's estimates should be treated for accounting purposes as a change in estimate.

Troubled Debt Restructuring

FASB 15 prescribes the debtor's accounting for troubled debt restructurings, while **FASB 114** presents the standards for the creditor's accounting for these restructurings. Not all renegotiations of debt covenants are covered by these standards; the restructuring must be a concession granted by a creditor to a debtor in financial difficulties. Renegotiations between a debtor and a creditor because of changes in the competitive general economic environment are not troubled debt restructurings and are not included in these standards.

The most common form of troubled debt restructuring is a modification of the debt terms to alleviate the short-term cash needs of the debtor. For example, the creditor may reduce the current interest rate, forgive some of the accrued interest or principal, or modify some other term of the debt agreement. Another common form of troubled debt restructuring is the creditor's acceptance of assets or equity with a fair value less than the amount of the debt, because the creditor feels it is the best alternative to maximize recoverability of the receivable from the debtor in financial difficulty. For example, the creditor may accept land with a fair value of $50,000 in exchange for extinguishing a debt of $65,000, because the creditor feels the $50,000 is the maximum amount it will be able to collect. The key issue is how to account for and report the troubled debt restructuring on the books of the creditor and the debtor companies.

For the Debtor.   Under **FASB 15,** the debtor compares the carrying value of the debt with the total future cash flows related to the debt, or with the fair value of the consideration exchanged in extinguishment of that debt. This comparison is made to determine if a gain or loss should be recognized on the transaction as follows:

$$\text{Restructuring difference (debtor)} = \text{CV} - \text{TFCF } or \text{ CV} - \text{FV}$$

where

$\qquad$ CV = carrying value of the debt

$\quad$ TFCF = total future cash flows

$\qquad$ FV = fair value of noncash items

The carrying value of the debt is the book value of the debt on the books of the creditor or debtor plus accrued interest as of the date of the restructuring. If the debtor and creditor agree to extinguish the current debt through an immediate payment of cash, transfer of noncash assets, or transfer of an equity interest, a *restructuring difference* is computed as the difference between the carrying value of the debt and the fair value of the consideration exchanged. The debtor recognizes a gain and the creditor a loss for the amount of the restructuring difference. The debtor's gain, if material, should be reported as an extraordinary gain in its income statement. The debtor's legal fees and other direct costs incurred are accounted for in the following manner: If an equity interest is transferred, the fees and direct costs incurred reduce the amount recorded for the equity interest; in other restructurings, the fees and direct costs are deducted in measuring the gain on the restructuring.

In a debt restructuring involving a modification of terms, the total future cash flows are the aggregate of all cash payments after the restructuring takes place as specified in the restructuring agreement. Any immediate cash payments or transfers of assets or equity reduces the book value of the debt prior to computing a gain or loss. The following decision rules are then used:

1. *CV ≤ TFCF: No gain or loss; future interest.* If the carrying value of the debt is less than, or equal to, the total future cash flows, no gain or loss is shown and the debtor's future effective interest expense on this debt is the restructuring difference between the carrying value and the future cash flows.

2. *CV > TFCF: Debtor gain; no future interest.* If the carrying value of the debt is greater than the total future cash flows, then the debtor recognizes a restructuring gain for the amount of the restructuring difference. In this case the current book value of the debt is greater than the total amount of cash that will be paid—obviously, the book value must be reduced. The debtor's gain, if material, is reported as an extraordinary item. Once a gain has been recognized, no future interest expense on this debt is reported by the debtor.

For the Creditor. Under **FASB 114,** the creditor accounts for a troubled debt restructuring as an impairment of a loan as presented earlier in this chapter. The major difference between the debtor's and creditor's measurement methods is that the creditor must determine the present value of the estimated total future cash flows to compare with the carrying value of the loan, as follows:

$$\text{Restructuring difference (creditor)} = CV - PV\text{ (TFCF) } or\ CV - FV$$

where

$$CV = \text{carrying value of the debt, including both principal and} \\ \text{accrued interest}$$

$$PV(TFCF) = \text{present value of total future cash flows}$$

$$FV = \text{fair value of property}$$

Remember that the present value is computed using the loan's original effective interest rate. If an impairment is recognized by the creditor, a contra-valuation allowance account is credited for the reduction from the carrying value of the debt down to its present value. A creditor typically provides for uncollectibles with an allowance for uncollectibles, and the creditor's impairment loss is charged against the allowance. If the creditor has not anticipated adequately for uncollectibles, the impairment loss is recognized as an increase in bad debts expense for the period.

Illustration of Troubled Debt Restructurings

The following illustration demonstrates the accounting for various forms of a troubled debt restructuring. This example is independent of the earlier illustration of creditor recognition of loan impairment. Peerless Products Corporation is financially distressed and is evaluating a variety of restructuring alternatives. Following are observations about Peerless Products Corporation:

1. On December 31, 20X6, the company has an unsecured current liability of $30,000 to the Creditor Company, on which $3,000 interest has been accrued and is unpaid.
2. Peerless Products Corporation has been negotiating with Creditor Company to restructure the current debt of $33,000 ($30,000 + $3,000). The three alternatives are presented below.

Alternative 1: Transfer of Cash in Full Settlement of Debt. The first alternative is the immediate transfer of $27,000 in full settlement of the carrying value of the debt. The restructuring difference between the carrying value of the debt and total cash flow of the restructuring agreement is computed as follows:

Carrying value of the debt:		
Principal	$30,000	
Accrued interest (10% for 1 year)	3,000	$33,000
Cash flows		(27,000)
Restructuring difference (debtor = creditor)		$ 6,000

The total cash flows of $27,000 are less than the $33,000 carrying value of the debt. If the creditor agrees to the restructuring, the debtor recognizes a restructuring gain of $6,000 and the creditor recognizes a restructuring loss in the same amount. No present value computation is needed by the creditor for the immediate cash flow alternative.

The entry required for Peerless Products Corporation, the debtor company, is as follows:

December 31, 20X6
(5)	Notes Payable	30,000	
	Accrued Interest Payable	3,000	
	Cash		27,000
	Gain on Restructuring of Debt		6,000
	Restructure and settle debt.		

The gain on restructuring of debt, if material, is reported as an extraordinary item on the debtor's income statement, according to **FASB 4**.

The entry required for Creditor Company is as follows:

December 31, 20X6
(6)	Cash	27,000	
	Allowance for Uncollectibles	6,000	
	Notes Receivable		30,000
	Accrued Interest Receivable		3,000
	Restructure and settle receivable.		

If Creditor Company had not provided adequately for uncollectible receivables, the bad debts account is debited instead of the allowance for uncollectibles.

Alternative 2: Transfer of Noncash Assets in Settlement of Debt. In the second alternative, Peerless Products Corporation agrees to transfer inventory with a book value of $45,000 and a fair value of $26,000 to Creditor Company in full settlement of the $33,000 debt. When noncash assets are transferred in a restructuring agreement, the assets must be revalued to their fair values *before* determining the restructuring difference. The gain or loss is shown on the debtor's income statement as an operating item resulting from the disposal of assets. Therefore, Peerless Products Corporation recognizes a loss on disposal of its inventory for the $19,000 decline in its inventory from its book value of $45,000 to its fair value of $26,000. The revaluation is typically made in the journal entry summarizing the troubled debt restructuring.

The restructuring difference is computed as follows:

Carrying value of the debt:		
Principal	$30,000	
Accrued interest	3,000	$33,000
Fair value of assets transferred		(26,000)
Restructuring difference (debtor = creditor)		$ 7,000

The carrying value of the debt is greater than the fair value of the assets transferred; therefore, the debtor recognizes a restructuring gain of $7,000, and the creditor recognizes a $7,000 loss.

The entry made on Peerless Products' books is as follows:

December 31, 20X6

(7)	Notes Payable	30,000	
	Accrued Interest Payable	3,000	
	Loss on Disposal of Inventory	19,000	
	Inventory		45,000
	Gain on Restructuring of Debt		7,000
	Restructure and settle debt.		

The $19,000 loss on the disposal of inventory reduces the inventory from its $45,000 book value to its $26,000 fair value before the restructuring difference is computed. The $33,000 carrying value of the debt is extinguished by the $26,000 fair value of the inventory. Therefore, a restructuring gain of $7,000 is recognized by the debtor company.

The entry on the creditor's books is as follows:

December 31, 20X6

(8)	Inventory	26,000	
	Allowance for Uncollectibles	7,000	
	Notes Receivable		30,000
	Accrued Interest Receivable		3,000
	Restructure and settle receivable.		

The noncash asset is recorded at its fair value. The allowance for uncollectibles is charged for the difference between the $26,000 value received and the $33,000 book value of the debt.

The creditor may also accept the debtor's common stock or other equity as settlement of the debt. The stock is recorded at its fair value, and the restructuring difference is computed as in the case of the transfer of a noncash asset. It may seem unusual that a creditor would accept stock of a company that is experiencing financial difficulty, but the creditor may feel that the company is viable and that the stock is a reasonable long-term investment.

Alternative 3: Modification of Terms.   A common technique of debt restructuring is to modify some of the terms of the original debt contract. Modification of terms may include the following:

1. Reduction of the stated interest rate for the remainder of the original debt.
2. Extension of the maturity date of the original debt at a lower rate of interest.
3. Reduction of part of the face amount of the original debt.
4. Reduction in the accrued interest.

The debtor's accounting for a modification of debt terms is included in **FASB 15.** The restructuring difference is computed as the difference between the carrying value of the debt and the total future estimated cash flows under the new terms. If the carrying value of the debt is greater than the total future estimated cash flows, the debtor recognizes a gain for the restructuring difference. If the carrying value of the debt is less than the total future cash flows, no gain or loss is recognized and the debtor's new effective interest rate is determined based on the amount of the restructuring difference. The following cases illustrate these points.

Case A. Carrying Value of Debt Greater than Modified Total Future Cash Flows—Debtor Gain and Creditor Loss (Expense) Recognized. Peerless Products Corporation, the debtor, owes $30,000 principal plus $3,000 accrued interest to Creditor Company. On December 31, 20X6, the two entities agree to the following modification of terms on the debt contract:

1. Forgive accrued interest of $3,000.
2. Reduce the interest rate from 10 percent to 5 percent.
3. Extend the maturity for one additional year to December 31, 20X7.

The restructuring difference as of the date of the modification of terms is as follows:

		Debtor	Creditor
Carrying value of the debt:			
Principal	$30,000		
Interest	3,000		
Carrying value of the debt	$33,000	$33,000	$33,000
Total future estimated cash flows:			
Total future principal	$30,000		
Total future contractual interest ($30,000 × .05 × 1 year)	1,500		
Total future estimated cash flows	$31,500	(31,500)	
Present value factor, 10%, 1 year	×.90909		
Present value of total future cash flows	$28,636		(28,636)
Restructuring difference		$ 1,500	$ 4,364

For the debtor, the $33,000 carrying value of the debt is greater than the $31,500 total future estimated cash flows and the debtor recognizes a $1,500 restructuring gain. Because a restructuring gain is recognized by the debtor, **FASB 15** states that the debtor will not recognize any interest expense on the debt in future periods. Therefore, although the restructuring agreement calls for contractual interest of 5 percent for a one-year period, the debtor includes this amount in the remaining book value of the debt as of the restructuring date.

The entry required for Peerless Products Corporation, the debtor, on December 31, 20X6, the date of the modification of terms agreement, is as follows:

```
December 31, 20X6
(9)  Accrued Interest Payable                        3,000
     Notes Payable (10%)                            30,000
         Restructured Debt Payable (5%)                       31,500
         Gain on Restructuring of Debt                         1,500
       Restructuring of terms of debt.
```

The total future cash flows of $31,500 are recorded as restructured debt, and the original debt and accrued interest are written off. The gain, if material, is shown as an extraordinary item on Peerless Products Corporation's income statement.

When Peerless Products Corporation repays the debt on December 31, 20X7, it makes the following entry:

December 31, 20X7

(10)	Restructured Debt Payable (5%)	31,500	
	Cash		31,500
	Pay restructured debt.		

Although the terms of the restructuring agreement specify a contractual interest rate of 5 percent, no interest expense is recorded.

The creditor must recognize a loss (expense or charge to the allowance for uncollectibles) in the amount of $4,364, the restructuring difference between the carrying value of the debt and the present value of estimated total future cash flows. Under **FASB 114,** the creditor recognizes future interest revenue using the effective interest method. The entries are as follows:

December 31, 20X6

(11)	Allowance for Uncollectibles	4,364	
	Accrued Interest Receivable		3,000
	Valuation Allowance for Impaired Loans		1,364
(12)	Impaired Notes Receivable (5%)	30,000	
	Notes Receivable (10%)		30,000

Note that the December 31, 20X6, balance sheet will report the following:

Impaired Notes Receivable	$30,000
Less: Valuation Allowance for Impaired Loans	(1,364)
Present Value of Impaired Notes Receivable	$28,636

The creditor's entries on December 31, 20X7, are as follows:

(13)	Cash	1,500	
	Valuation Allowance for Impaired Loans	1,364	
	Interest Revenue		2,864
	$1,500 = $30,000 × .05 contractual interest rate		
	$2,864 = $28,636 present value × .10 effective interest rate		
(14)	Cash	30,000	
	Impaired Notes Receivable		30,000

Case B. Carrying Value of Debt Less than Modified Total Future Cash Flows: No Gain Recognized by the Debtor. Peerless Products Corporation, the debtor, and Creditor Company agree to the following modification of terms for the debt of $30,000 and $3,000 of accrued interest:

1. Forgive $500 of accrued interest.
2. Reduce contracted interest from 10 percent to 5 percent.
3. Extend maturity for one additional year to December 31, 20X7.

The first step is to determine the restructuring difference on December 31, 20X6, the date of the troubled debt restructuring:

		Debtor	Creditor
Carrying value of the debt:			
Principal	$30,000		
Interest	3,000		
Carrying value of the debt	$33,000	$33,000	$33,000
Total future estimated cash flows:			
Total future principal	$30,000		
Remaining accrued interest not forgiven	2,500		
Total future contractual interest ($30,000 × .05 × 1 year)	1,500		
Total future estimated cash flows	$34,000	(34,000)	
Present value factor, 10%, 1 year	×.90909		
Present value of total future cash flows	$30,909		(30,909)
Restructuring difference		$(1,000)	$2,091

The debtor will not recognize a gain in this case, because the $33,000 carrying value of the debt is less than the total future estimated cash flows resulting from the restructuring. The entry required on Peerless Products Corporation's books on December 31, 20X6, the restructuring date, is as follows:

```
December 31, 20X6
(15)  Accrued Interest Payable                          3,000
      Notes Payable (10%)                              30,000
          Restructured Debt Payable (5%)                       33,000
          Restructuring of terms of debt.
```

Note that under this approach, the restructured debt payable (5 percent) is stated at the carrying value of the old note ($30,000) plus all accrued interest ($3,000) even though the creditor forgave $500 of the accrued interest as part of the restructuring. Because the total future estimated cash flows ($34,000) exceed the carrying value of the debt ($33,000), no adjustments are made to the total amount of the carrying value of the debt. The restructured payable is stated at $33,000 and a total of $1,000 of interest expense will be recognized over the term to maturity of the restructured debt representing the difference between the total of $34,000 of future cash flows and the $33,000 carrying value of the restructured debt.

On December 31, 20X7, Peerless Products Corporation must pay a total of $34,000, which includes $33,000 to extinguish the restructured debt and $1,000 of interest expense. The entry on December 31, 20X7, is as follows:

```
December 31, 20X7
(16)  Interest Expense                                  1,000
      Restructured Debt Payable (5%)                    33,000
          Cash                                                   34,000
          Pay restructured debt and interest expense.
```

The debtor's actual interest rate for the restructured debt may be found by solving the present value formula for the interest rate, as follows:

$$\text{Present value} = \text{Present value factor} \times \text{Future amount}$$

where the present value is the present book value of debt; the present value factor (PVF) is the factor from the "present value of $1" table for one period, which is the term of the debt; and the future value is the total future cash flows. Therefore

$$\$33,000 = PVF \times \$34,000$$

and

$$PVF = \frac{\$33,000}{\$34,000} = .9705$$

In a present value of $1 table, the factor .9705 is found for one year in the 3 percent column. Therefore, the interest rate is approximately 3 percent. For this one-year example, the interest rate may be approximated by a more direct manner, as follows:

$$\frac{\$1,000}{\$33,000} = .0303, \text{ or } 3.03 \text{ percent interest rate}$$

Although the restructuring agreement shows the contractual interest rate as 5 percent, the interest expense reported on the debtor's income statement is reported at an effective interest rate of 3.03 percent. The difference between the 5 percent and the 3.03 percent becomes part of the restructured debt principal. For notes payable of more than one year in length, the computed effective rate of interest would be used to determine the amount of interest expense to be reported for each year.

The creditor's entries are as follows:

December 31, 20X6

(17)	Allowance for Uncollectibles	2,091	
	Accrued Interest Receivable		500
	Valuation Allowance for Impaired Loans		1,591
(18)	Impaired Notes Receivable (5%)	30,000	
	Notes Receivable (10%)		30,000

December 31, 20X7

(19)	Cash	4,000	
	Valuation Allowance for Impaired Loans	1,591	
	Accrued Interest Receivable		2,500
	Interest Revenue		3,091

$4,000 = $30,000 × .05 contractual interest rate plus accrued interest not forgiven of $2,500
$3,091 = $30,909 present value × .10 effective interest rate

(20)	Cash	30,000	
	Impaired Notes Receivable		30,000

Other Considerations

Some restructuring agreements contain provisions for contingent payments. For example, the agreement may specify that the debtor must pay an additional amount if its future net income exceeds a certain level. At the time of the restructuring agreement, contingent amounts should be included in the estimated total future cash payments by both the debtor and creditor if the conditions established in **FASB Statement No. 5,** "Accounting for Contingencies" (**FASB 5**), for a recognition of a loss contingency have been met. This standard requires contingencies to be recognized as payables in the first period in which it is probable that a liability has been incurred and the amount can be reasonably estimated.

At the time of a debt restructuring, the debtor is required to make supplementary footnote disclosures in its financial reports describing the major features of the restructuring plan, the aggregate gain on restructuring the payables and any related income tax effects, the net gain or loss on transfers of assets in accordance with the plan, and the per-share effects of the aggregate gain on restructuring of the payables net of related income tax effects. For periods after the restructuring, the debtor must disclose amounts that are contingently payable and the terms under which these contingencies become payable.

Creditors must disclose, either in the financial statements or in the notes, specific information about impaired loans. These disclosures include the recorded investment in the loans for which impairment has been recognized and the total valuation allowance related to those loans. In addition, the creditor must disclose both the beginning and ending balance for the period in the allowance for uncollectibles, including any direct write-downs during the period and any recoveries recorded during the period. Finally, the creditor must disclose its income recognition policy and the amount of interest income recognized in the period.

The next section of the chapter presents corporate reorganizations administered under the Bankruptcy Act. Troubled debt restructurings are often a part of the reorganization effort as the debtor attempts to rehabilitate itself and return to profitable operations.

Chapter 11 Reorganizations

Chapter 11 of the Bankruptcy Reform Act of 1978 allows for legal protection from creditors' actions during a time needed to reorganize the debtor company and return its operations to a profitable level. Reorganizations are administered by the bankruptcy court, and trustees are often appointed by the court to direct the reorganization. Reorganizations are typically described by the four Ps of reorganization. A company in financial distress *petitions* the bankruptcy court for *protection* from its creditors. If granted protection, the company receives an order of relief to suspend making any payments on its prepetition debt. The company continues to operate while it prepares a ***plan of reorganization,*** which serves as an operating guide during the reorganization. The *proceeding* includes the actions that take place from the time the petition is filed until the company completes the reorganization.

The petition must discuss the alternative of liquidating the debtor and distributing the expected receipts to the creditors. The plan of reorganization is the essence of any reorganization. The plan must include a complete description of the expected debtor actions during the reorganization period and how these actions will be in the best interest of the debtor and its creditors. A *disclosure statement* is transmitted to all creditors and other parties eligible to vote on the plan of reorganization. The disclosure statement includes information that would enable a reasonable investor or creditor to make an informed judgment about the worthiness of the plan and how the plan will affect that person's financial interest in the debtor company. The bankruptcy court then evaluates the responses to the plan from creditors and other parties, and either confirms the plan of reorganization or rejects it. Confirmation of the plan implies that the debtor, or an appointed trustee, will fully follow the plan. The reorganization period may be as short as a few months or as long as several years. Most reorganizations require more than one year; however, the time span of the proceeding depends on the complexity of the reorganization.

Statement of Position No. 90-7, "Financial Reporting by Entities in Reorganization under the Bankruptcy Code" (**SOP 90-7**),[1] provides guidance for financial reporting for companies in reorganization. The financial statements issued by a company during Chapter 11 proceedings should distinguish transactions and events directly associated with the reorganization from those associated with ongoing operations. Companies in reorganization are required to present balance sheets, income statements, and statements of cash flows, but **SOP 90-7** requires these three statements to clearly reflect the unique circumstances related to the reorganization.

The balance sheet of a company in reorganization has the following special attributes:

1. Prepetition liabilities subject to compromise as part of the reorganization proceeding should be reported separately from liabilities not subject to compromise. Liabilities subject to compromise include unsecured debt and other payables that are incurred before the company entered reorganization. Liabilities that are not subject to change by the reorganization plan include fully secured liabilities incurred before reorganization, and all liabilities incurred after the company enters its petition for reorganization relief.

2. The liabilities should be reported at the expected amount to be allowed by the bankruptcy court. If no reasonable estimation is possible, then the claims should be disclosed in the footnotes.

The income statement of a company in reorganization has the following special requirements:

1. Income statement amounts directly related to the reorganization, such as legal fees and losses on disposals of assets, should be reported separately as reorganization items in the period incurred. However, any gains or losses on discontinued operations, or extraordinary items, should be reported separately according to **APB Opinion 30,** "Reporting the Results of Operations."

2. Some of the interest income earned during reorganization is a result of the debtor not being required to pay debt and thus investing the available resources in interest-bearing sources. Such interest income should be reported separately as a reorganization item. The extent to which reported interest expense differs from the contractual interest on the company's debt should be disclosed, either parenthetically on the face of the income statement, or within the footnotes.

3. Earnings per share is disclosed, but any anticipated changes to the number of common shares or common stock equivalents outstanding as a result of the reorganization plan should be disclosed.

The statement of cash flows of a company in reorganization has the following special features:

1. **SOP 90-7** prefers the direct method of presenting cash flows from operations, but if the indirect method is used, then the company must also disclose separately the operating cash flows associated with the reorganization.

---

[1] *Statement of Position No. 90-7,* "Financial Reporting by Entities in Reorganization under the Bankruptcy Code," American Institute of Certified Public Accountants (New York), 1990.

2. Cash flows related to the reorganization should be reported separately from those from regular operations. For example, excess net interest received as a result of the company's not paying its debts during reorganization should be reported separately.

Fresh Start Accounting

The basic view of a reorganization is that it is a fresh start for the company. However, it is difficult to determine if a Chapter 11 reorganization results in a new entity for which fresh start accounting should be used, or if the reorganization results in a continuation of the prior entity. **SOP 90-7** stated that fresh start reporting should be used as of the confirmation date of the plan of reorganization if both the following conditions occur:[2]

1. The reorganization value of the assets of the emerging entity immediately before the date of confirmation is less than the total of all postpetition liabilities and allowed claims.
2. Holders of existing voting shares immediately before confirmation receive less than 50 percent of the voting shares of the emerging entity. This implies that the prior shareholders have lost control of the emerging company.

Fresh start accounting results in a new reporting entity. First, the company is required to compute the *reorganization value* of the assets of the emerging entity. Reorganization value represents the fair value of the entity before considering liabilities, and approximates the amount a willing buyer would pay for the assets of the entity. The reorganization value is then allocated to the assets using the allocation of value method in **APB 16** for purchase accounting. Any reorganization value in excess of amounts assignable to identifiable assets is reported as an intangible asset called "reorganization value in excess of amounts allocable to identifiable assets." This excess is then amortized in conformity with **APB 17,** "Intangible Assets." Liabilities of the emerging company are recorded at the present values of the amounts to be paid. Any retained earnings, or deficit, is eliminated. A set of final operating statements is prepared just prior to emerging from reorganization. In essence, the company is a new reporting entity after reorganization.

Companies Not Qualifying for Fresh Start Accounting.   Those companies not meeting the two conditions for fresh start accounting should report liabilities at the present values of amounts to be paid, with forgiveness of debt reported as an extraordinary item as specified by **FASB 15.** These companies should continue their accounting for assets, as used prior to entering reorganization; however, any necessary write-downs of assets should be recognized in accordance with **FASB Statement No. 121,** "Accounting for the Impairment of Long-Lived Assets and for Long-Lived Assets to Be Disposed Of" (**FASB 121**). **FASB 121** specifies that assets to be held and used should be evaluated for impairment through a two-step process. The first step is to determine if the carrying amount of a long-lived asset is recoverable. This step is performed by comparing the carrying amount of the asset with the total estimated expected future

---

[2]*Statement of Position No. 90-7,* para. 36.

cash flows over the life of the asset. If the total estimated future cash flows is less than its carrying amount, the asset should be considered as impaired. The second step is to determine the amount of the loss to be recognized. An impairment loss should be recognized for the difference between the carrying amount and the fair value of the asset. If the asset being tested for recoverability of its carrying amount was acquired in a business combination accounted for using the purchase method of accounting, any goodwill recognized as part of the acquisition should be included in determining recoverability. In those cases in which goodwill is being included in the recoverability test, the carrying amount of the identified goodwill should be eliminated before making any reduction of the carrying amounts of impaired long-lived assets and identifiable intangibles.

For assets to be disposed of, the valuation to be used is the fair value of the assets. The company should have an approved plan in place to dispose of the assets, whether by sale or abandonment. In addition, assets to be disposed of should be separated in the balance sheet from the assets that will continue to be used, and no depreciation should be recorded on the assets held for disposal. If the fair value of the asset held for disposal should increase in a subsequent accounting period, the carrying amount of the asset should be increased to the new fair value except that the adjusted carrying amount cannot exceed the initial carrying amount of the asset at the time at which it was classified as held for disposal. Any subsequent decreases in fair value of assets held for disposal should be recognized in the period in which the value decreased.

FASB 15 does not apply to troubled debt restructurings in which debtors restate their liabilities generally under the purview of the bankruptcy court. **FASB 15** applies only to specific debt restructuring transactions. This exception is not an issue in the immediate settlement of debt in which the debtor's gain or loss is the difference between the fair value of the consideration given and the carrying value of the debt. The gain or loss is the same under **FASB 15** as under a general restatement of liabilities in a reorganization. However, in cases of modification of terms in a reorganization involving a general restatement of liabilities, the debtor's restructuring gain would be computed as the difference between the carrying value of the debt and the new principal after restructuring of the debt. The future cash flows from interest payments are not included in the computation of the new principal. Thus, in most cases of debt restructuring of companies in reorganization proceedings, the debtor's gain from the debt restructuring is greater than it would have been under **FASB 15.**

Plan of Reorganization

The plan of reorganization is typically a detailed document with a full discussion of all major actions to be taken during the reorganization period. In addition to these major actions, management also continues to manufacture and sell products, collect receivables, and pursue other day-to-day operations. Most plans include detailed discussions of the following:

1. Disposing of unprofitable operations, through either sale or liquidation.
2. Restructuring of debt with specific creditors.
3. Revaluation of assets and liabilities.
4. Reductions or eliminations of claims of original stockholders and issuances of new shares to creditors or others.

The plan of reorganization must be approved by at least half of all creditors, who must hold at least two-thirds of the dollar amount of the debtor's total outstanding debt, although the court may still confirm a plan that the necessary number of creditors do not approve, provided the court finds that the plan is in the best interests of all parties and is equitable and fair to those groups not voting approval.

Illustration of a Reorganization

A balance sheet for the Peerless Products Corporation on December 31, 20X6, is presented in Figure 20–1. On January 2, 20X7, Peerless's management petitions the bankruptcy court for a Chapter 11 reorganization in order to obtain relief from debt payments and time to rehabilitate the company and return to profitable operations.

The following time line presents the dates relevant for this example:

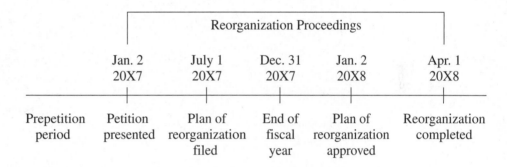

The bankruptcy court accepts the petition and Peerless Products prepares its plan of reorganization. The plan is filed on July 1, 20X7, and the disclosure statement is sent to all creditors and other affected parties. On December 31, 20X7, the company presents its financial statements for the 20X7 fiscal period in which it was in Chapter 11 proceedings. The bankruptcy court approves the reorganization plan on January 2, 20X8, and the reorganization is completed by April 1, 20X8.

Peerless Products Corporation files the plan of reorganization presented in Figure 20–2, together with audited financial statements and other disclosures requested by the bankruptcy court.

Prior to the approval of the plan of reorganization, Peerless Products Corporation continues to operate under the protection of the granted petition of relief. The company makes only court-approved payments on the prepetition liabilities. The only court-approved payment on prepetition liabilities is a $2,000 payment on the mortgage payable. On December 31, 20X7, the company issues financial statements for the fiscal year. **SOP 90-7** prescribes the reporting guidelines for companies in reorganization proceedings. A most important reporting concern is that the reorganization amounts be reported separately from other operating amounts. Peerless Products Corporation prepares the following financial statements as of December 31, 20X7: balance sheet (Figure 20–3), income statement (Figure 20–4), and statement of cash flows (Figure 20–5). Note that "Debtor-in-Possession" indicates that Peerless Products continues to manage its own assets rather than being managed by a court-appointed trustee.

FIGURE 20–1   Balance Sheet on the Date of Corporate Insolvency

Peerless Products Corporation
Balance Sheet
December 31, 20X6

Assets

Cash			$ 2,000
Marketable Securities			8,000
Accounts Receivable		$20,000	
Less: Allowance for Uncollectible Accounts		(2,000)	18,000
Inventory			45,000
Prepaid Assets			1,000
Total Current Assets			$ 74,000

Property, Plant, and Equipment:

	Cost	Accumulated Depreciation	Undepreciated Cost	
Land	$ 10,000	$ –0–	$10,000	
Plant	75,000	20,000	55,000	
Equipment	20,000	4,000	16,000	
Total	$105,000	$24,000	$81,000	81,000

Goodwill			20,000
Total Assets			$175,000

Liabilities

Accounts Payable			$ 26,000
Notes Payable:			
Partially Secured		$10,000	
Unsecured, 10% interest		80,000	90,000
Accrued Interest			3,000
Accrued Wages			14,000
Total Current Liabilities			$133,000
Mortgages Payable			50,000
Total Liabilities			$183,000

Shareholders' Equity

Preferred Stock		$40,000	
Common Stock ($1 par)		10,000	
Retained Earnings (Deficit)		(58,000)	
Total Shareholders' Equity			(8,000)
Total Liabilities and Shareholders' Equity			$175,000

On January 2, 20X8, the bankruptcy court approves the plan of reorganization, as filed. Peerless Products Corporation carries out the plan as shown in Figure 20–6.

An important concept for determining the appropriate accounting for entities in reorganization is the determination of reorganization value. Reorganization value is the fair value of the assets of the entity. Typical methods of determining reorganization

FIGURE 20–2   Plan of Reorganization

Peerless Products Corporation
Plan of Reorganization
Under Chapter 11 of the Bankruptcy Code
(Filed July 1, 20X7)

a. The accounts payable of $26,000 will be provided for as follows: (1) $6,000 will be eliminated, (2) $4,000 will be paid in cash, (3) $12,000 of the payables will be exchanged for subordinated debt, and (4) $4,000 of the payables are to be exchanged for 4,000 shares of newly issued common stock.

b. The partially secured notes payable of $10,000 will be provided for as follows: (1) $2,000 will be paid in cash, and (2) the remaining $8,000 will be exchanged for senior debt secured by a lien on equipment.

c. The unsecured notes payable of $80,000 will be provided for as follows: (1) $12,000 are to be eliminated, (2) $14,000 are to be paid in cash, (3) $49,000 are to be exchanged to senior debt secured by a lien against fixed assets, and (4) $5,000 are to be exchanged into 5,000 shares of newly issued common stock.

d. The accrued interest of $3,000 will be provided for as follows: (1) $2,000 will be eliminated, and (2) the remaining $1,000 will be paid in cash.

e. The accrued wages of $14,000 will be provided for as follows: (1) $12,000 will be paid in cash, and (2) the remaining $2,000 will be exchanged into 2,000 shares of newly issued common stock.

f. The preferred shareholders will receive 8,000 shares of newly issued common stock in exchange for their preferred stock.

g. The present common stockholders will receive 1,000 shares of newly issued common stock in exchange for their present common stock.

value are discounting future cash flows, or appraisals. After extensive analysis, a reorganization value of $195,000 is determined for Peerless Products' assets. Recall that fresh start accounting is appropriate only when both of the following conditions occur: (1) Reorganization value is less than total postpetition liabilities and allowed claims, and (2) holders of existing shares of voting stock immediately before the plan of reorganization is approved retain less than 50 percent of the voting shares of the emerging entity. To determine the first condition for Peerless Products Corporation, a comparison is made on the date the plan of reorganization is approved:

Postpetition liabilities	$ 73,000
Liabilities deferred pursuant to Chapter 11 proceedings	133,000
Total postpetition liabilities and allowed claims	$206,000
Reorganization value	(195,000)
Excess of liabilities over reorganization value	$ 11,000

Note that the first condition for fresh start accounting is present. The second condition for fresh start accounting also occurs, as shown in Figure 20–6. The common shareholders immediately before the plan of reorganization is approved hold only 5 percent of the common stock of the emerging entity. Therefore, fresh start accounting is used

FIGURE 20–3   **Balance Sheet for a Company in Reorganization Proceedings**

Peerless Products Corporation
(Debtor-in-Possession)
Balance Sheet
December 31, 20X7

Assets

Cash		$ 40,000
Income Tax Refund Receivable		12,000
Marketable Securities		8,000
Accounts Receivable	$ 6,000	
Less: Allowance for Uncollectibles	(1,000)	5,000
Inventory		37,000
Total Current Assets		$102,000
Property, Plant, and Equipment:	$85,000	
Less: Accumulated Depreciation	(26,000)	59,000
Goodwill		19,000
Total Assets		$180,000

Liabilities

Liabilities Not Subject to Compromise:		
Current Liabilities (post-petition):		
Short-Term Borrowings	$15,000	
Accounts Payable—Trade	10,000	
Noncurrent Liability:		
Mortgage Payable, Fully Secured	48,000	
Total Liabilities Not Subject to Compromise		$ 73,000
Liabilities Subject to Compromise (prepetition):		
Accounts Payable	$26,000	
Notes Payable, Partially Secured	10,000	
Notes Payable, Unsecured	80,000	
Accrued Interest	3,000	
Accrued Wages	14,000	
Total Liabilities Subject to Compromise		133,000
Total Liabilities		$206,000

Shareholders' Equity

Preferred Stock	$40,000	
Common Stock ($1 par)	10,000	
Retained Earnings (deficit)	(76,000)	
Total Shareholders' Equity		(26,000)
Total Liabilities and Shareholders' Equity		$180,000

for Peerless Products Corporation. If both conditions for fresh start accounting are not met, the emerging company is not a new reporting entity.

After intensive study of risk-equivalent companies, the profit potential of the emerging company, and the present value of future cash flows, the capital structure of the emerging company is established as follows:

FIGURE 20–4   **Income Statement for a Company in Reorganization Proceedings**

Peerless Products Corporation
(Debtor-in-Possession)
Income Statement
For the Year Ended December 31, 20X7

Revenue:		
Sales		$120,000
Cost and Expenses:		
Cost of Goods Sold	$110,000	
Selling, Operating, and Administrative	21,000	
Interest (contractual interest $6,000)	3,000	134,000
Loss before Reorganization Items and Income		
Tax Benefit		$ (14,000)
Reorganization Items:		
Loss on Disposal of Assets	$(10,000)	
Professional Fees	(8,000)	
Interest Earned on Accumulated Cash		
Resulting from Chapter 11 Proceeding	2,000	
Total Reorganization Items		(16,000)
Loss before Income Tax Benefit		$ (30,000)
Income Tax Benefit		12,000
Net Loss		$ (18,000)

Postpetition current liabilities	$25,000
Postpetition mortgage payable	48,000
Senior debt	57,000
Subordinated debt	12,000
Common stock (new)	20,000
Total post-reorganization capital structure	$162,000

Note that for purposes of the illustration, the newly issued common stock is no-par stock; therefore, no additional paid-in capital is carried forward to the emerging entity. If the assigned value of the newly issued stock is greater than its par value, an additional paid-in capital account would be credited for the excess. The $162,000 of post-reorganization capital is the reorganization value of $195,000 less the $33,000 paid out for the prepetition liabilities as part of the plan of reorganization.

Peerless Products Corporation prepares entries to record the execution of the plan of reorganization as it transpires between January 1, 20X8, and April 1, 20X8. Figure 20–7 presents a worksheet illustrating the effects of executing the plan of reorganization on the balance sheet accounts of Peerless Products Corporation. The first journal entry (21) records the debt restructuring and the retained earnings adjustment for the gain on the discharge of debt:

FIGURE 20–5   **Statement of Cash Flows for a Company in Reorganization Proceedings**

Peerless Products Corporation
(Debtor-in-Possession)
Statement of Cash Flows
For the Year Ended December 31, 20X7

Cash Flows Provided by Operating Activities:	
Cash Received from Customers	$133,000
Cash Paid to Suppliers and Employees	(109,000)
Interest Paid	(3,000)
Net Cash Provided by Operating Activities before Reorganization Items	$ 21,000
Operating Cash Flows Used by Reorganization Activities:	
Professional Fees	$ (8,000)
Interest Received on Cash Accumulated Because of Chapter 11 Proceeding	2,000
Net Cash Used by Reorganization Items	$ (6,000)
Net Cash Provided by Operating Activities and Reorganization Items	$ 15,000
Cash Flows Provided by Investing Activities:	
Proceeds from Sale of Assets Due to Chapter 11 Proceeding	$ 10,000
Net Cash Provided by Investing Activities	$ 10,000
Cash Flows Provided by Financing Activities:	
Net Borrowings under Short-Term Financing Plan	$ 15,000
Principal Payments on Pre-petition Debt Authorized by Court (Mortgage Payable)	(2,000)
Net Cash Provided by Financing Activities	$ 13,000
Net Increase in Cash	$ 38,000
Cash at January 1, 20X7	2,000
Cash at December 31, 20X7	$ 40,000

January 1, 20X8–April 1, 20X8

(21) Liabilities Subject to Compromise	133,000	
Cash		33,000
Senior Debt		57,000
Subordinated Debt		12,000
Common Stock (new)		11,000
Gain on Debt Discharge		20,000
Record debt discharge.		

The second journal entry (22) records the exchange of stock for stock. The prior preferred shareholders receive 8,000 shares of newly issued common stock. The prior common shareholders receive 1,000 shares of the newly issued common stock:

January 1, 20X8–April 1, 20X8

(22) Preferred Stock	40,000	
Common Stock (old)	10,000	
Common Stock (new)		9,000
Additional Paid-In Capital		41,000
Record exchange of stock for stock.		

The third and last journal entry (23) records the fresh start adjustments of the assigned values of the assets of the emerging entity, and elimination of any retained

Figure 20–6 Recovery Analysis for Plan of Reorganization

Peerless Corporation
Plan of Reorganization
Recovery Analysis

		Recovery							Total Recovery	
		Elimination of Debt and Equity	Surviving Debt	Cash	Senior Debt	Subordinated Debt	Common Stock %	Common Stock Value	$	%
Postpetition Liabilities	(73,000)		(73,000)						(73,000)	100%
Claims/Interest:										
Accounts Payable	(26,000)	6,000		(4,000)		(12,000)	20%	(4,000)	(20,000)	77
Notes Payable, partially secured	(10,000)			(2,000)	(8,000)				(10,000)	100
Notes Payable unsecured	(80,000)	12,000		(14,000)	(49,000)		25	(5,000)	(68,000)	85
Accrued interest	(3,000)	2,000		(1,000)					(1,000)	33
Accrued wages	(14,000)			(12,000)			10	(2,000)	(14,000)	100
Total	(133,000)	20,000								
Preferred Shareholders	(40,000)	32,000					40	(8,000)	(8,000)	
Common Shareholders	(10,000)	9,000					5	(1,000)	(1,000)	
Retained Earnings Deficit	76,000	(76,000)								
Total	(180,000)	(15,000)	(73,000)	(33,000)	(57,000)	(12,000)	100%	(20,000)	(195,000)	

Note: Parentheses indicate credit amount.

1131

Figure 20–7   Effect of Plan of Reorganization on Company's Balance Sheet

	Pre-confirmation	Debt Discharge	Exchange of Stock	Fresh Start	Company's Reorganized Balance Sheet
		Adjustments to Record Confirmation of Plan			
Assets					
Cash	$ 40,000	$(33,000)			$ 7,000
Income Tax Refund Receivable	12,000				12,000
Marketable Securities	8,000			$ 2,000	10,000
Accounts Receivable (net)	5,000				5,000
Inventory	37,000			(4,000)	33,000
Total	$ 102,000				$ 67,000
Property, Plant, and Equipment (net)	59,000			26,000	85,000
Goodwill	19,000			(19,000)	
Reorganization Value in Excess of Amounts Allocable to Identifiable Assets				10,000	10,000
Total Assets	$ 180,000	$(33,000)		$15,000	$ 162,000
Liabilities					
Liabilities Not Subject to Compromise:					
Current Liabilities:					
Short-Term Borrowings	$ (15,000)				$ (15,000)
Accounts Payable	(10,000)				(10,000)
Noncurrent Liability:					
Mortgage Payable	(48,000)				(48,000)
Total	$ (73,000)				$ (73,000)
Liabilities Subject to Compromise	(133,000)	$133,000			
Senior Debt		(57,000)			(57,000)
Subordinated Debt		(12,000)			(12,000)
Total Liabilities	$(206,000)	$ 64,000			$(142,000)
Shareholders' Equity					
Preferred Stock	$ (40,000)		$40,000		
Common Stock (old)	(10,000)		10,000		
Common Stock (new)		$ (11,000)	(9,000)		$ (20,000)
Additional Paid-In Capital			(41,000)	$ 41,000	
Retained Earnings (deficit)	76,000	(20,000)		20,000	
				(76,000)	-0-
Total Shareholders' Equity	$ 26,000	$ (31,000)	–0–	$(15,000)	$ (20,000)
Total	$(180,000)	$ 33,000	–0–	$(15,000)	$(162,000)

Note: Parentheses indicate credit amount.

earnings, or deficit. A comparison between the book values and fair values of the company follows. The fair values are determined according to the procedures in **APB 16,** which include requirements for appraisals and reallocations of "negative goodwill." Note that Reorganization Value in Excess of Amounts Allocable to Identifiable Assets is debited for any amount not assignable to other assets. The reorganization value excess is reported as an intangible asset and amortized according to **APB 17.**

Figure 20–8 *(Continued)*

Book Values			Estimated Amount Unsecured
Liabilities and Stockholders' Equity			
	(1) Fully secured creditors:		
$ 50,000	Mortgage Payable	$50,000	
	(2) Partially secured creditors:		
10,000	Notes Payable—Partially Secured	$10,000	
	Less: Marketable Securities	(9,000)	$ 1,000
	(3) Creditors with priority:		
-0-	Estimated liquidation expenses	$ 4,000	
14,000	Accrued wages	14,000	
		$18,000	
	(4) Remaining unsecured creditors:		
26,000	Accounts Payable		26,000
80,000	Notes Payable—Unsecured		80,000
3,000	Accrued Interest		3,000
	(5) Stockholders' equity:		
40,000	Preferred Stock		
10,000	Common Stock		
(58,000)	Retained Earnings (Deficit)		
$175,000			$110,000

meet these claims. Therefore, the estimated dividend to general unsecured creditors is 41 cents on the dollar ($45,000/$110,000). The estimated deficiency to unsecured creditors is $65,000.

7. The stockholders will not receive anything upon liquidation of the Peerless Products Corporation. Stock is a residual claim to be settled only after all creditors' claims are fully settled. Stockholders typically do not receive anything from a bankruptcy liquidation.

The statement of affairs is a planning instrument prepared only at the beginning of the bankruptcy process. It provides important information to creditors and the bankruptcy court as to the expected monies available to each class of creditors. Once the bankruptcy is underway, the debtor records the transactions on its accounting records as they occur.

Additional Considerations

Presented now are the accounting and reporting practices for trustees who act as fiduciaries for the creditors' committee or for the bankruptcy court. Trustees' reports are different from the traditional financial statements because the trustees' legal rights and responsibilities differ from those of the debtor company's management.

Also included is a brief presentation on the bankruptcy provisions applicable to individuals. The area of individual bankruptcies is undergoing constant change, and the presentation is only a general guide.

Trustee Accounting and Reporting

Bankruptcy courts appoint trustees to manage a company under Chapter 11 reorganizations in cases of management fraud, dishonesty, incompetence, or gross mismanagement. The trustee then attempts to rehabilitate the business. In Chapter 7 liquidations, the trustee normally has the responsibility to expeditiously liquidate the bankrupt company and pay creditors in conformity with the legal status of their secured or unsecured interests. In some cases under Chapter 7, the court appoints a trustee to operate the company for a short time in an effort to obtain a better price for the company in entirety rather than selling it piecemeal.

Trustees examine the proofs of all creditors' claims against the debtor's bankruptcy estate, that is, the debtor's net assets. Sometimes the trustee receives title to all assets as a *receivership,* becomes responsible for the actual management of the debtor, and must direct a plan of reorganization or liquidation. A trustee who takes title to the debtor's assets in a liquidation must make a periodic financial report to the bankruptcy court, reporting on the progress of the liquidation and on the fiduciary relationship held. When the trustee accepts the assets, the trustee usually establishes a set of accounting records to account for the receivership. The trustee's accounting records include a liability of the trustee which is created to recognize the debtor's interest in the assets accepted by the trustee. This new account is credited for the book value of the assets accepted and is usually named for the debtor company in receivership. The trustee does not transfer the debtor's liabilities, because these remain the legal responsibility of the debtor company. The general form of the trustee's opening entry, accepting the assets of the debtor company, is as follows:

Assets	XXX	
Debtor Company—In Receivership		XXX

The actual entry details the individual asset accounts and includes the debtor's company name.

Statement of Realization and Liquidation.   A monthly report, called a *statement of realization and liquidation,* is prepared for the bankruptcy court. It shows the results of the trustee's fiduciary actions beginning at the point the trustee accepts the debtor's assets. The statement has three major sections: assets, supplementary items, and liabilities. The debtor's liabilities are not transferred to the trustee, but the trustee may incur new liabilities that must be reported in the statement of realization and liquidation.

The assets section of the statement is divided into the following four groups:

Assets	
Assets to be realized	Assets realized
Assets acquired	Assets not realized

The assets to be realized are those received from the debtor company. The assets acquired are those subsequently acquired by the trustee. The assets realized are those sold by the trustee; the assets not realized are those remaining under the trustee's responsibility as of the end of the period. Cash is usually not reported in the statement of realization and liquidation because a separate cash flow report is typically made.

The supplementary items section of the report consists of the following two items:

Supplementary Items	
Supplementary charges	Supplementary credits

Supplementary charges include the trustee's administration fees and any cash expenses paid by the trustee. Supplementary credits may include any unusual revenue items.

Although the trustee does not record the debtor's liabilities, the trustee settles some of the debtor's payables and may also incur new payables during the receivership. The liabilities section of the statement is divided as follows:

Liabilities	
Liabilities liquidated	Liabilities to be liquidated
Liabilities not liquidated	Liabilities incurred

The liabilities liquidated are creditors' claims settled during the period. The liabilities not liquidated are those outstanding at the end of the reporting period. The liabilities to be liquidated are those debts remaining on the books of the debtor company for whose liquidation the trustee is responsible as of the date of appointment. Finally, the liabilities incurred are new obligations incurred by the trustee.

Illustration of Trustee Accounting and Reporting. On December 31, 20X6, D. Able was appointed trustee in charge of liquidating Peerless Products Corporation. D. Able will be allowed to operate the company for a short period of time to determine if the company can be sold in entirety as opposed to piecemeal. During this time, the trustee must reduce the current short-term debts of Peerless Products Corporation. If a sale in entirety is infeasible, Able is directed to liquidate the company. Able accepts the assets on December 31, 20X6, and makes several transactions during January 20X7. The transactions and the entries made on the books of Peerless Products Corporation and on the books of the trustee are presented in Figure 20–9 and discussed here:

1. Entry (24) eliminates goodwill by Peerless Products Corporation before transfer of the assets to D. Able, Trustee.
2. Entry (25) records the transfer of assets from Peerless Products Corporation to D. Able. D. Able recognizes the assets at their book values as reported by Peerless Products Corporation. Accounts receivable are dated as "old" to note that these were part of the transferred assets. The credit for $155,000 to

Figure 20–9 Trustee and Debtor Company Entries during Liquidation

Trustee D. Able's Books

Write off goodwill of $20,000:
(24) (No entry)

Transfer of Peerless's assets to trustee:
(25)
	Debit	Credit
Cash	2,000	
Marketable Securities	8,000	
Accounts Receivable (old)	20,000	
Inventory	45,000	
Prepaid Assets	1,000	
Property, Plant, and Equipment	105,000	
Allowance for Uncollectibles (old)		2,000
Accumulated Depreciation		24,000
Peerless Products Company—In Receivership		155,000

Purchases of inventory of $20,000 on account by trustee:
(26)
	Debit	Credit
Inventory	20,000	
Accounts Payable (new)		20,000

Sales on account by trustee, $85,000. Cost of sales is $50,000, including all the inventory transferred from Peerless Products Corporation.
(27)
	Debit	Credit
Accounts Receivable (new)	85,000	
Sales		85,000

(28)
	Debit	Credit
Cost of Sales	50,000	
Inventory		50,000

Receivables collected by trustee: Old $12,000   New 44,000
(29)
	Debit	Credit
Cash	56,000	
Accounts Receivable (old)		12,000
Accounts Receivable (new)		44,000

Disbursements by trustee: Old current payables $30,000
New current payables 4,000
Operating expenses 13,000
Trustee's expenses 5,000
(30)
	Debit	Credit
Peerless Products Company—In Receivership	30,000	
Accounts Payable (new)	4,000	
Operating Expenses	13,000	
Trustee's Expenses	5,000	
Cash		52,000

Peerless Products Corporation's Books

(24)
	Debit	Credit
Retained Earnings	20,000	
Goodwill		20,000

(25)
	Debit	Credit
D. Able—Receiver	155,000	
Allowance for Uncollectibles	2,000	
Accumulated Depreciation	24,000	
Cash		2,000
Marketable Securities		8,000
Accounts Receivable		20,000
Inventory		45,000
Prepaid Assets		1,000
Property, Plant, and Equipment		105,000

(26) (No entry)

(27) (No entry)

(29) (No entry)

(30)
	Debit	Credit
Accounts Payable	20,000	
Notes Payable	10,000	
D. Able—Receiver		30,000

Sales of marketable securities for $9,000:

(31) Cash   9,000   (No entry)

     Marketable Securities   8,000

     Gain on Sale of Securities   1,000

Adjusting entries at end of period:

Provision for bad debts:

   Old receivables $ 1,000

   New receivables   2,000

   Old receivables written off   2,000

   Depreciation expense   10,000

   Prepaid expenses expired   1,000

(32) Uncollectibles Expense   3,000   (No entry)

Depreciation Expense   10,000

     Allowance for Uncollectibles (old)   1,000

     Allowance for Uncollectibles (new)   2,000

     Accumulated Depreciation   10,000

(33) Allowance for Uncollectibles (old)   2,000

     Accounts Receivable (old)   2,000

(34) Prepaid Costs Expense   1,000

     Prepaid Assets   1,000

Closing entries at end of period:

(35) Sales   85,000   D. Able—Receiver   4,000

Gain on Sale of Securities   1,000   Retained Earnings   4,000

     Cost of Sales   50,000

     Operating Expenses   13,000

     Receiver's Expenses   5,000

     Prepaid Costs Expense   1,000

     Bad Debts Expense   3,000

     Depreciation Expense   10,000

     Peerless Products Company—In Receivership   4,000

Peerless Products Corporation—In Receivership is a liability of the trustee. On Peerless's books, the reciprocal account, D. Able—Receiver, is a receivable. Note that no liabilities are transferred. These remain on Peerless's books because they are legal responsibilities of Peerless Products Corporation.

3. The trustee's transactions are recorded in the normal manner in entries (26) through (29). The only difference is the differentiation between "old" accounts, which were part of the assets transferred, and "new" accounts, which result from the trustee's transactions.

4. The trustee pays $20,000 of Peerless Products Corporation's accounts payable and pays $10,000 for the partially secured note payable. In entry (30), the debit of $30,000 is made to the liability account Peerless Products Company—In Receivership. Peerless Products Corporation makes a corresponding entry to reduce its accounts payable and notes payable, and to reduce the receivable, D. Able—Receiver.

5. The remaining entries (31) through (35) complete the transactions, adjust the books, and close the books at the end of the first period of receivership. Operations resulted in a net income of $4,000 for the period. The closing entry transfers the net income to the receivership account on the trustee's books. A corresponding entry on Peerless Products Corporation's books increases the receiver's account and the retained earnings account.

The entries are the basis of the statement of realization and liquidation for the month of January 20X7. This statement is reported to the bankruptcy court to show the current state of the liquidation process and to report on the fiduciary responsibility of D. Able, the trustee. The statement of realization and liquidation for Peerless Products Corporation, as reported by D. Able, is shown in Figure 20–10.

Following are observations on this statement:

1. The statement begins with an accounting of the assets received from Peerless Products Corporation and those acquired by the trustee. The assets realized section reports the proceeds of the sale of assets. For example, the marketable securities were sold for $9,000, which is $1,000 more than their book value. Sales of inventory are also reported for the amount of the total proceeds. This is the traditional approach used most often in practice, although an alternative sometimes found is to recognize the disposal of the assets at their book values, with the profit or gain element recognized as a supplementary credit. Either method, using gross proceeds or using book value, is allowed in practice. The assets not realized shows the ending book values of remaining assets as of January 31, 20X7. Cash is not included on the statement, because it is already a realized asset. Cash is reported in a separate statement by the trustee.

2. Supplementary items include $13,000 of operating expenses paid, receiver's expenses of $5,000, and the net gain of $4,000 as a balancing item. It is important to note that cost allocations are not included in the supplementary items. For example, the trustee recognized depreciation expense of $10,000, bad debt expense of $3,000, and expiration of prepaid assets of $1,000. These do not appear directly in the statement, but they are shown indirectly. For example, under assets to be realized, depreciable assets are reported as $81,000, while under the assets not realized, the depreciable assets, net, are

Figure 20–10   Receiver's Statement of Realization and Liquidation

Peerless Products Corporation
D. Able, Receiver
Statement of Realization and Liquidation
December 31, 20X6, to January 31, 20X7

Assets

Assets to Be Realized		**Assets Realized**	
Old receivables (net)	$ 18,000	Old receivables	$ 12,000
Marketable securities	8,000	New receivables	44,000
Old inventory	45,000	Marketable securities	9,000
Prepaid assets	1,000	Sales of inventory	85,000
Depreciable assets (net)	81,000		
Assets Acquired		**Assets Not Realized**	
New receivables	85,000	Old receivables (net)	5,000
New inventory purchased	20,000	New receivables (net)	39,000
		New inventory	15,000
		Depreciable assets (net)	71,000

Supplementary Items

Supplementary Charges		**Supplementary Credits**	
Operating expenses paid	$ 13,000		
Receiver's expenses	5,000		
Net gain from operations	4,000		

Liabilities

Debts Liquidated		**Debts to Be Liquidated**	
Old current payables	$ 30,000	Old current payables	$133,000
New current payables	4,000	Mortgage payable	50,000
Debts Not Liquidated		**Debts Incurred**	
Old current payables	103,000	New current payables	20,000
New current payables	16,000		
Mortgage payable	50,000		
	$483,000		$483,000

shown as $71,000. The $10,000 difference is the depreciation expense for the period. Bad debts expense and prepaid expense are treated in a similar way.

3. The last part of the statement is a report on the liabilities. The trustee is responsible for liquidating the preexisting debts of $183,000 and has incurred additional debt of $20,000 during the month. A total of $34,000 of debts has been liquidated, leaving $169,000 still to be liquidated.

4. The statement balances at a total of $483,000, indicating all items are reported.

The trustee provides a statement of realization and liquidation to the bankruptcy court on a monthly basis. In addition, a short cash flow statement is provided which summarizes the cash receipts and cash disbursements during the period.

The fact that various bankruptcy courts are accepting alternative forms of the statement of realization may create some consternation for accountants providing professional services in several judicial districts. For example, should assets realized be shown at their gross proceeds, or should a net amount be shown with the gain or loss shown in supplementary items? The report format presented in this chapter is the traditional approach accepted by a large majority of courts. Some courts, however, are currently experimenting with other forms of trustee reporting. The experiments now taking place in trustee reporting may eventually lead to a new report that will be a modification of the present statement. Until then, accountants serving as trustees or advising trustees should ascertain from the specific bankruptcy court administering the estate which reporting form to use.

Bankruptcy Provisions for Individuals

In addition to Chapter 7 bankruptcies, individuals have the opportunity to use the provisions of Chapter 13 of the Bankruptcy Reform Act, entitled "Adjustment of Debts of an Individual with Regular Income."

An individual may file for bankruptcy only once every seven years. In addition, an individual is allowed to retain only the bare minimum of personal properties through a bankruptcy, and certain forms of debts are not dischargeable in bankruptcy.

An individual entering bankruptcy under any of the current provisions is allowed to exempt certain limited property from the bankruptcy estate; that is, the person may retain these properties after bankruptcy. Federal exempted property guidelines for an individual, as listed in Section 108 of the Bankruptcy Reform Act of 1994, include the following:

1. Real property or personal property used as a residence, not to exceed $15,500.
2. One motor vehicle, not to exceed $2,400.
3. Household items and wearing apparel for personal use, not to exceed $400 in any particular item.
4. Personal, family, or household jewelry, not to exceed $1,000.
5. Professional books or tools of trade, not to exceed $1,500.
6. Accrued dividend, loan value, and so forth of unmatured life insurance contract, not to exceed $8,000.
7. Professionally prescribed health aids.
8. Selected payments such as Social Security, retirement benefits, disability benefits, alimony, and the like. Some of these are limited to the extent reasonably necessary to provide essential support of the debtor and the debtor's dependents.

Individual judicial jurisdictions may have guidelines that differ from the federal statutes; an attorney should be consulted prior to any personal bankruptcy filing.

In personal bankruptcy, the court uses all the individual debtor's nonexempt assets to liquidate the debtor's liabilities. The debtor is then discharged from all remaining debts except those listed below. In other words, the debtor must repay the following debts even after being declared bankrupt:

1. A tax that was willfully evaded.
2. Debts obtained by false pretenses, false representations, or actual fraud.

3. Debts that were not scheduled by the debtor in time to permit timely action by the creditors.

4. Debts for fraud or defalcation while acting in a fiduciary capacity, for embezzlement, or for larceny.

5. Alimony, maintenance, or support obligations.

6. Debts due to willful and malicious injury to another entity or its property.

7. Most educational loans, unless the loan first became due more than five years before the petition date or if an undue hardship would be imposed.

Individuals with regular income from wages or a small business and total unsecured debts of less than $250,000 and secured debts of less than $700,000 may file for bankruptcy under Chapter 13. A trustee is appointed by the court to work directly with the debtor to schedule all debts and derive a plan for settling all priority claims. A three-year limit is imposed on any payment plan unless specially extended by the bankruptcy court to a maximum of five years. The advantage of a Chapter 13 bankruptcy is its greater flexibility than afforded by Chapter 11. Chapter 13 allows the debtor to retain control over assets and to work with the trustee under the order of relief given by the bankruptcy court. After completing payments under the plan, the debtor is discharged from all remaining debts except those listed earlier. In addition, the debtor may remain liable for certain long-term secured claims that cannot be exhausted within the duration of the plan, such as the mortgage for a personal residence.

Summary of Key Concepts and Terms

A variety of actions are available to companies in financial difficulty. A debtor may restructure its existing debt by agreeing to settle its obligation at less than current value or to modify some of the terms of the debt agreement. The debtor's payable may be settled with the transfer of equity or assets, or the terms of the debt may be modified. Not all troubled debt restructurings result in a gain to the debtor or loss to the creditor. A debtor recognizes a gain if its debt is settled for an amount less than the debt's book value or if all future cash flows on the restructured debt are to be less than the book value of the debt at the date of the restructuring. The creditor compares the carrying amount of the debt principal and accrued interest with the present value of the estimated total future cash flows. If the present value is less than the carrying amount, the creditor recognizes a loss (bad debts expense or allowance for uncollectibles) for the amount of the restructuring difference. In addition, the creditor may record a credit to the valuation allowance for impaired loans account. The creditor uses the effective interest method to recognize interest income over the remainder of the note's term. The interest rate used is the loan's original effective interest rate. Alternatively, if the loan is collateral-dependent and the creditor expects to foreclose on the collateral, then the fair value of the collateral is used to measure the amount of impairment.

In some cases, creditors may form a committee to manage the debtor's business. In this nonjudicial action, the debtor agrees to comply with the creditors. The creditors' committee may attempt to rehabilitate the business or may find that liquidation is the best course of action.

Two judicial remedies are available under the Bankruptcy Reform Act of 1978. The first is Chapter 11 reorganization, in which the debtor is given some relief from creditors' claims and can attempt to rehabilitate the business and return it to profitable operations. A trustee is sometimes appointed by the bankruptcy court to advise the debtor. **SOP 90-7** requires that financial statements produced during reorganization proceedings clearly separate the reorganization items from operating items. In addition, **SOP 90-7** prescribes the two conditions that must occur before fresh start accounting may be used by firms emerging from reorganization proceedings: (1) The postpetition liabilities, plus prepetition liabilities allowed as claims by the court, must be greater than the reorganization value assigned to the company's assets, and (2) the holders of voting shares immediately prior to confirmation of the plan of reorganization must hold less than 50 percent of the voting shares of the emerging company. Fresh start accounting includes the revaluation of assets and the elimination of any retained earnings, or deficit.

The second judicial remedy is a Chapter 7 liquidation. At the beginning of a judicial action, a statement of affairs is prepared as a planning document to show the expected amounts that will be realized on the liquidation of the business and the order of the creditors' claims against the debtor's assets. During liquidation, the debtor's assets are sold, and the creditors' claims are settled in the order of priority defined by the Bankruptcy Act. Secured claims are satisfied with proceeds of the sale of the corresponding collateral; unsecured claims with priority are then settled. Any remaining cash is distributed to the general unsecured creditors.

Trustees are sometimes appointed by bankruptcy courts to administer the reorganization or liquidation process. A trustee provides a statement of realization and liquidation to the bankruptcy court to report on the progress of the judicial action and on the fiduciary actions of the trustee. The statement presents the assets transferred to the trustee, the additional assets acquired by the trustee, and the ending balance of unrealized assets still to be converted into cash. The statement also reports on the debtor's liabilities discharged by the trustee as well as the additional liabilities incurred by the trustee. Some minor variations of the statement format are found in bankruptcy courts.

Accounting statement of affairs	Receivership
Creditors' committee management	Reorganization under Chapter 11
Creditors with priority	Reorganization value
Fresh start accounting	Restructuring difference
General unsecured creditors	Secured creditors
Liquidation under Chapter 7	Statement of realization and
Order of relief	liquidation
Plan of reorganization	Troubled debt restructurings

Questions

Q20–1 What are the nonjudicial actions available to a financially distressed company? What judicial actions are available?

Q20–2 What is the difference between a Chapter 7 action and a Chapter 11 bankruptcy action?

Q20–3 Under what circumstances may an involuntary petition for relief be filed? Who files this petition?

Q20–4 What is a troubled debt restructuring? Are all debt restructurings accounted for in the same manner?

Q20–5 Summarize the procedures for determining if a gain or loss from debt restructuring is reported.

Q20–6 Explain the two steps involved with accounting for the transfer of noncash assets in settlement of a restructured debt.

Q20–7 How is a gain from a troubled debt restructuring reported on the debtor's financial statements? How is a loss reported on the creditor's financial statements?

Q20–8 Under what circumstances will a gain be shown by a debtor in a modification of terms of the debt agreement?

Q20–9 How is interest expense computed by the debtor after a modification of terms in which the carrying value of the debt is less than the modified total future cash flows?

Q20–10 What is usually included in the plan of reorganization filed as part of a Chapter 11 reorganization? Does **FASB 15** apply to debt restructurings that are part of a reorganization plan? Explain.

Q20–11 Explain the use of the account Reorganization Value in Excess of Amount Assigned to Identifiable Assets during a Chapter 11 reorganization.

Q20–12 What conditions must occur for a company in reorganization to use fresh start accounting?

Q20–13 What financial statements must be filed by a company during a Chapter 11 reorganization?

Q20–14 What are the rights of creditors with priority in a Chapter 7 liquidation?

Q20–15 Describe the statement of affairs used in planning an anticipated liquidation.

Q20–16* What are the financial reporting responsibilities of a trustee who accepts the debtor company's assets in a Chapter 7 liquidation?

Q20–17* How are the sales of assets reported on the statement of realization and liquidation?

Cases

C20–1 **Restructuring of Debt**

Elec-Tric Inc. is experiencing financial difficulties and is seeking ways to settle a $100,000 debt with one of its creditors. The creditor is willing to accept $70,000 in cash or accept land that cost Elec-Tric Inc. $20,000 but was recently appraised at $90,000. The controller of the company wishes to settle the debt by transferring the land, while the president of the company feels the debt should be settled by transferring the $70,000 in cash.

Required

Discuss the accounting procedures and financial statement disclosures to be used by Elec-Tric Inc. to account for and report the settlement of the debt with the (*a*) transfer of the land and (*b*) transfer of the $70,000 cash.

C20–2 **Creditors' Alternatives**

The creditors of the Lost Hope Company have had several meetings with the company's management to discuss the financial difficulties of the company. Lost Hope currently has a significant deficit in retained earnings and has defaulted on several of its debt issues. The options currently open to the creditors are to (1) form a creditors' committee, (2) work with the company in a Chapter 11 reorganization, or (3) go through a Chapter 7 liquidation. The creditors have come to you to seek your advice on the advantages and disadvantages of each of the three options from their viewpoint.

Required

Discuss the advantages and disadvantages to the creditors of each of the three options available. Include a discussion of the probable recovery of each of the creditors' claims and the time period of that recovery.

C20–3 **Research Related to Bankruptcy**

You are working in your office late on a report regarding bankruptcies. You need to locate more information and have heard that the American Banking Institute (ABI) has a website that would be useful. Locate the website using a search engine. (*Hint:* Helpful search terms may be "Bankruptcy" or "ABI.") Locate the following information, and incorporate it into a one- to two-page report.

a. Provide a brief history or discussion of the ABI.

b. Summarize two current bankruptcy headlines.

c. Locate and summarize the following bankruptcy statistics:

   1. Most recent quarter.

   2. Most recent calendar year.

   3. Nonbusiness bankruptcy filings by chapter of the Bankruptcy Act for the most recent calendar year.

---

*Indicates that the item relates to "Additional Considerations."

Exercises

E20–1   **Multiple-Choice Questions on Debt Restructuring [AICPA Adapted]**

Select the correct answer for each of the following questions:

1. On January 1, 20X1, Kalb Company purchased at par 500 of the $1,000 face value, 8 percent bonds of Lane Corporation as a long-term investment. The bonds mature on January 1, 20X9, and pay interest semiannually on July 1 and January 1. Lane incurred heavy losses from operations for several years and defaulted on the July 1, 20X4, and January 1, 20X5, interest payments. Because of the permanent decline in market value of Lane's bonds, Kalb wrote down its investment to $400,000 on December 31, 20X4. Pursuant to Lane's plan of reorganization effected on January 1, 20X5, Kalb received 5,000 shares of $100 par value, 8 percent cumulative preferred stock of Lane in exchange for the $500,000 face value bond investment. The quoted market value of the preferred stock was $70 per share on January 1, 20X5. What amount of loss should be included in the determination of Kalb's net income for 20X5?

    a. $0.

    b. $50,000.

    c. $100,000.

    d. $150,000

2. Carling Inc. is indebted to Dow Finance Company under a $600,000, 10 percent, five-year note dated January 1, 20X1. Interest, payable annually on December 31, was paid on the December 31, 20X1 and 20X2, due dates. However, during 20X3, Carling experienced severe financial difficulties and is likely to default on the note and interest unless some concessions are made. On December 31, 20X3, Carling and Dow signed an agreement restructuring the debt as follows:

    Interest for 20X3 was reduced to $30,000, payable March 31, 20X4.
    Interest payments each year were reduced to $40,000 per year for 20X4 and 20X5.
    The principal amount was reduced to $400,000.

    What is the amount of gain that Carling should report on the debt restructuring in its income statement for the year ended December 31, 20X3?

    a. $120,000.

    b. $150,000.

    c. $200,000.

    d. $230,000.

3. For a troubled debt restructuring involving only modification of terms, it is appropriate for a debtor to recognize a gain when the carrying amount of the debt:

    a. Exceeds the total future cash payments specified by the new terms.

    b. Is less than the total future cash payments specified by the new terms.

    c. Exceeds the present value specified by the new terms.

    d. Is less than the present value specified by the new terms.

4. Hull Company is indebted to Apex under a $500,000, 12 percent, three-year note dated December 31, 20X1. Because of Hull's financial difficulties developing in 20X3, Hull owed accrued interest of $60,000 on the note at December 31, 20X3. Under a troubled debt restructuring, on December 31, 20X3, Apex agreed to settle the note and accrued interest for a tract of land having a fair value of $450,000. Hull's acquisition cost of the land is $360,000. Ignoring income taxes, on its 20X3 income statement Hull should report as a result of the troubled debt restructuring:

		Other Income	Extraordinary Gain
a.		$200,000	$ 0
b.		$140,000	$ 0
c.		$ 90,000	$ 50,000
d.		$ 90,000	$110,000

E20–2   **Impairment Entries by Debtor and Creditor**

On January 2, 20X7, Tristar Bank determined it was probable that a $400,000 note receivable from Johnson Corporation was unlikely to be paid in full at maturity. The note had been issued December 31, 20X2, and will mature on December 31, 20X8. The note pays interest of 8 percent per year each December 31. After reviewing all available evidence at January 2, 20X7, Tristar Bank determined it was probable that Johnson Corporation would pay back only $250,000 of the principal at maturity. As a result, Tristar Bank decided that the loan was immediately impaired. Interest at 8 percent on the original value of the note will continue to be paid until maturity.

Required

Prepare the journal entries (if any) by Tristar Bank and Johnson Corporation at January 2, 20X7, December 31, 20X7, and December 31, 20X8.

E20–3   **Settlement of a Debt: Debtor's and Creditor's Entries**

On December 15, 20X5, Thom Corporation informed Linco Company that Thom would be unable to repay its $80,000 note due on December 31 to Linco. Linco agreed to accept title to Thom's delivery equipment in full settlement of the note. The equipment's carrying value was $30,000 and its fair value was $35,000. Thom's tax rate is 35 percent.

Required

Prepare journal entries on the debtor's and creditor's books on December 15, 20X5.

E20–4   **Creditor's Entries for a Modification of Terms [AICPA Adapted]**

On December 31, 20X2, Clark Company entered into a debt-restructuring agreement with Astro Company, which was experiencing financial difficulties. Clark restructured a $90,000 note receivable as follows:

Reduced the principal obligation to $50,000.
Forgave all $9,000 of accrued interest.
Extended the maturity date from December 31, 20X2, to December 31, 20X4.
Reduced the interest rate from 10 percent to 5 percent.

Interest was payable annually on December 31, 20X3, and 20X4. In accordance with the agreement Astro made payments to Clark on December 31, 20X3, and 20X4. Present value factors are as follows:

Present value of a single sum, two years at 5 percent	.90703
Present value of a single sum, two years at 10 percent	.82645
Present value of an ordinary annuity of two years at 5 percent	1.85941
Present value of an ordinary annuity of two years at 10 percent	1.73554

Required

Prepare journal entries on Clark Company for December 31, 20X2, December 31, 20X3, and December 31, 20X4, that are related to the restructured debt.

E20–5   Multiple-Choice Questions on Chapter 11 Reorganizations [AICPA Adapted]

Select the correct answer for each of the following questions.

1. A client has joined other creditors of Jet Company in a composition agreement seeking to avoid the necessity of a bankruptcy proceeding against Jet. Which statement describes the composition agreement?

    a. It provides for the appointment of a receiver to take over and operate the debtor's business.

    b. It must be approved by all creditors.

    c. It provides that the creditors will receive less than the full amount of their claims.

    d. It provides a temporary delay, not to exceed six months, in the debtor's obligation to repay the debts included in the composition.

2. Hardluck Inc. is insolvent. Its liabilities exceed its assets by $13 million. Hardluck is owned by its president, Blank, and members of his family. Blank, whose assets are estimated at less than a $1 million, guaranteed the loans of the corporation. A consortium of banks is the principal creditor of Hardluck, having lent it $8 million, the bulk of which is unsecured. The banks decided to seek reorganization of Hardluck, and Blank has agreed to cooperate. Regarding the proposed reorganization:

    a. Blank's cooperation is necessary since he must sign the petition for a reorganization.

    b. If a petition in bankruptcy is filed against Hardluck, Blank will also have his personal bankruptcy status resolved and relief granted.

    c. Only a duly constituted creditors' committee may file a plan of reorganization of Hardluck.

    d. Hardluck will remain in possession unless a request is made to the court for the appointment of a trustee.

3. Among other provisions, a Chapter 11 plan of reorganization must:

    a. Rank claims according to their liquidation priorities.

    b. Not impair claims of secured creditors.

    c. Provide adequate means for the plan's execution.

    d. Treat all claims alike.

4. A condition that must exist for the filing of an involuntary bankruptcy petition is:

    a. The debtor must have debts of at least $10,000.

    b. If the debtor has 12 or more creditors, a majority of the creditors must sign the petition.

    c. If the debtor has 12 or more creditors, only one creditor need sign the petition, but that creditor must be owed at least $5,000.

    d. If the debtor has 12 or more creditors, the required number of creditors signing the petition must be owed at least $5,000 in total.

5. The plan of reorganization must be approved by:

    a. At least one-third of all creditors who hold at least half of the total debt.

    b. At least half of all creditors who hold at least half of the total debt.

    c. At least half of all creditors who hold at least two-thirds of the total debt.

    d. At least two-thirds of all creditors who hold at least two-thirds of the total debt.

E20–6   Recovery Analysis for a Chapter 11 Reorganization

The plan of reorganizing for Taylor Companies, Inc., was approved by the court, stockholders, and creditors on December 31, 20X1. The plan calls for a general restructuring of all debt of Taylor Companies. The liability and capital accounts of the company on December 31, 20X1, are as follows:

Accounts Payable (postpetition)	$ 30,000
Liabilities Subject to Compromise:	
Accounts Payable	80,000
Notes Payable, 10%, unsecured	150,000
Interest Payable	40,000
Bonds Payable, 12%	200,000
Common Stock, $1 par	100,000
Additional Paid-In Capital	200,000
Retained Earnings (deficit)	(178,000)
Total	$622,000

A total of $30,000 of accounts payable has been incurred since the company filed its petition for relief under Chapter 11. No other liabilities have been incurred since the petition was filed. No payments have been made on the liabilities subject to compromise that existed on the petition date.

Under the terms of the reorganization plan:

1. The accounts payable creditors existing at the date the petition was filed agree to accept $72,000 of net accounts receivable in full settlement of their claims.

2. The holders of the 10 percent notes payable of $150,000 plus $16,000 of interest payable agree to accept land having a fair value of $125,000, and a book value of $85,000.

3. The holders of the 12 percent bonds payable of $200,000 plus $24,000 of interest payable agree to cancel accrued interest of $18,000, accept cash payment of the remaining $6,000 of interest, and accept a secured interest in the equipment of the company in exchange for extending the term of the bonds for an additional year at no interest.

4. The common shareholders agree to reduce the deficit by changing the par value of the stock to $2 per share and eliminating any remaining deficit after recognition of all gains or losses from the debt restructuring transactions specified in the plan of reorganization. The deficit will be eliminated by reducing additional paid-in capital.

Required

a. Prepare a recovery analysis for the plan of reorganization, concluding with the total recovery of each liability and capital component of Taylor Companies.

b. Prepare the journal entries to account for the discharge of the debt and the restructuring of the common equity in fulfillment of the plan of reorganization.

E20–7   **Multiple-Choice Questions on Chapter 7 Liquidations**
Select the correct answer for each of the following questions.

1. Lear Company ceased doing business and is in bankruptcy. Among the claimants are employees seeking unpaid wages. The following statements describe the possible status of such claims in a bankruptcy proceeding. Which is the *incorrect* statement?

 a. They are entitled to priority.

 b. If a priority is afforded such claims, it cannot exceed $2,000 per wage earner.

 c. Such claims include wages earned within 180 days before the filing of the bankruptcy petition, but not to exceed $2,000 in amount.

 d. The amounts of excess wages not entitled to a priority are mere unsecured claims.

2. The highest priority for payment of unsecured claims in a bankruptcy proceeding is:

 a. Administrative expenses of the bankruptcy.

 b. Unpaid federal income taxes.

 c. Wages up to $2,000 earned within three months before the petition.

 d. Wages owed to an insolvent employee.

3. The order of payments for unsecured priority claims in a Chapter 7 bankruptcy case is such that:

   a. Tax claims of government units are paid before claims for administrative expenses incurred by the trustee.

   b. Tax claims of government units are paid before claims of employees for wages.

   c. Claims of employees for wages are paid before administrative expenses incurred by the trustee.

   d. Claims incurred between the filing of an involuntary petition and appointment of a trustee are paid before the claims for contributions to employee benefit plans.

4. Narco is in serious financial difficulty and is unable to meet current unsecured obligations of $30,000 to some 14 creditors who are demanding immediate payment. Narco owes Johnson $5,000, and Johnson has decided to file an involuntary petition against Narco. Which of the following is necessary in order for Johnson to file validly?

   a. Johnson must be joined by at least two other creditors.

   b. Narco must have committed a fraudulent act within one year of the filing.

   c. Johnson must allege and subsequently establish that Narco's liabilities exceed Narco's assets upon fair valuation.

   d. Johnson must be a secured creditor.

5. Your client is insolvent under the federal bankruptcy law. Under the circumstances:

   a. So long as the client can meet current debts or claims by its most aggressive creditors, a bankruptcy proceeding is *not* possible.

   b. Such information—that is, insolvency—need *not* be disclosed in the financial statements reported on by your CPA firm so long as you are convinced that the problem is short-lived.

   c. A transfer of assets to a creditor less than 90 days before filing a petition may be a voidable transfer.

   d. Your client *cannot* file a voluntary petition for bankruptcy.

E20–8   Chapter 7 Liquidation

The carrying values and estimated fair values of the assets of Penn Inc. are as follows:

	Carrying Value	Fair Value
Cash	$ 16,000	$ 16,000
Accounts Receivable	60,000	50,000
Inventory	90,000	65,000
Land	100,000	80,000
Building (net)	220,000	160,000
Equipment (net)	250,000	100,000
Total	$736,000	$471,000

Debts of Penn Inc. are as follows:

Accounts Payable	$ 95,000
Wages Payable (all have priority)	9,500
Taxes Payable	14,000
Notes Payable (secured by receivables and inventory)	190,000
Interest on Notes Payable	5,000
Bonds Payable (secured by land and building)	220,000
Interest on Bonds Payable	11,000
Total	$544,500

Required

a. Prepare a schedule to calculate the net estimated amount available for general unsecured creditors.

b. Compute the percentage dividend to general unsecured creditors.

c. Prepare a schedule showing the amount to be paid each of the creditor groups upon distribution of the $471,000 estimated to be realizable.

E20–9   Chapter 7 Liquidation

The book values and estimated realizable values of the assets of Royal Company on May 31, 20X1, are as follows:

	Book Value	Realizable Value
Cash	$ 14,700	$ 14,700
Accounts Receivable (net)	65,000	52,000
Inventory	75,000	40,000
Land and Building (net)	190,000	120,000
Equipment (net)	340,000	180,000
Total	$684,700	$406,700

Equities of Royal Company are as follows:

Accounts Payable	$105,000
Wages Payable (all have priority)	24,000
Note Payable (secured by receivables)	40,000
Note Payable (secured by inventory)	80,000
Note Payable (secured by equipment)	150,000
Bonds Payable (secured by land and building)	200,000
Common Stock	160,000
Retained Earnings (deficit)	(74,300)
Total	$684,700

Required

a. Prepare a statement of affairs.

b. Compute the percentage dividend to unsecured creditors.

E20–10*   Statement of Realization and Liquidation

A trustee has been appointed for Pace Inc., which is being liquidated under Chapter 7 of the Bankruptcy Reform Act. The following transactions occurred after the assets were transferred to the trustee:

1. Sales on account by the trustee were $75,000. Cost of goods sold were $60,000, consisting of all the inventory transferred from Pace.

2. The trustee sold all the marketable securities of $12,000 for $10,500.

3. Receivables collected by the trustee:

Old: $21,000 of the $38,000 transferred
New: $47,000

---

4. Recorded $16,000 depreciation on the plant assets of $96,000 transferred from Pace.

5. Disbursements by the trustee:

Old current payables: $22,000 of the $48,000 transferred
Trustee's expenses: $4,300

Required

Prepare a statement of realization and liquidation according to the traditional approach illustrated in the chapter.

Problems

P20–11　Debt Restructuring

Davis Inc. is in serious financial trouble and enters into an agreement with White Company, one of its creditors. Davis has a 8 percent note payable due to White Company for $80,000 plus $6,400 accrued interest. Under the terms of the agreement, White will receive computer equipment that cost $50,000 and has a book value of $32,000 and a fair value of $37,000. White agrees to forgive the accrued interest, reduce the note to $40,000, extend the maturity date two years, and reduce the interest rate to 6 percent. Interest is due at the end of each year.

Required

a. Record the journal entries on the books of Davis Inc. for the modification of terms and the future interest payments. Prepare supporting schedules in good form.

b. Assume that instead of Davis giving the equipment to White, Davis issues to White 25,000 shares of its $1 par common stock, which has a market value of $2 per share. All other modifications remain the same.

　　1. Record the entry on the date of restructure on the books of Davis Inc.

　　2. Explain how the new interest rate and the interest expense each year will be determined.

P20–12　Chapter 11 Reorganization

During the recent recession, Polydorous Inc. accumulated a deficit in retained earnings. Although still operating at a loss, Polydorous posted better results during 20X1. Polydorous is having trouble paying suppliers on time and paying interest when it is due. The company files for protection under Chapter 11 of the Bankruptcy Reform Act of 1978, and has the following liabilities and stockholders' equity accounts at the time the petition is filed:

Accounts Payable	$160,000
Interest Payable	20,000
Notes Payable, 10%, unsecured	340,000
Preferred Stock	100,000
Common Stock, $5 par	150,000
Retained Earnings (deficit)	(80,000)
Total	$690,000

A plan of reorganization is filed with the court, and after review and obtaining creditor and investor votes, the plan is approved by the court. The plan of reorganization includes the following actions:

1. The prepetition accounts payable will be restructured according to the following: (*a*) $40,000 will be paid in cash; (*b*) $20,000 will be eliminated; and (*c*) the remaining $100,000 will be exchanged for a five-year, secured note payable, paying 12 percent interest.

2. The interest payable will be restructured as follows: $10,000 of the interest will be eliminated, and the remaining $10,000 will be paid in cash.

3. The 10 percent, unsecured notes payable will be restructured as follows: (*a*) $60,000 of the notes will be eliminated; (*b*) $10,000 of the notes will be paid in cash; (*c*) $240,000 of the notes will be exchanged for a five-year, 12 percent secured note; and (*d*) the remaining $30,000 will be exchanged for 3,000 shares of newly issued common stock having a par value of $10.

4. The preferred shareholders will exchange their stock for 5,000 shares of newly issued $10 par common stock.

5. The common shareholders will exchange their stock for 2,000 shares of newly issued $10 par common stock.

After extensive analysis, the reorganization value of the company is determined to be $510,000 prior to any payments of cash required by the reorganization plan. An additional $10,000 in current liabilities have been incurred since the petition was filed. After the reorganization is completed, the capital structure of the company will be as follows:

Current liabilities (postpetition)	$ 10,000
Notes payable, 12%, secured	340,000
Common stock ($10 par)	100,000
Post-reorganization capital structure	$450,000

An evaluation of the fair values of the assets was made after the company completed its reorganization, immediately prior to the point the company emerged from the proceedings. The following information is available:

	Book Value	Fair Value
Cash	$ 30,000	$ 30,000
Accounts receivable (net)	140,000	110,000
Inventory	25,000	18,000
Property, plant, and equipment (net)	405,000	262,000
Goodwill	40,000	–0–
Total	$640,000	$420,000

Required

a. Prepare a plan of reorganization recovery analysis for the liability and stockholders' equity accounts of Polydorous Inc. on the day the plan of reorganization is approved. (*Hint:* The liabilities on the plan's approval day are $530,000, which is $520,000 from prepetition payables plus $10,000 in additional accounts payable incurred postpetition.)

b. Prepare an analysis showing if the company qualifies for fresh start accounting as it emerges from the reorganization.

c. Prepare journal entries for execution of the plan of reorganization with its general restructuring of debt and capital.

d. Prepare the balance sheet for the company on completion of the plan of reorganization.

P20–13   Chapter 11 Reorganization

The balance sheet of Solo Inc., a company in reorganization proceedings, on March 31, 20X1, is as follows:

Solo Inc.
Debtor-In-Possession
Balance Sheet
March 31, 20X1

Cash	$ 25,000
Accounts Receivable (net)	95,000
Inventory	160,000
Land	70,000
Plant and Equipment (net)	400,000
Patents	60,000
Goodwill	30,000
Total Assets	$840,000
Liabilities Not Subject to Compromise:	
Accounts Payable—Trade	$ 65,000
Liabilities Subject to Compromise:	
Accounts Payable	190,000
12% Notes Payable, Unsecured	200,000
15% Bonds Payable	400,000
Preferred Stock	50,000
Common Stock ($5 par)	100,000
Additional Paid-In Capital	25,000
Retained Earnings (Deficit)	(190,000)
Total Liabilities and Equity	$840,000

The plan of reorganization was approved on March 31, 20X1, by the court, the stockholders, and the creditors. The plan included the following:

1. The accounts payable creditors subject to compromise agreed to accept the $95,000 of net accounts receivable, and 6,000 shares of newly issued no-par common stock having a value of $36,000 in settlement of their claims of $190,000.

2. The holders of the 12 percent unsecured notes payable for $200,000 agreed to accept the land with a fair value of $100,000, and 6,000 shares of newly issued no-par common stock having a value of $36,000.

3. The holders of the 15 percent bonds payable agreed to reduce the principal of the bonds to $380,000. Interest at 9 percent will be due annually on December 31 of each period from the date the plan of reorganization is approved onward, and the bondholders agreed to extend the maturity date of the bonds for an additional four years.

4. The preferred shareholders agreed to accept 1,500 shares of newly issued no-par-value common stock having a value of $9,000 in exchange for their preferred stock.

5. The common shareholders agreed to accept 1,500 shares of newly issued no-par-value common stock having a value of $9,000 in exchange for their prereorganization shares of common stock.

After extensive analysis, the reorganization value of the company at the date the plan of reorganization is approved is determined to be $730,000 before the payment of any assets as required by the plan of reorganization. The plan of reorganization is then completed and the remaining identifiable assets have fair values as follows:

Cash	$ 25,000
Inventory	150,000
Plant and equipment (net)	255,000
Patents	90,000
Total	$520,000

After consultation among the creditors, the court, and the management of the company, the postreorganization capital of the company will be:

Accounts payable	$ 65,000
Bonds payable	380,000
Common stock (no-par)	90,000
Total	$535,000

Required

a. Prepare a recovery analysis for the plan of reorganization.

b. Prepare an evaluation to determine if the company meets the two conditions necessary for fresh start accounting as it emerges from the Chapter 11 reorganization.

c. Prepare the journal entries to record the execution of the plan of reorganization.

d. Prepare a worksheet presenting the effects of the plan of reorganization on the company's balance sheet.

P20–14 **Chapter 7 Liquidation, Statement of Affairs**
Name Brand Company is to be liquidated under Chapter 7 of the Bankruptcy Act. The balance sheet on July 31, 20X1, is as follows:

Assets	
Cash	$ 5,000
Marketable Securities	30,000
Accounts Receivable (net)	105,000
Inventory	160,000
Prepaid Insurance	7,000
Land	80,000
Plant and Equipment (net)	412,000
Franchises	72,000
Total	$871,000

Equities

Accounts Payable	$265,000
Wages Payable	20,000
Taxes Payable	12,000
Interest Payable	37,000
Notes Payable	280,000
Mortgages Payable	220,000
Common Stock ($20 par)	240,000
Retained Earnings (deficit)	(203,000)
Total	$871,000

Additional Information

1. Marketable securities consist of 1,000 shares of Wooly Inc. common stock. The market value of the stock is $22. The stock was pledged against a $28,000, 10 percent note payable that has accrued interest of $1,400.

2. Accounts receivable of $50,000 are collateral for a $40,000, 12 percent note payable that has accrued interest of $4,000.

3. Inventory with a book value of $79,000 and a current value of $75,000 is pledged against accounts payable of $105,000. The appraised value of the remainder of the inventory is $76,000.

4. Only $1,500 will be recovered from prepaid insurance.

5. Land is appraised at $110,000 and plant and equipment at $340,000.

6. It is estimated that the franchises can be sold for $30,000.

7. All the wages payable qualify for priority.

8. The mortgages are on the land and on a building with a book value of $162,000 and an appraised value of $150,000. The accrued interest on the mortgages is $14,600.

9. Estimated legal and accounting fees for the liquidation are $13,000.

Required

a. Prepare a statement of affairs as of July 31, 20X1.

b. Compute the estimated percentage settlement to unsecured creditors.

P20–15 **Chapter 7 Liquidation, Statement of Affairs [AICPA Adapted]**

Tower Inc. advises you that it is facing bankruptcy proceedings. As the company's CPA, you are aware of its condition. The balance sheet of Tower Inc. on December 31, 20X1, and supplementary data are presented here.

Assets

Cash	$ 2,000
Accounts Receivable (net)	70,000
Inventory, Raw Materials	40,000
Inventory, Finished Goods	60,000
Marketable Securities	20,000
Land	13,000
Buildings (net)	90,000
Machinery (net)	120,000
Goodwill	20,000
Prepaid Expenses	5,000
Total Assets	$440,000